INTRODUCTION TO SOCIOLOGY

Second Edition

INTRODUCTION TO

SOCIOLOGY

MAVIS HILTUNEN BIESANZ
and
JOHN BIESANZ
Wayne State University

PRENTICE-HALL, INC., *Englewood Cliffs, New Jersey*

Library of Congress Cataloging in Publication Data

BIESANZ, MAVIS (HILTUNEN)
  Introduction to sociology.

  Previous ed. entered under J. B. Biesanz.
  Bibliography:
  1. Sociology. I. Biesanz, John Berry
Introduction to sociology. II. Title.
HM51.B483 1973   301   72–7298
ISBN 0-13-947420-4

INTRODUCTION TO SOCIOLOGY
Second Edition
MAVIS HILTUNEN BIESANZ and JOHN BIESANZ

Cover photo courtesy the United Nations

Printed in the United States of America

10 9 8 7 6 5 4 3

Prentice-Hall International, Inc., London
Prentice-Hall of Australia, Pty. Ltd., Sydney
Prentice-Hall of Canada, Ltd., Toronto
Prentice-Hall of India Private Limited, New Delhi
Prentice-Hall of Japan, Inc., Tokyo

To Mother,
HILJA LEMPIA HILTUNEN
with admiration, respect, gratitude, and deepest love

PHOTO CREDITS

Contents

20

PREFACE

This second edition is in many respects more than a revision; it is essentially a new book. We have strengthened many features and added new ones, striving to make the second edition even more "highly readable" than reviewers and users found the first, without sacrificing soundness of sociological content.

The chief innovations or additions are discussions of religion and education; treatment of the "environmental problem" along with population; a new chapter on "Collective Behavior and Social Movements;" the use of the systems model in various contexts; and, at the end of each chapter, a summary of its content and a set of "Questions for Further Thought." These questions, like much of the new content, reflect a stronger value orientation than formerly, and a greater concern with social problems and policies as well as with the quality and meaning of life. We try to make our values explicit and to encourage valuing in the student. Therefore questions are not designed to encourage simple recall, but rather to stimulate the student to think about his own life and its social context from the sociological perspective.

We present not only empirical data but also conflicting theories, as well as interpretations by social philosophers, observers, and critics. We employ several devices to make the book an integrated whole that reads smoothly and builds logically from beginning to end. We wrote the chapters in sequence and based each of them on the materials that preceded, so that a concept introduced in one section usually appears in other contexts. The Introduction to each of the five parts relates the chapters in that part to what has gone before and what is to come. We also use a simple analogy to emphasize the interrelationship of culture, society, and personality: "Society casts the players, culture writes the script, and 'one man in his time plays many parts'."

Recurrent themes, however, probably serve best to unify the book in content and point of view. These themes include the transformation of societies around the world through the interrelated changes that are part of "modernization"; the delicate balance of individual freedom and social cohesion and control in a complex and changing world; and the tension between social order and social change in our time of great unrest and conflict. Our essentially humanist orientation is evident in two other themes: the unity of the human race, and the right of each individual to live with a sense of freedom, dignity, and autonomy and to have a reasonable opportunity to choose how he can best realize his potential for learning, health, and happiness. Finally, we see sociology as one means of understanding, preserving, and improving human life on this small planet.

Our many years of travel and residence abroad, in both industrial and "emerging" societies, have made it easy for us to think in cross-cultural terms and in the perspective of social change, especially modernization. Our personal experiences as well as our research help to lend a global perspective to our discussions of human nature and the social order, and of the possibility of achieving a world community that would ensure the survival and freedom of mankind.

An innovation that appears on the cover and title page does not reflect the rebellion of women so much as the fact that the former "junior author" assumed major responsibility for this book, and is therefore, according to convention, now referred to as "the senior author."

We are most grateful to Herbert Blumer and Richard Biesanz for their careful reading of many chapters and their valuable suggestions and criticism. Others who contributed help and advice which we appreciate immensely are Karen Zubris Biesanz, Suren Pilafian, Helen Hause, Leon Warshay, John Perry, Lillian Fleischman, Ann Diemer, Norman Goldner, Charles Swan, and William Brindle. The senior author's courses and seminars with Alvin Rose, Robin Williams, Jr., Jesse Pitts, Louis Ferman, and Gilbert Shapiro were fruitful sources of ideas and insights.

Edward Stanford was unusually helpful and understanding in his role as Sociology Editor at Prentice-Hall. We thank Ann Levine for careful and perceptive copyediting and we thank Bruce Kennan, marketing manager for Prentice-Hall. Helen S. Harris, Senior Production Editor, Marvin Warshaw, Art Director, and Lorraine Mullaney, book designer, are responsible for the production and design of the book. It was a pleasure to work closely with all of them.

MAVIS HILTUNEN BIESANZ
JOHN BIESANZ

INTRODUCTION TO SOCIOLOGY

INTRODUCTION

The first team of astronauts to circle the moon saw the earth as a small, lovely planet floating in the immense blackness of space. They asked, at first jokingly and then reflectively, "Is it inhabited?"

Indeed it is. Earth would be an arid chunk of rock without its protective atmosphere and its cycle of rainfall and evaporation. Thanks to these, it sustains an almost infinite variety of living things, evolved over some 4 billion years. In this book we are concerned with one species—*Homo sapiens.*

Living on the red-brown earth of the continents and islands that spacemen glimpse through the planet's mantle of swirling clouds are almost 4 billion members of the human race. In tribal villages in deserts and jungles, in peasant communities in the Balkans and the Andes, in towns where community life centers on a marketplace, in teeming cities, every man lives and moves and has his being in the company of his own kind. He works and plays, eats and sleeps, loves and hates, laughs and weeps, is born and buried according to patterns dictated not only by his nature as a biological organism but by the ways his own social group considers right and proper. Because these ways are patterned, most daily and seasonal and yearly events are predictable. Because men are organized into groups with patterned ways of life we can speak of a "social order."

But every social order changes, and today the predictability of group life in most societies is threatened by disorder that seems ever greater and change that seems ever swifter and less controllable. The basic change may be called "modernization." New industrial technology, the shift from rural to urban living, the great increase in interdependence, and tremendous changes in family life, education, government, and beliefs and values are all aspects of this global revolution. It is far advanced in Europe, North America, Japan, and the U.S.S.R.—so far advanced that many observers speak of "post-industrial" or "super-industrial" society. But in crowded Asia, where half the earth's people live, in Africa, and in Latin America, dozens of societies are struggling to emerge from poverty, colonialism, and ignorance, to take men off the land and put them into factories. Western technology has made them aware of Western affluence; the movies, radio, television, and jet travelers show them things that they want for themselves and their children. Western medicine keeps more and more people alive long enough to bear more and more children, and their population grows so explosively that by the year 2006, at present rates of increase, there will be more than 7 billion people on earth. In the poorest countries, where birth rates are highest, productivity is lowest and economic growth hardest to achieve. Ten thousand people a day die of malnutrition or starvation, and worse famine threatens before the century is over.

Even in the richest societies the blessings of technology are mixed. Many homes are warmed in winter and cooled in summer, furnished with electrical and gas appliances, their cupboards laden with foods packaged in foil and plastic and tin and glass and cardboard. For these comforts men fell forests; fertilize and spray crops; mine coal, gas, and oil, the fossil heritage of forests that flourished 300 million years ago; keep factories humming; dart about over land and water and through the air in vehicles propelled by internal combustion engines. But they see a pall of smog over their cities; they taste noxious gases in the air; read of DDT in mothers' milk and mercury in fish; pour human and industrial waste, fertilizers, and insecticides into lakes and rivers; pile junkyards high with rusting cars, and garbage dumps with the rubbish of affluence. And they live with the knowledge that if they escape dying with a whimper as the life-giving earth is poisoned, they may die in a nuclear bang that will end the human story.

The social changes that have accompanied industrialization also trouble many members of modern societies. Their cities are crowded with people of different classes and ethnic backgrounds; highly specialized occupations; differing beliefs and values; and often clashing interests. They deal with huge organizations: big government bureaucracies, mammoth corporations, massive armies, large churches, schools numbering thousands

and universities numbering tens of thousands. In this complexity and bigness they often feel lost, anonymous, powerless. They are numbers on
licenses, social security cards, draft cards, credit cards, I.D. cards.

Their reactions range from apathy to extreme violence. Some ignore the
changes and problems of the times: "Get yours. Don't rock the boat. Go
along from day to day." Others find avenues of escape: "Have another
martini. Drop acid. Blow a joint. Nibble snacks in front of the TV. Chant
the Hare Krishna. Go on a shopping spree. Take a sleeping pill." Some
earnestly try to recapture lost human values in communes and encounter
groups where they feel less alienated from nature and from one another.
Many defend the status quo, saying either, "The system is fine, smash dissent, vote for law and order." Or, "The system isn't that bad; tinker with
it here and there, muddle through, patch it up."

But protest is making headlines, and not only in America. One form it
takes is the emergent youth culture that combines elements of escapism
and a search for new (or recaptured) values with protest against the older
generation and the mess it has made of things. Many young people play
guitars and sing about changing times, hypocritical and insensitive elders,
napalm on Asian babies, sex, loneliness, drugs; they turn up the decibels
and flash the strobe lights; wear peace signs; boycott bras and barbers;
wear jeans even though Dad makes $25,000 a year; experiment with dif-
ferent styles of life.

Political protest is often directly activist. Nonviolent demonstrations—
sit-ins at lunch counters, boycotts, marches—have been largely over-
shadowed by violence. The radical and alienated riot, loot, make and throw
bombs and Molotov cocktails, hurl bricks and cobblestones at policemen,
hijack planes, kidnap diplomats, assassinate leaders, and yell "Off the
pigs. Down with the Establishment. Smash the system." Both kinds of protest have been countered with force and violence on many occasions:
arrests, beatings, tear gas, water hoses, and bullets. Student–police confrontations such as once made headlines only from exotic places like

4

Guatemala and Indonesia have occurred on the green campuses of Ohio and Mississippi.

The Stars and Stripes, once the symbol of national unity, has become a symbol of polarization as some wear shirts made to look like flags and others stick decals of the flag in their car windows. Name-calling, too, indicates the conflicts in our society: honkies, niggers, male chauvinists, racists, Commies, Yankee imperialists, dirty hippies, Nazis, freaks, warmongers, Fascist pigs.

In such times, how can one speak of a social order? Because there are still patterns and regularities in social life—even in much of this disorder and conflict! We are still pretty sure that the newspapers with their headlines about disorder will appear tomorrow; that the mailman will come; that classes will meet and offices and stores will be open at the usual time; that traffic will be regulated and TV programs will appear as scheduled. Most people will do their jobs and act pretty much as we expect them to. It is easy to overlook the fact, too, when the angry and alienated loom so large in the news and in our awareness, that many people manage to lead active, satisfying, autonomous lives in the midst of all these strains and tensions. They find in modern society a wide range of opportunities for personal choice in work, play, and human relationships. They find identity and fulfillment not only in their occupations but also in raising children, growing roses, playing the cello, going to church, knitting, going bowling, taking pictures, reading, playing bridge, doing volunteer work at the hospital, working for their political candidates, acting, skiing, hiking, fishing, making love, cooking, sewing, talking with friends and family, painting, traveling, practicing yoga, browsing in antique shops, refinishing furniture, playing tennis. They are able to cope responsibly with problems, calmly accept circumstances beyond their control, and feel a sense of dignity and self-fulfillment.

In free societies there are also those who seek not to smash the system, nor escape it, nor defend it blindly, but to improve it and make it possible for more people to live in freedom, dignity, and autonomy. Much of their work is based on that of sociologists, whose basic task is to try to understand social order and social change. How, they ask, does society work? How do societies hang together? How do they meet, or fail to meet, human needs? How do they change; in what directions are they evolving? And how will these changes affect our ways of thinking, feeling, and acting?

This book is addressed to these questions. Part One reflects our belief that a firm grasp of the concept of culture is basic to sound sociological analysis; that the study of different manifestations of "human nature" and varieties of social arrangements opens up new perspectives.

In Part Two we examine social organization and social differentiation. Here we deal with social structure as a network of interdependent statuses with their accompanying roles prescribed by culture; with variations in social organization, and especially the contrast between traditional and modern societies; with the ways societies are divided into categories of people according to their share of wealth, power, and prestige, and according to their membership in racial and religious and ethnic groups.

In Part Three we turn to social psychology, the field of sociology that stresses the person *in* the group. We begin by outlining different theories of socialization—the process that turns a helpless infant into a functioning member of his society. The emphasis here is on the universals of human nature, the variations from group to group, and the uniqueness of each individual human being.

Social change and the social problems it produces or aggravates are our concern in Part Four. After a general discussion of the processes of social and cultural change, we take up the "great transformation" of modernization, emphasizing urbanization and the population explosion, and man's effect on the biophysical environment. We conclude with a chapter on the forms of collective behavior and social movements that are often produced by and in turn produce change.

Part Five examines the social institutions of the family, religion, and education—what they are and how they are changing. We conclude with a look at trends that are unifying the world—political and economic trends among others—and the promise these may hold for man's survival and freedom. We ask what insights sociology may contribute to the moral and ethical order upon which the future of spaceship Earth depends.

The book is bound together by several themes. One is that human social behavior occurs in a field of five groupings of systems, all simultaneously present and interacting: the physical and biological environment, the human organism, the personality, the cultural system, and the social system. Although for some kinds of sociological study we may take environment, the human body, and even individual personalities as "givens," for many vital problems they must be taken seriously into account.

Another pervasive theme is the problem of maintaining a delicate balance between individual freedom and social control as the world becomes ever more complex and various groups come into conflict with one another and threaten social cohesion. Closely allied with this theme is the paradox that although we are more interdependent than ever before, many of us feel increasingly lonely and alienated. Some people argue that our institutions have failed to meet our needs and must be renewed; others that if we would only give them the respect they are due things would get better. Most of us agree that technology—with its promises and its dangers —has gotten out of hand. This tension between social order and social change is another recurrent theme.

Underlying these themes is our belief in the intrinsic worth of every human being; in the possibility of achieving a society in which everyone has the opportunity to decide how he can best fulfill his potential and live with a sense of freedom, dignity, and autonomy; and in the usefulness of social science as a means to understand, preserve, and improve human life.

1

If man is to survive in the modern world he must learn how society works.

ABRAM KARDINER and EDWARD PREBLE

The fascination of sociology lies in the fact that its perspective makes us see in a new light the very world in which we have lived all our lives.

PETER BERGER

The unleashed power of the atom has changed everything except our way of thinking.

ALBERT EINSTEIN

THE
STUDY
OF
SOCIETY

People have always looked for patterns and meanings in the physical and social world, and still rely—to varying degrees in different societies—on age-old sources of explanation such as tradition, authority, and common sense.

Every society has some world view, some theory of the meaning of the universe and man's relation to it. Tradition provides explanations of birth and death, male and female roles, the movement of the stars and planets, the cycle of day and night, the waxing and waning of the moon, the misfortunes of crop failures and illness and accident. These traditional explanations—often expressed in myths and legends—may be taught as revealed truth from a supernatural being, or as the wisdom of elders and ancestors.

The scholars who looked to Greek philosophers for truth depended on another kind of authority. For centuries Aristotle's proclamation regarding the number of teeth in a horse's mouth was unquestioned; no one bothered to count the teeth or to consult a stablehand. Similarly, a small child takes on faith the explanations of his parents and teachers.

Another traditional source of knowledge is the obvious—what everyone knows, what can be taken for granted in the name of common sense or conventional wisdom. Much practical behavior rests on this kind of "truth," which constitutes the bulk of every culture. People must act as if some things are so in order to get along. For example, it was long obvious that the earth is flat; even now, when science tells us it is round, for most practical purposes we act as though it were flat.

Besides relying on tradition, authority, and common sense, people have faith in their own powers of ordinary observation, interpretation, intuition, introspection, and informal logic. People generalize or theorize all the time, seeing relationships between two or more factors: "The brighter a person is, the more likely he is to be maladjusted, or even crazy. Young rebels are just going through a phase; wait till they settle down and have to support a family." Explanations arrived at by these unsystematic methods are often invalid because of sheer ignorance of the facts, the narrowness of personal experience, self-interest, prejudice against certain ideas, and rigid stereotypes of groups of people.

Yet they seem self-evident, and the idea of subjecting them to scientific proof appears unnecessary, ridiculous, and even subversive.

> Suppose that a researcher in the field of the family had demonstrated the following set of facts. Would it have been worth doing? Or were the facts already known?
>
> 1. The present divorce rate in the U.S. is much higher than the rates in primitive societies, and higher than any other nation has ever experienced.
> 2. Because of the importance of the extended family in China and India, the average size of the household has always been very high, with many generations living under one roof.
> 3. In Western nations, the age at marriage among peasants was always low, since early marriage meant that children would soon be produced, and these were useful in farming. By contrast, the average age at marriage among the nobility was generally higher.
>
> Although these statements sound plausible to many people, and impressive arguments could be adduced to support them, in fact they are all false. A majority of primitive societies have higher rates of marital dissolution than our own, and several nations in the past have at various times equaled or exceeded our present rate—notably Japan in the 1880s, and even her official rate (certainly an underestimate) was over 300 divorces per 1000 marriages. Every survey of Chinese and Indian households has shown that they are relatively small (about 3.3 to 5.5, from one region to another). Peasant marriages were later, on the average, than the nobility, requiring as they did that the couple have land of their own.
>
> Thus we see that in the instances just cited, common beliefs *did* require testing. Of course, many popular beliefs about how families work *are* correct, but we cannot simply assume their correctness. We must examine many of our individual observations to see how well they fit other societies or perhaps the different family types in our own society.[1]

Another drawback of common-sense knowledge is that for many things everyone knows, he also knows just the opposite. He knows that "Absence makes the heart grow fonder," but he also knows, "Out of

---

[1]William J. Goode, *The Family* (Englewood Cliffs, N.J.: Prentice-Hall, Inc., 1964), pp. 3–4. Another study often cited as an example of the fallibility of informal logic is the survey of American soldiers in World War II by Paul Lazarsfeld and associates. Contrary to common-sense expectations, men with high education were less neurotic than those with little education, soldiers with urban backgrounds were better adjusted than those from rural areas, and Southerners were no more adaptable than Northerners to a hot climate. ["The American Soldier—An Expository Review," *Public Opinion Quarterly* 13 (Fall 1949): 380.]

sight, out of mind." However much consolation either of these bromides may provide him in a given situation, both cannot be true. But more important, the preconceptions of traditional knowledge are often blocks to acquiring further knowledge. Nonscientific ways of getting knowledge are not self-correcting; science is. The scientific spirit and the scientific method can be safeguards against the perpetuation of error.

In this first chapter we consider the meaning and goals of science in general and of social science in particular, with special reference to sociology. We discuss the three main orientations of early social scientists who were reacting to the industrial and democratic revolutions: social philosophy, social observation and criticism, and empirical research. Then we ask, What are the uses of sociology in a professional career, in personal life, and in society?

Science and Social Science

WHAT IS SCIENCE?

In the particular sense, **a science** is a body of organized knowledge, including a set of logically connected propositions concerning the behavior of certain phenomena as it repeatedly occurs under certain given conditions (sunspots, business cycles, the change in the volume of gases). The word **science**, in the general sense, refers to method rather than content, to a certain way of seeking—or more precisely, *creating*—knowledge. In the words of Andrei Sakharov, a Soviet physicist and champion of intellectual freedom, "We regard as 'scientific' a method based on deep analysis of facts, theories, and views, presupposing unprejudiced, unfearing open discussion and conclusions."[2] Scientific research is deliberate, careful, controlled observation of the empirical world; it is a search for the truth about some fragment of the empirical world—the world of testable realities, such as the action of gases, the motion of objects, the relationships of managers and workers.

But science is not a dull, plodding pursuit, though it has its share of drudgery. "Science at its highest level is ultimately the organization of, the systematic pursuit of, and the enjoyment of wonder, awe, and mystery. . . . Not only does science begin in wonder; it ends in wonder."[3]

[2]Andrei D. Sakharov, *Progress, Coexistence, and Intellectual Freedom*, trans. *The New York Times* (New York: W. W. Norton & Co., Inc., 1968), p. 25. Introduction, Afterword, and Notes by Harrison E. Salisbury. The original manuscript was circulated from hand to hand in the Soviet Union, but never published; as one of the creators of the H-bomb, however, Sakharov commands enough prestige to escape severe sanctions. (Interview with Harrison E. Salisbury, April 13, 1972.)

[3]Abraham Maslow, *The Psychology of Science: A Reconnaissance* (New York: Harper & Row, Publishers, 1966), p. 151.

The aims of science are usually identified as description, interpretation or explanation, prediction, and control. (In the social sciences, however, as we shall see later, the goals of prediction and control, especially the latter, are controversial, for we are dealing with human behavior, not such things as physical forces or the processes of plant growth.)

The findings of science are always subject to revision. They are not the last word, but merely the latest word. Newtonian physics was acceptable until Einstein came along. Scientific knowledge is made public so it can be retested and verified or rejected.

Ideally, the scientist abides by all the rules of the scientific ethic, which prescribe the proper attitude or spirit. He is patient and precise, striving for accuracy in his collection and interpretation of data. He is impartial and objective, taking all the available relevant data into consideration regardless of his own preferences. He assumes nothing except that there is a natural order of things and that this can be discovered and explained. Skeptical even about his own findings, he tests his propositions against the data before he arrives at generalizations, and is similarly skeptical about the findings of others, asking, "What's the evidence?" His impersonal devotion to truth is presumably so great that he is delighted to have his theories proved wrong, but "in practice this delight is often moderate."[4] The ideal scientist reports his findings fully, making them public so that others may check them and so that they will add to the cumulative body of knowledge in the discipline. Finally, he is a scholar, knowing what has already been established in his field, and he is a master of methods and techniques of research and interpretation. Great scientists also have outstanding powers of imagination and judgment.

THE EMERGENCE OF SCIENCE

Modern science began when astronomy, physics, and mathematics broke away from the mother of science, philosophy. These intellectual explorations were, at least in part, a response to the needs of the explorers of land and sea, such as navigators who wanted more precise ways to find directions. In the organic sciences, which developed somewhat later, mathematics and measurement were less important. Early botanists, geologists, zoologists, and paleontologists collected and classified specimens. An orderly classification of the immense variety of living things in the history of the planet was the essential basis for Darwin's theory of evolution, which would not have occurred to him if he had not been familiar with the empirical data others had compiled.

Although we associate great discoveries with great names, sci-

---

[4]Kenneth E. Boulding, *The Meaning of the Twentieth Century: The Great Transition* (New York: Harper & Row, Publishers, 1964), p. 45. A famous English scientist said of Herbert Spencer, "His idea of a tragedy is a theory killed by a fact."

ence is a collective enterprise. As it grew, scientists communicated across national borders and organized societies; one landmark in the institutionalization of science was the establishment of the Royal Society of London for Improving Natural Knowledge in 1662. In the twentieth century science has become "a substantial, organized part of society on a full-time professional basis."[5]

EARLY SOCIAL SCIENTISTS

Just as the origins of physical science can be traced to the need of explorers and navigators for exact observations, the development of social science can be seen as a response to the need for knowledge about new phenomena that appeared with the economic and political revolutions of the eighteenth and early nineteenth centuries. Tradition furnished no guide to the new social realities of urbanization, industrial working classes, and physical and social mobility that broke up families and long-established communities and challenged old values and patterns of human relationships. "Social science developed largely as a way of perceiving, evaluating, and correcting the frictions and tensions generated by the high rate of individual mobility and institutional change in modernizing society."[6]

Social philosophers. Among early students of society, we may distinguish three main approaches to the problems of "perceiving, evaluating, and correcting" these conditions. One is that of the grand theorist concerned with historical trends and human destiny, who works out a social philosophy that he claims will explain a broad range of phenomena, and often constructs, as well, a model of a future "good society." Among the most influential of the social philosophers were Adam Smith, Karl Marx, Auguste Comte, and Herbert Spencer.

Adam Smith (1723–1790), a Scottish moral philosopher, was the first modern economic theorist. His *Wealth of Nations* (1776), essentially a theory of economics—especially in relation to government control—has served as the basis for much economic theory and practice in capitalist societies. Influenced by Enlightenment ideas about the rationality of man, by the notions of force, motion and equilibrium in physics, and by the scientists' preference for measurable units (in this case, price), Smith developed a model of the free market as a self-adjusting mechanism in which numerous rational individuals, each motivated by self-interest, work—without realizing it—for the common good, as if they were guided by an "invisible hand."

Karl Marx (1818–1883) was a prophet and a revolutionary who sought to change rather than simply interpret the world. Moved by a

---

[5]*Ibid.*, p. 40.

[6]Daniel Lerner, ed., *The Human Meaning of the Social Sciences* (Cleveland: World Publishing Company, 1959), p. 7.

vision of a perfect, classless society, he was convinced it could come about only through the class struggle. The misery of the new industrial proletariat and the failure of the political revolutions of 1848 led him to believe that economic factors determine social structure and culture, and that just as capitalism had superseded the even worse system of feudalism, so its evils would give way to "scientific socialism." Not only have his doctrines shaken the world, but his influence is reflected in studies of class systems and power relationships even among those social scientists who find his theory in general untenable.[7]

Like Marx, Auguste Comte (1798–1857) believed in progress toward a perfect society. He insisted, however, that it would come about not by political revolution but by the proper application of a new moral science, the study of society, which he named "sociology." The highest of all sciences, it would use the "positivist" scientific method of observation, experimentation, and comparison to understand order and promote progress.[8] Thus, said Comte, a scientifically designed commonwealth could be built, with social control entrusted to the religion of humanity—with sociologists as its priests.

Like many others in the late nineteenth century, the English philosopher Herbert Spencer (1820–1903) was especially influenced by the idea of evolution. A believer in extreme individualism, he abhorred the authority of the state and favored letting natural forces work themselves out in society as they did in nature—ideas that many industrialists of the American "robber baron" era used to justify their policies.

Social observers. Two Frenchmen illustrate another approach to the study of society—the observation and description of what *is* rather than speculation about what ought to be. *L'Esprit des Lois* by Baron Montesquieu (1689–1755), published in 1748, has been called "the first great descriptive treatise in sociology."[9] Montesquieu abandoned the idea of any one best system of government, religion, family life, or morals, and toured many countries "to discover men, things, and constitutions." He was the greatest advocate of the method of observation and comparison (rather than bookish scholarship and speculation) who had appeared up to that time.

Another shrewd observer, Alexis de Tocqueville (1805–1859), was especially interested in the effects of popular government on a whole society, and studied the new nation of the United States to examine trends that he believed would later appear elsewhere. In *Democ-*

[7]Alvin W. Gouldner sees Marxism as the official social science of the Soviet Union, and American "Academic Sociology" as the other side of the fission of early sociology. Each increasingly displays the influence of the other. [*The Coming Crisis of Western Sociology* (New York: Avon, 1970), pp. 20–24.] See Chapters 9 and 14 for further discussions of Marxism.

[8]Howard Becker and Harry Elmer Barnes, *Social Thought from Lore to Science*, 2nd ed. (Washington, D.C.: Harren Press, 1952), pp. 564–94.

[9]*Ibid.*, p. 560.

racy in America, published in two parts in 1835 and 1840, he predicted such developments as the mass society sociologists perceive today, and even foresaw that an autocratic Russia and a freedom-based America would one day divide the lion's share of world power between them.

Social empiricists. Among today's social scientists, social philosophy and grand theory are rare, social description and criticism considerably more common. But the main direction of modern social science is *empiricism*, which goes back to early investigators in France and England who asked factual questions of ordinary people, especially in the new urban working class, rather than of authorities.

In the 1820s Adolphe Quetelet, a mathematician and astronomer of Brussels, began to collect good census figures and to extract laws or generalizations directly from the facts he had gathered rather than from the "facts" in history books and those gleaned from unsystematic observations. He was influential in establishing in 1834 the Statistical Society of London, whose members were concerned with the condition of the new urban masses. They collected facts and figures based on direct observation and interviews, even going down into the mines to investigate conditions at first hand.[10]

Frederic LePlay collected, classified, and analyzed first-hand data on the income and expenditures of over 300 working-class families in every European country and several Asian ones. In his reports LePlay related data he collected while living with many of the families to the policy problems and ideologies of the time. One of the first major empirical studies of society was his six-volume report published in 1855, *Les Ouvriers Européens*.[11]

Poverty was also the chief concern of Charles Booth, a shipowner who tried to collect "all the facts" about the people of London; to show the relationship of poverty, misery, and depravity in contrast to regular earnings, comparative comfort, and stability. He questioned hundreds of school attendance officers who knew the homes and families of East London, and he lived with various families, keeping notebooks on their activities and conditions of life. In the monumental work, *Life and Labour of the People in London*, finished in 1903, he challenged the current notions that wealth and poverty were somehow related to good and evil, and that charity and the dole perpetuated poverty. His generalizations were empirically grounded, in contrast to Marx's denunciation of capitalism as *the* cause of poverty.[12] Further, Booth's findings led to reform of the poor laws and of old age pensions.

[10]Nathan Glazer, "The Rise of Social Research in Europe," in Lerner, *The Human Meaning*, p. 47.

[11]Lerner, "Social Science: Whence and Whither?" in Lerner, *The Human Meaning*, p. 20.

[12]One of his associates in this investigation was a brilliant woman of an upper-middle-class family, Beatrice Potter (Mrs. Sidney Webb), whose autobiography is a fascinating account of her initiation into empirical research. See Beatrice Webb, *My Apprenticeship* (London: Longmans, Green & Co. Ltd., 1926).

Thus, in Daniel Lerner's words, "As the mode of self-observation evolved by dealing with the new human problems raised by the endlessly changing lifeways of modern society, social science developed primarily as an empirical, quantitative, policy-related *method of inquiry* (not as a system of beliefs)."[13]

Sociology and the Other Social Sciences

Sociology is one of the social sciences; as such it is distinguished from the natural sciences (such as biology, physics, and chemistry) on the one hand and from the arts and humanities (such as literature, music, and art) on the other. All social scientists deal with human behavior—with the relationships and interactions of people in groups. This emphasis on interaction is based on the idea that we cannot understand human relationships by studying individuals any more than we can understand water by studying hydrogen and oxygen. Groups have characteristics that are different from the characteristics of their various members; they have a nature of their own and must be studied on their own terms. Just as something new happens when hydrogen and oxygen are combined, so new things happen when people come together. Their behavior is not the action of A plus the action of B and so on; it is the *interaction* of A and B, which is difficult or impossible to predict from their separate personalities.

This interaction may take such forms as a wedding, a debate, a riot, an election, strike negotiations, a music lesson. No matter what form it takes, its most important feature is that the participants are taking each other into account.

In their common concern with group behavior, social scientists assume that man is part of the natural order, and like all of nature can be observed and understood by disciplined methods. They also assume that the actions of people are largely rational and purposeful; otherwise there would be no social order. The actions of people have *meaning* for themselves and for each other. Like all scientists, social scientists seek to generalize, to make broader sense out of accumulated facts. They believe it is worthwhile to work toward such generalizations, even though the delicate nuances of human behavior disappear in the careful abstraction and the cold statistic. Fiction, religion, poetry, music, painting, dance, and philosophy—the arts and humanities—deal with sorrow, joy, dreams, faith, good, evil, the death of innocence, the ultimate meaning of man's existence, the infinite variations of human emotions and relationships. They have their insights to contribute; the social sciences have theirs.

The various social sciences are all the academic disciplines that deal with men in their social context—anthropology, sociology, history,

[13]"Social Science" in Lerner, *The Human Meaning*, p. 19.

*"All I know is that he came here two years ago
on a Fulbright to do a study on 'Primitive
Society—Burden or Blessing?' "*

economics, and political science. (Geography is also in some respects a
social science.) These divisions did not arise out of logical necessity as
much as through a historical process. The field of "political economy,"
for example, became "economics" when capitalist societies, under the
influence of Adam Smith and the laissez-faire philosophy, came to
treat the economy as something quite independent of government and
politics. Today it is often impossible to determine whether a problem in
economic policy is a problem in economics or political science.

    Although they all study human social behavior and their concerns
often overlap, the various social sciences do have different emphases
and perspectives on group life. **Anthropology** is the study of biological
and behavioral similarities and differences among the various peoples
of the world. Physical anthropologists concentrate on the biological aspect, cultural or social anthropologists on the behavioral aspects. Traditionally, cultural anthropologists have investigated groups distinguished
"only by their lack of alphabet and breeches,"[14] but they have also
carried out field work in more complex urban societies, as in the classic
studies of Muncie, Indiana, made by Robert and Helen Lynd, which
served as the bases for their books *Middletown* and *Middletown in*

[14]Scott Greer, *The Logic of Social Inquiry* (Chicago: Aldine Publishing Co., 1969),
    p. 150.

Transition. The invaluable contribution of anthropologists to human knowledge is the concept of *culture*.

Economics emphasizes the activities of men as they use their environment to produce goods and services, and as they distribute and consume them. **Political science** is the study of political life and government, of the distribution of power in a society. It is concerned with the maintenance of social order and the achievement of social change by planning, reform, or revolution.

History is the study of man's past, of a sequence of events. It is as much an art as a social science, for the historian has to select and arrange the available data according to the way he perceives their relationships and significance. Historians may specialize by geographical areas, by time periods, or by approach to selected bodies of facts, such as political or economic history or the history of ideas or art forms. Increasingly they draw on the data and theories of the other social sciences for better understanding of their problems; in turn other social scientists use historical data.

Sociology is the systematic study of human relationships. The sociologist focuses on men in groups and on their relationships to one another, as well as on the relationships of groups to other groups, including the large, inclusive group called a *society*. He asks how these relationships arise, why they persist or dissolve, how they change, and what consequences they have for the people involved and for other individuals and groups.

All human interaction—the normal as well as the abnormal, the everyday as well as the exciting—is grist for the sociologist's mill. He is interested in bums as well as beauty queens, whores and holy men, rioters and respectable middle-class housewives.

With the world and all its human relationships as his beat, a sociologist cannot hope to master all the theories, concepts, data, methods, and procedures of the discipline. He may choose to concentrate on theory, on a specific social institution such as religion or the law, on some concrete group such as a juvenile gang, on group relationships such as those of minority–majority groups, or on some area such as the city or Latin America. He may be especially interested in social problems. Whatever his specialization, he studies it not only for the sake of knowledge about that specialty, but also in the hope of contributing to basic theories of social organization and social psychology.

The various fields within sociology are reflected in the courses given in the average university department: sociological theory, research methods, social problems, social psychology, race and ethnic relations, urban sociology, rural sociology, social stratification, marriage and the family, social causation and social change, deviant behavior, social statistics, sociology of education, sociology of religion, political sociology, and so on.

The Uses of Sociology

What are the uses—actual and potential—of sociology? What can it do for the person and for society? In this section we consider these questions from several points of view: sociology as a career, the value of the sociological perspective in one's personal life, and sociology's contribution to the society as a whole. We conclude the chapter with a brief consideration of an issue that flares up periodically and has burned hotter than ever in recent years—what should be the sociologist's role in bringing about (or impeding) social change?

SOCIOLOGY AS A CAREER

Perhaps four out of five American sociologists are affiliated with colleges and universities, and engaged primarily in teaching and independent research. Almost without exception they have advanced degrees (M.A.'s or Ph.D.'s) or are working toward them. Graduate programs for the doctorate begin with a year or two of courses in research, theory, and various fields, followed by a year or two of seminars devoted to more intensive study of particular areas of interest, and ending with an independent research project, which becomes the doctoral dissertation.

Other sociologists are professionals rather than academicians, employed by public and private agencies to do research or to serve as advisers and consultants. They work in independent research institutes, such as the Social Science Research Council and the Russell Sage Foundation; for governments at various levels; and in corporations, political parties, churches, newspapers, hospitals, school systems, and social agencies. Some sociologists combine academic and professional roles, or shift back and forth between them, as consultants on specific problems, urban planners, United Nations advisers on community development in foreign countries, advisers to the President, even mayors or city councilmen. Many feel they enrich their mastery of the academic discipline by applying their knowledge and methods in social action. Most sociologists belong to regional, national, and even international associations, and write for and subscribe to such professional journals as the *American Sociological Review*, the official publication of the American Sociological Association, as well as more specialized journals.[15]

PERSONAL USES OF SOCIOLOGY

You may never look through a microscope again after you finish a biology course, or speak French after passing the exam, but you will

[15]*A Career in Sociology*, The American Sociological Association (1001 Connecticut Ave. N.W., Washington, D.C. 20036). A pamphlet prepared by Prof. Raymond W. Mack.

probably live with people, vote, hold a job, pay taxes, and discuss social problems. To the extent that sociology contributes to a new way of looking at the person, the group, and culture, it may help you make sense out of the world and to handle your relationships with others in a more satisfying way. No matter what occupation you choose, and what role in community life, the knowledge and awareness that come with study of sociology may help you participate more successfully than you otherwise might. The public administrator, lawyer, doctor, architect, or businessman, as well as the parent or the community volunteer, finds greater satisfaction in performing his role if he can relate it to a broader view of how society works; he can make judgments and decisions, both personal and professional, in a broader context.

Sociology may also help you understand yourself. As C. Wright Mills insisted, "It is by means of the sociological imagination that men now hope to grasp what is going on in the world, and to understand what is happening in themselves as minute points of the intersection of biography and history within society."[16] New concepts such as culture, status, role, reference group, institution, class, mobility, and the self-conception may help you order the events of your life, reinterpreting the past and giving direction to the future. You may become aware of yourself as a participant in the social order, helping to make group decisions, aware that institutions have not always been as we know them here and now, but are instead the products of time, culture, and man's actions—and that as such they are subject to change. This knowledge of alternatives may lead to a sense of patience and perspective toward the process of change—or perhaps to increased impatience about some long-standing problems that seem amenable to solution.

The senior author, for example, thinks of her life not just as a series of events idiosyncratic to her, but also as a sociological story including immigrant ancestry; upbringing in a community more "folk" than "urban"; social mobility through education; migration to cities; life in a number of other societies; a growing consciousness of heterogeneity and change in American society as the years went by and the two "clans" joined by marriage displayed varying political beliefs, social class statuses, religious affiliations, and patterns of conformity and deviance, and as children grew up and were socialized or resisted socialization.

SOCIOLOGY AND SOCIETY

Each of the various sociological approaches contributes to information and direction within a society. Social philosophers open up new alternative visions of the future. Social critics and observers interpret trends and changes, predicting the possible consequences of alternative

[16]The Sociological Imagination (New York: Oxford University Press, 1959), p. 7.

actions or policies. Empirical research adds to a growing body of solidly based knowledge upon which to base decisions.

The growth of social science knowledge. A team of two political scientists and a biophysicist identified sixty-two major accomplishments in the behavioral and social sciences since 1900, using two basic criteria: Did the achievement lead to a new perception or a new operation? Did it open up a new sector of knowledge (although not necessarily new social practice, which lags 10–15 years behind knowledge in application)?

Their list includes such varied items as Keynesian economic theory, community studies like those of Middletown, studies of the relationship of authoritarian personality to family structure, attitude surveys and opinion polling, Pavlov's work on conditioned reflexes, content analysis of texts and writings to infer thought and intention, computer simulation of social and economic systems, and general systems analysis.

Among their major conclusions were the following: Social science has not flourished under totalitarian governments of either the left or right. The United States accounted for 75% of the advances since 1930; Great Britain for 15%. Practical social demands stimulated most of these advances, and nearly all involved quantitative problems or findings. Significant contributions, once made by lone scholars like Max Weber and Sigmund Freud, are increasingly the product of team research in a few major intellectual centers (Cambridge, Chicago, London, and New York, for example) where social scientists have ready access to such resources as mathematics, computers, laboratories, specialists in other fields, and complex urban cultures. Many of the advances have had profound effects on society—for example, linear programming, a mathematical technique for allocating resources, is used in budgeting, inventory control, and modern weaponry. The authors conclude that there is unmistakable evidence of cumulative growth in the social sciences and of the need for constructive application of their findings to social problems.[17]

Many social scientists might argue with the list, declaring that it is biased in favor of team and quantitative studies, and does not do justice to the impact of interpretative theory and social criticism on society—and yet it includes the theories and accomplishments of Lenin, Gandhi, and Mao.

Government uses of sociological knowledge and methods. From the founding of our country, government leaders have recognized that social science information is basic to democratic government. The Con-

[17]Robert Reinhold, "Social Science Gains Tied to Big Teams of Scholars," *The New York Times* (March 16, 1971): C26, citing a study by Karl W. Deutsch, John R. Platt, and Dieter Senghaas.

stitution provides for a census to be taken every 10 years; its primary purpose is to ensure fair representation in Congress, but it has lent itself to many other uses as well. In September 1929 President Hoover, often thought of as a staunch conservative, appointed a Research Committee on Social Trends—directed by sociologist William Fielding Ogburn— to anticipate the consequences of technological change and provide a basis for planning. President Franklin Roosevelt's Secretary of Agriculture, Henry Wallace, asked psychologist Rensis Likert to find out how much government regulation farmers would accept during the Depression; public opinion polling has been very much a part of politics and policy ever since.

After World War II, the Carnegie Corporation and the Ford Foundation asked the Social Science Research Council to support studies of the Soviet Union as a prelude to better understanding; in 1959 the Ford Foundation and other philanthropic agencies asked the Council to do the same regarding China.

In recent years some social scientists have become identified with a new role, that of "social accountant." Work toward a system of social accounting—that is, measuring the welfare of citizens through such "social indicators" as infant mortality—has proceeded under private foundations as well as government agencies. Sociologists urge that a Board of Social Advisers be established and charged with delivering to America's citizens an annual social report comparable to the annual economic report, thus fulfilling the Constitutional duty of the president to keep the people advised on "the state of the nation."[18]

Sociology and social change. Sociology and the other social sciences are "potentially some of the most revolutionary intellectual enterprises ever conceived by the mind of man."[19] Insofar as they question conventional wisdom, destroy old myths, suggest alternative ways of patterning social relationships, and provide new perspectives on human nature, they threaten comfortable habits and vested interests. Sociologists can hardly avoid touching on controversial subjects when they deal with group conflicts and special problems, and with such "private" and intimate subjects as religion and sex relations.

Because sociology views any given social arrangement as only one of a number of alternatives, it is inherently "radical" in the original sense of getting at the "root" of things. It can, however, just as truly be "conservative" in the sense of conserving what is worthwhile. By

[18]John Lear, "Where Is Society Going? The Search for Landmarks," *Saturday Review* (April 15, 1972): 34–39. See also Eleanor Sheldon and Wilbert E. Moore, *The Human Meaning of Social Change* (New York: The Russell Sage Foundation, 1972). A further discussion of social indicators appears in Chapter 14.

[19]Behavioral Science or Electioneering?" excerpt from a 2-year study completed in 1969 by a National Academy of Sciences panel, *Saturday Review* (Nov. 1, 1969): 65–67.

analyzing the possible consequences of various alternatives, sociologists can contribute to orderly change and prevent needless conflict and violence. But their warnings and predictions are not always heeded in time. Twenty years before the long hot summer of 1967, for example, Robin Williams, Jr., noted the conditions that would eventually lead to mass riots in urban ghettos, but little or nothing was done to correct those conditions.[20]

By testing propositions about man and society, then, social scientists provide us not only with a multitude of social facts, but also with knowledge of trends and of possible courses of action and their probable consequences, justifying the definition of social science as "man's working tool for continually rebuilding his culture."[21]

THE SOCIOLOGIST AND PUBLIC POLICY: INVOLVEMENT OR NEUTRALITY?

But who is going to use this instrument? Sociologists disagree sharply on their proper role. Is it enough to use the classroom to teach students ways of understanding social problems? And to conduct careful investigations and make the findings public for whatever use others might make of them? Or should sociologists actively engage in the political process through which goals and policies are decided?

This issue is often stated in terms of values. Sociology, say many, should have no value except truth; a true scientist is objective, value-free, ethically neutral. He studies problems with the aloofness of a man from Mars. At the opposite extreme are self-styled radical sociologists who believe all their work should be action-oriented, and are concerned with values and goals, with policies or the means to those goals, and with the political process in which goals are chosen and means worked out.[22]

The third position is more complex, and even those who take it do not agree on all its premises. They insist that sociology can never be completely value-free, for to do is to choose, and values guide choices. The very choice of a problem reveals a value orientation. If we limit our concerns to what *is* rather than studying what might be and ought to be, then we are by default supporting the status quo. And if

[20]*The Reduction of Intergroup Tensions* (New York: Social Science Research Council, 1947), pp. 60–61.

[21]Robert Lynd, *Knowledge for What? The Place of Social Science in American Culture* (Princeton, N.J.: Princeton University Press, 1948), p. 200.

[22]A similar debate is going on in the other social sciences, and in the natural sciences as well; biologists, chemists, and physicists increasingly question the potential applications of their research to warfare, repression, and "human engineering."

the status quo includes war, crime, discrimination, injustice, and repression, we are exhibiting moral indifference—we're copping out.

The greatest social scientists combine "moral vision" with a devotion to careful research. Gunnar Myrdal insists that, since one's values inevitably pervade research, a good social scientist must state and pursue the ethical goals he treasures most highly. His concern with human integration and human equality is reflected in *An American Dilemma*, an analysis of the race problem a generation ago, and currently in books on world poverty.[23] Durkheim, who thought of himself as an objective scientist, made a clear moral commitment to social cohesion or solidarity and a preference for the kind of society that helps each individual to maximize his potential.[24] Alvin Gouldner argues that sociologists should make a conscious moral commitment in their work, and have the courage to be continually aware of the moral and political relevance of that work.[25] Thomas Ford Hoult insists that, since social scientists are *the* specialists in the principles of human behavior, it is "not an indication of scholarly detachment for a sociologist to refuse to indicate which of a variety of alternatives seems most likely, on the basis of available evidence, to contribute to the good society . . . ; it is a cheap avoidance of responsibility."[26]

The authors' position is that a social scientist who ignores the urgent issues of the day is "lecturing on navigation while the ship is going down," in W. H. Auden's phrase. Applications of social science knowledge to problems and policies cannot wait until some distant and unlikely day when grand theories and immutable laws of human behavior are established.

> We can see around us a multitude of problems that call for action, and a multitude of people torn by their imperfect understanding of the situations in which they have to act. What they need are not absolute truths and watertight theories but the skills to guide themselves toward realistic truths and sensible decisions. In this tormented world, the clarifications of which our social science is capable should be thrown productively into the scales.[27]

[23]*The Challenge of World Poverty: A World Anti-Poverty Program in Outline* (New York: Pantheon, 1970).

[24]Leon Bramson, "Social Theory," in Norman MacKenzie, ed., *A Guide to the Social Sciences* (New York: New American Library, 1966), pp. 169–71.

[25]"Anti-Minotaur: The Myth of a Value-Free Sociology," *Social Problems* 9, No. 3 (Winter 1962): 199–213. See also numerous passages (indexed) in his *The Coming Crisis of Western Sociology*.

[26]". . . Who Shall Prepare Himself to the Battle?" *American Sociologist* 5, No. 1 (Feb. 1968): 3–7. For a different point of view see Walter R. Gove, "Should the Sociology Profession Take Moral Stands on Political Issues?" *American Sociologist* 5, No. 3 (Aug. 1970): 221–23.

[27]Madge, *The Tools of Social Science*, p. 294.

Summary

Trying to find meaning and pattern in the world, people have long relied on such sources of explanation as tradition, authority, common sense, unsystematic observation, intuition, and informal logic—and still rely on them to varying degrees in different societies.

Science, in contrast, is systematic, deliberate, and controlled observation of the empirical world—the world of testable realities. Its aims are description, interpretation, prediction, and control of phenomena in that world. Unlike other sources of knowledge, science is self-correcting; it is always tentative, public, cumulative, and collective. The scientist is ideally objective, precise, honest, open-minded, scholarly, and imaginative. He works best in dynamic, open societies, but even there he is guided by the problems presented him by social institutions.

The systematic study of human society began in the nineteenth century as a response to the change and turmoil of the industrialization process. Three main approaches are exemplified by early social scientists: Karl Marx and Adam Smith were grand theorists or social philosophers; Montesquieu and de Tocqueville were careful observers who described whole societies; Quetelet, LePlay, and Booth were empiricists who used survey and statistical methods.

Although all the social sciences deal with the interactions of people in groups, the various disciplines have developed somewhat different perspectives and emphases. Anthropologists are concerned primarily with culture; sociologists with patterned group relationships; economists with the production, distribution, and consumption of goods and services (wealth); and political scientists with the use of power in keeping social order and effecting social change. Historians contribute perspectives on social order and social change that can be gained only through studying the past.

Sociology takes all human interaction and human relationships as its field, but individual sociologists typically concentrate on some aspect of that field. Increasingly, social science research tends to be quantitative, conducted by teams working in major intellectual centers, and limited to relatively free societies.

A sociologist may adopt an academic or professional role. A nonsociologist may find his personal, professional, and community life enriched by an understanding of the field.

Sociologists and other social scientists contribute to society by testing propositions about man and society, providing a multitude of social facts, identifying trends, and pointing out alternative policies and their likely consequences. They disagree, however, on the proper role of the sociologist in the arena of social and political action.

Our position is that the choice of a problem is guided by values;

the process of investigation should be as objective and dispassionate as possible; but once the conclusions are reached, social scientists have a moral obligation to make clear their implications for the future course of events, and even to recommend alternatives.

We turn, next, to the methods of social inquiry and the content of sociology.

QUESTIONS FOR FURTHER THOUGHT

1. To what extent are prediction and control legitimate aims of social science? Maslow said social science might make the individual *less* predictable to others, but perhaps more predictable to himself. Discuss.

2. Sociologist Alfred McClung Lee insists that we must separate facts and evaluations by dividing scientific curiosity into two questions: "Oh, yeah?" and "So what?" ["Can the Individual Protect Himself Against Propaganda Not in His Interest?" *Social Forces* 39, No. 1 (Oct. 1950): 56–61.] Relate this to the controversy over ethical neutrality.

3. How does the description of sociology presented in this chapter differ from your conception of sociology before you entered the course?

4. Do natural scientists, like sociologists, face a dilemma of ethical neutrality *vs.* involvement? Consider atomic scientists such as Oppenheimer and Teller.

5. In 1964 Alvin Gouldner and Timothy Sprehe polled the members of the American Sociological Association; 27.6% of those who responded had thought, at one time or another, of being clergymen. Gouldner links this finding to Comte's vision of a religion of humanity. Discuss.

6. Why does science flourish best in free, open societies?

7. Whom do you consider today's leading social philosophers? Are they social scientists? To what extent do they base their theories on empirical findings?

8. What disciplines or arts other than the social sciences do you think should be used to guide policy making? Why?

9. It has been observed that almost nothing appeared in sociological journals about Russia during the 1920s and 1930s, about Nazism during the rise of Hitler, and about The People's Republic of China until very recently. Discuss possible and probable reasons for this.

10. There has been a reaction against science and intellectualism among many students, and even professors, in recent years. Maslow points out that "In the political realm, antiscience could wipe out mankind just as easily as could value-free, amoral, technologized science." Discuss Nazism, Fascism, and the counterculture in this connection.

2

The primary research instrument would seem to be the observing human intelligence trying to make sense out of experience.

JOHN DOLLARD

The tremendous growth of sociology in the United States is one manifestation of the continuing efforts of American culture to explore, to cope with, and to control its changing environment.

ALVIN W. GOULDNER

Not everything that can be counted counts, and not everything that counts can be counted.

WILLIAM BRUCE CAMERON

THE CONDUCT OF SOCIAL INQUIRY

THE PROGRAMS OF SOCIOLOGY CONVENTIONS make interesting reading for anyone who wants to know what sociologists think about. At a recent convention of the American Sociological Association, for example, a very random sampling of the seventy-seven sessions (at each of which three or four papers were read and discussed) included "Problems of Getting Sociological Data In and Out of a Computer," "Relative Deprivation as a Force in Ghetto Riots," "Television in the Lives of Disadvantaged Children," "Self-Conceptions in India and the United States," and "The Hippie Community: Deviance and Social Control."

How do sociologists go about investigating such topics? Is sociology primarily a science? What do studies of race relations, the effect of television on children, hippies, Indian and American self-conceptions, and riots have in common with studies of planetary movements, chemical reactions, and biological mutations? How are they different?

In this chapter we shall consider the main philosophies that guide social scientists, the ways in which knowledge is organized in a "social science" such as sociology, and the methods and techniques of research. In succeeding chapters we shall use many of the concepts and generalizations introduced here, and this chapter will serve as a convenient reference for identifying the approaches, methods, and techniques employed in specific studies.

Approaches to Social Inquiry

Social science embraces a variety of approaches. One sociologist may take all of human history as his field of inquiry; another may conduct meticulous studies of the interaction of three or four people. One may try to emulate the precise measurements of the physicist; another may strive to depict group life in all its richness and complexity. Each approach—and those that fall somewhere in between—may be fruitful if properly applied.

DIFFERENCES OF SCALE

Some sociologists take a broad view, examining such things as total societies, world-wide trends (e.g., modernization), historical phenomena, or the relationship between personality types and cultural differences. Thus Max Weber related the rise of capitalism to noncomformist Protestant religions; David Riesman associated different character types with social trends; Robert MacIver focused on the competing claims of social order and individual conscience; and Robin M. Williams, Jr., analyzed American society.[1]

Reacting against the fact that many large-scale or "macroscopic" studies shade into social philosophy (à la Comte and Marx), American sociologists have typically concentrated on smaller, "microscopic" problems: family relationships, juvenile delinquency, the social roles of waitresses and doctors, the self-conceptions of executives and convicts, the relationship between patterns of childrearing and class status. Sometimes these studies are effectively related to broader themes and theories. Robert Merton has suggested that the most profitable course for some time to come is to attempt to combine low-level empirical generalizations with "theories of the middle range," rather than trying to construct "grand theory." In recent years many younger sociologists have objected to small-scale studies, arguing that they do not come to grips with the great problems of modern society.

POSITIVISM AND HUMANISM

For centuries Western thought has tended toward one or the other of two main approaches: humanism, which stresses individuality and freedom, and positivism, which stresses control over nature by means of dispassionate observation and experimental analysis. Many sociologists try to fuse the two; others argue passionately for one of the two. A **positivist** stresses the need for exact measurement, verifiable propositions rather than speculations, and "hard" data, the things you can see, hear, touch, taste or feel—and measure. Consciously or unconsciously, he often looks to the natural sciences for his methods, and

[1]Weber, *The Protestant Ethic and the Spirit of Capitalism*, trans. Talcott Parsons (New York: Charles Scribner's Sons & Company, Inc., 1948); Riesman, with Nathan Glazer and Reuel Denney, *The Lonely Crowd: A Study of the Changing American Character* (Garden City, N.Y.: Doubleday & Company, Inc., 1955); MacIver, *The Web of Government*, rev. ed. (New York: The Macmillan Company, 1965); Williams, *American Society: A Sociological Interpretation*, 3rd ed. (New York: Alfred A. Knopf, 1970).

tries to be a "no-nonsense, brass-instrument, experimental scientist."[2]

In contrast, a humanistic sociologist makes the most of the fact that he is a man studying his own kind, and thus has an inside track to knowledge that is unavailable to the physicist or chemist. He can feel empathy for those he studies, take their roles imaginatively, adopt their point of view, and thus arrive at a subjective understanding of their lives. Champions of this approach argue that the use of sympathetic understanding compensates for the fact that the human studies can never achieve the formal precision of physics. Without empathy, they insist, we cannot understand the meaning, value, and purpose of human behavior.

The positivist and humanistic approaches are both valuable; indeed they are complementary. "Certainly we need logical thinking and scientific techniques if we are to be effective social scientists; but we also need insight, imagination, an ability to respond to our feelings as well as to understand our observations, a recognition that art and science are components of the same reality."[3] Studies of some social phenomena seem to profit from the positivist, scientific techniques (population studies, ecology, formal organization); others seem more amenable to the humanistic approach (personality, socialization, institutions, culture, social processes). By recognizing both approaches and bringing together the natural and moral worlds of man, sociology may serve as a "third culture" to bridge the gap between the two cultures of science and the humanities noted by novelist C. P. Snow and others.[4]

It should be noted that even the strictest positivist—and even in the more "exact" sciences—may make discoveries or connections and arrive at explanations by means other than painful and plodding calculation. He may have an illuminating flash of insight, a dream, or a sudden inspiration or hunch; and it often comes after he has been fruitlessly pondering a puzzling phenomenon and feels frustrated with the results of the more prosaic means of investigation. Archimedes' leaping out of the bathtub yelling "Eureka!" when the implications of the displacement of water struck him has had many echoes in "Aha!" moments of scientific inspiration.

Furthermore, while predictability and precision are greater in physical than in social science, they are not perfect. Propositions are stated with such qualifiers as: under certain circumstances, so far as we know, other things being equal, at sea level. They are also stated in terms of probabilities: Given A, the probability is from 90 to 95% that B will occur.

[2]George C. Homans, *The Nature of Social Science* (New York: Harcourt Brace Jovanovich, Inc., 1967), p. 4.

[3]Norman MacKenzie, ed., *A Guide to the Social Sciences* (New York: New American Library, 1966), p. 32.

[4]Severyn T. Bruyn, *The Human Perspective in Sociology: The Methodology of Participant Observation* (Englewood Cliffs, N.J.: Prentice-Hall, Inc., 1966), p. 279. The suggestions of Dr. Leon Warshay were most helpful in this section.

The Content of Social Science

DATA

Each social science comprises a body of data, of social facts or findings. Facts are empirically verified (and re-verifiable) statements about phenomena. Some social science facts are "benchmark information," defined as "very comprehensive types of data [that facilitate] the *interpretation* of large amounts of commonly encountered factual information."[5] Data about the distribution of the three major religious groups in the United States, for example, serve as benchmark information against which to measure their distribution in New York City. Other social facts useful to sociologists include examples of data on income distribution, years of schooling, birth and death rates, marriage and divorce rates, the distribution of population, and the composition of the population by age, sex, racial, and ethnic groups.

Facts by themselves are of little use. They gain significance from evaluation, interpretation, definitions, and classifications. The researcher does not seek *all* the facts, but chooses relevant and useful ones, trying not to miss any of them. He has some notions, however, about how the facts fit together, and these lead him to perceive some phenomena and ignore others. If he is more concerned with finding "truth" than with proving his assumptions, he will modify his assumptions on the basis of new facts.

But a science is more than a collection of facts. Data in a science are *organized* by means of concepts, propositions, theories, models, and typologies.

CONCEPTS

A concept is a word or phrase abstracted from concrete experience; it represents a class of phenomena. For example, the concept "chair" represents a wide variety of objects constructed to hold one person with his back supported and his feet (usually) on the floor. Concepts serve to make perceptual experience intelligible. Before Galileo's time, motion was thought of as an inherent property of particular objects. Galileo and his contemporaries abstracted the idea of motion from the objects themselves. "Motion, as such, became a subject of experimental and reflective study resulting in the law of falling bodies, Kepler's law of planetary motion, leading eventually to the law of

[5]James L. Price, *Social Facts: Introductory Readings* (New York: The Macmillan Company, 1969) p. v.

gravitation."[6] Similarly, until Pasteur fashioned the concept of the infinitely small—bacteria—anthrax in cattle was a puzzling and problematic phenomenon.

Concepts such as culture, social class, reference groups, and values help sociologists to perceive and explain the workings of social order. (It is fascinating to hear a person who has acquired "the sociological imagination" discuss a commonplace event—say, a party you both attended—using concepts that illuminate processes of interaction, interpersonal relationships, and human motives.) Without concepts, sociology would be merely a catalogue of isolated phenomena.

Many sociological concepts are taken from everyday usage. They are, however, refined by careful definition, so that they can serve as sharp tools for analysis. Such ordinary words as class, society, status, role, and race all have special, precise meanings in sociological thinking, and to present them and their relations to one another is one of the chief tasks of an introductory course.

Although these basic concepts are simple enough, the feeling persists that it is somehow wrong to define them in simple language and to delineate their interrelationships in straightforward prose. In every science there are some who resemble Gladstone, who, according to Disraeli, was "inebriated with the exuberance of his own verbosity." Like the lyricist W. S. Gilbert's young man in the operetta *Patience* (1881), the person who writes obscurely perhaps wants people to think of him,

> "If this young man expresses himself in terms too deep for me,
>
> Why, what a very singularly deep young man this deep young man must be!"

There is also the possibility that he cannot express himself clearly because he cannot think clearly. A good idea can usually survive statement in simple words. In fact, many a high-flown theory, when deflated by simple language, collapses like a pricked balloon.

PROPOSITIONS

A **proposition** is a statement of a relationship between two or more facts or concepts. To be scientific, a proposition must be open to proof or disproof. The proposition that an Indian rain dance, when properly performed, will produce rain, is unscientific because it isn't susceptible to proof: A failure to bring rain simply means to the tribe that it was not properly performed.

There are several kinds of propositions. One is a hypothesis that has not yet been tested but is testable: If A, then B (and, perhaps,

[6]Herbert Blumer, *Symbolic Interactionism* (Englewood Cliffs, N.J.: Prentice-Hall, Inc., 1969), p. 159.

because of C). Another is an empirically verified generalization—for example, The rate of intergenerational mobility between classes is currently about the same in all industrialized nations. This is the most common usage. A proposition referring to invariant associations is a law; it is universally agreed upon within a science and accepted with confidence. The most often-cited example is Boyle's law: The volume of gas in an enclosed space is inversely proportional to the pressure on it. There are, as yet, few laws in the social sciences, but this does not mean that human behavior is, in principle, unpredictable.

THEORY

Facts, then, are verified statements about phenomena; concepts enable us to perceive or think about phenomena and communicate about them; and propositions are statements of relationships among concepts and/or facts. None of them, however, *explains* the phenomena and their relationships. What do the facts *mean*? Answering this question—explaining or making sense of facts—is the main function of theory.

A **theory** is a set of systematically related propositions. It may be empirically grounded, interpretative, or philosophical. In the first type, "Theory, inquiry, and empirical fact are interwoven in a texture of operation with theory guiding inquiry, inquiry seeking and isolating facts, and facts affecting theory. The fruitfulness of their interplay is the means by which an empirical science develops."[7]

Interpretative theory may or may not be firmly related to empirical findings; typically it is less rigorous, but it is also legitimate and important, for its aim is

> not to form scientific propositions but to outline and define life situations so that people may have a clearer understanding of their world, its possibilities of development, and the directions along which it may move. In every society, particularly a changing society, there is a need for meaningful clarification of basic social values, social institutions, modes of living, and social relations. This need cannot be met by empirical science, even though some help may be gained from analysis made by empirical science.[8]

David Riesman's interpretation of the changes in character and personality in changing societies is an example of this kind of theory.[9]

---

[7]Blumer, *Symbolic Interactionism*, p. 141.

[8]*Ibid.*, p. 140. Blumer also mentions policy theory, concerned with analyzing a given situation, structure, or action as a basis for policy or action. It is related to concrete situations, such as racial integration in a certain city.

[9]See p. 468 for a discussion of his theory.

Social philosophy is not generally considered social *science* theory, for it typically deals not with what is but with ideas of what *ought* to be, of the ideal society. Marxism and Comte's positive philosophy are examples. But such theories play a useful role in stimulating thinking about social goals.

Whether empirically grounded or interpretative, a good theory not only gives meaning to facts and direction and purpose to research, but also helps us see what is similar about different things, and what is different about things that look alike. Emile Durkheim built a theory of suicide by relating it to the degree of social cohesion in different groups such as Catholics and Protestants, married and unmarried people, and other categories.[10] Erving Goffman shows us similarities in such different institutions as convents, marine boot camps, mental hospitals, and prisons, by applying a set of propositions regarding resocialization and self-identity.[11] Theory also promotes the growth of the body of knowledge in a science by serving as a framework into which bits of knowledge are fitted. It serves as a pattern that gives structure. If one piles up bricks haphazardly, he winds up with a pile of bricks; if he fits them into a pattern he helps build a house.

MODELS

A model is a "guiding metaphor" or analogy that serves as the skeleton of a theory; it is applied to some complex phenomenon and compared to it in *form* but not in content. The most common metaphors applied to society are the organism model, patterned after biology, and the machine model, patterned after physics. The organic model of society suggests that social groups and institutions are like organs with specialized functions that contribute to the health and survival of the society as a whole and are in turn nourished by it. In the machine model the individual is thought of as a part fixed by his social positions, moved by the specifications of his role, and controlled by interaction with other parts; society as a whole is seen as a machine moving through cycles, and fixed by tinkering. A third model is the cybernetic model, which stresses the processing of information and feedback as important elements in interaction. Other models use such analogies for social interaction as drama, ritual, and games.[12]

Models generate ideas, and guide conceptualization and research. The danger is that the analogy may be overworked, carried too far, even reified; society may be thought of as really *being* an organism rather than simply being *similar* to an organism.

[10]*Suicide*, trans. George Simpson (New York: The Free Press, 1951).

[11]*Asylums: Essays on the Social Situation of Mental Patients and Other Inmates* (New York: Doubleday & Company, Inc., 1961).

[12]For a more detailed discussion of these models and their application to questions of social interaction, see Chapter 7.

TYPOLOGIES

Another way of bringing order and meaning to facts is to classify them according to some typology. A **typology** is a way of grouping data and ideas, giving reference points that provide orientation for research and understanding.

Typologies may be logically constructed, or they may emerge naturally out of empirical observation. One kind of logical typology, which can be neatly fitted into a four-fold table, covers all the possible relationships between two variables (actions or attributes that can be measured or categorized). By constructing a table showing the relationship between sex and income we create four types: males with incomes under $9000 a year, females with incomes under $9000 a year, and so on. (The figures are not "social facts" but are purely illustrative.)

PERCENTAGE OF LABOR FORCE EARNING ABOVE AND BELOW
THE MEDIAN INCOME, ACCORDING TO SEX

	INCOME	
	BELOW $9,000 A YEAR	$9,000 A YEAR OR ABOVE
Male	45%	55%
Female	85%	15%

This typology suggests a number of problems. What does it mean? To what extent is it explained by sex discrimination? What are the "census characteristics"—other than sex—of the people in each of the four cells—i.e., their age, education, ethnic background? What further refinements of the table would be necessary to test hypotheses about comparative incomes for men and women doing the same work?

"Ideal types" are another kind of logical typology. They may be based on reality, but they need not correspond to any one instance and may not fit any single empirical observation. Ideal types may also be consciously constructed or deduced from ideas rather than empirically induced from reality.

An ideal type may stand alone: e.g., the "economic man" of classical economics—a person with perfect foresight, rationality, freedom, mobility, and communication with others (a deduction from ideas). Or two ideal types may be thought of as *polar types*, with opposite and contrasting characteristics, standing at the extreme ends of a line or continuum. Examples are extroverted and introverted personalities, and folk and urban societies.[13] While idealizations such as economic men

[13]Folk and urban societies are discussed in Chapters 8 and 15.

have no actual counterparts—economic men "exist only in the pages of certain books and journals, and in the professional conversation of economists"[14]—polar types may exist, and all concrete instances may be placed somewhere along the continuum between them. The folk–urban continuum, for example, provides a framework for the comparative analysis of societies and is useful in the study of social change in a modernizing society.

Natural typologies emerge from observation of a situation. The observer may group people or events as he sees likenesses and differences, or he may find that the group itself has already distinguished natural types. For example, in *The Ghetto*, Louis Wirth reports on various social types already labeled as such in the Jewish culture: the *Mensch*, who has proudly kept his identity as a Jew while achieving superior economic status; the "allrightnik," an opportunist who has thrown overboard the cultural baggage of the group; the helpless shiftless *schlemiel* who fails in everything he undertakes; the *Luftmensch*, who moves easily from one unsuccessful project to another, apparently living on air; the otherworldly Talmudic student; the elderly orthodox Jew whose conduct is exemplary, and so on.[15] Wirth saw this natural typology as a complete index of the cultural traits and patterns of the group, as direct expressions of group values. Natural typologies are richly suggestive and broad-ranging. Logical typologies, in comparison, must leave out a great deal in order to serve as reference points for very specific problems in research.

Methods and Techniques of Social Research

The words "method" and "technique" are often used interchangeably. Generally, however, method refers to a broad approach such as the quantitative or qualitative method, or to a general study design such as the case study or survey method. The word technique refers to a more specific procedure such as administration of a Rorschach test, the statistical technique called factor analysis, or a technique for administering a mass survey of public opinion.

The research process is often described as if it were clearly divided into a series of steps that follow, logically and chronologically, one after another. In actual practice—in any science—the process is not so neat: The phases are intertwined, and there may be backtracking as fresh insights are achieved and more interesting problems suggested. The following discussion, therefore, is not of a series of steps but of various aspects of the process, which *tend* to take place serially.

[14]Robert Brown, *Explanation in Social Science* (Chicago: Aldine Publishing Company, 1963), p. 181.
[15]*The Ghetto* (Chicago: University of Chicago Press, 1928).

EXPLORATORY RESEARCH

In all social inquiry, Herbert Blumer insists, the first step should be to develop a base of close familiarity with the area of social life under study. Human beings have a persistent tendency to build up separate social worlds. Whether he is studying the social world of ghetto-dwellers, corporation managers, adolescent drug users, religious cultists, soldiers, professional politicians, revolutionaries, or any other category of people, the investigator should get close to them, see how they meet a variety of situations, note their problems and how they handle them, join their conversations, watch their life as it flows along.[16]

Such exploratory study is indicated even when an experimental or mathematical method is planned for the actual collection of data. By immersing himself in the social world, the investigator will choose problems and select and analyze data on the basis of what is actually taking place and what it means to the people involved, rather than on the basis of his preconceived notions and ideas; he will be less likely to overlook something important or to impose his own meanings on what he sees. Sometimes such a naturalistic inquiry will by itself answer the problems that come up, but often it is a preliminary to more formalized inquiry.

CHOICE OF A PROBLEM

The investigator usually chooses a problem that he considers important and that he feels he can get involved in; his choice, then, arises out of his particular interests or values. Throughout his study a core problem or set of problems guides and focuses his work and helps him avoid wasteful and aimless data-gathering.

Somehow he must justify his choice. Is there a shortage of data for some theory, or a shortage of important knowledge about some area or social world? He searches the books and journals to see what has already been done, to avoid duplication of research and to find new leads. In some cases a policy-making agency or a professional group may set the problem for him. He may wish to test the validity of some generalization (whether common-sense or scientific) or to try out a new technique.[17]

FORMULATION OF HYPOTHESES

Many nonsociologists explore other social worlds and think about the same problems as do sociologists. What, then, marks off the

[16]Blumer, *Symbolic Interactionism*, p. 40.

[17]Much of this section draws on a course in Methods of Social Research taught by Dr. Louis Ferman at Wayne State University in 1960.

sociologist from other observers of human behavior? James A. Davis
puts it this way:

> Some students find it hard to think like a sociologist, not because a
> sociologist's thought is so eccentric, but because at first glance it ap-
> pears so similar. By and large, sociologists think about the same
> things everybody does: friends, family, personal opinions, groups,
> organizations, money, and sex. What is different is the intellectual
> framework: The professional sociologist tends to think in terms of a
> *structure of probabilistic relationships among operationally interpreted
> variables.*[18]

A **variable** is an action or attribute that can be measured (degree
of modernism) or categorized (sex). A **hypothesis** is a statement of a
probable or expected relationship between two or more variables: If A,
then B. Thus variable A may be the attribute of education, B the act of
voting. The hypothesis may be stated as a cause-and-effect relationship
—A causes B—or as a statistical correlation—A is associated with B.
It may also be stated as a *null* hypothesis: A, education, and B, voting
behavior, are *not* associated; the degree of education makes no difference
in voting. Null hypotheses lend themselves well to statistical testing.
    When two variables are being tested, one is termed the depen-
dent variable, the other the independent one. Thus in the preceding hypothesis, voting behavior, the dependent variable, is assumed to be
related (or not related) to education, the independent variable. But it
might also be related to sex, rural or urban residence, age, income, or
occupation. The sociologist tries to control the variables, making sure
he screens out the effects of all other independent variables on voting
behavior so that he comes close to the truth about its relation to education. Scholarship in the field and scrutiny of the empirical social world
are especially important in helping the scientist to realize what possible
variables might be associated with the variable he is trying to understand. And knowledge of statistical techniques helps him to unscramble
the effects of these variables.
    The hypothesis may also include an intervening variable: If A,
then B, because of C. We may find that Catholics tend to vote Democratic more often than do Protestants. But is this a direct correlation
between religion and politics, or is there an intervening variable? Perhaps, we hypothesize, the foreign-born tend to vote Democratic more
than the native-born, and the foreign-born are also more likely to be
Catholics; ethnicity, then, is the intervening variable, the explanatory
connection in the reformulated hypothesis.
    It is necessary, especially with quantitative studies, to state the
variables in terms of indices or operational definitions that are measur-

[18]*Elementary Survey Analysis* (Englewood Cliffs, N.J.: Prentice-Hall, Inc., 1971),
    pp. 1–2.

able and testable. Ideally, an *index* is perfectly correlated with what it signifies and more perceptible than the variable for which it stands. Suppose we advance the hypothesis, The higher a person's social class, the greater will be his intelligence, or vice versa. We may operationally define intelligence in terms of score on IQ tests, social class in terms of income. Although both are controversial and crude measures, they are frequently used as indices because they are numerical and easily measured. The rate of absenteeism may be taken as an index of morale in a work group; the number of housing starts as an index of economic prosperity. In surveys concerned with such abstract variables as prejudice, happiness, or modernism, the measures may be indirect.[19] A doctor does not ask a patient if he has heart disease; he asks a series of questions about shortness of breath, pain in the chest, and other indicators which are part of his operational definition of heart disease.

A good hypothesis is simple, tight, and concise, capable of disproof as well as of proof. It is a plausible, educated guess, but not too ridiculously self-evident or obvious. In the early stages of research, the investigator may brainstorm a dozen or more hypotheses, choose several working hypotheses, and as he goes along, refine and narrow them down to one or two research hypotheses. As he begins his work, theory helps him formulate hypotheses; as he analyzes his data, theory helps him explain why research has confirmed or negated his hypothesis.

RESEARCH DESIGN

While exploring the social world and choosing problems for study, the social scientist must also choose a research design. He may decide that his hypotheses can best be tested by means of a sample survey, a case study, an experiment, or a combination of two or all three methods.

The **sample survey** is very popular among sociologists, social psychologists studying attitudes, political scientists, and economists in certain fields, such as market research. The "sample" is a statistical term for a number of people chosen from a "population" such as freshman college students, voters, farmers, adult females, and so on. A trained statistician selects the sample so that he can, with very little error, draw conclusions about the whole population from a small portion of it. The "survey" is the collection of data on the relevant variables—the career ambitions of freshmen, the probable presidential choice of voters, the income of farmers, the number of children born to females of a certain age. The questionnaire must be very carefully drawn up, however, so that it is *valid*—that is, it measures what it purports to measure. There

[19]See Joseph A. Kahl, *The Measurement of Modernism: A Study of Values in Brazil and Mexico* (Austin: The University of Texas Press, 1968), for lucid explanations of the research process, including the use of operational definitions of values.

Handelsman in the *Saturday Review*.

*"I'm doing a survey of lower-middle-class life.
May I come in and unobtrusively plug in
my tape recorder?"*

are also problems of *reliability*: Is it measuring accurately? Perhaps some people will not or cannot answer correctly or at all, and the results are thrown off.

The questions asked in a sample survey—which is essentially a mass interview—are usually simple and direct: Their aim is to discover objective facts or indices of attitudes and opinions. Usually "census data" are sought, so that whatever the dependent variables of the study, they may be correlated with some or all of the following independent variables: sex, age, race, rural or urban residence, education, income, occupation, religion, marital status, and so on. The questions relevant to the dependent variables must be carefully phrased in ways that have been demonstrated to elicit valid and reliable responses.

Sample surveys are especially useful in measuring changes over time; repeating them provides information about social change. Surveys also supply information about the correlation of variables, such as income and political affiliation. They measure large numbers of people on a few characteristics. The most familiar example is the public opinion poll.

A **case study**, in contrast, is an "in depth" examination of one person, group, or culture, usually over a long period of time. Community studies such as *Middletown* are essentially case studies, as are studies of changing neighborhoods, street corner gangs, or the life histories of psychotics. Because they are based on a sample of one person, group, or area, case studies rarely *prove* anything, but they are rich sources of ideas and provide insights that come only with intensive probing.

In an **experiment** the investigator intervenes in the situation to control or manipulate a variable and observe or measure the result. Usually he seeks to keep all other variables constant; often he introduces the variable into one group but not into a "control group." A student of nutrition might give two groups of rats the same diet, except that he deprives one group of Vitamin B-12. A social psychologist may attempt to determine the effect of propaganda by measuring the attitudes of two groups with matched characteristics, then exposing the experimental group to some propaganda, and remeasuring attitudes.

The experiment is a highly efficient method of research, especially in untangling cause-and-effect relationships. Experimental intervention in the social sciences, however, is limited by moral and humanitarian considerations. We can hardly bring up one group of children one way and another quite differently under laboratory conditions. But experiments may occur naturally. Psychologists have compared the health and intelligence of babies brought up by their own mothers in prison and babies brought up by nurses in a foundling home. Two Paraguayan villages may be much alike; when one becomes the site of a cotton mill, we can measure the effects of industrialization by comparing the two.

Intervention, even when morally acceptable, may alter the situation being studied in such a way that one must ask whether the change occurred because of the variable being manipulated or because of the investigator's presence. In the famous Hawthorne experiment, a group of women who worked together in a factory for a long period constantly increased their output regardless of whether they had more light or less, more rest periods or fewer, piecework or straight wages. The causal variable, as it turned out, was the feeling that the experimenter was interested in them, and their morale was consequently high.[20] Despite its precision, then, the experimental method is best used in combination with other methods.

COLLECTION OF DATA

A social scientist is above all an asker of questions. He asks them informally in face-to-face conversation, especially in exploratory

[20]Elton Mayo, *The Human Problems of an Industrial Civilization* (New York: The Macmillan Company, 1933).

studies of other social worlds, in case studies, and in anthropological field work; he asks them more formally in questionnaires and structured interviews. Richard Biesanz reports that the people of a Costa Rican village he studied for 7 months called him "El Yanqui Preguntón"— the Yankee who is a great asker of questions.

The investigator also poses questions to himself as he ponders possible problems for study, considers various hypotheses, and checks his understanding of situations. And he takes and files notes. He may take notes on the scene of action, or keep a journal, recording hunches and reflecting on the meaning of his observations. He may use a tape recorder for interviews, as Oscar Lewis did to great advantage in his case studies of Mexican and Puerto Rican families.[21] He may also make a photographic record of his observations.

In some kinds of studies, data are collected primarily by **participant observation**, which is *the* method of social anthropology. The social scientist immerses himself in the situation and, so far as possible, becomes part of it, living with an Australian tribe, joining funeral processions and fiestas in a Panamanian village, becoming a precinct delegate, standing on the street corner with a gang, merging into the hippie subculture. This method is especially valuable for discovering meanings and values and patterns of personal relationships. Unlike the survey method, it focuses on behavior as it is occurring rather than as it is recalled, and thus reveals the continuity of events. Participant observation has drawbacks, however. The group may behave differently because an outsider is present, although chances are that he will soon be taken for granted. If he is successful in participating, he may even learn to think as they think, but if he becomes too involved he may lose his objectivity. He must decide whether to be straightforward about the fact that he is investigating them, or to adopt a "cover" role at the risk of being exposed and accused of bad faith. He must also decide when to participate actively and when to observe passively.

Nonparticipant observation is more easily structured, and in some cases, as in indirect observation of nursery-school groups through a one-way window, the observed are unaware of the observer. The observer carefully notes the time, the people involved, regularities in interaction and deviations from these regularities, indices of group cohesiveness, and many other factors. Categories have been constructed into which observations of small-group interaction, for example, may be fitted. Behavior in disasters, riots, classrooms, and playgrounds has been observed by similar methods.[22]

Whether one is studying a person, a group, or a whole society,

[21]Oscar Lewis, *The Children of Sánchez: Autobiography of a Mexican Family* (New York: Random House, Inc., 1961) and *La Vida: A Puerto Rican Family in Culture of Poverty—San Juan and New York* (New York: Random House, Inc., 1965).

[22]See John Madge, *The Tools of Social Science* (London: Longmans, Green & Co., 1953), Chap. 3, "Observation," pp. 117–43, for an excellent discussion.

the art of watching and listening—and taking systematic notes—is essential to fruitful investigation. When one of Ernest Burgess's students complained to him about the talkative landlady in the rooming-house where he was living while collecting data about homeless men, Burgess pointed out that instead of being bored when she told her life story, the student should see it as an invaluable opportunity to find out what kind of person becomes a rooming-house keeper and why, what her problems are, and how she keeps her house orderly in a slum area.[23]

In addition to observing, listening, asking questions, and recording observations and the answers to questions, the sociologist may turn to documentary sources—public records such as census statistics, economic data systematically gathered by special agencies, minutes of meetings, organizational records, election records, historical archives, books, periodicals, newspapers, and manuscripts. In community studies, maps, telephone books, and city directories are also useful.

To grasp a situation of any depth and complexity, the investigator usually finds that a combination of research designs and techniques is most likely to assure him of valid conclusions. The camera and tape recorder (figurative or literal) of exploratory research may well be supplemented by the telescope of a sample survey, the microscope of a case study, and the test tube of an experiment. It is tempting to use survey methods alone, simply because they provide numerical data that are easily fed into a computer. But there is a danger that the conclusions, though precise, will be trivial or meaningless or both. "Not everything that can be counted counts, and not everything that counts can be counted."[24]

ANALYSIS, INTERPRETATION, AND PUBLICATION

The process of analysis and interpretation is continuous; it does not begin when the data are in. Analysis is the means of finding the relationships of variables, the connections between the data. They may be established by judicious reflection or by statistical correlation. The formulation of hypotheses anticipates the analysis; the more precise they are, and the better the operational definitions, the easier the analysis.

[23]Ernest W. Burgess and Donald J. Bogue, eds., *Urban Sociology* (Chicago: University of Chicago Press, 1967), p. 9. Other sources of data for an intensive case study of a person might include interviews with people who know him, personality tests, diaries, and letters. In their study *The Polish Peasant in Europe and America*, Vols. 1 and 2 (New York: Dover Publications, Inc., 1971) W. I. Thomas and Florian Znaniecki paid special attention to the subjective factor, finding their data in "human documents," especially life histories.

[24]William Bruce Cameron, *Informal Sociology: A Casual Introduction to Sociological Thinking* (New York: Random House, Inc., 1963), p. 13.

Interpretation relates the findings to theory; it suggests why the connections between data exist. Here most of the work goes on above the eyebrows. "Why?" is not automatically answered. The data must be interpreted if they are to add to the fund of social science knowledge and lead to further hypotheses and research.

Finally, the data and interpretations, complete with an account of procedures, must be made public. Research findings are often presented at professional meetings, published as books or as articles in scholarly journals, or filed as graduate theses. In each case they are available for scrutiny and criticism. The growth of science depends less on the cool objectivity of individual scientists than on the fact that their work is open to the appraisal of and use by others.

Summary

Some sociologists study world-wide phenomena, such as modernization; others concentrate on smaller problems, such as juvenile delinquency. Most research is either positivist and modeled after research in the physical sciences, or humanistic, a qualitative approach stressing empathy and insight. Both approaches are useful; they may be complementary.

A science is more than a collection of facts. In sociology as in the natural sciences, data are organized by means of concepts, propositions, theories, models, and typologies. The functions of social science theory are to explain facts, guide research, sharpen our perception of reality, and serve as a conceptual framework for the systematic accumulation of knowledge.

The research process consists of several steps that tend to take place serially. Through open-minded exploratory research the sociologist becomes familiar with the area of his concern, and thus is more likely to choose a significant problem. He states this problem in terms of one or more hypotheses, which he tests by means of a sample survey, a case study, an experiment, or a combination of methods. He collects data by various means, above all by asking questions, both formally and informally; by observing, as either a participant or a nonparticipant; and by taking notes and keeping records. Throughout this process he analyzes and interprets data. His final account, with his conclusions, is made public so that other sociologists may criticize it and profit from it.

QUESTIONS FOR FURTHER THOUGHT

1. A statesman once said he did not worry about intelligent, active generals, about intelligent, lazy generals, or about

stupid, lazy generals; the dangerous ones, he said, are the stupid and active ones. Construct a four-fold table according to these variables.

2. What kinds of sociological research would you consider unethical? Why?

3. Speaking of the empirical attitude, Maslow says a child can be scientific watching an anthill. Discuss.

4. Do you think the same person might be temperamentally suited to be equally good as a sociologist or as a physicist? Discuss.

5. Robin Williams says that when we see a paradox or a contradiction, a variable has been left out. Look for examples and try to supply possible missing variables.

6. The two major tools of the scientist are theory and empirical research. What would the state of science be if some scientists ignored one of these tools? How do they complement each other?

7. Name some situations in which it would be wiser to use indirect observation rather than participant observation. Why is this?

8. Formulate two hypotheses using each of the three formats suggested on page 40 of the text.

9. State Goode's "facts" about the family (p. 11) in the form of a hypothesis. What methods and techniques would you employ to investigate them?

10. Is an empiricist necessarily a positivist?

Part One

MAN
AND
CULTURE

Human society is a complex system of relationships among individuals and groups, based on shared values, beliefs, and behavior patterns—that is, on culture. Society (a system of relationships) and culture (a system of common understandings) together form a "social order" with structure, pattern, stability, and adaptability.

Society casts the players, culture writes the script, and "one man in his time plays many parts." In Part One we discuss the scripts that are handed to the players as they come on stage. These scripts are often referred to as "blueprints" or "designs for living." But beware of reifying culture, of making it real rather than abstract, a force that does things by itself. Powerful as it is, culture is no more than a guide. It is *people* who learn the script and either play their roles accordingly, or ad lib, or forget, or change the lines as the drama proceeds. Keep this in mind when you read that "culture is" this and "culture does" that.

A thorough grasp of the culture concept is essential to sociological understanding. It helps the student avoid extreme ethnocentrism, the habit of thinking and judging strictly in terms of the ideas, beliefs, and values of his own group. It sharpens awareness of alternative ways of arranging things, different from those that we take for granted. Robert Lynd sees the common task of all social scientists as understanding a culture in all its ramifications, past and present. American social scientists, for example, can most fruitfully state their research problems in terms of "the whole context of our fumbling institutional past and of our but rudely coordinated present" (*Knowledge For What?*).

Anthropology and sociology are the most closely related of the social sciences, and cover much the same ground. "Anthropology" comes from Greek words meaning "the study of man." (Bronislaw Malinowski added, "the study of man, embracing woman.") It tends to emphasize the qualitative-humanistic approach far more than does most sociological research. Nothing human is alien to the anthropologist, whether or not it lends itself to measurement. He is concerned with human beings all over the world, with man's past, with his biology, psychology, knowledge, actions, tangible and intangible products, relationships, dreams, emotions, the way he walks, eats, sleeps, and talks, and what he believes and wants and values.

Early anthropology was conducted mostly by "armchair" scholars who relied on the reports of travelers and explorers and missionaries. In the early eighteenth century, many believed primitive tribes were remnants of a lost Paradise in which men were noble savages, not yet corrupted by civilization. Later, the overwhelming concept of evolution dominated anthropological thought, and scholars sought evidence that man progressed from savagery through barbarism to civilization.

Modern anthropologists are typically "field workers" at least part of the time. They live for long periods in a community, whether a jungle or peasant village, a small town in Mississippi or Quebec, Hollywood or a ghetto. They gather their material at first hand, largely by participant observation. They are, in Walt Whitman's words, "both in and out of the game, and watching and wondering at it." They seek answers to two main questions: How and why is human nature alike all over the world? How and why is it different? They also ask what consequences these differences have for society and personality, and how anthropological insights can contribute to the enrichment of human life.

As you read Part One, you will become aware that almost everything you do is culturally conditioned, even though you take your own culture as much for granted as the air you breathe. In Chapter 3 we deal with the biological basis of culture and with the patterns and understandings that make up the content of culture: with their similarity and diversity from group to group, and with language as the indispensable basis of culture. We discuss the elements of culture: norms, understandings, material things, and social structures.

The unity and continuity that result from the organization of culture traits into configurations of related elements and from the integrating force of common values and beliefs are the subject of Chapter 4. Chapter 5 is concerned with the functions of culture, and Chapter 6 with the significance of the concept of culture for the student and for mankind as a whole.

THE NATURE AND CONTENT OF CULTURE

Man is the toolmaking, the talking, the symbolizing animal . . . not just the producer of culture but, in a specifically biological sense, its product.

CLIFFORD GEERTZ

Man is the only animal that eats when he is not hungry, drinks when he is not thirsty, and makes love at all seasons.

ANONYMOUS

Don't Be a Litterbug.

AMERICAN STREET SIGN

Please throw your garbage out the window.

SIGN IN A COSTA RICAN BUS

Man's natures are alike; it is their customs that carry them far apart.

CONFUCIUS, c. 500 B.C.

All men are baked of the same dough.

ROMANIAN PROVERB

THE SUBJECT OF CULTURE interests most of us even before we learn to think about it systematically. We like to be "hip" to what is "in." We consider the latest fashions in clothing and music terrific or repulsive. We study foreign languages and ancient civilizations. We tease our parents about funny clothes and hairdos in old picture albums, but search the attic for antique dresses. We read books on Tibet and Polynesia. We admire Indian saris and wonder about the red marks Indian women wear on their foreheads. We compare White House styles of life under different presidents. We buy dresses from Pakistan, ponchos from Mexico, American Indian jewelry; we eat in Italian, French, and Chinese restaurants. We tour museums and markets abroad, and, in the more familiar atmosphere of our own country savor regional differences in speech, food, and dress. We sprinkle our speech with the catchwords of the moment. All these things are part of culture, which the English anthropologist E. B. Tylor defined nearly 100 years ago as "that complex whole which includes knowledge, belief, art, morals, law, custom, and any other capabilities and habits acquired by man as a member of society."[1]

We can define culture in both a general and a specific sense. In the general sense, **culture** is the *learned* portion of human behavior, the patterned ways of thinking, feeling, and doing that man himself has developed and made part of his environment. Culture adapts man to his physical environment, his biological nature, and his group life. In the specific sense, **a culture** is the distinctive way of life of a society; it is that combination of behavior and beliefs that makes one society different from another. It is learned and shared by members of the group, and presented to the growing child as the social heritage of past generations. Although highly stable, a culture changes through time, and it spreads from group to group.[2]

In this chapter we stress the learning and sharing of culture, made possible by man's biological nature and his group life. We pay

[1]*Primitive Culture* (London: John Murray, 1871), p. 21.
[2]Not until Chapter 14 will we deal with the processes of cultural change, after we have explored at some length the idea that society, personality, and culture are all bound together in the human situation and that we can pull them apart only in the abstract, for analysis and study.

particular attention to language as the basis of learning and sharing. Then we consider the major elements of culture: norms; knowledge, beliefs, and values; material objects; and social structures. We consider some similarities and differences in cultural systems and ask why they exist.

Culture as Learned Behavior

In our general definition of culture we stated that it is the learned portion of human behavior. All animals learn to some extent, but it is man's superlative learning abilities that make him the only animal able to acquire and build culture. In this section we look first at the human species and at the biological characteristics that enable man to adapt through culture. Then we consider language, man's chief mechanism for learning and hence for acquiring culture.

THE HUMAN SPECIES

Man is a biological organism that, like other animals, takes in organic food and oxygen, moves, reproduces, and dies. Biologists classify man in the *phylum* CHORDATA because he, like the other chordates, has a group of cells along the back that help to stiffen the body and serve as the central cord of the nervous system. Like other members of the *subphylum* VERTEBRATA he has a bony spinal column. The Vertebrata are further subdivided into *classes*, including the MAMMALIA, which embraces man and other warm-blooded animals that bear live young and suckle them. Of the various *orders* of mammals, man, along with apes, monkeys, lemurs, and tarsiers, is placed in the PRIMATE order. The *suborder* ANTHROPOIDEA includes the great apes, such as the chimpanzee and the gorilla, as well as man. Within this suborder, man belongs to the *family* HOMINIDAE, or "man-like," which includes only modern man and his ancestors. Within this family man is the only member of the *species* SAPIENS (wise) of the *genus* HOMO (man).[3]

[3]A biological species may be defined as "an evolutionary unit composed of continuing populations, that regularly interchange genes by interbreeding and that do not or cannot have such regular interchange with other species." [George Gaylord Simpson, "The Biological Nature of Man," in S. L. Washburn and Phyllis C. Jay, eds., *Perspectives on Human Evolution* (New York: Holt, Rinehart & Winston, Inc., 1968), pp. 6–7.] The earth is thought to be about 4 or 4.5 billion years old. The first organic life may have appeared about 3.5 billion years ago; the first vertebrates, 550 million years ago; mammals, perhaps 200 million years ago; Hominids, probably 12 to 14 millions years ago, and maybe earlier. Manlike creatures certainly lived in Africa 2 million years ago.

Drawing by Ton Smits; © 1968 The New Yorker Magazine, Inc.

"Me Homo sapiens."

Although there is disagreement on dates and classifications of early man and his ancestors, and they are constantly being revised in the light of new discoveries, it is generally agreed that the species *Homo sapiens* is the result of a long, long process of evolution, and that this process began in Africa, when a creature ancestral to man came down out of the trees and began to walk upright, thus freeing his hands to use tools.

THE EVOLUTION OF CULTURE

Culture did not begin when *Homo sapiens* made his appearance, but long before. Anthropologists used to think that evolving man reached some "critical point" at which his brain was sufficiently large for him to develop language and other cultural forms—in short, that organic evolution preceded cultural evolution. The present view, however, is that man's cultural evolution accompanied his biological evolution, and each contributed to the other. As man made culture, so culture made man; as he manipulated tools, his hands and eyes fed messages back to the brain. Natural selection favored those who had the greatest manual dexterity and foresight, the greatest success in the hunt.[4]

[4]Clifford Geertz, "The Impact of the Concept of Culture on the Concept of Man," in Yehudi A. Cohen, ed., *Man in Adaptation: The Cultural Present* (Chicago: Aldine Publishing Co., 1968), pp. 16–29.

HUMAN LEARNING CAPACITY

Homo sapiens differs from all the other members of the animal kingdom in his capacity for learning, for communicating, and for manipulating physical objects. This capacity is due both to his lack of some biological traits that other animals have, and to traits he has that others lack.

Man is highly flexible and adaptable because he *lacks* (1) the fixed, inborn patterns of behavior and (2) the specific biological adaptations to environment that other animals have. He is born with only a few reflexes, or automatic responses, each attached to a given stimulus. His pupils contract in strong light. His salivary glands "water" when he is hungry and when food is placed before him. His muscles contract when he feels pain. His nervous system governs his breathing, heartbeat, digestion, and excretion with relatively little voluntary modification on his part. But aside from these few reflexes he inherits no fixed patterns of response. Much animal behavior is governed by instincts— inherited modes of behavior that have a physiological basis, clearly determine behavior, and are universal in expression in the species.[5] Human behavior is not. The old idea that war stemmed from man's "pugnacious instinct," for example, does not explain why man is not constantly at war, nor why some tribes never fight others. Even the "maternal instinct" is learned. Little girls and childless women act maternal; surgery and old age, which eradicate or atrophy the childbearing organs, do not alter a mother's love for her children as they would if the love depended only on a physiological basis. Moreover, some mothers reject their children, and infanticide is practiced in many societies.

We also said that man lacks specific biological adaptation to environmental conditions. The polar bear's heavy coat, the elephant's tusks, the rabbit's protective coloring, and the fish's fins and gills are all extremely useful under certain conditions. But few animals are fitted for more than one kind of climate, food supply, or life situation. Their remarkable adaptation to one set of surroundings makes them unable to live in many others. The lack of specific biological adaptations allows man to be highly flexible because he is free to create his own adaptations (in the form of culture) to different conditions. In fact evolving man *had* to create culture in order to adapt.

On the positive side, what biological characteristics does man possess that help him to build and acquire culture, the human means of adapting to the environment? For one thing, he has a *prehensile* (grasping) *hand*, and a *thumb* that he can oppose to each of his four long fingers. Thus he can manipulate and create with his hands. His hands, moreover, are freed for doing work by his *upright posture*. He can stand

[5]We may note here that even in the lower animals much behavior is the result of early and rapid learning—but always in the presence of the object.

on his two long legs because his *curved spine* and his *arched foot* cushion the shock of walking and prevent injury to his brain. He also has *binocular vision,* and can focus his eyes for different distances.

The great apes and monkeys, man's distant cousins, share these three attributes with him to some degree, and they have been seen by trained observers and experimental psychologists to make and use rudimentary tools to reach food. The use of tools is one of the *necessary* bases for society and culture—in fact, for the evolution of *Homo sapiens* himself from prehuman forms of man. But it is not a *sufficient* basis for culture. Culture is based primarily on language; and only man, it seems clear, has the biological traits that make it possible to speak and write and think abstractly.

The crucial biological differences between man and the rest of the animal kingdom, then, are those that make language possible. First, man's *vocal apparatus* enables him to articulate a variety of sounds. Compared to the primates, his jaws are smaller and less protruding, and he has no obstructions to interfere with the free movement of his tongue. But far more important, he has a *complex nervous system* including a large and complex *brain.* About three times as large as the gorilla's, man's brain is even larger in relation to his body weight. It is composed of three main parts, each evolved at a different stage. One is essentially reptilian, the second is mammalian, and the third—the neocortex—is the human "thinking cap" containing the areas responsible for language, and for abstract and symbolic thought. The neocortex contains perhaps 10 billion nerve endings, each connected with hundreds and sometimes thousands of other nerve cells. Fast as computers can solve problems (fed them by man), no machine is remotely like the brain in complexity and versatility. (It is reported that a sign on the wall of the IBM office in Tokyo reads: MAN—SLOW, SLOVENLY, BRILLIANT; IBM—FAST, ACCURATE, STUPID).[6]

Experimenters have failed to stimulate any vocalization in animals by touching neocortical areas; but they have brought forth regular sounds—emotional cries, for example—by stimulating the limbic system, the older part of the brain. "Speech and language," it is therefore concluded, "clearly depend upon . . . areas for which there simply are no analogues in the brain of any other animal. . . . Man's brain, and man's brain alone is a language-supporting brain."[7] In the words of W. Grey Walter, "No other animal is equipped for being *sapiens.*"[8]

[6]*Saturday Review* (June 1, 1968): 7.

[7]David Krech, "Coming—A New Breed of Brain Changers?" *Current* (Sept. 1969): pp. 55–64; reprinted from "Psychoneurobiochemeducation," *California Monthly* (June–July, 1969). See also John Paul Scott, *Animal Behavior* (Chicago: University of Chicago Press, 1968), especially Chap. 9, "Communication: The Language of Animals," pp. 189–205.

[8]*The Living Brain* (New York: W. W. Norton & Co., Inc., 1963), p. 16.

LANGUAGE AND CULTURE

Language ability is the "real, incomparably important, and absolute distinction" between men and other living organisms.[9] The very limited success of experiments in teaching chimpanzees to communicate in gestures or to recognize words and even create sentences with plastic tokens representing words only points up the enormous gap between human and nonhuman communication.[10]

The Nature of Language. Every culture has a "silent language" of meanings conveyed by gestures, postures, facial expressions, tones of voice, uses of time and space, and even smells.[11] But "language" usually means *words*. To define language more precisely, we must distinguish between natural and conventional signs.

Natural signs derive their meaning from concrete situations— the red glow of burning wood, the falling barometer, the click of a Geiger counter in the presence of radioactive materials, a child's fever at the onset of an illness. Animal cries to warn of danger or to express anger, however, are somewhat different kinds of signs, for they communicate meanings to other animals and thus approach the nature of conventional signs, which are the building blocks of human language.

Conventional signs, or symbols, derive meaning from usage and mutual agreement. They are not naturally and inextricably linked to the things they stand for. There is nothing inherent in a carrot, for example, that demands it be called a "carrot"; it can just as well be called a potato or a proverb if everyone in the group agrees that this combination of sounds refers to a particular elongated, orange-colored, edible root vegetable. Moreover, since the meanings of symbols are not inherent, different cultures can assign different meanings to the same words or gestures. *Hell* means "light" or "bright" in German; the gesture that Americans interpret as beckoning "Come here" is understood by Guatemalans as waving "Goodbye."

All words, then, are symbols. And **languages**, whether spoken or written, are systems of symbols that are voluntarily produced and have a specific and arbitrary meaning in a given society. *Every* human society has a well-developed language. Anthropologists report no tribe

[9]Simpson, "The Biological Nature of Man."

[10]For an account of two such experiments, see John E. Pfeiffer, *The Emergence of Man* (New York: Harper & Row, Publishers, 1969), pp. 396–401. See also *Time* (Sept. 21, 1979).

[11]Edward Hall, *The Silent Language* (Garden City, N.Y.: Doubleday & Co., Inc., 1959) and *The Hidden Dimension* (Garden City, N.Y.: Doubleday, Anchor Books, 1969).

with a vocabulary of fewer than 5,000 to 10,000 words; many "primitive" languages have a grammatical structure far more complicated than that of "civilized" societies. In what ways do these systems of symbols make culture possible?

Functions of Language.   Language is, first of all, a means of communication, of sharing thoughts and feelings. It is not the only one, nor is it a perfect one, but it is a remarkable instrument. It is also the main vehicle of thought, or problem solving. We think in words, the "significant symbols" of our culture, reflecting, weighing alternatives, imagining possibilities.

Language extends and enlarges experience in time, enabling man to remember, to imagine, and to foresee. These abilities are essential to morality and ethics. We can imagine the consequences of various alternative acts. "It is the capacity to predict the outcome of our own actions that makes us responsible for them and that therefore makes ethical judgment of them both possible and necessary."[12] Similarly, language transcends the world of concrete sense experience. Words may stand for something as tangible as one's own hand; they may also stand for abstract ideas such as souls, culture, honesty. Words enable us to visualize an angel with a flaming sword guarding the gates of Paradise; atoms with protons, electrons, neutrons, and nuclei; voodoo rituals; Napoleon's retreat from Moscow; Hobbits; an underground city on a far-off planet. Without language we would have little art, and even less science.

A language guides, even "programs," perception and action. As we saw in Chapter 2, we tend to perceive only those things we have concepts for. A language names and classifies things and people in terms of their significance for behavior: A child learns that the persons called father, friend, enemy, priest, teacher, and customer are each to be treated differently, and that food is to be eaten and poison to be avoided. Eskimo children learn numerous words for different states of what we consider one substance—snow. The Hanunóo of the Philippine Islands have ninety-two words for rice, their staple food.

A common language binds a social group together. Often a language itself is emotionally charged, a symbol to be preserved and defended. In bilingual Paraguay, Spanish is the neutral, necessary language of government, commerce, and schooling. But the old Indian language, Guaraní, is the language of home and friendship, and because it is freighted with emotion it is far more a symbol of nationalism than the flag. The street dialect of the black ghetto is another example. To "speak the same language" is to have a strong bond, whether this language is professional jargon, a criminal's argot, or merely a set of attitudes toward the world.

12Simpson, "The Biological Nature of Man."

Finally, language enables man to preserve and transmit culture, to build a cumulative tradition and pass it on.

Culture as Shared by Members of a Human Group

We have said that culture is learned. To this we must add the essential words "from others." For culture is shared, and socially transmitted. It exists only in a human group.

MAN AS A SOCIAL ANIMAL

Certain evolutionary biological changes contributed to the desire and need of prehumans and humans to live in groups of mixed ages and both sexes. The female is handicapped by pregnancy, and perhaps became more so as her pelvis enlarged to bear an infant with a large brain. But this infant's brain had to grow tremendously in size and power before it could acquire a culture of any complexity, and evolutionary processes therefore favored a longer and longer childhood. During this period humans need protection and nurturing if they are to survive; and their immobilization and dependence permit them to observe, learn, and listen.

The mother, too, needs help and protection not only during pregnancy and lactation but while she is caring for small children. The male wants to stay with her, possibly in part because she (unlike other animals) has no specific season of sexual attractiveness. And she wants to care for her infant because holding, nursing, fondling, and playing with it give her a great deal of pleasure. Attachment, affection, respect, and love were crucial in human evolution. "Social life is rooted in emotion and is basic to survival."[13]

Natural selection favored groups that were effectively organized to find food and water, and to avoid predators. Many anthropologists believe that when man turned to hunting, he greatly increased his adaptability by becoming more mobile, and by learning to cooperate and divide labor, and to establish bonds with other groups. Control of fire increased his adaptability and his attachment to his group even more.[14]

---

[13]David A. Hamburg, "Emotions in the Perspective of Human Evolution," in Sherwood L. Washburn and Phyllis C. Jay (Dolhinow), eds., *Perspectives on Human Evolution* (New York: Holt, Rinehart & Winston, Inc., 1968), pp. 246–57.

[14]For further discussion of early cultural and social evolution see S. L. Washburn and C. S. Lancaster, "The Evolution of Hunting," in *ibid.*, pp. 213–28; Marshall D. Sahlins, "The Origin of Society," in Yehudi A. Cohen, ed., *Man in Adaptation: The Biosocial Background* (Chicago: Aldine Publishing Co., 1968), pp. 108–14; and Kenneth P. Oakley, "Man as Tool-maker," *ibid.*, pp. 13–34; C. Loring Brace, *The Stages of Human Evolution* (Englewood Cliffs, N.J.: Prentice-Hall, Inc., 1967); and Pfeiffer, *The Emergence of Man*.

THE NECESSITY OF THE HUMAN GROUP

In spite of his biological potentialities, and even given his unique capacity to use language, no man would acquire culture if he were not nurtured by a functioning social group. He would never use his prehensile hands to hit a home run or weave a basket, or his brain and vocal apparatus to learn a language. In the social scientists' sense of the word, he would not even be human.

The first years of man's long childhood are especially crucial for his acquisition of culture and personality—in short, of human nature. His slow maturation and extreme dependence on others[15] would be disadvantages for other animals; they become advantages for man. For during his long period of dependence, he is flexible and adaptable; his immature organism is highly capable of learning. In addition, this helplessness compels him to be in close and continued contact with those who can teach him the culture—his parents and siblings and his neighborhood play group.

Cases of people who lived in extreme isolation from social contacts help to prove that human nature is a product of social life. Kingsley Davis has investigated two such cases—Anna and Isabelle.[16]

Anna was an illegitimate child whose stern grandfather kept her isolated in an upstairs room, where she received only enough care to keep her alive and little or no friendly attention or instruction. When she was found and removed from the room at the age of six, she could not walk, talk, or feed herself. She was extremely emaciated and apathetic, "lying in a limp, supine position and remaining immobile, expressionless, and indifferent to everything. She was believed to be deaf and possibly blind."[17]

For the next 4½ years, until she died of hemorrhagic jaundice, Anna was exposed to socializing influences. Before she died she had learned to walk, to talk in phrases, to practice habits of cleanliness, to follow directions, to identify a few colors, to string beads, and to build with blocks. In short, she had the abilities of a normal 2–3-year-old.

Isabelle was also an illegitimate child, kept in seclusion for 6½ years. She spent most of her time in a dark room with her deaf-mute mother, with whom she communicated by means of gestures. When she was found, she exhibited the behavior traits of a 6-month-old child. Lack of sunshine and proper diet had left her with rickets, and she was thought to be deaf and feeble-minded.

Nonetheless, those in charge of her began a systematic program of training. After she finally began to respond, she went through the

[15]Primates generally have a proportionately longer infancy than other mammals, mammals longer than reptiles, etc.

[16]Kingsley Davis, *Human Society* (New York: The Macmillan Company, 1949), pp. 204–8.

[17]*Ibid.,* p. 205.

usual stages of socialization that a child experiences from ages one to six in proper succession and far more rapidly than normal, learning in 2 years what ordinarily takes a child 6 years to learn. Only about 2 months after she first began to speak, she was putting sentences together, and by the 11th month she was reading, writing, counting, and retelling stories. When she entered school, she took a normal part in all activities.

These cases show how little purely biological resources contribute to personality, and how all-important communicative contact is to the process of becoming human. Anna's comparative slowness might be explained by a lower innate intelligence and the haphazard character of her socialization; but another important factor is that she did not have any friendly contact such as Isabelle had with her mother. Isabelle's rapid acquisition of culture invites speculation. Just how long could a person be kept in seclusion before he lost his capacity to acquire culture? Davis speculates that it might be only 10 years, and certainly no more than 15.

The Elements of Culture

Suppose a member of a New Guinea tribe, trained as an anthropologist, is doing field work in a suburb of Minneapolis. Sitting in a large building with windows of many bright colors, he observes women in shiny gowns and fur jackets being escorted up the aisle by young men. Other men, mostly in dark suits, accompany them and sit on the long benches. Up in front a man in a long robe and two young men in dark suits and white shirts appear and stand looking down the aisle toward the entrance. Soft music has been playing; suddenly it is louder. Heads turn to watch several young women wearing long pastel gowns and carrying flowers move slowly up the aisle. The music changes; everyone rises and there are whispers and rustles as a young girl in a long white gown, her head covered with a sheer white veil, comes slowly along the aisle on the arm of an older man. A complicated procedure ensues, with much bowing of heads and kneeling, and repeated incantations. One of the young men places a gold ring on the third finger of the left hand of the girl in white. They kiss. There is another burst of music, and they come down the aisle smiling. As they enter a shiny black automobile, waving and smiling, some of the guests, now standing at the entrance of the building, throw handfuls of rice at them. Several women are wiping away tears and blowing their noses.

What does it mean, this melange of actions and things, in this place? Why are there tears as well as smiles? Why are old shoes and tin cans tied to the back of the automobile? What are the roles and relationships of the various actors? The anthropologist may consult some of those present, attend similar affairs, and arrive at some generalizations.

He must, like all scientific observers, settle on some way of teasing out the component elements of a total situation and classifying them. While there are any number of ways to do it, he might settle on an explanation in terms of (1) norms or behavior patterns, (2) understandings, including knowledge, beliefs, and values, (3) material things and their meanings and functions, and (4) the social structures, including institutions—in this case, the family and religion. Let us consider each of these aspects of culture and the similarities and differences among cultures.

Norms

Norms are rules or patterns for behavior, defining what is expected, customary, right, or proper in a given situation. They are guides to what a person must, may, or should think, do, and feel. They are enforced by *sanctions*, or rewards for correct and punishments for incorrect behavior.

Norms are *ideal* patterns, carried in the minds of participants in a culture as expectations of one's own and others' behavior and sometimes explicitly formulated as laws or regulations. They serve as guides, much as do maps or blueprints. *Real* behavior may deviate considerably from the norms. Consider American weddings. Many weddings do conform to the ideal pattern, as did the one observed by our hypothetical New Guinea anthropologist. But there are also many variations—shotgun weddings, elopements, simple ceremonies before a justice of the peace, even weddings on horseback, on TV, in the woods, at home before the fireplace.[18]

FOLKWAYS

The most familiar scheme for classifying norms was developed by William Graham Sumner in his classic book *Folkways*, written in 1906. Sumner called *all* group customs folkways, but he labeled as *mores* those particular folkways that a society regards as essential to its

---

[18]In addition to the gap, great or small, between ideal and real behavior, there may be a gap between both of these and what people *think* others do—that is, *presumed behavior.* [Cara E. Richards, "Presumed Behavior: Modification of the Ideal–Real Dichotomy," *American Anthropologist* 71, No. 6 (Dec. 1969): 1115–16.] This distinction would seem to apply especially to actions, thoughts, and feelings that might be kept secret, such as stealing, violating sexual norms, doubting a religious doctrine, or hating one's mother.

welfare and enforces with great rigor and intense feeling. For convenience, however, the terms are often used as if they did not overlap, and we shall use them that way here.

Both folkways and mores are norms of long standing that define the proper, accepted ways of doing things. Passed from one generation to another, they have acquired the authority of tradition.

Folkways are usages that govern most of our daily routine and ordinary contacts with other people. They define what is socially correct, and are enforced informally, nondeliberately (but nonetheless effectively). Violations of folkways, however, are not considered a threat to the group at large.

Folkways may be purely arbitrary conveniences, like weights, measures, and monetary systems. Some folkways are rituals, like the pattern for eating or for celebrating a girl's coming of age or birthday. The proper way to greet friends is a folkway, whether it be very casual (the "Hi!" Americans so often use) or very elaborate (the hat-doffing, handshaking, shoulder-patting routine, accompanied by inquiries after one's health and that of one's entire family, typical of encounters between middle-class Latin Americans) or anything in between. Such greeting patterns are special rituals for behavior that we call *convention* and *etiquette*. Although they have no deep meaning, these sets of mutual expectations are convenient in social relations.

Other folkways define proper behavior in various roles: They distinguish "men's work" from "women's work," for example, and set up ideals for ladylike and gentlemanly conduct. Folkways also govern our general style of housing, dress, recreation, childrearing, courtship, and so on; and they define what is beautiful and pleasant. They compose the large underlying body of custom that is strongly rooted in tradition. By no means superficial or transitory, folkways are often charged with considerable emotional fervor. Let a woman try to do a "man's work" in most societies; or worse, let a man be found doing a woman's! Most young men who wear their hair long know how strong an emotional reaction this arouses in some of their elders.

Nonetheless, folkways change. Women now do many things that were once "men's work"; they are doctors, professors, lawyers, ambassadors, cab drivers. Britain has changed its ancient and unwieldy system of weights and measures to the metric system. (But Americans, who pride themselves on being progressive, have fewer women in the professions than most other Western countries and are only now beginning to adopt the metric system).

Folkways are effectively enforced by such rewards as praise, approval, and acceptance in a group, and by such punishments as ridicule, gossip, and nonacceptance. A child who politely shakes hands with guests is rewarded with smiles and praise. If he hangs back or is rude he is punished by his mother's displeasure or his sister's ridicule. The adult who betrays ignorance of the proprieties may feel punished by a raised eyebrow or an amused glance. Most people do not want to be considered rude, queer, ignorant, or uncouth by the standards of their group. They want to belong, to be accepted. Therefore they conform, usually without even thinking about alternative ways.

MORES

Mores are norms that are considered vital to the welfare of the group. They are not simply proper, like folkways; they are *obligatory*, and the sanctions that enforce them are invested with greater emotional content. They are supported by the dominant values of the culture. Mores define right and wrong—moral and immoral—actions, thoughts, and feelings. They may be expressed in terms of "must-behavior" ("Thou shalt"), or they may be negative ("Thou shalt not")—in which case they are called *taboos*.

In our culture long-standing mores include wearing a certain amount of clothing, having only one husband or wife at a time, and being loyal to our country. Bigamy, murder, theft, treason, and incest are among our taboos.

It is often said that mores can make anything right. Behavior that is sternly prohibited in one culture may be permitted or even encouraged in another. In some cultures it is moral to have several wives, to kill unwanted baby girls or helpless old people, to wear only a string of beads, or to take whatever has been left unguarded. Cannibalism has been considered moral in some cultures.

The sanctions that enforce the mores are invested with greater emotional content than are those that enforce the folkways. Respect and approbation reward those who obey the mores. Public esteem and praise reward those who personify them to the society. The Congressional Medal of Honor, the Order of Lenin, and the Victoria Cross reward patriotism and courage. A person is less likely to risk jeopardizing a reputation as an honest employee, a faithful wife, or an obedient son than he is to disregard rules of etiquette or fashions in dress.

Those who violate the mores may feel shame if they are discovered, and guilt whether or not they are discovered; these emotions vary from one society to another. Their reputations may suffer from gossip or from news stories in the mass media. They may be ostracized by their peers; they may be demoted, whipped, pilloried, excommunicated, stoned, imprisoned, exiled, or killed. A deserter is made an example to other soldiers. A rapist, too, though he may be seen as psychologically unbalanced and therefore not truly responsible for his act, is nonetheless frequently held accountable for it. For unless individuals are held accountable for their behavior, the web of mutual expectations crumbles, and with it the social order. Wrongdoing is punished not so much to teach the guilty person as to remind others that the norms must be obeyed.

Whereas the folkways of other cultures are apt to strike us as interesting and colorful, the mores, if they differ sharply from our own, are likely to shock and horrify us. We cannot conceive of such behavior: It is wrong, sinful, immoral. Other peoples often feel the same way about our customs, though anthropologists have found that some presumably primitive peoples are much more tolerant of strange customs than we are—perhaps because they consider only themselves really human.

Mores, like folkways, are subject to change, but somewhat more painfully and slowly. Slavery, once considered moral, is now considered highly immoral in most cultures. But bitter conflict tore American society apart while the change in attitude was taking place. Periods of strictness regarding sexual relations have alternated with periods of permissiveness over the centuries of Western history.

TECHNICWAYS

Some behavior patterns are so closely associated with technological developments—and so new—that they have none of the "right and proper" connotation of folkways. **Technicways**, as they are called, are simply the skills or habits associated with some material, utilitarian object. Most job skills in modern industrial society are technicways. There is, of course, a "right and proper" way to drive an auto, type a manuscript, use a dishwasher, and land an airplane, but it is a matter of technique, rather than of cultural custom. In simple societies, the cultivation of crops is governed by custom and often imbued with sacred meanings; in modern societies, it is considered a matter of technical know-how. The attitude that there are efficient and scientific techniques for doing things has, moreover, appeared in other areas of behavior such as child care and even sexual relations!

The sanctions for the technicways are simple. Getting and keeping most jobs depends on mastery of technical skills. Modern life is full of delay, awkwardness, inconvenience—and yes, even ridicule—for those who cannot drive a car or tune a TV set.

FASHIONS

A **fashion** is "any relatively shortlived folkway in a given society with which there is widespread, conscious, and voluntary conformity because of the status value associated with such conformity."[19] We usually think of fashions in women's clothing, and consider changes in style rather irrational and superficial. Herbert Blumer points out, how-

---

[19]Thomas Ford Hoult, *Dictionary of Modern Sociology* (Totowa, N.J.: Littlefield, Adams & Co., 1969), p. 131.

ca. 1900.

1881.

ever, that fashion operates in many areas of modern life. Fashion influences the content of the pure and applied arts such as painting, sculpture, music, drama, architecture, dancing, and household decoration; entertainment and amusement; childraising; medicine; business management; literature; philosophy; political doctrine; and even science, including social science as well as the physical sciences. Those who fail to abide by fashion are labeled oddballs or misfits, out of date. Fashion is respectable. "It carries the stamp of approval of an elite—an elite that is recognized to be sophisticated and believed to be wise in the given

1928.

1947.

area of endeavor."[20] But the elite does not arbitrarily and irrationally set patterns for others to follow. Fashion is a process of "collective selection" among alternative social forms in areas where the merit of competing possibilities cannot be demonstrated objectively; this selection is endorsed by persons of prestige who are emulated because they are felt to be "up to date."

Fashion serves a useful purpose in modern society. It is "a very adept mechanism for enabling people to adjust in an orderly and unified way to a moving and changing world which is potentially full of anarchic possibilities. . . . It facilitates detachment from a receding past, opens the door to proposals for the future, but subjects such proposals to the test of collective selection, thus bringing them in line with the direction of awakened interest and disposition."[21]

FADS

Fads are fashions that come and go very quickly. They are usually associated with amusement or adornment, and exercise an irrational and intense fascination. Some hit songs become "golden oldies," but most go the way of "Mairzy Doats" and "Open the Door, Richard." Some slang phrases win a permanent spot in the dictionary, but what was "groovy" yesterday and is "outasight" today will probably be

[20]"Fashion: From Class Differentiation to Collective Selection," *The Sociological Quarterly* 10, No. 3 (Summer 1969): 275–91.
[21]*Ibid.*

1969.

1971.

something else tomorrow. During the 1930s college boys swallowed goldfish and sat on flagpoles; in the early 1960s they crowded into telephone booths and pushed beds along highways. The turkey trot, the Big Apple, and the twist each had its short period of glory. Chinese fashions appeared in display windows after President Nixon's Peking visit. In spite of their transitory nature, fads, like fashions, are part of culture, for they are learned and shared patterns of behavior.

LAWS

In a small and unified society, informal sanctions are enough to keep most behavior in line with the norms. But in a complex society more formal norms and sanctions are necessary to coordinate the behavior of the society's members so that it can continue to function in an orderly fashion.

Laws are deliberately formulated rules of behavior enforced by a special authority. The sanctions that enforce them are specific and formal, and are carried out by designated personnel such as court and penal officials. Fines, damage penalties, imprisonment, and even execution are the lot of people convicted of violating laws.

Laws serve several purposes: They enforce the mores accepted by the dominant cultural group in the society; they regulate new situations not covered by custom; they fill the gap when old ways prove ineffectual in meeting a crisis; and they bring real cultural patterns more into line with the ideal patterns and dominant values. Let us consider some examples of each of these functions of law.

Mores enforced by law in our society are monogamy, a man's responsibility for his wife and children, and the taboos against murder, theft, and rape. New situations not defined by custom arose with the invention of railroads, automobiles, airplanes, radio, the telephone, and TV. The government had to pass laws to control the use of these new inventions—regulating traffic, licensing radio and television stations, etc.—to prevent chaos. Governments also enacted laws during the Great Depression of the 1930s, when many people were hungry and ill-clothed, and old ways of regulating business and labor proved inadequate.

The fourth function—bringing real patterns more closely into line with ideal patterns—is served by any law aimed at "social reform." For example, Americans believe in equality of opportunity, but in reality the white majority practices discrimination in housing, education, employment, and other fields. Fair employment acts and Supreme Court decisions against state-upheld discriminatory practices have operated to bring real behavior more closely in line with ideal patterns. (Of course some laws perpetuate the advantages of the powerful members of society. Thus tax and inheritance laws favor the rich and super-rich in

American society and enable them to give their children many opportunities.)

Laws are most effective when they are firmly grounded in the mores. At present traffic regulations are not regarded as part of the mores, which explains why so many people boast about getting away with violations. When laws that enforce the mores of a minority are enacted, they generally do not last. Drinking, for example, was not considered immoral by a majority of Americans, so the prohibition law was a failure. There is some evidence that widespread use of marijuana will lead to a relaxation of laws prohibiting its use.

CONFORMITY TO NORMS

The fact that norms or patterns for behavior exist does not mean that they are always understood and obeyed. For one thing, the norms themselves are not always clear and explicit. We hear folkways and mores debated every day: "It's no sin!" "You'd think I had committed a crime!" "Should I wear black to the funeral?" "Mother, all the other girls go camping with their boyfriends!" Even laws, which presumably are carefully written, are subject to debate among lawyers as to interpretation and application, and to deliberation by judges and juries as to whether or not they have been violated, and, if they have, what sanctions are appropriate. Particularly in a swiftly changing, heterogeneous society, the lines of the cultural map seem to blur and shift under our very eyes. We may belong to groups with different norms (we behave one way with our parents, another with our friends), and find ourselves in situations where no known norms apply (college administrators weren't sure how to react to widespread student protest in the late sixties). During periods of rapid social change, norms may be widely violated even when they are ritualistically given lip service. And once they are openly questioned, their power over behavior is virtually nil. Mores that are questioned are no longer mores. Laws may not be taken seriously if they make previously acceptable behavior criminal, as do many laws regulating banking, tax levies, traffic, and pollution; or if they equate actions that differ greatly in their consequences, as do shooting heroin and smoking marijuana.

Cultural norms, together with the formal and informal sanctions for enforcing them, comprise the system of social control in a society. But norms themselves do not control anything. *People* interpret and define and enforce norms as they act in groups, and in the process of interaction new norms or new definitions of old norms constantly emerge. People also consider the possible consequences of alternative courses of action, especially in modern societies; they consider their chances of being found out and punished, or of feeling guilty even if no one knows. "So conscience doth make cowards of us all," says Hamlet.

Knowledge, Beliefs, and Values

Norms are based upon and justified by what people know, believe, and value, by their shared understandings as to what is real, true, and important. Each culture contains a body of **knowledge**, of lore or science that involves intellectual awareness and technical control of matter, time, space, and events—of "reality." People in every culture also "know" a great many things that they seldom if ever formulate in so many words. "Thus one group unconsciously assumes that every chain of actions has a goal and that when this goal is reached tension will be reduced or disappear. To another group, thinking based upon this assumption is meaningless: they see life not as a series of purposive sequences but as made up of experiences which are satisfying in and of themselves, rather than as means to ends."[22]

Every culture also provides some answers to the mysteries of human existence—man's place in the universe, the meaning and purpose of life, the why of misfortune and death. These answers are expressed in religious doctrines, myths, legends, superstitions, philosophy, folklore, and proverbs. They are **beliefs** about what is not known, and—even in a highly sophisticated culture—*cannot* ultimately be known. They provide some relief from uncertainty and anxiety, and although regarded as just as real and true as science or lore, they are matters of faith and emotion rather than intellectual or scientific "truths" and "realities."

What is known and believed is imparted to new members of a society both formally and informally by parents and peers, by special teachers and religious leaders, in secular and ceremonial teaching. The unstated cultural premises and assumptions aside, knowledge and beliefs are usually explicitly stated in the lessons of elders, in the chief's chants, in textbooks and encyclopedias and bibles.

Values, on the other hand, may be explicit or implicit. **Values** are the underlying standards or principles by which social and individual goals are chosen and the criteria by which ends and means are judged and evaluated. They determine what is considered desirable, important, and worthwhile; they explain and justify behavior. The proverb "Cleanliness is next to godliness" is an explicit statement of this value, by which generations of American mothers explained why they enforced the norm of washing thoroughly.

But not all values are equally important. Many of these same mothers were Christians who put salvation first; cleanliness came only

---

[22]Clyde Kluckhohn and William H. Kelly, "The Concept of Culture," in Ralph Linton, ed., *The Science of Man in the World Crisis* (New York: Columbia University Press, 1945); reprinted in Alan Dundes, ed., *Every Man His Way: Readings in Cultural Anthropology* (Englewood Cliffs, N.J.: Prentice-Hall, Inc., 1968), pp. 188–211.

after godliness, and they admonished their children, "Seek ye first the kingdom of God." Cultural values are arranged in a scale on which several core values dominate and others are subsidiary. The core values determine the chief goals of the society or group, or at least justify and give meaning to them. All other values and goals tend to be measured in terms of these basic values and goals and to be directed toward their fulfillment. Harmonious values (such as work and material success) reinforce and complement one another; contradictory values (humanitarianism and rugged individualism) check and limit one another.[23]

Members of a society are expected to accept its dominant values without question, and the values tend to endure because they are grounded in emotion. Indeed, a society may regard a verbal attack on its dominant values as a greater threat than actual deviation from the norms they support.

CLUES TO VALUES

Many of the most important values in a culture are implicit. They have an "of course" quality; they are taken for granted. (The premise that distribution must be determined by money and the market —the value of "free enterprise"—was so thoroughly accepted in American culture that even during the Depression, unsold food was destroyed while people went hungry.) Only philosophers, artists, and bohemians (or beatniks or hippies) put basic values into words, question them, defend or attack them, seek their sources, or urge their abandonment in favor of other values. Most people feel disturbed when their basic values are challenged, but rarely can they express them articulately.

To understand any society, nonetheless, we must determine what its members value most highly. "For the value system relates not only to matters of prestige, but also defines status and the nature of social class, acts as a basis for leadership and power within the society, and sets the tone of behavior that dominates the culture."[24] How can we discover the values of a society or group?

There are a number of clues to the values implicit in a culture, and to their importance. One is choice. What do members of the society choose to do, to say, and to buy? Do they carefully preserve old buildings because they value tradition, or do they tear them down because they value modernity and progress? What words recur in such rituals as national anthems, pledges of allegiance, holiday orations? Do these words glorify war, conquest, national superiority, faith, work, peace,

[23]Robin M. Williams, Jr., *American Society: A Sociological Interpretation*, 3rd ed. (New York: Alfred A. Knopf, 1970), p. 463.

[24]Walter Goldschmidt, "Values and the Field of Comparative Sociology," *American Sociological Review*   18 (June 1953): 287–93.

progress, ancestors? What words of approval and disapproval, what explanations of their actions, do people employ? Do they spend their money on land, stocks, jewelry, charity, pilgrimages, fun? Do they stress past, present, or future? Here follows one example of choices as clues to values. The British government in 1970 debated a proposal to increase the maximum length of trucks from 32 to 44 feet, which is the size of Continental loads and would increase economy and efficiency. They rejected it in response to protests that the cost in fumes and noise and intrusion on the villages was too high, that "some things are more important than money in deciding what makes life worth living."[25] Another: The city of Hamburg gives more money each year to its Opera House and resident ballet than the United States government gives to all the performing arts.

But the yardstick of choice is tricky, mainly because people may say one thing and do another. Americans value education, but they spend more money each year on tobacco and liquor than they do on schools. Another disparity between real and ideal culture patterns appears in our national budget, where the lion's share is earmarked for defense and only a small fraction for health, education, and welfare.

The folklore, history, religion, and literature of a culture are useful sources of information about values. How might each of these help a foreign anthropologist understand American culture? The legend cf Paul Bunyan would suggest to him we admire things done on a big scale. Our elevation of Abraham Lincoln to the status of a culture hero is a clue to our values of honesty and compassion, traits most Americans believe Lincoln to have had. The Jewish and Christian religions offer the Ten Commandments as a set of norms expressing the values of worship of one God, love for our "neighbors," chastity, honesty, respect for parents, and so forth. But if he assumed that Americans really live by them, the foreigner would be bewildered by "sexploitative" movies, books, and magazines, the generation gap and youthful protest, militarism, poverty, and discrimination.

The system of rewards and punishments may be examined for further clues to values. What actions result in feelings of guilt, shame, or loss of self-respect? What infractions are most severely punished? In one society a mother will spank a child for stealing but not for "sassing" her; in another, stealing is not considered immoral, but lack of respect for elders is unthinkable. Public reaction to the "guilty" verdict in Lieutenant Calley's trial for his actions at My Lai revealed much about American values. As for rewards, professors are much more deferentially treated and saluted with titles in Europe and Latin America than in the United States. We can also ask who makes the most money in a society: statesmen? poets? movie stars? scientists? writers? doctors? business executives?

[25]Anthony Lewis, *The New York Times* (Dec. 21, 1970): 35.

But it is one thing to examine a foreign culture and quite another to analyze our own. Even a trained anthropologist would find it almost impossible to discover all the values of his own culture. "If one could bring to the American scene a Bushman who had been socialized in his own culture and then trained in anthropology, he would perceive all sorts of patterned regularities of which our anthropologists are completely unaware."[26]

Things and Their Meanings

Culture developed as man learned to use symbols and make things. We live surrounded by **material culture**—artifacts (man-made things) and man-made alterations in the natural environment—and can hardly do much more than contemplate our navels without their aid. At the moment I (the senior author) am using a typewriter and paper to express my ideas, glasses to correct for nearsightedness, a lamp to enable me to see the paper, a desk to hold other necessary items, a chair to hold me in a comfortable position, a house to keep me warm and dry and give me privacy, a jump suit and slippers to keep me warm and respectable. On the walls are paintings and photographs that give me pleasure and evoke many memories. Outdoors I see trees being pruned, sidewalks being swept, lawns raked, cars driven, dogs walked, kites flown, groceries carried in. Elsewhere in the house someone is playing a Vivaldi concerto on a stereo set, a washing machine is churning away, a pot of soup is simmering on the stove, some branches of forsythia are being forced. Whether for protection, work, play, sustenance, beauty, or pleasure, all these things have meaning for me; but the meanings of some of them might be hard for the New Guinea anthropologist to arrive at.

Like actions, things are part of *overt* (visible) culture, but have no cultural meaning aside from the *covert* (not readily observable) ideas people share about their proper forms, uses, and purposes. Every culture has a concept of property that includes norms regarding ownership of things, how one gets and gives. Cultural norms and knowledge, including skills or technicways, dictate the way things are to be made and used, while cultural beliefs and values give things meaning. A thing may be seen as purely secular, having a strictly utilitarian meaning. "A chair is to sit," in a child's pragmatic definition. It may have a purely esthetic value, affording pleasure to the senses; a Louis XV chair may be preserved only to look at in a museum. It may have symbolic meaning or value, whether sacred (a papal throne), sentimental-emotional (Grandmother's rocker), or status-indicative (the chair at the head of the table). It may, like these chairs, have two or more meanings. Art is almost as old as tools; from the time early men chipped flints with

[26]Clyde Kluckhohn, *Mirror for Man* (New York: Fawcett World Library, 1964), p. 36.

extra care, taking pleasure in their symmetry, men have designed useful objects with a concern for esthetic values. The Great Pyramids were only incidentally utilitarian burial places; they were also sacred, symbols of royal status, and treasure-houses of art. Even things with primarily personal or sentimental-emotional meanings have cultural meanings: baby pictures in our society. Things are so intimately interwoven with thought, feeling, and action that—much as we may abstract and analyze —we cannot imagine a specific culture without its distinctive material elements.

Many anthropologists, particularly those interested in "cultural evolution" and "culture as adaptation," see technology as central to the total complex of a culture. The technology of a society is the body of knowledge and skills and the tools and machines involved in producing goods (such as food and clothing) and services (such as transportation). So many other aspects of culture are related to technology that societies are often classified by "levels of technology." One common classification distinguishes five levels: hunting and gathering societies, which depend mostly on muscular energy; horticultural societies, in which the digging stick and the hoe supplement muscle power; pastoral societies, which herd animals for food and clothing; agricultural cultivators, who turn over the soil with animal-drawn plows, and irrigate and terrace land; and industrial societies, which apply scientific knowledge to production and thus harness such sources of energy as steam, electricity, and atomic fission.

Social Structure and Institutions

An important aspect of every culture is its social structure, the web of organized relationships among individuals and groups that defines their mutual rights and responsibilities. This structure is based on differentiation—at the very least on the basis of age and sex, and usually according to other criteria as well. Differentiation is expressed in the system of stratification and in the major social institutions of a society.

The system of stratification is diffuse and pervasive, cutting across all the groups in a society, and ranking relative positions in terms of prestige, power, and privilege. The main types of stratification are estate, caste, and class systems. While social strata are not organized into groups or units as are institutions (families, business firms, city councils, schools, churches), the consequences of stratification are very real and very important in all but the simplest communities and societies, as we shall see in Chapter 9.

Most of the social structure of a society is found in its major institutions. Institutions are clusters of norms organized and established for the pursuit of some need or activity of a social group, and supported by the group's knowledge, beliefs, and values, as well as by meaningful aspects of the material culture.

The pivotal institutions that are found in all cultures are: the economic system, the government (or other agencies of group decision-making and social control), religion, the family, education, and the expressional and esthetic institutions, including recreation and the arts. Each of these institutions is an established way of meeting a central and universal need that arises out of man's biological, psychological, and social nature.

What are these needs? Every society must provide for the survival and adequate biological functioning of its members; for the birth or recruitment and socialization of new members; for the production and distribution of goods and services; for the maintenance of order within the group and protection of the group from outsiders; for the motivation of members through a system of beliefs and values that define the meaning and purpose of life; and for play and self-expression. In meeting these needs, the pivotal institutions define relationships among and within social groups, thus forming the essential structure of the social order. In addition, they provide the individual with socially acceptable ways of satisfying biological needs and desires (as well as other needs he acquires from living in his society and culture).

Let us look at the cultural pattern of the family as a pivotal institution—a cluster of folkways, mores, and laws that fulfills basic biological, psychological, and social needs. The functions of mating, reproduction, and childrearing are essential to the perpetuation of society, as are orderly gratification of the individual's sexual drives and of his need for security and affection. The norms of courtship, marriage, and parenthood are designed to meet those needs in socially acceptable ways. In our culture dates, weddings, and homes apart from the in-laws are among the folkways associated with marriage. Long-standing mores include monogamy, postmarital fidelity, and the rights and duties of husband and wife with regard to each other and to their children. A legal framework has grown up to support the mores: licenses, legal ceremonies, laws against bigamy and nonsupport, laws providing for divorce under certain conditions, laws against marriage of close relatives, and laws against marriage under a certain age without parental consent. The meaningful things associated with the institution range from rings worn on the third finger of the left hand through all the paraphernalia of housekeeping and childrearing, licenses, documents, insurance policies, keepsakes, photographs, and gifts.

The noun "institution" can be turned into a verb, "institutionalize." To institutionalize an activity is to formalize and stabilize it, to accord it social recognition as the established way of doing something. A casual love affair is not institutionalized; a marriage is. A dip in the old swimming hole is not institutionalized; a swimming meet at the "Y" is. A friend's newsy phone call is not institutionalized; the evening

paper is. If many segments of human behavior were not institutionalized there would be very little order in modern society.

Similarities in Culture

The six pivotal social institutions found in every society are part of
what anthropologist Clark Wissler called "the universal culture pattern," a single fundamental plan along which all cultures are constructed. Other aspects of this pattern are language; materials; knowledge, beliefs and values; and ways of handling time, space, quantity,
and sequence. Some anthropologists believe that war is also a universal
phenomenon, but it seems that the Hopi Indians, among others, have
never engaged in violent conflict with any other group.[27]

Besides these broad general similarities, George Murdock listed
at random a number of more specific elements found in all cultures.
Among them are age-grading, athletic sports, bodily adornment, calen-
dars, cleanliness training, courtship, dancing, division of labor, dream
interpretation, ethics, feasting, folklore, funeral rites, games, gift giving,
greetings, joking, luck superstitions, modesty concerning natural functions, obstetrics, personal names, propitiation of supernatural beings,
soul concepts, surgery, visiting, and weather control.[28]

Because of such universals, Linton observed that "Any individual who is willing to observe and imitate can orient himself in any
human society."[29] What is the explanation for this "psychic unity of
mankind"?

First of all, mankind is one species. All men have the same basic
needs and drives, though there is no general agreement on a list of them.
But certainly all human beings must eat, drink, and breathe, urinate,
and defecate; all are helpless infants for a long time; all have sexuality,
reproduce and give birth in essentially the same way; all feel and try to
avoid pain and excessive heat and cold; and all feel anger, frustration,
anxiety, love, and fear. Yet there are so many different norms associated

[27]As Ralph Linton points out, this "universal culture pattern" is essentially a matter
of convenience for comparison, like any system of classification based on recognized resemblances; it is inadequate for any deep penetration into the nature of
culture. "Actually, there are no universal patterns, only a series of universal
needs which each society has met in its own way. These needs can be grouped
under three headings, biological, social, and psychic." [The Study of Man (New
York: Appleton-Century-Crofts, 1964), p. 394.]

[28]"The Common Denominator of Cultures," in Linton, The Science of Man, pp. 123–
42. This article has been reprinted in many books of readings, including Washburn and Jay, Perspectives on Human Evolution.

[29]"Universal Ethical Principles," in Ruth Nanda Anshen, ed., Moral Principles of
Action (New York: Harper & Row, Publishers, 1952); reprinted in James Fadi-
man, The Proper Study of Man: Perspectives on the Social Sciences (New York:
The Macmillan Company, 1971), pp. 7–14.

with all these functions and emotions that they are not sufficient to account for universal patterns; and many institutions, such as the family, provide for more than one need.

A further explanation may be sought in the universal conditions of human existence. These provide similar stimuli the world over. One is the physical environment, the facts of the earth, sky, water, sun, moon, and stars. Another is the anatomy and physiology of the human species, aside from its needs and drives: Men everywhere have beliefs about blood, hair, the genitals, menstruation, childbirth, sickness, and death. Furthermore, men everywhere live in groups of people of two sexes and varying ages.

The range of responses to these stimuli is wide, to be sure, but there are limits to the likely, and even the possible, responses. Nature puts limits on such things as the ways pottery can be made, cows milked, diseases cured. There are only a few satisfactory ways to dispose of the dead; and only three possible ways of affiliating a child with relatives through a rule of descent (by father, mother, or both). For these reasons, there are cultural similarities among peoples who have had no contact with one another.

A further reason for similarities, according to Murdock, is the human tendency to generalize, identifying one situation with another. Supernatural beings are typically conceived of in human terms, political organization often follows the model of the family, and menstruation is frequently identified with the moon because of its similarity to the lunar cycle.[30]

Variations in Culture

Cultures vary greatly in specific details, in the size and complexity of their cultural inventory, and in emphasis on one aspect or another of culture. "Traditional custom, taken the world over, is a mass of detailed behavior more astonishing than any one person can ever evolve in personal acts no matter how aberrant," said Ruth Benedict, who was more intrigued by the diversity than by the similarity of human cultures. Taking adolescence as an example, she cited societies that ignore it (the Samoans); societies that make an elaborate ceremony about it (the Masai); societies that treat it as a magic occasion, or one marked with horror and torture, or of consecration to the gods, or of magic that will guide all of later life ("a girl will pick each needle carefully from a pine tree that she may be industrious, or a boy will race a stone down the mountain that he may be swift of foot").[31]

Although food is a universal need, eating habits differ greatly.

[30]Murdock, "The Common Denominator."

[31]"The Science of Custom," *The Century Magazine* 117 (1929): 648–49; reprinted in Dundes, *Every Man His Way*, pp. 180–88.

Some people loathe milk and canned foods but eat fried snails or de-cayed wood or head lice with gusto. Hindus shun beef. There are many ways of giving directions. Americans name and number streets, and number houses by location. The Japanese name intersections rather than streets, and number the houses in each neighborhood according to when they were built.

Voodoo dances and the formal ritual of the mass both deal with the supernatural; gold nose-rings and false eyelashes both beautify the female countenance; cock-fights and Shakespearean dramas both help people pass leisure time; tom-toms and violins both produce pleasing sounds; the chants and potions of the medicine man and the penicillin and oxygen of a modern physician are both means of coping with disease; and hundreds of languages and dialects testify to the flexibility of man's tongue.

Cultural emphases also vary. One culture may stress acquisition of material goods, whereas another concentrates on the supernatural. The whole life of the Todas of India centers around their buffalo herds, and on the ritual of perpetuating and renewing the soured buffalo milk; the dairymen are the priests, the holy of holies is the sacred cow bell, and most of the taboos have to do with the sacredness of milk. While all cultures have some incest avoidance, one Australian tribe extends the taboo to almost everyone around!

Cultures also vary in the size and complexity of the cultural inventory. An Australian aborigine may own nothing but a couple of spears and a boomerang; he may nonetheless have a rich oral lore of poetry and myth. A modern industrial society has an immense material culture, a tremendous store of scientific knowledge, and numerous pat-terns of belief or lack of belief and styles of living. An Oriental society may have a small and simple material culture in comparison, but a large and varied pantheon of gods and a variety of rituals throughout the year.

Why this immense variety in culture? Two answers frequently given—and refuted—by social scientists are (1) that each group in-herits its culture as part of its biological heritage from the race to which it belongs, and (2) that habitat, or geographic setting, determines human behavior, that is, culture. These fallacies are so commonly believed that they deserve some attention.

RACIAL DETERMINISM

If it were true that culture is biologically transmitted along racial lines, then each culture would belong to a different race. But anthropol-ogists now distinguish about a thousand cultures—and *no one* claims that there are a thousand races. True, we can distinguish any number of "races" we care to make classifications for, by differences in such things as skin color, hair texture, and eyelid formation. But these racial types have no proven differences (such as "superiority" and "inferiority") in mental or physical capacity or in organic drives. They are, moreover, so intermingled that only a minority of each group conforms to the group's "ideal" physical type, and there are greater differences among individuals within a "race" than among "races." The notion of any inherent connection between physical type and culture is also disproved by the fact that a person of any racial background can learn any culture into which he is born. Furthermore, over the centuries no one group has displayed a greater capacity for culture-building than any other. While the Europeans were still wearing bearskins, the Chinese were building palaces and producing highly sophisticated art and literature, and the Egyptians were enjoying bronze plumbing. Finally, the racial determinist would have to explain cultural change—which constantly occurs in all societies—by genetic change, which we know to be far slower.

GEOGRAPHIC DETERMINISM

The second fallacy, that geographic environment—the natural setting or habitat—determines culture, appears on the face of it to be a more reasonable explanation for the diversity of cultures. It seems obvious, for example, that Eskimo culture could not exist anywhere but in the Arctic, that rainfall, temperature and soil affect crops, that topography is related to trade routes and settlements. Some observers have gone so far as to say that habitat *determines* the culture. These "environmental determinists" are easily proved wrong by two complementary observations. First, different cultures are found in similar settings. The Eskimos hunt animals and build igloos; the Siberians, in a similar habitat, herd reindeer and build huts of wood and skins. The Pueblo Indians are cultivators; the Navahos, in the same desert setting, are sheepherders. Second, similar cultures are found in different settings. Essentially similar Polynesian cultures are spread over such different habitats as the Hawaiian Islands and New Zealand.

What, then, is the relationship of habitat to culture? Habitat is but one of a number of forces that shape culture. Its impact is greater on some aspects of culture than on others: Technology and economics are more closely related to natural resources, for example, than are art, religion, and the family system. The habitat thus exercises a *selective limitation* on behavior. Men cannot make pottery if there is no clay to be had or weave baskets if there are no reeds, rushes, or young willow trees. The influence of habitat is greatest where primitive people cope with a harsh environment, as in the Arctic or the desert.

As their technology becomes more efficient, however, men become less dependent on the physical environment; they can even alter the habitat to a great degree. The building of the Panama Canal illustrates how both physical environment and culture can be changed. Medical scientists largely eliminated the hazards of tropical disease by discovering how malaria and yellow fever were caused and how they could be prevented; in doing so they cleared the way for a gigantic alteration of the natural environment.

We may say, in short, that culture and habitat stand in a reciprocal relationship. Habitat exercises a selective limitation, but culture is not passive. It acts upon the very environment that serves as its physical setting, and this action intensifies as technology becomes more efficient.[32]

ORIGINS OF CULTURAL VARIATION

If neither man's physical make-up nor his physical environment explain the great variety in cultures, what does? The answer appears to be a combination of the effects of his *adaptability*, his *creative energy and intelligence*, and *the accidents of original choices and their further elaboration*.

Man, we have seen, is highly flexible and adaptable; his basic needs can be satisfied in any number of ways. His digestive system, for example, will tolerate an enormous variety of foods; and his need for clothing can be met by grass, bark, animal or vegetable fibers, furs, skins, and synthetics, in a limitless array of styles. His housing need not even conform to our image of four walls and a roof; it may be a lean-to, a sampan, a round hut, or a cave. He builds strikingly different social arrangements around the needs for reproduction and protection of the group. His original solution to a problem may be a combination of accident and the possibilities afforded by the natural environment. In time, the procedure comes to seem right and natural. And once man has solved his basic problems, he has a great deal of creative energy and intelligence left over, for he is a restless animal and finds pleasure in experiment and play.

He selects from the "great arc of potential human purposes and motivations," to use anthropologist Ruth Benedict's phrase, and elaborates certain aspects of his culture at the expense of others. He may elaborate his technology and science, as Americans have, or his religious ceremonials, as do certain Australian tribes, or his art and architecture, as did the Mayans of Central America. Once he has selected an area of special interest and elaboration, he continues to develop it; thus differences pile upon differences. "The bulk of all cultures consists of what are, from the practical point of view, embroideries upon the fabric of

[32]This discussion is based on Melville J. Herskovits, *Man and His Works* (New York: Alfred A. Knopf, 1948), pp. 153–65. In Chapters 16 and 17 we consider some of the ways man's culture has altered his environment for the worse—in "dysfunctional" ways.

existence."[33] It is of these very embroideries that man is proudest, and it is these that make him most distinctly human.

These influences account, then, for variation in general, and for the different emphases in different cultures. But what explains the variation from simple cultures to highly complex ones? Contacts with other cultures are important sources of innovation. The stronger the links with the past, the greater the cumulative tradition that is preserved, passed on and built upon. The number of people in a society is also related to complexity; the more people, the more likely there are to be specialists and innovators. And finally, the greater the quantity of food available, the more some members of the society can specialize in various nonagricultural occupations.[34]

Differences in culture are fascinating, but in the long run the basic similarity of human behavior all over the world is more impressive. It is human nature everywhere not only to eat, sleep, seek shelter, and have sexual intercourse—like many other creatures—but also to think about one's behavior, judge it, set up rules and institutions, communicate with others in many ways, and create languages, art, religion, and philosophy. Man alone can conceive of himself as a rational and moral creature, with a "mind" and a "soul."

Summary

Homo sapiens is the result of a long process of evolution that probably began in Africa. Lacking the instincts and specific biological adaptations of other species, man is flexible and adaptable. The crucial difference between man and other creatures is his capacity for speech and thought —for language.

Every society has a silent language of natural signs, which are linked to concrete situations, as well as conventional signs, which derive their meaning from usage. Language, a system of conventional signs, is a means of communicating and a vehicle for thought. Language allows man to extend his experience in time and foresee consequences. It affects the way people perceive the world, binds groups together, and allows them to transmit culture.

Culture is learned. Despite his biological capacities, man cannot acquire human nature unless he is nurtured by a functioning social group, as was demonstrated by Anna and Isabelle. The first years are especially crucial in the acquisition of culture.

Every society has a system of norms or patterns for behavior, and rewards and punishments to enforce them. These norms include folkways defining right and proper ways of doing things, and mores

[33]Ralph Linton, *The Study of Man*, p. 310.
[34]John J. Honigmann, *Understanding Culture* (New York: Harper & Row, Publishers, 1963), pp. 309–10. See Chapter 14.

defining right and wrong, moral and immoral behavior. Especially important in modern industrial society are technicways, or skills and habits associated with the use of things; laws, or formal rules enforced by a special authority; fashions, relatively temporary folkways operating in areas of behavior where various possibilities are not subject to objective testing; and fads, superficial and transitory patterns typical of amusement and adornment.

Norms are based upon knowledge, which defines reality; beliefs that provide answers to the mysteries of human existence; and values, or guiding principles that establish the relative desirability and worth of various goals.

Both observable actions and material things may be regarded as overt expressions of the covert ideas, beliefs, and habits of a society's members. Neither actions nor things have meaning apart from the covert aspects of culture.

The chief means of organizing social relationships in any society are found in six pivotal institutions: marriage and the family, the economic system, the political system, education, religion, and the expressive institutions of play and the arts. An institution is a cluster of norms, organized and established for the pursuit of some need or activity of a social group, and supported by the group's knowledge, beliefs, and values, as well as by meaningful aspects of its material culture.

Besides these six institutions, the "universal culture pattern" includes language, materials, knowledge, beliefs and values, and ways of handling time, space, quantity, and sequence. War is well-nigh universal, but there are enough exceptions to make some anthropologists doubt that aggression against other groups is necessarily part of basic human nature. Similarities in culture the world over are attributed to the fact that mankind is one species, to the universal conditions (social, geographic, and physiological) of human existence, to the limits of possible responses to these conditions, and to the psychological tendency to generalize.

Cultures vary not only in detail, but in emphasis, and in the size and complexity of the cultural inventory. Neither physical differences usually considered "racial," nor geographic differences—except for the limitations imposed by habitat—account for cultural variety. Instead, anthropologists find the answers in man's great adaptability, his creative energy and intelligence, the accidents of original choice and their further elaboration, the possibilities for new ideas afforded by contacts with other groups, the accumulation of ideas made possible by links with the past, and the opportunities for specialization and innovation encouraged by sheer numbers of people and by an adequate food supply.

In discussing the content of culture, it has been impossible to neglect entirely the considerations that we will elaborate on in the next three chapters: the patterning and integration of culture, and the functions and consequences of culture for mankind. In considering these topics, we seek answers to two fundamental questions: How flexible is human nature? What are its limits?

QUESTIONS FOR FURTHER THOUGHT

1. It has been suggested that some social and psychological problems arise from the lack of coordination among the three levels of the human brain; that the areas controlling the emotions are primitive compared to those that control speech and reason. Discuss.

2. Sociologist Harold Garfinkel has lent his name to an experiment you might conduct: breaking a cultural norm in order to observe the reactions aroused and the sanctions employed. Examples: Act like a polite guest in your own home; dress like a hippie and shop in one of the "best" clothing stores, then go back in conventional clothing and see if you are treated differently.

3. With whom do you argue about norms? Parents? Your peer group? Do you recall arriving at new norms through discussion? Through tacit agreement?

4. Why *must* man create culture? What *enables* him to create it?

5. Imagine a culture in which the ideal and the real norms do not converge closely. What might such a society be like? Think of the current changes in American sexual patterns in these terms.

6. "Human nature is the same all over the world." In the light of the discussion of the uniformity and variability of culture, how would you qualify this statement?

7. Is culture everything people do? What do you do that is not culturally patterned?

8. The quotation from an anonymous wit on the opening page of this chapter suggests several relationships between biological needs and cultural patterns. Discuss.

9. What types of people in our society are able to violate some mores without being punished? Why?

10. Ralph Linton said we may assume that a culture element is present "if the response of a society's members to a repetitive situation is also repetitive." Discuss.

11. Man has been defined not only as *Homo sapiens* (wise) but also as *Homo faber*, the toolmaker, and *Homo ludens*, the man who plays. Richard L. Means suggests, however, that "the essence of man par excellence may be *Homo ethicus*, man the maker of ethical judgments." [*The Ethical Imperative: The Crisis in American Values* (Garden City, N.Y.: Doubleday & Company, Inc., 1970), p. 10.] Do you agree? Why or why not?

12. Theft is taboo in our society, but are all varieties of stealing defined as equally criminal? Discuss, for example, the different reactions in American society to "street crime," white collar crimes like income tax evasion or embezzlement, etc.

4

What really binds men together is their culture—the ideas and the standards they have in common.

RUTH BENEDICT

There is a "philosophy" behind the way of life of every individual and of every relatively homogeneous group at any given point in their histories.

CLYDE KLUCKHOHN

[In Middletown, U.S.A.,] thought and sentiment pass from person to person like smooth, familiar coins which everyone accepts and no one examines with fresh eyes.

ROBERT S. LYND and
HELEN MERRELL LYND

THE ORGANIZATION AND INTEGRATION OF CULTURE

A CARTOON DEPICTS A WORRIED-LOOKING ENGLISHWOMAN standing in the hall of her house with her children, surrounded by luggage. The caption reads, "I can't imagine what happened to your father. He went out hours ago to practice driving on the right-hand side of the road."

For any group to function effectively, there must be a certain minimum fit among behavior patterns, such as the norm that in England one drives on the left-hand side of the road. There must also be a certain minimum harmony of understandings. What would happen if half the country believed in slavery and half did not? We know the answer: The feeling of unity, identity, and belonging vanishes; the cohesion of society is seriously threatened. However, half the members of a society can be Protestants and half Catholics if all agree on the value of religious freedom.

More than other social scientists, the anthropologist conceives of his subject in terms of whole systems, rather than two or more variables isolated from their context. He sees culture as both organized and integrated—organized into patterns, and integrated by beliefs, values, and assumptions. In looking at culture as a set of patterns, he asks, "What goes (fits) with what?" In studying cultural integration, he asks, "What binds the various patterns together and gives them some harmony?"

Fit and harmony are never complete in a culture. There is always innovation and decay, conflict and discord. Even the stablest culture changes, and change requires readjustment of interrelated elements, which proceeds unevenly. Moreover, no society is made up of completely interchangeable units; members share differently in the culture —according to age and sex in the simplest society, and by numerous other statuses in more complex ones.

Are perfect fit and harmony desirable? How are cultural elements organized into a system? How do various members of a society share in its culture? What aspects of culture promote integration and harmony? What are the principal beliefs and values of American culture? These are the questions we consider in this chapter.

Traits, Complexes, and Patterns

A culture is more than the sum of the norms, understandings, and artifacts a group shares. These elements of culture are interrelated and organized in various ways, and this organization gives new meaning to the parts.

One concept often used to indicate an interrelated group of culture elements, as we saw, is "institution." Another is the scheme of traits, complexes, and patterns.

A **trait** is the smallest unit of culture—one item of behavior, one idea, or one object. Some traits tend to stand alone, as part of a "great 'loose' mass of material . . . that is not bound together by any strong tie but adheres and again dissociates relatively freely."[1] Fads are an example. But most traits are related to others, and fit into larger meaningful wholes called trait complexes; a number of complexes in turn come together in a culture pattern. A **complex**, then, is a system of interrelated traits that functions together as a unit; a **pattern** is a specific and enduring system of culture complexes. To return to the example of a wedding: The act of slipping a gold band on the third finger of the left hand of a girl in a long white gown involves two culture traits—a norm of behavior and a meaningful object. These in turn are part of a trait complex called a wedding, which in turn forms part of the culture pattern we call "marriage and the family," an institution that includes such other complexes as courtship and childrearing.[2]

Culture complexes are systematically organized, and tend to persist and cohere as units. Each complex is limited to some one aspect of the culture—weddings to the family, monotheism to religion, plow agriculture to subsistence, for example. Some complexes, such as marriage and the family, have so much coherence that we can trace them through history and compare them across cultures, for the basic plan persists relatively unchanged over long periods.

It is not only differences in traits, but differences in the organization of traits that makes one culture different from another.

A culture consists of elements or single traits, but the significance of a culture is less in its inventory of traits than the manner of integration of the traits. It is theoretically possible for two societies to possess identical inventories of culture elements, and yet so to arrange

[1]A. L. Kroeber, *Anthropology* (New York: Harcourt Brace Jovanovich, Inc., 1948), p. 313.

[2]There is no hard-and-fast rule for the use of these terms. Depending on the purposes of the analysis, traits may be further broken down into "items" or even into other traits; the words "complex" and "pattern" are often used interchangeably.

the relationships of these elements to each other that the complexes within the two cultures and the total forms of the two cultures will be quite unlike. By simple analogy, a mason may take two identical piles of bricks and equal quantities of mortar. Yet according to the manner in which he lays his bricks, he may produce a fireplace or a garden wall.[3]

Cultural Systems

Because traits are interrelated and organized into complexes and patterns, we may think of culture in terms of systems. We may look at any group and its culture as a system, whether it is a nation-state, a tribe, or small community; a minority enclave in a city, a hospital, business office, factory, or foreign aid mission.[4] We may also consider institutional systems, such as the economic system, the belief system, the educational system, the family and kinship system, and the political system.

At one extreme, the systems approach sees every culture trait as ultimately related to every other, so that one could begin an analysis of a culture with any trait in any sector and find threads leading to all the rest of the culture. This extremely "holistic" approach is typical of some *functionalists*, who insist that every item of culture contributes in some way to fulfilling the needs of society, and that no trait can be understood outside of its full context. They see all cultural patterns as beautifully logical and functional. A more realistic approach recognizes that there is indeed a "strain to consistency" among cultural traits, but that "a single culture may comprise a very large number of deeply contradictory, contrasting, discrepant themes."[5] Although traits are best understood in context (a doll is one thing if it is a child's plaything, quite another if it is a tool for witchcraft, a fertility symbol, or an item in a collection of historical interest), they may also be conveniently abstracted from context and compared to similar traits from other cultures for various purposes (the norm of behavior that symbolizes a marriage, the way pottery is made). Furthermore, the interrelatedness of various aspects of culture may be rather loose and distant; some spheres of activity are relatively autonomous. In modern society, par-

[3]Harry L. Shapiro, ed., *Man, Culture, and Society* (New York: Oxford University Press, 1956), p. 177.

[4]George M. Foster, *Applied Anthropology* (Boston: Little, Brown and Company, 1969), p. 58. "A *system* is an organized collection of interrelated elements characterized by a boundary and functional unity." [Amitai Etzioni, *A Sociological Reader on Complex Organizations*, 2nd ed. (New York: Holt, Rinehart & Winston, 1969), pp. 110–11.]

[5]Margaret Mead, *Anthropology: A Human Science* (Princeton, N.J.: D. Van Nostrand Company, Inc., 1964), p. 135.

ticularly, people tend to regard religion, art, and economic activity, for example, as very separate things.

Degrees of Sharing and Participation

The term **cultural integration** refers to the extent to which various people share common norms, understandings, and material cultures. One way of considering the extent of sharing is by measuring the scope of a cultural system.

Thus, we may speak of the "great traditions," such as Western civilization. By Western culture we mean the ways of life common to Europe, the modern sector of the Western hemisphere, and Australia, and rooted in the Greco-Roman and Judeo-Christian traditions. Western civilization obviously embraces a number of societies with different national traditions and languages. We may also speak of "culture areas," in which a number of neighboring societies have certain elements in common. This is a useful way of classifying various American Indian cultures, for example: Plains, Pacific Northwest Coast, Eastern Woodlands, Southwestern, and so on.[6]

When we speak of a culture, however, we ordinarily refer neither to the great cultural traditions of the world nor to geographic areas, but rather to the way of life of a society, a group with one dominant language and clearly delimited boundaries. This may be as small as a hunting–gathering band, or as large as a modern nation–state. Modern societies are characterized by heterogeneity—that is, they include groups with their own feeling of identity and unity, their own distinctive norms, and often a distinctive material culture as well. These groups we may call **subsocieties**, and their ways of life **subcultures**. In American society, class status, ethnic background, rural or urban residence, religious affiliation, and region are major subcultural influences, shaping the ways of life of various Americans. Thus we might speak of the urban middle-class Jewish subculture or of the rural Southern black subculture as distinct forms of American culture. Subcultures may be cross-cultural, that is, similar groups in several societies feel a sense of identity and have similar norms and understandings. The international "jet set" and the youth counterculture are current examples. Further, a person may belong to more than one subculture—in fact, to as many as any one sociologist cares to distinguish. He may, for example, be urban, black, intellectual, and of Puerto Rican ancestry. The concept of subculture has proved useful to sociologists studying various groups and associations such as juvenile gangs, hippies, hospitals, and convents.

[6]For a map of the world's culture areas see John J. Honigmann, *Understanding Culture* (New York: Harper & Row, Publishers, 1963), pp. 320–21.

UNIVERSALS, SPECIALTIES, AND ALTERNATIVES

Within both the society and the subcultural group, different members share the culture in varying degrees. Theoretically, all of the culture is there for a child to learn, but he will not learn all of it by any means. Variations in innate capacity and motivation to learn limit participation in a culture, particularly a literate and complex one, and cultural definitions of status limit *opportunity* to learn. The most erudite philosophers of the prescientific age, with what they considered "all knowledge" at their command, certainly did not master the specialized skills of the housewife and mother, the blacksmith, the sailor, the sculptor, and the musician. Even in a simple, primitive society a person's age and sex limit his participation in the culture.

Ralph Linton classified the customs and understandings of a culture into three categories—universals, specialties, and alternatives—according to how widely they are shared among the members of a society.

Universals are the customs and understandings shared by all normal adult members of the society. There are many universals in a simple and unified society, fewer in a larger and complex one. They include the basic ideas of how people are to behave toward one another and toward property—the ideal social relationships. Language is also a universal in every group with a distinct culture or subculture. The most important universals are the "core" values of a culture.

Specialties are understandings and patterns of behavior shared by particular kinds of people. They are born with or grow into some of these patterns, and choose others voluntarily. In most societies sex is the clearest basis of specialization and differentiation, not only in biological roles such as childbearing, but also in culturally determined personality differences and in the division of labor. In many societies age groups are clearly demarcated, with "rites of passage" at the various stages signifying new privileges and obligations. In some, such as the traditional caste system of India, each status group has its specialties.

More clearly voluntary, in most societies, are occupational specialties and particular recreational, scientific, artistic, or academic interests. Although many of these specialties require such a high degree of knowledge and skill that others cannot share them without long training, nonspecialists have the culturally-defined right to expect certain definite results from specialists—such as doctors and cooks. Like universals, most specialties are accepted by the members of the society, for they allow the development of skills that produce greater satisfactions in the forms of goods and services than would be possible without specialization.

Alternatives, like specialties, are not common to all members of a society; they differ from specialties in that they are not even common to any special categories such as occupations. Rather they are acceptable ways of thinking, believing, and doing from which the members of the society may choose more or less freely. A couple may develop its own patterns for sex relations and childrearing, for example, from within the broad limits set by modern society. Some alternatives entail free choice at any time: Given the means to do so, a man may travel by plane, rail, bus, automobile, horse, or bicycle, or foot. Choices between or among mutually exclusive alternatives are more limiting. A person cannot be both a Baptist and a Buddhist; a Roman Catholic priest and a husband.

But what about the ideas and behavior patterns a person develops for himself, without learning them from some group or category of which he is a member? Individual peculiarities, although frequently learned, are not shared, and thus are not a part of the culture. You may have learned an abnormal fear of thunder because of some harrowing experience, but almost everyone else in the society considers thunder harmless. Or you may have a notion that red blankets are warmer than those of any other color. In Costa Rican culture this notion was until recently a folk belief shared by people of many categories, though not by all Costa Ricans. But if an American believes that red blankets are warmest, his belief is likely to be an individual peculiarity.

In general, the cultures of complex societies are less uniform and predictable than the cultures of simple societies, which embrace a larger proportion of universals. When a person refers to a middle-aged Navaho man, for example, almost everything about this man's interests, habits, activities, and beliefs can be inferred. Such is not the case in complex cultures marked by subcultures. The statement "He is an American" tells us something, but to say "He is a Midwestern American farmer" reveals even more for we have placed him in occupational and regional subcultures. Additional clues complete the picture: "He is the son of Swedish immigrants . . . a Lutheran . . . a prosperous dairy farmer. . . . He is 40 . . . a high-school graduate." As we shall see later, cultures and subcultures shape personality to such an extent that we already know a great deal about this one man. Of course we do not know exactly what he looks like or what his individual peculiarities are; but knowing what each of these clues means in American life, we are fairly confident of knowing a great deal about his habits, attitudes, and beliefs.

Sources of Cultural Integration

Margaret Mead, in speaking of the discrepancies and contradictions in every culture, says they do not matter "provided some over-all recognition of commonality or community makes each individual member feel that all these behaviors, in spite of their diversity, are parts of the same over-all culture to which he gives his allegiance."[7] We may look, then, for the sources of cultural integration in those things that produce, not simply a meshing of overt behavior patterns into a functioning system of interaction, but also feelings of belonging, unity, security, and allegiance to a system.

Integration is fostered by consensus regarding certain basic and dominant ideas, beliefs, and values concerning the nature of things, the purpose of existence, and the comparative desirability of various actions or states of being. These dominant understandings cluster in integrative principles or themes and in cultural myths, and are expressed in symbols, rituals, and ceremonies that appeal to the emotions.

INTEGRATIVE THEMES OR PRINCIPLES

Cultural patterns tend to be integrated around **central themes** or principles—the fundamental attitudes, perceptions, or preoccupations of a society. While many themes are expressed in such overt patterns as folklore, others are implicit and operate largely on the unconscious level. They are the taken-for-granted premises of each culture.

According to Ruth Benedict, in some societies all patterns express one central principle. Thus Pueblo Indians tended to orient all their cultural patterns around the value of moderation, an "Apollonian" view of life. In the search to establish a relationship with a supernatural power, they learned to practice their rites in mild and orderly fashion, faithfully rendering traditional prayers. In contrast, the Pacific Northwest Indians and many other North American tribes valued excess carried to the point of frenzy, the "Dionysian" view. The Kwakiutl of the Pacific Northwest, for example, sought visions through fasting, self-torture, and violent dancing.[8]

But few cultures are so dominated by one integrative principle. In most several principal themes limit and balance one another. Morris Opler mentions three themes of Chiricahua Apache culture: "Men are physically, mentally, and morally superior to women"; "Long life and old age are important goals"; and the principle of "validation by participation." Each is expressed in many patterns, but where two conflict one must give way somewhat to the other: Although the old are respected, the principle of "validation through participation" demands that leaders

[7] *Anthropology*, p. 135.
[8] *Patterns of Culture* (Boston: Houghton Mifflin Company, 1934), pp. 78–87, 175–82.

must be physically fit and active as well as wise and experienced; most leaders, therefore, are middle-aged men.[9]

MYTHS, SYMBOLS, RITUAL, AND CEREMONY

Another way of looking at the integrative principles or values of a culture is to examine their embodiment in myth and their expression in symbols, rituals, and ceremonies. Social scientists use the word "myth" with no derogatory intent, no connotation of truth or falsehood. A cultural **myth** embodies a society's values, hopes, and fears; it is more or less sacred, being grounded in emotion and taken on faith. We may identify three levels of myth: stories or legends; myths of the origins and place of man and society in the universe, and of the events of each life and of the society as a whole; and the more abstract complexes of beliefs and values that are the taken-for-granted assumptions of a culture.

Legends of Gods and Heroes. The simplest kind of myth is a story, with or without a factual basis, that expresses some one cultural value in terms of a folk hero or god, who represents some virtue or flaw. Such myths are built not only around history book heroes but also about those who embody the dominant values of a period, whether they are business titans, kings, movie stars or other popular idols, or religious figures. The myth of George Washington and the cherry tree brings the value of honesty down to a child's level of understanding, provides him with a model, and appeals to emotion as well as reason. Similarly, Nathan Hale stands for patriotism; Andrew Carnegie for thrift, hard work, and material success; Thomas Edison for technological progress. Minerva represented wisdom; Diana, chastity. Aaron Burr means treason, Cain murder, Narcissus vanity.

Myths of Social and Personal Meaning. Myths also evolve around the origins of a people, the great events in their history, and the recurrent crises of the life cycle. These myths are often expressed in symbols, dramatized in rituals and ceremonies, and celebrated in festivals. The British regard their queen as a symbol of their highest values and dearest traditions. To Soviet citizens the embalmed body of Lenin symbolizes the Communist Revolution. The hammer and sickle, the Stars and Stripes, the Union Jack, the tricolor—each has a profound and emotion-packed meaning for the citizens of the country it represents. An American child internalizes our nationalist myth during the ritual and ceremony of raising the flag, reciting the Pledge of Allegiance, and singing "The Star-Spangled Banner."

[9]Morris E. Opler, "Themes as Dynamic Forces in Culture," *American Journal of Sociology* 51, No. 3 (Nov., 1945): 192–206.

Italy.

Woodstock, New York.

Ritual and ceremony are powerful means of sustaining the social order, for they dramatize traditional beliefs and values and invest them with emotional content. A **ceremony** is a formal, dignified procedure that impresses observers and participants with the importance of an occasion. A wedding, a funeral, a church service, even a Boy Scout Awards Night are lifted above ordinary events by ceremony. Ceremony, being out of the ordinary, satisfies what seems to be a basic human need, escape from boredom.

The most distinctive element of ceremony is usually **ritual**—a formal, rhythmic series of symbolic acts that are repeated on appropriate occasions. The wedding procession, the exchange of vows, the giving of rings, the smashing of the wine glass, or the nuptial blessing and the pronouncement that the two are now man and wife—whatever the religion, its wedding ceremony is as stylized as classical ballet. Like rituals surrounding birth, initiation or confirmation, and death, the marriage ceremony restates a culture's definition of man's relationship to nature, society, and the supernatural. Each of these rituals dramatizes the meaning of a major crisis in the life cycle.

Ritual has its roots deep in the past and serves to keep traditional meanings alive. The ritual of the Passover, which commemorates the Exodus of the Jews from Egypt, contributes to the coherence of Jewish culture and creates a feeling of unity among Jews. The richly symbolic ritual of the Mass, a reenactment of the Last Supper, impresses Catholics with its importance to their lives. Participants in such rituals may experience awe, gratitude, and rapture, and a renewed sense of personal identity and of group belonging.

96

We belittle ritual, says Orrin Klapp, if we think of it as some kind of rigmarole or fanfare. It is, rather, a gestural language that states sentiments and mystiques a group needs, and adds to the solidarity and fullness of emotional life. It says, "We are together; Don't worry, something you do not understand is working for you; Congratulations, you made it; We repent and will try to do better; Help us, O Lord." "Ritual is not only pleasant but absolutely necessary for giving people a full sense of themselves, of their place, of belonging; it fills the emotional void of mechanized and routinized life."[10]

Festivals—times or days of joyous feasting and celebration— also contribute to cultural integration. Celebrating the Fourth of July —at least as it used to be done in small towns, with orations and parades—reminds Americans of the myth of national origins. Christmas, Thanksgiving, and Easter, secularized and commercialized as they are, still provide common bonds, annually reinforced. The puberty rites of the Cuna of Panama involve feasting, drinking, and dancing as well as chants recounting the myths about tribal origins and the life cycle. Theologian Harvey Cox, commenting on the emptiness of many American "celebrations," says festivity and fantasy (the capacity to imagine alternatives) "help make man a creature who sees himself with an origin and a destiny, not just an ephemeral bubble."[11]

Central Cultural Myths. It is on a third, and probably the most important, level that the concept of myth is most elusive. The great central myths of a culture are pervasive complexes of values and beliefs

[10]*Collective Search for Identity* (New York: Holt, Rinehart & Winston, 1969), p. 137.
[11]*The Feast of Fools* (Cambridge: Harvard University Press, 1969).

Colorado Springs, Colorado.

Mexico.

that are generally so deep that they are rarely if ever verbalized, but are experienced unconsciously and taken for granted. It is often difficult to perceive the prevailing myths until they have disintegrated and are being replaced by new ones.

> Myth is the all-pervading atmosphere of society, the air it breathes. . . . Wherever he goes, whatever he encounters, man spins about him his web of myth, as the caterpillar spins his cocoon. Every individual spins his own variation within the greater web of the whole group. The myth mediates between man and nature. Inside his myth he is at home in his world.[12]

What are some central cultural myths? "The American Dream" or "the American Way of Life," the classless Utopia of Chinese communism, are myths that tend to bind whole societies and give them a sense of mission. The myth of the Frontier, which provided heroes and goals in the late nineteenth century, continues to operate—with outer space the new frontier. Psychoanalyst Rollo May sees the main myths of modern, Western societies as rationalism and individualism, along with nationalism, competition, and the faith that problems can be solved by amassing and analyzing technical data. These replaced the Christian myth that prevailed through the Middle Ages, and are in turn being questioned as men seek new values: a myth of one world, collectivism, cooperation, and the value of inner or subjective experience.[13]

Dr. May sees myth as essential to social integration and mental health. Myths give meaning and value to experience, answering the questions: Who are we? Where did we come from? Where are we going, and why?—for the society as a whole as well as for individual members. Thus the dominant myth of nationalism helps orient many collective and individual decisions. People choose their goals by the myths in which they place their faith. The myth system interprets reality and gives people a sense of identity in relation to others and to the world. Myths help a person to handle anxiety, face death, deal with guilt, and find an identity and a purpose. Through its expression in rituals, myth helps people negotiate the crises of life.[14]

ETHOS

Each society has its own characteristic quality, or **ethos**, that springs from many contributing factors, particularly from the beliefs

[12]R. M. MacIver, *The Web of Government* (New York: The Macmillan Company, 1949), pp. 5, 39.

[13]Rollo May, "Reality Beyond Rationalism," presented at Concurrent General Session of the 24th National Conference on Higher Education, Chicago, March 3, 1969.

[14]*The New York Times* (Nov. 25, 1968): C 49.

and values around which its culture is integrated. Comparable to what we would call a person's disposition or character, a society's ethos is rather elusive. It is those "qualities that pervade the whole culture—like a flavor."[15] The ethos of the Italian Renaissance was sensuous and passionate, that of the north European Reformation puritan and ascetic; Hindu civilization is mystical and otherworldly; Chinese civilization is temporal and matter-of-fact.[16]

The ethos of a culture may be predominantly *sacred* or *secular*. A sacred culture is based on a systematic theology; it is conservative and stable, reveres tradition, and provides dogmatic answers to all questions. Everything that happens has a religious motivation or explanation; nothing is simply a means to a practical end. Deviation from traditional behavior is severely punished. In a secular culture, on the other hand, ideas and things and people are evaluated in utilitarian terms. Change is readily accepted; in fact, it is sought and encouraged—and called "progress." Instead of passively bowing to divine will, members of the secular society believe that "God helps those who help themselves."

Secularization, the trend toward secular values, began in the fourteenth and fifteenth centuries. The Renaissance and the age of invention and discovery were characterized by a new interest in life on this earth and a belief in the scientific approach to human problems. Although this trend has continued, many customs and institutions are still sacred to us, so that Western culture is a mixture of sacred and secular elements.

Integration and Adaptability

Is a highly integrated culture a good thing for a society? On one hand a harmonious culture tends to produce a sense of security and satisfaction among its members (unless the culture itself, like that of the Dobuans of New Guinea, contains elements that make them feel hostile and insecure).[17] But on the other hand, thorough integration may mean that change, even if it begins in only one aspect of culture, may cause the whole culture to disintegrate like a house of cards. When the British abolished headhunting in Melanesia, for example, the results were disastrous. The people lost their interest in living, and the birth rate dropped precipitously; on one island the number of childless marriages increased from about 19% to 46%, on another from 12% to 72%. Why? Headhunting was the center of social and religious institutions; it pervaded the whole life of the people. They *needed* to go on headhunting expedi-

[15]Kroeber, *Anthropology*, p. 294.

[16]*Ibid.*, p. 4.

[17]Ruth Benedict, *Patterns of Culture*, pp. 78–87, 175–82. See Chapter 11.

tions because they needed heads to propitiate the ghosts of their ancestors on many occasions, such as making a new canoe, building a house
for a chief, or making a sacrifice at the funeral of a chief. Although their
expeditions lasted only a few weeks, and fighting itself only a few
hours, preparations lasted for years. They had to build new canoes and
to celebrate numerous rites and feasts, which stimulated horticulture
and the breeding of pigs. They held festivals as the date for the expedi-
tion neared, and still others when the successful hunters returned. With
the integrating pattern of their lives denied them, the Melanesians lost
interest in living.[18] Something similar is presumed to have happened
to the Mayans of Central America, whose culture centered around the
cultivation of maize, and crumbled when some event, perhaps a drought,
made it impossible to grow maize any longer.

Apparently a culture with a lower degree of integration, in
which the various themes and patterns are less perfectly coordinated,
adapts more easily to circumstances that bring about change. In a society
in which there is very little harmony and integration of cultural norms
and understandings, however, there will be much conflict, confusion,
waste, insecurity, and social unrest. When the prevailing myths lose
their power, many people become disoriented, alienated, and unsure
of their identities and goals. The disintegration of the myth system, says
May, is a sign but not a cause of disunity and trouble. But he believes
man can create new myths and symbols to meet new needs.[19]

American Cultural Themes

The American world view is essentially that of the Western tradition,
rooted in the Greek and Roman civilizations and the Judeo-Christian
heritage. It sees life as work and effort through which one can satisfy
his needs and dreams, and the material universe as orderly and predictable enough to be explored. From the religious tradition comes the
underlying premise that all creation must be of intense interest and
value since it is God's work, and a messianic hope that the future will
be better than the present, that man progresses toward new possibilities.
In contrast, the Hindus see the world as Maya or illusion, "a fevered
dance of fleeting appearances which mask the pure reality of uncreated
being." Like most traditional societies, Hindus "feel themselves bound
to a 'melancholy wheel' of endless recurrence," and thus are fatalistic
rather than optimistic.[20] The Western emphasis on individualism, espe-

---

[18]W. H. R. Rivers, ed., *Essays on the Depopulation of Melanesia* (New York: The
   Macmillan Company, 1923), pp. 101–2; cited in Ashley Montagu, *Man Observed*
   (New York: G. P. Putnam's Sons, 1968), p. 94.

[19]*The New York Times* (Nov. 25, 1968).

[20]Barbara Ward, *The Rich Nations and the Poor Nations* (New York: W. W. Norton
   & Co., Inc., 1962), p. 21.

cially marked in the United States, springs from the idea that all souls are equal in the sight of God. We also draw many of our ideas from the Enlightenment philosophers and classical economists.

Ours is a large, diverse society with many subcultures—racial, geographic, ethnic, religious, and socioeconomic. It is a dynamic and changing society, whose history has paralleled the history of modern democratic ideology, industrialism, and capitalism. Pioneering, promise, and action have been the flavor of its culture—its ethos—for Americans had a fresh start if ever a people had one. There was a frontier to push back; a wealth of natural resources to exploit; and a vast land to explore, "conquer," and populate—with a diverse population constantly swelled by floods of immigrants to be "Americanized," believers in the myth of the land of opportunity if not of gold-paved streets.

What are the great American myths? What is the American Dream? Values, we have said, are not always obvious or easy to analyze. And Americans, unlike the Chinese, have no explicit ideology. But most Americans do hold sacred a vague myth we call "The American Way of Life." Numerous observers have analyzed our culture from colonial days on to the present time—visitors such as Crèvecoeur, de Tocqueville, James Bryce, and D. W. Brogan, as well as Americans such as historian Henry Steele Commager, sociologists Robert and Helen Lynd (who studied "Middletown" in the 1920s and 1930s) and Robin M. Williams, Jr.[21] They generally agree that the following clusters of values and beliefs are characteristic of American culture, particularly of middle-class culture. Some of them may seem painfully obvious to you, others you may deny, others you may never have thought of. Still others are traditional values that are being challenged in our time of rapid social change. In discussing each value constellation or myth we first state it as a traditional or long-standing one. Then we consider some of the ways in which it is being questioned, challenged, eroded, and reinterpreted, most conspicuously by those who have been alienated from the mainstream of American life by such events as the Vietnam War and the urban crisis.

DEMOCRACY–FREEDOM–EQUALITY–INDIVIDUALISM

The democratic myth is paramount in America. Democracy itself is highly valued, even when its meanings are various and confused. It embraces several other values: freedom, equality, and respect for the individual personality. It is embodied in the myth of the Founding Fathers, symbolized by the flag, the Constitution, and the Declaration of Independence. "One nation indivisible [social cohesion itself is a value]; Liberty and justice for all; All men are created equal." Its mythic

[21]*American Society: A Sociological Interpretation*, 3rd ed. (New York: Alfred A. Knopf, 1970).

character is indicated by the fact that these things are held sacred by the most conservative super-patriot and the radical alike.

Spokesmen for the counterculture charge, however, that the real behavior of most Americans does not fit these ideals. They question the "frontier freedoms" of past generations, who felt free to push West, decimate the Indians, despoil the land, and run businesses for profit alone. They interpret freedom as liberty to deviate from conventional norms. They apply the ideal of equality perhaps more stringently than their elders, insisting that racial and ethnic barriers and even class differences are essentially meaningless, that racism, poverty, and "sexism" deny the democratic myth. They tend to interpret respect for the individual personality as letting everyone "do his own thing," and as providing everyone with the opportunity to fulfill his potential through education and satisfying work.

LAISSEZ-FAIRE–THE PROTESTANT ETHIC–FREE ENTERPRISE

In American history, the democratic theme has come to be associated with the attitude toward economic and political institutions generally called *laissez-faire*.[22] The two chief sources of the laissez-faire theme are the Protestant ethic and the classical economic theories expounded by Adam Smith.

The "Protestant ethic" is a term used to refer to a cluster of values long accepted by Americans of all faiths. According to the theory of the famous German sociologist Max Weber, members of nonconformist Protestant sects, especially in England and Holland, contributed greatly to the rise of industrialism and capitalism because their religions emphasized *individual striving, progress, self-discipline*, and *thrift*.[23] To them, *material success* was not merely a proof of diligence, virtue, and respectability, but a sign of God's grace, an indication that the person who was successful in this world had been chosen by God to live in Paradise in the next. The early settlers of New England brought these values into our culture. The maxims of Ben Franklin in *Poor Richard's Almanac*—taught to generations of Americans—are the clearest expression of these values: for example, "Early to bed, early to rise, makes a man healthy, wealthy, and wise"; "A penny saved is a penny earned."

The Protestant ethic combined in the United States with Adam Smith's theories of *free enterprise*. As they came to be understood in American culture, these theories and beliefs emphasized *"rugged individualism"*—each person's responsibility for his own well-being. Any-

[22]The origin of the term laissez-faire has been traced to a seventeenth-century French merchant who, when asked what government policy toward businessmen should be, replied, "Laissez faire," which translates into English as "Let them do as they please."

[23]Max Weber, *The Protestant Ethic and the Spirit of Capitalism*, trans. Talcott Parsons (New York: Charles Scribner's Sons, 1948).

one who was willing to work could make a living and prosper. He had only to save, be punctual and self-reliant, and show initiative, and by his own effort he could get ahead. The novels of Horatio Alger and the idealization of Abe Lincoln as the great culture hero who went from log cabin to White House expressed this myth as "The American Way."

This individualism, combined with our frontier history, helped to create a preference for *direct action* rather than for the slower processes of government legislation and administration; for local rather than central government, for the sheriff and the posse rather than federal troops. It may also help to explain Americans' high valuation of personal consumption expenditures and their reluctance to finance collective goods, and the carelessness that allows them to strip forests and mines, ruin farmlands, and pollute air and water.

A natural consequence of laissez-faire values and the Protestant ethic has been the enshrinement of THE JOB as the measure of a person's excellence, the goal of his education, the factor governing where he lives, the key to his social status. He is evaluated according to what he does (by achievement), and to some extent by what he *has* (by "success" measured in material rewards).

Along with these economic values has gone a myth of abundance, a belief that we could have everything. Not until recent years have Americans been forced to face problems resulting in part from this myth, to examine priorities, weigh values, and try to fashion policies accordingly.[24] (This constellation of economic myths does not fit real patterns, for ours is in many respects a planned economy rather than a free market economy.)

The counterculture rejects or questions most of these economic values, stressing cooperation rather than competition, denying that money and the job are the measures of personal excellence, and severely challenging the system of national priorities. Even well-to-do young people avoid such signs of material success as fashionable clothing and big cars; and many seek "really basic" values by experimenting with subsistence agriculture, communal living, and the crafts as a way of life.

RATIONALISM–KNOWLEDGE–SCIENCE–TECHNOLOGY

Another strong theme in American culture is the belief in rationalism, objective knowledge, science, and technology. In work and production, Americans emphasize technique, practicality, efficiency, inventiveness, resourcefulness, rationality, and order. They are oriented to the material world, not to the inner world of meditation or esthetic appreciation, nor to a utopian world or a heaven to come. And Americans are pragmatists, dealing at short range with the problem at hand, reject-

[24]J. Irwin Miller, "Changing Priorities: Hard Choices, New Price Tags," *Saturday Review* (Jan. 23, 1971): 36 ff.

ing long-range planning based on any single ideology or philosophy. They have a "mechanistic" world view, that is, they tend to see the physical and social world as made up of parts that fit together like those in a machine. When the parts in the social system don't mesh properly Americans do not theorize, plan, or abandon the system for another. They act. They tinker with the machine until it works better.

Some critics of American priorities turn this whole value system around, charging that science and rationalism have created a monstrous technology that threatens to destroy human values, that makes men into things. They often turn to Oriental religions and philosophies, to occult and mystic ideas, to meditation and psychedelic drugs in a search for inner knowledge; they seek spontaneity, beauty, and a sense of community.[25]

Still another viewpoint is that science and technology are not bad in themselves; they have simply been misapplied. "When we want to build as sound a society as we do a spaceship, our technology is able to lead us. Only, first, we must be willing to lead it, and not be led."[26]

FUTURE ORIENTATION–PROGRESS–OPTIMISM

Americans are oriented to the future; they tend to ignore the past and to use the present for future gains. They believe in progress; change is understood to mean change for the better, especially if it is change in material things, in technology. Americans are optimistic, confident in themselves and their system. They have long believed that, through a spontaneous process of unguided social change, everything will turn out well for America in the long run.

But the events of the 1960s eroded that confidence in many Americans, and not only those in the counterculture. Many now question the application of this value-cluster to individual goals, the idea of a career for which one is willing to sacrifice enjoyment of the present moment. They prefer expressive, spontaneous experience in the here and now. They also refuse to measure progress by material standards such as economic growth.

VALUES GOVERNING INTERPERSONAL RELATIONSHIPS

The norms guiding interpersonal relationships in America stress equality and the peer group rather than authority and subordination. They are based on a cluster of values that includes fair play, generosity, hospitality, gregariousness, informality, and external conformity in dress, attitudes, and beliefs. This conformity, much criticized by foreign observers from de Tocqueville on, is interpreted by Robin Williams as

[25]Theodore Roszak, *The Making of a Counter Culture* (Garden City, N.Y.: Doubleday, Anchor Books, 1969), p. 233.

[26]Sydney J. Harris, "Technology Holds Key to Social Gains," *Detroit Free Press* (July 1, 1970): 13-A.

useful in a heterogeneous society, "a sort of 'social currency' making it possible to continue the society in spite of many clashes of interests and basic values."[27] Thus Americans tend to employ clichés in most social interaction, avoid controversial subjects, and save personal opinions for those whom they know to be like-minded. Dissent and nonconformity make many Americans uneasy; they see them as a threat to society itself.

Americans are joiners; they associate to get any number of things done, whether to have fun, do good, or solve a social problem. They are also humanitarian; in spite of many contradictory values, they do have a sense of personal responsibility for the welfare of others. They feel they *should* give to the March of Dimes, send CARE packages, and ring doorbells for the Community Chest.

The youth culture shares the emphasis on peer group relationships, carrying hospitality, sharing, and informality even further; but it stresses sensitivity rather than superficiality in human relationships. Young people experiment with unconventional styles of life, and often seem to wind up conforming to their own nonconformist norms—and they have influenced "straight" fashions in the process.

MORALISM–RELIGION–SIMPLISM

American culture has a markedly moralistic orientation. Americans tend to see things in terms of right and wrong, good and bad, with little regard for nuances; they tend to hate and fear complexity. Religion —monotheistic religion—is held to be good in itself, and everyone is expected to have a religious identity. Morality is usually narrowly interpreted to mean sexual morality. A strong puritanical urge to impose one's own standards on others was most clearly demonstrated by passage of the prohibition amendment to the Constitution in 1919.

The counterculture also has a marked moralistic flavor, but instead of being oriented toward religion and sex—areas in which many old values are questioned or ignored—it denounces war, poverty, racism, and environmental pollution as immoral, charging the "older generation" with hypocrisy.

THE PURSUIT OF HAPPINESS

A complex of values concerning the importance of personal happiness and the means of pursuing it runs counter to the Puritan ethic of work, action, and thrift. It includes material comfort, fun, taking it easy, hedonism, self-indulgence, and security. Americans tend to ride when they might walk, to watch rather than to do; to overheat and overcool houses and public buildings; to eat refined and luxury foods; to use a great deal of alcohol, tobacco, and other drugs; to take expen-

[27] *American Society*, p. 486.

sive vacations; to choose jobs with an eye to security. They are willing consumers in an affluent society. Their "fun morality" is evident; conversations are liberally sprinkled with "fun" as a measure of the worth of time spent doing almost anything. One MUST have fun, pursue it earnestly. "Come on, live a little."

Yet, observes Harvey Cox, Americans seem to have lost the capacity for unapologetically unproductive festivity, for pure expression, genuine revelry, and joyous celebration. Only a few pallid rituals mark birth, puberty, marriage, and death. How many really enjoy New Year's Eve parties? How many more find them empty?[28]

Increasingly, happiness is being defined as self-expression and joyful, natural communion with others. Many Americans are active participants rather than passive spectators, in sports, dramatics, music, and the visual arts. There is a growing concern for an improvement in "the quality of life," an emerging and not yet clearly defined value. In the counterculture, the American habit of seeking euphoria and oral gratification involves marijuana and sometimes other drugs. Sensuality is replacing luxury and comfort.

YOUTH

Still another American myth is that youth is the best time of life. The child is the center of the family; his education and future are of intense concern to the parents. The lovely young woman in her teens and early twenties is the center of attention in many aspects of the culture; the young playboy-athlete is her male counterpart. Young people are admonished to enjoy themselves; time enough later to settle down into a rut.

The youth theme is obviously strong in the counterculture, too; but it takes a different direction. The slogan popular in the 1960s "You can't trust anyone over 30" is heard less often as the years go by and Abbie Hoffman and others pass that milestone. Many feel that the older generation simply cannot understand that Hiroshima and Nuremberg made nationalism obsolete; that materialistic values have brought little satisfaction. Their elders counter that the young cannot appreciate what their parents had to struggle for; and indeed many youths in underprivileged groups fail to sympathize with a rejection of material comforts.

SENTIMENTALITY–ROMANCE–LOVE

Sentimentality and romance are also reflected in many aspects of American culture. Love is glorified—especially romantic love, which makes the world go 'round. A glance at a rack of greeting cards reveals our sentimentality about home, mother, children, dogs, the good old days, friendship, and marriage.

[28]*Feast of Fools.*

In the counterculture "love" is more broadly defined as a kind of universal brotherhood; the relations between the sexes are freer and more casual; and homosexual relationships are far more tolerated.

SUPERIORITY OF "THE AMERICAN WAY"

The idea that "ours is the best way" has recurred throughout our history. This theme appears in most societies, but in this country it seems especially strong, and any questioning of America's superiority in any area of life whatever is met with resentment. Most Americans believe in a myth of omnipotence as well (and are sure this country has never lost a war), and in a myth of moral superiority (they are sure America has never waged an aggressive war, and fights only from the purest motives). They are certain they have the highest standard of living in the world, although some social indicators, such as those connected with health, show other countries far ahead. At least a dozen other countries, for example, have lower rates of infant mortality, and a number have greater life expectancies. They are also sure America has the best system of government, the best education, the most freedom. The American way of life, many believe, is so superior it should be adopted elsewhere. This sense of mission is "both an index of the

strength of nationalistic feeling and a potent source of misunderstanding and resentment in international affairs. In peace as well as in war, many citizens have believed that the United States must have a mission as a crusader for righteousness."[29]

A feature of the counterculture that intensely irritates many older Americans is its seeming contempt for nationalism and patriotism, its cross-national character, its frequent expressions of indifference to or contempt for such symbols as the flag, and its openness to "alien" philosophies and ways of life. "America—love it or leave it" is one pole of patriotism; but the counterculture says "Love it and improve it, or leave it" or suggests that a nation is an improper object of love. They construe dissent to be in accord with the highest American values: democracy, equality, freedom, and individualism, as well as direct action. They often part company, however, on whether or not dissent may be violently expressed.

This is not the first period of tension among values; they are always hammered out during periods of rapid change. The ways of the counterculture may never become "the American way," but it seems clear that the traditional American style of life is changing in fundamental ways. Mainstream Americans feel uneasy because by challenging ideas, beliefs, and values—bringing myths out into the open—the counterculture seems to threaten unity and security, to destroy cultural integration. But sheer consensus on values and beliefs is not the only source of social integration. We shall see in our discussion of social organization (Chapter 8) that structural arrangements, as well as cultural integration, foster stability and unity in a society.

Summary

Culture traits are organized into interrelated complexes, which in turn are part of larger cultural patterns. There is a strain to consistency of the various culture elements in any given system, but their fit and harmony are never complete. In general, the more completely integrated a culture, the less adaptable it is, although no culture is ever totally static.

The scope of cultural systems varies depending on whether we are concerned with traditions, such as Western civilization, geographic areas in which several societies share a number of cultural patterns, societies as large as nation-states and as small as hunting–gathering bands, or the subcultures of groups within a society. Participation in culture and the degree to which items are shared may be analyzed in terms of universals, specialties, alternatives, and individual peculiarities.

A society must have a certain minimum of fit and harmony among its elements: sufficient agreement on overt behavior patterns and

[29]Williams, *American Society*, p. 491.

procedures to permit functioning, and sufficient consensus regarding beliefs and values to promote a feeling of unity and belonging. The integrative values and beliefs of a culture are embodied in myth, expressed in symbols, rituals, and ceremonies, and celebrated in festivals. Myth has a sacred quality, being grounded in emotion and taken on faith. A myth may embody one value in a folk hero or god; it may give a society a sense of its origins and its mission, and provide individuals with answers to questions of identity, especially at crises in the life cycle; or it may consist of a deep, underlying complex of values and beliefs that are taken for granted.

American culture is pervaded by an ethos of action, pioneering, and promise. Its chief myths and value constellations include democracy, freedom, equality, and individualism; laissez-faire, the Protestant ethic, and free enterprise; rationalism, knowledge, science, and technology; emphasis on the future, progress, and optimism; informal, egalitarian peer group relationships, external conformity; humanitarianism; moralism; distrust of complexity; belief that religion is a good thing; pursuit of happiness through fun, material comfort, self-indulgence, and security; a belief that youth is the best time of life; sentimentality, romance and love; and above all, a strong belief that the American way is the best way, and others should adopt it. These values are being rejected and reinterpreted during the present period of rapid social change; the most conspicuous challenge comes from adherents of the cross-national youth culture or counterculture. By bringing long-accepted myths out into the open for examination, they upset many Americans, who believe they endanger the unity and security of the society.

In the next chapter we shall consider what culture "does" for society and for its individual members—how "it serves to adapt man to his physical environment, his biological nature, and his group life."

QUESTIONS FOR FURTHER THOUGHT

1. Pick some culture trait at random—some custom or material object. List other traits with which it is related, and the complex and pattern of which it is a part.

2. To what subcultures do you belong? List the chief ones in order of their importance to your life.

3. List several universals that you believe you share with most others in your society. List several alternatives. Are they subcultural? What are your specialties? Your individual peculiarities? Examine the latter to see if they might, after all, be culturally influenced.

4. The word "myth" is used in social science without any necessary connotation of falsehood. Do you find this meaning hard to accept? To what extent do you think some of our cultural myths actually are false? True?

5. Were the British justified in abolishing headhunting in Melanesia? What functional alternatives might they have introduced?

6. Which traditional values do you accept? Which emergent ones?

7. Why is it hard to question core values?

8. What problems would be created if all values were equally important to a person?

9. If you arrived in a strange society not knowing its language or values, how could you discover what some of its values were?

10. How does ritual keep traditional meanings alive? Give examples.

11. Construct a scale of your personal values, based in part on the discussion of American values, and add any other values you hold. How do they determine your goals? Your daily schedule? To what extent are they different from your parents' values?

12. Analyze the elements of symbol, ritual, and ceremony in your routine day. In your observance of the Sabbath and holidays. In what ways do they affect your emotions?

5

THE FUNCTIONS OF CULTURE

Custom is custom; it is built of brass, boiler iron, granite; facts, reasonings, arguments have no more effect upon it than the idle winds have upon Gibraltar.

MARK TWAIN

Each specific culture constitutes a kind of blueprint for all of life's activities.

CLYDE KLUCKHOHN

We do not see the lens through which we look.

RUTH BENEDICT

Custom in the end becomes men's nature.

EVENUS, 450 B.C.

If TODAY ISN'T VERY DIFFERENT from most days and you are a person not very different from most others, one small event has followed another pretty much as you expected when you woke up. You haven't had to make any major decisions. You chose between scrambled eggs and pancakes for breakfast with a slight shrug signifying that it did not matter much; dressed without thinking about how to tie your shoelaces or button your coat; took the usual route to the usual bus or subway or car rather automatically; and found yourself in class without any great surprise that other students were there and the instructor arrived more or less on time and picked up about where he left off in the previous discussion.

Habit has been called "the shackles of the free." Almost all our minor actions are patterned so that we are barely conscious of them; and major decisions, like the choice of a mate, are more patterned than most of us realize. If we really think about the impact of culture on our lives, we can hardly avoid a sense of wonder; we marvel at its power and pervasiveness.

In this chapter we ask: How does culture adapt man to his physical environment? Does it ever work against survival and adaptation? How does culture foster group cohesion and survival? How is culture related to an individual biological organism? Does it free him or control him, or both?

A few reminders are in order. No list of "needs" on the one hand and culture elements that satisfy them on the other is more than a classificatory device. There is no one-to-one correspondence between a culture element and the purpose it serves. Culture is a complex and interrelated whole, and any one aspect may have many meanings for the complex human beings who interact in a society. To take a simple example, a birthday cake is food in the strictest sense, but to classify it as serving the need for nutrition is obviously ridiculous. It also gives pleasure to children, and perhaps ego gratification to the mother who baked it, and is part of a ritual celebration marking what Americans (but not all peoples) see as a special day in life and giving it meaning and value.

Furthermore, when we say "culture does this and that," we do not mean that culture is an entity in itself, something superhuman that pushes people around. It is always *people* who behave according to cultural patterns and understandings, deviate from them, enforce them by means of sanctions, and pass them on to their children. Even so, culture is a useful abstraction for the regularities in the behavior of members of a group. In a more general way, we think of it as man's means of adapting to his physical environment, the imperatives of group life, and his biological and psychological nature.

Culture as Adaptation to Environment

Culture is mankind's survival kit on earth. Other animals come equipped with the right protective coats and the genetic programming or instincts that enable them to find food and shelter and perpetuate the species. "Genetic sources of information order their actions within much narrower ranges of variation, the narrower and more thorough-going the lower the animal." But man, as we saw in Chapter 3, is born with only very generalized capacities and tendencies to action. "Between what our body tells us and what we have to know in order to function, there is a vacuum we must fill ourselves, and we fill it with information (or misinformation) provided by our culture. . . . Undirected by culture patterns . . . man's behavior would be virtually ungovernable, a mere chaos of pointless acts and exploding emotions, his experience virtually shapeless."[1]

Culture extends man's powers and senses. Stone hammers and bulldozers are extensions of his hands; tamed horses and 747s of his feet; spectacles and television of his eyes; telephones and radio of his ears; books and newspapers of his speech; abacuses and computers of his brain. But none of these extensions is specifically linked to biological features; all can be changed as conditions change. The slow processes of biological evolution have been almost entirely replaced by swift and cumulative cultural adaptation.

Man can find food, clothing, and shelter in even the harshest environment. His clever hands, his fertile brain, and his capacity for speech combine to enable him to make tools and weapons, discover fire and metals, invent machines and containers, domesticate plants and animals. Language enables him to accumulate information, generation after generation, in an ever-growing storehouse of knowledge from which his descendants can draw.

This versatility more than makes up for the fact that man is a weak, slow-moving animal; it has allowed him to dominate and use the

[1]Clifford Geertz, "The Impact of the Concept of Culture on the Concept of Man," in Yehudi A. Cohen, ed., *Man in Adaptation: The Cultural Present* (Chicago: Aldine Publishing Company, 1968), pp. 16–29.

strength and speed of the horse, and then to invent the jet plane and space capsule. His capacities make up for his thin skin and the exposure of his highly vulnerable visceral region when he stands upright: He learns to utilize skins, fibers, bark, wood, stone, sod, leaves, reeds, sand, mud, and metals for housing and clothing, and eventually to live in gas-heated skyscrapers and wear dacron suits.

Man's adaptability more than makes up for his lack of instincts about desirable food; he learns through trial and error which berries and roots are edible, where to find fish, how to stalk animals, how to soften corn, and finally how to fill supermarket shelves with cans and packages of processed food. Perhaps some day he will use this same versatility to adapt himself to life on another planet—unless he chokes on poisoned air or finds himself back in a cave hiding from a radioactive cloud, a victim of his own inability to control the forces leading to war. Cultures or, more strictly speaking, culture-bearing animals not only solve problems; they create them. Not everything in man's survival kit serves the purpose.

Culture and Society

If culture in the general sense is the means of adaptation for the species as a whole, what consequences does each specific culture have for the society? Ralph Linton warns that we cannot speak of societies as having *needs* of their own apart from the needs of their individual members,[2] and Dorothy Lee remarks that too often social scientists simply assume that the ultimate goal of a society is survival.[3] Yet many culture patterns are oriented toward the maintenance of society rather than the satisfaction of individual needs. And *if* a society is to function successfully and endure through time, certain conditions must be fulfilled. What are they?

(1) First, individual psychological and biological needs must be met, and pivotal institutions emerge to do so. (2) New members, usually newborn babies, must be socialized, indoctrinated with the social values and trained to occupy positions in the social structure. "The new recruits to the society learn how to behave as husbands or chiefs or craftsmen and by so doing perpetuate these positions and with them the social system as a whole."[4] (3) Behavior must be guided toward what is socially desirable, through norms and sanctions. Every society must have a system of control to regulate the expression of aggression,

[2]*The Cultural Background of Personality* (New York: Appleton-Century-Crofts, 1945), pp. 23–24.

[3]"Are Basic Needs Ultimate?" in James Fadiman, ed., *The Proper Study of Man* (New York: The Macmillan Company, 1971), pp. 38–42.

[4]Linton, *The Cultural Background of Personality*, pp. 21–22.

sexual behavior, and property distribution. There is no known society where people are allowed to rape, rob, or kill.

(4) For individuals to function in a society, interaction must be largely regular and predictable. Norms are expectations, common definitions of possible actions.

> The common definition supplies each participant with decisive guidance in directing his own act so as to fit into the acts of others. Such common definitions serve, above everything else, to account for the regularity, stability, and repetitiveness of joint action in large areas of group life; they are the source of the established and regulated social behavior that is envisioned in the concept of culture.[5]

There is always an element of uncertainty in interaction, but it is minimized insofar as the participants accept established norms or arrive at a consensus on new ones.

(5) Another imperative is that the members of society feel they belong to the group and are motivated to act according to its rules. The constellation of beliefs and values we call myth tends to meet this imperative; it sets social and individual goals, gives a sense of origin and purpose, and invests experience with meaning and value.

The institutionalized meeting of individualized needs, indoctrination of new recruits, social control of behavior, predictability of interaction, and the sense of belonging and purpose enable a society to function and endure. Its common culture is a society's survival kit. Even this generalization, however, has exceptions. People continue to fight, kill, get sick, go mad. Some cultures have actually led to the extermination of the society: The Kaingang of Brazil, for example, had a cult of force and blood revenge that led to their progressive annihilation; the Shakers, who prohibited sexual relations, failed to recruit enough new members to keep the group going. Do technologies and social structures that include provisions for atomic, bacteriological, and chemical warfare promise any better for modern societies?

Culture and the Individual

The newborn baby enters a social group that already has a culture. He learns it almost as naturally as he breathes, for his parents, siblings, and playmates transmit its patterns to him as if there were no others. Partly through deliberate instruction, but largely through unconscious imitation and absorption of value orientations and even of ways of walking and standing, he adopts the society's ways. For most of us the

[5]Herbert Blumer, *Symbolic Interactionism* (Englewood Cliffs, N.J.: Prentice-Hall, Inc., 1969), p. 71.

main form and content of our personalities reflects that early experience. Let us consider what culture does for a person.

The culture provides an established pattern for satisfying biological needs. We need not individually work out ways to keep warm, to satisfy hunger and thirst, to fulfill sexual desires, to get our rest. Patterns that regulate and channel these elemental functions are present in the culture and guide us from infancy on. We are taught how, when, where, and with whom we may satisfy these needs. We learn the diet pattern of our culture and the modesty and hygiene of elimination. A person

> takes the bait of immediate personal satisfaction, and is caught upon the hook of socialization. He would learn to eat in response to his own hunger drive, but his elders teach him to "eat like a gentleman." Thus, in later years, his hunger drive elicits a response which will not only satisfy it but do so in a way acceptable to his society and compatible with its other culture patterns.[6]

Besides providing patterns for satisfying our elemental needs, each culture sets goals and creates desires that come to be regarded as needs. Group living appears to create a need to belong, to feel accepted, and this is an effective basis for socialization in the norms of the group. Some desires are not biologically beneficial, even though a person's "need"—for cigarettes and alcohol, for instance—may seem just as strong to him as his requirements for food or sleep. In a culture where esthetic satisfaction or success or spiritual commitment or wealth is highly valued, the desire of some people for these things is often stronger than their sexual drives. Even physical survival itself may seem less important than honor or freedom or country.

The language of each culture is a distinctive way of codifying reality; as he learns it, the child comes to perceive and interpret the world largely from its perspective and within its limitations. The language guides him not only to observe the world in a certain way, but also to express himself and react to it in a certain way. "A language is, in a sense, a philosophy. [It] says, as it were, 'notice this,' 'always consider this separate from that,' 'such and such things belong together.'. . . Every language has an effect upon what the people who use it see, what they feel, how they think, what they can talk about."[7]

Various societies codify reality differently. Dorothy Lee compared the concepts of the Trobriand Islanders concerning the relationships of events to our own.[8] The Trobrianders have no tenses—no lin-

[6]Linton, *The Cultural Background of Personality*, p. 25.

[7]Clyde Kluckhohn, *Mirror for Man* (New York: Fawcett World Library, 1964), pp. 164–67.

[8]"Codification of Reality: Lineal and Nonlineal," in Dorothy Lee, ed., *Freedom and Culture* (Englewood Cliffs, N.J.: Prentice-Hall, Inc., 1959), pp. 105–20.

guistic distinction between past and present—nor do they arrange activities and events according to causes, or means and ends. In contrast, we are extremely conscious of time, and use many tenses to express various time relationships. We are also conditioned to think of each event as followed by another in a series of stages leading to some goal or climax. To the Trobrianders, each "stage" has its own meaning. They have a different name for a yam at each of its stages; when it is ripe and round it is no longer considered the same yam as when it was small and green. What we would call a ripe yam is to them a *taytu*; when it is overripe, it is a different being, a *yowana*. But it does not *become* a sprouting *yowana*. "When sprouts appear, it ceases to be itself; in its place appears a *silasata*."[9]

In Western society we see lines in nature, lines between material points, and, metaphorically, lines between days and actions. What to the Trobrianders would be an aggregate of anecdotes we organize as history or narrative. We feel that "one thing leads to another"; they see acts in whole patterns, as indispensable parts of clusters (rather than sequences) set by tradition.

Cultural patterns guide and channel our interactions with others. Culture defines situations and outlines expectations for whatever role we play. The child learns how a good son acts—and a good father, a good friend, a good teacher, a good warrior. At a wedding he is expected to behave in one way; at a funeral, in another. He greets friends, disciplines his children, and meets strangers with actions prescribed by the culture. The rules of social interaction help him adapt to the group. In a more general way, we may say that institutions channel human actions into patterned grooves, much as instincts channel the actions of insects. They present a limited number of alternatives and bar other options so effectively that to the members of any one society the available patterns seem to be the only right and proper ones. In our society, for example, a young man attracted to a girl does not think of making her one of a harem, or of rejecting her because his parents have chosen another mate for him. Our system of norms lays out a path for him. "To desire is to love is to marry" is the institutional formula that channels his actions.[10]

As we said in discussing myth, culture gives meaning and value to experience. It defines what the child should regard as normal and abnormal, good and bad, pleasant and unpleasant, beautiful and ugly, interesting and uninteresting. It even defines the emotions a person should feel in different situations—love, pride, fear, anger, guilt, shame. Men must *learn* to love flags, worship stones, feel sexual jealousy. In some Moslem societies a person is grievously insulted if someone touches him with a shoe or with his left hand. In some, a strong

[9]*Ibid.*, p. 109.

[10]Peter Berger, *Invitation to Sociology* (Garden City, N.Y.: Doubleday & Company, Inc., 1963), p. 89.

warrior may lie down and die because a witch has predicted his death. Cultural patterns also guide the expression of emotions. In one society loud voices and violent motions express anger; in another the only visible sign may be a cold stare through narrowed eyelids. In some societies it is proper for men to weep for the dead, or weep for joy when reunited with a friend; in others only women may weep.

Finally, culture and group living combine to make a human being of the infant, to give him personality. As Geertz says, man without culture would not be a mindless ape, but a mental basket case, an unworkable monstrosity. Man with culture is human—and not just human in a general sense, but human by the specific definitions of his own society.

> When seen as a set of symbolic devices for controlling behavior . . . culture provides the link between what men are intrinsically capable of becoming and what they actually, one by one, in fact become. Becoming human is becoming individual, and we become individual under the guidance of cultural patterns, historically created systems of meaning in terms of which we give form, order, point, and direction to our lives. . . . One of the most significant facts about us may finally be that we all begin with the natural equipment to live a thousand kinds of life but end in the end having lived only one.[11]

Culture and Personal Freedom

The processes of socialization and continuing social control operate largely below our level of awareness. Edward Hall calls culture

> the hidden dimension. No matter how hard man tries it is impossible for him to divest himself of his own culture, for it has penetrated to the roots of his nervous system and determines how he perceives the world. Most of culture lies hidden and is outside voluntary control, making up the warp and weft of human existence. Even when small fragments of culture are elevated to awareness, they are difficult to change, not only because they are so personally experienced but *because people cannot act or interact at all in any meaningful way except through the medium of culture.*[12]

Are we, then, prisoners of culture? If we recognize the great power of culture, do we deny free will and individual initiative? That is an enormously controversial question, debated over the centuries.

[11]Geertz, "The Impact of the Concept of Culture." See Chapter 12 for a discussion of studies of culture and personality.

[12]Edward Hall, *The Hidden Dimension* (Garden City, N.Y.: Doubleday & Company, Inc., Anchor Books, 1969), p. 188.

The romantic philosophers of the Enlightenment saw man as the "noble savage," innately pure and good until corrupted by society. Man in his glorious, pure, unsullied original nature was the ideal. He was to be looked for "behind," "under," or "beyond" his customs. Then anthropologists came along who looked for man *in* his customs, seeking a universal human nature by classifying and comparing the content of different cultures. Still others divorced man from culture, denying that man himself had anything to do with the course of cultural evolution once he had given it the original push by starting to make tools and use language. These cultural evolutionists or determinists see that beginning as "the last creative act in which man ever engaged," and regard culture as having a dynamism of its own quite apart from people: It proceeds automatically, by laws of its own.[13]

In contrast Morris Opler and other humanist anthropologists insist that "Culture is the work of humanity; we have the impression that it is autonomous only because it is anonymous. It is the story, not of impersonal forces or prime movers and shakers, but of countless millions, each of whom has left a trace. Our subject is the study of *man*, of the human being, in every possible cultural context."[14]

Quite aside from the debate over whether man is simply the creature of culture or its creator, what about individual freedom? We have seen already that an individual growing up alone and provided in some fantastic fashion with food and warmth would not really be free. Because of his lack of instincts and biological adaptations, he would not even be free in the sense that an animal is free; he would be the prisoner of his own helplessness. Robinson Crusoe survived alone on his island because he was an adult who remembered a store of culture that he ingeniously applied to the problems of survival and comfort. But a lone infant, like Anna or Isabelle, would not be free to develop his potentialities as a human being.

Culture and society provide that freedom. Paradoxically, culture does so precisely because it is a set of ready-made patterns for behavior, "a map of beaten paths through the jungle of living."[15] We learn the accepted ways of satisfying our needs: We master the routines of dressing, eating, walking, getting to and from our place of work, and using language in speech and reading and writing, and we make them so habitual that they require little conscious thought and effort. Habits free our minds and energies for more creative thought and action and for enjoyment of life. Furthermore, by patterning the behavior of many individuals and groups within a society, culture makes it possible for any one of us to predict the behavior of others with varying degrees

[13]Morris E. Opler, "The Human Being in Culture Theory," *The American Anthropologist* 66, No. 3 (June 1964): 507–28; reprinted in Morton H. Fried, ed., *Readings in Anthropology*, vol. 2: *Cultural Anthropology* (New York: Thomas Y. Crowell, 1968), pp. 19–42.

[14]*Ibid.*

[15]Lee, *Freedom and Culture*, p. 45.

of accuracy. When we know what to expect of others, we eliminate much wasted effort and many possible sources of conflict. Conformity has its very real uses, and one of these is furthering personal freedom.

> Unless they are informed of it by an anthropologist, human beings seldom are aware that they have a culture and that they are supposed to act and re-enact its terms. What they are really trying to do is to live as fully and as well as they can. The symbols, tools, and understandings that constitute the culture act in a multiple capacity for the human being. They acquaint him with the ordinary possibilities. . . . They indicate to him the outer limits of permissible conduct. . . . They provide him with materials and avenues by means of which he can fashion something personal and unique for himself. . . . Man manipulates and uses his culture for his own ends quite as much as he is subject to it.[16]

But the degree to which specific cultures allow personal autonomy and provide freedom to the individual varies greatly. "In some societies, we find what amounts to a dictatorship; in others, the group may demand such sacrifice of individual uniqueness as to make for totalitarianism. On the other hand, in some societies we encounter a conception of individual autonomy and democratic procedures which far outstrip anything we have practiced or even have conceived of as democracy."[17]

Some American Indians show the individual absolute respect from birth, and value the child "as sheer being for his own uniqueness." No adult would presume to make choices or decisions for him. A mother in the Sikh tribe of British Columbia, for example, took excellent care of her 18-month-old baby, but did not cut the hair that fell over his eyes. Her reason? He had not asked her to. The language of the Wintu of California expresses this respect for others: Instead of saying, "I took the baby," they say, "I went with the baby"; instead of "The chief rules the people," they say, "The chief stood with the people."

Dr. Lee concludes that "law and limits and personal autonomy can coexist effectively, that spontaneity is not necessarily killed by group responsibility, that respect for individual integrity is not an end to be achieved by specific means, but that it can exist only if it is supported by deep conviction and by the entire way of life."[18]

There is a margin of free play, experiment, and innovation in every culture. Some people make more use of it than others. Margaret Mead sees in this fact hope for the survival of mankind. "There is little doubt that among our living populations as mankind is constituted— without resort to controlled eugenic manipulation—there is a sufficient

[16]Opler, "The Human Being in Culture Theory."
[17]Lee, *Freedom and Culture*, p. 6.
[18]*Freedom and Culture*, p. 4.

number of highly gifted individuals who, given the proper cultural conditions in which to work, could go on to make the necessary innovations" to assure the survival of the species.[19]

Summary

Because man is born with generalized and diffuse capacities and tendencies, he could not survive without culture, which is the uniquely human form of adaptation to the environment. Cultural evolution is far swifter than the biological evolution by which all animals adapt.

If societies are to endure, cohere, and function successfully, they must satisfy individual biological and psychological needs, socialize new recruits to fill their positions in the social structure, guide behavior to what is socially desirable, provide for regularity and predictability in interaction, and instill a feeling of belonging and a desire to work toward group goals. The system of norms, sanctions, beliefs, knowledge, and values fulfills these social imperatives, especially through institutions.

A society's culture provides patterns by which the individual can fulfill both elemental needs and culturally created desires; presents a codification of reality, primarily through language, which shapes his thoughts and perceptions; guides and channels his interaction with others; gives meaning and value to his experience; and makes a human being out of a helpless biological organism. The individual absorbs the culture of his group largely through subtle processes of which he is unaware.

Cultural determinists insist that culture is governed by its own laws and develops independently of human initiative. Humanist anthropologists stress the active, innovative role of individuals. There is a great difference among cultures in the degree to which individual autonomy and personal freedom are valued and encouraged.

In describing its nature, content, and functions, we have expanded on the definition of culture in Chapter 3. Now we sum up what culture is and does:

Culture in the general sense is man's system of adapting to the physical environment, his biological nature, and his group life. Each specific culture is a configuration that includes norms or behavior patterns with accompanying sanctions; understandings, including knowledge, beliefs, and values; material things given meaning by norms and understandings; and a social structure defining the relationships among people on the basis of various kinds of differentiation. Culture defines the meaning and value of things, ideas, emotions, and actions. It arises out of language communication within a social group, and is learned

[19]Margaret Mead, *Continuities in Cultural Evolution* (New Haven, Conn.: Yale University Press, 1964), p. 247.

and shared by its members. Its various elements or traits are organized into complexes and patterns. Its degree of integration, or fit and harmony among elements, varies according to the degree of consensus on overt patterns and on cultural myths or constellations of values. Culture is highly stable and continuous, yet it changes through time and spreads from group to group. It divides and unites, frees and constrains the human race.

In the concluding chapter of Part One, our concern is the significance of this concept of culture for the person, society, and relationships among persons and groups.

QUESTIONS FOR FURTHER THOUGHT

1.   What decisions did you make this week that you believe were not patterned by culture? Reflect on the cultural elements that helped you make your decision. Were they communicated to you by others? Were they part of your childhood socialization? Did they include some new elements you had to seek out, through advice from others, library research, or careful weighing of pros and cons? How much freedom did you have to decide among alternatives?

2.   If habit is the shackles of the free, may it not also be the shackles of the enslaved?

3.   Things in "man's survival kit" that do not serve the purpose are called "dysfunctional." What cultural patterns in your personal life do you consider dysfunctional? In the society as a whole? In the world?

4.   Have you recently entered a social relationship with a member of another subcultural group? Did you have difficulty knowing what was expected of you and what to expect of the other person? How did you arrive at mutual agreement on norms?

5.   Is it difficult for you to grasp the Trobrianders' conception of states of being as opposed to stages, of clusters of events rather than narrative? What consequences do you think such an outlook has for behavior? (See *Argonauts of the Western Pacific* by Bronislaw Malinowski if you wish to pursue the subject.)

6. If you feel there is a "generation gap" either specifically between you and your parents, or between you and the "older generation" in general, try to analyze it in terms of different definitions of situations and expectations of behavior.

7. Do you think the sanction against males' weeping in our culture and a few others is functional or dysfunctional? Why?

8. Elaborate on Geertz's comment that man without culture would not be comparable to a "mindless ape" but would be a completely unworkable monstrosity.

9. "As a simple unit in the social organism," said Ralph Linton, "the individual perpetuates the status quo. As an individual he helps to change the status quo when the need arises. New social inventions are made by those who suffer from the current conditions, not by those who profit from them." (*The Cultural Background of Personality*, pp. 22–23.) Discuss.

10. Although man adapts more by cultural than by biological evolution, the two still go hand in hand to some extent. People today, for example, may be physically weaker than their early ancestors because of various "cushions" against the environment. Occasionally biologists predict that men may lose their teeth, or that their legs may atrophy, and other less startling mutations. Speculate about what will happen to man the organism if some innovations now limited to fantasy and experiment occur, e.g., personal rocket propulsion from place to place.

11. The leading cultural evolutionist Leslie White believes that culture is governed by its own laws and men "are merely the instruments through which cultures express themselves." Do you agree with him or with humanist anthropologists like Morris Opler?

All good people agree,
    And all good people say,
That all nice people like Us are We,
    And everyone else is They;

But if you cross over the sea,
    Instead of over the way,
You may end by (think of it!) looking on We
    As only a sort of They!

                    RUDYARD KIPLING

In ancient Greece, the navel of the earth
was marked by a monolith at Delphi.

                    ARNOLD TOYNBEE

Those who know no culture other than their
own cannot know their own.

                    RALPH LINTON

THE
IMPORTANCE
OF
THE
CULTURE
CONCEPT

AMERICAN CULTURE AND PERSONALITY has been observed and criticized by many foreigners, including the astute de Tocqueville and the bitterly critical Charles Dickens. Here is a more recent sample:

> All Americans, without exception, make an effort to smile. In America, a person can learn to smile in short courses at special schools. Americans are unable to avoid three topics of conversation: automobiles, the state of their digestion and insomnia. Americans drink coffee without end, anywhere and at any time. If they don't drive themselves with this 'whip' they quickly go sour, lose their ability to work and become irritable. All of Hollywood's movies are filled with a clear, sometimes deeply concealed but always detectable, aim of strengthening and propping up the capitalist system. Under the guise of 'patriotic films' there is concealed a yearning of American monopolists for world domination. Americans are an unusually practical people, even though they use a surprisingly impractical and frightfully inconvenient system of weights and measures. Americans are punctual. When staying in an American hotel, one need not present any kind of documents. All one has to do is write his name on a registry card, his profession and home address. In America people live without passports.[1]

How did you react to these generalizations by a Soviet journalist? Do you think he was an objective critic? Did he irritate you by lack of understanding? Do you understand his remark about passports? Does he reveal anything about Soviet culture?

The concept of culture is as important to understanding human behavior as are the concepts of evolution to biology, of gravity to physics, and of disease to medicine.[2] But to use the concept fruitfully, a person must be aware of the tendency to believe that his "own usages far surpass those of all others"—a tendency noted by Herodotus, the

---

[1]From "Why the Statue of Liberty Looks to the East, Etc.," *The New York Times Magazine* (Dec. 25, 1966): 8–9 ff. A report on Soviet journalist Albertas Laurinchikas's book on American life, *The Third Side of the Dollar.*

[2]Clyde Kluckhohn, *Mirror for Man* (New York: Fawcett World Library, 1964), p. 18.

much-traveled historian of ancient Greece. He must try to acquire an attitude of respect for cultural differences. In this final chapter on culture, we shall concern ourselves with these conflicting attitudes (ethnocentrism and cultural relativity), their sources, and their significance for human behavior and society. In addition, we shall sum up the implications of the concept of culture in order to anticipate its uses in the rest of the book and in the broader context of group life.

Ethnocentrism

As a person is socialized, he comes to feel that "the axis of the earth runs right through his home town." The tendency to judge other groups and cultures by the norms and values of one's own, and therefore to regard them as inherently inferior, is called **ethnocentrism** (from the Greek word *ethnos* or "nation.").

Ethnocentrism is a universal phenomenon; every group sets "us" off from "them." "We" are the center, and all others are scaled in reference to us; *our* ways are "human nature," *our* motivations obvious. The Greeks thought that people who spoke no Greek "babbled," hence our word "barbarian." Finnish immigrants in Minnesota and Michigan refer to people who do not speak Finnish as *toiskielinen*, meaning "other-tongued." The Cuna of Panama (and many other tribes) call themselves "The People."

A team of researchers studied this attitude in five neighboring communities in Rimrock, an area of western New Mexico. A different ethnic group lives in each community: Navaho and Zuñi Indians, Mormons, Texan homesteaders, and Spanish-Americans.

> Although propinquity leads to some intercultural borrowing and to some pattern of intercultural communication, it is also a first-rate preservative of uniqueness and difference. The intercultural dynamics of the Rimrock area appear to lead to a tenacious retention of distinctive values. The self-image of each cultural group is ethnocentrically flattering. All refer to themselves in terms that define them as "persons" or "people," and to the others as excluded from or inferior to true humanity.[3]

Members of each community were asked to suppose that a 10-year drought drove everyone away, and then the rains returned and God allowed one group to come back to build a good new community. Which one should it be? Each thought his own group would be by far the most desirable for the area.[4]

[3]Evon Z. Vogt and Ethel M. Albert, eds., *People of Rimrock: A Study of Values in Five Cultures* (Cambridge: Harvard University Press, 1966), p. 26.
[4]*Ibid.*, pp. 27–28.

Nationalism is the most prominent form of ethnocentrism today. A person's belief in the superiority of his group may also include pride in and loyalty to his community or home town, his school, his fraternity, or his state. And this same belief may take such socially disruptive forms as racism, sexism, religious bigotry, and the over-zealous and belligerent patriotism called jingoism.

THE INEVITABILITY OF ETHNOCENTRISM

The assumption that one's own group is superior and the tendency to judge others by one's own standards are practically inevitable. A social group *teaches* its members to be ethnocentric, both through the informal processes of socialization and social control and through deliberate instruction by school, church, and government. The ways of our own group seem natural and right, because our own morals and values are the only standards we have for judging behavior. As we become aware that there are other groups with other ways, we may be willing to think in terms of their cultural values; but we are able to do so only to a limited extent. Our thinking stems from certain premises; members of other societies think according to different premises. So with equal logic we and they arrive at different conclusions.

The practice of bride-purchase among the cattle-raising Guajiro Indians of her country disturbed a Colombian anthropologist, who "felt terribly sad that a Colombian woman could be sold like a cow." But her Indian informant in turn lost all respect for her when she learned her husband had not given even a single cow for her: "You must not be worth anything."[5]

ADVANTAGES AND DISADVANTAGES IN ETHNOCENTRISM

Ethnocentrism is not altogether objectionable. It has certain definite advantages for the "we group" and its individual members. It makes for social integration, reduces conflicts within the group (by deflecting many frustrations outward), and promotes cultural stability and uniformity (if what we do is right and natural and human, why change?). In a nation at war ethnocentrism is obviously an asset, and is fostered by various means.

Besides holding the group together, ethnocentrism is psychologically satisfying to the individual. He participates vicariously in all sorts of wonderful things that other members of his group have or do. The

[5]Virginia Gutiérrez de Pineda, quoted in George M. Foster, *Traditional Cultures and the Impact of Technological Change* (New York: Harper & Row, Publishers, 1962), p. 69.

lowly substitute's ego is enhanced if he is a member of a championship team, however little he may personally have had to do with the team's success. A nationality gives a person an identity, a sense of belonging.

But in the modern world the harmful effects of ethnocentrism outweigh its advantages. First, ethnocentrism, especially in its more extreme manifestations, tends to be accompanied by a sense of satisfaction with the status quo—with things as they are—and by a resentment of anyone who questions conditions or suggests ways to improve the cultural and social order. Social changes, when they come, prove to be far more disruptive and violent than a gradual process of intelligently guided change would have been. Second, modern societies such as ours are highly complex, with their parts interdependent, and no group within such a society can live in a vacuum. Extreme ethnocentrism in subcultural groups in our society incites conflict among these groups, or at best prevents them from working together as effectively as they might for the good of the whole society. Intolerance and misunderstanding among racial, religious, and nationality groups stem largely from each group's conviction of its own "rightness."

Most important of all, ethnocentrism hinders nations from solving mutual problems and settling their disagreements. Narrow nationalism is the chief stumbling block to a really effective world organization. Ethnocentrism breeds ill will whenever members of one society display it in their dealings with members of another. Only a deep belief in the superiority of English culture over "native" cultures enabled the British to rationalize their imperialism in terms of "The White Man's Burden." In their contacts with so-called underdeveloped areas, Europeans and Americans have been especially prone to tread roughshod over the cultures of other peoples, and as a consequence to produce confusion and disorganization in many societies. Disdain and contempt for the ways of others breed resentment and in time often provoke aggression.

ETHNOCENTRISM AND PERSONALITY

Although everyone is ethnocentric to some degree, extreme ethnocentrism in our society has been found to correlate with a person's general orientation toward authoritarian rather than democratic values. T. W. Adorno and his associates constructed an opinion-attitude scale for measuring ethnocentrism. Respondents were asked to rate their agreement or disagreement with such statements as the following on a scale of six degrees: (1) To end prejudice against Jews, the first step is for the Jews to try sincerely to get rid of their harmful and irritating faults. (2) Negroes have their rights, but it is best to keep them in their own districts and schools and to prevent too much contact with whites. (3) The worst danger to real Americanism during the last 50 years has come from foreign ideas and agitators. (4) America may not be perfect, but the American Way has brought us about as close as human beings can get to a perfect society.[6]

Adorno found that a person who is ethnocentric in one of these areas (a white racist) is very likely to be ethnocentric in the others as well. He is hostile to each outgroup, though he dislikes some more than others; he tends to idealize the ingroup as superior in morality, ability, and general development, and to give it blind obedience and loyalty. The irrationality of extreme ethnocentrism, especially in America, is apparent. "Thus, in a context of international relations ethnocentrism takes the form of pseudopatriotism; 'we' are the best people and the best country in the world. . . . [But the pseudopatriot] actually regards most of America as an outgroup: various religions, nonwhites, 'the masses,' too-educated people and too-uneducated people, criminals, radicals, and so on, tend largely to fall in the outgroup category."[7]

Culture Shock

No matter how willing a person may be to understand the ways of another group, he is bound to experience some culture shock—to feel like "a fish out of water"—when he first visits a strange country or even a subcultural group. Despite many pleasant experiences in Paris, we also recall being annoyed because no one at the hotel had warned us that all ordinary business comes to a halt on Pentecost. A French visitor to American factories was surprised to find that all of them were nationalized; after all, he saw the American flag flying over each one!

Peace Corps volunteers experience culture shock in spite of intensive training, and after their 2 years in the field they suffer a "re-entry crisis." A volunteer home from Pakistan and wearing the national dress was recognized in an elevator as the heroine of a Peace Corps recruiting film. When everyone in the car turned to look at her, she was so embarrassed that she became dizzy and nearly fainted. Why? Women do not get that kind of attention in Pakistan, and she was reacting like a Pakistani. The typical returnee sees his own country differently: as "a crowded, car-jammed, commercialized mess—surfeit and superabundance everywhere. His friends and relatives seem none too clear on where he had been or what he did there or why it was important. They don't appear much interested in the rest of the world."[8] Perhaps the chief difference between him and them is that he has acquired an attitude of cultural relativity.

[6]T. W. Adorno et al., *The Authoritarian Personality* (New York: Harper & Row, Publishers, 1950), p. 142.

[7]Daniel J. Levinson, *ibid.*, pp. 147–48.

[8]Richard B. Stolley, "The Re-Entry Crisis," *Life*, p. 98 ff.

Cultural Relativity

The concept of **cultural relativity** refers to an attitude of respect for cultural differences. The concept includes the ideas (*1*) that every culture must be seen intact, with its values inseparably interwoven into the whole; (2) that each body of custom has an inherent dignity and meaning as the way of life that one group has worked out for adapting to its environment, answering the biological needs of its members, and ordering group relationships; and (3) that our own culture is but one among many, one that most of us happen to prefer primarily because we grew up in it.

Cultural relativity does not imply that "all systems of moral values, all concepts of right and wrong, are founded on such shifting sands that there is no need for morality, for proper behavior, for ethical conduct."[9] Morality, truth, and beauty are values in every culture, though they may take different forms. Margaret Mead demonstrates vividly that an act we consider unthinkably immoral can be moral within another cultural context:

> Among the Arapesh of New Guinea, children are valued and welcomed. Parents make every sacrifice that their children may thrive and grow, and the whole culture is oriented toward the needs of the next generation. Yet infanticide is part of the standard cultural behavior. If, in spite of rigorously observed lactation taboos on sex relations until at least a year after each child's birth, a woman bears more children than she and her husband can care for, or if the next oldest child is still sickly and needs great care, then it is the duty of the parents to put the new baby to death. Living on very poor land, with a most meager technology, infanticide is a moral act for the Arapesh. If, however, they were transplanted to more fertile land, their scanty supply of food crops augmented with new and more nourishing food plants, their inadequate technology improved, infanticide would cease to be compatible with the central value in their culture, the stress on the importance of producing and raising children.[10]

Although cultural relativity means respect for other ways, it does not necessarily mean loss of respect for our own. A person may decide, after rational reflection, that his ways are *the* best, or the best for his group or the best for him (because he wants to adjust to his

[9]Melville J. Herskovits, *Man and His Works* (New York: Alfred A. Knopf, 1948), p. 75.
[10]*Anthropology: A Human Science* (Princeton, N.J.: D. Van Nostrand Co., Inc., 1964), p. 96.

group). As Clyde Kluckhohn says, anthropology does not destroy the need for standards, "the useful tyranny of the normal."[11] It does teach us, Ruth Benedict points out, to recognize that other cultures are as significant to their members as ours is to us.[12] It may also suggest ways, we might change our own culture or life style.

In any case, culture has such a hold on us that most of us never escape our own, established patterns to more than a limited extent—and relatively few of us try to do so. Even anthropologists are rooted in their own cultures. Besides, one "who was truly and utterly free from his own culture would be no more competent to study other ways of life than an individual who has lost his memory is able to grasp what is going on around him."[13]

While most anthropologists believe that cultural relativity enriches even familiar experiences by increasing our level of awareness, some social scientists think one pays a penalty for being self-conscious. When his own society is no longer the center of things, he feels a bit shaken up and seeks new moorings. Aware of cultural myths that others take for granted, he may no longer enjoy such "tribal rites" as weddings and Christmas.[14]

Acquiring an Attitude of Cultural Relativity

A study of anthropology is one way—perhaps the quickest way—to overcome extreme ethnocentrism and acquire an attitude of cultural relativity. Perhaps nothing the anthropologist can tell us is more convincing than the realization that much of our own culture is the result of contact over time with other cultures. Ralph Linton's classic description of a "100% American" drives home the point that ignorance of a culture's many and varied sources fosters ethnocentrism:

> There can be no question about the average American's Americanism or his desire to preserve this precious heritage at all costs. Nevertheless, some insidious foreign ideas have already wormed their way into his civilization without his realizing what was going on. Thus dawn finds the unsuspecting patriot garbed in pajamas, a garment of Indian origin; and lying in a bed built on a pattern which originated in either Persia or Asia Minor. He is muffled to the ears in un-American ma-

[11]*Mirror for Man*, p. 41.

[12]*Patterns of Culture* (Baltimore, Md.: Penguin, 1946), p. 37.

[13]Clyde Kluckhohn, "Common Humanity and Diverse Cultures," in Daniel Lerner, ed., *The Human Meaning of the Social Sciences* (Cleveland, Ohio: World Publishing, 1959), pp. 245–84.

[14]Kenneth Boulding, *The Meaning of the Twentieth Century* (New York: Harper & Row, Publishers, 1964), pp. 65–66.

terials: cotton, first domesticated in India; linen, domesticated in the
Near East; wool from an animal native to Asia Minor; or silk whose
uses were first discovered by the Chinese. All these substances have
been transformed into clothes by methods invented in Southwestern
Asia. If the weather is cold enough, he may even be sleeping under an
eider-down quilt invented in Scandinavia.

On awakening he glances at the clock, a medieval European invention, uses one potent Latin word in abbreviated form, rises in haste,
and goes to the bathroom. Here, if he stops to think about it, he must
feel himself in the presence of a great American institution; he will
have heard stories of both the quality and frequency of foreign
plumbing and will know that in no other country does the average
man perform his ablutions in the midst of such splendor. But the in-
sidious foreign influence pursues him even here. Glass was invented
by the ancient Egyptians, the use of glazed tiles for floors and walls
in the Near East, porcelain in China, and the art of enameling on
metal by Mediterranean artisans of the Bronze Age. Even his bathtub
and toilet are but slightly modified copies of Roman originals. The only
purely American contribution to the ensemble is the steam radiator.

In this bathroom the American washes with soap invented by the ancient Gauls. Next, he cleans his teeth, a subversive European practice
which did not invade America until the latter part of the eighteenth
century. He then shaves, a masochistic rite first developed by the
heathen priests of ancient Egypt and Sumer. The process is made less
of a penance by the fact that his razor is of steel, an iron-carbon alloy
discovered in either India or Turkestan. Lastly, he dries himself on a
Turkish towel.

Returning to the bedroom, the unconscious victim of un-American
practices removes his clothes from a chair, invented in the Near East,
and proceeds to dress. He puts on close-fitting tailored garments
whose form derives from the skin clothing of the ancient nomads of
the Asiatic steppes and fastens them with buttons whose prototypes
appeared in Europe at the close of the Stone Age. This costume is
appropriate enough for outdoor exercise in a cold climate, but is quite
unsuited to American summers, steam-heated houses, and Pullmans.
Nevertheless, foreign ideas and habits hold the unfortunate man in
thrall even when common sense tells him that the authentically American costume of gee string and moccasins would be far more comfortable. He puts on his feet stiff coverings made from hide prepared
by a process invented in ancient Egypt and cut to a pattern which can
be traced back to ancient Greece, and makes sure they are properly
polished, also a Greek idea. Lastly he ties about his neck a strip of
bright-colored cloth which is a vestigial survival of the shoulder
shawls worn by seventeenth-century Croats. He gives himself a final

appraisal in the mirror, an old Mediterranean invention, and goes downstairs to breakfast.

Here a whole new series of foreign things confronts him. His food and drink are placed before him in pottery vessels, the popular name of which—china—is sufficient evidence of their origin. His fork is a medieval Italian invention and his spoon a copy of a Roman original. He will usually begin the meal with coffee, an Abyssinian plant first discovered by the Arabs. The American is quite likely to need it to dispel the morning-after effects of over-indulgence in fermented drinks, invented in the Near East; or distilled ones, invented by the alchemists of Medieval Europe. Whereas the Arabs took their coffee straight, he will probably sweeten it with sugar, discovered in India, and dilute it with cream; both the domestication of cattle and the technique of milking having originated in Asia Minor.

If our patriot is old-fashioned enough to adhere to the so-called American breakfast, his coffee will be accompanied by an orange, domesticated in the Mediterranean region, a cantaloupe domesticated in Persia, or grapes, domesticated in Asia Minor. He will follow this with a bowl of cereal made from grain domesticated in the Near East and prepared by methods also invented there. From this he will go on to waffles, a Scandinavian invention, with plenty of butter, originally a Near-Eastern cosmetic. As a side dish he may have the egg of a bird domesticated in Southeastern Asia or strips of the flesh of an animal domesticated in the same region, which have been salted and smoked by a process invented in Northern Europe.

Breakfast over, he places upon his head a molded piece of felt, invented by the nomads of Eastern Asia, and, if it looks like rain, puts on outer shoes of rubber, discovered by the ancient Mexicans, and takes an umbrella, invented in India. He then sprints for his train— the train, not the sprinting, being an English invention. At the station he pauses for a moment to buy a newspaper, paying for it with coins invented in ancient Lydia. Once on board he settles back to inhale the fumes of a cigarette invented in Mexico, or a cigar invented in Brazil. Meanwhile, he reads the news of the day, imprinted in characters invented by the ancient Semites by a process invented in Germany upon a material invented in China. As he scans the latest editorial pointing out the dire results to our institutions of accepting foreign ideas, he will not fail to thank a Hebrew God in an Indo-European language that he is a one-hundred per cent (decimal system invented by the Greeks) American (from Americus Vespucci, Italian geographer).[15]

[15]Ralph Linton, "One Hundred Per Cent American," *The American Mercury* **40** (April 1937): 427–29.

Evaluating Cultures

It is a precarious thing to judge cultures, but people do it constantly. We often hear cultures called high or low, barbaric or civilized, decadent and imitative or active and innovative. Usually such judgments reflect the observer's own culture. Americans tend to judge other nations by their attainment of the things in which we take most pride—bigness, speed, material abundance, comfort, and efficiency. Latin Americans are more likely to judge in terms of art, literature, music, courtesy, and enjoyment of life.

Often we comment on special aspects of culture, admiring something about this one, something else about that. We may admire the Plains Indians for devising special norms for men who did not fit the masculine warrior role. An expert on preliterate art and myth admires the magnificent songs of the Navahos, while noting that the Pueblos have few songs but elaborate ceremonials, and that Australian aborigines have a high order of myths. Similarly, England has always had an abundance of great writers, but fewer painters proportionately than the Flemish, and fewer composers than the Germans. The Polynesian account of the Creation "makes Genesis read like the comic strip *Tales from the Great Book.*"[16]

Sometimes our favorable judgments of another culture are as false as our unfavorable ones. An Iranian objects to the American idea of the mystical Orient as a romantic illusion. "The East they glorify is a famished, ailing man sprawled on the side of the road who is struggling to arise while they stand around congratulating him and his ancestors on being spiritual, and living so close to the earth."[17]

Some cultures, insists Morris Freilich, *are* inferior—witness that of Nazi Germany. Although it is not easy to devise "measuring rods" for evaluating cultural rules, he argues, the attempt should be made.[18] What might we tentatively suggest as guidelines for such an attempt?

First, we might ask how well a society fulfills the basic functions of protecting the individual and preserving the social group. How well does it cope with the environment? How well does it adapt to change? How well does it reconcile conflicts? Does it provide for health and safety? Is it on a self-destructive path, like the Kaingang of Brazil, and like the nuclear powers? In today's interdependent world, we cannot be content to judge a culture strictly in terms of its inner function-

[16]John Greenway, "Conversations with the Stone Age," *Saturday Review* (Feb. 16, 1964).

[17]F. M. Esfandiary, "The Mystical West Puzzles the Practical East," *The New York Times Magazine* (Feb. 5, 1967): 22–23 ff.

[18]Morris Freilich, ed., *Marginal Natives: Anthropologists at Work* (New York: Harper & Row, Publishers, 1970), p. 582.

ing; it must adapt not only to geography and climate but also to other societies.

> The era of world history has begun. The scale of functional dependence between societies expands, drawing together the histories of different parts of the planet. The several cultures of mankind become subcultures, subsystems, differentiated parts of a larger complex of cultural relations. . . . [No culture] is intelligible in isolation, apart from its adaptation to others in the world-cultural net. As each . . . society becomes an environment of every other, it becomes for us common sense and necessity to learn how to interpret cultures as much from the outside, from their environmental contexts, as from their inner values.[19]

Adaptability and successful functioning may be measured by such social indicators as economic distribution, infant mortality, life expectancy, political stability, and mental health. Attempts to measure "the quality of life"—what makes one society happier than another—include these and more elusive indicators, such as availability of outdoor recreation, opportunities for participation in creative arts, and freedom from anxiety about illness, violence, and crime.

The social order is based on trust. We venture out on the road trusting hundreds of other drivers; we trust that stores will be open, that the mail will be delivered, that we can safely go about our business. Does the culture support or erode this trust? Swiftness of communication, ever-increasing with the development of communications satellites, is usually held to be a good thing, uniting more and more people. But some fear that the mass media tend rather to *divide* people and destroy their sense of community and communion. "As we hear and read much about the acts of violence and injury men perpetrate upon one another, year after year, with so little emphasis placed on the loving, caring, and humanitarian acts of man, we begin to trust our fellow men less, and we thereby diminish ourselves."[20]

Second, we might ask how well a society lives up to its own cultural values and goals. Does it provide opportunities to satisfy the desires it creates and achieve the goals it sets for its members? "Social problems" are indications that something is out of gear: racism and inequality of educational opportunity in a democracy, poverty in an affluent society, militarism on the rise in a nation that prides itself on being peace-loving.

Third, we might ask what kind of people result from the socio-

---

[19]Marshall D. Sahlins, "Culture and Environment: The Study of Cultural Ecology," in Sol Tax, ed., *Horizons of Anthropology* (Chicago: Aldine Publishing Co., 1964), pp. 132–47.

[20]Herbert A. Otto, "New Light on the Human Potential," *Saturday Review* (Dec. 20, 1969): 14–17.

cultural patterning. Abram Kardiner insists that the *only* adequate measure of a culture is its effect on the individual personality. "There is a penalty for bad social patterning; the effects on the human unit are disastrous, and the entire culture is put into jeopardy sooner or later."[21] The Alorese of Indonesia, for example, bring up children in a way that produces unhappy and spiteful adults. Children are teased, frightened, tolerated, half-abused, and neglected by their mothers, who must work in the garden. As adults they are suspicious, mistrustful, fearful, and anxious, lacking in confidence and self-esteem, and nonaggressive, (preying on their neighbors with lies, deception, and chicanery). They are unable to sustain a love relationship or friendship based on voluntary interest. They are chronically unhappy, frustrated, and confused, convinced that they can expect only the worst from life; they have a limited capacity to master or enjoy their social world.[22]

Finally, we might ask to what degree does the culture realize human potential—innate intelligence, length of life, and the capacity for love and joy, for spiritual and esthetic experience? Does the process of socialization stifle or develop sense awareness, empathy, imagination, and creativity?[23]

Uses of the Culture Concept

An attitude of cultural relativity and an understanding of the concept of culture and its implications can be of value to the student and to society in a number of ways. To be very practical, both are essential to fruitful study of the remaining chapters of this book, as well as of further courses in the social sciences. We have already touched upon the concepts of society, personality, and institutions, placing them in the context of a human group with a particular way of life we call its culture. In the rest of the book we shall expand upon these concepts, and we shall call upon our knowledge of norms, beliefs, and values in many other connections.

In a broader and less immediate sense, cultural relativity is essential to a liberal education. It helps to close "the gap between our small ethnocentric, narrowly racial, class and time bound senses of identity and the grandeur of our membership in one human species, now bound together as denizens of one planet."[24] Differences in phys-

[21]Kardiner and Preble, *They Studied Man.*

[22]Cora DuBois, *The People of Alor* (Minneapolis: University of Minnesota Press, 1944).

[23]We consider these questions further in Part Three, "The Person in Culture and Society," and in Chapter 19.

[24]Margaret Mead, "Anthropology and an Education for the Future," in Jesse D. Jennings and E. Adamson Hoebel, eds., *Readings in Anthropology*, 2nd ed. (New York: McGraw-Hill, 1966), pp. 3–5.

Operation Crossroads.

ical appearance, customs, and language come to seem less important than our common humanity.

An understanding of the culture concept also makes us more at home in a world where intergroup contacts steadily increase. We learn to predict the behavior of others somewhat successfully as we become more familiar with their culture or subculture, and more aware of our own. We learn how to ask ourselves what cultural basis there is for some difficulty or misunderstanding.

American families at a military post in a small French town, for example, found the community unfriendly. By chance, one day an officer who enjoyed gardening approached his neighbor with some questions. This broke the ice, and when his wife arrived some weeks later, she was met by a delegation of French ladies carrying flowers. The block to friendly interaction was simple: Americans who move into a neighborhood expect their neighbors to make friendly overtures; French people expect newcomers to do so. If the Americans had verbalized their own customs, saying "In our country the established residents break the ice," and then gone one step further, "But maybe it is the other way around here," they would probably have discovered the source of the difficulty much earlier.[25]

A thorough grasp of the culture concept also makes us more objective toward our own culture. "The last thing a dweller in the deep sea would be likely to discover would be water. He would become conscious of its existence only if some accident brought him to the surface and introduced him to air. . . . Those who know no culture other than their own cannot know their own."[26] Comparing our own culture with others in an open-minded way, we may find that things we regard as fundamental seem minor to others, and we see alternative ways of doing things—alternatives an ethnocentric attitude would prevent us from considering. Britain, for example, does not treat drug addicts as criminals, but as sick people whose habit need not lead to crime; addiction is a matter for doctors and health authorities.[27] Where an ethnocentric person is rigid in his judgments of others even in his own society, a culturally aware person is more tolerant of harmless deviations from cultural patterns.

A delightful parody of anthropological reports, written by Horace Miner and titled "Body Ritual Among the Nacirema," depicts the personal hygiene and grooming of a backward (try spelling it that way) group from an anthropological perspective. "The magical beliefs and practices of the Nacirema present such unusual aspects that it seems desirable to describe them as an example of the extremes to which human behavior can go."[28]

As we come to recognize the oneness of humanity, to feel more at home in the world, to regard our own culture more objectively, and to tolerate differences and harmless deviations, we may also come to understand ourselves better. Perhaps this understanding will not be as intense as that of the field worker in a strange tribe, who "discovers

[25]Edmund S. Glenn, "Across the Cultural Barrier," *The Key Reporter* 31, No. 1 (Autumn 1965).

[26]Ralph Linton, *The Cultural Background of Personality* (New York: Appleton-Century-Crofts, 1945), p. 125.

[27]Amitai Etzioni and Fredric L. Dubow, *Comparative Perspectives: Theories and Methods* (Boston: Little, Brown and Company, 1970).

[28]Horace Miner, "Body Ritual Among the Nacirema," *American Anthropologist* 58, No. 3 (1956): 503–7; reprinted in Alan Dundes, ed., *Every Man His Way: Readings in Cultural Anthropology* (Englewood Cliffs, N.J.: Prentice-Hall, Inc., 1968), pp. 433–37.

Drawing by W. Miller; © 1968 The New Yorker Magazine, Inc.

"I see your people putting down roots. I see them becoming renowned for cheeses, buffet-style dinners, sexy blondes and modern furniture."

how he [himself] stands, walks, and gestures, the patterns of logical forms of his thoughts, his assumptions of order, progress, and time."[29] Yet an awareness of alternative norms and values gives us an opportunity to choose, to guide our own lives; we gain greater control of our own behavior, more autonomy.

How does the study of culture serve society? Largely through the changes in attitudes outlined above, which instill patience, perspective, objectivity, and optimism about social change; and also through the application of cultural understandings to various specific problems.

Patience comes from appreciation of the strength and persistence of cultural patterns. The would-be reformer who takes customs, values, and beliefs into account knows that radical changes cannot be accomplished overnight. In human affairs there is no such thing as a completely fresh start; no one can wipe clean the slate of tradition and past experience. Foreign aid consultants and Peace Corps workers in other

[29]Thomas Rhys Williams, *Field Methods in the Study of Culture* (New York: Holt, Rinehart & Winston, 1967), p. 62.

countries quickly realize that "no reform can ever bear fruit unless it is grafted successfully to the living tree of culture."[30]

Once we understand the role of culture in human behavior, we become more optimistic about the eventual solution of social problems. If the people of a warlike nation were "born that way," little could be done to change them. But such people are aggressive because their culture has shaped them that way; and culture does change. The ancestors of today's neutral, pacifist Swedes were the warlike Vikings. The murderer and the thief are not following instincts; they are shaped largely by their life circumstances, important parts of which are their culture and subculture. Under different circumstances each criminal might have been a law-abiding citizen.

Knowledge of specific cultures has helped us to avoid misunderstandings among allies (British girls and American men in World War II had different norms of dating, for example); to understand "the enemy" (Ruth Benedict's study of Japan, *The Chrysanthemum and the Sword*, and other studies helped make American occupation peaceful and constructive); and to guide foreign aid and Peace Corps workers.

The Vicos project in Peru is a famous example of "applied anthropology," a laboratory of social change. This project, in which anthropologists tried to stimulate self-help within the local culture, has been so successful it is a model for many others. Some 2250 Quechua Indians living on the Hacienda Vicos high in the Andes were abjectly poor, sickly, almost entirely illiterate, and suspicious and antagonistic after years of exploitation by government officials. After studying the Indians for 5 years, Allan Holmberg of Cornell set up a self-help project in 1952. The project supplied better seed potatoes on a sharecropping basis; only seventeen families joined the first year, but when others saw that these families had not been cheated, eighty-five more families joined the following year. The Indians supplied labor for a six-room school to replace a miserable hut. They accepted the idea of branding cattle as a way of ending disputes over ownership. Holmberg says that, like psychoanalysts, anthropologists who thus "intervene" are dealing with people who desire change but are held back by social obstacles, by "man's inhumanity to man, . . . the countless tragedies of ignorance and misunderstanding. . . . Anthropology, the science of man, is shaping weapons to reduce inhumanity, to lessen the tragic ignorance of this world. It remains to be seen whether we are willing to use them."[31]

Summary

A mastery of the culture concept is essential to understanding human behavior. Ethnocentrism blocks such understanding. It is the tendency to

[30]Stuart Chase, *The Proper Study of Mankind* (New York: Harper & Row, Publishers, 1956), p. 66.

[31]H. R. Hays, *From Ape to Angel: An Informal History of Social Anthropology* (New York: Alfred A. Knopf, 1965), p. 427.

regard one's own group as superior and to judge all others by its norms and values. To some extent it is inevitable, and it makes for group cohesion; but extreme ethnocentrism bars intelligently guided change and fosters misunderstanding and conflict. A classic study by Adorno and associates found that authoritarian personalities are more likely to be ethnocentric than democratic ones, and that their ethnocentrism extends to numerous "outgroups."

An attitude of cultural relativity, in contrast, includes a respect for cultural differences and a belief that each culture is valid as a more or less satisfactory way of adapting to environmental, biological, and social needs. It does not preclude evaluating cultures—if one is aware of his criteria. Among guidelines for judging cultures are adaptability, success in preserving the group and meeting biological and psychological needs, provision of opportunity to satisfy the desires and reach the goals set by the culture itself, the kind of personality produced by the culture, and the extent to which a culture promotes the human potential for learning, health, and happiness.

The study of anthropology helps one acquire an attitude of cultural relativity. The anthropological point of view is essential not only to fruitful study of human behavior in all the social sciences, but also to a liberal education. It makes a person more at home in a world where intergroup contacts steadily increase, more objective toward his own culture, more aware of the oneness of humanity, and more conscious of his own identity. It also is useful in guiding attempts to solve social problems, especially those arising from ignorance and misunderstanding.

QUESTIONS FOR FURTHER THOUGHT

1. Prejudice is disliking all members of a specific group, despite individual differences. Distinguish from ethnocentrism.

2. What groups do you feel ethnocentric about? (Who are your "we groups"?) To what extent are you proud of them? Defensive about them? To what outgroup do you feel most hostile? Why? What outgroups do you admire? Why?

3. Adorno and his associates said a nonethnocentric person can be supportive of other groups without necessarily identifying with them; critical without a sense of alienness and categorical difference. Discuss.

4. How much do you employ your sense of smell? Do you frequently try to "turn it off"? Why? In what cultural circumstances would cultivation of this sense be an advantage? Do the same observations apply to sight, taste, touch, and hearing?

5. "You are a violent country, with an extraordinary attachment to legal niceties. . . . It is well and good to have a system that protects the innocent, but surely there must be something wrong with a system that also protects the criminal. As I see it, you are a strange people, with strange habits—but I suppose that any people is strange when seen by an outsider. I might suggest that you change your legal system, but I am not an American. Nonetheless, I find some of your habits almost absurd." These are the words of Raymond Aron, a famous French sociologist. Compare his comments to those by the Soviet journalist at the beginning of the chapter. Do you have different impressions of the two writers?

6. When we say that most people can escape the limitations of their culture only to a limited extent, we leave room for some who escape more completely. Can you think of examples? To what extent do cultural influences help explain dramatic changes of "personal culture," such as religious conversion? To what extent are changes due to adoption of a new subculture? (Keep in mind that culture grows and changes largely through personal innovations; see Chapter 13.)

7. What qualities come to mind when you think of Englishmen? Frenchmen? South Sea Islanders? Cubans? Swedes? Chinese? South Africans? To what extent do your characterizations betray ethnocentrism? Which, if any, do you consider "inferior" to Americans? Superior? Why? What do you think they think of Americans? Why?

8. Psychologist Herbert Otto believes Americans tend to be more conscious of their faults and weaknesses than of their strengths and potentialities; he considers news reports in the mass media evidence of this tendency. Discuss.

9. It is often said that most human beings function at only a fraction of their potential capacity: Some put the figure as low as 5 to 10 percent. Do you agree? What blocks do you see to fuller use of human potential in our culture?

10. Go back over the chapters on "Man and Culture" to find examples of theory, empirical research, social observation and criticism, benchmark information, and the use of various methods and techniques of social inquiry.

Part Two

MAN
AND
SOCIETY

We turn now from the concept of culture to that of society. We are still talking about human behavior, but our emphasis shifts from the "blueprints for living" to the structures fashioned in part according to those blueprints. These structures are the groups in which we live—casual friendship groups, families, churches, schools, clubs, corporations, nations, and many more.

"There is," says Robert Lynd in *Knowledge for What?*, "no social science other than the science of persons interacting in groups." In Part One we discussed the cultural blueprints or patterns for that interaction, and in the next one we shall emphasize the individual *person* in the group. In the first two chapters of this part we consider *interaction* and *groups*, the basic concepts of the area of sociology called "social organization."

These concepts are systematically and coherently related to still others, such as the large and inclusive group we call a *society*. We shall look at the *structure* of groups—the network of *statuses* or positions occupied by their members and the *roles* these members are expected to play according to the cultural norms that provide patterns for their interaction. Society casts the players; culture writes the script; and "one man in his time plays many parts."

The second chapter of this part deals with several dimensions of social organization that affect interaction within a group—its *size*, the nature of the *social relationships* within it (whether intimate or impersonal, formal or informal), and its degree of *integration* or cohesiveness. After a look at the nature and consequences of various kinds of social organization such as *bureaucracy*, we shall compare and contrast two polar types of societies—*traditional* or folk society and *modern* or urban-industrial society.

Class and race are two aspects of social organization that have tremendous meaning for all of us. Chapter 9, on *social stratification*, examines social inequality and its consequences for society and its members. Chapter 10, which deals with *intergroup relations* in multigroup societies and summarizes the meaning of racial, religious, and ethnic backgrounds from the viewpoint of sociology, necessarily stresses ideas of "race" as a principal source of tensions in modern society. Both our class and our "race" —although they are categories rather than interacting groups—have much to do with the groups to which we belong or aspire, the way those groups interact with others, the opportunities open to us, and the choices we are likely to make.

We proceed, then, in these four chapters, from abstractions of social structure and function to two areas of social organization replete with pressing problems and controversial issues. Sociological theories and the findings of sociological research can illuminate these areas for those who make policy; and in a democracy this ideally incudes all of us who discuss issues and express our opinions at the ballot box and elsewhere.

7

Man seeketh in society comfort, use, and protection.

FRANCIS BACON

Status and role serve to reduce the ideal patterns for social life to individual terms.

RALPH LINTON

Groups are as real as the interdependence of their parts. In this respect they are not at all different from stones and stars. They are as real as rocks; rocks are as real as groups.

SCOTT GREER

SOCIAL INTERACTION AND SOCIAL STRUCTURE

W̲E MEMBERS OF THE HUMAN SPECIES are constantly acting, thinking, and feeling—and interacting with others. We send and receive signals with shrugs, smiles, frowns, movements toward or away from another person. But most often we use language signals to tell others how we feel, to ask them what to do, to soothe, hurt, inform, deceive, amuse, persuade. This symbolic interaction is the basic social process.

The cultural norms that our society has developed serve as guidelines for interaction. These norms help us to define the situation, to guess what others intend to do and what they expect us to do. Much of the time there is no problem. We know the script calls for us to act gay at a wedding, subdued at a funeral, civil, serious, diligent, and interested in a classroom or office, relaxed and affectionate at home.

We usually know what norms to apply because we recognize the cast of players—the statuses of the people involved in the relationship. Family relationships, for example, are defined by the status labels of father, mother, husband, wife, son, daughter, brother, sister. We have learned the corresponding roles: "Shame on you for hitting your little brother." "You don't speak to your mother like that, young lady." "How was your day, honey?"

Interaction in most situations is cooperative, but we also compete—for prizes, jobs, grades, mates, prestige, and other scarce values. Sometimes, too, we feel hostile and fight, seeking to destroy or hurt the others involved; then we accommodate our differences and resume peaceful interaction.

We find ourselves in groupings and in categories. Often, as in clusters of shoppers, pedestrians, or passengers, we do not feel we *belong* to these groupings. Nor do we always feel we belong to the various pigeonholes into which we are often placed according to such categoric differences as age, race, nationality, education, or the fact that we are diabetic or overweight or color blind.

But we *do* feel we belong to families, communities, nations, street gangs, congregations, women's clubs, softball teams, string quartets, the Black Panthers or the John Birch Society, and to our friends and lovers. We *live* in groups.

Much of our action and interaction occurs in large formal organizations, to many of which we feel little or no allegiance. We are born in General Hospital (Babies may be seen 3–4 P.M. and 7–8 P.M) and are mourned in the Friendly Funeral Home (Dignity and Service Since 1894). In between we study at Fitzgerald Elementary School (The tardy bell rings at 8:30), Embarrass High School (16 credits are required for graduation), and the University of Iowa (Registration September 6–9); attend the Puritan Heights Lutheran Church (Turn to Hymn No. 305); read *The New York Times* (Entered as second-class matter at the U.S. Post Office); work for General Motors (Do not fold, spindle, or mutilate your check); shop at Sears (Will that be cash or charge?); vote for city clerks and Presidents (Do not vote for more than one); and fill out forms for the Internal Revenue Service (If line 48 is equal to or greater than line 46, check this block ☐ and omit lines 49 through 56). Formal organizations deliver our milk, sweep our walks, broadcast our radio and TV programs, make our clothes, arrange our travel, and perhaps even provide our cleaning women and baby sitters.

Concepts of Social Organization

All these aspects of our lives involve social organization, for they are patterned relationships that guide social interaction. In this chapter and the next we shall examine some of the concepts that sociologists use in analyzing social organization. Since it is impossible to "say everything first" about the subject, let us begin with a bird's-eye view.

Social organization—the coordination of relationships among persons and groups—is a matter of degree; that is, groups and societies are organized *to the extent that* there are patterns and regularities in social interaction. Several fundamental concepts help us to discern these patterns and regularities. *Norms*, as we said, are rules or guidelines for interaction. The various *processes of interaction*, such as cooperation, competition, and conflict, are in part guided by norms, but they also give rise to new norms and to new interpretations of existing norms. *Social relationships* are patterns of more or less recurrent, regular, and expected interaction between two or more social actors, which may be persons or groups. *Status*, or position in a group, and *role*, the bundle of norms associated with a status, define expected behavior in social relationships. Statuses and roles form the *social structure* of a group or *society*. Let us begin our discussion of social organization with the central concept of society.

What Is a Society?

Society, unlike culture, is not limited to mankind. In the general sense *society* refers only to the association of living creatures functioning in organized relationships of mutual dependence. Specifically, *a society* is a population aggregate that (*1*) is organized into a division of labor that persists in time, (*2*) lives in a certain territory, and (*3*) shares common goals.

By this definition, almost all animals and insects show some degree of social behavior and social organization.[1] But, as we have already seen, the human group is very different from other animal groups because of man's capacity for building culture. Culture enables men to live in societies based not only on division of labor and interdependence but also on shared values and beliefs. It enables them to have many different kinds of social relationships and to interact with their fellows in many different ways. Once culture was introduced, society and culture grew more complex together. As language and the use of tools developed, society became more efficient in its basic functions of protection, nutrition, and control of reproduction; it thereby enabled men to live in larger and more complex groups and to elaborate their cultures.

Starting with our broad definition of society and adding the effect of culture, we can define **human society** as a complex system of relationships among individuals and groups, based on shared symbolic values and common beliefs and norms—that is, on culture. Society, a system of relationships, and culture, a system of common understandings, together form a *social order* or a *social system* that has structure, pattern, stability, and adaptability.

Whether it be a nonliterate jungle tribe or a modern nation-state of several hundred million members, any specific human society will have these distinguishing characteristics:

1. It is not a subgroup of any other group; it has a definite territory, within which its members have a common life, their needs being provided for by a system of interdependence based on division of labor.

2. It has a distinctive culture, and most or all of its members accept and abide by the universal or core values and norms of the culture.

3. Its members have a sense of belonging to it, a "we-feeling" that sets them off from nonmembers; it is the largest group within which most or all of them have this feeling of common identity.

4. Most or all of its recruitment of new members occurs through biological reproduction and the socialization of the

[1]See Sherwood L. Washburn, Phyllis C. Jay, and Jane B. Lancaster, "Field Studies of Old World Monkeys and Apes," *Science* 150, 3703 (Dec. 17, 1965): 154–157; reprinted in Morton H. Fried, ed., *Readings in Anthropology*, vol. 1, 2nd ed. (New York: Thomas Y. Crowell, 1968), pp. 277–91. See also Marshall D. Sahlins, "The Social Life of Monkeys, Apes and Primitive Men," in Fried, *Readings in Anthropology*, vol. 2, pp. 263–76; and John Paul Scott, *Animal Behavior* (Chicago: University of Chicago Press, 1958).

newborn. Thus it is self-perpetuating: Both sexes and all ages live out their lives within it.

5. Its organization as a functioning whole encompasses all the social groups and individuals within its bounds.

Models of Society

In analyzing societies and the groups within them, sociologists make use of several different models. As noted in Chapter 2, a model is essentially a "guiding metaphor" and should not be taken literally. No sociologist seriously believes that societies are machines, but for a long time many thought societies were *like* machines, and this analogy had a definite influence on the way they perceived such things as social change.

Basic to all of the models we will discuss is the idea that societies are systems,[2] and the groups within them subsystems, that can be understood in terms of structure and function. Amoebas, the planet Earth, and social groups all have structure, a relatively stable relationship between their various parts. The functioning of their parts is coordinated sufficiently so that their behavior is largely predictable. We can predict the amoeba's division into two cells, the tides of the Earth, and the likelihood that classes will meet tomorrow as scheduled.

In describing the relationships among the various parts of societies and attempting to predict their behavior, sociologists have most often used the mechanical and organic models; currently a cybernetic model is gaining favor.

THE MECHANICAL MODEL

Taking their cue from physics, early sociologists (and some modern-day ones) thought of a society more or less as a machine, much like a mechanical clock, whose various parts work together like cogs or gears. The ideal state for such a system is equilibrium. This analogy suggests that "energy" is the means of interaction or interchange among parts, and that "forces" such as momentum and inertia affect the workings of the system, which moves through cycles and is changed by tinkering.

THE ORGANIC MODEL

A more fruitful model, dominant in anthropological and sociological thinking for decades, has been the model of society as an organism whose interrelated parts or organs have one ultimate function: to

[2]See pp. 88 and 155 for definitions of a system.

meet "system needs" and thus keep the organism as a whole functioning properly. The ideal state of an organism is the biological equilibrium
called homeostasis, signified in the human body, for example, by a
temperature of 98.6° F. In this functional school of thought, the worth
of any individual or group is measured by its contribution to the preservation of the society as a whole. Functionalists are inclined to assume
that if a pattern is present in a system, it must be there to fill some
system need. Class systems, for example, are seen as necessary ways of
getting a society's work done; ceremonies as functioning to reinforce
"social solidarity."

Talcott Parsons is generally recognized as the most prominent
sociologist in the structural-functional school of theory. Answering the
age-old question "How is social order possible; why does society not
disintegrate into chaos?" he posited four "system problems" that a
society must solve. (1) Pattern maintenance and tension management:
Every society, Parsons said, must somehow motivate and mobilize its
members, socialize them to accept its world view, and continually reinforce this socialization in order to maintain its social patterns. Some
"organs," such as the family and recreational patterns, operate to relieve
tensions and thus help maintain the integrity of the society. (2) Goal
attainment: Values must be translated into goals to guide day-to-day
interaction; usually political institutions are in charge of meeting this
need. (3) Adaptation: No social unit functions in a vacuum. It must be
able to adapt to changes in other units and the physical environment as
well as to changes in the society as a whole. (4) Integration: Every
society must somehow regulate internal competition and conflict, avoid
arousing a sense of social injustice within any of its units, and maintain
a workable division of labor.[3]

Guided by the organic model, functionalist theories stress cooperation, consensus, and harmony, underplaying the positive role—
even the existence—of strain, conflict, and change in social systems.
They tend to assume that social processes unfold in a kind of natural
history without active intervention or control; thus Robert Park traced
a natural history of race relations from conflict through competition and
cooperation to assimilation. But sociologists have recognized the need
for a model that takes into account complexity, conflict, change, and
the role of social actors as decision-makers. Some find it in the cybernetic model.

[3]Among statements of Parsons's theory are *The Structure of Social Action* (New
York: McGraw-Hill, 1937; reprinted by The Free Press, 1949); and *The Social System* (New York: The Free Press, 1951). For discussions of his theory and influence
see Max Black, ed., *The Social Theories of Talcott Parsons* (Englewood Cliffs, N.J.:
Prentice-Hall, Inc., 1969); and Alvin W. Gouldner, *The Coming Crisis of Western
Sociology* (New York: Avon Books, 1970), Part 2, "The World of Talcott Parsons,"
pp. 167–338.

THE CYBERNETIC MODEL:
SOCIETY AS A COMPLEX ADAPTIVE SYSTEM

The cybernetic or "dynamic systems" model draws on process models, modern systems theory, and especially on that part of systems theory called cybernetics.

Process models stress action, interaction, and change, rather than static structure. "Symbolic interactionists," for example, see structure as the pattern grasped at any one moment in a fluid reality, much as a snapshot freezes one instant of a moving scene. They see social actors as decision-makers who define the situation as they go along, in part according to cultural norms, but *also* according to the demands of the situation, their perception of the definitions of others, and what they feel these others expect of them.[4]

This view of social organization is compatible with modern systems theory, which focuses on organization in general. A system is seen as being more or less continuous, more or less stable, and more or less clearly defined by boundaries. It may be seen as an entity in itself or as a set of interrelated subsystems. But it is not simply the sum or aggregate of its parts; it has properties as a system that are not found in the parts. Thus water is not just hydrogen plus oxygen; it is an entity in itself, with its own properties. We may also think of it as a system made up of interrelated molecules of hydrogen and oxygen, which in turn are systems made up of interrelated atoms, and so on.[5]

Similarly, a social group is more than the sum of the individual members; it has emergent properties arising from the way members interact.[6] "When we say that 'the whole is more than the sum of its parts' . . . the 'more than' points to the fact of *organization*, which imparts to the aggregate characteristics that are not only *different* from but often *not found in* the components alone."[7]

Thus far, the description of systems fits the mechanistic and organic models. What are the distinguishing features of the dynamic systems model of society? First of all, it takes into account the com-

[4]See Chapter 11 for a detailed discussion of symbolic interaction.

[5]Walter Buckley, *Sociology and Modern Systems Theory* (Englewood Cliffs, N.J.: Prentice-Hall, Inc., 1967), p. 42. "A system is something that divides the universe into all that is inside the system as distinct from all that is outside of it. Your body is such a system. So is a tomato can. So is the earth." [R. Buckminster Fuller *et al.*, *Approaching the Benign Environment* (Tuscaloosa, Ala.: University of Alabama Press, 1970), p. 83.]

[6]*Emergence*: [Biol., Philos.] "the appearance of new properties in the course of development or evolution that could not have been foreseen in an earlier stage." (*Random House Dictionary of the English Language*.)

[7]Buckley, *Sociology and Modern Systems Theory*, p. 42.

plexity and variety of social life. Human social behavior is seen as occurring in a field of five groupings of systems, all of which are simultaneously present and interacting: the ecosystem, which is the physical and biological environment; the human organism itself; the personality, which embraces psychological systems; cultural systems; and social systems. "Every social act . . . is accordingly at once physical, biological, psychological, cultural, and social."[8]

Second, the model stresses information and communication, recognizing that "whereas the relations of parts of an organism are physiological, involving complex physico-chemical *energy* interchanges, the relations of parts of society are primarily psychic, involving complex communicative processes of *information* exchange, and . . . this difference makes all the difference."[9]

This difference brings us to cybernetics. Norbert Wiener chose the word *cybernetics* (derived from the Greek *kubernetes* or "steersman") to refer primarily to "the study of communication among men, animals, and machines, with particular emphasis on the *feedback* of information and the function of feedback in the process of control."[10]

"Feedback control loops" in computers and automated machinery are built-in mechanisms that compare input against a goal. If there is a mistake or discrepancy, they pass this information on to a control center that activates appropriate corrective behavior in the system. Similarly, learning in the individual (or even such a simple act as reaching for a pencil) and decision-making in the group benefit from positive feedback, which reinforces correct choices, and from negative feedback, which penalizes incorrect ones or at least alerts the actor to the fact that his action is not leading to his goal. Feedback, then, is a way of checking and guiding goal-directed action. (Examples of feedback in a modern social system are protest, voting, consumer choices, and criticism of the political elite by intellectuals.)

Thus we come to the third and perhaps the most significant feature of the cybernetic model of society—the fact that a modern society is seen as a complex adaptive system which can persist or develop by changing its own structure, sometimes in fundamental ways.[11] Where the mechanical model suggests blind forces and inertia, and the organic model suggests that somehow all things work together for the good of the system defined in terms of an ideal equilibrium, the

[8]Robin M. Williams, Jr., *American Society: A Sociological Interpretation*, 3rd ed. (New York: Alfred A. Knopf, 1970), p. 24. See also Bertram M. Gross, "The State of the Nation: Social Systems Accounting," in ed. Raymond A. Bauer, *Social Indicators* (Cambridge, Mass.: The M.I.T. Press, 1967), pp. 154–271.

[9]Buckley, *Sociology and Modern Systems Theory*, p. 43.

[10]George A. Theodorson and Achilles G. Theodorson, *A Modern Dictionary of Sociology* (New York: Thomas Y. Crowell, 1969), p. 101. See also Norbert Wiener, *The Human Use of Human Beings: Cybernetics and Society* (New York: Avon Books, 1950), p. 23, for a broader usage of the term.

[11]Buckley, *Sociology and Modern Systems Theory*, p. 206.

cybernetic model suggests the possibility of a self-guiding or active society. It thus has tremendous implications for planned social change.[12]

Adaptive systems are open systems, that is, they engage in exchanges with the environment. They continually process information from within and without in an attempt to adapt. Thus a socio-cultural system "continually attempts to 'map' the variety of its external environment through science, technology, magic, and religion, and its internal milieu through common understandings, symbols, expectations, norms, and values."[13] Closed systems, in contrast, are subject to entropy, that is, they run down, much as a mechanical clock runs down; their final state depends on initial conditions.[14] If environmental systems intrude, closed systems lose organization or even break down and dissolve. For open systems, conflict, stress, and disturbance are sources of dynamics. They become more complex and elaborate as they engage in exchanges with the environment and adapt to strains and pressures from within. According to cybernetic theory, modern societies are open systems.

Social systems are not, however, *infinitely* adaptive. They operate under constraints: the coercive power of other social systems, the demands and limitations placed on them by the ecosystem and the nature of the human organism, the scarcity of resources such as the means of subsistence, and the limited energies and capacities of individuals. Furthermore, not every possible element of social structure is compatible with every other. It seems, for example, that the traditional extended family and the modern industrial corporation do not work well together. Nonetheless, there is always some free play, some alternative arrangement within any given social system at any given time. No social system is as rigid as a machine, with only one possible way its parts may be linked together in order to function satisfactorily.

The systems model of society helps social scientists relate variables to their total context and assess their relative importance more satisfactorily than is possible when only two or three variables are taken out of context. Thus Jay Forrester performed computer simulations of what would happen to cities (seen as total social systems) on the basis of certain programs; he found that piecemeal planning would only exaggerate current urban problems, that some proposed reforms

[12]See Warren Breed, *The Self-Guiding Society* (New York: The Free Press, 1971). This is a shorter version of Amitai Etzioni, *The Active Society* (New York: The Free Press, 1968). The central thesis, that "the post-modern society has the option to change its course," is discussed in Chapter 14.

[13]Buckley, *Sociology and Modern Systems Theory*, pp. 128–29.

[14]"Physical universe is forever expanding and multiplying in ever more disorderly ways. This is called entropy. Biological life is forever sorting, selecting, compacting, and producing more orderly chemical substances. This is called antientropy. Human mind is the most powerful selector and order formulator thus far evidenced in the universe." [R. Buckminster Fuller, *Utopia or Oblivion: The Prospects for Humanity* (New York: Bantam Books, 1969), p. 344.]

would have unintended side effects, and that many assumptions about trends are invalid.[15] Similarly, Leo Srole and his associates used systems analysis to illustrate the complexity of interrelated variables in mental health. They found that "dependent" variables may influence "independent" ones; variations in marital status, socio-economic status, religion, and rural-urban migration may be *consequences* of mental health (or illness) rather than independent antecedents.[16]

Summing up the potential power of this model of society, Walter Buckley insists that:

> only the modern systems approach promises to get at the full complexity of the interacting phenomena—to see not only the *causes* acting on the phenomena under study, the possible *consequences* of the phenomena, and the possible *mutual interactions* of some of these factors, but also to see the *total emergent processes* as a function of possible positive and/or negative *feedbacks* mediated by the *selective decisions*, or "choices," of the individuals and groups directly or indirectly involved.[17]

Thus the cybernetic model allows sociologists to deal with more complex patterns of interaction than is possible with either the mechanical or organic models of society. We turn now to the basic medium of social organization, interaction.

Processes of Social Interaction

Social organization emerges from social interaction and, in turn, guides further interaction. As people come into contact with one another, and as they become aware of one another as more than mere physical objects, their behavior both modifies and is modified by the behavior of others. Each defines the situation partly in the light of cultural norms and past experiences; each has an idea (reinforced or corrected by feedback) of what the situation means to the others involved, and what they intend to do and expect him to do.

Social interaction is the reciprocal influencing of behavior through symbolic communication between persons. It always involves communication by means of gestures or language, although we are not always conscious of sending or receiving signals. It does not necessarily involve face-to-face contact; it can take place through phone calls, letters, books, paintings, and even a piece of music, although here the reciprocity of influence is less evident.

The processes of social interaction have been categorized in var-

[15]Jay Forrester, *Urban Dynamics* (Boston: M.I.T. Press, 1969).
[16]Leo Srole *et al.*, *Mental Health in the Metropolis* (New York: McGraw-Hill, 1962).
[17]Buckley, *Sociology and Modern Systems Theory*, p. 80.

ious ways.[18] Here we focus on behavior—Who does what to (or with) whom?—and its consequences—Is the process *associative*, bringing people together, or *dissociative*, dividing them?

COOPERATION

Cooperation is the combined effort of two or more social actors to reach a shared goal. Clearly an associative process, it pervades all forms of group life and is indispensable to its existence; it is an element in all situations except overt personal conflict. Cooperation may take the form of shoulder-to-shoulder effort in a common task, such as harvesting a crop; direct exchange for the benefit of both ("You scratch my back and I'll scratch your back"); or conformity to the norms of overt behavior that make it possible for a society to function.[19]

Most interaction in the routine of daily life is cooperative simply because of the interdependence of persons that results from the division of labor. In a small face-to-face group, one is often aware of cooperating as he helps with the dishes, assists a younger brother with math, works on the school paper, or catches a pass in a football game. In small non-literate societies, cooperation is often a chief cultural value, consciously used to regulate the interaction of members in farming, fishing, hunting, and housebuilding.

In a highly complex society such as ours, division of labor is carried to such extremes that cooperation may be less apparent; but it is just as necessary as in a simple society. Members of the society may not often be aware of cooperating as they go about their daily routine; but all the traffic of a city, the schedule of a university, the buying and selling in stores, depend on cooperation. When you stop for a red light, when you appear in class at the same hour as your instructor and classmates, when you answer the telephone or doorbell, even when you reply to an acquaintance's greeting, you are cooperating.

COMPETITION

Competition is the striving of two or more social actors for the same goal, which is limited in quantity. Each wants the whole pie or the lion's share of it, whether it consists of money, power, prestige, safety, public office, a certain girl, or some other scarce value. What-

---

[18]We may distinguish "social processes" from "the processes of interaction." In the latter, persons and groups, even whole societies, are reacting to the behavior of others. Social processes are more general; we speak of processes of social change, social control, stratification and differentiation, evolution, modernization, urbanization, and so on.

[19]A special form of cooperative interaction is more asymmetrical and episodic: giving (charity) or helping behavior (the Good Samaritan); here the emphasis is more on the social relationship between giver and taker than on a common goal. Deviant behavior may be defined as noncooperation, and its forms are as varied as are the forms of cooperation.

a. Competition.   b. Conflict.

ever the prize, their primary aim is to get it for themselves, not to injure or destroy their competitors. Unlike conflict, competition is carried on within an accepted system of rules which limit the acceptable means of trying to gain the prize. It is often impersonal: The farmer selling wheat on the Chicago exchange does not know his competitors, nor does the person taking a civil service exam. When competitors *are* aware of one another—candidates for the Presidency or for a girl's hand in marriage —we term their relationship one of rivalry. In such situations, as in games and contests, the group has laid down certain cultural rules of fair play, and losers are supposed to bow to the decision with good grace—to congratulate the President-elect or to dance at the wedding.

Like cooperation, competition is present in all cultures. In any society, people will compete for status according to the cultural values. In a monastery where piety and austerity are the chief values, status may be won by the monks who most zealously deny themselves physical comforts and who spend the most time in devotions. In a middle-class suburb status may depend on visible signs of wealth, the husband's occupation, the colleges that accept his children.

Competition is a conspicuous element in much interaction occurring in a society where many statuses can be achieved, whether in jobs, politics, business, school and college, sports, and even in the family ("Mommy, do you love me best?"). Our culture is distinguished for making competition a positive value, a "good thing." Americans are convinced that although cooperation gets things done, competition assures that they will be done *well*.

CONFLICT

"Social **conflict** consists of interaction in which one party intends to deprive, control, injure, or eliminate another, against the will of that

160

(Courtesy of New York Rangers)

c. Accommodation.

other."[20] Conflict may be normatively regulated, and its goals may be limited. In games, the parties are primarily bent on winning, and play by the rules; in debates, their chief goal is to convince or persuade their opponents and others that their views are right and justified. But "pure conflict is a *fight*; its goal is to immobilize, neutralize, destroy, or otherwise harm an opponent."[21] Unlike cooperation, conflict must by nature be intermittent; unlike competition, it always involves awareness of the other parties in interaction.

The scope of conflict ranges from marital discord to total war. But when we refer to "social conflict" we usually think of intergroup conflict within a society. Such collectivities as racial and religious groups, students, workers, and revolutionaries fight against other groups and against the control system of the political Establishment, the police, soldiers, and national guardsmen. Collectivities engage in riots, strikes, lynchings, pogroms, gang fights, guerrilla warfare, confrontations, and violent demonstrations met with violent countermeasures. For reasons obvious to anyone who follows the news, sociologists are currently very much concerned with the study of conflict.

What are the sources of conflict? There are many different theories. Ethologists say aggression is programmed into man in his genetic make-up; that like other animals he fights to defend his territory against intruders. Some sociologists suggest that ethnocentrism—not merely hostility to others, but loyalty, even blind devotion, to one's own group —is the main cause of conflict, and that it is learned in the socialization process. Psychoanalytically-oriented theorists believe the inevitable

[20]Robin M. Williams, Jr., "Social Order and Social Conflict," *Proceedings of the American Philosophical Society* 114, No. 3 (June 1970): 217–25. This section on interaction draws in part on a seminar on Social Conflict conducted by Dr. Williams at Wayne State University, Fall Quarter, 1970.

[21]*Ibid.*

frustrations of living in society lead to feelings of aggression, which may or may not be overtly expressed. Adorno associated aggressiveness with authoritarian personality traits.[22] Marx believed conflict is built into society in the class system, which in turn depends on economic structure.

Robin Williams sees three classes of opposition as the main sources of conflict: (1) incompatible claims to scarce things of value, such as money; (2) incompatible beliefs, values, and norms, including loyalties and obligations to different collectivities and individuals; and (3) affective (or emotional) dispositions and impulses that are expressed in anger toward some vague antagonist, such as the Establishment.[23] A society *guarantees* conflict, he suggests, if rewards for work are unpredictable; if work is unsatisfying; and if central aspirations are blocked (all of which "add up to an operational definition of hell").

Conflict may have positive results. The baby coming into conflict with his mother is developing his sense of self and learning cultural norms. The group fighting another group is strengthened in its "we" feeling. If it is confined to issues, conflict (between husband and wife, for instance) may clear the air of tension. During a period of rapid social change, conflict serves to define the status of persons and groups, as did the labor-management conflict of recent decades. It may force awareness of injustice. And it may (like recent wars) spur technological innovation and scientific research.

Much conflict, however, is destructive and dissociative, and breeds more problems than it solves. Riots may deepen differences between collectivities and increase alienation of one group from another. Strikes and lockouts result in loss of income, production, and profits. And war "is unhealthy for children and other living things."

ACCOMMODATION AND ASSIMILATION

Conflict may result in annihilation of one of the parties, or in subjugation, slavery, or some other form of dominance or repression. But it may be resolved or even avoided through the social process called accommodation, the reduction of conflict and the restoration of peaceful interaction through such measures as compromise, arbitration, mediation, truce, toleration, contract, or adjudication. Examples are labor–management agreements, the racial etiquette of the old South, and the peaceful coexistence of essentially hostile nations. Similarly, incompatible beliefs and values may be reconciled through debate, persuasion, a mutual agreement to live and let live, or mutual withdrawal from interaction. Or the party against whom aggression is directed may define the others' behavior as neurotic, psychotic, mistaken, or accidental, thus denying any valid attempt to injure and refusing to respond in kind.[24]

[22]See Chapter 6.
[23]"Social Order and Social Conflict."
[24]*Ibid.*

None of these measures really eliminates potential sources of conflict, but they do enable persons and groups to go about their business without overt conflict. In one sense, accommodation is the basis of all formal social organization. Government, for example, is designed to harmonize the interests of different groups sufficiently so the society can function effectively. Because the incompatible values and goals still exist, accommodation has been called "antagonistic cooperation."

Experimenting with groups of boys in summer camps, Muzafer Sherif and his associates were able to produce two integrated and cooperative groups, create hostility and conflict between them, and then bring about a friendly and cooperative relationship. During the period of competitive games, hostilities erupted, but the solidarity of each group increased. Bringing the hostile groups into close association under pleasant circumstances, instead of reducing conflict, provided opportunities for further name-calling and fighting. Then the experimenters created a series of urgent natural situations to challenge the boys. Water came to the "Robbers Cave" camp in pipes from a tank about a mile away; the flow was interrupted, and both groups worked together to locate the break. A truck that was to bring food to an outing broke down ("accidentally on purpose"); the groups helped start it by pulling it with a rope. Further cooperative acts gradually reduced friction and conflict, until finally the groups actively sought opportunities to mingle, entertain, and "treat" each other. "In short, hostility gives way when groups pull together to achieve overriding goals which are real and compelling to all concerned."[25]

Assimilation is the social process whereby individuals and groups come to share the same sentiments, values, and goals. It commonly refers to the absorption of immigrants into the social order of a large modern society such as the United States. It can with equal accuracy be used to describe the process of adjustment in a successful marriage or even the socialization of the growing child. The cultural assimilation of new members of a society may or may not be accompanied through the years by a process of biological *amalgamation* in which the physical differences of the incoming groups also disappear through intermarriage with members of the receiving group.

Cultural assimilation and biological amalgamation occur most frequently in multigroup societies such as ours. Cooperation, competition, conflict, and accommodation occur in every society, but they are found in varying proportions depending on the complexity of the soci-

[25]"Experiments in Group Conflict," *Scientific American* 195, No. 5 (Nov. 1956): 54–58; reprinted in Edgar A. Schuler *et al.*, eds., *Readings in Sociology*, 4th ed. (New York: Thomas Y. Crowell, 1971), pp. 543–47. For a more complete account, see M. Sherif et al., *Intergroup Conflict and Cooperation: The Robbers Cave Experiment* (Norman: University of Oklahoma, Institute of Group Relations, 1961); and M. Sherif, *In Common Predicament: Social Psychology of Intergroup Conflict and Cooperation* (Boston: Houghton-Mifflin, 1966).

ety and the value placed on any one process. The Zuñi of New Mexico stressed cooperation; the Kwakiutl of the Pacific Northwest built their culture around competition; the Comanches glorified the warrior and conflict. Counterparts in modern society might be found in Scandinavia, where cooperation is important, in the United States, where competition is believed to promote efficiency, and in Russia, where the idea of class conflict on a world-wide basis long justified and motivated public policy.[26]

Similarly, we find varying blends of the different social processes in the interaction of groups and organizations within a society. Cooperation and assimilation are essential to family life, but the very intimacy of family relationships intensifies hostility and conflict when these arise. Accommodation in parent–child and husband–wife relationships permits peaceful interaction in spite of conflicting interests and values.

Social Relationships and Social Groups

The more often social interaction of whatever type is repeated, the more fixed and predictable becomes the behavior of the actors. A pattern arises, based on the participants' mutual expectations regarding one another's behavior; this pattern is a social relationship. Such social relationships as father and son, policeman and speeder, employer and employee, even unfriendly neighbors, are meaningful only in terms of the reciprocal expectations that pattern interaction.

A relationship may be chiefly normative, utilitarian, or coercive. Normative relationships are based on shared norms and values; they predominate in families, religious groups, and small stable communities in which members treat one another as important for their own sake. In utilitarian relationships, actors treat one another as means to their own ends; exchanges may lead to mutual profit, as in the market, but competition and contained conflict may arise. Coercive relationships involve the use or threat of violence; the social actors treat one another as objects, and conflict may occur uncontained by norms.[27]

The network of social relationships is the structure of a group; it organizes behavior. But before exploring the subject of groups and social structure further, let us take note of unorganized behavior and nongroups.

UNORGANIZED BEHAVIOR

Not all human behavior is social behavior, and not all social behavior is organized behavior. Organization may be entirely or almost

---

[26]For a comparative anthropological study, see Margaret Mead, ed., *Cooperation and Competition Among Primitive Peoples* (Boston: Beacon Press, 1961), a revised version of the 1937 McGraw-Hill edition.

[27]Breed, *The Self-Guiding Society*, p. 21.

entirely lacking when people are thrown together in new and undefined situations where existing cultural norms that might guide interaction do not apply. This is the case with some crowds and mobs, which engage in what sociologists call "collective behavior."

Organization is also lacking in behavior that is not coordinated by a system of social relationships, but shows a certain regularity because it occurs in response to common stimuli. If 10 million people are watching the Flip Wilson Show at a given moment, they form a mass audience, not an organized group. If a water engineer observes a heavy drain on water supplies during a commercial, it is due to individual behavior that happens to coincide, not to organized behavior. Other regularities within a social system are the result of many uncoordinated decisions rather than of organization. Birth rates are one example; while they fluctuate over the years, any extreme changes are easily explained, usually by social influences that affect many potential parents.

NONGROUPS: AGGREGATES AND CATEGORIES

We often find ourselves in *physical aggregates*, collections of people who happen to be in physical proximity. Examples are clusters of people waiting for a bus or walking along Main Street, or people who happen to live as neighbors on a block. While aggregates are not social groups, they may have sociological meaning, for the spatial distribution of people has various effects on social organization.[28]

Statistical aggregates or categories are logical classifications of people based on the existence of one or more common characteristics: the same age, sex, race, religion, marital status, hair color, hobbies—the list can be expanded almost indefinitely. People in a category may or may not have a "consciousness of kind" with other members, but ordinarily they do not interact on the basis of their categorical similarity. Some social groups, however, are consciously formed on such a basis: tall young men and women, for example, may join the Tip Toppers Club. And categories such as class and race are recruiting grounds for the formation of interacting groups.[29] When a statistical category is based on one or more statuses in the social structure (such as class, race, parenthood, etc.) we may refer to it as a *social category*.

Quite aside from any interaction among the people who compose them, social categories may be highly significant for sociology in that they enable researchers to discern patterns that might not be visible in individual cases. For example, Durkheim related suicide rates to various social categories and found that the suicide rate is higher among Protestants than among Catholics, among single than among married

[28]See Chapters 15 and 16 on urbanization and population.

[29]Such groups are called *collectivities* when they are not genuine groups but have some social structure and some collective consciousness of shared values and interests and easily engage in interaction. American blacks and college youth, for example, are collectivities in this sense, and readily form interacting groups.

people, and among army officers than among enlisted men. (Of course he did not stop there; he also related his findings to other factors affecting the categories, such as the degree of group integration within them.)[30]

WHAT ARE SOCIAL GROUPS?

Significant as many aggregates and categories are, they are not social groups. A social group is a plurality of persons (two or more) who interact, take one another into account, are aware that they have something significant in common, feel a sense of identity that sets them off from others, and have social relationships consisting of interrelated and reciprocal statuses. Their interaction may be momentary or long-lasting. They may relate to one another with varying emotions. What they have in common may be some task, territory, interest, belief, or value, but to form a genuine group, they must believe that it makes a difference. The group boundary takes in all those the members refer to as "we" or "us" ("You and I, darling," or "My fellow Americans"). Their relationship may be as direct, close, and egalitarian as that of two friends, or as indirect, distant, and unequal as that of the President of General Motors and a janitor in his office building.

The Structure of Groups: Status and Role

The network of interrelated statuses, the pattern of relationships sufficiently regular and enduring to be perceived, is the *social structure* of a group. Recurrent behavior suggests a pattern and allows an observer to arrive at a consistent interpretation of transitory events in the history of a group, just as it does in the life story of a person. Thus a political scientist discerns patterns in party politics as well as in the more formal organization of government. And thus a friendship group of two or three, or even a pair of lovers, behaves in fairly predictable ways as its members establish lasting relationships.

STATUS

A teacher named M. B. Smith will serve to illustrate the various concepts we use to analyze social structure. The word "teacher" is a label (conventional symbol) that identifies a status, a position in a social structure. As the basic element in social structure, status is a key concept in sociology, and therefore merits our detailed consideration.

A status is independent of any one person. The status of teacher

[30]Emile Durkheim, *Suicide*, trans. George Simpson (New York: The Free Press, 1951).

does not depend on Smith's occupying the position: Teacher is a unit of the social structure of a school system. The status exists even though the school board may have trouble filling the position and may not have employed Smith until school had been in session for a week.

A status is always *relational* or *reciprocal*; that is, it has meaning only in terms of at least one other status. Teacher as a status is meaningless without students, President without citizens. So too, with doctor-and-patient, boss-and-employee, mother-and-child, husband-and-wife, friend-and-friend.

A person's statuses are *multiple*. We may now identify our teacher as a woman, Mary B. Smith, and further, as a wife, Mrs. John Smith, and further, as a mother, a daughter, a daughter-in-law, and a homemaker. Obviously she has the status of adult. She also is a member of the American Association of University Women, a secretary of the local chapter of Phi Beta Kappa, a Democrat, and a member of the First Congregational Church. On occasion she occupies still other statuses: She is captain of a bowling team, a patient of a certain doctor and dentist, a customer at the corner drugstore and a nearby supermarket, a taxpayer, a voter, a tourist.

But each person has a *key status*, a position by which he is chiefly identified. In the case of most women, it is probably the status of wife-and-mother. In modern society nearly all men are identified first in most situations by their occupations.

Some of a person's many statuses are *compounded* or clustered; that is, they go with other statuses. Mrs. Smith's statuses as mother, wife, and homemaker are compounded with her status as adult female; although males or children can be bowlers, tourists, and customers, only an adult female (by our cultural norms) is a mother, wife, or homemaker—and if she is one, she is likely to be all three.

Some statuses are *sequential* in that we fill them in a fixed order. We cannot avoid being infants before we are children, teenagers before we are adults, then "senior citizens"—and finally, perhaps, "ancestors." Mrs. Smith was a student before she was a teacher, a high school graduate before she could be a college graduate.

Some steps from one status to another are ceremonially celebrated by rites of passage, especially in sequential statuses related to age and sex and the life cycle; a wedding ceremony is an example. Almost everywhere the change in status from single to married life is an occasion for ritual and ceremony, to impress the community at large as well as the couple with the implications of their new status. In many societies only married persons are considered fully adult; in others, only parents.

Statuses may be classified as communal or associational. A *communal* status is defined by the general culture: Everyone in our society has a general idea of what it means to be a woman, an adult, or a member of a general occupational category such as teacher, doctor, or writer. However, within a special group—an association—status is more precisely defined. To others in the school system, Mrs. Smith has not only the communal status of teacher, but also the *associational* status of fourth-grade homeroom teacher at Oakland Elementary School.

Statuses are *ranked* within a group. Each carries with it a certain freight of prestige, privilege, and power in relation to the other statuses in the group. In most formally organized groups there is an explicit pattern or hierarchy that indicates who has authority over whom and to whom he in turn owes obedience and deference. The hierarchy of an army or a church is a direct line of authority. A principal has authority over Mrs. Smith. He owes obedience in turn to legitimate instructions from the school board and the superintendent. Mrs. Smith has authority within her classroom; the pupils are subordinate to her.

Even in a group with no formal structure and explicit rules there is a rank order of personal influence. In his book *Street Corner Society*, William Foote Whyte relates that the slum gang called The Nortons— a group of thirteen Italians in their twenties—had a clear social structure. By noting who suggested ideas for common activity and who had to agree before the action could be carried out, Whyte was able to chart lines of influence from the leader, Doc, and his childhood friends, Mike and Danny, to the other members, and to place each person in a definite position relative to the others.[31]

Each person also has a "total status" in his community or society, a ranking relative to others that takes into account various indices considered important in the culture—wealth, education, aristocratic ancestry, athletic prowess, and so on. This system of *social stratification* refers to a special kind of status ranking, and is the subject of Chapter 9.

ROLE

Every status in a social structure implies a role—a minimum pattern of behavior that is expected (and perhaps demanded) of anyone occupying the status. The concepts of status and role have often been likened to the cast of characters and script of a play. The list of characters provides the network of statuses; the script outlines their interaction in terms of the role of each player.

Roles are composed of norms, which are the ideal patterns for action, thought, and feeling, the mutual understandings regarding the right and proper behavior in different situations, the standards of what is socially acceptable. They define the conventional expectations that people hold regarding the behavior of others.

A **role**, then, is a bundle of norms that defines the rights, obli-

[31]*Street Corner Society* (Chicago: University of Chicago Press, 1943). Even in a formally structured group such a rank order may not correspond perfectly to the explicit hierarchy.

"Never mind, Walter. You may be only number four at the office, but here you're number two."

Drawings by Chon Day (reprinted from *Look*)

"Of course I love you. I'm your husband. That's my job."

gations, and privileges of a person who occupies a particular status. It is not identified with him personally, however; it is attached to the status. Roles are elements of culture, just as statuses are elements of one aspect of culture, social organization. To understand the distinction more clearly, imagine the status of teacher as part of the social organizations of Sweden and of The People's Republic of China. Then go on to the concept of role, and you will realize that in the two societies the norms attached to the status of teacher are very different, the beliefs, values, goals, and degree of modernization are very different, and the teachers are expected to teach different things.[32]

[32]J. Milton Yinger, *Toward a Field Theory of Behavior* (New York: McGraw-Hill, 1965), includes lucid discussions of social structure.

Institutionalization of roles.   Although the roles of friend and lover are largely culturally defined (though often implicitly), these roles are subject to the judgment of the other person involved alone. But some roles are institutionalized, that is, they are subject to explicit rules laid down by duly constituted authorities or by customs that have the force of law. Institutionalization is a matter of degree. The roles of clergyman and teacher are highly institutionalized, that is, very much subject to formal and informal control by others. But only flagrant neglect of the parental role brings on formal sanctions: lack of support, refusal to send a child to school, unmerciful beating.

We sometimes assume roles that are institutionalized for others but not for ourselves. Mrs. Smith may play nurse to a sick child, but she does not have the status of nurse, and there are no formal sanctions for the way she goes about it. A stranger on a plane may play the role of confidant, and often does, because the person who unburdens himself feels sure he will not see the stranger again. He is not, however, an institutionalized confidant, as are family doctors, lawyers, clergymen, and psychiatrists. In many social structures a person playing a deviant sex role has no corresponding status; in others the role is institutionalized. Among the Plains Indians a male transvestite assumed the status of *berdache*; he was allowed to dress as a woman after going through a ceremony analogous to marriage.[33]

Institutionalized roles are firmly attached to statuses and applied to certain situations. Just as the mores can make anything right in a culture, so a certain status can make behavior right that would be improper or even illegal for someone occupying another status. When a man is functioning in his status as a doctor and is playing the accompanying role (as in his office, in a hospital, or on a house call), it is perfectly all right for him to ask a woman to undress. He might be tempted to do so at a party when a guest asks for free medical advice, but the norms do not permit it. Under certain circumstances a policeman can deprive a person of his freedom to move about—by force if necessary.

Communal and associational norms.   Just as there are communal and associational statuses, so there are communal and associational norms defining roles. Communal norms are present in the general culture—sex, age, and kinship roles are typically communal—whereas associational norms are peculiar to a group smaller than the society as a whole. They may arise in the course of interaction, as in a group of friends or a gang of criminals, or they may be specified when a group is formally organized, as in the constitution of a club or the rules and regulations of a business.

A member of any formally organized group brings to it certain

[33]Michael Banton, *Roles: An Introduction to the Study of Social Relationships* (New York: Basic Books, 1965), p. 8.

norms to guide his behavior, but there are also associational norms he must learn. Our teacher, Mrs. Smith, knows in a general way what American society expects of her as a wife and mother, and she knows somewhat more specifically what it expects of her as a teacher. In the course of interaction with her husband and children, more specific associational norms arise, concerning mutual rights and obligations, mealtimes, chores, allowances, errands, and the like. These are not as clearly spelled out, however, as the associational norms of her school, where a series of memos and meetings keeps her informed about her hours and duties. Some norms are never verbalized; without ever being told, Mrs. Smith learns that the principal expects teachers to laugh at his jokes.

Assignment of Status and Role: Ascription and Achievement

The statuses into which a person is born and those to which he is automatically assigned with the passage of time—those over which he has no control—are ascribed statuses. Those he *attains* by his own efforts or by a stroke of good fortune are achieved statuses.

ASCRIBED STATUSES

All our lives, from the moment of birth, *sex* is the first fact noted about us. The accidental chromosome combinations occurring at the moment of conception determine many things about one's life in any society. Sex is almost never changed; it almost always provides a clear-cut distinction on which cultural norms that prescribe much of a person's behavior are based.

The only known significant biological differences between the sexes are the reproductive role and the greater physical strength of the male in matters calling for muscular exertion (females may have greater long-range endurance). In societies with less advanced technologies, and to some extent everywhere, these differences call for a division of labor that keeps the woman close to home and engaged in fairly routine tasks, such as cooking, cleaning, foraging for food, gardening, and sewing, and perhaps weaving and pottery making, which do not interfere very much with pregnancy and childrearing. The man is typically assigned duties that demand physical strength and long periods away from home; he is the hunter, fisherman, warrior, and herder of cattle.

But aside from these general distinctions, each society uses sex as an arbitrary peg on which to hang many other assignments of status and role that have little or nothing to do with physical capacities. The definitions of men's and women's roles include not only division of labor but also many norms regarding appropriate behavior. Among some Australian aborigines, for example,

> Men and women consider it improper to perform tasks appropriate to the other sex. Women are not supposed to handle a man's spears or arrows for fear a female touch will weaken their power. Women have to sit on the left-hand side of the fire, men on the right. If a man sits on the woman's side, or where some woman has previously been sitting, then he will lose his power to hunt. If a woman sits in a man's place she will suffer from a mystic disease. A man wears his skin cape differently from a woman, and only a woman wears ostrich shell beads. Such ideas as to the proper behavior of the sexes are worldwide and few people dare wear clothing appropriate to the other sex.[34]

Age serves as another universal basis for ascription of status and role. Unlike sex, age is a continuum rather than a dichotomy: Most societies identify infancy, childhood, adulthood, and old age as distinct statuses, but the lines of demarcation vary noticeably. The transition from childhood to adulthood is easy and gradual in one society, marked with impressive ritual, ceremony, and trial by ordeal in a second, and ambiguous and difficult in a third. Among the Masai of Africa, every male passes through three clear-cut stages: boy, warrior, and elder. In the United States, in contrast, there is no clear definition of status by age. The age of legal maturity is an arbitrary one unmarked by rites

[34]*Ibid.*, p. 8. The Chinese "unisex" clothes are a notable exception.

Without knowing who this is, we can identify this person's *ascribed* statuses: She is a woman, an Indian, a Hindu, a member of the upper class.

of passage or tests of civic judgment or legal responsibility. Puberty is a private affair; sexual maturity comes long before economic independence; schooling is extended longer and longer. Much of the strain of adolescence in American culture is thought to be a result of the ambiguity that keeps the "teenager" a child in one situation and an adult in another.

Kinship also universally ascribes a number of statuses and roles. The child grows to learn a series of rights and obligations in relation to his parents and siblings. In a number of societies the kinship structure embraces many other relatives, defines a person's status in relation to the whole clan or tribe, and governs his behavior toward them throughout his life. In such a system marriage rules are tied to the kinship structure: They may state that a man may marry only his mother's brother's daughter, for example, or prescribe marriage outside the clan or other kin group in order not to blur kinship lines. Noble, royal, or aristocratic status is also assigned at birth, and the order of birth frequently determines the right of succession to a title.

Several statuses may be assigned the newborn infant simply because they are those of his parents. In a *caste* system he keeps his parents' caste status for life; it usually determines his occupation as well as many other aspects of his life. In a *class* system his initial position is that of his parents, and although he may go up or down the social ladder, whether he has a head start or a handicap in life depends upon where he starts. His *citizenship* and *religion* are also those of his parents, and are infrequently changed. And the newborn infant is assigned his parents' *racial* or *ethnic* status, where such distinctions are made.

ACHIEVED STATUSES

Ascription is a convenient way to begin the task of training different people for the different functions that must be performed in a society. Even in a complex modern society, statuses ascribed on the basis of sex, age, kinship, and (in a world of nation-states) nationality or citizenship continue to be very important.

An increasing number of statuses open to achievement as a society industrializes, largely because there are so many new occupations in the specialized system of production and distribution. How does one achieve a status? Typically, he learns the role (the communal and associational norms of the status) through education, training, and experience. Then he convinces others—voters, perhaps, or audiences or employers—that he deserves the status and can perform the role satisfactorily. Examples of achieved statuses are club secretary, gang leader, movie star, college graduate, chemist, teacher, guitarist, minister, and President of the United States. Achieved statuses require some decision and action, such as a marriage proposal and ceremony to achieve the statuses of husband and wife.

Revealing the mystery lady on p. 172 as
Indira Gandhi, we learn her *achieved*
status: Prime Minister of the largest
democracy in the world.

Few statuses are gained or held entirely by ascription or entirely by achievement. Although occupational status in modern society is largely achieved, a doctor's son has an initial advantage in a medical career, and a farmer's son is much more likely to be a farmer than is a lawyer's son. Aspirants to the position of President of the United States are limited by Constitutional provision to those occupying the ascribed statuses of natural-born citizen over 35 years of age, and by practical politics to white males.

ROLE PERFORMANCE

Once we know the social structure of a group—its network of statuses and their attached roles or norms—we can outline the general pattern of interaction within the group without reference to any specific actors and their particular personalities. Thus we can describe a baseball game in terms of each player's position and role and the general rules of the game—what the pitcher, catcher, basemen, fielders, and batter are supposed to do, under what circumstances a team scores or fails to score, when the teams change sides up at bat, and so on.

But it is **role performance** that brings a baseball game or stage play to life and constitutes the ongoing social interaction of any group. In the performance of roles we see the dynamic interplay of culture, society, and personality. We do not usually go to see just any movie or any baseball game; we go to see Barbra Streisand or Willie Mays performing a role. Our interest in what goes on around us, fun, novels, movies—and social change—all have their roots in the great variety of role performances that can occur within statuses that are culturally defined as the same.

No role can be more than a *guide* to the behavior of a performer, for it can never describe the nuances of a specific person's role behavior. Several variables affect role performance: the latitude of its interpretation, its compatibility or conflict with other roles, the performer's degree of internalization of norms and commitment to their underlying values, and the degree of enforcement of sanctions by others, as well as the unique personality of the performer.

Latitude of interpretation. Certain kinds of roles permit a wider range of interpretation than others. Among these are *diffuse* roles, which apply to many situations, as compared to the *specific* roles of a special occupation. The interaction of friends and family in most societies is governed by very diffuse norms, as opposed to the narrow and rigid role requirements of an occupation. For example, the half-humorous reference to a "Jewish mother" indicates a particular interpretation of the role of mother fairly prevalent within a subcultural group. But given the more precisely defined role of plumber, we find that a Jewish plumber plays his role just about like any other plumber. New and undefined roles—such as television producer—that arise as a society changes and becomes more complex are defined by the role performances of the first incumbents. There is also great latitude in the performance of roles in which interaction with others is infrequent and reciprocal expectations few: An artist or novelist is much more free to experiment than a physician or teacher.

Role conflicts. Performance of a role is reinforced if a person's other roles are compatible with it; it is often weakened when a person has assumed incompatible or conflicting roles.

> The structure of a society can be viewed as a set of rules about which roles should be linked together and which ones are to be kept apart. But because circumstances change more rapidly than the rules, it regularly happens that individuals have to play two or more roles that do not combine well. Role conflicts have been the very stuff of tragedy from the earliest days of drama.[35]

The "working" mother—that is, one employed outside her home —may experience role conflict. Mrs. Smith, for example, may have chosen to be a teacher in part because her schedule would conform pretty well to that of her school-age children. But if one of them is sick at home, she suffers from a feeling that if she goes to work she is not a good mother, while if she stays home she is not a good teacher. Then

[35]*Ibid.*, p. 167.

she may not perform well in either role. Black policemen feel they are trapped in the middle and "get it from both sides." Some statuses are defined by legal or other norms as incompatible: A Secretary of Defense should not be chairman of the board or a large stockholder in any industry that might have contracts with the government; a doctor should not own a drugstore.

Even where role conflicts are not clearly evident, a person may experience "role strain" simply because, in modern society, his total role obligations demand too much of him, and there just isn't enough time, money, or energy to meet all the demands of all the roles. He seeks a "role bargain"—a balance among roles that permits him to fulfill the major ones, at least, satisfactorily and some of the others passably; in the process he may have to abandon one or two roles entirely. Thus, a writer who is also a wife and mother experiences considerable role strain; occasionally something has to "give."

Internalization of roles.   The internalization of a role occurs as part of the process of socialization, which is most intense in childhood but continues throughout life as learning, punishment, and reward continue. As a role is internalized, the person comes to accept its norms as right, to distinguish in a general way between mandatory and permissive norms, and to feel emotionally committed to the values underlying them.

We may say that a role is thoroughly internalized when a person feels guilty or uncomfortable if he does not conform to its norms; he is then emotionally committed to adequate role performance. This strong inner sanction tends to ensure such performance. But even when a role is less thoroughly internalized, a person may still conform so long as he wants to avoid the consequences of nonconformity—the sanctions imposed by those in reciprocal relationships or in the more extended group. On the other hand, he may not conform at all because he cares about neither the values nor the sanctions.

Mutual reinforcement of role performance.   A person's role performance is also affected by the way others in a situation play their reciprocal roles and the degree to which they enforce sanctions. If Mrs. Smith does not care how well or badly her students perform on homework, class recitation, and tests, she will exert no influence toward good performance. On the other hand, even if she does not really care how much they learn, and yet she wants to be considered a good teacher by her superiors, keep her job, and gain tenure, she will encourage them to do well. This pressure from "third parties" acts as a powerful social control: What will people say? What will the neighbors think? What will Principal Jones say if my pupils do badly on the Stanford Achievement Tests? The more specific and closer the third party in a situation, the more effective he is in reinforcing role performance. Thus the principal may exert pressure both on teacher and pupils.

Because roles are reciprocal, they tend to reinforce each other: An actor who fails to perform adequately makes it difficult for his opposite number to do so. Often roles are so interrelated that failure or success in one role imposes similar results on another: A student who fails displeases his parents as well as his teachers.

Ralph Linton succinctly summed up what social structure means for human behavior: "Status and role serve to reduce the ideal patterns for social life to individual terms."[36]

Summary

Social organization is the coordination of relationships among persons and groups. The largest unit of organization, the largest group in which men interact and feel a sense of belonging, is a society. Both nonhuman and human societies are organized into a continuing division of labor, live in a certain territory, and share common goals, such as protection, nutrition, and reproduction of members. Culture enables human societies to become increasingly large and complex.

Various models of society have guided sociological theory and research. The machine analogy depicts a society as a set of interrelated moving parts that work together, connected by energy and subject to such forces as momentum and inertia. The organic model, the framework of functional theory, depicts a society as a system whose parts contribute to its healthy functioning and survival and are in turn nourished by it. Both suggest a state of equilibrium as the goal of social action.

The cybernetic model of a society as a complex adaptive system stresses interaction, variety, and change, and the use of information and communication to adapt to external and internal constraints, demands, and disturbances. The concepts of feedback and decision-making suggest that a society is not subject to blind forces and natural history and therefore can become self-guiding.

Social interaction is the reciprocal influencing of behavior through symbolic communication between persons. The main processes of interaction are cooperation, competition, conflict, accommodation, and assimilation.

A social relationship is a pattern of interaction between two or more social actors—persons or groups—based on their mutual expectations of behavior. Not all human behavior is social behavior, and not all social behavior is organized behavior, that is, some is not coordinated by a system of social relationships. Neither are all groupings genuine

[36]Ralph Linton, *The Study of Man* (New York: Appleton-Century-Crofts, 1936), p. 114.

social groups; they may be physical or statistical aggregates, or social categories.

Genuine social groups consist of people who feel they belong together because of something significant they have in common, interact according to mutually accepted norms, and have interrelated and reciprocal statuses.

Social structure refers to a pattern of social relationships, a network of reciprocal statuses with their accompanying roles. A status is a position in a social structure; a role is the pattern of expected behavior accompanying a status. A person has one key status among multiple statuses, which tend to be clustered or compounded. Some statuses are sequential; some are communal, others associational. Statuses are often ranked within a group. Some are ascribed (age, sex, kinship, caste, nationality, race); others are achieved (occupations and public offices in modern society).

A person's performance of a role varies according to the permissible latitude of its interpretation, its compatibility or conflict with his other roles, the degree to which he has internalized its norms and feels committed to their underlying values, the degree of enforcement of norms by others in the role set as well as their performances, and his unique personality.

Statuses, then, are the positions that can be mapped, as in the organizational chart of a corporation or bureau, according to the lines of authority and influence flowing down a hierarchy or horizontally from one person or subgroup to another. Roles are the "job descriptions" attached to these positions, the bundles of norms that outline the behavior expected of each status occupant and the rewards and rights he can in turn expect. Role performance is the "play-by-play account" of actual behavior in the role, of actual interaction in a given situation. With these basic units of social organization and social interaction in mind, we turn next to such aspects of social organization as the various kinds of groups and group relationships, and the kinds of societies in which we find them.

QUESTIONS FOR FURTHER THOUGHT

1. A good actor is said to lose himself in his role, to be unconscious of playing one. What phrases in everyday language refer to good role performance in life, to poor role performance, to unauthorized or false role performance?

2. Roles are said to be situational, yet a mentally healthy person keeps a certain consistency among his roles even as he shifts from one to another. Have you ever experienced difficulty in shifting roles with different situations? Why?

3. We have used a number of concepts in a general or abstract sense and a specific or concrete sense. Review science, culture, and society as both types of concepts.

4. Which process of interaction do you engage in most often during a normal day? What kinds of competition and conflict have you been aware of recently? What are the sources of conflict in your own experience? Identify accommodation of conflict in your family or friendship groups. Does it resolve conflict, or merely call a truce?

5. Give examples of normative, utilitarian, and coercive relationships from your own experience.

6. List a number of categories in which you might be placed. Try to arrange them in order of significance for your life. Do the same for a number of groups to which you belong. Which ones are "recruited" from or otherwise related to the categories you listed?

7. Why does assimilation of immigrants often take three generations?

8. What social processes are present in a football game?

9. Are the following social groups? If not, what would you call them? The population of Houston. Your sociology class. French males age 40. The family next door. Passengers on an airplane. Children playing in the back yard. Divorcees.

10. What do you consider the proper roles for a female of your age? List appropriate actions and traits. Do the same for a male. Do any items on the lists overlap?

11. What is the first question an adult male American is likely to ask another upon being introduced? What does this suggest to you about American social structure?

12. Distinguish between status and role. Which is more clearly related (for purposes of analysis) to culture? Which to society? Use the analogy of a play to illustrate the distinction further.

13. In our society, do ascribed or achieved statuses generally carry more prestige? Explain your answer.

14. How do clear symbols of status facilitate social interaction and social control?

15. Would cooperation or competition be more likely to prevail in a society where most statuses are ascribed? Where they are achieved?

16. List the roles you have played in the past week. What inner sanctions affected your performance in various roles? What external sanctions, formal and informal? Did you experience role conflict or role strain? How did you arrive at a role bargain?

8

A crowd is not company; and faces are but a gallery of pictures; and talk but a tinkling cymbal, where there is no love.

FRANCIS BACON

When in charge, ponder; when in trouble, delegate; when in doubt, mumble.

MOTTO OF THE NATIONAL ASSOCIATION OF PROFESSIONAL BUREAUCRATS

In the United States; associations are established to promote the public safety, commerce, industry, morality, and religion. There is no end which the human will despairs of attaining through the combined power of individuals united into a society.

ALEXIS DE TOCQUEVILLE

TYPES OF SOCIAL ORGANIZATION

THE GLAMOR GARMENTS COMPANY makes women's dresses. This corporation has a president, a board of directors, stockholders, executives, office workers, designers, salesmen, foremen, workers who actually make the dresses, and janitors. A clear chart of organization indicates lines of authority. Company rules are posted in prominent places. Employees punch in at a time clock as they arrive and leave.

Five dress finishers have a work area to themselves. Their job of clipping threads and checking buttons is so automatic they can talk almost constantly. They use first names, joke, tease, argue, know all about one another's families, share snacks, and sometimes see one another outside work. Each produces about the same amount of work per day; no one wants to outshine the others or lag too far behind. They feel like a unit against the badgering of the supervisor, and they set themselves off from women doing other kinds of work.

The contrast between the large firm and the small group within it illustrates the three closely related aspects of social organization that we shall consider in this chapter: the size of a group, the nature of the social relationships within it, and the degree to which its structure is formalized. We shall also consider the cohesion of groups, the ties that bind them. Finally, we shall compare two polar types of societies in terms of these four aspects: folk or traditional society and industrial or modern society.

The Importance of Group Size

Kin groups and small cliques of friends are present in every society, and account for almost all social interaction in small, preliterate societies. In modern society we find a proliferation of groups of all sizes, including giant organizations such as business corporations, armies, universities, and government agencies. What consequences does size alone have for group interaction?

SMALL GROUPS

A **small group** consists of two or more persons who repeatedly interact face-to-face. The passenger who boards the same bus every morning and the driver who wishes him "Good morning" do not constitute a small group in spite of recurrent contact; the five dress finishers do. No more than fifteen or twenty members fit the definition, for even before a group reaches that size, it tends to break down into subgroups, cliques, and factions. Friends, lovers, families, play groups, adolescent gangs, committees, athletic teams, seminars, work groups, and professionals such as a psychiatrist with each of his clients—all these and many more come under the definition. If each of the 3.7 billion people in the world belongs to five or six groups on the average, and we allow for overlap, it is estimated that there may be 4 or 5 billion small groups in existence at this moment. *Most* social groups consist of seven persons or less; nine out of ten, in fact, consist of only two or three people.[1]

Small groups interest social scientists because of what they mean to the individual and society. They are a primary source of social order, mediating between society and a person, socializing and motivating him. Because of their psychological hold over members they are a powerful means of social control. A person is likely to conform to small-group pressures because he wants the emotional satisfactions, the sense of belonging, identity, and self-esteem they can provide. Cohesiveness (unity) and morale tend to be higher in small groups than in large ones. The more cohesive a work group in a factory, the less absenteeism and turnover among its members. Small groups are very effective in producing decisions and action: They decide whether or not to have babies and whether or not to wage war.

Sociologists also study small groups to learn about social behavior in general, for they exhibit many features of larger groups and societies. They evolve status structures with differentiated roles, including leadership, and differences in prestige, power, and influence. They evolve subcultures—group norms and values enforced by group sanctions, perhaps even their own set of material things. Studying them, we can see how individuals react to social pressures; how personality develops in interaction; how motivations are developed, maintained, and changed; how cooperation, competition, conflict, assimilation, and accommodation occur; what holds a group together and what breaks it apart; how they make decisions and solve problems.

The study of small groups is part of group dynamics, "the field of inquiry dedicated to achieving knowledge about the nature of groups, the laws of their development, and their interrelationships with individuals, other groups, and larger institutions."[2] It may be carried on in laboratories or in natural settings, where investigators systematically observe the everyday chaos of "organisms making noises at one another."[3]

[1]John James, "A Preliminary Study of the Size Determinant in Small Group Interaction," *American Sociological Review*   16 (Aug. 1951): 474–77.

[2]Dorwin Cartwright and Alvin Zander, *Group Dynamics: Research and Theory*, 3rd ed. (New York: Harper & Row, Publishers, 1968), p. 4.

[3]Michael Olmsted, *The Small Group* (New York: Random House, 1959), p. 94.

"Interaction process analysis" is one example of such systematic methods. An observer classifies behavior act-by-act according to a predetermined scale as it occurs in the face-to-face interaction of small groups. He decides, for example, if an act of Person 3 directed toward a certain other person or the group at large comes under Category 1, "Shows solidarity, raises other's status, gives help, reward," or 7, "Asks for orientation, information, repetition, confirmation," or 11, "Shows tension, asks for help, withdraws out of field," or any other of twelve categories. Each category is related to problems of orientation, evaluation, control, decision-making, tension management, or group integration.[4]

Sociometric tests, which measure interpersonal attraction in a group, are widely used. In the original test, delinquent girls in a "training home" were given questionnaires asking them to write down the names of the other girls with whom they liked and disliked to live, work, study, and spend leisure time. Although such questionnaires may rely too much on verbal reports, they do provide clues to a group's internal structure, and have been used to assign people to dormitories, bomber crews, and other diverse groupings.

Other studies have concentrated on such problems as the effects of group atmosphere (democratic, authoritarian, laissez-faire), the subculture of street gangs, communication networks, conformity, leadership, and the emergence of a status structure. What are some of the findings of such studies?

Even within the limits of two to twenty, variation in size is significant. When the number of persons in a group increases arithmetically, the number of possible channels of interaction increases geometrically. There are four possible relationships in a group of three, but the addition of just one person increases the number of possible relationships to eleven.[5] By the time the group numbers seven, there are *120* possible relationships.

The smaller the group, the more intense interaction tends to be. *Dyads*, or groups of two, and *triads*, groups of three, have characteristics that are not only different from those of larger groups but also different from each other. Dyads are conscious of their mortality; if one member withdraws, the group no longer exists. Group opinion must be unanimous. Dyads such as husband and wife are "characterized by high tension and emotion, a high tendency to avoid disagreement, a tendency for one to be the active initiator and the other the passive controller with veto—all because of the delicate balance involved in the situation

[4]Robert F. Bales, "A Set of Categories for the Analysis of Small Group Interaction," *American Sociological Review* 15 (1950): 257–63.

[5]In a group made up of Tom, Dick, and Harry, for example, we have the relationships of all three, of Tom and Dick, of Tom and Harry, and of Dick and Harry. If Ed joins the group, seven more relationships are added: that of all four; of Tom and Ed; of Tom, Dick, and Ed; of Tom, Harry, and Ed; of Dick and Ed; of Dick, Harry, and Ed; and of Harry and Ed.

In triads, one person is often left out.

where there is no other support within the group for either participant in case of disagreement and where getting along is necessary for survival."[6]

A dramatic change in a husband–wife relationship occurs when the first child is born. Unlike a dyad, a triad is potentially immortal; it can persist by replacing one member at a time (like the Kingston Trio). Its most significant property is the tendency to break into a coalition of two against one, as any mother who has watched her children with playmates knows. Each member serves to unite and to separate the other two. He may act as an intruder (even though, like a baby, he may be welcome), as a mediator, as an "enjoying third" who exploits and benefits from the dissension of the other two, or as an oppressor who instigates conflict for his own purposes.

Much of the world's work is done by hierarchical triads, such as leader-lieutenant-follower and manager-foreman-worker. "Each of these has a man in the middle who bears the brunt of the tension between discipline and freedom by sustaining nearly incompatible relationships with his superior and his subordinate. In general, the presence of a person who witnesses the interaction of a pair of unequals tends to increase their inequality, and his departure reduces the status difference."[7] The concept of triads may also be applied to social systems of three interacting groups: "two triads of the same type may behave very similarly, although one consists of three small boys and the other of three large bureaucracies."[8]

Social psychologists who have conducted experiments in group size suggest that perhaps the optimum size of a group is five or seven people (note the uneven numbers); perhaps no more than seven people

[6]Bernard Berelson and Gary A. Steiner, *Human Behavior*, shorter ed. (New York: Harcourt Brace Jovanovich, 1967), pp. 63–65. Based on the research of Robert F. Bales and Edgar F. Borgatta.

[7]Theodore Caplow, *Two Against One: Coalitions in Triads* (Englewood Cliffs, N.J.: Prentice-Hall, Inc., 1968), p. 6.

[8]*Ibid.*, p. 1.

can really take account of one another as individuals, and members of a group of five find more personal satisfaction than in smaller or larger groups. Why? Because "there is ease of movement within the group, a two-to-three division provides support for the minority members, and it is large enough for stimulation but small enough for participation and personal recognition."[9] A division into equal numbers on opposite sides of a question hinders compromise.

Small groups also serve some instrumental purposes better than do larger ones. John James found that action-taking committees in a large bank averaged six or seven members, while committees that did not take action but discussed questions and served as sounding boards averaged fourteen members.[10] Subcommittees of the House of Representatives average about eight members.

LARGE GROUPS

If a small group consists of no more than twenty persons, then a large group must consist of more than twenty persons, and may be as large as a nation-state. What happens as a group grows larger? First of all, it tends to *split into subgroups*. Consider what happens at a party:

> When just a few people are present, they usually talk with one another as a single group. But as people continue to arrive at the party, an interesting change takes place. Some of the members come to dominate the discussion, and others do not speak at all. This process usually sets in when half a dozen to a dozen people are present. Some members, dissatisfied with the group life because they cannot involve themselves in it as much as they like, strike up conversations with the person on either side of them. As the evening progresses, the original group fragments into a series of smaller groups in which the individual has ample opportunity to relate to others.[11]

Second, as the number of possible channels of interaction increases geometrically with the addition of new members, interaction becomes chaotic and unwieldy; if the group is to persist and function, a *structure of authority* that blocks off some of the channels of interaction and facilitates the use of others must emerge. The ideal educational group may be a student on one end of a log and a teacher on the other, but most schooling goes on in classrooms with twenty, thirty, or more students. If all the possible channels of interaction were open, the syllabus would be neglected and any learning that occurred would be un-

[9]Berelson and Steiner, *Human Behavior*, p. 63.

[10]"A Preliminary Study of the Size Determinant."

[11]Paul E. Mott, *The Organization of Society* (Englewood Cliffs, N.J.: Prentice-Hall, Inc, 1965), pp. 50–51.

planned and incidental. To accomplish the group's purpose, the teacher must have authority to block or regulate interaction among the students and to direct their attention to her. The situation becomes "structured" —that is, statuses become differentiated and explicit, their accompanying roles are clearly defined, and a rank order of authority emerges.

As a group comes to include two or more subgroups, this authority structure may become a hierarchy, more or less pyramid-shaped, with one person or a small committee at the top and several distinct levels of authority down the line. Thus all the teachers in a school system would be the leaders of subgroups at the same level; all the principals would be a level above them, each with his staff as a subgroup below; and so on up to the superintendent.

Third, *roles tend to become more specialized*; the functions of persons and subgroups become more differentiated and more interdependent. In a small restaurant, for example, the same person might take your order, cook it, serve it, and accept payment. In a large one, there are many specialized roles such as cook, waitress, pantry worker, kitchen helper, dishwasher, bartender, hostess, and cashier, all under the authority of a manager.

Fourth, as the group thus becomes more fragmented, specialized, and interdependent, the need for *coordination of interrelated parts* arises. A change in any subgroup may affect many or all of the others. A deprived group in a community or society, for example, may have accepted their status for years; but if they grow rebellious, all other groups are affected, and some new form of accommodation must be arrived at if the society is to function and achieve its goals.

Fifth, the larger and more complex the group becomes, and the greater its need for coordination, the more essential is *communication* among the parts—and at the same time the more possibilities arise for this communication to be blocked. Subgroups may be separated by physical distance: The members of a community may live more or less unaware of one another in suburbs, ghettos, and ethnic enclaves; or the field units of an army may be widely dispersed. Then, too, people in the same subgroup or category tend to interact more with one another and thus to share the same values and norms, and to adopt ethnocentric attitudes. In effect they develop subcultures whose understandings and behavior patterns may be at variance with those of other subgroups to such an extent that they act as barriers to communication. (This principle will be evident in our discussions of class and race in the next two chapters.) Subgroups may also seek different and conflicting goals within the larger group. A labor force may seek only job security, higher wages, and fringe benefits, while management expects employees to share concern for production and profits.

Two more things occur as a group gets larger: Personal relationships tend to become less intimate, and organization becomes more formal. We shall consider these dimensions of social organization at some length.

Primary and Secondary Relationships

Sociologists often analyze complex social phenomena by means of polar types, pairs of opposites regarded as the extremes of a straight line or continuum. Because they are ideal or abstract, polar types seldom describe any one situation perfectly, but they permit the investigator to analyze a "case" by placing its various elements in positions along the continuum.

Primary and secondary relationships are polar types. Human groups, including whole societies, may be characterized as primary or secondary groups according to which relationships predominate.

Primary relationships are "personal, spontaneous, sentimental, and inclusive."[12] The groups in which they predominate are typically small and homogeneous, the result of intimate association over a long period of time. Primary group interaction is expressive rather than instrumental; it is not a means to some specific goal, but is valued for itself, for the feelings of companionship, affection, and security that arise from it. Each person cares what happens to the other or others. Primary relationships involve deep, but not necessarily positive, emotions (both "I love you, darling," and "Shut up, you make me sick" indicate a primary relationship). If a person's primary relationships are unsatisfactory, he feels tense, unhappy, and frustrated. He may feel trapped, inhibited, and smothered by too close a one, and lonely and isolated if he has no close ones at all.

[12]Kingsley Davis, *Human Society* (New York: The Macmillan Company, 1949), p. 294.

Drawing by Scott Val Taber. Copyright 1969 Saturday Review, Inc.

Membership in a primary group is nontransferable. Each person is valued for himself; he is unique, and interaction would be different with a different person. He is not seen in terms of his race, class, or occupation, but as a person with a personal meaning to *me: my* friend Emily, *my* brother Bob.

The family, the play group or circle of close friends, and the neighborhood are the primary groups that are fundamental to every society. They are, as the pioneer sociologist Charles Horton Cooley said, "the nursery of human nature." Every person starts life in them; they transmit the culture and shape his personality when he is young and plastic. Throughout life they serve as the principal sources of motivation and social control.

Secondary relationships, in contrast, are impersonal, superficial, transitory, and segmental. Even though secondary contacts may involve face-to-face interaction, this interaction is not intimate. It involves only the particular segment of the personality—the status and role—relevant to the situation. Unique personal attributes are not ordinarily taken into account.

Secondary relationships are instrumental: They are means to ends. The license clerk is there only to serve us (and to earn money); we are there only as clients who want to be served. The relationship between license clerk and applicant would be changed little if at all were another person to perform the role. The applicant interacts with the clerk, not with Susan Anderson, the girl known to family and friends as affectionate, warm-hearted, idealistic, hard-working, thrifty, and subject to blue moods on rainy days.

Secondary relationships are especially prevalent in large groups and in modern societies. We could not possibly know intimately all the people with whom we come into contact in city living. When we go out to work or shop, most of our contacts are fleeting and impersonal. In a single day, we may rub elbows with hundreds of people. We may engage in minor transactions or brief conversation with dozens without knowing their names, their family backgrounds, or anything at all about them except their function in relation to us and what they look like (and often we don't notice even that). Most of the people around us are merely obstacles to be avoided as we walk along, or fellow passengers to be classified and dismissed with a glance. Others are means to ends—the bus driver who lets us out at the proper stop, the salesgirl who helps us match a color, the bank teller who cashes a check, the policeman who untangles the rush-hour traffic jam.

As a rank-and-file member of a secondary group such as a political party, student body, or audience, an individual acts not as a "whole person" (which he more nearly does in the primary group), but in a segmental or partial role based on his particular status as voter, student, or spectator. His membership is transferable. When he leaves the scene the people who remain will experience no sense of loss, nor will

there be bereavement or loneliness; the group will simply be smaller by one, and anyone else can fill the gap and make up the loss to the party's registration rolls or the theater's profits. Instead of the intimate sharing of common values that characterizes the primary group, the secondary group involves a rational pursuit of common interests, or at least of interests members happen to share at a certain point. Secondary groups are typically larger than primary groups, and as we saw, large groups manifest a far greater differentiation of roles and clearer social structure than do small ones. Sanctions are formal and explicit.

Whole communities and societies have been characterized as "primary" or "secondary," depending on the proportion of warm, personal contacts to impersonal ones. The trend toward larger, more highly urbanized societies has inevitably meant that secondary groups become increasingly important. Groups such as governments, schools, churches, and business corporations grow larger, more formal, and more elaborate. Associations spring up around specific interests.

Within these secondary groups, however, primary relationships evolve out of repeated face-to-face interaction. The soldier has buddies; members of a work group become friends; even a long-standing relationship between a housewife and her butcher or hairdresser typically acquires elements of a primary relationship. In all large organizations

Dinner begins with the *secondary* relationships of the supermarket and ends with the *primary* relationships of the family.

cliques form and communication proceeds by grapevine as well as through formal channels. Persons see one another as persons, not just as functionaries.

The converse is also true. Primary groups often have purposes and goals other than merely the pleasure of interaction. The family, for example, performs basic social functions such as reproduction, socialization, and regulation of consumption, as well as providing affection and security. The various roles in the family's social structure are not completely open to definition in the course of interaction; they are culturally defined. The father punishing his son for violation of a norm is performing a culturally defined duty—that of socializing the child, which, in some situations, takes precedence over the demonstration of affection.

Formal and Informal Organization

All social groups are organized in the sense that they have a structure consisting of coordinated social relationships. But some are more organized than others. In long-standing social units such as the family and the tribe, this structure is defined by traditional folkways and mores. In other units, where people are thrown together by circumstance, a structure emerges in the course of social interaction. We see such informal organization when children who happen to be growing up in the same neighborhood form play groups and street gangs. It is also apparent when soldiers or factory workers are assigned to a task force or work group. In contrast to these groups that "just happen," formal organizations are deliberately created for a specific purpose, and their structures are clearly outlined.

INFORMAL ORGANIZATION

The Hawthorne Experiments at the Western Electric Company in Chicago provide classic examples of the emergence of **informal organization** within large formal organizations. The experiment in the Relay Assembly Room, conducted by Elton Mayo of Harvard, was based on these assumptions: that the worker must be studied as an isolated unit; that he resembles a machine whose efficiency can be measured scientifically; and that his efficiency depends on his motions, his fatigue, and the physical environment—light, heat, humidity, seating, and so on. But the results of the experiment upset every assumption.

The investigators set out to study the effects of illumination on productivity. In both the control group, in which lighting was unchanged, and the experimental group, in which various kinds of changes in lighting were made, output went up. Why? A second series of experiments was necessary. Two girls were asked to choose four more girls to join them in a workshop where they would assemble telephone relays, small mechanisms of about forty separate parts. For 5 years an experimenter sat with the team in the workshop, observing them, keeping them informed about the experiment, listening to their talk and complaints, and asking them for advice and information.

Productivity was recorded at the outset. Then one condition after another was changed, each for a period of 4–12 weeks. The girls were put on piecework and then returned to straight wages. They were given longer and shorter rest pauses or more frequent ones, dismissed ½ hour earlier, given a free hot meal. Output went up with each change. It remained the same, however, when numerous rest pauses were introduced (the girls complained that their work rhythms were broken) and when the group was dismissed 1 hour early. Then during the final 12 weeks the girls were returned to their original hours and working conditions—a 45-hour, 6-day week, at straight wages, with no piecework, no rest pauses, and no free meal. Output was the highest ever recorded![13]

The investigators concluded that their own interest was one factor in high morale. The other was the emergence of a cohesive group with a sense of purpose and belonging.

Another experiment in the Bank Wiring Room disproved the managers' idea that workers would work extra hard for bonuses. It was the time of the Depression; the workers feared that if they worked too fast someone would be laid off. They evolved a code whereby a "rate buster" was not a good guy; but neither was a "chiseler" who worked much less than the others, nor a "squealer" nor a "snob." In both groups, a social structure appeared, with differentiation of roles—leaders and followers, a clown, a taskmaster, and so on. The larger group of fourteen in the second experiment divided into two cliques, which differed in work habits and status. Members of both groups developed loyalty and a sense of belonging.

The phenomenon of informal organization is universal. Although its rules and roles are not institutionalized, they are real. Group pressure enforces norms; force or other coercion is seldom necessary. A subculture of patterned behavior emerges, "a subtle blend of overt activity, speech, gestures, feelings, and ideas which comes to serve as an identifying badge for the 'insider' as against the 'outsider.' "[14] The Soviet term for this phenomenon, "familyness," conveys this feeling of the "we-group."

[13]*The Human Problems of an Industrial Civilization* (New York: The Macmillan Company, 1933).
[14]Olmsted, *The Small Group*, p. 30.

Formal Organization

A formal organization is a social group deliberately created to reach an explicit goal by means systematically planned by those in authority. Such a group does not, like families or friendship or tribes, "just happen"; it is "organized" at a given time. It is given a name or title, such as The Cornerville Social and Athletic Club or The Republic of Panama. Its goals are outlined, perhaps in a constitution; means for reaching them, including a division of labor, are planned. A set of rules and regulations is spelled out, with explicit sanctions for good or bad role performance: wages or loss of a job, honorable or dishonorable discharge, and so on. Property is acquired in the name of the group; this may be as simple as a notebook for records, as complex as a world-wide chain of offices and factories.

The existence of a formal organization does not hinge on particular members. This, in fact, is the infallible test of a formal organization: Can it substitute personnel, and even survive a complete turnover in membership? Because its purpose is instrumental rather than expressive, members are typically not emotionally involved in the interaction needed to carry out group goals; they interact in segmental roles.

In small societies dominated by tradition, the formally organized group is a rarity. But as societies grow and become more complex, formal organization increases; without it there could have been no Roman Empire, no Catholic Church, no conquering armies. However, domination of social life by formally organized groups, both large and small, is something quite new.

We can get an idea of the dominant role of formal organization by thinking for a moment of how many needs in modern complex society are met through different voluntary associations. Such groups as sports or country clubs, bridge clubs, lodges, civic luncheon groups, alumni associations, and church circles not only serve their explicit purposes, but also are substitutes for declining primary group relationships. Many formal organizations with specifically commercial goals also allow face-to-face association. The small businessman knows all his employees, and interaction among them proceeds on a basis of primary as well as secondary relationships.

But it is the *large-scale* formal organization that dominates much of modern life. A formal organization may be called large-scale when most of its members are not in face-to-face contact with one another. Its rise has been called "the most striking development in social structure in the twentieth century."[15] In the United States the trend began after the Civil War, with the emergence of a few giant

[15]Don Martindale, *Institutions, Organizations, and Mass Society* (Boston: Houghton Mifflin, 1966), p. xiii.

"What do you mean you're taking up a collection for good ole Hal Cooper—I'M good ole Hal Cooper."

producers in such heavy industries as oil, steel, and railroad transportation. Before long, most industrial manufacturing was similarly consolidated, and conducted by a few huge financial organizations. Advertising the products of large-scale industry called for mass media: Chains of newspapers appeared, and the number of independent papers in each city dwindled. The growth of radio and TV was followed by their coordination into large networks. To regulate all these organizations, government had to grow correspondingly. Labor, professions, and farmers organized to defend their special interests. Education, too, became increasingly subject to large organizations, of which the "multiversity" is the epitome. Even charity has become a matter for coordinated "community chest" drives, and philanthropy for nonprofit foundations.

BUREAUCRACY AND LARGE-SCALE ORGANIZATION

Because large-scale organizations are oriented toward specific goals and must coordinate the actions of many different people toward reaching them, their paramount values are efficiency, rationality, expertise, and discipline. To realize these values, they create a clear social structure, an explicit division of labor in which each status has a name or "job title" and each accompanying role is spelled out in a "job description" that includes clearly assigned tasks, responsibilities, and privileges. Each status is analyzed in terms of rationality and efficiency —the contribution it makes toward reaching the goal of the organization. Statuses are coordinated in a hierarchy, a chain of command that indicates who has authority over whom. It is possible to make a life career of climbing within such a hierarchy: The parish priest may dream of becoming a Monsignor, a Bishop, an Archbishop, perhaps a Cardinal or even Pope. A junior executive knows just which rungs of the ladder he must climb before he can aspire to be chairman of the board.

Impersonal, secondary relationships predominate in large-scale organizations. Interaction is supposed to occur between statuses, not persons (a norm impossible to achieve but most closely realized, perhaps, when a subject curtsies to the Queen or a private "salutes the rank, not the man"). The rules for interaction are spelled out; one must "go through channels" or "by the book."

The administration of large-scale organizations is typically bureaucratic. We usually think of bureaucracy in connection with government, where it is established to meet a demand for order and protection of rights without regard to party affiliation, social class, or heredity. Once established, it is enduring; it is one of the hardest social structures to destroy. Parties and rulers come and go, but the officials in a typical bureaucracy stay on and work much the same way with one regime as with another. No new set of rulers can afford to replace all the bureaucratic officials, for their expertise is necessary to the functioning of a modern nation, as it is to a modern corporation or army.

The great German sociologist Max Weber described the model type of government bureaucracy as an administrative structure under legal authority, made up entirely of appointed officials, except perhaps for the supreme chief, who may be designated by election or succession.[16] The bureaucracy, and each official within it, has a clear-cut area of jurisdiction, both geographically and as a sphere of competence. It has a set of files and records. It also has a set of rules and regulations which are supposed to cover all problems that arise in the course of administration, and which are to be applied impersonally and equally to all.

In bureaucracies a clearly defined hierarchy of offices with a graded system of centralized authority exercises strict and systematic discipline and control over each official's conduct of his office. Office holding is a career with definite steps upward; it demands the entire work capacity of the office holder for a long period of time. Officials are selected on the basis not of personal relationships but of examina-

---

[16]*The Theory of Social and Economic Organization*, trans. A. M. Henderson and Talcott Parsons (New York: The Free Press, 1957).

tions or certificates of technical training. There is much to know, and the official becomes an expert; he concentrates on one small area, and the hierarchy coordinates his expertise with that of others.

The bureaucratic official normally has life tenure, with guarantees against arbitrary dismissal, and a pension plan. He is paid a fixed salary at each level of the hierarchy. His official life is supposed to be entirely divorced from his personal life; any violations of this rule are considered graft, corruption, or nepotism. In other words, primary relationships should not influence his behavior in the secondary group.

Bureaucracy may have negative consequences. Its stability may be seen as rigidity, its regard for rules and proper procedure as red tape, its impersonality as lack of concern for human problems. Changing conditions and unusual cases are typically not allowed for, and initiative is stifled. Bureaucrats may not see the forest of organization goals for the trees of its minor regulations. Spoofing the negative side of the bureaucratic personality, the National Association of Professional Bureaucrats, founded by a United States government employee, adopted a rampant duck snarled in red tape as their seal. They came out in favor of the status quo and buck passing, use executive pencils with erasers at both ends, and urge due recognition of "the inarticulate fingertappers of the world who, by their steadfast dedication to the principle of dynamic inactivism, have kept things from happening, and thereby have prevented mistakes from being made."[17]

Robert Merton observed that the "bureaucratic personality" is highly conformist, and suggested that graded careers encourage conformity and even timidity. Bureaucracy's need for "methodical, prudent, disciplined employees" may lead them to consider adherence to the rules an end in itself. And professional bureaucrats may band together to defend their own interests rather than those of clients, sometimes making things difficult for elected officials whom they dislike.[18] An extreme case of bureaucratic man is the so-called Eichmann phenomenon, "the individual who can be a major cog in a machinery designed to exterminate people and yet maintain his innocence since he 'only obeyed orders.' "[19]

But the technical advantages of bureaucracy are similar to the advantages of machinery as compared to manual labor: precision, speed, reduction of friction, economy, efficiency. In addition, the bureaucratic

[17]Al Blanchard, *Detroit Free Press* (Oct. 16, 1970).

[18]Robert Merton, *Social Theory and Social Structure*, 1968 enlarged edition (New York: The Free Press), Chap. 8, "Bureaucratic Structure and Personality," pp. 249–60. Recently this view has been challenged. Melvin L. Kohn argues that the bureaucrat is more likely to be flexible, open, and self-directed than the non-bureaucrat, perhaps because he is better educated, better paid, and more secure, and his work is more complex. ["Bureaucratic Man: A Portrait and an Interpretation," *American Sociological Review*   36 (June 1971): 461–74.]

[19]Steven E. Deutsch and John Howard, *Where It's At: Radical Perspectives in Sociology* (New York: Harper & Row, Publishers, 1970), p. 482.

official is ideally discreet (as well as impersonal), and familiar with the files and the rules. His very impersonality tends to ensure that he will apply the rules equally to all, a democratic tendency which levels social differences. For these reasons, Max Weber called it "the most rational known means of carrying out imperative control over human beings. . . . For the needs of mass administration today, it is completely indispensable."[20]

Regulative authority in professional organizations. Certain kinds of formal organizations do not lend themselves to bureaucratic forms as well as do industry, commerce, and government. Education, medicine, social work, and psychiatry, for example, depend on professionally (rather than technically) trained persons, and deal with human complexities. The task of dealing with these problems professionally does not lend itself to infinite specialization, coordination, and standardization. Files cannot be freely accessible, for example; there must be professional secrecy. Therefore these professions and the organizations through which they work (hospitals, universities, and the like) are regulated somewhat differently from corporations and government bureaus. First of all, the profession itself has an ethical code. All members of the profession are considered colleagues, equals; all are expected to uphold the dignity and mystique of the profession in return for the protection of their colleagues. Second, professionals are trained by established members of the profession, who also exert control over licensing of new members and continue to sanction members' behavior by means of professional control (for example, a review board checks on the need for operations and thus exerts some control over a knife-happy surgeon). Even though control is collegial (by a body of equals), there are a few at the top of the profession who by virtue of superior skill and experience assume responsibility for continual supervision and enforcement of behavior. They also may have control over facilities (salaries of professors, grants, budgets, admission to a hospital staff, and so on). Advancement in a profession is not automatic, as it tends to be in a bureaucracy. In the case of college and university teachers, however, security and academic freedom are guaranteed by granting tenure; the teacher can presumably then be discharged only for grave cause.

Interrelationship of Group Dimensions

The three dimensions of social organization we have been discussing are closely interrelated. In general, the smaller the group, the more likely it is to be informally organized and characterized by primary

[20]*The Theory of Social and Economic Organization*, p. 337.

relationships, and the larger the group, the more likely it is to be formal and secondary. But while all primary groups are small, not all small groups are primary: Committees, boards of directors, and small firms may be both formally organized and characterized by secondary—that is, essentially impersonal and segmental—relationships. The members of fairly large tribes and peasant communities may all be able to share primary relationships, yet interact on a secondary basis in some areas such as the market. And to know the score in a formal organization of any size, one must be aware not only of the charted social structure and division of labor but also of the informal friendships and loyalties, power cliques, and external commitments of various members.[21]

For a full life in modern society, we need both small primary groups and larger, rational units. Each of us needs friends and relatives who accept us for our own sake, soothe our hurts, listen to our tales of woe, laugh at our jokes and puns, and allow us to relax. But we also need[22] formal organizations to fill supermarket shelves, run airlines, train doctors, stage plays, staff schools, and build houses.

Cohesion and Control

Why do groups—societies in particular—endure as identifiable units? That is one of the central questions of sociology. In this section we discuss sources of group cohesion: consensus, control, coordination, and individual commitment.

CONSENSUS

Consensus or agreement on norms, values, and goals is essential to cohesion. It depends first of all on what the members of the group have in common, and on their belief that what they have in common is important, whether it is language, religion, occupation, race, locality, kinship, political ideology, sex, caste, or class status, the fact that they are set off in a certain part of a factory or office, or simply that they like each other. But they must also agree on a certain amount of overt conformity to behavior patterns if they are to interact smoothly and know what to expect of others. Even in the most complex society, they must agree on certain core values. For such agreement to arise and endure, there must be a flow of communication among members.

Milton Yinger suggests four possible degrees of consensus and dissensus. The first is *cultural unity*, with no disagreements, or so few

[21]Amitai Etzioni, *A Sociological Reader on Complex Organizations*, 2nd ed. (New York: Holt, Rinehart & Winston, Inc., 1969), p. 23.

[22]The verb "need" is used here to refer to culturally-instilled needs.

that they do not disrupt interaction and are not cumulative. Where this condition prevails, the system of shared expectations is effective in guiding interaction—that is, norms and values are clear, accepted, and followed. In the second condition, *cultural pluralism*, there are some disagreements, but they are at the very least tolerated, or they are considered legitimate, or they are even considered desirable. Examples in the United States are political parties, ethnic differences in language, food, and customs, and perhaps religious differences.

The other two possibilities are different kinds of *anomie*. Defined as "a loss of pattern in the *mutual* expectations for social action,"[23] anomie refers to a lack of agreement on norms and values so severe that behavior becomes more or less unpredictable. Where the third pattern, *subcultural anomie*, exists, "the differences make a difference." Disagreements disrupt the pattern of mutual expectations. The norms in each subcultural group are clear, and its members "know how to behave." But these norms are different from those in other subgroups, and when persons from different groups interact, conflict and misunderstanding occur. They may agree on goals but not on means. Yinger sees much of the interaction at the United Nations as anomic in this sense, as well as much interracial conflict. The fourth possibility is *full anomie*. Confusion over values occurs within persons as well as among them; they are in doubt about what are appropriate ends and legitimate means.[24]

CONTROL

Groups **control** the behavior of members through three kinds of power: normative, utilitarian, and coercive. Normative rewards are emotional satisfactions. When a primary group distributes or withholds response, affection, approval, and esteem, it is using normative power; a formal group employs such power through prestige rewards, ritual and ceremony, persuasion, and manipulation of the mass media. Utilitarian power refers to material rewards and appeals to self-interest. A mother denies dessert if a child misbehaves; a father gives a new bicycle if grades improve; formal organizations allocate different amounts of salaries and wages, fringe benefits, and so on. The emotional cost of leaving a family and the financial cost of leaving a firm may keep a member within the group.

But many groups are held together by the possibility or actual-

[23] *Toward a Field Theory of Behavior: Personality and Social Structure* (New York: McGraw-Hill Book Company, 1965), pp. 188–97.

[24] *Anomie* is often used to refer both to the normlessness of a group or the breaking of the sense of morale or belonging of an individual. We use it to refer to the normlessness of a group, a breakdown in its consensus or morale, the lack of predictability in its interaction. We use other concepts to indicate the degree of belonging or identification which an individual feels.

ity of coercion or force. Prisons and armies obviously depend on such power; the state relies ultimately on the fact that a citizen who disobeys the law may be subject to pain, death, imprisonment, discomfort, and denial of access to many satisfactions such as sex and good food. Most groups employ a combination of controls. Parents use the carrot and the stick, the promise of candy and the threat of spanking; but in social units such as the family and the school, normative rewards are more appropriate and effective in the long run. To pay a child for being "good" confuses him about utilitarian and normative rewards.

COORDINATION

Although groups must have something important that all members hold in common, they also require role differences among members, and these differences must be coordinated so that each role contributes to achievement of the group goal. Leaders emerge or are appointed (or self-appointed) to assign functions and power to the occupants of various statuses. To mobilize skills, there must be a chain of command that integrates specialized roles. The chief task of leaders and managers is that of delegating responsibilities. When this delegation is formal and institutionalized, that is, firmly attached to statuses rather than to persons, the formal group is highly rational and subject to manipulation; occupants of statuses are judged by performance, and can be replaced. Coordination is especially vital to the cohesion and productivity of formal organizations.

COMMITMENT

The cohesion of a group rests ultimately on the willingness of its members to remain within it and contribute to it. The more members feel they have something important in common with others (a sense of belonging), and the more satisfied they are with the rewards of participation as compared to the costs of leaving, the more highly *committed* they will be.

Even without a firm sense of belonging and identification, a person may participate in a group for instrumental (utilitarian) rewards. But if he does not feel involved or identified with the group, and yet nominally a member of it, he is *isolated*. If he has once felt the power of group ties and then feels cast adrift, turns against the group, or resents its coercive power, he is *alienated*. When he is denied admission to a group to which he feels he has a right to belong (and especially if the core values of the culture agree with his own), he is said to be *segregated* or discriminated against. Feelings of isolation, alienation, and segregation are obviously disruptive to the cohesion of a group or society.

CHANGING BASES OF SOCIAL SOLIDARITY

Emile Durkheim, observing the process of industrialization in Europe, was concerned with its effects on group cohesion, but he came to the conclusion that in complex as well as simple societies members may have a strong sense of belonging. Simple societies have a "mechanical solidarity" based on likenesses; complex ones have an "organic solidarity" based on the coordination of differences in a marvelous system of functional interdependence in which each person and group, like the organs of the body, contributes to the health and functioning of the whole system and in turn depends on the others for its own needs.

All modern societies depend to a large extent on *symbiosis*, the mutual satisfaction of needs that rests on a division of labor, specialization, heterogeneity, and functional interdependence. As Durkheim saw it, this symbiosis produces greater moral solidarity than would be expected from the exchange of tasks and products. The division of labor "creates among men an entire system of rights and duties which link them together in a durable way," and gives rise to rules which assure peaceful and predictable interaction.[25] He denied that the heterogeneity of modern society inevitably results in disorganization and anomie, dehumanization and alienation, a "mass" or atomized society almost devoid of meaningful interpersonal relationships.

Totalitarian nations have tried to extend to the large industrial nation the cultural unity and the sense of belonging of the small group. Thus all Chinese learn "The Thoughts of Mao" as a guide to all aspects of life, and everyone in China and Cuba is required to do some manual labor. In contrast, pluralistic nations, such as democracies, have achieved social cohesion by various means besides the division of labor: They have allowed or even encouraged both structural and cultural diversity. While insisting on a certain basic loyalty to the nation-state and its core values, they have allowed a multiplicity of autonomous groups to exist, many of them voluntary associations (which a totalitarian state dissolves or turns to its own ends). Their memberships overlap and crosscut one another, as well as the racial and class divisions of the society, and thus prevent deep rifts from appearing along any one line. For example, in the small cities where civic service clubs such as Rotary and Lions meet, they draw their memberships from the three or four top classes of the five or six in the community, from various religious groups, and a number of businesses and professions. No monolithic blocs based on several lines of cleavage that coincide are likely to arise and confront one another in such a society.

Pluralistic societies have also developed systems of coordinating

[25]Emile Durkheim, "The Division of Labor in Society," reprinted in Schuler *et al.,* *Readings in Sociology,* 4th ed. (New York: Thomas Y. Crowell, 1971), pp. 384–92.

roles that bring people in various statuses together, and interlock or mesh their claims and expectations and coordinate their overt behavior. The intermediary puts people in touch with one another in a large and complex world and thus promotes functional integration. For example, the advertiser brings the buyer and seller together; the political party strikes a bargain among the competing convictions of citizens; the government balances the interests of different groups and guards the basic rights of all citizens. We may see these linking and coordinating (or "triadic") roles as a contrast to the direct "dyadic" relationship of buyer and seller, lord and vassal, plantation owner and cotton hand. As we saw in our consideration of bureaucracy, this type of relationship promotes objectivity in judgment, and thus justice and fairness; these in turn prevent isolation, alienation, and segregation.

In discussing the relationships, degree of formality of organization, and cohesion of groups, we have, a number of times, compared small and large groups, including small and large societies. Let us attempt now to summarize the essential differences between such societies.

Traditional and Modern Societies

The polar concepts of traditional and modern societies represent ideal types. These types have also been called folk and urban, pre-industrial and industrial, *Gemeinschaft* and *Gesellschaft*, status and contract, primary and secondary, communal and associational. Perhaps a few isolated tribal societies and peasant communities are near the traditional pole, but most societies are moving ever closer to the modern type.

THE FOLK OR TRADITIONAL SOCIETY

Robert Redfield constructed a model of the folk society after years of comparing many societies, and an intensive study of four communities in Yucatan, which varied in the degree of urban influence from a tribal village in the deep forest to the city of Merida.[26]

The folk society is small. It may consist of a few families, or as many as 2000 people; at any rate, all its members can have face-to-face interaction. It is isolated from other societies, and therefore is economically self-sufficient. Because it is small and isolated, its members are biologically homogeneous, relatively speaking (there are still individual differences, of course). It has a highly integrated culture

[26]Robert Redfield, *The Folk Culture of Yucatan* (Chicago: University of Chicago Press, 1941). For a critique arguing that this model is too idyllic, and overlooks elements of strain, change, secularity, and conflict, see Oscar Lewis, "Tepoztlan Revisited," in Alex Inkeles, ed.; *Readings in Modern Sociology* (Englewood Cliffs, N.J.: Prentice-Hall, Inc., 1966), pp. 51–64.

THE POLAR CONCEPTS OF TRADITIONAL AND MODERN SOCIETIES

VARIABLE	TRADITIONAL SOCIETY	MODERN SOCIETY
Size	Small; maximum of about 2000	Large
Composition	Homogeneous	Heterogeneous
Relation to other societies	Isolated; self-sufficient	Interdependent
Degree of division of labor	Low; simple	Extensive; intricate
Group memberships	Few; ascribed	Many; voluntary
Character of social organizations	Small; informal	Large-scale; formal
Dominant form of social organization	Kinship	Citizenship in nation-state
Dominant type of social relationships	Primary	Secondary
Nature of institutions	Interrelated	Formal and distinct
Assignment of status	Ascription	Achievement
Scope of roles	Diffuse; clustered	Specific; fragmented
Nature of norms	Constraining; prohibitive	Permissive in primary relations, prescriptive in secondary ones
Type of sanctions	Informal	Formal
Orientation to change	Resistant; values tradition; static	Innovative; dynamic; oriented to the future
Predominant values	Sacred; traditional	Secular; scientific
Basis of cohesion	Consensus	Symbiosis
Functions of social organization	Expressive	Instrumental
Degree of cohesion	High; cultural unity	Low; tends to anomie

which imparts great meaning to action and makes a person feel that what he is moved to do is well worth doing. Its institutions are so interrelated that religion, for example, is inseparable from making a living. "Life, for the member of the folk society, is not one activity and then another and different one; it is one large activity out of which one part may not be separated without affecting the rest."[27]

[27]Robert Redfield, "The Folk Society," *American Journal of Sociology* 52 (1947): 293–308; reprinted in Peter I. Rose, ed., *The Study of Society*, 2nd ed. (New York: Random House, 1970), pp. 256–73.

The folk society is characterized by a strong sense of community—identification with the group, belonging. (That is why we refer to it as *communal*.) It is a familial society, based on the extended family: Even when its members are not all relatives, kinship terms are ceremonially extended to them, by means of blood brotherhood, godparenthood, and so on.

In such a society, the family or the group rather than the individual is thought of as the basic unit. The group structure is composed of ascribed statuses with clearly defined roles. These outline all rights and obligations; no special arrangements or contracts are necessary. Nor is there any need for legislation; the folkways and mores govern all relationships, and informal controls keep members in line. The norms are (in the ideal type, but never in reality) unchanging; tradition rules. There is no written language; the elders are the respected storehouses of folk wisdom.

There is little or no division of labor in folk society, except on the basis of sex and age. Although the technology may be admirably adapted to its purpose, as is the case with Eskimo tools, it is simple in the sense that no machines are used to make tools or other machines, and natural power is untapped. Every adult male or female does just about the same things as others of the same sex, and shares essentially the same life experiences.

The members of a traditional society take its culture and social organization as "given." They do not question, criticize, or analyze. There is no institutionalized science. Consensus is (again ideally) so complete that cultural values and goals need never be formulated in words. Behavior is "traditional, spontaneous, and uncritical."

Behavior is also personal. No person is ever treated as a "thing" to be used, as is the case in secondary contacts. Personalization extends to the natural environment: trees, rocks, winds, waters, sun, moon, and stars are given human attributes. Not even the distribution of goods and services is treated impersonally: It "tends to be an aspect of the conventional and personal relationships of status which make up the structure of the society; goods are exchanged as expressions of good will and, in large part, as incidents of ceremonial and ritual activities."[28]

Patterns of behavior are clear and unchanging. The few ascribed statuses are compounded: adult male-hunter-warrior, for example. Their accompanying roles are diffuse; they apply to many situations. The norms are not permissive; they are constraining and prohibitive. But precisely because there are no alternatives, they do not seem burdensome; they seem right and meaningful.

The folk society is a sacred society. Ritual acts are no empty conventions; they are freighted with meaning. Sacred objects are regarded with awe and protected from profanation. Just as nature is per-

---

[28]*Ibid.*, p. 268.

sonalized, it is also sacred. A Navaho Indian regards a cornfield as a holy place, a stray kernel of corn as a lost and starving child. In a folk society, such activities as planting and harvesting are not simply practical and instrumental; they are holy acts, expressing the ultimate values of the society.

THE URBAN OR MODERN SOCIETY

At the other extreme of the continuum is the modern society, based on an advanced technology and a highly developed store of knowledge, written and otherwise recorded. It is large and heterogeneous, with a far weaker sense of community and less consensus than the folk society. Highly urbanized and industrialized, it depends on other societies for raw materials and markets. It is never self-sufficient, nor is any one of its members. An extensive division of labor makes everyone dependent upon many others for most of his needs, and the various specialties are coordinated in a vastly complicated system of production and distribution. Being highly specialized, statuses and roles are specific and narrow rather than clustered and diffuse. Being based on training and experience, most statuses are achieved rather than ascribed.

The diversity of occupations is accompanied by diversity of interests, expressed in a great variety of voluntary associations. (In actual fact, but not essential to the model of an associational society, modern industrial societies tend also to be multigroup societies, made up of peoples of diverse cultural, racial, and religious backgrounds.) This diversity results in a variety of values and norms, and widely different patterns of behavior are tolerated. The culture is thus "secular." Few objects are regarded as meaningful in themselves, few activities as more than means to ends. Much behavior is rational and calculating. Each institution is allotted its special function. Religion is set apart from everyday affairs; sacredness is confined to religion and to a few values such as patriotism, the flag, the king, the constitution. Science and progress are highly valued; change is regarded as good.

The size, diversity, secular values, and rapid change of a modern society mean that tradition and informal controls are insufficient to maintain order: Legislation and formal sanctions are needed. The nation-state is the social organization that exercises ultimate power and controls all other associations and institutions.

Other large-scale formal organizations dominate in business and industry, and, to a smaller extent, in education, religion, medicine, and other areas. Bureaucratic administration characterizes business and government. Impersonality, rationality, and efficiency are positive values in such organizations. People are evaluated on the basis of effective performance of their roles. Secondary relationships in fragmented roles are the basis of much social interaction.

The cohesion of a modern society rests on symbiosis. Because cultural unity is lacking, there are tendencies to anomie.

The transition from traditional to modern society is part of the "great transformation" that is occurring throughout the world. This transformation is manifest in many ways—in scientific and technological changes and their effects, in changes in the numbers and distribution of population, in the class structure, in relations among various groups, in personality types and problems, and in changes in the institutions of the family, education, religion, economy, and government. This transition and its consequences will be a recurrent theme in the rest of this book.

Summary

Three closely interrelated aspects of social organization are variations in the size of groups, in the kinds of relationships within them, and in the degree of formality of organization.

Most interaction occurs in small face-to-face groups, which are important because of their psychological hold over members, their effectiveness in producing decisions and action, and their role in mediating between individuals and the larger society. They are also interesting sociologically because they exhibit many features of larger groups: They evolve cultural codes and social structures. Social processes can be easily observed in such groups. There are striking differences in interaction in dyads, triads, and larger groups.

As a group becomes larger, it tends to split into subgroups. A structure of authority emerges, roles become more specialized, and there is a need for coordination of interrelated parts of the system. The proportion of secondary (segmental, impersonal, and instrumental) to primary (personal, expressive, spontaneous) relationships rises. Organization also becomes more formalized. However, informal organizations often arise within large-scale formal organizations.

The test of a formal organization is that it can survive a turnover of personnel. Bureaucracy is typical of the administration of large formal organizations; it is an impersonal means of exerting social control in modern society.

The cohesion of a group depends on consensus on norms and values, effective control of members, coordination of interdependent functions, and a sense of commitment and involvement that keeps members participating.

Much of the world is undergoing a transformation from a form of social organization that fits rather closely the polar type of folk society toward an increasingly modern society. The folk society is small, isolated, and homogeneous. It has a highly integrated culture in which sacred values predominate. Although its technology is simple, it is self-sufficient. Folk societies are ruled by tradition, and there is complete consensus on core values among its members, who feel a strong sense of community. Primary relationships predominate.

Modern societies, in contrast, are large, heterogeneous, and highly interdependent. Their cultures are secular; change is regarded as good; formal organization and secondary relationships predominate. Cohesion rests on symbiosis, and there are tendencies to anomie.

In the next two chapters we consider two aspects of social organization that threaten the cohesion of modern societies—differentiation by social classes and by ethnic groups.

QUESTIONS FOR FURTHER THOUGHT

1. Georg Simmel, a pioneer sociologist, observed that there is a much sharper difference between dyads and triads than between triads and larger groups. Test this generalization on the basis of the text and of your experience.

2. Watch for a "natural experiment" to occur: You are engaged in dyadic interaction, and a third person enters the scene. What happens? Observe children at play in a similar situation.

3. What are some of the barriers to communication in large groups? How do you think they might be overcome?

4. Make parallel lists comparing the characteristics of primary and secondary relationships. What would human relationships be like if all groups were secondary groups? What effect might this have on personality?

5. Why is Max Weber's description of bureaucracy referred to as a "model" type?

6. Would you say that the advantages of bureaucracy outweigh the disadvantages? Why? Can you think of some ways of minimizing the disadvantages without dysfunctional consequences?

7. Why do some large organizations not lend themselves well to bureaucratic administration? What elements of bureaucracy may be present nonetheless?

8. It is said that before making a decision, bureaucrats ask, "Who will be mad? How mad? Who will be glad? How glad?" Relate this to Weber's model of bureaucracy.

9. In what type of society would gossip be a strong social pressure? Why?

10. Discuss Robert Redfield's model of the folk society as a product of the complementary nature of theory and empirical research.

11. List the social groups in which you have participated in the last two days. Do not overlook groups of two or three persons that fit the definition of a social group, nor large-scale formal organizations such as corporations and government agencies, even if interaction was not face-to-face, but was carried on by mail or telephone. Characterize each group as small or large, primary or secondary, formal or informal. Which types predominate?

12. Durkheim believed that interdependence or "organic solidarity" holds modern societies together; but he also indicated that members of such societies must be aware of and value this interdependence, and not do anything to upset it. Richard Means gives examples of such disruptive actions: "suburban builders who create housing without giving thought to the future water supply, . . . the congressman who votes only for the special interests of his district" (*The Ethical Imperative*, p. 31). Discuss. If you agree, give further examples and propose policies for preventing such disruptive acts.

13. If Durkheim's concept of organic solidarity holds for modern societies, why is there a tendency to anomie?

14. "Familyness" is considered unfavorable to production in Soviet factories. Under what circumstances might this be true? False?

15. This chapter has made extensive use of ideal types. List some explicit ones. Look for implicit ones (totalitarian *vs.* democratic, for example). Examine the polar types of traditional and modern societies critically, and try to think of exceptions to various generalizations about each.

9

SOCIAL STRATIFICATION

Let me tell you about the very rich. They are different from you and me.

F. SCOTT FITZGERALD

O let us love our occupations,
Bless the squire and his relations,
Live upon our daily rations,
And always know our proper stations.

CHARLES DICKENS

In Boston, they ask, How much does he know? In New York, How much is he worth? In Philadelphia, Who were his parents?

MARK TWAIN

Such poverty as we have today in all our great cities degrades the poor, and infects with its degradation the whole neighbourhood in which they live. And whatever can degrade a neighbourhood can degrade a country and a continent and finally the whole civilized world, which is only a large neighbourhood.

GEORGE BERNARD SHAW

The sons of mandarins will one day be mandarins. The sons of the poor will spend their days lighting coals.

VIETNAMESE PROVERB

For DECADES THE SENIOR AUTHOR thought that the Finnish word *meikäläisiä*, which her father often used, meant "poor farmers." Recently she learned that it simply means "our kind of people." It was nearly always used when there was talk of what we could reasonably expect to do and have—go to the movies, buy new clothes, attend high school and college, associate with "rich" townspeople—and it generally meant "not a chance." The poor are low on the scale of "life chances."

But this was not stubborn, hopeless poverty; it was part of the general poverty of the Depression (and of immigrant farmers). The booming economy since World War II has boosted many members of Western societies up the social ladder and given them far better life chances than their parents had, helped in most cases by schooling and the shift from farms to cities. The average level of living has nearly doubled in the United States, and many believe that the land of equality and opportunity has no social class distinctions, or if it does, that most of us are middle class.

Yet just as Panamanians speak of those "inside" and "outside" the wall (a real one in colonial days) as good families and nobodies, Americans use a number of terms that indicate awareness of class differences: rich and poor, the country-club set and people from the wrong side of the tracks, good respectable people who are the salt of the earth, social climbers, the power structure. Perhaps we come up against rebuffs, snubs, or slights if we aspire too high, and feel ill at ease if we are thrown into close proximity to those who use poorer grammar and less soap than we do. We easily understand what the author of a play, novel, or movie means by such clues to social class as manners, dress, diction, ideas, occupation, education, and home furnishings. Although one of our core values as stated in the Declaration of Independence is that "All men are created equal," we recognize that "Some are more equal than others."

The Meaning of Social Stratification

We may define social stratification as an institutionalized system of social inequality in a community or society that ranks families[1] in categories or strata according to their share of scarce and desirable values such as wealth, prestige, and power. We refer to it as institutionalized because it is part of the social structure, given stability and relative permanence by support from cultural beliefs, values, and norms, and by the fact that each person is initially (and in some systems permanently) assigned to the stratum of his parents. Such a system is pervasive, cutting across all other differences in the community or society. The *strata* or different levels in the system are perceived as real by members of the society, and their relative statuses[2] in the system have important consequences for their life chances, their behavior, their values and attitudes, and their personalities.

How does stratification occur? All human beings tend to *differentiate* among different objects, including people and groups, to assign labels to them, and to *evaluate* them according to these differences. It is theoretically possible for us to see each person as unique and value him for himself without comparing him to others; but differentiation and evaluation generally lead to *ranking* in terms of superiority, equality, and inferiority. Students are ranked by grades, girls by beauty and charm, warriors by bravery, athletes and hunters by skill. But these are individual rankings; they do not lend themselves to a system of stratification.

Nor do all categorical rankings. Perhaps most members of a society believe that men are superior to women, rich people to poor, whites to blacks, doctors to doormen, aristocrats to peasants, college graduates to high school graduates, the old to the young. Some of these distinctions can be made criteria for a system of social stratification; others cannot. Wealth, for example, can be a means of assigning and transmitting social status, for it can be measured, stored, and passed on to others. What about age and sex?

In every society, age and sex divide the population and influence behavior. And there are great inequalities of wealth, power, and prestige along these lines. In most traditional societies the wisdom of the elders is unquestioned; some are age-graded, and it is very clear when one may expect a new and higher rank. In many modern societies, power, wealth, and prestige tend to be concentrated among the middle-aged. Seniority rules in legislatures, bureaucracies, and labor unions discriminate against younger people. Similarly, the really old feel powerless and neglected; their productive years are over, and the rapidly changing technological society does not value their kind of experience and wisdom. Many have little money and less prestige. But age cannot serve as a basis for stratification simply because everyone

[1]For many purposes, such as the census, the units for classification are "families and unrelated individuals," the latter including people who live alone. When we refer to families in connection with class, we also mean such individuals.

[2]Note that "status" is used in this chapter to refer to position in the system of social stratification, and more narrowly to prestige. It often serves as shorthand for "social class status." See Chapter 7 for a more general definition.

passes through about the same cycle. And although women are often thought of and treated as naturally inferior beings, sex (like age) cannot be used to categorize whole families, and thus cannot serve as the basis for a system of social stratification.

Race, ethnic background, and religion, however, often do serve such a purpose; in fact, some sociologists see American society as divided by *two* systems of social stratification, one based on class criteria, the other on racial, religious, and ethnic criteria. In this chapter, we shall concentrate on the first type; the second is the subject of Chapter 10.

IS SOCIAL STRATIFICATION UNIVERSAL?

Like the pecking order of chickens, a ranking order is found in all known human societies. But not all are stratified in the sense of hereditary ranking of families. In many simple societies, chieftains or elders may hold office only temporarily and are not permitted to pass it on to their sons. Kwakiutl society included many different ranks and titles, but each was passed on from person to person, and during his lifetime one man might be anything from a commoner to a chief.[3] Using the files of the Cross-Cultural Survey at Yale University, Murdock found no system of stratification (except by age and sex) in 74 of 250 societies.[4]

As a society becomes larger, however, it also becomes more complex and breaks up into subgroups. Theoretically, these, like individuals, could also be regarded as different but equal categories; but "in no large-scale or long-continued social grouping have they been equal; the differential evaluation of men as individuals and as members of social categories is a universal, formal property of social systems."[5] As statuses and roles become more specialized, rewards become more unequally distributed. A structure of authority emerges to direct and coordinate action; some have power to direct and command, others must follow and obey. In every complex society throughout history there has been an unequal distribution of wealth, prestige, and power to the members of different social strata. If the upper classes were overthrown, a new system of stratification emerged, but never a classless society.

WHY STUDY STRATIFICATION?

Inequality has preoccupied philosophers since the Enlightenment, economists since Adam Smith, social critics—with special intensity

[3]Helen Codere, "Kwakiutl Society: Rank Without Class," *American Anthropologist* 59 (June 1957): 473–586.

[4]George Peter Murdock, *Social Structure* (New York: The Macmillan Company, 1949), pp. 87–88.

[5]Robin M. Williams, Jr., *American Society: A Sociological Interpretation*, 3rd ed. (New York: Alfred A. Knopf, 1970), p. 100.

—since the beginnings of the Industrial Revolution, and empirical investigators since Quetelet, LePlay, and Booth surveyed the living conditions of the urban poor.

Sociologists are especially interested in social stratification for several reasons. First of all, it is an explosive and controversial subject, for inequality is reflected in different opportunities for "health and wealth, knowledge and experience, wisdom and happiness";[6] the cohesion of a society depends on whether those who feel left out seek social change through peaceful or violent means, and whether or not those in the upper classes are willing to share scarce and desirable values more equitably. All revolutions and most social movements seek to erase some kind of inequality.

Second, the system of stratification affects education, family life, religion, politics, and the economy. Third, because the members of each stratum share many attitudes, values, and norms, social class status serves as an excellent tool for predicting behavior. Finally, the system of stratification gives an excellent overall picture of the social structure—the pattern of social relationships—of a whole community or society. All individuals and subgroups fit somewhere in the hierarchical system. Like other patterned relationships, those associated with this system serve as guides to interaction: We know what to expect of others in certain strata, and how we are expected to behave toward them.

In this chapter we look first at variations in systems of social stratification, and ask how modernization affects them. Then we briefly examine three leading theories about the origins and consequences of stratification. Next we ask how money power, social prestige, and power over personal and group decisions are distributed, and how we can measure them.

How are these three variables correlated? What are their consequences for life chances, group interaction, ways of life, and personality? After considering these general questions, we sketch the class structure of the United States as sociologists see it at the level of the local community, the large city, and the nation. Finally, we consider the ways in which people and groups change their status, and the possibilities of a new kind of class system in post-industrial society.

Variations in Systems of Stratification

Three ideal types of stratification systems are caste, estate, and class. At one extreme is the caste system, in which the strata are hereditary, endogamous (with a rule that mates must be chosen from within the group), and permanent; a person is born into his caste, marries in it,

[6]Kurt B. Mayer, *Class and Society*, rev. ed. (New York: Random House, 1955), p. 1.

and dies in it. At the other extreme is the **open-class system**, in which only individual achievement matters, and one rises or falls in social class according to his own merits; but even here, an infant is assigned his family's status at birth, and thus has an initial advantage or disadvantage in life. In the **estate system**, strata are defined by law and are relatively rigid and permanent, but there is some opportunity to shift one's status. The best-known caste system is that of traditional India; the United States is considered by many of its citizens to have the most open and mobile class system in the world; and feudal Europe is the most notable example of an estate system. Both ideal types and actual systems vary in many ways.

Number of strata.   There may be only two broad categories, such as slaves and freemen, or the elite and the masses. More commonly, however, there are three or more broad categories. Ancient tradition classified all Hindus into four chief castes: priests and teachers of the sacred lore (Brahmans); warriors (Kshatriyas); peasants, craftsmen, and merchants (Vaisyas); and manual laborers and servants (Sudras). Outcastes or untouchables were considered to be outside the Hindu spiritual community. In medieval Europe, the various estates included the secular feudal aristocracy, the clergy, and the serfs or peasants who worked the land and labored for the manor. Sociologists find from three to six major classes in modern industrial societies.

Criteria of rank.   Property, authority, "blue blood," prestigious occupations, learning—whatever the society values most, the upper strata have (or are thought to have) more of it than the lower. The three highest Hindu castes may wear the sacred thread symbolizing spiritual rebirth and ritual purity; the Sudras exist only to serve them; the untouchables perform "unclean" tasks such as scavenging, skinning dead animals, and tanning hides. Feudal distinctions were based on hereditary relationships to land. In caste systems, status is permanently ascribed for everyone; in estate systems, for almost everyone (the clergy, being sworn to celibacy, recruited its upper orders from the nobility and its lower orders from promising members of lower estate). In class systems, in contrast, although one's status is initially that of his parents, things that can theoretically be achieved by anyone with the necessary talent and drive are the main criteria of social status— occupation, income, education, political power.

Complexity.   The complexity of a system depends on the number of strata and the number of criteria. Even the caste system is complex. There are actually about 3000 castes in India, most of which are further divided into subcastes; any one village or locality may contain 20 or 30 caste groups. In the estate system, too, there were various degrees of aristocracy and of freedom or servitude.

Reprinted by permission of Cartoon Features Syndicate.

"Don't bother to get up—I'm just passing through."

Stratification systems in heterogeneous modern societies—notably that of the United States—are especially complex. Ascribed statuses coexist with achieved ones. Gerhard Lenski, in fact, sees a number of class hierarchies based on different criteria of rank, and believes every member of American society can be rated in occupational, property, racial-ethnic, educational, age, and sexual class systems. (Women are lower class!) In some societies, such as the Soviet Union and the People's Republic of China, political status is extremely important, and may even replace the property hierarchy; in many new states, bureaucrats occupy a commanding position. In Lenski's view, "the struggle for power and privilege involves not only struggles between individuals and classes, it also involves *struggles between class systems, and thus between different principles of distribution.*"[7] Social movements aiming to raise the status of certain groups—for example, to increase recognition of educational and occupational accomplishments and diminish

[7]*Power and Privilege: A Theory of Social Stratification* (New York: McGraw-Hill Book Company, 1966), p. 81.

the importance of aristocracy or sex or race—are all, in this sense, class struggles.

Most views of the class structure, however, see it as one complex system, in which a family's social status depends on a number of variables. This results in a certain blurring of lines between strata, and in a number of cases of *status inconsistency*—of high standing by one or more important criteria and low standing by another or others. For example, if one rates blacks low and Supreme Court Justices high (surveys show this to be the most prestigious position in the United States),[8] then how does he rank Thurgood Marshall? Where does a wealthy racketeer or an impoverished member of the "First Families of Virginia" stand? Nonetheless, the view of a single complex class system is valid insofar as people actually think and act in terms of one system with several broad levels of social stratification—and, as we shall see, the evidence is overwhelming that they do.

Sharpness of stratum boundaries. Castes and estates are discrete strata, clearly marked off from one another; everyone knows exactly where he and others belong in the system. Each Indian subcaste has its own religious cult, distinctive dress, food customs, and linguistic usages; and each is identified, in its community, with an exclusive hereditary occupation. The estate system, too, was a clear hierarchy in which each lord's standing was symbolized by knightly trappings and by acts of deference[9] to those above and from those below. In modern class systems, differences in dress, manners, diction, and possessions are more subtle, and there are no sharp breaks in the distribution of property, prestige, and power. Class lines are blurred, and even when categories are delineated with some degree of confidence, there are many marginal cases not clearly assigned to one stratum or another. Some sociologists, therefore, conceive of a class system as a continual gradation of social statuses rather than a set of categories. On the local level, however, personal knowledge of others permits categorical placement of most people, and intimate interaction promotes the formation of distinct status groups. Both locally and nationally, boundaries appear to be sharpest at the highest and lowest levels of the system.

Degree of mobility. In closed systems of stratification there is no legitimate way for a person to rise to a higher stratum—all one

[8]Robert W. Hodge, Paul M. Siegel, and Peter H. Rossi, "Occupational Prestige in the United States, 1925–1963," in Reinhard Bendix and Seymour Martin Lipset, eds., *Class, Status, and Power: Social Stratification in Comparative Perspective*, 2nd ed. (New York: The Free Press, 1966), pp. 322–34.

[9]*Deference* is expressed in actions that indicate respect or honor or yielding to the wishes of one regarded as superior; the norms and symbols of deference include etiquette, titles or modes of address, such as "sir," and "Mr. Ambassador," uniforms, medals, and insignia. One may claim deference by his bearing, dress, possessions, and actions, if his superior status is not clear in a given situation.

can do is accept his lot in life and hope to be born into a higher caste in the next incarnation. But as India modernizes, it is increasingly common to marry across caste lines and otherwise deemphasize ritual status, and to put more emphasis on secular (economic and political) status, especially in the larger cities. Movement up and down the social ladder is frequent in modern class systems, for industrialization demands a skilled labor force that is not bound by traditional occupations; here education is the main avenue to social advancement.

Range of inequality and stratification structure.   Aside from societies in which slaves are property, inequality is most glaringly obvious in societies where the enormous gap between the very rich and the abysmally poor is not filled by a middle class of any significant size. The Maharajah and the Indian peasant were like creatures from different planets. But is the range of inequality any less in modern societies? Sociologists disagree. Modernization, says Alex Inkeles, reduces the gap between top and bottom, and changes the social pyramid, with a broad base of peasantry, to a trapezoid or even diamond shape as more and more people become middle class.[10] Lenski believes that as technology advances, stratification systems become more rigid and inequality increases; but industrialization reverses this trend, because knowledge becomes an increasingly important source of power and must be widespread in an advanced industrial system.[11] Kaare Svalastoga says that statistical measures of the distribution of income, total wealth, years of formal education, power, and social prestige all have a skewed distribution; that is, the upper class is much farther from the mean than is the lowest class.[12]

Social distance.   Social distance is "a feeling of separation or actual social separation between individuals or groups. The greater the social distance between two groups of different status or culture, the less sympathy, understanding, intimacy, and interaction there is between them."[13] Eating together, visiting one another, and intermarrying indicate the absence of social distance. In India a complicated set of rules governs interaction among persons of different castes: A person of high rank shuns inferiors because he believes their touch (or even their

[10]"Social Stratification in the Modernization of Russia," in Cyril Black, ed., *The Transformation of Russian Society* (Cambridge, Mass.: Harvard University Press, 1960), pp. 338–39; reprinted in abridged form in Paul Hollander, ed., *American and Soviet Society: A Reader in Comparative Sociology and Perception* (Englewood Cliffs, N.J.: Prentice-Hall, Inc., 1968), pp. 150–53.

[11]*Power and Privilege*, pp. 308–18.

[12]"Social Differentiation," in Robert E. L. Faris, *Handbook of Modern Sociology* (Chicago: Rand McNally, 1964), pp. 530–75.

[13]Theodorson and Theodorson, *Modern Dictionary of Sociology*, p. 388.

shadow) will pollute him and make it necessary to take a long ritual bath; he accepts food only from the hands of certain castes; endogamy is so strong that each subcaste is in effect an extended family or kin group. In class systems, even in the absence of such rules, intimate interaction and intermarriage are most frequent among social equals. Although any Costa Rican maid has a strong sense of her own worth and dignity, it makes her uncomfortable to eat with those she considers her superiors, particularly if they are Costa Ricans, whom she knows to be as class-conscious as she is.

Class consciousness and class conflict. As the previous example indicates, in many societies there is sharp awareness of one's own status as compared to that of others; this is especially true where feudal systems once prevailed and have left some cultural legacies, as in Europe and Latin America. It is less true in societies with a strong cultural belief in equality. Class awareness may or may not be accompanied by a feeling of solidarity with those in one's own stratum and of hostility to others. Class conflict, however, is endemic to all stratified societies, though it may rarely break out in overt violence or revolution; it may occur through established channels such as political parties and pressure groups.

Means of institutionalization. The degree of class consciousness and hostility is closely related to the means of institutionalizing and justifying the system of stratification—the beliefs, values, norms, and sanctions that uphold it. Though some systems originated in conquest or slavery, force alone does not suffice for long. Religion, law, cultural myths, the inertia of established folkways and mores—any or all of these help perpetuate a system by making it seem somehow right and fair, and by dissipating the resentment of the lower strata enough to allow the system to keep functioning.

The justification may be that the ranking system is part of the natural order of things, whether that order be religious, biological, or social. The caste system of India is deeply rooted in the Hindu religion and village culture. The belief that a person who faithfully fulfills the duties of his status enters the next higher caste when he is reborn acts as a powerful sanction to uphold the system. The institutionalization of interaction within and among castes also helps to perpetuate it. The members of each caste group help one another build houses, till fields, and meet life crises of various kinds; and being highly specialized occupationally, the various subcastes are interdependent. For these reasons the abolition of castes by the constitution of 1949, with special reference to the one in seven Indians classed as untouchable, has hardly changed the system.

Similarly, in medieval Europe the estate system was institution-alized by hereditary relationships to land, sanctioned by law and pri-vate contract in which an oath of fealty to one's lord was a holy vow. The preachings of the Church also justified the system: "Some fight, some work, some pray." The custom of the manor fixed individual rights and duties, and protected serfs from unusual exploitation. Work on the manor was for subsistence only, not for profit. A man aimed not to grow wealthy but to maintain himself in the position or estate into which he was born and then pass into eternal life.

In modern class systems, social inequality is usually justified on the basis of rewards for achievement. Both the United States and the Soviet Union set out to accomplish goals of equality or classless-ness; both have modified this goal and replaced it with a cultural myth of equality of opportunity. Each person is held to be in the position he deserves. This encourages people who have not achieved a high position to blame themselves, or other groups, rather than the system as a whole. Such an explanation, however, is much more vulnerable to criticism than those that hold social inequality to be part of the nat-ural order of things. Many deny that there really is equal opportunity. Many feel unjustly deprived; others find no stopping place in the quest for further achievement and ever greater rewards. And, as in any sys-tem of stratification, those in positions of power use it, deliberately or otherwise, to perpetuate the status quo. But as long as most people are convinced that the system is fair, inequality poses no serious threat to social cohesion.

Modernization and Stratification

Rigid systems of stratification such as caste and estate tend to crumble under the impact of modernization. An industrial society requires an educated, skilled labor force, not bound by occupational inheritance and free to move from job to job. Therefore, as we have already sug-gested, modern class systems tend to be open, to stress achievement rather than ascription, and to allow mobility, especially through educa-tion. Class boundaries tend to blur, and the proportion of those in the middle range grows.

Class systems in modern society are not rooted in religion, tra-dition, or law. They are informal and unofficial, the result of many judgments that place people in categories according to certain segmen-tal criteria that reflect societal values. Income, education, occupation, and style of life are perhaps the clearest bases for these judgments.

People, then, define a class system in their own thoughts and actions. The description of a class society does not depend on what a person is permitted to do or made to do, but on what he *in fact* does, to whom he in fact feels superior and inferior, and the reasons why. Most people think in terms of perhaps three to six broad categories, and the distinctions they make are clearest with respect to those just above and just below them. Members of a particular stratum also make distinctions among themselves. The tendency to differentiate and evaluate, as well as to generalize and categorize, finds abundant material in modern societies, even in those defined by cultural myth as "classless." As we shall see, social stratification is not just a sociological concept; it has real consequences for culture, society, and personality.

Theories of Stratification

Because it deals with the unequal distribution of scarce and desirable values, social stratification is a thorny subject. Few if any modern thinkers agree with Aristotle that there are by nature freemen and slaves, and that slaves find their condition just and agreeable. Some see stratification as an evil to be attacked and destroyed, others as an aspect of social organization essential to the survival of a society, and others as a complex phenomenon that must be analyzed and understood if one is to understand human social behavior.

Is stratification inevitable? Useful? Necessary? Just and fair? How does it arise? What are its functions and dysfunctions for society in general and for its individual members? These questions are not only sociological: They are moral, ethical, and political, and they are at the core of conservative and radical ideologies. The views sketched here represent three basic orientations that have guided theory and research on the subject and have, to varying degrees, influenced action and policy in the industrial era.

MARXISM: THE CLASS SYSTEM IS ECONOMIC AND EXPLOITATIVE

The class system, Marx insisted, is inevitable as long as private property exists. It is the key to history, social organization and social change, and individual behavior. Society is divided into distinct and *hostile* classes under slavery, feudalism, and capitalism. Only through class struggle can a society work toward the perfect classless society of communism. No one can help belonging to a certain class and sharing its motivations; we are all prisoners of the system. Even the capitalist exploiter acts as he does simply because of his status. But when

the proletariat, tired of oppression, overthrows the capitalists' bourgeois government and eliminates private property, inequality and exploitation will vanish. Thus Marxism promises a heaven on earth, where
conflict and suffering will be no more. But it is also a call to revolution,
for although change is inevitable, men must act to bring it about:
"Workers of the world, unite!"

"There may be few sociological hypotheses that have been
tested at such a high human cost" as Marx's proposition that inequality
will disappear with the abolition of private ownership of the means
of production.[14] That a clear system of social classes has emerged in
the Soviet Union and class lines in capitalist countries are blurred con-
tradicts Marx the prophet. His influence, however, is apparent in the
social sciences as well as in the revolutions that have shaken the world
since 1917. By stressing the fundamental importance of class systems
in urban industrial societies, he stimulated a great deal of thought and
investigation. His emphasis on the dynamic relationships between economic fact, class, and culture has influenced social scientists, even
though most of them deny his thesis that economic facts determine all
other aspects of the social order. His central insight was that "conflicts
between unequally rewarded groups and a sense of injustice on the
part of the less privileged may be just as endemic in society as the
necessity for unequal rewards itself."[15]

FUNCTIONALISM: SOCIAL INEQUALITY
IS ESSENTIAL AND DESIRABLE

The "necessity for unequal rewards" is the main theme of the
functionalist interpretation of social stratification. Most functionalist
sociologists believe that each item of culture and social organization
somehow contributes to the survival of society and the accomplishment
of its tasks. Their theory may be summarized as follows:

Because stratification is universal, it obviously performs a vital
function for society. There are certain things a society must have done.
Some of them require scarce talents and demand much training; some
are freighted with responsibility. The society rates positions according
to these criteria and gives the highest rewards to those that are most
important and demand the greatest talent and sacrifice. Thus people
are motivated to train themselves for these positions and to accept
heavy responsibilities. The rewards may contribute to comfort and
sustenance, provide humor and diversion, or enhance self-esteem.

[14]Svalastoga, "Social Differentiation."

[15]Dennis H. Wrong, "The Functional Theory of Stratification; Some Neglected Considerations," *American Sociological Review* 24 (December 1959): 772–82; reprinted in Jack L. Roach, Llewellyn Gross, and Orville Gursslin, eds., *Social
Stratification in the United States* (Englewood Cliffs, N.J.: Prentice-Hall, Inc.,
1969), pp. 32–45.

Social inequality, then, is not only universal; it is essential, inevitable, and functional, "an unconsciously evolved device by which societies insure that the most important positions are conscientiously filled by the most qualified persons."[16]

This calm, harmonious theory, stressing cooperation and consensus, is in sharp contrast to Marxism. But does it hold water? Critics charge that it is a theory of individual ranking—of differentiation and evaluation, but not of stratification. And even so, it does not account for the fact that some people do the dirtiest work of a society for meager rewards. Nor does it answer such questions as: Why does a Prime Minister or President, responsible for war and peace, get a fraction of the salary of a corporation executive? Is there truly an open channel for talent, a free competition with an equality of opportunity that ensures the use of each person's potential and places the most qualified person in each position?

Any inequality, point out critics of this theory, tends to increase over time and to diffuse to other situations besides the original sequence of task-reward-status. A person may become rich and honored in the first place because he performs an important task demanding unusual talents and great responsibility; but then he gains more prestige and power (as well as more money) for reasons that cannot be explained on functionalist premises; and he passes this consolidated status on to his heirs. Inheritance of position may be seriously dysfunctional for society by discouraging productivity, the use of talents, and the assignment of status according to merit. Furthermore, how does one establish the importance of a task for the survival of a society, except, perhaps, by relating it to maintenance of the status quo? How, within this framework, does one account for initial ascription, for the use of power to gain wealth and prestige, and for other aspects of the stratification system that are a heritage from the past and resist change? Like the economic theory that market price is based on supply and demand in a situation of free competition, functionalism is a neat package explanation that assumes natural order and rationality; it disregards the Biblical maxim "Unto everyone that hath shall be given."

MAX WEBER: SOCIAL CLASS
IS MULTI-DIMENSIONAL

Many sociologists base their ideas about stratification on the theories of Max Weber, who saw class as consisting of three interre-

[16]Kingsley Davis, *Human Society* (New York: The Macmillan Company, 1949), pp. 367–68. Davis and Wilbert Moore are the sociologists most closely identified with this theory. See also Melvin Tumin, "On Inequality," *American Sociological Review* 28, No. 1 (Feb. 1963): 19–26, for a criticism of this theory, and Moore, "But Some Are More Equal Than Others," 13–18, for a rejoinder to Tumin. See also Roach, Gross, and Gursslin, *Social Stratification in the United States*, pp. 13–50.

lated dimensions of the stratification system. "Class" is money power; "status" is social power; and "party" is political power in a community or society. A person's share of each of these variables has enormous consequences for his "life chances" and his "style of life."

Class or money power is determined by competitive skill in the labor or commodity markets. It is rational, impersonal, and objective, measurable by fixed criteria of wealth and income. *A class*, in Weber's definition, is any grouping or category of people in the same situation with respect to their *life chances*—their chance for "a supply of goods, external living conditions, and personal life experiences, in so far as this chance is determined by the amount and kind of power, or lack of it, to dispose of goods or skills for the sake of income in a given economic order."[17] But membership in a class is not enough to impel class action. Nor does money power necessarily confer status honor or social power.

Weber defines status as the degree of prestige within a community. Economic class is cold, impersonal, objective; status is subjective, the result of personal judgments. It can exist only where people know one another and where the members of a community agree on what criteria confer or deny prestige and command deference.

This estimation of honor or prestige may or may not be linked with economic class. In any case, "it normally stands in sharp opposition to the pretensions of sheer property."[18] What those with similar prestige in a community always have in common is a similar *style of life*—activities, possessions, speech patterns. Because they live in similar style and enjoy the same amount of prestige, they associate with one another and regard themselves and their intimates as "better" than those with less prestige and "inferior" styles of life. As they continue to interact they form "status groups." Most noneconomic social interaction—leisure time activities and intermarriage in particular—occurs within such groups, and there is social distance between one group and another. Class, then, is more concerned with production or "getting," and status with consumption or "spending."

Party, Weber's third dimension of social stratification, refers to power over the actions of others in any organized group or over the collective decisions of the community or society. In industrial society, such power flows largely from position in the bureaucratic hierarchies of such large-scale formal organizations as business corporations and government.

Where Marx saw prestige and political power as simple outgrowths of economic positions, Weber showed that the three kinds of power are interrelated in complex and subtle ways. The same people often do have similar amounts of economic power, status honor, and

---

[17]"Class, Status, and Party," in *Max Weber: Essays in Sociology*, trans. H. H. Gerth and C. Wright Mills (New York: Oxford University Press, 1946), pp. 180–95.

[18]*Ibid.*

socio-political power, and possession of one helps them attain and keep the others. In general, those in a status group must have roughly the same economic position to support similar styles of life. In turn, members of status groups (especially at the upper levels) try to restrict opportunities to their own group; often they use "party" power to this end. One may also use such power to acquire wealth and honor.

In all three theories, stratification is seen as inevitable. Marx believed it is inevitable because of the nature of the historical process that will lead to a classless society. Functionalists regard it as necessary for the workings and survival of society. Weber implied that it occurs because of differential success in the competition of the market and differential distribution of prestige and power.

Turning now from general theories of stratification to empirical research and to middle-range theories regarding certain aspects of class systems, we take up the distribution of wealth and income, the assignment of status honor or prestige, and the power to make or influence decisions and action, plus the two variables that are consequences of the interrelationships of these three: life chances and subcultural styles of life.

The Distribution of Wealth and Income

Residents of the United States received a per capita income of $4134 in 1971, and a median income of $9867 per family in 1970.[19] By these indices, Americans are the richest people in the world. But other figures reveal great inequalities in the distribution of wealth and income.[20]

There is no gradually rising curve of income by different economic classes. When the population was divided into five equal parts by family income, the poorest fifth received 5.6% of aggregate income; the second, 12.3%; the third, 17.6%; the fourth, 23.4%; and the top fifth, 41%. The top 5% of families (1 out of 20) received 14.7% of income, and the top 1% received 5%.[21] Measured in terms of wealth

[19]*Information Please Almanac*, 26th ed. (New York, 1972).

[20]Being numerical, wealth and income appear offhand easy to measure and compare; but there are many pitfalls in the process and much disagreement on how figures should be interpreted. One scholar uses them to prove that inequality is decreasing, and more income than formerly goes to the lower income groups; another draws the opposite conclusion. See Herman P. Miller, *Rich Man, Poor Man*, 2nd ed. (New York: Thomas Y. Crowell, 1971); Gabriel Kolko, *Wealth and Power in America: An Analysis of Social Class and Income Distribution* (New York: Praeger Publishers, 1962); Robert J. Lampman, *The Share of Top Wealth-Holders in National Wealth, 1922-1956* (Princeton, N.J.: Princeton University Press, 1962); and Ferdinand Lundberg, *The Rich and the Super-Rich: A Study in the Power of Money Today* (New York: Bantam Books, 1968).

[21]Census Bureau figures for 1969.

rather than income, concentration is even greater. A tiny fraction—
0.2 to 0.3%—of the population owns 22% of all privately held wealth
and 60–70% of all privately held *corporate* wealth.[22] Few of these
fortunes are accounted for by the "rags to riches" stories of the nine-
teenth-century classics; almost every holder of wealth in the upper
0.5% of the population inherited it.

AMERICAN MYTHS REGARDING
ECONOMIC DISTRIBUTION

Many Americans believe that "we are all becoming middle
class" because our general level of living has improved and the distribution of economic rewards is increasingly equitable. True, median
income in constant dollars was 90% higher in 1969 than in 1947. But
the share of each fifth of the population has changed little since then,
although there was some decline in inequality during the previous
decade.

Another myth is that our system of taxation and of such benefits as social security redistributes the wealth and redresses income
inequalities. Census Bureau expert Herman P. Miller says that although
federal income taxes are progressive, taking a higher percentage of their
incomes from the rich, state and local taxes (such as the sales tax, property tax, and fixed-percentage income tax) do just the reverse; they are
regressive, taking a higher percentage of their income from the poorer
classes. In 1965, people at all income levels between $2,000 and $15,000
paid about 27% of their income in taxes. In 1966, 7 out of 10 dollars
paid for personal income taxes came from people earning less than
$20,000. Those with incomes less than $2,000, according to the Council
of Economic Advisers, paid 44% in taxes, and those with incomes over
$15,000, 38%. There are numerous loopholes for the rich in the tax
system: Capital gains are taxed at a low rate, there are depletion allowances on oil and depreciation on real estate, expense accounts, and other
nontaxable kinds of income.[23] The Biblical verse "Unto everyone that
hath shall be given, and he shall have abundance" continues, "but from
him that hath not, shall be taken away even that which he hath" (Mat-
thew 25:29).

A third myth, thoroughly exploded in recent years, is that no
one goes hungry in America.

POVERTY IN THE UNITED STATES

In any system of inequality, some people are bound to be at
the bottom of the heap. Are they necessarily poor? To answer, we must

[22]G. William Domhoff, "The Power Elite," *The Center Magazine* 3, No. 2 (March 1970).
[23]*Rich Man, Poor Man.*

With the rediscovery of the poor in the
1960s America began to realize that
hunger isn't confined to the Third World.
These children live in Chicago.

distinguish between absolute and relative poverty. Absolute poverty refers to extreme inadequacy in the essentials of food, clothing, and shelter. It means malnutrition or starvation, chronic ill health, low life expectancy, rags and hovels and slums. Relative poverty is comparative; it is measured against the greater plenty of others. It may persist even when the standard of living of all groups in the society improves, for it is a question of inequality.

Depending on the yardstick used, 10 to 20% of Americans are living below the poverty line. Using an income of $3,743 for a nonfarm family of four as the poverty threshold, there were 24.3 million poor Americans in 1969. And some of these know absolute poverty: About 10 million are chronically malnourished; 13.5 million were on welfare in 1971, a rise of 70% in 5 years.

Who are the poor? We can answer in two ways: by the *incidence* of poverty in any one category of the population—how hard it hits blacks, or the old, or children, for example, in terms of percentages; and by the *composition* of the poor—that is, what percentage of all the poor falls into a given category. "It is possible for a high percentage of female-headed households to be poor (incidence) but to contribute a much lower percentage of all the poor (composition)."[24]

Poverty hits the elderly increasingly hard. One of every three Americans over 65 is poor—almost one-fourth of elderly whites and one-half of elderly blacks. One child in five (and according to some estimates, one in three or four) is growing up in poverty, and nearly half of these live in families of five or more children. One of every ten whites and one of three blacks is poor. But of all population groups, households with dependent children headed by a woman have the highest likelihood of being poor—among whites, 36% in 1968, among nonwhites, 62%.

[24]S. M. Miller and Martin Rein, "Poverty, Inequality, and Policy," in Howard S. Becker, ed., *Social Problems: A Modern Approach* (New York: John Wiley & Sons, 1966), p. 445.

When we consider the composition of the poor, some categories overlap. For example, a family head may be female, unemployed, and nonwhite, or an aged farmer. Two-thirds of the poor are white; 60% are urban; nearly half are 21 or younger; one-fourth are 65 or older; 40% of poor families have female heads. And more than one-third of the poor live in families headed by a person who is employed full time! Minimum wage laws cover less than three-fourths of the labor force.

How do these figures compare to previous years? During the Depression nearly half of American families had less than a minimum subsistence income; now only one in ten (by government estimates) falls in this category. We often think of the years before the 1929 stock market crash as years of great prosperity. But in that year, half the families lived on less than $3,000 a year (in 1962 dollars) and seven out of ten on less than $4,000. (Both these figures are often used to mark the poverty line today.) "In 1966, the poverty level for a nonaged, nonfarm, male-headed family of four was $3,335. Using this standard, the poor numbered some 40 million persons in 1960. By 1967, that number had dropped to 26 million."[25] Economic expansion and a government War on Poverty helped most to reduce the incidence of poverty in families headed by an able-bodied workingman.

But poverty is persistent among the elderly, the unemployed, and families headed by females; and it is not likely to fall below 4 million even in families headed by a nonaged working male by 1974, when the total number of poor will probably still be at least 17 million.[26]

How do we account for the prevalence and persistence of poverty in the United States? Three related factors appear to explain much of it: the rapidly changing requirements of our technological society, the nature of today's poverty as compared to that of half a century ago, and the failure of government policies to deal with the swift transition from rural to urban living, from subsistence to commercial farming.

There is little or no room for unskilled labor in advanced industrial society, and less and less for semi-skilled labor; automation creates unemployment that may be offset by greater opportunities in the long run, but only for those who are technically trained. Cotton-picking machines are symbols of the agricultural revolution that has displaced millions of tenant farmers and sharecroppers.

Today's poverty is not like that of immigrants who worked themselves out of the slums in a generation or two, or the "all-in-the-same-boat" poverty of the Depression. It is the poverty of those who feel left behind and hopeless. It is largely self-perpetuating, in that seven out of ten poor families have four or more children, and many of the mothers bring them up alone, with such meager chances for schooling, health care, and jobs that they grow up to repeat the pattern.

[25]*Toward a Social Report* (Washington, D.C.: U.S. Department of Health, Education and Welfare, University of Michigan Press, 1971), p. 46.
[26]*Ibid.*

Some poverty, as has always been the case, is due to personal misfortunes and handicaps, and is aggravated by discrimination against certain categories of people.

American poverty is not so different from poverty in developing nations where an agricultural revolution pushes people off the land into city slums. While we have produced a surplus and paid farmers not to grow crops (the bulk of these payments going to the wealthiest farmers), we find hunger and malnutrition in rural slums and urban ghettos, and especially among the most neglected group of all—the migrant laborers who pick fruits and vegetables. Thinking in terms of tractors, chemicals, and "efficiency," agricultural policy-makers have failed to modernize or rehabilitate farm families left behind by the new technology.[27] And in comparison to most other industrialized nations, including those with largely capitalist or free-market economies, our government provisions for public assistance are inadequate; we do not really have a "welfare state."[28]

Status Honor and Social Interaction

The distribution of economic rewards does not coincide entirely with the distribution of "status honor" or prestige. The town's richest man is not necessarily the most respected. Empirical studies of status honor have relied largely on the evaluations of "prestige judges" and on observation of social interaction. Numerous studies have been made in fairly small towns for decades; more recently attempts at subjective evaluations of status have also been made in large cities and the nation as a whole. The "status" approach to stratification harmonizes with American beliefs and values, for it is based on the idea that classes are what people say they are; we tend to reject ideas of economic class and power as somehow Marxist or medieval.

COMMUNITY STUDIES

Among the most notable studies of status honor in local communities are those conducted by William Lloyd Warner and his associates in "Yankee City" (Newburyport, Massachusetts, a town of 17,000

[27]See Sidney Baldwin, *Poverty and Politics* (Chapel Hill, N.C.: University of North Carolina Press, 1969), for an account of what went wrong in America's transformation from hand-craft-and-labor farming to modern capital-intensive agriculture. Subtitled "The Rise and Fall of the Farm Security Administration," it relates the story of a short-lived effort to aid families as well as production by providing counseling and guidance to poor farm families and communities during the Depression of the 1930s.

[28]Hyman Lumer, "Why People are Poor," in *Poverty: Its Roots and Future* (New York: International Publishers, 1965), pp. 13–32: reprinted in Maurice Zeitlin, ed., *American Society, Inc.* (Chicago: Markham, 1970), pp. 207–21.

in the 1930s), and by A. B. Hollingshead in "Elmtown," a Midwestern city of 10,000 in the 1940s.[29] In long interviews, informants were asked how many strata they perceived, what characterized each stratum, and what standards they used to measure status. Researchers observed who associated with whom and compared the styles of life of the different status groups.

Informants agreed closely on ratings of individuals and families, and on the criteria for these ratings. Both Warner and Hollingshead concluded that even those who deny the reality of classes act as if they exist. A class system, said Warner, "is a social reality rather than an individual one, a rank order that exists in the minds of people as a social map which directs and organizes the activities and lives of the people of the town."[30]

The use of subjective evaluations by prestige judges is limited to fairly small communities. "The placement of individuals by personal knowledge, the class meaning of street names and neighborhoods, and the class significance of cliques, clubs, and associations were criteria that could only have meaning within relatively limited geographic boundaries."[31] The test of social status in communities like Elmtown and Yankee City is "What is the highest status group in which I am accepted as a social equal, an intimate friend?" Other studies have demonstrated that intimate interaction—eating together, visiting, intermarriage—is closely bounded by the lines of local prestige classes, even in larger communities, and that the smallest class unit is the friendship group or clique. Most people are far more interested in local prestige than in broader systems; they can perceive their own status honor in the judgments of others; they feel more comfortable when they stick with their own kind.[32]

In addition to subjective evaluations by "prestige judges," Warner constructed a more objective "Index of Status Characteristics." This included four weighted indicators of status: *occupation* (with a weight of 4); *source of income* (3); *type of house* (3); and *dwelling area* (2). (He originally used *amount of income* and *amount of education* as well, but found that they correlated almost completely with the other four indicators.) A person's status according to each indicator was placed somewhere on a seven-point scale. Source of income, for example, ranged as follows on a scale of 7 down to 1: inherited wealth, earned wealth, profits and fees, salary, wages, private relief, public re-

[29]W. Lloyd Warner and Paul S. Lunt, *The Social Life of a Modern Community* New Haven: Yale University Press, 1941), and A. B. Hollingshead, *Elmtown's Youth* (New York: John Wiley & Sons, 1949).

[30]*American Life: Dream and Reality* (Chicago: University of Chicago Press, 1953), p. 62.

[31]Leonard Reissman, *Class in American Society* (New York: The Free Press, 1959), p. 388.

[32]For a summary of findings and citations of various studies, see Williams, *American Society*, pp. 140–42.

lief, and nonrespectable income. A salaried person rated 4; this was multiplied by the weight of 3 given "source of income" to arrive at 12 for this indicator; and the total of all four indicators was his ISC score. Even these numerical measures, however, Warner cautioned, depend ultimately on evaluations placed "in the backs of all of our heads . . . by our cultural tradition and our society."[33] Using similar methods, Hollingshead found a very similar ranking in Elmtown except that he outlined five classes and Warner, six; in the New England town a self-conscious old aristocracy still existed and formed an "upper-upper class."[34]

STATUS HONOR IN LARGE CITIES

Richard P. Coleman and Bernice L. Neugarten believed that status honor could be judged in large urban communities by using both the "evaluated participation" techniques of Warner and Hollingshead and more objective socio-economic indices. They first interviewed a sample of 200 residents of Kansas City for the relative rankings of "residential address, occupational titles, club membership," and so on, regarding this approach as the urban equivalent of asking small-town people to rate one another directly.[35] They found high agreement on ranking of neighborhoods, and even streets and blocks, and that churches, clubs, schools, houses, clothing, the stores one patronized, and the car one drove also served as clues to social status. After interviewing 462 people aged 40 to 69, they composed an Index of Urban Status that combined occupation, income, housing, neighborhood, club memberships, community participation, ethnic identity, educational background (including that of a man's wife), and church affiliation. They concluded that face-to-face contacts are not necessary to judge social prestige. "In a metropolis, social class is evaluated in terms of the observable social characteristics of hypothetical equals, rather than by reference to specific individuals. As a consequence, status in a city can be assessed in almost the same way that residents themselves assess it."[36]

[33]W. Lloyd Warner, M. Meeker, and Kenneth Eells, *Social Class in America: A Manual for Procedure for the Measurement of Social Status* (Chicago: Science Research Associates, 1949).

[34]Warner's class structure: Upper-upper class, 1.4%; lower-upper class, 1.6%; upper-middle class, 10%; lower-middle class, 28%; upper-lower class, 33%; lower-lower class, 25%. Hollingshead: Class I, only a few families; Class II (corresponding to Warner's upper-middle class) 6 to 8%; Class III, 35 to 40%; IV, 40%; and V, 12 to 15%.

[35]*Social Status in the City* (San Francisco: Jossey-Bass, 1971), p. 8.

[36]*Ibid.*, p. 83. The authors saw Kansas City as divided into thirteen strata, with two in the upper class, three each in the upper-middle class, the lower-middle class, and the working class, and two in the lower class.

SOCIAL STATUS AT THE NATIONAL LEVEL

Coleman and Neugarten then compared Kansas City with seven other communities studied by anthropologists and sociologists, and concluded that "people of similar characteristics are perceived, both by their fellow citizens and by the social scientist, as equal to each other in status from community to community. Thus we can speak meaningfully of a nationwide status system."[37] The average person does not think in terms of a status system, however; he recognizes people as equal or superior or inferior, whether they are specific people in his own community or people in abstract categories identified by various clues and criteria.

> He translates social status in his local community into social characteristics, then he observes equivalence of social characteristics across communities; and then he retranslates into presumed equivalence of status across communities—a process, incidentally, not unlike that which the social scientist himself follows. In generalizing from the local to the national level, the social characteristics by which status is evaluated change somewhat in their relative importance.[38]

Among fairly well-established generalizations about status honor at the national level are these. The most important distinction is still, as it was in the Lynds' Middletown in the 1920s and 1930s, that between those who work with their hands and those who do not. Another touchstone is the attitude toward a college education. Talcott Parsons distinguishes the upper-middle from the lower-middle class by this criterion: If a family takes it for granted that its children will go to college, it is upper-middle class. Finally, sociologists agree that the occupation of the head of the family, while not synonymous with class, serves as the best single indicator of social status, and it is the one most often used to delineate a national class system. In industrial society a person's occupation is his major role, governing the rewards he receives and the power he exercises. Americans, especially, consider work their most important activity. The first question after an introduction is likely to be, "What do you do?" or "What business are you in?" It has been demonstrated repeatedly that occupation correlates very highly with income and education, which in turn are correlated with a style of life. Thus occupation is a valuable clue to social class status.

The National Opinion Research Center conducted two studies, in 1947 and 1963, to measure the comparative prestige of ninety occupations. The highest were Supreme Court Justice, physician, nuclear physicist, scientist, and college professor; farther down and rating

37[Ibid., p. 26.
38[Ibid., p. 264.

about the same were novelist, electrician, and farm owner and operator; policeman, carpenter, plumber, and barber were about equal; coal miner and shoe shiner were at the bottom. The findings were substantially the same in both years, and studies in twenty-three other countries, including several underdeveloped ones, had very similar results.[39]

The Distribution of Power

While income levels are under constant study, and evaluations of status honor have been numerous for decades, Weber's third dimension of social stratification—"party," or power over collective decisions and actions—has received relatively little attention. Americans find the idea of power or of a "ruling class," especially at the national level, distasteful, Marxist, and un-American; serious research into the subject has been taboo. We prefer to think of our equality at the ballot box, and of decisions being made by formal systems of government. But sociologists and political scientists are taking an increasing interest in the nature and distribution of power, and a number have concluded that it tends to be more concentrated than wealth and prestige.

What is **power**? It is control over the decisions that affect the way people live, and over the allocation of scarce and desirable values. Power is exercised through economic and social institutions as well as through government structures. It is thus "the capacity [though not necessarily the *right*] to mobilize resources for the accomplishment of intended effects with recourse to some type of sanction(s) to encourage compliance."[40] When power is regarded as legitimate and right, it is **authority**, and people voluntarily obey; when it is not, they are either coerced or manipulated.

How is power distributed in American society? Two opposing points of view are that it is (1) pyramidal, with a power elite at the top, or (2) pluralistic, with many groups struggling for advantage, and checking and balancing one another. Theoretically, there could also be (3) equal distribution of power throughout society, a sort of "mass democracy" of one-man-one-vote regarding all important decisions and policies affecting freedom of choice and allocation of values (anything scarce and desirable, including free time, education, etc., as well as goods). If the first were true in any one community or society, the same leaders would make all or nearly all the significant decisions, would

[39]Hodge, Siegel, and Rossi, "Occupational Prestige in the United States: 1925-1963," and Robert W. Hodge, Donald J. Treiman, and Peter H. Rossi, "A Comparative Study of Occupational Prestige," in Bendix and Lipset, *Class, Status, and Power*, pp. 309–21.

[40]John Walton, "The Vertical Axis of Community Organization and the Structure of Power," in Willis D. Hawley and Frederick M. Wirt, eds., *The Search for Community Power* (Englewood Cliffs, N.J.: Prentice-Hall, Inc., 1968), pp. 353–66.

agree on them, and would not be responsible to an electorate. If the second were true, the leaders would vary from issue to issue, and any concentration of decision-making would be in the hands of duly chosen public officials. If there were a mass democracy, the community would be ruled by the people, with a majority influential in all or almost all cases.[41]

COMMUNITY POWER STUDIES

Social scientists studying community power have generally ignored formal positions in government and used one of two approaches: the reputational approach, in which informants are asked who are the leaders; and the participational or decision-making approach, in which an attempt is made to find out who actually decides important issues.

Most early studies, such as those of Middletown and Elmtown, indicated that some people with wealth and prestige chose to exercise power, but they preferred to remain behind the scenes. A typical instance was an attempt by business leaders to influence public officials to keep their taxes and assessments low. Floyd Hunter studied "Regional City" (Atlanta, Georgia) by the reputational approach and also found business leaders exercising covert power. He identified forty top leaders, interviewed them, and observed them in action. All of them, he concluded, are known to one another; few wish to be singled out as leaders, but rely on government officials to carry out their wishes. "They are able to enforce their decisions by persuasion, intimidation, coercion, and, if necessary, force."[42] The mayor, the county treasurer, and the heads of various government departments consult the economic leaders before making any major decision. One of the leaders is said to be the power behind the governor of the state. Several make frequent trips to Washington and foreign countries, and are part of a broader network of power and influence.[43]

Believing that a reputation for power may not coincide with

[41]Aaron B. Wildavsky, "Leadership in a Small Town," in Hawley and Wirt, *The Search for Community Power,* pp. 115–24.

[42]*Community Power Structure: A Study of Decision Makers* (Chapel Hill: University of North Carolina Press, 1953), p. 24.

[43]Of these 40 top "influentials" 11 direct or administer large commercial enterprises, 7 direct and supervise banking and investment operations, and 5 have major industrial responsibilities. The other leaders include 5 lawyers, 1 dentist, 2 labor leaders, and 5 social or civic leaders who have no business offices. Only 4 are in government positions. Coleman and Neugarten found the leaders of Kansas City more heterogeneous and more visible. Delbert Miller found businessmen dominate "Pacific City," but in a comparable English city the "key influentials" came from a broad representation of various sectors of community life; he suggests businessmen have less prestige in English than in American culture. ["Industry and Community Power Structure: A Comparative Study of an American and an English City," *American Journal of Sociology* (1958); reprinted in Roach, Gross, and Gursslin, *Social Stratification in the United States,* pp. 299–307.]

actual power, others have tried to study "instances in which power was actually employed, by individuals or groups, to influence the outcome of a decision in the direction desired."[44] While the reputational approach apparently leads to a conclusion favoring the theory of a "power elite," the decisional approach leads to the conclusion that power is pluralistic. Robert Dahl studied New Haven, Connecticut, and concluded that middle-class leaders take over decision-making roles; different ones are influential in different areas; and the top leaders are not a monolithic and covert elite but "a coalition of public officials and private individuals who reflect the interests and concerns of different segments of the community. [and] "it would be unwise to underestimate the extent to which voters may exert *indirect* influence on the decisions of leaders by means of elections. . . . If the leaders lead, they are also led."[45] Although Aaron B. Wildavsky found that businessmen do predominate in leadership roles in Oberlin, Ohio, there is considerable conflict over issues among them.[46]

Even New York City is not governed by a powerful machine. Its "huge and diverse system of government and politics is a loose-knit and multi-centered network in which decisions are reached by ceaseless bargaining and fluctuating alliances among the major categories of participants in each center, and in which the centers are partially but strikingly isolated from one another."[47]

But power involves much more than political decision-making. It involves social control through the mass media, through manipulation of credit, hiring and firing, social approval or ostracism.[48] Robert Presthus found that the eighty leaders (0.005% of the population) in two communities were essentially divided into two different decision-making systems, political and economic. The economic leaders, not being subject to the electoral process, enjoy greater continuity in the power structure, and their bases of power are "more extensive, constant, and durable."[49] Some decisions are arrived at through cooperation and competition between the two elites. A third elite, "the specialists," participate in some decisions, but they are rarely nominated as "influentials" when the reputational method is used; they are welfare-oriented, highly educated, have professional statuses, and play active, highly visible roles in community affairs. But "despite high levels of popular educa-

[44]Hawley and Wirt, *The Search for Community Power*, p. 148.

[45]*Who Governs?* (New Haven, Conn.: Yale University Press, 1961).

[46]*Leadership in a Small Town* (Totowa, N.J.: Bedminster Press, 1964).

[47]Wallace S. Sayre and Herbert Kaufman, *Governing New York City* (New York: Russell Sage Foundation, 1960), p. 716. By centers the authors mean the agencies and bureaus of various levels of government; e.g. the City Council, the Board of Education, the Housing Authority.

[48]Thomas J. Anton, "Power, Pluralism, and Local Politics," *Administrative Science Quarterly* 7 (March 1963): 448–57; reprinted in Hawley and Wirt, *The Search for Community Power*, pp. 180–88.

[49]*Men at the Top: A Study in Community Power* (New York: Oxford University Press, 1964).

tion, economic stability, a fair degree of social mobility, a marvelously efficient communication system, and related advantages usually assumed to provide sufficient conditions for democratic pluralism, the vast majority of citizens remains apathetic, uninterested, and inactive in political affairs at the community level."[50]

Presthus also found that community power is declining; higher levels of government and industry make more and more decisions, reducing local autonomy. Where resources are of local origin (schools, hospitals, and new industry) local power still operates; but in other spheres pluralism is declining because of nation-wide centralization in both political and economic decision-making.

POWER AT THE NATIONAL LEVEL

Empirical studies of power at the national level have been few, but theory, speculation, and debate have been lively, centering around the opposing views of a power elite and pluralism. Our formal system, as outlined in the Constitution and as practiced in theory through the party system, is pluralistic. Champions of this view hold that power is widely diffused among "veto groups" that balance one another; some hold that this discourages effective decision-making and leadership,[51] others that this ensures a democratic consensus.

The leading advocate of the "power elite" school of thought was sociologist C. Wright Mills. He defined power as control over "whatever decisions men make about the arrangements under which they live, and about the events which make up the history of our times."[52] He argued that American society is dominated by a power elite that is quite different from other ruling classes in history because our society is very different. Its members have not *seized* power by design; they occupy the positions of power in large-scale formal organizations that have grown ever stronger and make or influence decisions about "the size and shape of the national economy, the level of employment, the purchasing power of the consumer, the prices that are advertised, the investments that are channeled."[53] There is an "interlocking directorate" of top-ranking military, political, governmental, and business leaders. They know one another; cliques and "crowds" overlap among them. Like the changing inner circles of Soviet Russia, the American power elite exerts influence undreamed of by the Caesars, because economic corporations are so huge, the nation-state controls

[50]*Ibid.*

[51]See James MacGregor Burns, *The Deadlock of Democracy* (Englewood Cliffs, N.J.: Prentice-Hall, Inc., 1963).

[52]*Power, Politics, and People: The Collected Essays of C. Wright Mills*, Irving Louis Horowitz, ed. (New York: Oxford University Press, 1963), Chap. 1, "The Structure of Power in American Society," pp. 23–28; reprinted in Roach, Gross, and Gursslin, *Social Stratification in the United States*.

[53]*The Power Elite* (New York: Oxford University Press, 1956), p. 125.

such giant armies and lethal weaponry, and the masses are so power-less. Mills anticipated the Eisenhower phrase about the "military-indus-trial complex" in these words: "There is no longer, on the one hand, an economic, and on the other, a political order containing a military establishment unimportant to politics and to money-making. There is a political economy numerously linked with military order and deci-sion."[54]

Mills believed that the interest group and political party con-flicts so emphasized by pluralist theorists do not occur at the top level of power, but at the middle levels. Here professional politicians, mem-bers of Congress and pressure groups, and "the new and old upper classes of town and city and region" arrive at "an organized stalemate" in bargaining over lesser decisions. The middle classes find their careers in large formal organizations dominated by the power elite. These white-collar people, though ever more numerous and indispensable, are neither politically aware nor politically organized. At the bottom of the power structure is a "mass-like society," fragmented and im-potent.[55]

An attempt to assess the validity of Mills's much-debated thesis by empirical methods was made by Floyd Hunter, who concluded that Mills was essentially correct. Using a reputational method similar to that he employed in Atlanta, he developed a list of 100 leaders who are reputedly highly influential in national affairs. He then documented the network of relationships among them and found that politicians, the wealthy, and the top military "brass" do tend to know one another personally and to have close social, political, and business connections.[56]

G. William Domhoff agrees that there is a power elite, "persons who are in command positions in institutional hierarchies controlled by members of the upper class." He also believes that there is a governing class—"a social upper class which owns a disproportionate amount of the country's wealth, receives a disproportionate amount of the coun-try's yearly income, and contributes a disproportionate number of its members to positions of leadership." Some members of this class oc-cupy positions of power, but members of the power elite may or may not belong to this class. The governing class is an "establishment," an "American business aristocracy." But it is not unified and monolithic; it has its antagonisms and conflicts. Some of its members seek to con-trol the shifting coalitions of the Republican party; others are active in the Democratic party. Neither is it omnipotent; there are opposing interest groups and classes—workers, farmers, small businessmen, con-sumers; and there are restraints on power in cultural values manifested in the Constitution and laws, as well as in our mores. "Most of all,

[54]"The Structure of Power in American Society."
[55]White Collar (New York: Oxford University Press, 1951).
[56]Top Leadership, U.S.A. (Chapel Hill, N.C.: University of North Carolina Press, 1959).

there is the right to vote, which means that the leaders are accountable to all the people."[57]

The governing class has different power at different levels.

Members of the upper class dominate major corporations, founda- tions, universities, and the Executive branch of the federal govern- ment, while they merely have influence in Congress, most state gov- ernments, and most local governments. This does not mean that they are never influenced in areas where they have control, nor does it mean that they never get their way where they merely exert influ- ence. However, the interesting thing about 'control' and 'influence' in a country where the concept of a governing class calls forth notions of sinister men lurking behind the throne, is that members of the American governing class in fact serve their interests from positions of authority. Authority-based control, rather than covert influence, is their dominant mode.[58]

Consequences of Stratification

Studies of our relatively open class system, then, demonstrate clearly that the three variables of money power, status honor, and decision- making power or party are differentially distributed among the various social classes and that they are, in general, highly correlated and tend to reinforce one another. What consequences does this differential dis- tribution have for life chances and styles of life?

LIFE CHANCES

Chances for "life, liberty, and the pursuit of happiness" are closely related to social class status. The farther down the scale one goes, the more limited are opportunities, the more restricted are choices, the greater are risks of illness, deprivation, and broken homes, the less is one's freedom or capacity to take a hand in his own development.

The most basic life chance is the chance to stay alive. Villerme computed life expectancy by occupation in the French city of Mulhouse in 1823–34, when the miserable conditions of early industrialization prevailed. Life expectancy was low for everyone, largely because babies died like flies: 7.5 years for the city, 20 at best for the country as a whole. The most well-to-do people in town had only a 28-year life expectancy, yet this was over twenty times that of the children of sim- ple weavers, which was a year and four months![59] The average life

[57]*Who Rules America?* (Englewood Cliffs, N.J.: Prentice-Hall, Inc., 1967), p. 151.
[58]*Ibid.*, p. 11.
[59]J. Fourastie, *The Causes of Wealth* (Glencoe, Ill.: The Free Press, 1960), cited in Svalastoga, "Social Differentiation."

expectancy in modern industrial societies is nearly ten times higher, and the gap between classes much narrower. One study found a difference of 7.6 years between the life expectancies of the highest- and lowest-income white groups in Chicago and 18 years between the highest-income whites and the lowest-income nonwhites. The gap apparently is being reduced by about 1 year each decade.[60]

The higher we go in the social scale, the taller, healthier, and heavier are the members of each class, and the higher they score on IQ tests. Infant mortality among the poor is twice the national average; active tuberculosis, four times. The poor have less dental care, more heart trouble, a higher incidence of illness and disability—both mental and physical—and poorer care in home and hospital when they are sick. The poor pay more for less, in housing, groceries, and furnishings (for which they pay a high rate of interest on loans or installments). The poorer a person, the greater his risks of being a victim of crime and of being charged with and convicted of crime.[61] The greater is their chance of military service under both draft and voluntary systems. They are more likely to suffer the stigma of public welfare, to be alienated from the mainstream of American life, and to feel hopelessness and despair. Their chances of getting out of this trap are low in today's pattern of self-perpetuating poverty.

> Being poor is not a choice for these millions; it is a rigid way of life. It is handed down from generation to generation in a cycle of inadequate education, inadequate homes, inadequate jobs, and stunted ambitions. It is a peculiar axiom of poverty that the poor are poor because they earn little, and they also earn little because they are poor.[62]

Because education is the chief avenue to advancement in modern industrial society, chances for schooling are among the most crucial life chances. The farther one goes up the social ladder, the more years of schooling children are likely to receive, the better the schools, the greater the chance of professional graduate training. (One exception: The upper-middle class is more highly educated than the upper class.) Only 17% of the heads of poor families have graduated from high

[60]Albert J. Mayer and Philip Hauser, "Class Differentials in Expectation of Life at Birth," in *La Revue de l'Institut International de Statistique* 18, No. 200 (1950).

[61]See Hollingshead, *Elmtown's Youth*, pp. 102, 110, and 119–20, for a comparison of the public record of criminal charges and convictions by class status.

[62]From "The War on Poverty," A Congressional Presentation, March 17, 1964, cited in Louis A. Ferman, Joyce L. Kornbluh, and Alan Haber, eds., *Poverty in America: A Book of Readings*, rev. ed. (Ann Arbor: University of Michigan Press, 1968), p. 315. See also Robert E. Will and Harold G. Vatter, eds., *Poverty in Affluence*, 2nd ed. (New York: Harcourt, Brace, & World, 1970); Victor B. Ficker and Herbert S. Graves, *Deprivation in America* (Beverly Hills: Glencoe Press, 1971); and S. Kirson Weinberg, *Social Problems in Modern Urban Society*, 2nd ed. (Englewood Cliffs, N.J.: Prentice-Hall, Inc., 1970), Chap. 6, "Poverty: Deprivation and Stigma."

school, but the gap promises to be narrowed. It is estimated that by 1980 community colleges will be educating about 40% of the college-age population, and this share will come largely from the lowest economic level.[63] Quite aside from the intrinsic value of education to personal fulfillment, lifetime earnings are correlated with amount of schooling.

Where political loyalty is a determinant of status, it also necessarily affects life chances; in the Soviet Union a person branded as politically unreliable may lose his job, be transferred to a distant region, lose good housing, lose access to higher education or promotion. In addition, just as in the United States, a child's chances of getting a good education are affected not only by his native ability and the availability of schools, but depend largely on "the income, motivations, and values of his family and on the region where one was born. . . . A child born in a family of kolkhoz [collective farm] peasants, for example, in Kazahkstan, has a poorer chance to attend . . . any university than the child of a high civil servant, engineer, or scientist living in some of the urban areas of European Russia. The chances of such a child may not be quite as bad as those of an illegitimate child of a Negro mother living on welfare in Mississippi, but they are still rather dim."[64]

SOCIAL INTERACTION, SOCIAL PARTICIPATION, AND CLASS SUBCULTURES

When F. Scott Fitzgerald said that the very rich are different from you and me, Ernest Hemingway retorted, "Yes, they have more money." But most sociologists would agree with Fitzgerald. The people in various social strata *are* different: They have different styles of life, patterns of social participation, beliefs, values, and attitudes. This differentiation is not a direct consequence of variations in wealth, prestige, and power (except possibly for those lowest on the scale); rather it arises from the tendency of those in each stratum to associate more often and more intimately with those they perceive to be similarly situated. The more they limit their interaction to such people, the more they come to form "status groups" with similar styles of life, norms, and values—in short, subcultures. The more stable a society, the more marked are subcultural differences. But even in our rapidly changing society, members of the various class strata participate differently in social groups and carry out their institutional roles as family members, students, church-goers, voters, producers, and consumers in different ways. Inevitably such differences are correlated with variations in per-

[63]*The Center Magazine* (March 1970).
[64]Hollander, *American and Soviet Society*, p. 125.

sonality, in manners, speech, and traits, including modes of interpersonal relationships.

The members of stratified societies take account of such differences in "hanging people on the peg they belong on," to use an Elmtown phrase. Hollingshead's study of Elmtown's youth substantiated his hypothesis that "the social behavior of adolescents is related functionally to the position their families occupy in the social structure of the community." He studied 369 girls and 366 boys, and concluded that class is reflected "in every major phase of social behavior—the school, the church, the job, recreation, the clique, dating, and sex . . . [and that] this class system is far more vital as a social force in our society than the American creed."[65]

All over the world political affiliation is correlated with social class status, with the "right" generally associated with upper classes, the "left" with lower classes, and the "center" the middle classes. In every election in the United States since 1936, when such studies were first begun, "the proportion voting Democratic increases sharply as one moves down the occupational or income ladder."[66] Religious affiliation has also been shown to be class-linked, as have patterns of childrearing and husband–wife relationships.

The consumption patterns and activities of different classes serve as clues to status and thus as cues to guide interaction. Let us consider five women of about the same age, let us say thirty-five, from the five classes delineated in many community studies. We know without studying them personally which one has: a mansion furnished with heirlooms; a four-bedroom Colonial with two acres of suburban land on a ravine; a small "ranch" house with three bedrooms; a two-story house in an aging neighborhood; a rented upper flat in a slum. On the living room wall one hangs an original Picasso, one a watercolor picked up at the neighborhood art show, one a Van Gogh print, one a mail-order seascape, and one a calendar with cute kittens. One goes to a board meeting for the Symphony Society, one is more likely to belong to a book review group, another attends her church circle meeting, a fourth goes to a lodge auxiliary meeting, and the fifth belongs to no organized group at all, but visits her mother or sister when she has a free moment. We could make further guesses about their speech and manners, how they spend their evenings, what they read, where they shop, how they dress, how they entertain, how they spend their vacations, how they raise their children, and so on. But we have said enough to illustrate that an understanding of the class system does furnish us with "a map of social reality."

Although we have referred to differences in life chances and life

[65]*Elmtown's Youth*, pp. 439, 441, 452.

[66]Seymour Martin Lipset, *Political Man: The Social Bases of Politics* (Garden City, N.Y.: Doubleday & Company, Inc., 1960), Chap. 7.

styles as *consequences* of stratification, they are more than that. They also reinforce and perpetuate systems of stratification through their effect on social mobility and their influence in encouraging people to limit their intimate interaction to those of similar status.

The American Class Structure

We may now define a social class as a category of people with similar amounts of wealth, prestige, and power, and similar life chances and ways of life, who tend to recognize one another as social equals and those in other categories as superior or inferior. Some sociologists regard free intermarriage among people as a reliable index of equal social class status.

As noted in our discussion of "Social Status at the National Level," comparative studies indicate that the class systems of American communities are basically similar. Warner suggests that "a good test of this statement is that people who move from one region to another recognize their own and other levels in the new community and know how to adjust themselves."[67] But the national class system is not a conglomeration or composite of local systems, which vary somewhat and are based on fairly precise personal knowledge. It has a much larger range of inequality than most local systems, more anonymity, and, in the middle range, a stronger egalitarian bent.

Robin Williams finds that a nationwide system

> exists, first, in the enduring objective differentials of income, wealth, authority, and power. It exists also in the relatively high degree of consensus about categorical rankings of occupational prestige, extending even to fairly definite evaluations of specific conspicuous positions. It exists in the interpersonal knowledge, mutual acquaintance, and intimate association among persons in 'elite' circles of upper strata. Finally, it has reality in the web of communication and mobility that links together, in a great variety of ways, persons in similar rank positions in different regions and localities.[68]

Using the criteria of occupation, income, and education, Coleman and Neugarten made some rough estimates of the national class structure. They see an upper class of about 1%; an upper-middle class

[67]*American Life*, p. 53.
[68]*American Society*, p. 104.

of 10%; a lower-middle class of 32%; a working class of 39%; and a lower class of 18%.[69]

THE UPPER CLASS

The upper class, estimated at 1 or 2% of the population, is a clearly identifiable group, a truly national class that freely mixes and intermarries within its rather definite set of boundaries which are "guarded by social secretaries, private schools, social clubs, and similar exclusive institutions."[70] Its core is the "business aristocracy" of corporate fortunes, most of which originated after the Civil War. It is unlike the upper class of any other country, "for it alone grew up within a middle-class framework of representative government and egalitarian ideology, unhampered by feudal lords, kings, priests, or mercenary armies. Only the American upper class is made up exclusively of the descendants of successful businessmen or corporation lawyers—whatever their pretensions, few families are 'old' enough or rich enough to forget this overriding fact."[71]

Its members are active in business, law, and finance; a number are also physicians, professors, and architects. Most of them, says G. William Domhoff, do not fit the stereotype of the jet set or cafe society or the "functionless genteel"; they are not a leisure class, but hardworking and competent. They have been educated at exclusive private schools and elite universities. Attendance at these schools, membership in exclusive clubs, and listing in the various urban Social Registers are reliable indices of upper-class status. Intermarriage is national in scope; people meet at debutante parties and fashionable resorts. Many own farms or ranches; their distinctive—and expensive—sports include horseback riding, fox hunting, polo, yachting, and sailing.

The upper class, then, is more than a category; it is an interacting group whose members either know one another or know of one another. It is not entirely cohesive, however; it has its antagonisms and differences. The older families are largely Protestant, generally Episco-

---

[69]*Social Status in the City*, p. 273. By similar criteria, one student concluded that the Soviet class structure has an upper stratum of 3.8%; upper-middle 6.6%; lower-middle, 15.7%; upper-lower, 27.5%; and lower-lower, 46.4%. Boris Meissner, *Sowjetgesellschaft im Wandel* (Stuttgart: Kohlhammer, 1966); cited in George Fischer, *The Soviet System and Modern Society* (New York: Atherton Press, 1968). Although the elite have many special privileges, there is less conspicuous inequality and no affluent idleness. [Hollander, *American and Soviet Society*, p. 126.]

[70]Domhoff, *Who Rules America?*, p. 33.

[71]*Ibid.*, p. 12.

| John D. III | Nelson | Laurance | Winthrop | David |

If we accept the idea that there is a ruling elite *in America, we would certainly number the Rockefellers among them.*

John D. III: Chairman, the Rockefeller Foundation, National Policy Panel on World Population, Committee on Population and Growth and the American Future, Agriculture Development Council, Japan Society; Trustee, Princeton University, United Negro College Fund, Educational Broadcasting Corp., Lincoln Center for the Performing Arts, Phelps Memorial Hospital.

Nelson: Governor of New York (1958-   ); Assistant Secretary of State (1944-45); Undersecretary of Health, Education and Welfare (1953-54); Special Assistant to the President (1954-55); Director and Founder, the Museum of Primitive Art; Director, International Development Advisory Board.

Laurance: Chairman, Caneel Bay Plantation Inc.; Director, Rockefeller Center Inc.; Trustee, American Committee on International Wildlife Protection, Memorial Sloan-Kettering Cancer Center, National Geographic Society, M.I.T.

Winthrop: Executive Vice President, Chase National Bank (1937-38); Director, Rockefeller Brothers, Inc.; Director, Rockefeller Center, Inc.; Trustee, Industrial Relations Counsellors; Chairman of the Board, Colonial Williamsburg and Williamsburg Restorations, Inc.; Governor of Arkansas (1967-70).

David: Chairman, Chase Manhattan Bank, Council for Latin America; President, Sealantic Fund; Chairman of the Board of Trustees, Rockefeller University, the Museum of Modern Art; Co-chairman, Task Force on Housing of the Urban Coalition; Director and Vice President, Council on Foreign Relations, Inc.

palian or Presbyterian,[72] and their treatment of rich Jews and Catholics —many of whom were "new rich" and immigrants as well—in the first half of this century "was little short of incredible, the least cruel of their actions being . . . exclusion from social clubs and summer resorts."[73] These antagonisms appear to be declining, but there is some trace of them in party alignments. The "staunchly Protestant, Anglo-Saxon industrialists and bankers" clearly dominate the Republican party; old-time aristocrats, the "ethnic rich," and smaller big businessmen dominate the Democratic party. Many of the power elite come from the upper class; others are dominated by the upper class, according to Domhoff. Thus the upper class, though neither monolithic nor omnipotent, is a governing class.

THE MIDDLE CLASSES

Below the clearly defined upper class and above those engaged in manual labor is a large amorphous middle class, perhaps half the population. Its core beliefs and values are those generally identified with "the American Way of Life." But within it sociologists (and ordinary citizens as well) distinguish at least two strata.

The Upper-Middle Class. Perhaps one American in ten is a member of the upper-middle class, the proportion being larger in big cities. Its core are "college-educated, managerial level businessmen and successful professionals. In large cities managers and professionals are the archetypes; but in smaller communities, and among the older generation especially, the independent businessman is more nearly the typical man of this class."[74]

Members of the upper-middle class are the prototype of "modern man."[75] They have a rational, purposeful, manipulative world view, a sense of personal responsibility for what happens to them, an emphasis on doing and achieving, an orientation to the future, a tendency to self-control and to impersonality in social interaction. Career advancement is a central value. They are socially and geographically mobile, willing to move if greener pastures beckon. They are extremely active in voluntary associations and community activities. They train their children to delay gratifications and work for future benefits. They em-

---

[72]E. Digby Baltzell, *The Protestant Establishment* (New York: Random House, 1964), and *An American Business Aristocracy* (New York: The Free Press, 1958).

[73]Domhoff, *Who Rules America?*, p. 29.

[74]Coleman and Neugarten, *Social Status in the City*, p. 262.

[75]See Chapter 15 for a discussion of modern (as distinguished from traditional and transitional) man.

phasize individual competitiveness and disciplined effort. Often they emulate the life style of the upper class and associate with them in formal organizations. In many American cities this class, like the upper class, is made up largely of WASPs (white Anglo-Saxon Protestants).

The Lower-Middle Class.   Historically the class of clerks, salesmen, and small businessmen, the lower-middle class now has as its core "families in the white-collar world who will never reach full-fledged managerial status in their respective corporate or governmental bureaucracies . . . and is coming to include both the blue-collar technician and the well-educated, well-housed gray-collar service worker."[76] A generation ago a high school education distinguished them from the working class, but this index is no longer reliable. Among their core values are respectability, thrift, hard work, honesty, and decency. They are also strongly family-oriented. Hollingshead found that in Elmtown members of this class were more active, although less influential, in political and church affairs than their superiors, and that they supported lodges and women's auxiliaries.

Some sociologists lump the lower-middle class with the upper-lower class of such community studies as Elmtown and Yankee City into a "working class," with the same values, life styles, and income, calling them the class of the "white majority," or the average or common man. Others believe the blurring of this class line by material things and income is illusory, that even when manual workers have "things" long considered symbolic of middle-class status, they remain working-class in values, attitudes, and actions.

THE WORKING CLASS

Roughly two Americans out of five are "working class"; they work in skilled or semi-skilled manual jobs and form the stable element of the blue-collar labor force. They believe such work is *real* work, white-collar jobs and supervisory jobs are not; they prefer working with things to working with people. They have a level of living above subsistence; although many have a hard time making ends meet, they "get by."

Many are of recent foreign background. Louise Kapp Howe reminds us that the "average man" is not the blond, blue-eyed WASP of the TV commercial, but what sociologists soberly call a "white ethnic" of Italian, Irish, Polish, Greek, Lithuanian, German, Hungarian, Russian "or any one of the still amazing number of national origins represented in this country."[77] Many belong to Catholic or salvation-

[76]Coleman and Neugarten, *Social Status in the City*, pp. 262–63.
[77]Louise Kapp Howe, ed., *The White Majority: Between Poverty and Affluence* (New York: Random House, Vintage Books, 1970), p. 4.

ist-cult churches as well as to an array of Protestant denominations.

Things and home ownership are symbols of success. Bennett M. Berger, in a study of a new working-class suburb, found its residents exhilarated at being better off, "homeowners in a bright new world of lawns, patios, electrical appliances, and pastel bathroom fixtures."[78] But despite our myth of suburbia, they are not middle class. Both before and after moving to the suburbs about half identified themselves as working class, and those who think of themselves as middle class do so because our society sanctions this as a term for a decent, comfortable standard of living that includes home ownership. Nor is their style of life middle class; it did not automatically change with the move to suburbia.

Working-class patterns of social participation are different from middle-class patterns. Few join voluntary associations. Berger found that 70% do not belong to any club, organization, or association, and only 8% belong to more than one. Few have really close friends; nine did not know the occupations of those they called their closest friends. Almost half the sample spends more than 16 hours a week watching TV. Their social interaction centers around relatives, neighbors, and the informal work group. In a study of an Italian working-class neighborhood, Herbert Gans found sociability restricted largely to "a routinized gathering of a relatively unchanging peer group of family members and friends that takes place several times a week." Most social relationships are with people of the same sex, age, and life-cycle status.[79]

Traditional sex roles prevail: A man goes out with "the boys" while his wife is "limited to a small circle of parents, relatives, and two or three friends who set her standards in life—from food and house furnishings to politics, sex, and religion—and the moral universe seems to have the unity of the simple society of the past. It would appear that it is the working-class girl, rather than her middle-class sister, who leads the sheltered life."[80]

What are the consequences of this limited social participation? There is less of a generation gap in the working class because young people are not exposed to the currents of contemporary thought. Women are unself-conscious, certain, and single-minded, with a simple view of their place as compared to the complexities and uncertainties of college-educated women. Avoidance of voluntary associations and organizations, and limitation of participation almost exclusively to primary groups, protect a member of the working class "from the encroachments of an associational society with its impersonality and its stringent role requirements," but limit his ability to cope with the complex mod-

[78]*Working-Class Suburb: A Study of Auto Workers in Suburbia* (Berkeley and Los Angeles: University of California Press), p. 80.

[79]*The Urban Villagers* (New York: The Free Press, 1962).

[80]Mirra Komarovsky, "Blue-Collar Marriages and Families," in Howe, *The White Majority*, p. 40.

ern world.[81] "The restricted environment and the low cultural level of the home hinder the development of working-class children from the first years of life on, retard the development of intellectual interests and motivation, and diminish the children's chances for higher education. [Until this situation is corrected] the working class will live on the fringe of society."[82]

Not only the life style, but the personality traits, values, and attitudes of the working class differentiate them from the middle and lower classes. Mirra Komarovsky found the most surprising aspect of the blue-collar world not in the manners and morals reminiscent of the past, but in the typical cognitive style. In 6-hour interviews meant to focus on psychological relationships, she found that the respondents almost without exception "thought in terms of the situational and material conditions of life," focusing on sensory, concrete details and using a low level of abstraction. Women were asked, for example, if their mothers could help them when they were feeling depressed. A standard answer was, "No, she doesn't have any cash to spare."[83]

Working-class young people do not expect much out of life. They want to do good, to do well, and to be well-liked; they plan to carry on their lives in simple comfort, marry and raise their families, and retire on small pensions plus social security. They do not think in terms of sacrificing present pleasures to work toward future careers; many want the "bird in the hand" of a job that seems, to an 18-year-old, to pay well, or they may see military service as promising travel, training, and money. Perhaps less than a quarter of high school graduates who are children of factory workers go on to college.[84] They take pride in working and supporting themselves; in home ownership and possessions; and in courage, loyalty, and endurance. Most are afraid of slipping into the lower class.

In recent years there are signs of a growing feeling of alienation among members of the working class. They feel trapped and insecure, unable to control their own lives, ignored or treated with disdain by those who look on them as bigoted "hardhats." They resent the feeling that they are neglected while other groups get their demands. Unemployment and inflation have contributed to this feeling; and statistics disprove the myth that they are middle class and sitting pretty. Between 1965 and 1970 the real incomes of blue-collar workers declined.[85]

[81]Roach, Gross, and Gursslin, *Social Stratification in the United States*, p. 180.

[82]Komarovsky, "Blue-Collar Marriages and Families," p. 44.

[83]*Ibid.*, p. 38.

[84]Brendan Sexton, "Workers and Liberals: Closing the Gap," in Howe, *The White Majority*, pp. 230–45.

[85]The average industrial worker with a wife and two children got $96.78 a week in 1965, $116.58 in 1970. But with inflation his real annual income declined by $209.56. The Labor Department reported that the financial needs of a family with growing children rose by 61% in the 1960s, while the average earnings of skilled workers increased only 41%, as compared with 64% for blacks as a group and 61% for executives. [*Christian Science Monitor* (Feb. 6, 1971).]

THE LOWER CLASS

So many different kinds of people make up the 16 to 20% in the "lower class" that we might say there are any number of lower classes. Unskilled workers (including domestic servants and migrant workers) who are often unemployed, who work part time, are paid little and often have to resort to public assistance; mothers on Aid to Families of Dependent Children; the disreputable poor such as petty thieves and skid row bums; the most disadvantaged members of minority groups; the unfortunates who are poor because of age, sickness, or accident—are they a "class" or a heterogeneous mass, outcasts who are not part of the American class hierarchy at all?

Regardless of our answer, most of us would call lower class those people who live in urban and rural slums, are deprived of wealth, prestige, and power, and are stigmatized and discriminated against. Most live all their lives at or below subsistence level, and raise their children that way.

They live with danger as well as poverty; people around them are out to hurt or exploit them in petty or significant ways. They learn that in their neighborhoods "they can expect only poor and inferior service and protection from such institutions as the police, the courts, the schools, the sanitation department, the landlords, and the merchants."[86] Under these circumstances there seems no point in adopting the goals of the good life and career success that guide most Americans. They seek strategies for sheer survival. One is the "expressive life style," either seeking to elicit rewards by making oneself interesting and attractive through benign forms such as fun, singing, dancing, lively slang, and spontaneous gratification of impulse, or turning to more destructive forms such as dope addiction, drunkenness, and dropping out. When the expressive strategy fails, some of the more desperate turn to "violent" strategies. Older people are more likely to adopt "depressive" strategies for coping with life, retreating into isolation and constricting their goals to surviving as a simple organism rather than as a human being.[87]

Lee Rainwater, who has studied the lower class extensively, does not believe they "reject" middle-class values; they simply know that given their conditions and opportunities they cannot gain a sense of self-esteem in terms of those values. They have a low level of social participation and few informal contacts; physical distance limits their choice of friends. They are not only almost completely isolated from formal community organizations but also from friendship cliques, except in their youth. They "interact minimally and lack identification even with those of their own kind."[88]

[86]Lee Rainwater, "A World of Trouble: The Pruitt-Igoe Housing Project," in Ficker and Graves, *Deprivation in America*, pp. 102–11.
[87]*Ibid.*
[88]Roach, Gross, and Gursslin, *Social Stratification in the United States*, p. 200.

A profile of a more or less typical lower-class person (outside of criminals and other outcasts) might include these traits and attitudes: He lives from day to day; he does not plan; he acts on impulse and seeks immediate gratification; he is not concerned with status advancement but with subsistence. He is fatalistic, seeing himself as trapped in a cruel, unyielding system. He profoundly distrusts the world, and is full of fears and worries.[89] He is poor not only in goods but also in interests, ambition, self-confidence, and self-esteem. He has a low level of aspiration and a low degree of confidence in his ability to control his own life. If he is religious, he is likely to be a member of a fundamentalist sect or a magical cult.

These traits have their genesis in the mother–child relationship. Middle-class mothers, says psychologist Jerome Kagan, who play with their infants and children constantly, tend to raise joyful, affectionate, parent-oriented children who are able to develop intellectually and work persistently at a given task. They lavish praise on every achievement; "The day the kid stands is like V-J Day." Lower-class mothers, in contrast, feel depressed and harassed, fatalistic about their children's potential, and only lightly committed emotionally. They do little touching and talking.[90]

Is there a "culture of poverty" that characterizes the lower class? This has been much debated. Oscar Lewis studied poor families in many countries and wrote richly detailed accounts of their lives and personalities based on numerous taped interviews. He believed there is a culture (or more strictly speaking, a subculture) of poverty, with similar traits in many nations, a "distinctive way of life, remarkably stable and persistent, passed down from generation to generation along family lines." It is cross-national because it results from "common adaptations to common problems." In London, Glasgow, Paris, New York, San Juan, and Mexico City, Lewis found "remarkable similarities in family structure, interpersonal relationships, time orientations, value systems, spending patterns, and the sense of community" among the poor.[91] The poor do not participate effectively in the major institutions of the larger society: They hate the police, distrust the government, and are cynical about the church. They evolve informal institutions as functional alternatives: Informal credit without interest, for example, is a substitute for banks and usurious money-lenders; herb cures and midwives for the mistrusted hospitals; a saint's shrine at home for the priest. Families tend to be mother-centered.

This culture of poverty, according to Lewis, is not found among peasants, primitives, or the working class; it flourishes under colonial-

[89]See Jack L. Roach, "The Crawfords: Life at the Bottom," in *Ibid.*, pp. 213–18, for a report of taped interviews with a lower-class family.
[90]*The New York Times* (April 8, 1969).
[91]*La Vida: A Puerto Rican Family in the Culture of Poverty—San Juan and New York* (New York: Random House, 1965), pp. xlii–xlviii.

ism and the early stages of industrial capitalism. It does not include all the poor, but only those whose poverty is persistent and self-perpetuating; in the United States it might include, he surmised, perhaps 20% of the poor. He saw this as a hopeful augury for the eventual elimination of poverty, because the culture of poverty is much harder to eliminate than poverty itself.[92]

Social Mobility

Social mobility is the movement of persons or groups up or down the ranking order of a social stratification system. It is the dynamic aspect of stratification, and may be seen as a source, a consequence, and an index of social change. A person who achieves complete social mobility (up or down) changes his degree of prestige and his style of life as well as his more objectively determinable occupational and economic ranking.

All systems of stratification have some degree of stability because each child is assigned his family's status at birth. And all have some mobility. Even in Imperial China, there was a saying, "It takes three generations to go from rags to riches, and three more to go from riches to rags."

People's attitudes toward social mobility vary. In Corsican villages, a man can rise to a prominent position (perhaps elsewhere) but if his grandfather was a goatherder, old-timers still regard him as a goatherder and he cannot sit in the same cafe as the landowners.[93] As Weber noted, status groups try to limit power and privilege to themselves. In a stable society they may be quite successful; an aristocracy develops and effectively controls wealth, power, and honor. If someone gains an entering wedge through wealth, he is looked down on as a parvenu, nouveau riche, a bourgeois gentilhomme. In most industrial societies, however, the self-made man is a hero, and "getting ahead" is a core value.

STRUCTURAL SOURCES OF MOBILITY

Changes in social structure that open up opportunities for mobility may have their source in violent revolution, in large-scale but peaceful revolutionary changes such as modernization, in demographic

[92]For a clear critique of the concept of a culture of poverty, see Jack L. Roach and Orville R. Gursslin, "An Evaluation of the Concept 'Culture of Poverty,'" in Roach, Gross, and Gursslin, *Social Stratification in the United States*, pp. 202–13. Roach warns against concluding in effect that "the traits of the poor are the cause of the traits of the poor."

[93]John L. Hess, "Lo, the Poor Corsican Landowner," *The New York Times* (Aug. 23, 1969).

trends, and in deliberate attempts to change the system of inequality through collective action or government policy.

Before 1917, Russia was an estate society; the rights and duties of the clergy, the hereditary nobility, urban merchants and workers, and peasants were all defined by law. The revolution destroyed this system, and there was a great deal of sudden mobility, both upward and downward, as properties were expropriated, aristocrats and intelligentsia killed or exiled. The country was changed into a vast bureaucracy under central planning. In every revolution, "the surge and sweep of power is partly directed against the family inheritance of class advantages."[94]

The peaceful revolutions of modernization inevitably change the system of stratification toward more openness and mobility. As a country industrializes, the skills it demands—its occupational structure —the skills it demands—keep changing. In the early stages, the peasantry becomes an urban proletariat, working in factories, and a middle class emerges to guide and administer the process. There is considerable mobility; farmers become urban proletarians; ambitious sons of low status families, not tied to traditional notions of prestige, may take over important positions, while the old middle or upper class may cling to traditional ways and lose status.[95] Education and training become the keys to advancement; more and more jobs open up, requiring more and more specialized training. In fifteen Latin American countries, Germani found that the relative size of the middle class was closely related to the degree of industrialization, urbanization, and literacy.[96]

This process continues in the advanced stages of industrialization. In the United States, for example, the shift from lower-class and working-class to middle-class occupations in the last two decades is illustrative. Of every 100 working adults, 49 were in unskilled or semi-skilled labor in 1950, but only 38 in 1970. While the percentages of managers, proprietors, and officials (11) and skilled workers (13) remained the same, the percentage in clerical, sales, and other white collar jobs rose from 19 to 24, and in professional and technical jobs from 8 to 14. The number of farmers and farm managers (included in managers, proprietors, and officials, above) dropped from 10 to 4 per 100 between 1957 and 1969, a substantial shift for such a short period.[97]

[94]William J. Goode, "Family and Mobility," in Bendix and Lipset, *Class, Status, and Power*, p. 582.

[95]Neil J. Smelser and Seymour Martin Lipset, eds., *Social Structure and Mobility in Economic Development* (Chicago: Aldine Publishing Company, 1966), p. 48.

[96]Glaucio Ary Dillon Soares, "Economic Development and Class Structure," in Hodge, Siegel, and Rossi, *Class, Status, and Power*, p. 196.

[97]Based on *Statistical Abstract of the United States, 1970*, pp. 225–226. Using census data on occupations for urban and rural men, Coleman and Neugarten estimate that the proportion of Americans in the middle class or higher increased from 32% in 1900 to 43% in 1960. The upper class has remained at about 1%; the upper-middle class increased from 5 to 10%; the lower-middle class from 26 to 32%. The working class decreased from 42 to 39%, and the lower class from 26 to 18% [*Social Status in the City*, p. 273].

Urbanization also contributes to the degree of mobility. Freed from local knowledge of his ancestral status, the new urban dweller finds it easier to achieve more prestige; in the anonymity of the city, old ascriptions tend to lose their power. "City air makes free."

Differential reproduction opens up opportunities. In general, the higher one goes in the social scale, the smaller the number of children per family. Even if every rich man's son stepped into his father's shoes, there was room at the top as population grew and the society became industrialized. These new high statuses had to be filled from below.

Groups may organize and struggle for a collective gain in status, as workers do through labor unions. Reformers may gain enough political power to initiate policies that improve conditions and opportunities. The franchise has been extended to more and more citizens of modern societies, as have educational systems. Governments alleviate the condition of the lowest strata through legislation providing social security, tax reforms, family allowances, medical care, unemployment insurance. Such measures reduce both inequality and *resentment* of inequality. Sociologists are studying not only the facts of mobility, but alternative policies for promoting it on the assumptions that stratification bars many with badly needed talents from achieving the positions they merit, and that political institutions should be used to create greater equality of opportunity and greater motivation for achievement.[98]

COLLECTIVE MOBILITY

Changes in the wealth, power, and prestige of whole strata or of substantial groups within them may occur through such structural changes as revolution, modernization, and reform, as well as the "class struggle" of unionization. Or a whole group may decide to change its way of life and thus rise in status according to cultural values. Some disadvantaged Indian subcastes take on the customs, rituals, and symbols of higher castes, becoming "Sanskritized." They stop eating pork or beef and change to fish or mutton, which are considered less degrading, and substitute fruit and flowers for blood offerings to their gods. Thus the Brahman way of life spreads through the society.[99]

INDIVIDUAL MOBILITY

When opportunities for individuals to rise in social class status open up in the society, who takes advantage of them? Who has the

[98]John Porter, *The Vertical Mosaic: An Analysis of Social Class and Power in Canada* (Toronto: University of Toronto Press, 1965). See also S. M. Miller and Pamela Roby, "Strategies for Social Mobility: A Policy Framework," *The American Sociologist 6*, Supplementary Issue on Sociological Research and Public Policy (June 1971): 18–22.

[99]M. N. Srinivas, "A Note on Sanskritization and Westernization," in Hodge, Siegel, and Rossi, *Class, Status, and Power*, pp. 552–60.

ability and the motivation? How does he go about the climb? How do we measure the amount of mobility?

Individual mobility may be intergenerational or intragenerational. In the first instance, a son advances or falls one or more strata from that of his father. In the second, he climbs or skids dramatically; it is a matter of individual "rags to riches" or vice versa rather than the more normal pattern of a slight shift or a steady climb up a career hierarchy.

Numerous empirical studies of intergenerational mobility based on occupational indices have established a number of generalizations. There is considerable mobility in the United States, and more of it is upward than downward. Between one-half and three-quarters of the men in professional, business, clerical or skilled jobs have climbed relative to their fathers.[100] There is also considerable mobility in other industrialized urbanized nations. In France, Germany, Switzerland, Sweden, and Japan, as in the United States, roughly a third of the sons of men in the industrial labor force achieve nonmanual positions.[101] Most upward mobility, however, occurs within the middle range of the stratification system. The sons of men in top business and professional positions "have from five to eight times more opportunity to succeed their fathers than would be the case if the structure were completely open."[102] At the extremes of upper and lower class, it is much more likely that the son will stay at the same level as his father. Most mobility is limited in extent—for example, from the working class to the lower-middle class. An unskilled worker's son rarely becomes a professional man. In an industrial society, advances in occupational status typically occur step by step through the clearly defined bureaucratic hierarchies of large formal organizations. Most upwardly mobile women, being largely dependent on their husbands for their social status, try to "marry well," and may choose "careers" as nurses or white-collar workers with one eye on opportunities for meeting desirable men. Studies reveal that daughters of manual workers who marry "upward" have already achieved education or white-collar jobs on their own.

The best predictor of mobility or lack of it is one's initial class status, for this affects not only opportunities but motivations. Only as children do we have trouble choosing between becoming an astronaut or the President; by adolescence, most of us have adjusted our sights more realistically. But in a society committed to equality of opportunity, the most serious defect of the system of social stratification is that lower-class and working-class youth lack motivation and awareness of opportunities that may actually be open to those with native ability.

[100]Joseph A. Kahl, *The American Class Structure* (New York: Holt, Rinehart & Winston, 1965), p. 272.

[101]Bendix and Lipset, *Class, Status, and Power*, p. 17.

[102]Kahl, *The American Class Structure*, p. 272.

Their aspirations are low; they seek jobs not for the satisfactions of the work itself but for quick material rewards, and measure their success by things: job security, home ownership, and money. The middle classes, in contrast, take material rewards more or less for granted, and seek education, friends, and prestige.[103]

This low level of aspiration, learned in the family and peer group, may explain the fact that even where educational opportunities have been greatly expanded, the lower classes fail to take advantage of them, as shown in studies in Great Britain and the United States.[104] One study in the Netherlands showed that even when IQ is held constant, working-class youth are greatly underrepresented in college. Forty-five per cent of male university students and 66% of females come from the upper 5% in occupational prestige; 9% of the males and 3% of the females come from the 68% of the population with the lowest occupational prestige.[105]

While the lower classes aspire not at all or only a step higher, the middle classes live in a milieu of continuous striving. Their goals beckon them ever onward, but seldom is there any assurance that they have "arrived." And if they do not arrive, achieve, accomplish, the burden of failure is their own, for they believe that they live in a land of opportunity.[106]

How does the upwardly mobile person, the "status striver," go about climbing? First of all, he seeks education and a prestigious occupation with a high income. But the economic dimension alone does not give him status honor; he must win it through changing his life style. This is easier to achieve in our swiftly changing society than in older, more stable societies. "Money must be translated into socially approved behavior and possessions, and they in turn must be translated into intimate participation with, and acceptance by, members of a superior class."[107] Physical mobility may facilitate social mobility, especially in the anonymity of large cities; in smaller places such as Elmtown, newcomers undergo a thorough grilling designed to place them socially. The striver often moves to a better neighborhood as he achieves economic success, cultivates a new group of friends, joins new clubs, and perhaps switches his religious and political affiliations as well. He may even change his name to play down his ethnic background. His wife may be an asset or a liability in his striving, depending on how well she manages their style of life. Coleman and Neugarten found "education of wife" highly correlated with social status and upward mobil-

[103]Ephraim Mizruchi, *Success and Opportunity: A Study of Anomie* (New York: The Free Press, 1964), pp. 61–90.

[104]Miller and Roby, "Strategies for Social Mobility."

[105]Study by F. van Heek in 1961, cited in Svalastoga, "Social Differentiation."

[106]Mizruchi, *Success and Opportunity*.

[107]Warner, Meeker, and Eells, *Social Class in America*, p. 21.

ity. Corporation executives usually judge the acceptability of a prospective junior executive's wife before hiring or promoting him.

An aspirant to upper-class status, perhaps newly rich, first joins charitable and cultural organizations; then he perhaps hires a social secretary who is usually a member of the upper class. He knows he has "made it" when he is nominated for membership in an exclusive club and his wife makes the Junior League. Their parents may have sent them to private schools and elite universities; in any case they consolidate their status by sending their own children to such schools. Newcomers to higher classes abandon their old values and attitudes as well as their old styles of life; in fact, strivers use the class to which they aspire as a reference group, adopting their values and attitudes and insofar as possible emulating their life styles even before they have quite been accepted.[108]

The social escalator moves down as well as up. Low intelligence and motivation, addiction to drugs and alcohol, and ill health, especially on the part of such workers as carpenters, plumbers, electricians, and painters, who work by the job or the hour, account for much downward mobility. Structural factors such as unemployment and occupational obsolescence also contribute.

Class in the Post-Industrial Society

What will happen to the system of social stratification in the post-industrial society? Social scientists have hazarded a number of guesses about the impact of automation, increased affluence, and continued rapid change.

Education will be increasingly important; the educational differences now blamed for much "class conflict" in the United States may become wider, as knowledge and up-to-date information and skill become ever more important and demand continued retraining. The proportion of technical and professional workers will continue to rise. As affluence increases, income may not serve as a reliable criterion of status. People will work fewer hours as industry becomes increasingly automated, and their work will be relieved of much of the dirt and physical effort that now distinguishes manual from nonmanual labor. Their roles as consumers will be more important than their roles as producers, but in a swiftly changing society with much physical mobility, status groups will not form; perhaps people will evolve their own distinctive styles of life. The use of leisure time rather than occupation and similar income will draw people of common interests together. New service industries, creative arts, recreation, and entertainment will employ many more people proportionately than in our present work-and-production—oriented society.

[108]Domhoff, *Who Rules America?*, pp. 22, 140.

As expertise becomes more important and the scale of economic and political organization continues to increase in size, power will become more concentrated. Some foresee an unprecedented social structure of an elite of experts and a huge mass of nonspecialized machine-tenders who can easily be switched from job to job. Others see a diamond-shaped social structure, with an elite of experts and executives comprising about 12 to 15% of the population, a small lower class of unskilled or unemployed workers and welfare recipients, and a huge, amorphous middle class without important differentiations.

The one thing no one predicts is perfect equality of wealth, power, and prestige. Does anyone really want it? The upper classes obviously want to hang on to their privileges. The middle classes think in terms of individual achievement and rewards. The working class wants things to be better, but fears equality. Robert E. Lane, in extensive interviews with stable blue-collar workers, found that they tended toward a functionalist view: "If everyone were equal," said one, "who would bother to train to be a doctor?" Said another, "Who would dig our sewers?" The lower classes live from day to day, seeing themselves trapped in a hopeless system. Who, then, champions equality? Very few, says Lane, and they are mostly professionals—lawyers, ministers, and teachers; but most of them preach equality of *opportunity* rather than perfect equality.[109]

Inequality, in fact, according to one point of view,

> is the dynamic impulse that keeps social structures alive. Inequality always implies the gain of one group at the expense of others; thus every system of social stratification generates protest against its principles and bears the seeds of its own suppression. . . . There is certainly reason to regret that children are ashamed of their parents, that people are anxious and poor, that they suffer and are made unhappy, and many other consequences of inequality. There are also many good reasons to strive against . . . arbitrary forces that erect insuperable barriers of caste or estate between men. The very existence of social inequality, however, is an impetus toward liberty because it guarantees a society's ongoing, dynamic, historical quality.[110]

Only through totalitarianism can the appearance of a classless society be created; a free society must have both equality of citizenship and inequalities of status. And such inequalities need not mean that anyone lacks such basic necessities as adequate food, shelter, and health care.

[109]"The Fear of Equality," from *Political Ideology: Why the American Common Man Believes What He Does*, reprinted in Louise K. Howe, *The White Majority: Between Poverty & Affluence* (New York: Random House, Inc., 1971), pp. 119–47. Many blacks, students, and women appear to have equality as their chief goal.

[110]Ralf Dahrendorf, "On the Origins of Inequality Among Men," in Edward O. Laumann, Paul M. Siegel, and Robert W. Hodge, eds., *The Logic of Social Hierarchies* (Chicago: Markham Publishing Company, 1970), p. 30.

Summary

Social stratification is an institutionalized system of social inequality in a community or society that ranks families in categories or strata according to their share of scarce and desirable values such as wealth, prestige, and power. It arises from the processes of differentiation and evaluation according to criteria that can be applied to families. It is found in all societies except some small and simple ones.

In caste systems, strata are hereditary, endogamous, and permanent, sanctioned by religion and mores, and upheld by economic interdependence. Estate systems depend on hereditary relationships to land, defined by law, and ascription of status is nearly as permanent as in caste systems. Open-class systems stress individual achievement; they have considerable mobility and blurring of stratum boundaries, and are justified by belief in equality of opportunity. Modernization generally breaks up estate and caste systems and moves a society toward an open-class system.

Karl Marx saw stratification as based on the institution of private property, which will be abolished in the class struggle that will eventually and inevitably bring about the classless utopia of communism. Functionalists consider inequality a device by which societies achieve the best division of labor according to ability; their theory has been criticized as one of differentiation rather than stratification. Max Weber saw stratification as multi-dimensional: Class is objective economic fact, and largely determines life chances; status is honor or prestige within a community, and leads to the formation of status groups with similar life styles supported by similar incomes; and party is power over collective decisions. These three dimensions of stratification are often highly correlated and work to reinforce one another.

Most sociologists base their research on Weber rather than on Marx or the functionalists, but some are more interested in one dimension than another. Economic inequality, and especially poverty and the concentration of wealth, has received considerable attention in recent years; it appears that economic distribution in the United States has stayed about the same since the end of World War II, although the general level of living has risen. Studies of status honor find that people do think in terms of social classes and use them as a map of social reality. In small communities status judgments are personal and subjective, but in large cities very similar rankings are arrived at through more impersonal clues. On the national level, occupation is the best index of prestige. According to many scholars, the third dimension, party, or power over social and economic arrangements and political decisions, tends to be concentrated at the upper levels, especially in national economic and political affairs, and more pluralistic at state and local levels; but the majority of people have little power and take little interest in decision-making or policy.

One's life chances—opportunities for long life, health, education, safety, self-determination, and dignity—are directly correlated with social status. The various strata also have different subcultural patterns—consumption styles, patterns of social participation, values, and attitudes. Religious and political affiliations, recreational patterns, and family relationships also vary according to class status.

Bringing together the main stratification variables and their consequences, we may define a social class as a category of people with similar amounts of wealth, prestige, and power, and similar life chances and ways of life, who tend to recognize one another as equals and those in other categories as superior or inferior. In the class structure of the United States, boundaries are clearest for the 1% in the upper class and the 16 to 20% in the lower class. The upper class is mainly a business aristocracy, freely intermarrying and interacting across the nation. A power elite includes many of the upper class and others who have high positions in institutions controlled by the upper class.

About 10% of Americans are upper-middle class; career advancement is their central value. The lower-middle class of about 32% is concerned with hard work, respectability, thrift, honor, and decency. Middle-class values are the core American values.

The working class includes the 40% of Americans who work at skilled or semi-skilled manual jobs. They participate less than the higher classes in voluntary organizations and formal and informal groups, limiting their social interaction largely to peer groups and kin. They tend to think in terms of concrete and practical details, to limit their aspirations, and to feel increasing resentment and alienation because they believe they are losing ground in comparison to other groups.

The lower class includes many different kinds of people who have not made it into the industrial working class or have skidded down for various reasons. Although they distrust the world and are full of fears and worries, they live from day to day and do not plan ahead. Some exhibit the traits of a culture of poverty transmitted from generation to generation, manifesting itself in many countries through similar responses to similar conditions.

Social mobility, or movement up and down the system of social stratification, may be fostered by revolution; by industrialization with its demand for an educated, skilled labor force; by struggles for collective gains through such organizations as labor unions; and by political reforms. People rise or fall in the scale according to their level of aspiration and opportunities for education, both of which depend largely on initial class status. Most industrial societies have about the same amount of intergenerational mobility. Individual mobility is complete when one has achieved not only the education, occupational prestige, and income (whether less or more than formerly) of a different stratum, but has also adopted its values and life style.

Predictions of stratification in post-industrial society generally take account of the increased need for expertise, of the impact of automation, and of increased leisure and physical mobility. Pictures of future class structures differ, but only utopian ones portray a completely egalitarian society; and it appears that few if any people really want one. Our cultural myth and liberal values stress equality as citizens and equality of opportunity to rise as high in the social scale as one's abilities and motivations permit.

In the next chapter we shall look at the parallel and interrelated system of social stratification by criteria of race, religion, and nationality background.

QUESTIONS FOR FURTHER THOUGHT

1. Suppose you were stuck in an elevator with a stranger for half an hour. What clues would help you place him in the system of social stratification? What questions would you ask?

2. To what class do you belong? Has your family risen in social status? Fallen? Why? Do you aspire to another class? Why? How do you plan to change your status?

3. Some social commentators foresee an elite based on merit, especially education. Do you think such an elite would be preferable to an aristocracy? In such a "meritocracy," would people who failed to climb feel better or worse than in an ascribed or partially ascribed system?

4. European societies take public assistance to the poor for granted; United States citizens either attack it as "something for nothing" or rationalize it under the guise of providing more opportunities to climb. Relate this to cultural myths and values.

5. Theories are often time-bound and culture-bound. They are often also dialogues, attempts to provide alternative explanations and refute unsatisfactory ones. Discuss in connection with Marx, Weber, and the functionalists.

6. We often think of Sweden as a relatively classless society; but 70% of the Swedes say headwaiters treat them differently depending on class, and 45% say policemen do. Construct a small experiment to test this in your community.

7. The Prime Minister of Sweden said there are automatic forces that work to widen social and economic differences, and governments must always be dealing with them. What do you think these forces include? How can governments deal with them?

8. Study an issue of a weekly newsmagazine or a newspaper. Identify issues that have to do with social class conflict. Which of these are conflicts between different distributive systems, in Lenski's concept?

9. Some sociologists say the level of aspiration in the lower and working classes is too low to allow our society to use all its potential talent. Others say the level is realistic given the opportunities, and aspiration should not be too distant from actual chances. Are these views necessarily contradictory?

10. Psychologists report that poor black children ages 6 to 9 in Manhattan have no greater incidence of psychological impairment than other groups; but between age 9 and adolescence the rate rises sharply, from 4 to 28%. Has this chapter provided clues to the reasons?

11. Inconsistency between ascribed and achieved statuses has been correlated with mental illness. Which do you think might be more subject to personality disorganization and erosion of self-esteem—a poor white or a Negro surgeon? Why?

12. How do you account for the high prestige accorded a Justice of the Supreme Court? A physician? (For speculation on this subject, see Werner Cohn, in Roach, Gross, and Gursslin, *Social Stratification in the United States*, pp. 65–71.)

13. In the Soviet Union physicians rank low in prestige and earn less than skilled factory workers. They have no choice over where they work and no power to set fees;

70% are women. Are any of these facts related, in your opinion? An attempt to raise their prestige by inaugurating a Soviet version of the Hippocratic oath is reported; do you think this is an effective approach?

14. Drug abuse was not given much priority as a social problem until the middle classes became involved. Explain in terms of the stratification system.

15. Some social scientists object to the idea of class subcultures on the grounds that subcultures emerge from group interaction and not simply as common responses to similar conditions. Check back on the definitions of cultures and subcultures in Chapters 3 and 4 to decide which position you will take.

16. What picture of China's class structure has emerged since President Nixon's visit in 1972? How was the change from pre-revolutionary patterns brought about?

17. In what sense is power over collective decisions also power over individual decisions?

10

Remember when you say, "I will have none
of this exile and this stranger
For his face is not like my face and his
speech is strange,"
You have denied America with that word.

STEPHEN VINCENT BENET

Give me your tired, your poor,
Your huddled masses yearning to breathe
   free,
The wretched refuse of your teeming shore,
Send these, the homeless, tempest-tossed,
   to me;
I lift my lamp beside the golden door.

EMMA LAZARUS
Inscription on The Statue of Liberty

Our nation is moving toward two societies,
one black, one white—separate and unequal.
. . . The alternative is the realization of
common opportunities for all within a single
society.

*Report of the National Advisory
Commission on Civil Disorders*

All we want is for America to be what it
says it is.

THE HONORABLE JOHN CONYERS,
CONGRESSMAN FROM MICHIGAN

INTERGROUP
RELATIONS
AND
AMERICAN
MINORITIES

M̲OST MODERN SOCIETIES ARE MULTIGROUP SOCIETIES as well as class societies. And in most, people are far more intensely conscious of racial, religious, nationality, and cultural differences than of class differences—more aware they belong to such groups, more hostile to members of others. This ethnocentrism sets "us" off from "them"— believers from infidels, civilized men from savages, blacks from whites. Some of these antagonisms are the heritage of colonialism; many arise as the establishment of new nation-states brings under one flag different tribes, language groups, religions, and "races," and as modernization brings them into contact and competition.

Religious differences divide the Hindus and Moslems of northern India, who are alike racially and culturally. Canadians are divided according to Anglo-Saxon or French backgrounds. Language divides the Flemings and Walloons of Belgium. Race is the major line of cleavage in Rhodesia and South Africa as well as in the United States. According to Soviet authorities, the enormous expanse of the Soviet Union embraces 169 different national-cultural groups, including Buddhists, Mongols, desert nomads, about 12 million Moslems, the intensely ethnocentric Ukrainians, and Russians, who comprise half the population and hold most of the power, playing "elder brother" to the rest.

Such differences do not always lead to tension and conflict. Switzerland, with its three national divisions, and Hawaii, with its many "races," as well as the Netherlands, with a sizeable group of Asian immigrants, demonstrate that people of diverse backgrounds can live together peaceably. But in many other societies racial, national, and religious differences are expressed in prejudice and hatred; in discrimination, oppression, and even genocide; in riots and civil war. Nazi Germany exterminated 6 million Jews. When Pakistan was set up as a Moslem state in 1947, Hindus fled across the new border to India, Moslems to Pakistan—a total of 10 million refugees; and before the dust had settled, 1 million died. The same antagonisms led to war and the division of Pakistan in 1972. Catholics and Protestants live in hatred and terror in Northern Ireland. Three-and-a-half million Jews in the Soviet Union suffer various kinds of job discrimination and slurs, and are regarded as outsiders and even as potential traitors; they are not allowed to emigrate freely and do not enjoy cultural autonomy as do

Reprinted by permission of Cartoon Features Syndicate.

Armenians and Ukrainians. The new nation of Kenya had to set up twenty different tribal provinces. Even Israel, haven for millions fleeing persecution, suffers from misunderstandings among Jews from all over the world who look different, speak different languages, have brought different customs to their new home, and disagree on religious beliefs. And in the United States social cohesion and domestic tranquility are seriously threatened by the explosive mixture of racial discrimination with inequalities of class, status, and party.

The problem of intergroup conflicts, furthermore, is international in scope. Many of the two-thirds of the world's people who are nonwhite define the present situation as a gigantic conflict with the dominant whites who for centuries ruled their countries and treated them as "natives"—a conflict that may result not in equality and harmony, but in a turning of the tables.

In this chapter we can touch upon only the salient facets of this huge and pressing problem. First, we inquire into the nature and sources of prejudice and discrimination. We next examine several patterns of intergroup relations. Then we sketch the structure of intergroup relations in the United States—its division along the lines of national background, religious affiliation, and "race."

In the remainder of the chapter our attention will be focused on American minority groups, especially black Americans. After a brief sketch of their history in the New World and the consequences of their status, we inquire into the social structure and culture of the black subsociety. Finally, we outline possible goals in interracial relations, and various means for reaching them.

The reasons for this emphasis are perhaps obvious. Not only do blacks comprise 11% of the population; not only have they suffered discrimination more oppressive and pervasive than that accorded any other minority group (with the possible exception of Indians); but also their recent demands have challenged our social structure and our system of national priorities so sharply that many consider race relations our most urgent problem. In addition, the story of black–white relationships and of black Americans' struggle for equality throws into relief many aspects of culture and social structure, and the processes of cooperation, competition, conflict, accommodation, and assimilation. Above all it emphasizes the great importance of beliefs and values in guiding social interaction—that "The solid facts of life are the facts of the imagination."

Prejudice and Discrimination

Comparisons among groups, like those among classes, are rooted in the human tendency to differentiate among people, things, and ideas, to evaluate them, to put them in categories, and to rank them as equal, inferior, and superior. We are all bundles of prejudices in this sense: We pre-judge. Instead of withholding judgment of a person until we know him and can evaluate him on the basis of his individual qualities, we believe we know what he is like because he belongs to a category —"they're all like that."

Prejudice carries an emotional freight, favorable or unfavorable. Perhaps we are prepared to like all Englishmen and hate all Turks. And prejudice embodies an attitude, a readiness to act in a certain way toward all members of a category.

When we speak of intergroup relations we usually use the term "prejudice" to mean a *negative* pre-judgment of some group on the basis of its race, religion, or national background. **Intergroup prej-**

udice may be defined as an attitude of hostility or rejection based on faulty and inflexible generalizations about a group or category of people, every member of which is presumed to share the group's objectionable qualities. It is this kind of prejudice that produces fear, suspicion, revulsion, and hate.

The belief that all members of a category are "like that" is a **stereotype**, a picture we carry in our heads whether or not we know any members of the category. "Do not obtain your slaves from Britain," Cicero warned Atticus in the first century B.C., "because they are so stupid and so utterly incapable of being taught that they are not fit to form a part of the household of Athens." The ideas that all redheads are trigger-tempered, all fat men jolly, all professors absent-minded, and all Scots thrifty are stereotypes. So is the upper-middle-class liberal's idea that all white members of the working class are racist bigots.

Like other generalizations, stereotypes simplify our psychological processes by economizing on perception and cutting down on the labor of thinking. In intergroup relations, they also serve to justify and explain our behavior (favorable or otherwise) toward a group. The word "stereotype" is borrowed from the metal molds for printing and thus suggests something rigid; and indeed stereotypes are so persistent that they seldom yield to new knowledge. At the same time, the irrational, emotional content of prejudice makes us quite capable of admiring certain behavior in a group we like and condemning the very same behavior in a group we dislike. If Abe Lincoln worked far into the night, this testifies that he was industrious and resolute, determined to exercise his capacities to the fullest extent. If Abe Cohen or Abe Kurokawa does the same, says Robert Merton, this testifies to the sweatshop mentality of Jews and Japanese. "Is the in-group hero frugal, thrifty, and sparing? Then the out-group villain is stingy, miserly, and penny-pinching."[1] We also apply contradictory stereotypes to the same group, depending on the situation or even a minute shift in conversation. In almost the same breath an anti-Semite can with perfect comfort charge Jews with "clannishness" (sticking to themselves) and "pushiness" (wanting to intrude in other groups).

DISCRIMINATION

While prejudice refers to how we think of and are disposed to act toward the members of certain groups or categories, **discrimination** refers to overt behavior, to the way we actually *do* act toward them. It has been defined by the United Nations as "any *conduct* based on a distinction made on the grounds of natural or social categories which have no relation either to individual capacities or merits, or to the concrete behavior of the individual person."[2] It usually implies *unfavorable*

[1] *Social Theory and Social Structure*, rev. ed. (New York: The Free Press, 1968), p. 482.

[2] *The Main Types and Causes of Discrimination.* United Nations Publication 14, No. 9 (1949). Emphasis added.

conduct based on prejudice against some ascribed status group: women, youth, blacks, Moslems, untouchables.

Discrimination may involve political and legal barriers; it invariably involves social and economic barriers. Among forms of discrimination *officially* practiced in various societies, the United Nations lists inequalities in: legal rights, political participation, and personal security; housing, recreation, and health services; freedom of movement, residence, thought, religion, communication, and peaceful association; and finally choice of employment, enjoyment of the right to marry and found a family, and opportunity for education and "cultural" participation. In addition, the U.N. points to official approval of such indignities as forced labor, special taxes, sumptuary laws (forbidding the wearing of certain clothing, for example), public libel, and the forced wearing of distinguishing marks.

Officially outlawed, discrimination often continues unofficially. A personnel manager may tell a black applicant that he would not want him to be embarrassed by prejudiced employees, or he may "regret" that the requirements of the job have changed since the ad was placed—and yet the ad continues to run unchanged. A realtor may be reluctant to sell blacks houses in white neighborhoods, for fear of economic losses by loss of cooperation from other realtors.

Segregation—isolation of one group from another—sets up barriers to interaction. If extreme, this form of discrimination makes other forms "unnecessary," so to speak, for there are no opportunities for unwanted contacts. Such segregation characterizes colonialism: Parks and residential areas in Canton, for example, once bore signs, "Dogs and Chinese not allowed." Even when less extreme, segregation in housing, schools, churches, and clubs isolates groups and thus increases chances for the formation of unfavorable stereotypes. In their studies of Elmira, New York, where law and public policy are firmly set against public segregation and discrimination, a group of Cornell investigators found that the members of various categories "tended to follow beaten social paths that did not often intersect with the paths of other groups. . . . For most persons, such paths were narrow walks of life that exposed them to only a few limited social environments."[3]

THE RELATIONSHIP BETWEEN PREJUDICE AND DISCRIMINATION

There may be prejudice without discrimination; there may even be discrimination without personal prejudice, although this is not very common. As we saw in our discussion of status and role, pressures from third parties, real or imagined, guide conduct. A person may wish to

[3]Robin M. Williams, Jr., *Strangers Next Door: Ethnic Relations in American Communities* (Englewood Cliffs, N.J.: Prentice-Hall, Inc., 1964), pp. 141–42.

sell his house to blacks but hesitate because the neighbors would be angry with him; thus he may discriminate although he has little or no prejudice and even wants blacks to be free to buy wherever they find a suitable house. On the other hand, a prejudiced person may decide he "cannot afford" to discriminate. In the authors' neighborhood, where the first black residents caused a flurry of excitement, one woman admitted that she did not like the idea of black neighbors, but said that her husband's work required that he get along with blacks, and moving away could stigmatize him as prejudiced. (She later became good friends with her black neighbors, her prejudice declined, and after twelve years she still lives there—which illustrates one of the principles we shall discuss later concerning reduction of intergroup tensions!)

The looseness of the correlation between prejudice and discrimination is illustrated by a classic experiment by a white American social psychologist, Richard LaPiere. In the 1930s he traveled widely in the United States with a Chinese couple, stopping at 66 sleeping places and 184 eating places. They were refused service only once. Yet when the proprietors of these same places were asked in letters if they would take "members of the Chinese race" as customers, more than 9 out of 10 said they would not. A control group of places LaPiere and his friends had not visited gave similar replies.[4]

Other experiments corroborate the proposition that verbal expressions of discrimination may not result in actual discrimination. Most prejudiced people, when challenged with a face-to-face situation, prefer not to create a scene, especially where they do not have the support of a powerful group and are aware that they would be violating core values if they engaged in discriminatory behavior.

RACISM AND DISCRIMINATION

The words "racist" and "racism" have been rather commonly and loosely used in recent years, especially to account for the problems of American blacks. "White racism" is said to be the evil in men's hearts that permeates all institutions and is at the root of discrimination, conflict, and violent protest; the Kerner Report (the report of the President's National Advisory Commission on Civil Disorders, appointed after the destructive riots of the summer of 1967) used the term in this way. But there is danger of its becoming a catch-all epithet, and being regarded as the one cause of all the problems in the complex race-relations scene. It therefore bears analysis.

Michael Banton defines racism as "the doctrine that a man's behavior is determined by stable inherited characters deriving from separate racial stocks having distinctive attributes and usually considered to stand to one another in relations of superiority and inferiority."[5]

[4]"Attitudes versus Action," *Social Forces* 13 (1934): 230–37.
[5]*Race and Racialism* (London: Tavistock, 1970), p. 18.

The doctrine originated as a serious scientific theory in the 1800s, even though on present evidence it seems naive. It was seized upon as a convenient and conscience-easing justification of colonial exploitation and discrimination, which had to be reconciled somehow with the ideals of Western civilization—Christianity, equality, and democracy. It assured the dominant nations that the man of dark skin, who was also "native, barbarian, heathen, and slave,"[6] was naturally inferior to the white man, who was destined to rule and lead by inborn right of superior endowments. It justified their **racialism**, the expression of racist beliefs through discriminatory practices.

From belief in racist doctrine, it was only a step toward the following corollaries. Any individual of the superior race must be superior to any individual of the inferior race; biological crossing leads to degeneration or "mongrelization," and therefore it is safest to forbid social contact between the races. Racism also breeds a fear and suspicion that the inferior race, which is being held back, wants to encroach on the power and privileges of the master race.[7]

There *are* obvious physical differences among the earth's people—in the chemical composition that colors their skins, in hair texture and curl, in stature, in the shape of the eyelid fold, and so on. But there are no "pure" races, only arbitrary categories or pigeonholes man has constructed, with a great deal of overlapping. There is, furthermore, no proven relationship between race and innate intelligence, as diligently as some people have sought such proof. Cultural achievements are not related to inborn differences, for when the now-dominant Europeans were living in a comparatively primitive fashion, Africans were working iron and Chinese civilization astounded Marco Polo and other adventurers. People classified as belonging to the same "race" have great disparities in culture. Changes over time provide further proof: The warlike Vikings and the pacifist Swedes come from the same gene pool, perhaps slightly altered over the centuries by intermarriage. Men are, then, all one species, with no pure races but a few minor biological differences that have no correlation with intelligence or culture.

Why, then, do we treat these minor differences in a sociology text? Because people *think* they are important, and use them as cues to guide their interaction. The American definition of "Negro" is a prime example of the fact that racist fallacies can be sociologically important. Over the centuries, black women were subject to the sexual whims of men of the dominant caste, and as a result, many people now classed as black have more "white blood" than black. Yet if they have one known black ancestor they are said to be black. "In no other

[6]Robert Redfield, "Ethnic Relations, Primitive and Civilized," in Jitsuichi Masuoka and Preston Valien, eds., *Race Relations: Problems and Theory* (Chapel Hill: University of North Carolina Press, 1961), p. 36.

[7]Herbert Blumer, "Race Prejudice as a Sense of Group Position," in Masuoka and Valien, *Race Relations*, p. 217 ff.

area of biology would we reason similarly. Imagine a dog breeder saying, 'Most of this pup's forebears were cocker spaniels, but he's really a Doberman pinscher'—meaning that one of his great-grandparents was."[8]

Biological nonsense this may be, but as W. I. Thomas, a pioneer American sociologist, said, "If men define situations as real, they are real in their consequences." The social definition of a black puts all people with "Negro blood" in a category that is marked off as different and—in the minds of racists—inferior, and hence to be discriminated against. For the purposes of social interaction and social relationships, a person is a black, or a Jew, or a white man *if others in the society think he is.*

Because the once-scientific biological basis of racism has been quite thoroughly discredited, Banton would prefer to call racism "ethnocentrism." And, it is, obviously, one type of ethnocentrism. However, since prejudice by definition is based on an inflexible generalization that does not yield to new knowledge, people continue to think in terms of race. Many, in fact, still believe the racist doctrine of inborn and ineradicable differences; others, equally prejudiced and discriminatory, seek justification elsewhere. Even when they disavow racist doctrines, they point to cultural and class variations that threaten law and order, for example. Just as bits of biology were used 100 years ago (and still are by some), so bits of sociology, psychology, and anthropology are now used to justify discrimination.[9]

SOURCES OF PREJUDICE AND DISCRIMINATION

Where does prejudice come from? Why does it persist? Why is discrimination practiced and perpetuated? We have already suggested that the roots of prejudice lie in the human tendency to differentiate and evaluate, generalize, and categorize. We also suggested that racist doctrines were seized upon—as certain interpretations of Scripture had also been used—to justify colonialism and slavery.

Prejudice and discrimination do help to perpetuate the wealth, prestige, and power of a dominant group. Economic gains are obvious enough in the case of colonial exploitation and slave labor, and the high rents and low wages of a caste or pseudocaste system; the dominant group also escapes such drudgery as cotton picking or housework. The men of a dominant majority often enjoy sexual gains as well, for they have access to low-status women but shield their own. And finally, all members of the dominant caste experience a prestige gain; the poorest white coal miner feels superior to the best educated black.

[8]Raymond W. Mack, *Race, Class, and Power*, 2nd ed. (New York: American Book Company, 1968), p. 104.
[9]Banton, *Race and Racialism*, pp. 31–33.

Almost always, the minority serves as a scapegoat. Just as Aaron called down upon a goat all the sins of Israel and sent it off into the wilderness (Leviticus 16:20–22), so a dominant group places the blame for anything that goes wrong on a minority group. Whenever anything caused the Roman populace to grow restless and critical of its rulers, the cry was "To the lions with the Christians!" Hitler whipped a latent sentiment of anti-Semitism to such a frenzy that many of his followers really believed the Jews were responsible for all of Germany's problems.

Prejudice may persist because certain people or groups want it to persist. The British, for example, encouraged Hindu–Moslem hatreds, following the principle of "divide and rule," and established separate waiting rooms and drinking fountains for each group.

A sense of threat is often associated with intensified prejudice. A group may come to feel entitled to its advantages, fearful when another group competes for them. Panamanians, for example, have a racist prejudice against West Indian black immigrants and their descendants—although Panama itself has a large percentage of native-born, Spanish-speaking blacks—largely because the West Indians speak English and thus have an economic advantage with the Canal Zone Americans.

Once a prejudice is rooted, it has the inertia and persistence of any cultural belief. It tends to go on under its own power, so to speak. A person who has never seen a black man accepts the stereotype. And since the separate social worlds of the various groups keep interaction at a minimum, the "equal status contacts in pursuit of common goals" that are so effective in reducing prejudice just do not occur.

In discussing the persistence of prejudice and discrimination, it is impossible to escape the formula of the vicious circle. As a visiting Irish observer remarked, "The haughty American nation makes the Negro clean its boots and then proves the inferiority of the Negro by the fact that he is a bootblack." Merton has called such vicious circles "self-fulfilling prophecies."

Individuals and prejudice.   How do individuals become prejudiced? Why are some more intensely prejudiced and more actively discriminatory than others?

Although people all tend to differentiate and evaluate, prejudice against any one outgroup is not inborn. A group prejudice is learned in a natural, informal way, along with other items of culture, as part of the process of socialization in family, church, school, and peer group. A person may accept it uncritically along with other cultural or subcultural norms; he may adopt it because he aspires to a group that will not accept him if he does not conform. One sociologist remarked that it would take as much courage for the average white Mississippian to reject openly the idea of white supremacy as it would for him, a northern college professor, actively to oppose school integration.

The power of culture to shape prejudices and stereotypes was vividly demonstrated in the 1920s by the "social distance" tests devised by Emory Bogardus. Respondents were asked to indicate which of seven degrees of social intimacy they would accept for various groups. Would they admit them "to close kinship by marriage"; "to my club as personal chums"; "to my street as neighbors"; "to employment in my occupation"; "to citizenship in my country"; "as visitors only to my country"; and finally, would they "exclude them from my country"?

All groups across the country, regardless of such variables as region, income, occupation, and education, indicated about the same pattern of preference. True, each minority rated itself high on the list, but it rated all *other* groups just about the same way that white Gentiles rated them. That is, English, native white Americans, and Canadians were considered most acceptable, followed by French, Germans, Norwegians, Swedes, and other North Europeans; then Spaniards, Italians, South and East Europeans, and Jews; and finally, Negroes, Japanese, Chinese, Hindus, and Turks. Negroes rated Jews just about the same as did white Gentiles. Thus even for minorities, the standards of the dominant majority served as a frame of reference.[10]

Within each group, individuals vary in the emotional content of their prejudices and in why they discriminate. A "good gentle person who wouldn't hurt a fly" may calmly and uncritically accept the stereotype of an outgroup as an accurate description of fact and therefore accept and support the status quo. A hostile, authoritarian person may embrace the stereotype and enthusiastically engage in discriminatory behavior because it satisfies his emotional needs. Nonetheless, it appears that intergroup prejudice may more profitably be approached as a sociological rather than an individual problem, one based on cultural norms and having its roots in social structure.[11]

Patterns of Intergroup Relations

Turning now from beliefs, attitudes, and values, and the discriminatory actions often associated with prejudice, let us examine the patterns of social relationships among different groups in multi-group societies. We may distinguish four general patterns as ideal types: the melting pot,

[10]E. S. Bogardus, *Immigration and Race Attitudes* (Boston: D. C. Heath, 1928), pp. 13–29. Later studies by Bogardus and others have had substantially the same results.

[11]For a vivid portrait of a person whose emotional needs seem to coincide with the subcultural norms of his group, and especially those of the Ku Klux Klan, see Stewart Alsop, "Portrait of a Klansman," *Saturday Evening Post* (April 9, 1966): 23–27; reprinted in Howard E. Freeman and Norman R. Kurtz, eds., *America's Troubles: A Casebook on Social Conflict* (Englewood Cliffs, N.J.: Prentice-Hall, Inc., 1969), pp. 53–61.

majority dominance and minority subordination, pluralism, and integration. In modern societies various mixtures of these patterns exist, both as ideal goals and as actualities.

THE MELTING POT

Around the turn of the century, the "American dream" was that a new man would be forged in the crucible of a new nation through cultural assimilation, intimate interaction, and biological amalgamation. In 1908 Israel Zangwill wrote a drama, *The Melting Pot*, in which he portrayed the various poor and oppressed peoples of Europe come to the "fires of God" to be made into "the American." All distinctions were to be erased, and a homogeneous type would emerge through "Americanization." This myth was echoed recently in the Kerner Report, which stated as the American goal "the creation of a true union— a single society and a single American identity." To some extent Mexico has been a melting pot in which Spanish and Indian people and cultures have produced a new blend called "mestizo." But for most of the rest of the world the complete assimilation of a "melting pot" is considered an undesirable if not a nightmarish goal or an impossible dream.

MAJORITY-DOMINANCE SITUATIONS

The pattern of a dominant majority and a subordinate minority (or minorities) was typical of colonialism, and is perhaps the most prevalent pattern today, regardless of lip service to other ideals. It is the pattern from which American race relations are emerging, and hence demands our special attention.

A **minority** is a category of people in a political unit such as a nation-state who (1) are subordinate in power to the majority (even though, like the Bantus of South Africa, they may far outnumber them); (2) can be distinguished on the basis of physical or cultural characteristics; (3) are collectively regarded and treated as different and inferior on the basis of these characteristics; and (4) are excluded from full participation in the society and therefore have poorer life chances and fewer rights and privileges than the majority.

The dominant majority may adopt one of three policies, officially or unofficially. At one extreme it may seek to annihilate the minority, to drive them out, or to isolate them on reservations or in camps. At the other extreme, it may seek to incorporate them into the society, usually on condition that they abandon their own culture and conform to that of the dominant group. Cultural assimilation may then be followed by biological amalgamation. Americans treated the Indians (and the Japanese in wartime relocation camps) according to the first extreme, most European immigrants according to the other.

More commonly, however, the dominant majority seeks to "keep them in their place" through discrimination and segregation within the society. Slavery is an extreme version of this pattern, and still exists in Saudi Arabia and some African nations.[12] Another stringent policy is that of *apartheid* or separateness in South Africa, where blacks are restricted to certain areas, forced to carry passbooks, and subjected to severe sanctions for infringement of the rules against socializing and curfews (as are whites!). More informally, the Eta or Burakumin caste of Japan—physically indistinguishable from other Japanese—are kept in ghettos and confined to traditionally "defiling" occupations such as butchering and leather work by the custom of investigating family backgrounds before marriage.[13]

Pierre van den Berghe has constructed a typology that relates the discrimination–segregation policy of majority dominance to traditional and modern societies. He sees the *paternalism* of a traditional pre-industrial society as one end of a continuum, with the *competitive* relationships of an industrial society at the other. As a society modernizes, the accommodation of paternalism gives way to tension and conflict.

Under paternalism there is an unbreachable gap between the small ruling aristocracy and the subordinate minority (or lower caste) of black slaves, Indian peones in Latin America, or colonized "natives." Most of the minority are agricultural or pastoral workers with little division of labor; some are house servants in close contact with their masters. The upper caste are benevolent despots who believe that their inferiors are eternal children, lovable but irresponsible, to be treated kindly but firmly. An elaborate set of rules governing interaction serves as "the primary mechanism of social control to maintain intimacy of contact coupled with status inequality."[14]

The "racial etiquette" of the South was such a set of rules. John Dollard described the system as it persisted in small Southern towns in the 1930s, when a member of the white caste had "an automatic right to demand forms of behavior from Negroes which serve[d] to increase his own self-esteem."[15] For example, in a conversation with a white man, a black shuffled his feet, held his hat in his hand, agreed constantly: "Sho' nuff; yes, boss." Blacks could enter "white folks'" houses only by the back door, and had to step off the sidewalk as whites approached. They were addressed by name but never by titles

---

[12]"Slavery Still Plagues the Earth," editorial, *Saturday Review* (May 6, 1967): 24.

[13]George DeVos and Hiroshi Wagatsuma, *Japan's Invisible Race: Caste in Culture and Personality* (Berkeley and Los Angeles: University of California Press, 1967).

[14]"Paternalistic versus Competitive Race Relations: An Ideal-Type Approach," in Bernard Segal, ed., *Racial and Ethnic Relations: Selected Readings* (New York: Thomas Y. Crowell, 1966), pp. 53–69.

[15]*Caste and Class in a Southern Town*, 3rd ed. (New York: Doubleday & Company, Inc., 1957), p. 174.

of respect such as "Mr." or "Mrs.," although a preacher might be "Professor" and an old woman "Auntie." Blacks had to be more than polite; they had to be "actively obliging and submissive." This deference made the white man feel comfortable; it assured him there was no hostility toward him.

And indeed, under paternalistic patterns, most of the lower caste are accommodated to their status most of the time. But as agrarian economies move toward industrialization, interracial relations change toward the competitive type. An industrialized urban society needs skilled, technically trained people and cannot depend on ascribed statuses for supplying them.

Although caste is dysfunctional for an industrializing society, it does not disappear at once. There is still a color bar, but as differences in education, occupation, income, standards of living, death rates, etc., decrease, there is more and more class differentiation within each color caste. "The status gap *between* castes tends to diminish and the status range *within* the castes tends to increase."[16] This often creates a feeling of "status panic" among lower-class members of the upper caste, as reflected in the virulent race prejudice found among poor whites in the United States, who feel they are competing for scarce values, such as jobs and housing, and fear loss of prestige. The stereotype of the member of the inferior caste changes. Under paternalism he is regarded as "childish, immature, exuberant, uninhibited, lazy, impulsive, fun-loving, good-humored; inferior but lovable." In the competitive situation he is seen as "aggressive, uppity, insolent, oversexed, dirty; inferior, despicable, and dangerous."[17]

In such a mobile, changing society, the system of mutual expectations breaks down. Racial roles and statuses are not well defined. There is no "racial etiquette" in a Northern city, for example. Spatial and social segregation take its place as a preservative of social distance. Accommodation gives way to fear, suspicion, hatred, and even overt conflict. Miscegenation (which under paternalism occurs frequently between upper-caste men and lower-caste women) is severely condemned and infrequent. Although the law may not recognize the lower caste as different, the upper caste finds effective ways to "keep them in their place." They are largely restricted to menial jobs, excluded from intimate social interaction with the upper caste by the segregation of neighborhoods and institutions, and excluded from political participation by such means as literacy tests (and until recently by poll taxes, which have now been banned by constitutional amendment).

PLURALISM AND ETHNIC GROUPS

Pluralism, the third pattern of intergroup relationships, arises from the interaction within a society of a number of *ethnic* groups.

[16]van den Berghe, "Paternalistic versus Competitive Race Relations."
[17]*Ibid.*

All social groups that are based on the categories of race, religion, or nationality, says Milton Gordon, may be called **ethnic groups**, because the members of such groups share "a sense of peoplehood." (Ethnos, from which *ethnic* and *ethnocentrism* are derived, is the Greek word for "people.") This *sense of group identity and belonging* is one of the three major characteristics of the ethnic group. Second, it is a *subsociety* within the larger society. Within it each member finds most or all of his primary relationships and perhaps many of his secondary relationships as well. Third, the ethnic group has a distinctive *subculture*.[18]

Except where a whole minority group forms a distinct lower caste, the vertical walls of subsocieties are also crisscrossed by the horizontal class lines of the larger society. Members of the same class, as we saw in the previous chapter, share a similar style of life. Members of the same ethnic group share a sense of belonging or peoplehood. A person interacts most intensely, relaxes, and participates most easily with those who are in *both* the same class and the same ethnic group (and for them Gordon has somewhat apologetically coined the term *ethclass*). Here he finds his friends and chooses his mate. In this sense, even the dominant majority (the WASPs) form an ethnic group, in spite of their lack of a feeling of separateness from the larger society (they alone are unhyphenated Americans).

Ethnic groups of this kind may arise within the caste division of a majority–minority situation. More commonly we think of them as making up a **pluralist society**, in which various ethnic groups are considered as (1) different but equal, or (2) different and ranked in a loose hierarchy in which ethnic background serves as one determinant of social class. In either case, under a pluralist system groups are allowed to maintain their own identities as long as they are loyal to the larger society. They can retain much of their traditional culture and communal life as long as they participate as citizens in the political and economic systems of the society. Each group, then, is a subsociety with a subculture.

INTEGRATION

Pluralism is widely held to be the truly democratic pattern of intergroup relations. "Integration," though often used to refer to an ideal goal or the process of reaching that goal, is, in contrast, hotly debated. What does it mean? Can it coexist with pluralism, or is it synonymous with the loss of "peoplehood" in a melting pot?

Integration must be distinguished from *desegregation*, which refers to the achievement of civil rights and privileges for minority groups: the elimination of racial, nationality, or religious criteria in pub-

[18]Milton Gordon, *Assimilation in American Life: The Role of Race, Religion, and National Origins* (New York: Oxford University Press, 1964), pp. 29, 58–59. The term "ethnic" is more commonly used to refer to nationality background.

lic and quasi-public facilities, services, and institutions, such as schools and restaurants. Desegregation refers to behavior in *secondary* relationships.

Integration means much more. It involves, says psychologist Kenneth Clark, a change in "men's hearts and minds"—that is, the elimination of prejudice. In terms of social structure, integration means "the elimination of hard and fast barriers in *the primary group* relations and the communal life of the various ethnic groups of the nation. It involves easy and fluid mixture of people of diverse racial, religious, and nationality backgrounds in social cliques, families (i.e. intermarriage), private organizations, and intimate friendships."[19] People in an integrated society would choose their associates primarily on the basis of common interests rather than ethnicity.

Would desegregation inevitably lead to integration? Sociologists predict that the ties of "peoplehood" are so strong that intimate friendships and intermarriage would be infrequent among members of different subsocieties even if the desegregation process were completed. Most people, in other words, would still move within the narrow world of their "ethclass"—that is, society would still be pluralistic. But at the same time any person would be *free to* cross lines and make friends with, and even marry, members of other ethnic groups; his privileges and opportunities—or lack of them—would not be determined by or related to his ethnicity.

Patterns of Intergroup Relations in the United States

If America is neither a melting pot, nor an integrated social order where everyone has the same freedom of choice and opportunity—and if majority dominance is being repudiated—how can we describe its social structure? Is it a mass of more than 200 million atomized, unrelated individuals? A truly pluralistic democracy?

Sociologists see in America a pattern of remarkably stable and persistent group relationships, along the lines depicted by Milton Gordon. Most Americans find most of their primary relationships among people of the same social class, nationality background, racial category, and religious affiliation. The only notable exception is a small "intellectual subsociety" in which vertical boundaries mean little. The life style and incomes of intellectuals put most of them in the upper-middle class; but their interests make it easy for them to ignore race, religion, and nationality in making their friendships and to a lesser extent in choosing their mates.[20]

[19]*Ibid.*, p. 246. [Emphasis added]

[20]Andrew M. Greeley calls the "intellectual elite" an ethnic group—distrustful and ignorant of other groups, with a strong ethnocentric feeling that they are superior to all others. ["Intellectuals as an 'Ethnic Group,'" *The New York Times Magazine* (July 12, 1970).]

The members of each subsociety do not all live in one geographical area, but in many widely separated communities that are bound together by networks of friendships, publications, and voluntary associations. They can move from one city to another and easily find the group in which they feel at home. An intellectual, for example, like a lower-middle-class white Protestant or an upper-middle-class Jew, recognizes others of his kind wherever he goes and communicates with them easily on the basis of common assumptions. Region of origin is of minor interest: Within any one group, for example, there is little concern about where a daughter's suitor comes from; it is his class and ethnic background (including his religion) that matter.

The social worlds of the different subsocieties tend to be isolated; people seldom come into contact with members of other ethnic groups, particularly of different races. This lack of communication apparently blocks understanding (especially of minority problems) and results in anger, fear, and bewilderment when the social barriers are in danger of being breached. One source of misunderstanding is that sometimes ethnic associations appear to be exclusive—designed to keep people out—when on the whole they were originally designed to be *inclusive*—to keep people in, give them a sense of national culture, preserve the old language, confine marriage to the group, and keep the faith from being questioned or secularized.

But ethnic groups are not watertight compartments. There are many other groups and associations in American life whose multiple, overlapping memberships keep the lines from being drawn too sharply. For example, although they are a racial minority, blacks are "at the same time overwhelmingly Gentile, Protestant, native-born and English-speaking. As such they share significantly in dominant-group attitudes and behavior directed against the Jews, Roman Catholics, foreign-born and non-English-speaking people in American society."[21] And countless secondary contacts develop into primary relationships even though the persons involved have extremely different backgrounds. In political groups, hobby clubs, service clubs, military service, work groups, schools, and numerous other associations, both vertical and horizontal boundaries are often crossed. Movement across ethnic boundaries is much easier and more frequent with those on the same social class level.

The stories of how various ethnic groups became part of the larger society in America—some fairly complete, some still being written in daily headlines—have somewhat different plots. Have these groups lost or retained their unique cultural patterns? Have they been integrated into the social structure of the core population or do they interact primarily with members of their own group? Do they still feel a strong sense of identity with their ethnic group? Do they marry among themselves or intermarry freely with other Americans?

[21]Milton L. Barron, ed., *Minorities in a Changing World* (New York: Alfred A. Knopf, 1967), pp. 3–4.

Louis Wirth outlined four minority orientations: (1) pluralistic, a group's seeking toleration of its ethnic identity, in spite of its differentness; (2) assimilationist, desiring full integration; (3) secessionist or separatist, wanting political as well as cultural independence; and (4) militant, aiming to dominate other groups.[22]

Each ethnic story also varies according to the type of people who came, under what circumstances, and where they settled; whether they were biologically visible; whether their values were compatible with the core American middle-class values established during WASP domination; and whether they came in trickles or huge numbers. Let us trace, first, the story of diverse nationalities, then touch upon religious differences, and finally racial minorities.

Nationality Divisions

From the beginning, America embraced many nationalities. When the English took over New Amsterdam from the Dutch in 1664, they found eighteen nationalities; Pennsylvania, Benjamin Franklin estimated, was one-third German in 1776; of the fifty-six signers of the Declaration of Independence, eighteen were of non-English backgrounds; Irish and Germans made up much of the Revolutionary army; Jewish Americans helped fight and finance the war; Paul Revere was of French ancestry.

Even so, the dominance of Anglo-Saxon Protestant culture was established very early. The first census in 1790 showed that 90% of Americans were of Northern and Western European backgrounds, 64% of them from the British Isles. Between 1820 and 1970 over 45 million immigrants came to this country—at least 35 million of them from Europe. Most of those who came before 1882 were very similar in culture and appearance to the dominant majority, and many settled on midwestern farms rather than crowding into cities where differences might have been more visible. This "old immigration" included large numbers of Germans (who eventually totaled 6 million), as well as many British and Scandinavians.

The Irish and the "new immigrants" from Southern and Eastern Europe were not so fortunate. The potato famine that hit Ireland in 1846 produced an avalanche of immigrants that eventually brought a total of 4.5 million Irishmen to our shores. By 1859, 44% of our foreign-born were Irish—mostly Catholic; by 1865 they numbered nearly 2 million. Years before their heaviest influx, however, the Irish who had come to this country began to experience prejudice and violence. Crowded into the first urban slums, where they were highly visible and vulnerable to discrimination, they were attacked by virulently anti-Irish and anti-Catholic groups like the American ("Know-Nothing") Party.

[22]"The Problem of Minority Groups," in Ralph Linton, ed., *The Science of Man in the World Crisis* (New York: Columbia University Press, 1945), pp. 354–63.

Already in the 1830s churches and convents were being burned and pillaged. In 1844 Philadelphia was in chaos for three days: Thirteen persons were killed and scores injured. Whole blocks of dwellings as well as a seminary and two churches went up in flames. In 1854, ten men were killed in anti-Catholic riots in St. Louis. "A year later, on 'Bloody Monday' at Louisville, Kentucky, nearly a hundred Catholics were slain and scores of houses burned to the ground."[23] Only with the Civil War and the subsequent surge of industrial development and western settlement did antagonisms subside.

The "new immigration," which is usually dated from 1882, was different in culture, appearance, and religion from the dominant majority, who had come to think of themselves as "native whites." Between 1890 and 1920 came 4.5 million Italians, most wretchedly poor, set moving by the cholera epidemic of 1887. Eight million other immigrants from Southern and Eastern Europe—Poles, Hungarians, Bohemians, Slovenians, Ukrainians, and Russians—left their homelands as peasant economies broke down. Many of them were Jews.

Earlier arrivals and their descendants looked down on these "foreigners"; their prejudice had elements of racism, superpatriotism, anti-Catholicism, and anti-Semitism. Immigrants from the Balkans and the Mediterranean region were stigmatized as human flotsam who vulgarized American life. "Nordic" and "Aryan" doctrines gained favor. The rise of labor unions in the latter part of the nineteenth century aroused fear of foreign-born radicals. The Irish-American humorist "Mr. Dooley" (Finley Peter Dunne) satirized such sentiments by saying that, as "a pilgrim father who missed the first boat," he had to denounce the new immigrants as "paupers and anarchists."[24]

And what of the official policy? As early as 1818 the government had established a precedent that there was to be no official recognition or support of ethnic groups. When Irish organizations asked for land out West on which to settle Irish charity cases, Congress refused on the grounds that formally assigning territory to a particular ethnic group could lead to fragmentation of the nation and the establishment of territorial ethnic enclaves. Thus it served notice that the legal framework recognized only individuals, and that if groups wished to preserve ethnic community, they had to do so without official support.

This is exactly what happened, and the result was first the "cultural" and then the "structural" pluralism that successively character-

---

[23]Will Herberg, *Protestant-Catholic-Jew*, rev. ed. (New York: Doubleday & Company, Inc., 1960), pp. 141–42. German Catholics escaped such persecution, largely because they were not concentrated in urban slums.

[24]Since immigration laws were liberalized in 1965, immigration patterns have changed dramatically. In that year, Canadians and British far outnumbered other immigrants; in 1970 the largest influx was from the Philippines and Italy. Immigration accounted for about 20% of total population growth in the United States in the 1960s. Nearly 14% of the 3.9 million immigrants during the decade were nonwhite. [*The New York Times* (June 14, 1971), reporting Census Bureau figures.]

ized American nationality groupings. New immigrants, who were for the most part "peasants whose previous horizons rarely stretched beyond their native village, meagerly educated workmen and tradesmen, and refugees from medieval ghettoes,"[25] sought out earlier .arrivals from their own lands. Banding together for mutual protection and comfort in an indifferent and even hostile environment, they created "little Polands," "little Italies," and so on.

> And so came into being the ethnic church, conducting services in the native language, the ethnic school for appropriate indoctrination of the young, the newspaper published in the native tongue, the mutual aid societies, the recreational groups, and, beneath the formal structure, the informal network of ethnically enclosed cliques and friendship patterns which guaranteed both comfortable socializing and the confinement of marriage within the ancestral group.[26]

Thus, cultural pluralism developed without the assistance of government policy. Indeed, the dominant majority throughout the century of heavy immigration—and especially during the "new immigration" and the hysteria of World War I—stressed the importance of cultural assimilation in the sense of Americanization. This policy (sometimes called "Anglo-conformity") required that the immigrants abandon their native cultures and completely accept the language, behavior, and values of the core culture of America. Neither the dominant majority nor the new ethnic groups ever took seriously the theory of a "melting pot," in which the various cultural elements were to be blended into something new and genuinely American. Such integration and amalgamation would involve large-scale intermarriage, which both the "native whites" and new immigrants resisted. The immigrants clung to their ethnic groupings and to cultural pluralism as the only way to prevent the complete victory of the core culture and the loss of their own.

But their children experienced pressures toward assimilation and Americanization that led them to ignore or despise Old World cultures. The effect was to alienate them from their parents, whom they looked down on as "queer foreigners." They rejected much of the old culture as, through public schools and mass media, they rapidly learned the new. They found, however, that they were rebuffed when they sought intimate social relationships with "native white" Americans, or with members of other immigrant groups who felt more established and acculturated or otherwise superior. Therefore they had to return to their own ethnic communities to find their primary relationships. Many of the ethnic institutions endured because the Americanized third generation did not feel the same emotional need to reject them that their parents had felt. As a result our society does not now exhibit "cultural pluralism," but rather "structural pluralism."

[25]Gordon, *Assimilation in American Life*, p. 105.
[26]*Ibid.*, p. 134.

A young performer at the O-Bon Festival, held in New York City to pay homage to the dead as a traditional custom of Buddhists. The scene is being observed by New Yorkers of many ethnic backgrounds.

This heritage of the once culturally distinct ethnic communities is a collection of structurally distinct subsocieties, each of which contains not only its own primary groups of cliques and families, but also many of its own associations and organizations. Thus each is "a highly structured community within the boundaries of which an individual may, if he wishes, carry out most of his more meaningful life activities from the cradle to the grave."[27]

One example of a structurally distinct subsociety is the American Jewish community. While an ethnic group in Gordon's sense, Jewish-Americans are neither a nationality group nor, strictly speaking, a religious group. They do not identify themselves as Russians, or Poles, or Germans; they may not belong to any synagogue or temple; but they still think of themselves as Jews.

The United States has "the largest concentration of Jews in the world, more than two and a half times the size of the Jewish state of Israel, and accounts for nearly half of world Jewry."[28] The 6 million Jewish-Americans are about 3% of the nation's population. Most of them arrived when economic and educational opportunities were plentiful, especially for those with middle-class values such as the Jews shared with the dominant majority—"ambition, veneration for education, willingness to defer immediate gratification, urban mentality"[29]— and their children were extremely successful in achieving acculturation. Rejected by the dominant majority for primary relationships, they contributed to building a distinct subsociety. The third generation sought not only security and greater conformity to American patterns, but also continuity of their Jewish identity, largely through community organization, Jewish neighborhoods, education of children in the ancient language and traditions, and communication with Jews in other communities. The American Jewish subsociety, then, has achieved a blend of acculturation and ethnic identity, fitting into American life successfully and yet giving its members a strong "sense of peoplehood."

Is America today a genuinely pluralistic society? Recently some

[27]Ibid., p. 234.
[28]Sidney Goldstein and Calvin Goldscheider, *Jewish Americans: Three Generations in a Jewish Community* (Englewood Cliffs, N.J.: Prentice-Hall, Inc., 1968), p. 32.
[29]Ibid., p. 7.

"white ethnics" are protesting that Americans have always been intolerant of cultural differences at home and abroad, that they "have never confronted squarely the problem of preserving diversity." In an angry expression of this thesis, a professor of Slovakian descent charges that WASPs and Jews deny power and status and intellectual voice to "PIGS"—Poles, Italians, Greeks, and Slavs; that the history and literature taught in schools and universities are peopled almost exclusively by WASPs and Englishmen; that the loyalty of "white ethnics" to America is met with rejection; and that above all, the liberals and upper-middle class, who find it easy to feel sympathy for blacks, Mexican-Americans, Indians, and all the poor, do not even try to understand the fellow who drives a beer truck or wears a helmet at a construction site. These nationality groups, he declares, have a strong sense of family and community, stability and roots; they are not attracted to the modern, largely "Anglo-Saxon" model of freely mobile and highly individual living, and reject the melting pot as a "kind of homogenized soup."[30] As we saw in the previous chapter, the "white ethnics" are largely lower-middle class and working class; these "ethclasses" are increasingly resentful and alienated because they feel ignored or left behind, and believe they are not understood or respected. The answer to the question of whether America is truly pluralistic thus depends on one's vantage point.

Religious Groupings

Religious differences—as we saw in our discussion of Irish-Catholic immigration—once led to bitter hatreds and conflicts. In early New England, those who had fled the Old World to seek religious freedom were the first to deny it to others. Later the Constitution guaranteed religious freedom; but prejudice and discrimination die slowly. Although neither has completely disappeared, Jews have occupied high offices and won high honors, and Catholicism is no longer a barrier to the Presidency. Accommodation, acculturation, and even cooperation are the themes of interreligious relations today.

What generalizations do sociologists make about the role of religious differences in modern America? Among the chief ones are these.

Most Americans accept the three major religious divisions as part of the right and natural order of things. In a famous book-length essay called *Protestant-Catholic-Jew*, theologian Will Herberg observes, "The only separateness or diversity that America recognizes as per-

---

[30]Michael Novak, "White Ethnic," *Harper's* (Sept. 1971): 44–50. See also his *The Rise of the Unmeltable Ethnics: Politics and Culture in the Seventies* (New York: The Macmillan Company, 1972); and Louise Kapp Howe, ed., *The White Majority* (New York: Random House, Vintage Books, 1970).

manent, and yet also involving no status of inferiority, is the diversity or separateness of religious community."[31]

Not only is religious pluralism considered part of the American heritage, religion itself is regarded as "a good thing"—that is, believing or faith *as such*, without regard to the particular dogma or doctrine. All the major religions are felt to affirm the spiritual ideals and moral values of a greater whole called "The American Way of Life."

And indeed the churches of different faiths tend to reflect our culture, just as the different nationality groupings do. Observers have often commented that the religions of America are much more like one another than they are like their European counterparts. The structures, rituals, and social activities of both Catholic and Jewish congregations have become more and more "Americanized." In conservative and reform Judaism, for example, English is used in part of the service and in the business affairs of the synagogue; sermons are preached, the sexes worship together, and age- and sex-graded recreational and educational programs have been introduced—all of these being substantial breaks with orthodoxy in the direction of American middle-class norms.

Leaders and laymen of all the major faiths take part in social movements such as civil rights. They cooperate in interfaith activities, where—apparently for fear of controversy—the one taboo subject is religious belief! Such cooperation combined with such a taboo is possible in American culture but appears strange to Europeans.[32]

Almost all Americans regard religious identity as extremely important, regardless of whether or not they actually attend churches or temples. As national origins retreat farther and farther into the past, and as mobility and the mass media minimize the importance of regions, religious identity has come to be regarded as not only legitimate but necessary. Just as the question "What does he do?" is a clue to a person's social class, "What is he?" places him in one of the three social worlds of religion. His religious "brand name" gives him identity and social location. The army and the hospital, as well as the neighbors, want to know.

The social necessity of "belonging" is reflected in a spectacular rise in church membership. In 1969, about 63% of Americans were formally affiliated with a church, as compared with 36% in 1900.[33] Furthermore, 70 to 75% of Americans *regard* themselves as church members even if not all are formally on the rolls. Even more indicative of the feeling that one must have a religion is that 95% of Americans identify themselves as either Protestant (68%), Catholic (23%), or Jewish (4%).[34]

This stress on religious identity is part of what Gordon calls the "structural pluralism" of our society. Most primary relationships

[31] *Protestant-Catholic-Jew*, p. 38.

[32] *Ibid.*, p. 144.

[33] *American Almanac for 1971*, p. 4.

[34] Herberg, *Protestant-Catholic-Jew*, pp. 46–49.

take place within the boundaries of the three main religious divisions. Intermarriage among nationality groups is largely confined to each major religion. It is for this reason that America has been called a "triple melting pot."[35] Recent data on intermarriage are lacking, largely because the Census Bureau yielded to the pressure of some small groups and did not ask questions about religion in the 1960 and 1970 censuses. The last year for which adequate data exist, 1957, revealed that 7% of marriages involving at least one Jewish person were mixed, 9% of Protestant, and 22% of Catholic. But the data do not reveal trends, for they included all marriages, with an average age in the early or mid-forties. Furthermore, a careful study would distinguish between spouses brought up in different religions and those brought up in the same religion.[36]

A study of interfaith marriage in Canada indicates that it is increasing. Between 1927 and 1957 mixed marriages involving Protestants rose from 5% to 11.6%; Catholics, 7.2% to 11.5%; and Jews, 3% to 6.8%. The smaller the percentage of a religious group in a community, the greater the tendency to marry someone of another faith.[37]

Friendships also tend to be confined to the religious subsociety, especially during the years of adolescence, when many parents try to guard their children against the possibility of marrying outside their religion. A study of close friendships by Gerhard Lenski showed that 77% of the Jews in his Detroit sample said that all or nearly all their closest friends were of the same religion. Forty-four per cent of the Catholics and 38% of the Protestants reported similar in-group ties.[38] The rate of in-group friendship is highest—80%—among Catholics who attend parochial schools.[39]

Even Catholics who attend parochial schools, however, have been found to accept almost exactly the same values as the dominant majority. It is probably true of almost every American that "the social, cultural, and economic state he finds himself in is a better index to his

[35]In a study of intermarriage in New Haven, Ruby Jo Kennedy found that nationality-group endogamy had decreased from 91% in 1870 to 64% in 1940, but that 80% of Protestants, 84% of Catholics, and 94% of Jews married within their religious groups. ["Single or Triple Melting Pot? Intermarriage Trends in New Haven, 1870–1940," *American Journal of Sociology* 49, No. 4 (Jan. 1944): 331–39.]

[36]Because of conversion after marriage, the same group could show 85% of marriages of the same faith if present status only were used, and 68% if religion as children were used. [See Ira L. Reiss, *The Family System in America* (New York: Holt, Rinehart & Winston, 1971), chap. 19, "Deviance and the Family: Intermarriage."]

[37]David M. Heer, "The Trend of Interfaith Marriages in Canada, 1927–1957," *American Sociological Review* 27 (April 1962): 245–50.

[38]*The Religious Factor* (New York: Doubleday & Company, Inc., 1961).

[39]Joseph H. Fichter, S.J., *Parochial School: A Sociological Study* (Notre Dame, Ind.: University of Notre Dame Press, 1958).

thinking and behavior than his religion."[40] Only over a few issues that involve the relation of church and state—birth control, abortion, divorce, and public aid to parochial schools, for example—do Americans divide along religious lines.

Some studies, however, conclude that religious prejudices are, still forces to be reckoned with, and that religious beliefs may be associated with other types of intergroup prejudice as well. Although theologians and clergymen are prominent in interfaith projects and try to promote interracial amity, many laymen—70% in one survey—believe their priests and ministers should confine themselves to the private religious lives of their congregations.[41] Christian churches have officially denounced the notion that Jews continue to bear guilt for the crucifixion of Christ; yet half the American Christians polled and many clergymen continue to subscribe to it. From one-half to two-thirds of American Christians would deny civil liberties to a person who does not believe in God, bar him from holding public office, and remove him from a teaching position in the schools.[42]

Rodney Stark and Charles Y. Glock conclude from their studies that the image of man as having completely free will results in a tendency to blame the disadvantaged for their own plight. This is also true of the disadvantaged themselves. "The more committed a Negro was to Christian beliefs and institutions, the readier he was to see the lowly condition of Negroes as self-inflicted," and to trust that God will correct it in His own good time. People, in short, get what they deserve in this life and the next. But church members more strongly committed to New Testament ethics than to these ideas display less prejudice and more social concern.[43]

Racial Divisions

The once bitter antagonisms and violent conflicts between people of different nationalities and religions have given way, then, to a pattern of accommodation, assimilation, and even varying degrees of integration within a context of pluralism. The same cannot be said for several highly visible minority groups, who suffer prejudice and discrimination, whose life chances are far inferior to those of other groups, and who are currently reacting with increased group awareness and protest. Let

---

[40]John Leo, "The American Catholic Is Changing," in Milton L. Barron, ed. *Minorities in a Changing World* (New York: Alfred A. Knopf, 1967), pp. 305–18.

[41]Jeffrey K. Hadden, *The Gathering Storm in the Churches* (New York: Doubleday & Company, Inc., 1969).

[42]Rodney Stark and Charles Y. Glock, "Prejudice and the Churches," in Charles Y. Glock and Ellen Siegelman, eds., *Prejudice U.S.A.* (New York: Frederick A. Praeger, 1969), pp. 70–95.

[43]*Ibid.*

us look at some of the smaller minorities before we consider black Americans.

INDIANS AND ESKIMOS

Only Indians and Eskimos are truly "native" Americans. When Columbus discovered the New World, there were probably between 1 and 3 million Indians in what is now United States territory. Dispossession and genocide by the invading whites reduced them to about 340,000 by 1860 and an all-time low of 220,000 in 1910. The 1970 census, however, records 792,730 Indians, an increase of more than 100% in 20 years.

The first of 284 reservations was established in 1853; in 1871 Indians were made wards of the federal government and assured of the protection of the President—the Great White Father. Under a system of treaties with various tribes, they were to retain land and water rights and have the protection and help of their own bureaucracy, the Bureau of Indian Affairs (BIA). Thus they became the only territorially distinct minority, formally dependent on government paternalism. In 1924 Indians were granted citizenship; in the 1930s they were allowed to set up economic corporations and self-governing agencies. By the 1950s they were allowed and even encouraged to leave reservations for industrial cities, thus forfeiting their rights to tribal lands, which had been dwindling as treaty after treaty was broken and reservations could no longer support growing numbers of Indians. In 1887 they held 138 million acres; now they hold about 55 million.

When the "Americanization" movement was strongest in the late nineteenth century, the BIA often took children and placed them in boarding homes, forcing them to abandon Indian ways. This kind of treatment, plus the dubious paternalism of an unwieldy and generally slow-moving bureaucracy, has resulted in much personal and social disorganization, both on and off the reservations. Division into some 300 tribes has impeded awareness of common problems. The average income of families on reservations is $1500, less than half the minimum that marks the poverty line. The birth rate is about 2.2 that of whites;

A recent Tribal Council of the Devils Lake Sioux.

average age at death is 64.0 years as compared to 70.5 for all races in the United States.[44] Indians average 5.5 years of schooling. Unemployment is about 20% on the more affluent reservations, 80% on the poorest. Rates of alcoholism and suicide (even among teenagers) are high. But the dramatic increase in Indian population since 1950 reflects improved health: tuberculosis, long a scourge, has declined 75%, and infant mortality dropped from 63 per 1000 live births to 31 (as compared to 22 for whites) in 1968.

Another reason for the increase in numbers of Indians tabulated is increased pride in their identity. In former censuses, 26% Indian "blood" was the criterion; in 1970 self-identification was relied on. Many Indians are seeking a way to retain this identity and at the same time improve their life chances. Closing down reservations does not appear to be the answer; the incidence of suicide, crime, alcoholism, and registration for welfare is high among the 200,000 who have moved to cities. "Integrity, Not Integration" is a popular slogan. Among values the Indians stress are pride and dignity (which have impeded protest), their tradition of communal ownership, and closeness to nature. Their leaders seek more control over their own affairs—lands, schools, resources, businesses—and more efficient assistance from the BIA.[45]

Eskimo life chances are also meager. Native Alaskans have a life expectancy of only about 35 years, and a per capita income less than one-fourth that of white Alaskans. Unlike the American Indians, they were never conquered by either Russia or the United States and never signed away their rights to land. Therefore they stand to gain economically from the use of Alaskan territory by oil and mineral interests.

ASIAN MINORITY GROUPS

Asians on the United States mainland numbered about 600,000 in 1960; of these, 207,000 were Japanese-Americans, 200,000 Chinese-Americans, and 107,000 of Filipino ancestry. The differing stories of the Chinese and Japanese illustrate the play of such factors as the class of people that migrated, when they came, and under what circumstances.

Chinese contract laborers began to come to the West Coast in large numbers in the 1850s. Mostly poor villagers, they were highly visible because of their appearance, dress, language and writing, and their willingness to do domestic labor. Most came as "sojourners," planning to go back after earning some money. In the lawless setting of the frontier they were often subject to violence, especially in hard times,

[44]Average age at death for all races in the United States is 70.5. Data from "Facts on Indian Affairs," mimeographed bulletin from U.S. Department of the Interior; Bureau of Indian Affairs, July 1971.

[45]Based in part on Charles F. Marden and Gladys Meyer, *Minorities in American Society*, 3rd ed. (New York: The American Book Company, 1968), chap. 16, "Indians in the United States," pp. 356–77.

222222222222222222

to which they usually reacted with passivity and withdrawal. Immigration was highest in the 1870s; but in 1882 an exclusion act was passed, under which Asians were declared "unassimilable." Because of this exclusion (which ended in 1943), and because so many came as sojourners, Chinese-Americans now number only half the total of 400,000 that came. Although the Chinatowns of the large cities are in some respects slums, and young Chinese-Americans protest the aura of mystery and exoticism with which white stereotypes surround them, many members of the group have achieved middle- and upper-middle-class status, and many of these are Christian. Prejudice has declined, and acculturation is so nearly complete that young people complain of identity problems.

Although the Japanese also suffered from the exclusion act and were singled out for unreasonable treatment in World War II they have, on the whole, become a "model minority," often compared with the Jews because of their occupational and educational achievement; low rates of crime, delinquency, and mental illness; stable family life; community cohesion; and acculturation to American middle-class values. They began to emigrate later than the Chinese, when Japan was already modernizing; though highly respectful of authority, they were less passive and accommodated to technological and economic demands more easily. At first laborers and domestics, the Japanese found more opportunity and less discrimination in farming; having learned intensive agriculture in Japan, they were very successful with fruit and vegetable farms.

But suddenly in 1942 all West Coast Japanese were herded into ten hastily built concentration or relocation camps, and their property sold at about 10 cents on the dollar; this hasty and ill-considered action was intended to prevent sabotage. Although the government has never officially renounced this policy or made restitution, Japanese-Americans have adjusted successfully since then, and prejudice and discrimination have declined greatly. The third generation has largely discarded the old language and become quite thoroughly acculturated; many have achieved success in such prestigious occupations as architecture, the arts, and the academic world.[46]

MEXICAN-AMERICANS

In the 1970 census 9.2 million Americans, almost 5%, identified themselves as of Spanish-speaking origin; other estimates are as high as 12 million. Eight out of ten were born in the United States or Puerto Rico; half still speak Spanish at home.

The 5 million Mexican-Americans (Chicanos in the preferred usage of the more militant members of the group) are different from other minorities in many ways. We discuss them here as a racial minor-

[46]Harry H. L. Kitano, *Japanese Americans: The Evolution of a Subculture* (Englewood Cliffs, N.J.: Prentice-Hall, Inc., 1969).

ity, primarily because much prejudice and discrimination against them is racist in nature, even though it is directed largely at their cultural differences. Mexican-Americans themselves "have no very clear consensus on whether they are a racial group, a cultural group, or even if they are white or nonwhite," yet most of them have a strong feeling of ethnic identity.[47]

Mexicans settled in New Mexico a generation before the Pilgrims landed, and their descendants were incorporated into the United States through conquest and annexation. Thus they are one of the oldest minorities. But only recently have they come in huge numbers, and in a stream that still continues. Eight out of ten live in the five Southwestern states of California, Arizona, New Mexico, Colorado, and Texas, but many are migrating to Northern cities. Most came as agricultural laborers, legally or illegally, ambivalent about the new land and ready to return across the border. Their culture was extremely different from that of the almost entirely Protestant whites of the area, who stereotyped them as innately lazy, cowardly, and cruel, and at the same time (especially from contacts with "Spanish" white Mexicans of the upper class) as warm, charming, gay, and able to enjoy life.

Being territorially concentrated in a region with a long Spanish tradition, and constantly reinforced by new immigration, Mexican-Americans have retained many aspects of their cultural tradition. They celebrate "La Raza" (the race) or "The People" of Mexican culture, and especially the Spanish language and the Catholic religion as embellished by Mexican customs. Their world view is one of acceptance and appreciation of things as they are; the core values of La Raza are honor, dignity, manliness (machismo), courtesy, and fulfillment of obligations to family and friends.[48]

This very cultural cohesion, and especially the emphasis on language, places Chicanos at a disadvantage in schooling and employment. One in four has less than 5 years of schooling, the definition of functional illiteracy; one in five speaks no English. Those in the Southwest have a median of 6.2 grades of schooling as compared to 8.7 for blacks and 10.7 for whites in the area; their dropout rate is twice the national average. A Chicano child "starts dropping out the first day of kindergarten," when his chief learning tool, an amalgam of Spanish and English, is snatched from him; he gets a sense of inferiority and guilt when he is forbidden to talk his own language.[49] In Houston, only 2% of those entering first grade complete high school.

Families of Spanish-speaking origin had a median family in-

[47]Jean W. Moore with Alfredo Cuellar, Mexican Americans (Englewood Cliffs, N.J.: Prentice-Hall, Inc., 1970), pp. 158–59. Only in the 1930 census were their racial backgrounds tabulated, showing less than 5% as "white" and the rest as "colored." The population of Mexico has been described as 10% white, 30% Indian, and 60% mestizo (mixed). The U.S. Census classes them as white.

[48]Marden and Meyer, Minorities in American Society, pp. 134–35.

[49]The New York Times (April 18, 1971).

come of $7,330 in 1970 as compared with $6,280 for blacks and $10,240 for whites. And families are larger; the median age of their population is under 20 as compared to 28.6 for Anglos (as they call whites). Over a third of the poor in the Southwest are Mexican-Americans.

By 1975 it is estimated that there will be almost 20 million United States citizens of Latin American origin. Where they are concentrated—as in Texas, where 2 million Mexican-Americans live—they are increasingly conscious of "brown power" and are politically organized in such parties as La Raza Unida. The Chicano movement, which backed the grape strike to improve conditions for migrant workers, also indicates the growing cohesion and awareness of this minority.

Blacks in the New World

Twenty-three million Americans of African ancestry, 11% of the population, form the largest and most visible minority group in the nation. Only 24 of the more than 130 nation-states and self-governing territories have populations outnumbering Afro-Americans.

The history of the involuntary African immigrants and their descendants is not simply one of an era of slavery suddenly followed by an era of freedom. It goes back to the first explorers and settlers, and is interwoven with all of American history. Black Americans through the centuries have experienced ups and downs that were related not only to shifting patterns of prejudice and discrimination but also to economic conditions, political decisions, social movements, and broad social changes that affected the whole society.

EARLY BLACK AMERICANS

The first blacks who came to the New World did not come as slaves. Some accompanied Spanish explorers and settlers long before the English came. In 1619, a Dutch captain left twenty Africans at Jamestown, Virginia. They were, like a number of whites (and like many whites and blacks who came later), indentured servants. In colonial days there was interest in and curiosity about their physical appearance, but no racist prejudice.

As plantation agriculture developed—rice, indigo, tobacco, and later sugar and cotton—more Africans were brought; by the end of the seventeenth century, they were brought as slaves. At the time of the Revolutionary War (in which the first American casualty was a black) there were about 700,000 black slaves, 40% of them in the wealthy state of Virginia.

From early times there was opposition to slavery. Thomas Jefferson included a clause calling for the immediate abolition of slavery in the first draft of the Declaration of Independence, but Georgia and the Carolinas, which believed slavery had made Virginia prosperous and wanted similar prosperity, blocked its passage. Ironically, the American victory over the British may be one of those "if only" occurrences of history: Had we remained part of Britain, which abolished slavery in 1844, we might have been spared the agonies of interracial tension and conflict.

In 1808 Congress passed a law prohibiting the further importation of slaves. But by then it was too late. In 1793 Eli Whitney had invented the cotton gin, and now cotton was King. The law was ignored because Southern cotton growers needed an abundance of cheap labor if they were to cultivate cotton profitably; slaves were smuggled in and sold at high prices.

AMERICAN SLAVERY

Now racism and the caste system appeared and took firm root. Southern planters needed to rationalize their subjugation of millions of people at a time when liberty, equality, fraternity, humanitarianism, and progress were watchwords. Thus they readily believed that the Bible sanctioned slavery, that democratic Greece had been based on it, and that blacks were biologically inferior. They made the slave a piece of property, denied him the right to family life, and stripped him so thoroughly of the culture of his ancestors that survivals of African culture traits are almost entirely lacking in North America.[50]

In 1860 there were nearly 4 million black slaves, as well as half a million free blacks, in a population of about 31 million Americans. That they were not fully accommodated to the paternalistic (and often cruel) system was evidenced by numerous small uprisings and frequent runaways, and by the fear of massacre in which many whites lived. Nevertheless most slaves, utterly dependent on their white masters, seemed resigned to their status.

THE POST–CIVIL WAR ERA

Emancipation in 1863 "freed the slave but ignored the Negro," in the words of abolitionist Wendell Phillips. Blacks were still lower-caste and dependent on whites for jobs; but their former masters, on the whole, felt less responsible for them than when they were human

[50]The slavery of the American South was more brutal and degrading than that of the Spanish and Portuguese colonists, who considered slavery a misfortune that could happen to any human being, and did not affect his mind and soul, only his body. He could marry and family unity was respected. He might earn a little money and buy his freedom, and once free he had, on the whole, the same social status as other free men. [Charles E. Silberman, *Crisis in Black and White* (New York: Random House, 1964), pp. 84–93.]

chattels. Many were much worse off than before, for most of them were illiterate agricultural laborers. Both whites and blacks suffered from postwar economic and political disorganization. The former owners enacted a series of "black codes" that made a mockery of Afro-Americans' "free" status, and used force and intimidation to keep them as servile as possible. Only in 1867 did the federal government send in troops to enforce the new constitutional amendments that gave the slave freedom, citizenship, and the vote.

This "Reconstruction Era" has frequently been misrepresented in history books. It lasted at most 10 years, and in some states only 3. It was not a time of black domination. Only one state legislature had a black majority, and then for only 2 years. There was, to be sure, some corruption and manipulation of blacks; but there was also an attempt to set up the first public school system in the South, staffed largely by sympathetic and idealistic white Northern spinsters.

It was not long, however, before political expediency led to the removal of federal troops and ended the protection that blacks still needed. The Southern Democrats, in the Compromise of 1877, agreed to the election of Republican Rutherford B. Hayes as President on the condition that federal troops be withdrawn. Even so, for some years after the races lived in comparative peace and harmony. Then step by step black Americans' new rights were taken away and white supremacy was restored. Intimidation kept blacks away from the polls at first; then quasi-legal means such as poll taxes and literacy tests were used. By the turn of the century most Southern states had established a new caste system. They institutionalized racial inequality by means of Jim Crow laws segregating public facilities, and by the system of racial etiquette with elaborate rules of deference and avoidance.

From about 1890 to 1930 the condition of the black man was in general no better than it had been under slavery. In the North he was unemployed or poorly paid; in the South he was typically a debt-ridden tenant farmer, often a sharecropper, vulnerable to white exploitation and oppression. In the last 16 years of the nineteenth century, according to historian John Hope Franklin, there were more than 2500 lynchings; in the first 14 years of the new century, 1100. In Philadelphia and New York, as well as in other cities north and south, there were race riots, not of black protest but of white men pillaging, burning, and killing in the black sections.[51]

The federal government, in effect, upheld the caste system. In a famous decision, *Plessy* v. *Ferguson* in 1896, the Supreme Court ruled that the provision of "separate but equal" facilities in public transportation did not violate the "equal rights" amendment of the Constitution. The court declared that "legislation is powerless to eradicate racial instincts or to abolish distinctions based upon physical differences." This

[51]*From Slavery to Freedom: A History of Negro Americans*, 3rd ed. (New York: Alfred A. Knopf, 1967), pp. 439–44.

case and others cleared the way in the South for complete segregation of the races from the cradle to the grave in all but economic enterprises, in which they were interdependent. This low point of black status coincided with growing racism in the North, as Americans rationalized such adventures as the Spanish-American War and the building of the Panama Canal, which placed large numbers of nonwhites under American domination.

NEGRO LEADERSHIP BEFORE 1940

Three kinds of black leaders appeared during the era before the Second World War. The first stressed accommodation and conciliation. The church, typically oriented to the hereafter, and providing emotional release, was the center of cohesion in the black community. Because their congregations were vulnerable and dependent on the whites, black ministers served as conciliators and mediators.

A leading proponent of this kind of adaptation was educator Booker T. Washington, who preached hard work, self-help, self-improvement, and gradualism. He accepted the American philosophy of rugged individualism: Everyone had his future in his own hands; success comes to the deserving as a result of work, thrift, tact, and good manners. He urged blacks to forego political and legal rights and social equality, and to become good farmers and artisans, to find ways to be useful in the community. He urged cooperation with the "best white men." He was much applauded and quoted when he said in 1895, "In all things that are purely social we can be as separate as the fingers, yet one as the hand in all things essential to mutual progress." Some charge that he was a toady to the white man, an Uncle Tom. Others see his program as the only realistic and workable one, considering the temper of the times.

A second kind of leader was W. E. B. Du Bois, who took sharp issue with Washington. He stressed that the black should have full civil rights and be treated as a man, arguing that the Declaration of Independence and the Constitution did not require citizens to earn or to deserve equality. He saw what Washington failed to see—that industrialization and urbanization were making obsolete the kind of program that tied blacks to the soil and to primitive tools, and that ignoring legal and social rights made things easier for the segregationist and the black less of a man in his own eyes. "Manly self-respect," said Du Bois, "is worth more than land and houses." In 1909 this militant civil rights position was institutionalized in the National Association for the Advancement of Colored People (organized by white liberals and blacks), of which Du Bois served as the leader for 20 years. The NAACP worked, through test cases for example, to get the dominant majority to grant Afro-Americans equal legal rights.

Marcus Garvey was a third kind of leader—nationalist and secessionist, appealing to the impoverished blacks of the large cities. Coming to New York in 1916 from his native Jamaica, he declared that "black" stood for beauty and strength and honor rather than for inferiority and shame. He glorified the African past and promised blacks a home of their own in Africa. It was futile, he said, to appeal to whites, for race prejudice was too deeply rooted in their civilization. In 7 years he had established thirty branches of his back-to-Africa movement, and sold stock in a steamship line to take his followers to Africa; but the enterprise failed—apparently because he trusted dishonest subordinates. He was convicted of using the mails to defraud, jailed in 1923, and deported in 1927.[52]

CHANGES IN BLACK STATUS
SINCE WORLD WAR II

The decades since 1940 have witnessed the transformation of black Americans from an agricultural peasantry concentrated in the South into an increasingly urban minority, half of whom live in the North. Only traces of the paternalistic pattern of interracial relations remain; accommodation has given way to the tension and conflict of the competitive pattern. Caste barriers are no longer legal; depriving a person of his civil rights is now a federal offense.

Many blacks have achieved middle-class status. Black families with husband and wife both present earned 57% of average white income in 1960, and 72% in 1969. Most of this gain occurred among 532,000 Northern black families with husband and wife under age 35, who now average about $9,000 annual income, 91% of that of their white counterparts. This is a significant gain over the 62% figure in 1960 for similar families. In 1970 61% of blacks between 20 and 29 had completed at least a high school education as compared to 40% 10 years earlier. Proportionately more Northern blacks voted in the elections of 1966 and 1968 than did Southern whites. Nearly 1500 blacks held elective public offices in 1970; among them were Congressmen, state legislators, and mayors of cities as large as Cleveland and Gary.[53] A black man sits on the Supreme Court of the United States. The percentage of blacks who are professional and technical workers, teachers, medical and health workers, has risen steadily, and the percentage who are farm workers, domestic workers, and nonfarm laborers has declined.

How did these postwar gains come about? Not because prejudice declined and white Americans decided not to discriminate. They

[52]Franklin, *From Slavery to Freedom*, pp. 489–92. See also Edmund D. Cronon, *Black Moses: The Story of Marcus Garvey* (Madison, Wis.: University of Wisconsin Press, 1962).

[53]*The New York Times* (Feb. 12, 1971); *Current Population Reports*, Series P-20, No. 204 (1970); *Saturday Review* (April 4, 1970).

are due largely to impersonal social forces, some of which affected all Americans; a shift in government policy toward active support for civil rights; and pressures from blacks themselves.

Industrialization and urbanization led to the migration of rural Southern blacks to large Northern cities—one of the great migrations of history, with tremendous consequences. In 1940, 77% of the nation's blacks lived in the South; by 1970, only slightly more than half. In the first decade after 1940, 2 million blacks moved North; in the next, 1.7 million; in the 1960s, 1.4 million; and the shift promises to continue in the current decade. Better job opportunities, especially in wartime, and better schools attracted them, while mechanization of agriculture pushed them off the land in the South. In addition, federal measures such as social security, minimum wages, unemployment insurance, and Aid to Dependent Children gave all citizens a new measure of security.

Meanwhile, America's role, assumed during and after World War II, as the champion of freedom in the world, put a spotlight on her treatment of minorities. Gunnar Myrdal, hired to lead a group studying the race problem, set forth his analysis in 1944 in *An American Dilemma*.[54] Its central thesis was that there is a tension between our ideals and reality—between our core values of moral concern, rationalism, liberalism, equality of opportunity, and freedom, and the discrimination and inequality that exist.

Taking the lead in resolving this moral dilemma, the Supreme Court in 1948 declared unconstitutional restrictive covenants intended to keep neighborhoods white or Gentile or both. Then, on May 17, 1954, it handed down an epoch-making decision in the case of *Brown* v. *Board of Education of Topeka, Kansas* (and in several other cases involving other states). Reversing the *Plessy* v. *Ferguson* decision of 1896, the Court declared that separate school facilities were *inherently* unequal, and that to separate children "from others of similar age and qualifications solely because of their race generates a feeling of inferiority as to their status in the community that may affect their hearts and minds in a way unlikely ever to be undone." Other postwar government measures included an executive order desegregating the armed forces, laws to encourage registration of black voters, and a Court decision outlawing state laws against racial intermarriage.

The most striking result of these changes in economic class and legal status is an increase in black power, expressed not only in the vote but also in other forms of pressure. As blacks become a majority in the central city limits of many metropolitan areas, their votes are ever more eagerly sought. Led by such integrationists as Martin Luther King, Jr., blacks discovered the power of nonviolent demonstrations—boycotts, passive resistance, sit-ins, freedom rides. Many whites joined their attempt to enter the mainstream of American life, to achieve civil

---

[54] *An American Dilemma: The Negro Problem and American Democracy* (New York: Harper & Row, 1944).

rights. Other leaders rejected the idea of integration, and formed such separatist movements as the Black Muslims, and militant ones such as the Black Panthers, spurning white help, white values, and even white society. Such a trend toward militancy and extremism occurs in every revolution—and the transformation of black Americans is truly revolutionary.[55]

Another principle of revolutions is that they do not occur when a group is still in the depths of oppression, but rather when an advancing group is blocked and frustrated in its desire to advance faster and farther. The group measures its advances not against its former status, but against the status of other groups. Schools, magazines, newspapers, movies—and especially TV—show how middle-class whites live. Aspirations rise, and the feeling of relative deprivation increases. For even though blacks have gained on many fronts, there is still a considerable gap between their life chances and those of white Americans.

The Costs of Discrimination and Minority Status

Minority status not only is correlated with social class inequalities in wealth, prestige, and power, but also affects self-esteem and life chances. All racial minorities are in some sense deprived and excluded from participation in the rewards of the society, and, as Lee Rainwater says, "The lower-class Negro is doubly deprived and doubly excluded."[56]

LIFE CHANGES

Although the income gap is closing, it is still considerable. In 1965 the median income of black families was 54% that of whites; by 1969 it had risen to 61%. This discrepancy is attributed to lack of education. But after differences in education, class, and family size are all allowed for, there still remains a gap of about $1400 a year in the incomes of black and white men that can be accounted for only by discrimination.[57]

Although indices of educational attainment show that the gap between the races is narrow, the close relationship of education with social mobility that exists for Americans in general does not hold true for blacks. "The Negro man originating at the lower levels is likely to stay there, the white man to move up. The Negro originating at the higher levels is likely to move down; the white man seldom does."[58]

[55]There is no solid front among blacks, any more than there is among youth or women, in their protest movement. See Chapter 18, "Collective Behavior and Social Movements."

[56]*Behind Ghetto Walls: Black Families in a Federal Slum* (Chicago: Aldine Publishing Company, 1970).

[57]*Toward a Social Report*, p. 26. Rapid social mobility has been found to be associated with *increased* prejudice.

[58]*Ibid.*, p. 24.

Many black men, even if their fathers were in professional, managerial or proprietary positions, are operatives, service workers, or laborers.

The incidence of unemployment and poverty is high among blacks, especially recent migrants from the rural South, teenagers, and those who stay behind on farms where machines have taken their traditional jobs. One of three blacks lives in poverty, as do half of all elderly blacks. About one-half of all poor black families are headed by females. This situation is in part due to the disintegration of black families during the slavery era, but also to welfare policies that punish families for staying together; an unemployed man may leave his wife and children so they can qualify for welfare. "The United States is the only major industrialized nation that provides public welfare *after* the family has broken up rather than before to keep it together."[59]

All figures on health and mortality throw the gap in life chances into startling relief. There is still a gap of about 7 years in the life expectancy of blacks and whites (although this is an improvement from the 15-year gap in 1900). Black babies are about twice as likely to die in infancy as whites. The incidence of deaths from tuberculosis and syphilis is three times as high. Maternal mortality is six times greater.[60]

Blacks are much more likely than whites to be victims of crime. When suspected of crime, they are more likely than whites to be arrested, more likely to be convicted, and more likely to be penalized. Rates of drug addiction are also high, but appear to be declining even though white rates are rising.[61]

Housing discrimination makes it difficult for blacks to find a decent place to live. Fair housing measures and federal mortgaging are often nullified by attitudes and dodges of brokers and officials. When blacks do move into a pleasant neighborhood, most whites leave. They believe the neighborhood will soon be all black, and, in a classic example of the self-fulfilling prophecy, they flee to the suburbs. Slum rents are high. Urban renewal projects have been branded as "black removal," for slum clearance often makes room either for freeways or for housing the poor cannot afford. As a result, three out of ten blacks live in substandard housing.

Residential segregation produces *de facto* school segregation, which is just as real as the *de jure* segregation outlawed by the Supreme Court—except that, as writer James Baldwin puts it, "nobody did it." Most blacks attend predominantly black schools (except in Northern high schools), and these facilities are just as "unequal" as black schools in the South. Busing to achieve school integration has met resistance in all parts of the country. Schools in urban slums are usually physically

[59]Robert A. Liston, *The American Poor* (New York: Dell Publishing Company, 1970), pp. 102–3.

[60]Alphonso Pinkney, *Black Americans* (Englewood Cliffs, N.J.: Prentice-Hall, Inc., 1969), p. 43.

[61]*Ibid.*, p. 136. He warns that data on crime are inadequate and often contradictory.

inadequate and also difficult to staff. Teachers prefer well-behaved middle-class youngsters, and where there is choice of assignments slum schools must often make do with "permanent substitutes." Teachers also tend to share the race prejudice of the American community in general, or, if they are black, to have class prejudices against slum children. One white teacher found his colleagues so racist, cynical, condescending, unimaginative, and anti-intellectual that he wrote an angry book called *Death at an Early Age: The Destruction of the Hearts and Minds of Negro Children in the Boston Public Schools.*[62]

CONSEQUENCES FOR PERSONALITY AND SOCIAL RELATIONSHIPS

Members of a group subject to prejudice and discrimination suffer several kinds of consequences to their personalities, all of which are manifest among the blacks of our urban slums, where the problems appear most acute. Overcrowding, poor living conditions, and inadequate schools affect motivation. Children form a negative conception of themselves as they learn that they are considered second- or third-class citizens and become convinced that nothing they do will make much difference. They come to believe they really are inferior; they expect to fail, and so they do. In the words of Martin Luther King, Jr., blacks are "forever fighting a degenerating sense of nobodyness." They feel that whites do not look at or listen to them as people; that they are either invisible or, if they are noticed, are categorically rejected on the basis of skin color. Further, the skills young blacks must learn to survive on the streets are often penalized in school, where middle-class teachers interpret their behavior as defiant and disrespectful.[63]

Blacks in general, and especially the black youth of the slums, feel a sense of alienation, of being cut off from the mainstream of American life. Alienation has been defined as "the state of mind that can find a social order remote, incomprehensible, or fraudulent; beyond real hope or desire; inviting apathy, boredom, even hostility. The individual not only does not feel part of the social order; he has lost interest in being a part of it."[64] Feelings of powerlessness, feelings that no one hears, listens, or cares, are involved in such a sense of estrangement from the larger society. An Oakland, California, gang leader is quoted as saying, "I can't lose by rioting. Done lost. Been lost. Gonna be lost some more. I'm sayin' to the Man, 'You includin' me in this game or not?' And I know his answer, so I'm gettin' ready to get basic."[65]

[62]Jonathan Kozol (Boston: Houghton Mifflin, 1967).

[63]For a discussion of ghetto life styles see David A. Schulz, *Coming Up Black* (Englewood Cliffs, N.J.: Prentice-Hall, Inc., 1969).

[64]Robert A. Nisbet, *Community and Power* (New York: Oxford University Press, 1962), p. viii.

[65]*Newsweek* (Nov. 20, 1967).

Another consequence to personality, related to those already mentioned, is the corrosion of hate, anger, and frustration. These emotions may be expressed in self-destructive behavior such as alcoholism, drug addiction, gambling, withdrawal, or apathy. Or they may find an outlet in aggression against other blacks or the hated majority—in crime or mob violence. "Rioting," says psychologist Kenneth Clark (a black man), is "the expression of the anarchy of the profoundly alienated," who, being *systematically* excluded from middle-class life, can hardly be expected to feel bound by its constraints.[66]

Such attitudes and behavior tend to perpetuate the stereotype of blacks held by many whites, who react with fear and intensified suspicion and hostility. This, says Charles Silberman, is the *real* "American dilemma," and it has been so since long before the Civil War. He disagrees with Myrdal's thesis that white Americans are tortured by the discrepancy between their ideal of equality and the reality of discrimination. The real dilemma is the self-fulfilling prophecy: "white prejudice evokes Negro lawlessness, irresponsibility, and dependency—and these traits in turn nurture white prejudice."[67]

SOCIAL COSTS OF DISCRIMINATION

The social costs of discrimination are conspicuous in the higher incidence of poverty, disease, and crime in minority groups—and in the drain on public funds for palliative measures, and for the few measures aimed at correcting the underlying causes thus far taken. Less evident than money actually spent, but very real to economists, is the waste implicit in an untrained, unemployed, or underemployed group. They represent an untapped natural resource, one that cannot be stored for later use as oil reserves can. If the third of the poor who are black were fully employed, this alone would add $23.7 billion a year to our economy.[68]

But the problem of social costs goes much deeper. The final cost may be the cohesion of our society. The Kerner Report warns that unless the trend is reversed the United States will come to consist of two separate and unequal societies, a poor black one concentrated in the central cities and an affluent white one in the surrounding metropolitan areas. "The dark ghettoes now represent a nuclear stockpile which can annihilate the very foundations of America."[69]

[66]"The Wonder Is That There Have Been So Few Riots," *The New York Times Magazine* (Sept. 5, 1965); reprinted in Barron, ed., *Minorities in a Changing World*, pp. 249–57. See Chapter 18 for a discussion of riots.

[67]*Crisis in Black and White*, p. 13.

[68]*Newsweek* (Nov. 20, 1967).

[69]Clark, "The Wonder Is That There Have Been So Few Riots."

The Nature of the Black Subsociety

Why is racial division such a threat to the cohesion of American society? Why are not black Americans just another ethnic group, a subsociety with a subculture, accepted by themselves and others as part of the legitimate pluralism of our social system? More specifically, ask some whites, why don't they, like an immigrant group from Europe, pull themselves up by their bootstraps through patience, hard work, education, and thrift?

In a few respects American blacks in our large cities *are* like the earlier immigrant groups, in that their ancestors were also peasants struggling for a living from the land. They have the same problems of poverty, overcrowding, lack of continuity between the experiences of parents and children, and rejection of parents by children. Many immigrant groups also suffered discrimination and prejudice: Signs prohibited Irish-Americans from applying for jobs; negative stereotypes were expressed in epithets such as "Hunkies," "Wops," and "Polacks."

Like the immigrant groups whose descendants found they could not move freely in American society even when they became acculturated, the blacks confine most of their primary group interaction to their own separate social world. Like nationality groups, black Americans generally attend separate churches. They belong to separate voluntary associations such as fraternities and social clubs. To some extent they conduct separate businesses and patronize black doctors and lawyers. They have their own newspapers and magazines.

Like other subsocieties, blacks are further divided along class lines. In the days of slavery, there were distinctions among blacks, according to whether they were house slaves or field slaves, for example; and among free Negroes by white ancestry, shade of skin color, education, and occupation. Since Emancipation, many of the same criteria of stratification have been applied as among whites. The new black pride has deemphasized the importance of looking and acting like whites.

Before the great migration to the North, Southern blacks included a small upper class (perhaps 6%) of those with a known and respected family heritage, high educational status, and respectable occupations such as doctors, teachers, and successful landowners. A middle class of perhaps 12% included white-collar workers, small businessmen, teachers, and some skilled artisans. Most blacks were lower class, unskilled and semiskilled workers, sharecroppers, and tenant farmers.[70]

Being perceived by whites in general as "totally outside the white social order,"[71] today's urban blacks may be said to have a par-

---

[70]Allison Davis, Burleigh Gardner, and Mary Gardner, *Deep South* (Chicago: University of Chicago Press, 1941); Dollard, *Caste and Class in a Southern Town*; and Charles S. Johnson, *Growing Up in the Black Belt* (Washington, D.C.: American Council on Education, 1941).

[71]Richard P. Coleman and Bernice L. Neugarten, *Social Status in the City* (San Francisco: Jossey-Bass, 1971), p. 22.

allel class structure, with a larger lower class and an upper class corresponding to the white upper-middle class. Roughly 10% of blacks are upper class, 40% middle class, and 50% lower class. In addition to the criteria of education, income, and occupation, middle-class blacks stress respectability and communal activity.[72] This emphasis is seen as a consequence of the greater incidence of poverty among blacks.[73]

The black upper class centers around stable old families from the "safe six" occupations: doctors, lawyers, dentists, teachers, ministers, and social workers, as well as an increasing number of businessmen. They are likely to be Episcopalians, Presbyterians, and Congregationalists. Many mingle with whites socially, but few feel completely comfortable. Middle-class blacks come from a variety of occupations, including service workers and laborers as well as professionals, independent businessmen, and clerical workers; as long as they have fairly secure and adequate incomes and maintain a middle-class style of life, they qualify. They have a great concern for home ownership, education, stable family life, and keeping up appearances. They are likely to be members of Baptist and Methodist congregations. Both upper- and middle-class blacks are very active in social clubs and fraternities and sororities.[74]

A recent study finds that when socio-economic status and age are held constant, blacks are more likely than whites to participate in organizations—not only in the voluntary associations of the black community, but increasingly in areas that bring them into direct contact with whites—"the mass media, community activities, cultural events, voting, partisan political events, and contacts with the government." Participation is higher among those who identify as members of an ethnic community, which suggests that the new emphasis on "black pride" and "black power" stimulates increased social participation.[75]

The black lower class has probably been studied more than any other group in America in recent years. Despite this, certain stereotypes persist: The poor urban black is usually unemployed, prone to crime, and dependent on welfare, often deserting his family so that it can get public support. Although he agrees this is *sometimes* the case, Andrew Billingsley distinguishes three levels in the black lower class: the

[72]Andrew Billingsley, *Black Families in White America* (Englewood Cliffs, N.J.: Prentice-Hall, Inc., 1968), chap. 5, "Social Status in the White Community," pp. 122–46.

[73]E. Franklin Frazier, *The Negro Family in the United States* (Chicago: The University of Chicago Press, 1966), p.191.

[74]Pinkney, *Black Americans*, pp. 62–69, citing such studies as E. Franklin Frazier, *The Negro in the United States* (New York: The Macmillan Company, 1957); and *Black Bourgeoisie* (Glencoe, Ill.: The Free Press, 1957); and St. Clair Drake and Horace Cayton, *Black Metropolis* (New York: Harcourt, Brace, 1945). Recent studies indicate that blacks, like whites, increasingly rely on education, occupation, and income in determining class status.

[75]Marvin E. Olsen, "Social and Political Participation of Blacks," *American Sociological Review* 35, No. 4 (Aug. 1970): 682–97.

working nonpoor (families supported by a father who earns $5000 a year as a skilled craftsman, longshoreman, truck driver, etc.); the working poor (families headed by unskilled laborers and service workers); and the "underclass" (families who earn less than $2000 a year). Billingsley estimates that 50% of the black community belongs to one level or another of this class.[76]

Despite similarities with European immigrant groups, the history and visibility of blacks make their subsociety very different from other ethnic subsocieties. First, blacks cannot shed their blackness as Europeans could shed queer clothes and accents—if they should want to. Even those blacks who are middle-class Americans in every sense are still visible. Second, they "immigrated" late. They came to the Northern cities, not when everyone else was poor, but when affluence surrounded them. They immigrated, moreover, into an economy that no longer needed untrained men.

Finally, they are different from other immigrants because they are old Americans whose distinctive cultural patterns have long been considered inferior—often by blacks themselves. Centuries of slavery destroyed the black American's African heritage; he learned English, became a Christian, and often took his master's name. As he became urbanized he adopted the values of materialism, success, and comfort. Thus black culture has many elements in common with that of the white majority.

But centuries of oppression have left their mark on life style, religion, and the arts. Excluded from the mainstream, blacks developed a distinctive subculture, with its own churches and social organizations, its own forms of art and entertainment, and to some extent its own language. However, this culture has not always been a source of pride for blacks who aspired to higher status. (For years many blacks tried to lighten their skin and straighten their hair because status in the black community often was connected with degree of whiteness.)

In the last decade this attitude has changed. Somewhat like third- and fourth-generation immigrants whose parents had rejected Old World culture, blacks hark back sentimentally to the "old country," as Claude Brown explains in his autobiography, *Manchild in the Promised Land*:

> I suppose it's the . . . thing all Negroes have in common, the fat-back, chitterlings, and greens background. I suppose that regardless of what any Negro in America might do or how high he might rise in social status, he still has something in common with every other Negro. . . . In the fifties, when "baby" came around, it seemed to be the prelude to a whole new era in Harlem. It was the introduction to the era of black reflection. A fever started spreading. . . .
>
> I remember that . . . cats would stand on the corner and talk, just

76*Black Families in White America*, chap. 5.

shooting the stuff, all the street-corner philosophers. Sometimes, it was a common topic—cats talking about gray [white] chicks—and somebody might say something like, "Man, what can anybody see in a gray chick, when colored chicks are so fine; they got so much soul." This was the coming of the "soul" thing too.

"Soul" had started coming out of the churches and the nightclubs into the streets. Everybody was talking about "soul" as though it were something they could see on people or a distinct characteristic of colored folks. . . .

Everybody was really digging themselves and thinking and saying in their behavior, in every action, "Wow! Man, it's a beautiful thing to be colored." Everybody was saying, "Oh, the beauty of me! Look at me. I'm colored. And look at us. Aren't we beautiful?"[77]

The trend now is to "think black," let one's hair "go natural," study African history and art, to cultivate a feeling of solidarity with "black brothers" all over the world.

Since the emergence of independent nations in Africa, American blacks have begun to feel a sense of identity with the long-lost continent of their ancestors. For some, a pilgrimage increases the sense of being *Americans*; for others, it strengthens ethnic pride.

A Detroit artist and his wife, who works in the theater, reported, for example, that they

felt an almost urgent need to see our ancestral land. . . . Africans are, we found, a dignified and proud people with an immense devotion to their children and strong family loyalties. We felt an exhilarating—almost heady—sense of belonging to these proud and beautiful black people. It was like coming home to long-lost relatives. . . . Our trip to Africa deepened, strengthened, and intensified our feeling of "we are somebody." We only wish that every other Afro-

[77]Reprinted with permission of The Macmillan Company from *Manchild in the Promised Land* by Claude Brown. © by Claude Brown, 1965.

American could feel this way about himself. . . . The most amazing sensation was the feeling of belonging to and with these people—a feeling of binding ties never fully realized before; a sense of a proud, strong, and beautiful heritage.[78]

Like other strong ethnic subsocieties that resisted assimilationist policy, blacks have contributed in many ways to American culture. Much of Afro-American culture has its roots in suffering and oppression, which found release in work songs, spirituals, blues, and jazz, and in distinctive prose and poetry that often center around protest themes. The arts and sports were among the first areas in which blacks (as well as "white ethnics") distinguished themselves.

But, says Alphonso Pinkney, "Perhaps the single most important contribution (past, present, and future) of black people to American culture is to be found in the realm of social values." Their ability to endure makes some observers see in America's black people the ultimate salvation of America itself. Blacks, who in a sense are on the outside, can see the problems and faults of the social order more clearly and objectively than those in the mainstream; and they are more accepting of racial and cultural differences, more keenly aware of human suffering. Awareness of common problems has emphasized communalism among blacks—the idea of brotherhood, of sticking together. Thus black Americans set a moral example and are in the vanguard of social change.[79]

Goals and Means in Interracial Relations

While complete unity is impossible in a multi-group society, we have seen pluralism *is* possible and has allowed our religious and nationality subsocieties to remain distinct while sharing a strong undergirding of cultural unity on core values, a sense of belonging, and a sense of loyalty to the larger society. But interracial relations have been characterized neither by unity nor by pluralism; rather, there is what J. Milton Yinger calls "subcultural anomie," with a threatened drift to full anomie. That is, there is so great a lack of pattern in the mutual expectations for interaction that it threatens social cohesion. Whites and blacks disagree on or simply fail to communicate the nature of their goals. To the extent that they do agree in a general way on goals, they disagree on means for reaching them.

On one hand many blacks see the various ethnic divisions as having been designed not to keep members in but to keep them out. And whites in turn are bewildered and sometimes frightened by the

[78]*Detroit Free Press* (July 2, 1967).
[79]*Black Americans*, chap. 7, "Contributions to American Life," pp. 139–61.

more extremist, militant, and separatist factions of black protest. Do they really want to secede from American society? Do they really want to destroy it? Do they really want to join with the "colored" peoples of the world and dominate the whites?

Let us grant first of all that certain highly publicized black groups do proclaim these as their goals. But the great majority, it appears, agree with Representative John Conyers of Michigan, who said, "All we [blacks] want is for America to be what it says it is." They accept the core values of freedom, equality of opportunity, respect for the individual, and impartial justice, and want them for themselves as well as for whites. These, then, may be accepted as the fundamental goals of the black people in the United States. And, as we have seen, the inequalities in life chances, the costs of discrimination and prejudice to personality, and the threat to the cohesion of our society demand that the reality of interracial relations be brought closer to these goals.

Is pluralism compatible with racial desegregation and integration? Would not one or more of the groups always be singled out as a minority and discriminated against?

Yinger looks to Hawaii for clues. Our fiftieth state, he says, has preserved distinctive groups with visibly different subcultures, among which there is some hostility but relatively little stereotyping and discrimination. On the basis of the Hawaiian situation Yinger has developed four principles to help us distinguish between "arbitrary and discriminatory segregation" and "legitimate pluralism."[80]

First, segregation is undesirable when it is related in hidden ways to other lines of separation. For example, the principle that a man has a right to pick his friends may justify exclusion of some people from a men's club, and that he has a right to pick his neighbors may be used to justify neighborhood segregation. But if the men's club also has lines into political and economic power and not merely friendship, it is discriminatory; and if the neighborhood separates the excluded children from opportunities for schooling and any other cultural participation, this, too, is discriminatory.

Another principle is that "when separation is systematic or total it is undesirable segregation." Thus a city may have a few snobbish, exclusive, and lily-white neighborhoods (as does Honolulu); but if it does not also have massive ghettos, and provides its minorities with many "escape hatches" from the slums, it is perhaps providing freedom both to be snobbish and to buy wherever one can afford to buy. Third, when segregation is exclusive rather than inclusive—designed to keep certain groups *out* rather than certain groups *in*—it is unjust. Finally, the criteria of membership should have some cultural or functional significance. Jewish neighbors will not feel offended at not being invited to join the Methodist Mission Circle, nor sociologists to the Engineering Society. But if black Methodists are barred from the church or black

[80] *A Minority Group in American Society* (New York: McGraw-Hill, 1965).

engineers from the society, that is discrimination rather than legitimate separation based on functional or cultural criteria.

To Yinger's four principles, Gordon would add a fifth—that a proper blend of integration and pluralism means that any person may freely choose to stay within his ethnic subsociety or may with equal freedom cross its lines and make friends with, and even marry, members of other subsocieties. In Hawaii, most lines of separation are legitimate by these five tests; on the mainland they fail.

In sum, concludes Yinger,

> Separation is legitimate in a democracy when it is freely chosen and not coerced, when it does not deny any group access to the mainstream of the culture while giving others an advantage, when it does not so warp the personalities of some—by denying them hope and the opportunity to learn the skills and values of the society—that not only they but the whole nation suffers.[81]

ACHIEVING A BALANCE OF INTEGRATION AND PLURALISM

Let us assume, then, that a blend or balance of pluralism and integration would bring about the greatest improvement in life chances for black Americans and serve as the best guarantee of social cohesion. How can this balance be achieved?

The formula of the vicious circle or self-fulfilling prophecy—in which prejudice justifies discrimination, discrimination results in low status, and low status reinforces prejudice—suggests three angles of attack. These are: reduction of prejudice; reduction of discrimination; and improvement of status.

Reduction of prejudice. A direct attack on prejudice requires that parents, teachers, churches, the mass media, and other agencies attempt, formally and informally, to educate people on the facts of racial, religious, and nationality differences, and on the causes of tension and conflict. One aspect is preventive—a sort of immunization against the poison of prejudice, which, like smallpox vaccine, is best administered early in childhood and regularly thereafter.

Although prejudice is not innate, it is learned very early and very easily. Frances Ilg, a well-known psychologist, advocates a program that begins with the child at age 3, when he should play with children of other racial groups.[82] The 4- and 5-year-old can be told in

[81]Ibid., pp. 86–87.

[82]Judith D. R. Porter, Black Child, White Child: The Development of Racial Attitudes (Cambridge, Mass.: Harvard University Press, 1971), reports that actual interaction patterns of preschool age children do not reflect the racial prejudices they express. Instead, they choose playmates on the basis of sex, personality, and play style; thus integrated nursery schools may be able to counteract the negative effects of early and informal socialization in the family and neighborhood.

simple language about the world and its people, the 6- to 8-year-old guarded against absorbing stereotypes from the rhymes and clichés of the culture ("Eenie, meenie, minie, mo, catch a nigger by the toe"). The 9-year-old's horizons can be broadened by such activities as taking him to different churches and temples. At age 10 the "intellectual approach" can reinforce the emotional acceptance that earlier contacts have inculcated; he can be taught facts about race, minorities, discrimination, and scapegoating. Social scientists are giving serious study to training teachers in this area, for the teacher's role is crucial in any long-range program aimed at changing attitudes.[83]

But none of these attempts will be effective unless they are reinforced by reference groups,[84] which means that the problem cannot wait until a new and unprejudiced generation grows up. Adult attitudes need to be changed, partly through the intellectual approach but mostly through *equal-status contacts in pursuit of a common goal.* These do more to teach people their essential similarity than all the scientific research and formal teaching in the world. The factory worker who stands next to a black day after day soon sees him as an individual. The college student whose class is mixed is more likely to judge members of minority groups on the basis of individual traits and abilities than one whose school excludes minorities, no matter how many fine books both may read on race relations. A black who saw combat in Vietnam says, "At first the white guys in our unit were ashamed that they had to associate with you, but after our first combat, we were real buddies."[85] Another said that for the first time he found out that not all white people are geniuses and not all blacks are idiots.[86]

As interracial violence and brutality became increasingly appalling and flagrant in the early 1960s, the late President Kennedy asked Americans to put American values to work "in all our daily lives." Kenneth Clark expresses the effect of everyday contacts as follows:

> Every time a Negro sees a group of secretaries—white and Negro—chatting over lunch; or children—white and Negro—walking together to school, he feels that hope is possible. Every time his white friend shows he is not afraid to argue with him as with anyone else, he sees that freedom is possible, that there are some for whom race is irrelevant, who accept or reject a person not as a Negro or a white,

[83]See Lloyd Allen Cook, *College Programs in Intergroup Relations* (Washington, D.C.: The American Council on Education, 1950); and *Intergroup Relations in Teacher Education* (1951) vol. 1 and 2 of the College Study in Intergroup Relations.

[84]See Chapter 11 for a discussion of reefrence groups.

[85]*Newsweek* (Nov. 20, 1967).

[86]Whitney M. Young, Jr., "When the Negroes in Vietnam Come Home," *Harper's Magazine* (June 1967), p. 63 ff.

but in terms of himself. Only so can the real confinements of the ghetto be broken.[87]

Reduction of discrimination.   The attack on prejudice is primarily educational; the attack on discrimination depends largely on the power of government. It was long believed that legislation could do nothing to solve the problem of interracial relations because it could not "change men's hearts." But this belief did not take into account the formula of the vicious circle. Let us consider the effect of the court rulings, executive orders, and laws that have banned segregation in schools, public housing, and the army and that have outlawed discrimination in hiring and in the use of public and quasi-public facilities.

Frequently, the results have demonstrated that where discrimination is outlawed, prejudice actually declines. Legislation helps create a changed social climate and thus helps change attitudes. When people are asked, for example, what they think of fair employment practices, of having black mayors, doctors, teachers, nurses, or neighbors, they often object vehemently, predicting dire results and destructive conflicts. But if the policy is put into effect firmly and without fanfare, the results are almost always contrary to these predictions. Fair employment practices legislation and nonsegregated housing projects have been highly successful where they have been tried. "A *fait accompli* that fits in with our democratic creed is accepted with little more than an initial flurry of protest."[88] When whites realize, in other words, that busing and neighborhood integration may help bring reality closer to the American creed, many of them accept the policies philosophically. And the resultant contacts on a basis of equality help eradicate prejudice and encourage acceptance of individuals on their own merits.

The great majority of Americans, according to James Vander Zanden, fall into two categories: those who are not prejudiced but stand silently by or give discrimination passive support because it is expedient or profitable to do so; and those who are prejudiced but will not discriminate if it is made difficult to do so—who prefer to conform. Laws that punish discriminatory practices are highly effective with both kinds of people, and thus they can give a person a chance to be accepted—or rejected—on his own merits.[89]

Individuals, especially whites, can bring pressure to bear, challenging discriminatory practices that may be habitual and persist more

---

[87]Kenneth B. Clark, "Delusions of the White Liberal," *The New York Times Magazine*, April 4, 1965. © 1965 by The New York Times Company. Reprinted by permission.

[88]Gordon W. Allport, "Resolving Intergroup Tensions, An Appraisal of Methods," in Lloyd Allen Cook, ed., *Toward Better Human Relations* (Detroit: Wayne State University Press, 1952), p. 71.

[89]*American Minority Relations: The Sociology of Race and Ethnic Groups*, 2nd ed. (New York: Ronald Press, 1966), p. 512.

by inertia than on the basis of prejudice. Shoppers can remind a store-keeper that he would do well to employ blacks; invite black friends to church services; put pressure on local boards to reexamine school districting and housing credit; and, perhaps, forget the old "color-blind" ideal and appreciate black friends, as they might appreciate Japanese or Chilean or Swedish friends, on the basis of the spice diversity adds to life. They face the possibility of rejection, of suspicion of their sincerity, of being charged with "tokenism," for blacks often feel that these long-overdue recognitions of common humanity come too late. In Alan Paton's *Cry, the Beloved Country*, a black in South Africa says sadly, "I have one great fear in my heart, that one day when they [the whites] are turned to loving they will find we are turned to hating."

Improved status for black Americans.   The third angle of attack on the vicious circle is aimed at improving the status of black Americans. In the framework of Weber's analysis of social stratification, this in turn involves three dimensions: (1) *economic position*, which at present causes the life chances of most blacks to lag behind those of whites; (2) *status* or prestige, in their own eyes and those of others, thus diminishing self-hatred and aggressive tendencies on both "sides"; and (3) *power* to influence others and to determine the course of their own lives. Like other approaches to the problem, these are intricately interrelated. Success in one dimension facilitates and reinforces success in the other dimensions. A steady job for an unemployed father, for example, increases his self-respect, improves family stability, provides his children with a model for achievement, with better food and medical care, and with clothes to wear to school, and frees the family from dependence on public welfare funds.

The means to these ends are subjects of controversy. Quite aside from the "let-them-pull-themselves-up-by-their-bootstraps" school of thought, there are those who would prefer to attack the problem of poverty in general without any special reference to race. Others say the black subsociety is like an underdeveloped nation within our borders, lagging so far behind that it needs huge injections of "foreign aid" for schools, job training, housing, health, and welfare in order to break the self-perpetuating cycle of poverty. The precedent of 1818, which makes the government hesitate to single out any "ethnic group" for special help, is, the latter would insist, hardly applicable to a group that was held in slavery for two or three hundred years, and treated as peons or "untouchables" for a hundred more. Whatever the approach, however, the task of erasing the results of past discrimination is urgent and essential.

Economic improvement helps; reduction of prejudice and discrimination helps; but the growing strength of the black subculture may help even more.

Blacks are coming to terms with their collective self and celebrating ethnic being. Despite rhetorical excesses, the current Black self-pride can be as creative and positive as the past self-hate syndrome was destructive. It becomes creative when it is seen not as 'separatism,' as some of its advocates view it, but as a necessary phase through which Black Americans must go to achieve full equality in a pluralistic culture.[90]

And while some black nationalists are separatist rather than pluralist, "black power" need not be so interpreted. Although the concept arouses fear and distrust among whites, black power can help raise the status of blacks and ensure the cohesion of American society. For what do the vote and the dollar mean for other blocs in our society if not power? Democracy, said a group of black clergymen in a statement regarding black power, means the use of economic and political strength to influence the people with whom one interacts. Why should whites use it freely while blacks are expected to appeal only to conscience? Power in modern society is essentially *organizational* power. The whole group was oppressed, not just chosen individuals. "We will not find our way out of that oppression until both we and America accept the need for Negro Americans as well as for Jews, Italians, Poles, and white Anglo-Saxon Protestants, among others, to have and to wield group power. . . . We and all other Americans are one. We are indissolubly linked."[91]

The concept of black power, then, may be seen as a recognition of the reality of and the need for pluralism as well as for integration; and perhaps more and more Americans, black and white, will come to define it in these terms when the "tumult and the shouting die." And like the three main religions and the various nationality groups, blacks will see themselves, and be seen by others, as a subsociety that is part of a unified, yet diverse America—with freedom to remain within their group for their primary relationships and to cross its borders equally freely if they wish to do so.

Summary

Most modern societies are divided along the lines of race, religion, and nationality, which in many cases give rise to bitter conflict. Negative intergroup prejudices are based on faulty and inflexible generalizations or stereotypes of what all the people in an outgroup are like. Prejudice refers to how we think and feel about others, and to how we are disposed to act toward them; discrimination, to how we actually do behave toward them, depriving or excluding them according to their category

[90]James Farmer, "Toward Pluralism," *The Humanist* (Nov.–Dec. 1971): 21.
[91]*The New York Times* (July 31, 1966).

and not on the basis of individual qualities. Segregation, by setting up barriers to interaction, increases the likelihood of unfavorable stereotypes. Although discrimination is usually based on or "justified" by prejudices and stereotypes, prejudice does not invariably lead to discrimination. A particularly virulent form of prejudice is racism, the belief in inborn and ineradicable differences among categories of people, which places all members of one category in a position of inferiority or superiority in relation to others. Although no correlation between intelligence or cultural achievement and the inherited physical differences by which men are categorized into "races" has ever been proved, such beliefs are important because people *think* they are.

Discrimination and prejudice may persist because they bring one group gains in wealth, power, and prestige; because that group fears competition; and because cultural beliefs persist through inertia and through the operation of the vicious circle or self-fulfilling prophecy. Individuals acquire prejudice from the groups in which they are socialized and to which they aspire; social distance tests indicate that, even for minorities, the standards of the dominant majority serve as a frame of reference.

One pattern of intergroup relations is the melting pot, in which, presumably, all differences would be discarded and blended into something new. The most prevalent pattern is that of majority dominance of a subordinate minority or minorities. The majority commonly tries to keep the minority subordinate through discrimination and segregation, whether in a paternalistic caste system or a competitive situation, which arises as a society modernizes. Less commonly, the majority resorts to annihilation or complete segregation, or insists on acculturation in the dominant culture, which may be followed by assimilation and amalgamation.

In a pluralistic pattern, ethnic groups based on ascribed differences form subsocieties with subcultures that give their members a sense of peoplehood; as long as they are loyal to the political and economic institutions of the larger society, they are allowed to maintain their own identities. Most people find their primary relationships within an ethnic group and among members of the same social class. Desegregation means the achievement of civil rights for all; integration involves the elimination of prejudice and the achievement of freedom in primary relationships among all groups. The American social order is a mixture of pluralism and majority dominance, with some effort to achieve desegregation and integration, but a general abandonment of the dream of the melting pot.

This pattern is reflected particularly in the history of various nationality groups. The older immigrants established the dominance of white Anglo-Saxon Protestant culture; the new immigration, largely Catholic peasants from southeastern Europe, as well as Jews, suffered prejudice and discrimination, but over several generations became acculturated. Still they return to their own subsocieties for primary relationships and a sense of peoplehood, thus achieving "structural pluralism."

Religious antagonisms have largely subsided; Americans are very interested in a person's religious identity and tend to regard religion itself as a good thing. But interfaith cooperation and involvement in social issues are more common among theologians and clergymen than among laymen, who continue to harbor prejudices and encourage marriage within the ingroup.

Racial minorities continue to suffer discrimination, with its consequences of inferior life chances and costs to society and personality. Indians form a unique minority, almost annihilated under early settlers and the U.S. Army, then placed on reservations under the paternalistic administration of a special federal bureau. For complex reasons, especially a disparity in cultural values, communal living appears to offer them more promise of improved life chances than does assimilation. Japanese- and Chinese-Americans were long subjected to discrimination and even oppression and violence, but have become so thoroughly acculturated that many Chinese fear a loss of identity and the Japanese are seen as a "model minority" comparable to Jewish Americans. Mexican-Americans are a cultural and especially a linguistic minority, subject to racist prejudice and discrimination reflected in their life chances.

But the largest minority, the Americans of African descent whose ancestors came in chains and were stripped of their culture and denied family life, present the most serious challenge to social cohesion and implementation of core values. Although remarkable gains have occurred, partly as a result of the great migration to Northern cities since World War II, there is perhaps more consciousness of relative deprivation now than formerly. Gunnar Myrdal believed that gains would come about because of the "American dilemma"—the great disparity between our ideals and reality which tortures well-meaning white Americans. Silberman disagrees, saying the real American dilemma is the self-fulfilling prophecy by which some blacks react to white prejudice with lawless behavior, irresponsibility, and dependency, and thus evoke further prejudice and discrimination.

The black subsociety is comparable to other ethnic subsocieties in some respects, but different in others: visibility, a history of slavery, and their late migration to industrial cities. Blacks today are cultivating their distinctive subculture and gaining a sense of "black pride," and of identity with "brothers" all over the world.

Despite some extremist advocates of separatism and revolution, most blacks appear to want to work within the system, and achieve a blend of pluralism and integration that would improve their life chances and self-esteem, as well as their freedom to participate in many aspects of American life. No one approach appears adequate: Prejudice must decline, but will not decline unless discrimination is also attacked; and both are interrelated with improvements in material comforts, educational opportunities, and self-esteem. The concept of black power means essentially that blacks, like other groups, stand to gain within the pluralist structure of our society by working together to put political and economic pressure where it counts.

QUESTIONS FOR FURTHER THOUGHT

1. Who are you? What are you? Quickly jot down several self-identifying terms. Analyze your reaction to these questions. Which terms give you a "sense of peoplehood"?

2. Ask several others these questions. Note the order in which they use self-identifying terms. If they mention nationality background, find out which generation; how much of the ethnic culture they retain; if they are part of a structurally distinct subsociety. If they mention religion, ask them if they attend a church or temple. If they mention race, ask why they identify themselves as members of that race. The question of "Jewishness" is a difficult one, even in Israel. Ask your Jewish acquaintances why they consider themselves Jews.

3. Do you believe self-identification is the proper criterion for census classification? If not, what indices of race, ethnic background, and religion would you use, and why?

4. Do you believe American society is still WASP-dominated? If so, in what institutional areas? By what indices?

5. The black policeman is a classic example of the marginal man, part of two cultures but not completely at home in either. Why?

6. Do women fit the criteria of a minority group? Students? Young people? Elderly people?

7. Philip Wylie once said the world's problems would not be solved until everyone is the color of tea. Do you believe biological amalgamation would really solve the world's problems? Would it help? What other sources of conflict would remain?

8. Walter White, long head of the NAACP, looked white. Why did he identify himself as a black? If this question intrigues you, read his autobiography, *A Man Called White,* and you will find much about the importance of

identity, definitions of the situation, American racism, and the civil rights movement.

9. By the same reasoning that institutions are now charged with being "white racist," they might have been called "English" 100 or more years ago (but other nationalities joined them); "Christian" 50 years ago (but Jews joined them). Do you believe this charge is correct? Why or why not? Will racial minorities ever become part of them? How?

10. "Black English" is as much the language of home and friends, especially among ghetto blacks, as "Spanglish" is that of Chicano children. Relate this fact to the still-powerful "Americanization" or "Anglo-conformity" doctrine implicit in American education, and the middle-class orientation of most teachers.

11. Myrdal, some critics have charged, confused race prejudice with class prejudice, and believed a change in the socioeconomic status and education of blacks would eliminate prejudice. Is there evidence in this chapter for or against this argument?

12. Myrdal also believed riots would occur in the South rather than the North. Account for the fact that the most severe riots have been in Northern cities.

13. Myrdal predicted that labor unions would be prominent in acting to promote legal equality. Why have they failed to do so?

14. The mass media are charged with perpetuating stereotypes. Watch a number of programs. Is it true that Mexicans are the one minority still depicted according to stereotypes? Do you see any black family portrayed as going about its ordinary daily routine?

15. James Farmer says the idea of "color blindness" adhered to by blacks and their liberal allies until the mid-sixties has not served us well. It's a phony ideal; it is dishonest to pretend one is not aware of differences. The ideal of pluralism, Farmer says, is "He's black; how beautiful. He's white; how lovely. Or brown or red or yellow." Discuss. ["Toward Pluralism," *The Humanist* (Nov.–Dec. 1971): 21.]

16. Busing to achieve school integration and scatter-site housing (building small low-income housing projects in middle-class neighborhoods) have caused considerable controversy.

Those in favor of these projects argue that both racial and economic prejudice will decline if the races and classes mix. Opponents argue these plans will ruin suburban schools and neighborhoods. Which side do you take? Do you feel the federal government has a right to intervene in this way? An obligation?

Part Three

THE PERSON IN CULTURE AND SOCIETY

We have set the stage, cast the players, and studied the script. Now the actors come on stage. We have hinted at their arrival many times, mentioning their basic similarities and their infinite variety. We have spoken of the action of the play as social interaction, the reciprocal influencing of behavior through symbolic communication among socialized persons. We have emphasized that culture itself does nothing; it is *persons* who do things, more or less according to the cultural script that tells them how they may, must, or must *not* act, think, and feel. Each person gives a performance guided by this script and by the roles in which he is cast by the social structure.

How does a person accept a part and learn a role? Why are no two people, even in the same role, quite alike? Why do some give wooden performances and others create fresh interpretations? Why do some forget their lines, ad lib, stalk off the stage before their exit cue, rewrite the second act? What bits of byplay go on that are not in the script?

Like all analogies, that of the play is intriguing, but it goes only so far and then misleads us. There is, for example, no director in social interplay; everyone directs everyone else, and in the process they change the script and shift roles. Perhaps an extemporaneous performance or the theater of the absurd might be a more perfect analogy. But let us leave it now and pose our questions in sociological terms.

Culture, society, and personality (as the analogy suggests) are intimately bound up with each other. In Part Three we examine their interrelationships from the vantage point of personality. Social cohesion must rest on the willingness of each person to abide by cultural norms and to play the role that goes with his status in the group. How does the person come to feel part of the group? Why does he accept (or reject) social discipline? How does he come to feel that he is a unique being with an identity of his own, and a capacity to shape his own life?

In Chapter 11 we look at several theories of personality formation that are very different from one another and give us perspective on the social-psychological view. Instincts, inborn drives, cultural patterns, class status, the capacity to learn to respond in conditioned ways to external stimuli—each of these has been held to be the "master key" to human behavior. The social psychologist claims to have no master key; he relies on no single factor to explain the development of personality. Instead, he considers the biological organism inside the social group and examines the process by which a person *becomes* a person by interacting with others and learning the cultural patterns. The last section of the chapter discusses one of the great theories of human behavior—symbolic interactionism—which demonstrates the intricate relationship of culture, society, and personality as single-factor theories do not. This theory, first advanced by George Herbert Mead, explains how culture and society "get inside" the person; how the "self" arises; why the basis of the social order is the ability of each person to think about himself and his actions and to feel empathy with others. We shall see that each person's behavior may best be understood in terms of his conception of himself—his sense of identity and self-esteem. As he interacts with others, he seeks to arrive at a satisfactory self-conception, to live up to it, enhance it, and defend it.

While Chapter 11 deals with the process of becoming human—how any baby in any society becomes socialized—Chapters 12 and 13 are concerned with variations in personality—the things that make each of us unique and those that make all of us somewhat like other members of the various groups and categories to which we belong. We consider conformity to and deviance from cultural norms, and finally discuss the possibility and desirability of achieving personal autonomy—freedom to choose what to make of ourselves within the limits of our organic nature on the one hand and our socio-cultural order on the other.

We haven't all had the good fortune to be ladies; we haven't all been generals, or poets, or statesmen; but when the toast works down to the babies, we stand on common ground.

MARK TWAIN

We normally organize our memories on the string of our self.

G. H. MEAD

Through the Thou a man becomes I.

MARTIN BUBER

There is an organizing center in human beings that comes to grips with the outside world, forms it, and acts upon it. This psychic center we call the *self*.

RICHARD L. MEANS

THE
PROCESS
OF
BECOMING
HUMAN

W$_{\text{HAT IS A BABY? A BUNDLE OF INSTINCTS?}}$ A receptacle for culture and a pipeline through which it is passed on? A prisoner of the economic class of his parents? An infinitely plastic creature with equal potential for becoming a physicist or a filling-station attendant? A battlefield for the conflict between primitive inborn forces and social restrictions? Or an active, seeking member of *Homo sapiens*, who will acquire and express a universal human nature and a unique personality through interaction within a culture-possessing social group?

These questions are all part of a more comprehensive question: How does the red, damp, squally, squirmy newborn baby grow up to be a participating member of society? In this chapter we look at several answers to that question in its general sense: How does a baby acquire human nature—any baby, in any society? In the next two chapters we shall inquire into variations in human nature in different societies and subcultures. In all three, we will be talking about the individual version of human nature—personality.

Personality refers to the (more or less) organized ways of behaving that characterize a given individual, including his patterns of thought, feeling, and action. It embraces all his modes of adjusting to and attempting to master his environment—his habits and skills, his perspectives or frames of references, his style of interaction in interpersonal relationships, the things he "knows" as matters of fact and believes on faith.

When we think of personality we are generally thinking of its unique aspects, those that distinguish each of us from the other billions in the world. And it is true that in some respects each of us is like no one else. This infinite variety of personality lends the spice of unpredictability to social interaction. But in many respects each of us is also like some other men and all other men. This likeness results from similarities in the three main factors that shape personality: our biological organisms, our nurturing as infants, and the society and culture in which we are socialized. The many possible variations in each of these factors, and their dynamic interplay, plus the accidents and circumstances of life, all contribute to the uniqueness of the personality, which is not a result of passive reactions to their influence but rather "an effortful, striving, seeking unity."

The first theories into which we shall inquire, however, dismiss such complexities and claim to have the "master key" to the mystery of human nature and personality.

Biological Determinism

Human nature and personality depend on the original baggage babies bring into the world. That is the basic premise of theories of biological determinism, which appeared after Charles Darwin caused man to see himself in a new light—as a biological organism, a member of the animal kingdom. According to these theories, human behavior is simply an expression or unfolding of inborn drives or tendencies such as instincts, needs, constitutional make-up, or preprogrammed action patterns, some of which appear at certain ages, with maturation.

While the recognition that man is a biological organism helped to open the subject of human behavior to scientific study, the more extreme forms of biological determinism no longer command attention among social scientists and psychologists. The absurdities of classical instinct theory, for example, became apparent when one psychologist posited 2 instincts as the keys to behavior, while others compiled lists of 13, or 250, or even 1500. New versions of biological determinism, nonetheless, appear at intervals. A popular one these days is propounded by ethologists, who attribute such behavior as aggression to preprogramming in the genes (a new way of phrasing "instinct"), laid down millenia ago when early men and their ancestors lived much as ground apes do today. The main contribution of such studies, when they are not summarily rejected, is to remind social scientists that "in the beginning is the body."[1]

Cultural Determinism

Human nature and personality depend on the society into which a baby happens to be born. That is the basic premise of theories of cultural determinism. The individual is seen as a mere reflection of his culture, which is an irresistible, impersonal force. Leslie White sees the individual as a helpless slave of culture, a sort of puppet whose wishes, hopes, and fears have nothing to do with creating culture. At some point in the distant past, man did start the cultural ball rolling, but it has been out of his control ever since. White admits that "Man must

[1]Dennis Wrong, "The Oversocialized Conception of Man in Modern Sociology," in Robert Endleman, ed., *Personality and Social Life* (New York: Random House, 1967), pp. 39–50.

be there, of course, to make the existence of the culture process possible," but he is "merely the instrument through which cultures express themselves. . . . Culture makes man what he is and at the same time makes itself."[2]

Such a scheme does not explain the uniqueness of personality, and denies the capacity of persons to discover, interpret, and select alternative modes of behavior. It perpetuates the view that the individual and society are completely separate entities, and fails to explain how the person acquires culture.

Karl Marx was also a determinist, although he emphasized the influence of social structure rather than of culture in general. He regarded the occupation and social class into which a person is born as the basis of his motivation. Should a person offer verbal explanations of his actions that are contrary to his class interests, he is either ignorant of his true interests or covering up his motives. Under capitalism, worker and capitalist alike are enslaved by circumstances of their own making. The worker is alienated; his work does not belong to him but is an alien activity that dominates him, leaving him physically exhausted and mentally debased. Because work is so meaningless, man does not feel he has any power over the world. Industrial capitalism thus turns man into a thing and the slave of things; it destroys his individuality. According to Marx, only under full communism will man realize self-fulfillment, human nature blossom into perfection, and harmony and peace prevail.

Marxism is a classic example of those one-sided or "single-factor" theories that contribute a much-needed emphasis on a neglected factor—in this case by counteracting the assumption that human motivations are purely individual in origin and showing that men could be commonly motivated by shared circumstances.

Behaviorism

In sharp contrast to biological and cultural determinists, behaviorists focus on the individual organism and its capacity to learn. Although there are different schools of behaviorism, in general it may be said that they agree on the following principles:

1. Psychology is essentially the study of animal behavior, and experiments with "lower" animals can furnish knowledge directly applicable to human behavior.

2. Only overt behavior is a proper subject of scientific study; subjective experience that can be studied only by introspec-

[2]Leslie White, *The Science of Culture* (New York: Grove Press, 1949), pp. 340, 353.

tion is to be ignored. (Thought and speech, however, are considered organic behavior.)

3. Behavior can be understood in terms of stimulus and response. The process of learning consists of "conditioning" —attaching the proper responses to various stimuli through a system of reward, or "positive reinforcement," and punishment, or "negative reinforcement," which works because in general the organism seeks to avoid pain and experience pleasure.

4. Aside from narrow physiological needs such as those for food, water, and a mate (which provide the energy for all psychological processes), the newborn infant is infinitely plastic; he can learn anything.

This last belief was stated in extreme form by John B. Watson, whose book *Behaviorism* appeared in 1924:

> Give me a dozen healthy infants, well-formed, and my own specified world to bring them up in and I'll guarantee to take any one at random and train him to become any type of specialist I might select— doctor, lawyer, artist, merchant-chief and, yes, even beggar-man and thief, regardless of his talents, penchants, tendencies, abilities, vocations, and race of his ancestors.[3]

Many psychologists today are behaviorists in the sense that they believe that "Behavior, rather than mind, thoughts, and feelings, is the subject of psychology, because it alone can be observed, recorded, and studied. No one ever saw, heard, or touched a mind, but one can see, hear, and touch behavior."[4] They are, thus, positivist-empiricists. They believe that personality is nothing more than learned behavior; that behavior can be predicted on the basis of past conditioning, and changed or corrected by reconditioning in the present.

B. F. Skinner, a leading behaviorist, insists that societies must make desirable behavior "pay off." His arguments are based largely on years of experimenting with laboratory animals, which he taught to perform complex operations by rewarding correct movements with food. Skinner believes that human (like other animal) behavior is determined; it represents the consequences of past conditioning. He has no room for such concepts as consciousness, mind, imagination, and purpose; even when a person invents something or writes a poem or establishes a business he is simply expressing the determining effects of his past history.

[3]*Behaviorism*, rev. ed. (Chicago: University of Chicago Press, 1930), p. 104. Paperback version reprinted in 1962.

[4]Clifford T. Morgan, *Introduction to Psychology*, 2nd ed. (New York: McGraw-Hill, 1961), pp. 2–3.

Skinner even argues that freedom, in which the individual is subjected to arbitrary, unguided, and often contradictory experiences, is dangerous. In his Utopian novel, *Walden Two*, Skinner suggests that people would be much happier in a society where all behavior is controlled through "social engineering" (positive reinforcement of desirable actions) and everything runs smoothly.[5]

Critics of Skinner's Utopia ask who will be in charge of conditioning; who will control the controllers? Such a society, they say, must be authoritarian and even totalitarian. Critics of behaviorism in general believe that man's mastery of language sets him so far apart from rats and pigeons that any knowledge gained from laboratory experiments with them is extremely limited in application. They also quarrel with the behaviorists' dismissal of subjective and emotional phenomena as something to be ignored because they cannot be measured. Learning, they insist, is far more complex and dynamic a process than stimulus and response plus conditioning can explain. Society cannot be understood as a maze in which organisms are taught the rules of the game by judicious administration of rewards and punishments. Finally, while the infant is capable of learning, he is not infinitely plastic. There are innate differences in drives, temperament, and intelligence that affect the response patterns of the growing child.

But whatever its shortcomings, behaviorism did contribute to a de-emphasis on heredity, even among those who do not accept extreme environmental determinism. It encouraged sociologists as well as psychologists to develop theories derived from overt behavior, to formulate operational definitions, and to test their hypotheses in such a way that another scientist could repeat the experiment. It also focused the psychologists' attention on the learning process.

Psychoanalytic Theory

Sigmund Freud (1856–1939), one of the giants of personality theory, has influenced scientific and popular thinking tremendously. Whenever we accuse a friend of a "Freudian slip" of the tongue, label a person "an anal character," tell someone he should see a shrink, or worry about how to toilet train our children, we are reflecting the Freudian revolution in the image of man.

Freud was concerned with the unconscious, irrational, covert, and emotional aspects of human nature, and their roots in early childhood experiences. Where behaviorists stress the effect of environment or biological capacities, he stressed biological imperatives; where they

[5]B. F. Skinner, *Walden Two* (New York: The Macmillan Company, 1948). A nonfictional exposition of the same ideas is found in *Beyond Freedom and Dignity* (New York: Alfred A. Knopf, 1971).

stress external stimuli and reward, he stressed inner motivations and emotional attitudes. He also believed that "anatomy is destiny"; that women, for example, not only *feel* inferior because they lack a penis, but that they *are* inferior; he always viewed them as mysterious and problematic creatures.

THE FREUDIAN VIEW OF PERSONALITY DEVELOPMENT

Freud saw a personality as consisting of three parts—the id, the ego, and the superego—that develop during clearly marked stages in early childhood. The *id*, he said, is the primitive core of the unconscious, quite ignorant of good and evil. It seeks only to gratify two overwhelming instinctual drives, sex (or libido) and aggression, which are the sources of psychic energy. The *ego* is the rational, largely conscious portion of personality, which seeks to preserve the organism by reconciling the insistent pleasure seeking of the id with the "reality principle"—the demands of the outer world. The ego is subject to anxiety if it is unable to find a socially acceptable outlet for the impulses of the id. To relieve this anxiety, it resorts to defense mechanisms. The chief of these is repression of undesirable impulses, which are forced back into the unconscious. The third element of personality is the *superego*, which is comparable to character or conscience; "it observes the ego, gives it orders, corrects it, and threatens it with punishments."[6] Thus it is the source of guilt.

The sensuality of the id seeks expression from earliest infancy. Personality is formed during various stages of maturation or development; in each stage a different erogenous zone is the chief source of pleasure, and the child's interests and interpersonal relationships are also different. During the *oral* stage, the infant gets erotic pleasure from sucking. If his needs are not satisfied, insecurity, anxiety, and conflict develop. The differentiation of the id and the ego begins as the infant establishes relations with his mother and others about him and becomes aware of himself as separate from surrounding people and objects. During the *anal* stage, when he discovers the mystery of the defecatory process and enjoys soiling a diaper and otherwise thwarting his toilet-training, retention and elimination become the center of interest and the source of pleasure. If he cooperates with his parents' demands, he wins their love and approval. Toilet-training is thus the ego's first conscious struggle for mastery over an id impulse.

During the *phallic* or *Oedipal* stage, between the ages of two-and-a-half and six, the famous "Oedipus complex" emerges. The growing boy wishes to possess his mother completely and to destroy his

[6]Sigmund Freud, *An Outline of Psychoanalysis* (London: Hogarth Press, 1949), p. 77.

father. (The girl feels the same love-hate pattern in reverse.) The repression of these incestuous and parricidal impulses is the core of socialization. It is accomplished through the development of the superego, which incorporates the moral judgments of the parents through a process of emotional *identification* with the parent of the same sex. (Freud believed that women fail to develop strong superegos; therefore they remain inferior human beings, childlike and puzzling.)

All personality structure, Freudians believe, is based on what happens during these three stages. If the child is handled incorrectly or "arrested" at any one stage, he will bear the scars for life, in the form of anxieties, traumas, and perversions, unless psychoanalytic therapy rids him of them. In normal development, the working out of the Oedipus complex and the development of a mature superego take years.

The appearance of the superego at age six marks the beginning of the *latency* period, when sexuality is relatively dormant. The ego, mediating between the id and the superego and between the id and reality, represses sexual tendencies. During these years when sexual turmoil is absent, the child learns a great deal about the world, and the basic biological tendencies such as giving and taking, retaining and eliminating, continue to develop into more complex forms. The pleasure from oral reception now manifests itself as pleasure in receiving gifts, and pleasure from retention develops into a desire to collect things.

With puberty the *genital* phase begins; latent libidinal impulses are reawakened by physical maturation, and once again the ego tries to repress them. If sexual tensions prove too difficult to cope with, the adolescent may resort to infantile ways of seeking satisfaction; the superego may cause intense guilt feelings; or expansion of interests and achievements, perhaps into intellectual and esthetic pursuits, may indicate successful sublimation. The old Oedipal conflict is revived in new form, as the girl quarrels more with her mother and the boy with his father. If he achieves emotional maturity, the person accepts both the sexual drives and social regulation of them. Adulthood is presented in the Freudian scheme as simply a working out of earlier occurrences, and neurosis as a failure of the ego to satisfy both id and superego, because of influences dating back to childhood.

PSYCHOANALYSIS OR PSYCHOTHERAPY

Psychoanalysis is aimed at freeing the person from "the tyranny of the unconscious." Because, the Freudians say, the impulses and experiences that create neurotic anxiety are buried so deep in the unconscious, psychoanalysis may take years. The analyst proceeds by a process called "free association," encouraging the subject to recall everything he can, including his dreams. He tries to dredge up repressed impulses and anxiety-producing memories from the unconscious, to allow the ego to focus conscious attention on them, and thus to permit the person to rid himself of his anxieties.

THE FREUDIAN INTERPRETATION OF SOCIETY

Where Leslie White sees personality as a dependent variable, reflecting culture, Freud saw *culture* as a dependent variable, merely a reflection of individual psychology. All our prescriptions for living, he believed, are based on man's eternal effort to handle the problems of sex and aggression. The social roles people play are crystallizations of mechanisms they have collectively decided are acceptable for harnessing the id. But living in society exacts a toll from the individual; the price of civilization is discontent. Man is the helpless victim of pressures that frustrate his natural impulses and distort his personality. Yet the very frustration of his sexual impulses forces him to find new channels to express them; thus he sublimates them and builds culture.

Social cohesion, according to Freudian theory, is explained by the concept of *identification*. This concept implies not only forming oneself after an admired model (the parent of the same sex during the latency period, for example) but also reacting to the status and characteristics, the possessions and achievements, of another person or group as if they were one's own. This gives a sense of belonging and security. When social organization breaks down, as in mob behavior, the libido reigns supreme; the person relaxes his inhibitions in favor of a guiltless expression of desires and repressed impulses, and the superego is powerless to control him.

AN EVALUATION OF FREUDIAN THEORY

Freud believed his theory, based on his experiences with neurotic upper-middle-class Viennese of the Victorian era, was universally applicable. He did not recognize the importance of cultural factors. Much of his theory, it is true, has been accepted as applicable to modern Western culture: The Oedipus complex, for example, appears to describe Western parent-child relationships at a certain stage of development. But the Oedipus complex has not been found in many societies, and some psychologists suggest that, to the extent that it is found in ours, it may be an outgrowth of roles and relationships rather than an expression of primal urges. In our culture, for example, fathers tend to be severe and repressive with sons, and mothers with daughters, and both are more indulgent with children of the opposite sex.[7] To the ex-

[7]Ross Stagner, *Psychology of Personality*, 3rd ed. (New York: McGraw-Hill, 1961), p. 306.

tent that Freud did recognize the importance of culture and society, he saw them as rooted in individual psychology, and as repressing, constraining, and distorting the human personality. He saw man as a helpless victim, caught in the trap of his own nature on the one hand and the prison of society on the other, rather than as an active agent with any degree of autonomy.

Freud also overemphasized the infantile origins of human motivation; he accepted no explanation of adult behavior that did not tie it firmly to early childhood experiences. In so doing, he also overemphasized the irrational, morbid, emotional side of man's nature and almost ignored the role of language and reason in human affairs.

Another shortcoming of Freudian theory, say its critics, is that it is essentially unscientific; it must be taken on faith. It is based on clinical evidence from case studies of disturbed personalities, which is presented as raw data mixed with interpretations in such a way as to make empirical checking and testing impossible.

On the positive side, the genius of Freud did suggest new depths and dimensions of human behavior and did provide a corrective to the view that man was a completely rational creature. His theory also stressed the subtlety and complexity of human interaction and fostered a skepticism about explanations of behavior in terms of observable actions alone.

Neo-Freudian Theory

Neo-Freudian psychologists accept much of Freud's theory, but also recognize cultural influences, the importance of language, and the possibility that experiences during adolescence and adulthood may have significance in themselves rather than simply as reproductions or recapitulations of childhood experience.

Erik Erikson, a prominent neo-Freudian psychotherapist, studied with Freud in Vienna, but later came to realize the importance of socio-cultural influences; he studied anthropology and worked with people in different cultures, including the Sioux and Yurok Indians. Erikson insists that "personality [not anatomy] is destiny," that we live in a social order and a personal order as well as a somatic (biological) order. It is conflict among these three that shapes personality. When all are in tune, the experience of the body is vital, and not simply functioning; the person is uniquely expressive, and not simply adjusted; and social life is truly communal, and not just organized.

Erikson's central concepts are identity and the life cycle. All through life, the ego engages in a quest for identity, which is a sense of personal sameness and historical continuity. Like Freud, he divides the development of personality into stages, but he outlines growth from the cradle to the grave, and not just to adolescence. In each of the eight stages of life that he distinguishes, a new dimension of social interaction becomes possible; success in each one depends on success in the previous stages.

In the first year of life, the infant acquires a sense of either trust or mistrust, depending on his relations with others (especially his mother). In the next two years, he seeks autonomy, wants to do things "by himself," to feel he has some control over himself and the world; failing in this, he suffers shame and doubt. At ages four and five, he engages in motor play, fantasy, and continual questioning; if his initiative is discouraged, he feels guilty and stupid.

In the fourth stage, corresponding to latency, he learns to play games by the rules, how things are made, how they work, and what they do. Other adults besides his parents become important. If this stage goes well, he masters industry; if not, he feels inferior. Adolescence, ages twelve to eighteen, is typically a period of identity crisis, for he is neither a child nor an adult. If he has come through earlier stages well and has a sense of autonomy and trust, he achieves a solid identity. Unarmed with these, he suffers role confusion, and may withdraw from society or assume some sort of mob identity.

In young adulthood and early married life he seeks intimacy with mate and friends; failing in this, he suffers isolation. During middle age the person who has successfully negotiated earlier stages is less concerned with personal needs and comforts than with the future of society, the welfare of coming generations. Finally, as old age comes and death approaches, he looks back on his life and either enjoys a sense of integrity and satisfaction, or feels despair and regret about what might have been.[8]

Humanistic Psychology

Dissatisfied with both experimental-behavioristic psychology and Freudian theory, a number of present-day psychologists stress subjective experience and the search for meaning and value in existence. Abraham Maslow called this "Third Force" (which includes neo-Freudian, existential, Gestalt, and ego or personality psychologists, among other schools) Humanistic Psychology. It "is not purely descriptive or academic; it suggests action and implies consequences. It helps to generate a way of life, not only for the person himself within his own private psyche, but also for the same person as a social being, a member of society. As a matter of fact, it helps us to realize how interrelated these two aspects

[8]Erik H. Erikson, *Childhood and Society* (New York: W. W. Norton, 1950), and *Identity: Youth and Crisis* (New York: W. W. Norton, 1968).

of life really are."[9] Maslow equates the humanistic revolution in psychology, which is just beginning, with the Freudian. "It is as if Freud supplied to us the sick half of psychology and we must now fill it out with the healthy half."[10]

On the basis of pilot research, bits of evidence, personal observation, theoretical deduction, and sheer hunch, Maslow posited a hierarchy of "instinctoid" needs. The evidence that we need each of these—love, for example—is exactly the same, in Maslow's view, as the evidence that we need Vitamin C. We can tell if needs are inborn, he said, if their absence breeds illness, their presence prevents illness, their restoration cures illness, and healthy persons do not demonstrate a deficiency of those things that gratify these needs. The five basic needs, as he saw it, are life, safety or security, belongingness and affection, respect and self-respect, and self-actualization. Life takes precedence over the others; only when the first three are gratified does a person seek the other two.

Maslow and other humanist psychologists make use of everyday words that are often ignored or taken for granted in psychological inquiry. We should, he said, regard as miracles such things as decision, choice, responsibility, self-creation, autonomy, and identity itself. The "mystery of communication between alone-nesses via intuition and empathy, love and altruism, identification with others" traditionally has been a subject for poets and novelists; he considered its disciplined study essential to achievement of a full life in a world where much seems meaningless and absurd. Similarly, he was concerned with "the seriousness and profundity of living (or perhaps the 'tragic sense of life') contrasted with the shallow and superficial life, which is a kind of diminished living, a defense against the ultimate problems of life."[11] He saw humanness as a matter of degree, self-actualization as the achievement of full humanness.

Symbolic Interactionism

Social psychologists agree with biological determinists and Freudians that human behavior begins with a biological organism that has certain needs, drives, and capacities. They agree with cultural determinists that patterns exist before the newborn infant can have any part in creating them, and that they serve as guides to behavior. They agree with Marxists that a person's status and group memberships are very important

---

[9]Abraham Maslow, *Toward a Psychology of Being*, 2nd ed. (New York: Van Nostrand Reinhold, 1968), p. iii.

[10]*Ibid.*, p. 5.

[11]*Ibid.*, p. 14.

in shaping his behavior. They agree with behaviorists that the human organism has a tremendous capacity for learning a variety of behaviors. But they argue that neither the nature of the biological organism, nor cultural patterns, nor social structures, nor early life experiences, nor the capacity to learn to respond in conditioned ways to external stimuli is in itself a sufficient explanation of the process of becoming human.

An adequate and valid theory of personality development must take into account all these things—the biological organism, born with needs, drives, and a capacity to learn, especially through language; the socially structured groups that nurture and teach him, interacting with him as he plays various roles; and the cultural beliefs, values, and norms that pattern this interaction. Many social psychologists find the basic framework of such a theory in symbolic interactionism. Like humanists and neo-Freudians, symbolic interactionists consider a person's concept of self or identity crucial to his actions. And they see the emergence of the self as the process by which the newborn baby becomes a human being.

Every socialized person is aware of himself—his "self"—as distinct from others, as a being having unity and continuity. He can almost always distinguish between what "happens to" him and what he himself "does." It is the self that makes sense of the booming buzzing confusion of the world out there. It serves as a sort of reference center for planning and orientation, for sorting and assessing the issues of life in terms of their relative importance. The self, then, is the core of personality, which accounts for its unity and structure.[12]

But this "self" is not something in the organism at birth, waiting to be drawn out or developed. It emerges, rather, in the course of socialization, which is (1) the general process by which a baby becomes a human being, and (2) the process by which a member of a group is fitted into its social structure through interaction with family, peers, teachers, and others. How do these agencies "get inside" a person and socialize him? How do they contribute to the emergence of a self?

GEORGE HERBERT MEAD: "MIND, SELF, AND SOCIETY"

Philosopher George Herbert Mead (1863–1931) tried to answer these questions, and in so doing developed the framework of symbolic interactionism. Demonstrating the intricate interrelationship of culture, society, and personality, this theory outlines the process by which the newborn specimen of *Homo sapiens* becomes a human being, playing his culturally-defined roles in the social structure of his group.

[12]Gordon W. Allport, *Becoming: Basic Considerations for a Psychology of Personality* (New Haven, Conn.: Yale University Press, 1955), p. 43.

"Human society as we know it," said Mead, "could not exist without minds and selves."[13] He also insisted on the converse: that rational minds and conscious selves arise only in society. They are products of social interaction, and especially of symbolic communication through language. Mead emphasized meanings rather than stimuli, and saw the person as an acting and thinking agent rather than simply a reacting or responding organism. He recognized the presence of irrational impulses, but he stressed the rational and creative aspects of personality.

Mead saw self-control and empathy[14] as the psychological bases of social order. The process of socialization ideally produces a mature social being (1) who is self-critical and reflective, and therefore capable of controlling his own behavior, and (2) who has insight into the feelings and expectations of others, and therefore can participate successfully in social interaction and interpersonal relationships.

THE CONCEPT OF OBJECT

The key to the emergence of the self, in Mead's view, is the capacity of the person to think of himself reflexively, to be an *object* to himself. An "object" is not simply something that exists; it is something that can be referred to—a concept with meaning. In this sense, things existing in the natural environment are not objects until they are discovered and named; and things that do *not* exist in the natural environment can be objects. Thus to the nonliterate tribesman with influenza, the influenza virus, of which he has no concept, is not an object (although he is just as sick as the modern doctor who has a word for it). But the angry god he blames for his illness *is* an object. The primitive does not orient his actions toward destroying the virus, but toward appeasing the god.

An object, says Herbert Blumer:

> . . . may be physical as a chair or imaginary as a ghost, natural as a cloud in the sky or man-made as an automobile, material as the Empire State Building or abstract as the concept of liberty, animate as an elephant or inanimate as a vein of coal, inclusive of a class of people as politicians or restricted to a specific person as President de Gaulle, definite as a multiplication table or vague as a philosophical doctrine. In short, objects consist of whatever people indicate or refer to.[15]

[13]*Mind, Self, and Society*, Charles W. Morris, ed. (Chicago: University of Chicago Press, 1934), p. 227. Reprinted from *Mind, Self, and Society* by permission of The University of Chicago Press.

[14]*empathy*: Psychol. The intellectual identification with or vicarious experiencing of the feelings, thoughts, or attitudes of another. *Random House Dictionary of the English Language.*

[15]Herbert Blumer, "Sociological Implications of the Thought of George Herbert Mead," *American Journal of Sociology* 71 (Mar. 1966): 535–44.

The culture of each group consists of its world of meaningful objects; the mind of each person consists of *his* world of meaningful objects. These meanings serve to orient behavior. They are not simply stimuli, because one of the objects that a person acquires in the process of socialization is a self. As he comes to see himself as an object—a unique, separate object with unity and continuity—he can think about himself, love himself, hate himself, be ashamed of himself, be proud of himself. But above all, as compared to the monster that is an unsocialized toddler, he can *control* himself. This is because he can think— interact with himself and communicate with himself. He constructs his own action or conduct. His behavior is not simply reaction to stimuli: He copes with things, considers them, takes them into account, then acts or decides not to act (which is in itself an act).

THE THEORY OF SYMBOLIC INTERACTIONISM

Mead's theory involves a number of interrelated concepts woven into a coherent theory by a process of philosophical reasoning so subtle and complex that a brief account can only suggest the bare outline.

The conversation of gestures. Social interaction, said Mead, may be viewed as a conversation of gestures. This can occur on a nonverbal level, among humans as well as animals. A *conversation of gestures* consists of the mutual adjustment of behavior, in which each participant uses the initial gesture of another's action as a cue for his own action, and his response becomes a stimulus to the other, encouraging either a shift in his attitude or completion of the originally intended action. Mead used the dogfight as an example of a conversation of gestures on the rudimentary level. "One dog is attacking the other, and is ready to spring at the other dog's throat; the reply on the part of the second dog is to change its position, perhaps to spring at the throat of the first dog. There is a conversation of gestures, a reciprocal shifting of the dogs' positions and attitudes."[16]

Symbolic interaction. Some human action occurs on somewhat the same rudimentary level as the dogfight, as when two people going in opposite directions on the street shift positions to get by one another, or when one person unwittingly responds to a tone of voice or a facial expression of which the other may be unaware. This is an unconscious or nonsignificant conversation of gestures, consisting of simple stimulus and response. But most human interaction—increasingly so as a person becomes socialized—is symbolic, that is, it depends on *shared understandings about the meanings of gestures.*

Symbols are conventional signs that derive their meanings from

[16]Mead, *Mind, Self, and Society*, p. 63.

usage and agreement. For the purposes of Mead's theory, a *significant symbol* is a gesture that arouses the same response or attitude (tendency to respond) in the self that it arouses in the other. It conveys an idea and arouses the same idea in the mind of the other. This sharing is essential to communication. Vocal gestures or words (as well as written or sign language) are the most satisfactory kinds of significant symbols—the most reliable and versatile. When language is used, the conversation of gestures is conscious. Only to language does the person using the gesture respond in the same way as the other person. "We must be constantly responding to the gesture we make if we are to carry on successful vocal conversation. The meaning of what we are saying is the tendency to respond to it. . . . There cannot be symbols unless there are responses. There would not be a call for assistance if there was not a tendency to respond to the cry of distress."[17] Thus symbolic interaction is not only conscious, it is *self-conscious*. As we speak, we are aware of what we are doing and of the response we hope to arouse; we hear what we say, and are speaking to ourselves as well as to others. Each gesture, or word, serves as a stimulus to us as well as to the hearer. Its meaning lies in our adjustive response to it, as well as in the response of the hearer. Both the gesture and the response are directed toward or related to completion of the act.

Only man is capable of symbolic interaction through language. With it he builds the set of significant symbols called a culture, and the system of social relationships based on this culture called a society.

The emergence of the self.   The self is a social product, developed on the basis of the biological organism in the process of social interaction. The word "self" is reflexive; it indicates something that can be both subject and object. There can be no self except in relation to an "other." As Mead saw it, the process of acquiring a self is possible because a person can be an object to himself; and he becomes an object to himself through empathy—his ability to "take the role of the other," to imagine the attitudes and responses of others to his acts. Mead traced the process of acquiring a self through infancy and childhood.

The infant has no conception of himself as an individual, no notion that he is set apart from other individuals. Only as he interacts with his mother and others, bumps up against things, finds he has a name, is clothed and bathed, and feels the boundaries of his body, does he begin to be aware of a separate identity. Roughly at the age of two he begins to use the pronouns "I," "me," and "you," indicating that he is beginning to be conscious of himself and of other persons as separate individuals. This awareness grows as he acquires language and can participate in symbolic interaction. He can perceive roles and their relationships. As he observes and responds to his mother and others in the household, they become meaningful references to him, objects that

[17]*Ibid.*, pp. 67, 190.

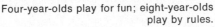
Four-year-olds play for fun; eight-year-olds play by rules.

bring him pleasure, frustration, security, and the like. Their reactions are important to him, and in order to win the responses he wants, he must anticipate what they are going to do by putting himself in their positions. He gradually takes on their attitudes and imagines their responses to him—that is, he "takes the role of the other." It is in doing this that he becomes an object to himself, first seeing himself through the eyes of others, and eventually being able to look at himself from outside himself, so to speak—to see himself from the perspective of others. Instead of experiencing only vague subjective sensations or emotions, he can be aware of, and think about, his wants, wishes, feelings, aches, pains, bad moods, and ideas, looking at them as if he were standing at some distance. He can act toward himself and guide himself.

Mead saw two main stages in the child's process of acquiring a self—the play stage and the game stage, in each of which he takes the role of the other in a different way. In the early years, the *play stage* of development, the process of role-taking is learned by "playing at" different roles. Anyone who has watched a small child at play knows that he "tries on" various roles, switching from one to another with ease. He addresses himself as storekeeper and answers himself as shopper, or he is parent and child alternately. A conversation of gestures is going on, and he is stimulating and responding to himself. He is assuming the attitudes of others through the self-stimulation of the vocal gesture. At this stage, however, his self is not yet a unity, an organized whole. It is made up of the particular attitudes of specific others to himself and toward one another as they participate in specific social acts.

It is in the *game stage* that an organized personality develops, and the person becomes capable of functioning in society. In his early school years, the child learns to participate in games with rules, in which each player is expected to respond in a certain way to a given stimulus—to play his assigned role properly. Playing baseball, for example, the child of eight or so finds he must carry in his mind a knowledge of the roles that all the others play in the game and the relationships of these roles to one another. In order to do what he should do, he must know what behavior to expect of them, and what they expect of him. *He must take the role of all the others on the team as an organized unit.* These are impersonal, conventional, standardized roles, defined by norms that do not take individual personalities into account. The player must not just take the attitudes of others toward himself; he must also consider their attitudes in general toward the common activity in which they are engaged and the goals to which it is directed.

Like the ball game, society is an organized system of interrelated roles. In the game stage, and in continuing socialization, knowledge of the roles and attitudes of others becomes more generalized—more abstract, less dependent on specific persons. The child becomes aware not only that "Mother says it's not right to do this," but also that "It isn't right to do this." In childhood, he is made to feel that he *must* do or not do things in order to avoid negative sanctions or enjoy positive sanctions from specific persons. As he grows older, a larger, more inclusive "other" comes to control his actions. He feels he *ought* or *ought not* to do things in order to avoid self-blame or to keep and enhance self-esteem. He has become aware of the moral voice of the community as a whole and has internalized its mores and values as a conscience or character. In short, he has acquired what Mead calls a "generalized other." Through the generalized other (expressed in self-control) the community exerts control on the person, and ensures the cohesion of society.

Structure of the self.   Mead recognized that the self is neither completely rational and responsible nor a mirror image of social structure. It also has an innovative, impulsive, unpredictable aspect. To account for both the stability and the unpredictability of personality, as well as its relationship to culture and society. Mead developed the concepts of three components of the self—the "I," the "me," and the "generalized other." (These three aspects of the self are roughly comparable to Freud's id, ego, and superego.)

The "*I*" is the impulsive, nonreflective, expressive portion of human nature. It is the acting self, which may be creative and innovative. The *me* is composed of the significant symbols internalized from the culture. It is conventional and habitual. It exists in remembered experience and thus can anticipate the consequences of various kinds of behavior, including impulsive actions. It can halt responses, deliberate, and select the appropriate way to behave. Nonetheless, the acting "I" at any given moment is always a bit unpredictable, and may surprise even the person himself. A common remark may illustrate the distinction: "I don't know why I did that; it was not at all like me." The "me" is the organized core of personality, the "I" is the sometimes errant actor, that gives a sense of freedom and spontaneity.

The self is different in different situations and relationships, but the generalized other—the conscience—gives it unity. Said Mead, "We divide ourselves up into all sorts of different selves with reference to our acquaintances."[18] In addition, the "I" and the "me" are not in similar balance at all times and in all selves. In some people and in some situations, as well as in some types of societies such as very stable traditional ones, the conventional, conforming "me" predominates, and there is little of the creative or innovative surprise of the acting "I." At other times and in other people—and particularly in changing societies —the expressing, asserting "I" is at the fore, and may bring about changes in responses. But both the "I" and the "me," said Mead,

> are essential to the self in its full expression. One must take the attitude of the others in a group in order to belong to a community: he has to employ that outer social world taken within himself in order to carry on thought. It is through his relationship to others in the community, because of the rational social processes that obtain in that community, that he has being as a citizen. On the other hand, the individual is constantly reacting to the social attitudes, and changing in this co-operative process the very community to which he belongs. Those changes may be humble and trivial ones. . . . And yet a certain amount of adjustment and readjustment takes place.[19]

Mind and thought.   Like the self, mind emerges in the process of social interaction, and by virtue of language communication. It is "an internalization of the conversation of significant gestures, as made possible by the individual's taking the attitudes of other individuals toward himself and toward what is being thought about."[20] It appears, then, through the apparatus of taking the role of the other and using it to control one's own conduct. Mind is social. Even in the "inner forum" of the mind, thinking is "a conversation carried on by the individual between himself and the generalized other,"[21] and it always implies expression of this inner conversation to an audience.

The essential characteristic of intelligent behavior is delayed response—a halt in behavior while thinking is going on. It is possible for man to delay response and to think because of the nature of his central nervous system and his command of language. Using the ideas or significant symbols of his culture, a person can foresee some possible consequences of various courses of action and guide his behavior accordingly.

[18]*Ibid.*, p. 142.
[19]*Ibid.*, pp. 199–200.
[20]*Ibid.*, p. 192.
[21]*Ibid.*, p. 254n.

IMPLICATIONS OF SYMBOLIC
INTERACTIONISM

Mead's highly abstract and complex theory has inspired a number of specific theories and hypotheses about the interrelationship of society, culture, and personality, suggesting new perspectives on the nature of human action and interaction, social control and social cohesion, social change, and the role of the self-conception as a guide to behavior.

Human action.   The human being is seen as an active organism in his own right, not merely one who responds or reacts to outside influences. He defines his world and constructs his action. He may not do so very well or rationally, but in coping with the world he must somehow "identify what he wants, establish an objective or goal, map out a prospective line of behavior, note and interpret the actions of others, size up his situation, check himself at this or that point, figure out what to do at other points, and frequently spur himself on in the face of dragging dispositions or discouraging settings."[22]

Social interaction.   Similarly, social interaction is not a neutral medium for the operation of outside factors. It is, rather, a dynamic and formative process in its own right. Participants in any situation must constantly interpret the gestures of others, and as they do so, "They have to arrest, recognize, or adjust their own intentions, wishes, feelings, and attitudes; similarly, they have to judge the fitness of norms, values, and group prescriptions for the situation being formed by the acts of others."[23] This process of interpretation and redefinition goes on in all kinds of interpersonal situations, whether they involve cooperation, love, and friendship; conflict, hostility, and anger; domination and subordination or equality; close identification or great social distance.

In recent years a number of sociologists have studied social interaction from an essentially symbolic interactionist viewpoint, stressing the *meanings*, both obvious and subtle, of behavior. Erving Goffman, for example, believes that the essential element of face-to-face interaction in every society is ritual, that this ritual is designed to protect or save "face" (for others as well as oneself), and that every society therefore needs members who are perceptive and considerate. The study of interaction rituals is a sociology of occasions or "encounters" rather than of social relationships, small groups, communications systems, and so on. These small ritual encounters are the cement of society, for each

[22]Blumer, "Sociological Implications of the Thought of George Herbert Mead."
[23]*Ibid.*

participant must cooperate, with tact and empathy, in saving the face of others.[24] Other sociologists stress not only those meanings that participants use to guide interaction, but those with which they reconstruct something that has happened and give "accounts" of it.[25]

Society and culture.   Society, it follows, is not a static structure nor even a system kept somehow in equilibrium. It is instead "a vast number of occurring joint actions, many closely linked, many not linked at all, many prefigured and repetitious, others being carved out in new directions, and all being pursued to serve the purposes of the participants and not the requirements of a system." Roles, statuses, norms, and values *are* important, but not as *determinants* of action. "Instead, they are important only as they enter into the process of interpretation and definition out of which joint actions are formed."[26]

Social change.   As people try to fit their developing lines of conduct to one another's and establish workable relationships, they may redefine statuses, roles, norms, and values. Thus social change is always present in group life. The stability of society rests in the habits and conventions of the "me" and the moral principles of the generalized other. Its fluidity and change emerge from the spontaneous "I" acting in ongoing situations.

Social control and social cohesion.   Social control and social cohesion depend on man's capacity to be an object to himself and to take the role of the other. This self-interaction and empathy make social control essentially a matter of *self-control.*

Because the person "takes the role of the other" he knows what is expected of him. He acts to live up to, defend, and enhance the image of himself that has been formed in social interaction. At maturity his conscience incorporates the generalized other as a set of principles by which he guides his acts; he feels guilt and shame if he fails to live up to these principles and thus tarnishes his self-image. Internal sanctions have replaced the fear of punishment for violating tribal taboos or parental prohibitions. "Experiences of fear, prohibition and 'must' give way to experiences of preference, self-respect, and 'ought.' "[27]

[24]*Interaction Ritual: Essays in Face-to-Face Behavior* (Chicago: Aldine Publishing Company, 1967), pp. 1–2. See also *Relations in Public: Microstudies in Public Order* (New York: Basic Books, 1972).

[25]These sociologists are often labeled existentialists or "ethnomethodologists." One book oriented toward the game-like features of social interaction, and emphasizing the fact that people must continually build and rebuild the social order by assigning meaning to action, is Stanford M. Lyman and Marvin B. Scott, *A Sociology of the Absurd* (New York: Appleton-Century-Crofts, 1971).

[26]Blumer, "Sociological Implications of the Thought of George Herbert Mead."

[27]Allport, *Becoming*, p. 73.

In symbolic interactionist theory, culture is seen not only as a set of significant symbols but also as shared perspectives arrived at through interaction and communication. These perspectives define situations and constitute agreed-upon conceptions of reality. To quote W. I. Thomas, "If men define situations as real, they are real in their consequences." Santa Claus, ghosts, and inherent racial differences are real to many people because they define them as real, and they act accordingly.

Men develop conceptions of reality in social interaction. As they participate in groups, they come to perceive reality as it is defined in the culture of the group. They check and test these views of reality as they communicate with others, and feel confident of their validity so long as others support and reinforce them and act according to them. This support of one's conception of reality by others may be called *consensual validation*. A member of a sect that believes the world is flat or that it will end next July 27 at two o'clock feels secure in his belief because it is shared by his reference group. Consensus makes it appear valid.

To the extent that the members of a group share the same perspectives, there is cultural unity. The effort of a society's members to arrive at a common definition of a situation, at least long enough to agree on a common course of action, is the effort to achieve consensus. Where perspectives are in sharp conflict—as in American society's division over the Vietnam War and the urban racial crisis—consensus is extremely difficult to achieve, and the society's course of action wavers. In any multi-group society, people interact—perhaps often and closely —with others who define situations very differently, and as a result there is tension and conflict. But learning and adjustment do go on. We observed a drugstore clerk who said to two black males in their early twenties, "What can I do for you boys?" Seeing their reaction as they laughed a bit and looked at each other, she hastily amended her words: "What can I do for you gentlemen?" She had succeeded in taking the role of the other, and revising her own conduct accordingly.

To the extent that there is reciprocal role-taking, there is sharing of the definition of the situation and thus consensus—and there is regularity, stability, repetitiveness, and predictability in joint action. But if the members cannot communicate and understand, their definitions of the situation continue to differ, and the attempt to arrive at workable relations suffers accordingly. This is why, in our discussion of culture, we stressed its nature as a set of shared understandings.

The Self-Conception

As we said above, an individual's image of himself is an essential part of his concept of reality. The **self-conception** has two chief elements: a sense of *identity*, which is his answer to the questions "Who am I?"

and "What am I?"; and a sense of *self-esteem*, which is his answer to the question "What am I worth?" He may measure both elements against an *ideal self*, which incorporates his aspirations or long-range goals as guided by the generalized other. The ideal self answers the questions "What would I like to be?" and "What would I like to be worth?"

The self-conception is the core around which personality is organized. Our memories and aspirations cluster around it as a continuing entity. Each of us has some sense of personal autonomy, some feeling of control over his own destiny, even if it extends no further than the random choices of the hour. Much of our behavior, as we said, is designed to arrive at, live up to, defend, and enhance our self-conception.

THE ORGANIC BASIS OF THE SELF-CONCEPTION

Each of us has a name, which seems an integral part of him. Each of us also has a body to which this name is attached. Our body has quite definite limits (if one does not get too technical about air and food and so on), and its sensations are peculiarly our own. We have an image of and an evaluation of its shape, size, strength, coloring, proportions, stamina, and skill. We try to enhance it to fit our ideal selves. We have our photos taken to commemorate special occasions; our names and faces appear in yearbooks and passports, confirming our identity to whom it may concern. When people recognize us and remember our names they validate our identity. They compliment us or

Drawing by Frascino; © 1968 The New Yorker Magazine, Inc.

criticize us on our appearance, admire our youthfulness or athletic skill, and inquire after our health, confirming our sense of identity with the body. Most of us feel our faces are unique, and find it somewhat disconcerting to be taken for someone else—unless it is a much-admired movie star or other personage after whom we have modeled our ideal self!

Thus our bodily sense is "a lifelong anchor for our self-awareness." Allport drives home the "warmth and importance" of our own bodies by asking us first to imagine swallowing our own saliva which has collected in the mouth, and then to imagine spitting it into a glass and swallowing it from the glass. "What I perceive as belonging intimately to my body is warm and welcome; what I perceive as separate from my body becomes, in the twinkling of an eye, cold and foreign."[28]

But the self-image transcends the body. It also includes our estimates of our characters and personality traits and of our intelligence and learning. It is extended into the possessions, causes, ideals, and groups we call our own, and into the people with whom we identify— people whose actions can cause us to feel pride or shame in much the same way we feel it for our own accomplishments and failures. It extends backward in time to our ancestors and forward to our descendants. The infant has a body but no self-conception; multiple personalities have two or more self-conceptions but only one body, as did the woman in *Three Faces of Eve*.

THE SELF-CONCEPTION AS A SOCIAL PRODUCT

The self-conception is a social product. It arises in social interaction and is continually tested, and confirmed or changed, in social interaction. Our sense of identity arises as we learn our statuses and roles. Our self-esteem (whether high or low) is established as we perceive the reactions of others to us. Later, when we have become objects to ourselves, self-esteem also depends on our own evaluations as we interact with ourselves and compare ourselves to others and to our ideal selves.

Status and role.   Statuses and roles are central to the self-conception. Some statuses can easily be dropped, but others are learned early and appear to be of great importance to self-identity. Among them are those ascribed by the groups and classes to which we belong— sex, ethnic group, religious affiliation, and position in the family. In one study, a group of 288 college students was asked to write 20 answers to the question "Who am I?" (an operational definition of the concept of "self"). The respondents tended to describe themselves in terms of their group and class memberships before listing any evaluations of themselves as individuals; that is, the first answers included such terms

[28]Allport, *Becoming*, p. 43.

Drawing by W. Miller; © 1971 The New Yorker Magazine, Inc.

"Shucks, Ma, you've got it all wrong. No drawers in a desk means a fella's got a very, very responsible position."

as girl, student, Catholic, and Negro, and only later in the list did they include such evaluative terms as happy, fat, and intelligent.[29]

Each culture has its own definition of masculine and feminine roles. Cases of mistaken sexual identity demonstrate that sex roles are learned long before a child is aware of primary sex differences. At the age of five "Frankie," who had been reared as a boy because of uncertain genital structure, was discovered to be a girl. Nurses and interns in the hospital found it difficult to treat Frankie as a girl because she considered girls' toys and activities to be "sissy," refused to wear a dress, and became extremely belligerent when anyone tried to treat her as a girl.[30] The socialization process had effectively organized her behavior along masculine lines quite independently of her feminine anatomy.

Some achieved statuses, such as marriage and certain occupations, are also crucial to the self-conception. A bride may feel strange with her new status and title, as often as she may have written her new name secretly, but the ritual and ceremony of a wedding, the support of the community, the use of her new name by tradesmen and correspondents, help her identify it with herself. Social recognition helps her to sustain her new status until it is firmly a part of her. Similarly, the rites of ordination, the garb and new title of a priest or min-

[29] M. H. Kahn and T. S. McPartland, "An Empirical Investigation of Self-Attitudes," *American Sociological Review* 19 (1954): 68–76.

[30] Alfred R. Lindesmith and Anselm L. Strauss, *Social Psychology*, 3rd ed. (New York: Holt, Rinehart & Winston, 1968), pp. 338–39.

Drawing by Lorenz; © 1971 The New Yorker Magazine, Inc.

*"I need reassurance, Miss Kimball. Send
someone in on his hands and knees."*

ister, are reinforced by the deference he is accorded. The role shapes a person's actions, and increasingly he "becomes" what he plays at being.

"The looking-glass self."   In the beginning, and to a great extent all through our lives, the perceived reactions of others influence our self-esteem. This aspect of the self-conception has been called the "looking-glass self" and is associated with Charles Horton Cooley. To a large extent, he said, the reference to other persons involved in the sense of self

> . . . takes the form of a somewhat definite imagination of how one's self . . . appears in a particular mind, and the kind of self-feeling one has is determined by the attitude toward this attributed to that other mind. A social self of this sort might be called the reflected or looking-glass self:
>
> > Each to each a looking-glass
> > Reflects the other that doth pass.
>
> As we see our face, figure, and dress in the glass, and are interested in them because they are ours, and pleased or otherwise with them according as they do or do not answer to what we should like them

to be; so in imagination we perceive in another's mind some thought of our appearance, manners, aims, deeds, character, friends, and so on, and are variously affected by it.

A self-idea of this sort seems to have three principal elements: the imagination of our appearance to the other person; the imagination of his judgment of that appearance; and some sort of self-feeling, such as pride or mortification. The comparison with a looking-glass hardly suggests the second element, the imagined judgment, which is quite essential. The thing that moves us to pride or shame is not the mere mechanical reflection of ourselves, but an imputed sentiment, the imagined effect of this reflection upon another's mind. This is evi-dent from the fact that the character and weight of that other, in whose mind we see ourselves, makes all the difference with our feel-ing. We are ashamed to seem evasive in the presence of a straight-forward man, cowardly in the presence of a brave one, gross in the eyes of a refined one, and so on. We always imagine, and in imagin-ing share, the judgments of the other mind. A man will boast to one person of an action—say, some sharp transaction in trade—which he would be ashamed to own to another.[31]

Significant others.   Not all "others," of course, are of equal importance to the self-conception. Each of us has some "significant others" whose judgments of us concern us far more than do the judg-ments of the rest of those with whom we come in contact. For a student trying to earn a good grade, his teacher is a significant other. Experts or colleagues within one's special field of interest—whether in work, sports, or hobbies—are significant others. The members of any refer-ence group are our significant others.

Most important to our self-esteem, however, is the disinterested love, approval, and acceptance of family and intimate friends. Being valued by the people we know intimately is essential to our emotional well-being. In such groups we have "personal status" as ourselves, not simply as occupants of statuses. Positive evaluation and disinterested love are especially important in infancy and early childhood, setting a level of self-esteem that is difficult to change for better or worse in later life, regardless of success or failure in conventional roles.

EMPIRICAL RESEARCH ON SELF-ESTEEM

Social psychologists have conducted a number of studies of self-esteem and interpersonal relationships.[32] Stanley Coopersmith, for

[31]Charles Horton Cooley, *Human Nature and the Social Order* (New York: Charles Scribner's Sons, 1903), pp. 151–53.

[32]A number of instruments for measuring such attitudes may be found in John P. Robinson and Phillip R. Shaver, *Measurements of Social Psychological Attitudes* (Survey Research Center, Institute for Social Research, University of Michigan, Ann Arbor, 1969).

example, set out to answer the question "What are the conditions that lead an individual to value himself and to regard himself as an object of worth?" He administered a self-esteem inventory of fifty items to a sample of 8- to 10-year old school children; a questionnaire regarding their behavior patterns to their teacher; and a questionnaire about their upbringing to their mothers. He also interviewed the mothers at length, and tested the children's behavior in tasks that indicated level of aspiration, selectivity of perception and memory, constancy and independence of judgment, and ability to tolerate stress and adversity.

High self-esteem, he concluded, is related to the following factors: total or near-total acceptance of the child by his parents; clearly defined and enforced limits of behavior; and respect and latitude for individual action within these limits. Parents who seem permissive because they are vague about rules for their children, but punish them severely when, in the parents' judgment, they misbehave, produce low self-esteem in their children.[33]

Summary

Personality is the individual version of human nature, the organized patterns of thought, feeling, and action that characterize a given individual. The process of becoming human, of acquiring a personality, is a complex one, and there are many theories of how it occurs.

Biological determinists find the master key to human behavior in inborn patterns or constitutional tendencies. Cultural determinists see individuals as mere reflections of their cultures or of the particular status into which they are born in the social structure.

Behaviorists see the newborn baby as infinitely plastic, and believe he can be conditioned to almost any conceivable kind of behavior, depending on the stimuli to which he is exposed and the rewards and punishments he perceives to be consequences of his actions.

Freudian psychoanalysts see personality as consisting of the id, with its powerful urges of sex and aggression; the ego, which tries to reconcile these urges with outer reality; and the superego or conscience. Early experiences in the oral, anal, and Oedipal stages leave scars on the personality if the ego cannot cope satisfactorily with impulses and represses them into the unconscious. Adolescence and adulthood are reflections and recapitulations of childhood experiences. Culture is a set of ways that the group has evolved for handling sex and aggression. Society always represses natural impulses; the price of civilization is discontent. Freud emphasized the irrational, emotional, and unconscious aspects of personality. While he made us aware of the complexity of human behavior, he neglected or underplayed the role of reason, language, and cultural variation.

[33]Stanley Coopersmith, *The Antecedents of Self-esteem* (San Francisco: W. H. Freeman and Company, 1967).

Neo-Freudians, in contrast, take these factors into account. Erik Erikson sees the life cycle as a series of stages, each of which is successful largely to the extent that previous stages were successful, especially if the identity crisis is satisfactorily resolved.

Humanist psychologists stress subjective experience and the search for meaning and value in existence. Abraham Maslow, for example, posits a hierarchy of needs, the highest being self-actualization or achievement of full humanness.

Symbolic interactionist theory as developed by George Herbert Mead demonstrates the intricate relationship of culture, society, and personality. Because a person can become an object to himself, he can control his own behavior through self-interaction; because he feels empathy, he can take the roles of others and know what to expect of them and what they expect of him. Minds and selves arise in the process of symbolic interaction. A culture is a set of significant symbols shared by a group; a person's mind is his set of significant symbols. The child acquires a self in two stages: the play stage, in which he takes the roles of particular others toward himself, and the game stage, where he acquires a generalized other, the moral voice of the community as a whole, which is his conscience or character. Two other aspects of the self are the acting, impulsive "I" which gives impetus or propulsion to behavior, and the reflective and remembering "me," which gives guidance and direction. Thought is a conversation between the "me" and the generalized other; the distinguishing characteristic of intelligent human behavior is delayed response while thinking goes on.

In symbolic interactionist theory, social control rests on self-control and empathy, social cohesion is based on common definitions of the situation, and social change arises from the dynamic nature of interaction in which the "I" may act outside the established framework of norms.

The self-conception is crucial to behavior. It includes a sense of identity, a level of self-esteem, and an ideal self. Although it has an organic basis, it is a social product, resulting from one's statuses and roles, his self-evaluation, and feedback from significant others.

In this chapter we have dealt with socialization as the general process of becoming a functioning member of the human race. Now we turn to socialization as the process of incorporating each of us into a specific social group, and the factors that make for similarities and differences in personality.

QUESTIONS FOR FURTHER THOUGHT

1. How would you answer the questions posed in the first paragraph of the chapter? Would you have answered them any differently before taking this course?

2. What theories of biological determinism exist in your culture as conventional wisdom or common-sense knowledge (concerning the relationship of body type to personality, for example)?

3. Would you prefer to believe that personality is biologically determined? Culturally determined? A consequence of many factors, including the capacity of the person himself to choose and decide?

4. Which of the theories discussed in the book agrees with the common saying "You can't change human nature"? Which disagrees most radically? How would you amend that statement after studying this chapter?

5. The development of various theories often proceeds as a dialogue or argument; thus Max Weber's theory of stratification was an attempt to refute that of Karl Marx. What evidence do you find for such a dialogue in this chapter? (If you wish to pursue the subject further, read some of the books referred to.)

6. What evidence do you find that Freud's theory, once thought a shocking innovation, was time-bound and culture-bound, as all theories are to some extent?

7. Observe friends and family to test the idea of eight stages in Erikson's life cycle. Have you suffered an identity crisis?

8. Could Mead be called a determinist? Why or why not?

9. "I don't care what people think." According to Mead, is this possible? What kinds of people might really not care?

10. Think about your feelings and motivations; how you were socialized at home and in your peer group, and perhaps in Sunday school; how you played as a pre-school child and a primary-school child. Does your introspection and reflection produce any contradictions to Mead's theory of how the agencies of socialization "get inside" a child and make him a human being? Does it corroborate them?

11. Reflect on daily interaction in your family, between you and your friends, and in the classroom. Do you find any indications that self-control and empathy are indeed the psychological bases of the social order?

12. Who are you? Describe your model or ideal self. Do you seek—or find—your chief identity in ascribed or achieved statuses? In work? Religion? Leisure? Who are your significant others?

13.   What has your body to do with your self-conception, both identity and self-esteem? Do you feel you *have* a body, *are* a body, or *live in* a body, or do you have some other conception of the relation of the body to your personality?

14.   How does the idea of a dynamic "self" that acts consciously and plans more or less rationally confirm the importance of values in the socio-cultural order?

15.   People may to some extent change themselves deliberately, by making objects (in the symbolic interactionist sense) of their traits, and perhaps seeking feedback from significant others. Relate this idea to New Year's resolutions, Ben Franklin's schedule for self-improvement (see his *Autobiography*), and your own experience.

16.   Robert Burns wrote, "Oh wad some Power the giftie gie us, To see oursels as others see us!" To what extent do we have that gift, and what is its significance for personality?

Each human being is unique, unprecedented, unrepeatable.

RENE DUBOS

The culture is sun and food and water; it is not the seed.

ABRAHAM MASLOW

The elements of which each of us is "made" are in themselves highly complex and variable and infinitely recombinable to produce infinite numbers of unique creatures.

MARY ELLEN GOODMAN

Every man is in some respects
   a. Like all other men
   b. Like some other men
   c. Like no other man.

CLYDE KLUCKHOHN and
HENRY A. MURRAY

Cada cabeza es un mundo (Each head is a world).

SPANISH PROVERB

12

FACTORS IN PERSONALITY DEVELOPMENT

I DON'T SUPPOSE THERE EVER WAS A CHAP QUITE LIKE ME BEFORE, said one of H. G. Wells's characters. And indeed each of us is an original, and wants to be accepted and appreciated as a separate, special person.[1]

Each of us has a unique combination of biologically-based attributes: sex, appearance, temperament, health, intelligence. For a relatively long period we are all dependent on adults, and the way they handle us affects our orientation to others and to life in general. The combination of inborn attributes and early nurturing apparently leads us to react differently and selectively to environmental influences. We grow up in a certain society, and within it there are great variations in physical environment, patterns of socialization, membership in subcultural and peer groups, and in the personalities, ages, number, and statuses of the members of our family. Finally, there are the happenstances of life: the people we meet; the opportunities we seize or miss; the accidents and coincidences that affect us; and the innovations, wars, economic conditions, and social movements of our particular times.

But some social psychologists warn us against thinking of the individual as the "product" or result of any combination of these factors and influences. Personality, says William Kolb, is "the most complex and dynamic system known to man. . . . It is an emergent from the interaction of the biological organism with society and culture, but it cannot be reduced to any one of them or to any interactional combination of them."[2] Because man has a self, capable of thought as well as empathy, his growth is a process of "creative becoming" as he perceives, selects, reflects, and acts. Man is not a helpless puppet of various influences, but rather a dynamic, selective agent, acting within the limits of his organic nature on the one hand and the boundaries set by his society and culture on the other.

Yet each of us is also like some other human beings and like all other human beings. We recognize this likeness when we compare, categorize, and label people according to similarities we perceive in their

---

[1] At least in Western societies with a cultural value of individualism.
[2] "A Social Psychological Conception of Human Freedom," *Ethics* 63, No. 3, Pt. 1 (April 1953): 182–83.

behavior. We describe them in terms of traits, or consistent patterns of perception, action, and interpersonal relationships. People, we say, are kind or cruel, shy or outgoing, clever or stupid, sophisticated or naive, warm or cold, cynical or trusting, and so on through hundreds of adjectives. We also describe them as social types, which are descriptions of role performance—"the-kind-of-person-who-acts-that-way."[3] One may be a go-getter, a drag, a back-slapper, a yes-man, a wet blanket, an eager beaver, an Uncle Tom, a tough guy, a cheapskate. Social types are shorthand for clusters of traits: a clinging vine, for example, is passive, dependent, trusting; an inside-dopester is gossipy, know-it-all, and boastful of his connections.

We also label people in terms of their orientation to norms, as respectable, immoral, straight, crooked, queer, nice, eccentric, "characters," dropouts, bad guys. We show that we operate according to some notion of health and illness in personality by calling people crazy, well-adjusted, "together," mixed up, solid, paranoid, and so on.

When we ask someone what another person is "like" we are answered in terms of such traits, types, and orientations to norms— all of which are largely styles of interaction. "Clue me in" means "Tell me more about him than just his formal statuses; give me some information about how I may like him and how I may best handle our relationship." These clues are especially valuable for effective participation in modern society, with its numerous secondary relationships.

Social psychologists do much the same thing, but more systematically. Seeking patterns and regularities, as all scientists must, they attempt to relate variations in personality to such factors as organic variables, infant nurturing, cultural and subcultural influences, and especially to patterns of socialization. They seek the sources and manifestations of conformity to and deviance from norms. They study commitment to the group and participation in its interaction from several points of view, including skill in interpersonal relationships and identification with or alienation from the group. They are interested in the sources and consequences of variations in the self-conception, and particularly in self-esteem. And finally, many are increasingly concerned with ideas long shunned as "unscientific"—happiness, the good life, realization of human potential. In this chapter and the next we inquire into these concerns.

Biological Variables

Men everywhere are born with the same involuntary reflexes—automatic responses, each attached to a given stimulus, which can be altered only slightly. They are also equipped with primary defense reactions;

[3]Orrin Klapp, "Social Types: Process and Structure," *American Sociological Review* 23, No. 6: 674–78.

on the simplest level are the startled crying and withdrawal of infants who are afraid of being dropped or of a sudden loud noise. Many psychologists believe emotions such as rage, disgust, shame, and grief, as well as fear, are based on such reactions. At any rate, emotions appear to be closely linked with the physiology of the organism, for under emotional stress there are measurable and often striking changes in body functioning. Emotions are subject to considerable conditioning through experience, however, as are such more distinctly primary or innate drives as sex and hunger. It also appears that people vary in the strength of innate urges and their capacities for emotion.

The way the genes happen to combine into a nuclear cell at the moment of conception determines all the "hereditary" aspects of an individual. *Sex* is fixed at this moment by the presence of an X or Y chromosome in the sperm cell. The particular combination of genes also determines a person's probable *appearance*—his eye and hair color, stature, and other physical features (although prenatal and subsequent environmental factors—nutrition in particular—affect his actual stature, weight, muscular development, and the like). Heredity also determines the limits of a person's *intelligence*, and probably has much to do with his *temperament* or prevailing mood. Closely related to growth, temperament, and behavior is the organism's *glandular balance*, which affects many bodily functions. Studies of infants show that they are different from birth. Alexander Thomas and associates conducted intensive studies of eighty infants from birth to age two. They found a "primary reaction pattern" characteristic of each child, which led him to react selectively to stimuli.[4] Thus the biological heredity of the individual apparently predisposes personality in certain directions and sets limits to possible development.

Some of the potential traits and capacities of the organism appear only with *maturation*, that is, physical growth to a given level of development. Until the eye is capable of discerning letters, for example, the child cannot learn to read. Until leg and back muscles are sufficiently developed, no amount of encouragement will persuade the infant to walk. Until the sphincter muscles have developed to the point where they can be controlled, toilet-training is futile. Although the rate of maturation varies from one individual to another, it always follows the same developmental sequence—a child sits before he stands, walks before he runs. He is never ready for any stage of development until his organism is ready.

The rate of maturation varies not only among members of a society at any given time, but also over long periods of time. Probably because of improved nutrition, sexual and physical development—and possibly mental development as well—come far earlier now than they did in previous generations. In the eighteenth century, boys continued to sing soprano in Bach's choir until age eighteen; now their voices

[4]*Behavioral Individuality in Early Childhood* (New York: New York University Press, 1963).

change at about thirteen. About 1900, European men did not stop growing until age twenty-six; now they reach their full growth by seventeen
or eighteen. The age of menarche, or first menstruation, has dropped 2
to 5 years since the seventeenth century, and even in recent decades in
the United States. Of four generations of Harvard men, each was taller
than the previous one, except that the increase stopped with the generation born about 1941.[5]

There is much debate about the degree to which intelligence
is "biologically determined." Intelligence may be defined in various
ways—as the capacity of the organism to adjust to its environment, as
"the ability to solve present problems on the basis of past experiences
in terms of possible future consequences,"[6] as the capacity for thought
and creativity.[7] As a potential of mankind in general, intelligence is the
basis of culture. As an attribute of individuals, intelligence varies
greatly among members of any society. The variation is a result of both
heredity and environment. The quality of the brain and nervous system
is the inborn potential; it does not depend, however, entirely on genetic
heritage, for the quality of the pregnant mother's diet has been shown
to be highly correlated with her child's intelligence, as has the infant's
diet during the first year of life.

Intelligence cannot be measured at all accurately; it can only
be guessed at from the way the brain functions as a result of an individual's experience. Nor is it yet clearly understood whether intelligence
is a general ability or a number of specific abilities. But it is clearly a
biological potential that emerges only as a result of social experience.

Innate intelligence sets limits to a person's capacity to learn.
However, men in fact rarely use their intelligence to its limits. A meager
culture, emotional blocks or anxieties, a narrow ideology, malnutrition,
or simply illness or lack of time may prevent a person from utilizing
all his intellectual potential.

Our biological equipment, then, is one factor that makes us
like all other men, like some other men, and like no other man.

Variations in Infant Nurturing

In recent decades scientists have come to believe that the very early
care of an infant has tremendous consequences for his personality. We
are speaking here of influences distinct from the potentials and urges
of the biological organism, and also distinct from the largely verbal

[5]Walter Sullivan, "Boys and Girls Are Now Maturing Earlier," *The New York Times* (Jan. 24, 1971).

[6]Tamotsu Shibutani, *Society and Personality* (Englewood Cliffs, N.J.: Prentice-Hall, Inc., 1961), p. 78.

[7]Mary Ellen Goodman, *The Individual and Culture* (Homewood, Ill.: Richard D. Irwin, 1967), p. 4.

socialization by which the child learns the culture and his place in the social structure: the way a mother holds her child, the way she feeds and later weans him, diaper-changing, toilet-training, and other infant disciplines. These are the infant's first experience of another organism, of the world around him.

Infant nurturing thus appears to be responsible for (*1*) universal human nature, (*2*) the basic orientation of the personality toward others, (*3*) health and survival, and (*4*) even the realization of potential intelligence. Cooley, who called primary groups "the nursery of human nature," speculated that it is because infants in all societies experience fondling, petting, and frustration in the intimate interaction of the family group that we can feel empathy for those from very different cultures, put ourselves in their places and understand their emotions and sentiments. That is also why folktales and literature from all over the world often have very similar themes and plots.

Studies show that the character of infant care—whether warm and loving or cold and mechanical—is directly related to an individual's ability to establish emotional relationships with others, to feel a sense of security and mastery, and to experience and understand such sentiments as love, sympathy, envy, and pity. Psychiatrists suggest, for example, that the psychopathic personality—completely self-centered, incapable of emotional ties with others, lacking both internalized standards of right and wrong and a sense of guilt—may be the result of inadequate primary-group relationships during infancy, especially the lack of a warm, nurturing mother.

As a result of his work with autistic children—children who have normal intelligence but who have shut themselves off from the world—psychologist Bruno Bettelheim is convinced that the way a child's first "spontaneous moves toward the world" are met during the crucial period of his first six months either frustrates or encourages him in his natural tendency to be an active, seeking agent.

> If a normal child is to develop initiative and have it take root, he must be given the chance to test out for himself that taking action really gets him what he wants. . . . [Time-clock feedings] rob the infant of the conviction that it was his own wail that resulted in filling his stomach when his own hunger timed it. By the same token, if his earliest signals, his cry or his smile, bring no results, that discourages him from trying to refine his efforts at communicating his needs. In time he loses the impulse to develop those mental and emotional structures through which we deal with the environment. He is discouraged from forming a personality. . . .
>
> Even among adults the joke that fails to amuse, the loving gesture that goes unanswered, is a most painful experience. And if we consistently, and from an early age, fail to meet the appropriate response

to our expression of emotions, we stop communicating and eventually lose interest in the world.[8]

"Tender loving care" is as important as food to the health and survival of an infant. René Spitz compared the handling of infants in an excellent foundling home, where each nurse gave seven babies nutritionally perfect food in hygienic surroundings, with the care imprisoned women gave their own babies in "inferior" conditions. Of the prison children, all survived the first year, while 30% of the foundlings died. The prison-reared children were normal or superior in height, weight, ability to walk, and vocabulary; the foundlings were distinctly below normal.[9] In other studies, it has been found that middle-class mothers who stressed hygiene and schedules and "crying it out" had sicklier babies than did warm, nurturing lower-class mothers who were indifferent to strict rules of baby care.[10]

Even more dramatic evidence of the importance of intensive emotional relationships in early childhood comes from a study of two groups of mentally retarded children. At age three, thirteen were placed in the care of women inmates in a state institution for the mentally retarded, one child to a ward, while a control group remained in an orphanage. In 1½ years the experimental group had gained 28 IQ points, from 64 to 92; the average of the control group had dropped 26 points. It was then possible to place the experimental group for adoption. A follow-up study 30 years later found all thirteen self-supporting; all but two had completed high school and four had 1 or more years of college. Members of the control group were all either dead or still institutionalized.[11]

Culture and Personality

Common-sense knowledge holds that there are differences in personality from one society to another; these differences are expressed, for example, in stereotypes of Germans as authoritarian and phlegmatic, Italians

[8]"Where Self Begins," *The New York Times Magazine* (Feb. 12, 1967), p. 65 ff. © 1967 by The New York Times Company. Reprinted by permission.

[9]"An Inquiry into the Genesis of Psychiatric Conditions in Early Childhood," *The Psychoanalytic Study of the Child* 1 (1945): 53–74. See also R. A. Spitz, "Hospitalism: A Follow-up Report," *The Psychoanalytic Study of the Child* 2 (1946): 113–17.

[10]Margaret Ribble, *The Rights of Infants* (New York: Columbia University Press, 1944).

[11]Harold M. Skeels, "Adult Status of Children with Contrasting Early Life Experiences," *Monographs of the Society for Research in Child Development* 31 (1966), Serial No. 105. Experiments have shown that monkeys raised without maternal closeness were never able to form normal adult sexual relationships, and if females nonetheless became mothers they rebuffed their offspring and often displayed extreme cruelty. See Harry F. Harlow and Margaret K. Harlow, "The Effect of Rearing Conditions on Behavior," *Bulletin of the Menninger Clinic* 26 (1962): 213–24.

as impulsive and emotional, Latin Americans as sensual and mercurial. Social scientists have explored this idea of a "modal" or "basic" **personality type** in various ways, ranging from pure speculation to rigorous empirical study, but as yet have arrived at few firm generalizations. Depending on their orientation, they attribute these differences to different patterns of infant nurturing and childrearing; to the world view, core values, and ethos of the culture; to definitions of sex roles; and to the handling of crises in the life cycle.

Sweeping generalizations about the relationship of socio-cultural patterns of infant nurturing to personality have been characteristic of some psychoanalytically-oriented anthropologists. They ascribe the "national character" of great modern nations to norms of swaddling, weaning, toilet-training, and other infant disciplines, sometimes with such great emphasis on these experiences that they have been called "chamber-pot determinists" or "the nipple-and-diaper school." Weston La-Barre, for example, based a theory of Japanese modal personality on descriptions of their presumably severe early training in bowel habits. Trauma at the anal level of development, he declared, produced a neurotic personality characterized by secretiveness, fanaticism, cleanliness, ceremoniousness, and other traits. The fit is suspiciously pat and neat.[12]

A landmark study by Cora DuBois was more firmly grounded in evidence. She applied psychoanalytic techniques—the collection of life histories; the administration of Rorschach, Thematic Apperception, and word association tests; and the analysis of drawings and dreams—to the Alorese of Indonesia, and had her material independently analyzed by several experts. As we saw in Chapter 6, the Alorese tend to be spiteful, suspicious, frustrated, and confused. She attributed these traits to the inconsistent, neglectful, and even abusive treatment of children.[13]

Dissenting from the psychoanalytic approach to the study of modal personality, Francis L. K. Hsu points out that since psychiatry deals with the abnormal, there is a tendency to view the traits of other cultures in terms of neuroses—because their behavior would be so defined in American society. "Infant and childhood experiences," he insists, "are much less important [to the anthropologist] than the roles, structures, and cultures of the societies in question. At best the early training of the individual may be used as a symptom of some of the cultural emphases."[14] Cultural influences on personality, then, continue throughout life.

[12]"Some Observations on Character Structure in the Orient: The Japanese," *Psychiatry* 8:319–42. The article was written during World War II, when it was impossible to collect empirical data, and when even behavioral scientists might have been more affected by ethnocentrism than under other conditions.

[13]*The People of Alor.*

[14]"Anthropology or Psychiatry: A Definition of Objectives and Their Implications," *Southwest Journal of Anthropology* 8 (1952): 227–50.

Chief among these cultural influences, in Ruth Benedict's view, are the dominant world view and values of a society. Each society, she believed, has a different conception of the ideal personality, and most people come to approximate that type naturally and easily. The warrior and visionary were the ideals of the Plains Indians, who rewarded self-reliance, initiative, individualism, and ability to see visions. As a result, men cultivated frenzies, and endured danger and discomfort in order to win approval and prestige. The Zuñi Indians of New Mexico, in contrast, discourage individualism, violence, and power. They value moderation and self-effacement and suspect that anyone who likes to wield power practices witchcraft. The Dobuans, who live on rocky volcanic islands off the New Guinea coast, make virtues of ill will and treachery. Existence appears to them an unending struggle for each of the goods of life against deadly antagonists. Suspicion, cruelty, animosity, and malignancy are common among Dobuans.[15]

In a study of three New Guinea tribes, Margaret Mead concentrated on cultural definitions of sex roles, especially in relation to temperament. Two, she found, make no personality distinctions between men and women. Among the mountain-dwelling Arapesh, the chief cultural goals are growing yams and raising children. Both men and women act in a fashion Americans would call "feminine." Both are cherishing, gentle, maternal, mild. Not far away live the fierce, cannibalistic Mundugumor. Both men and women of this tribe act in ways we would call predominantly "masculine." Both "are expected to be violent, competitive, aggressively sexed, jealous and ready to see and avenge insult, delighting in display, action, and fighting."[16] Every man is against every other, including his father and his brothers. The things that give him greatest satisfaction are fighting and the competitive acquisition of women. Children are unwanted. The world is charged with hostility and conflict.

Instead of ignoring sexual differences in personality, the third tribe, the Tchambuli, define male and female roles in a way that is the reverse of ours. Women manage and dominate. Men gossip, wear curls, and go shopping; they are emotionally dependent upon women and less responsible than them. The people live chiefly for art; the event celebrated means less to them than the elaborate and lavish ceremony itself.

One study of subcultural personality differences in the United States centers on differing reactions to a life crisis—an illness involving considerable pain. Among patients with similar problems in a veterans' hospital in New York City, both Jews and Italians were very emotional in their responses to pain; they were not ashamed to talk about their pain, groan, complain, and cry. The Italians, however, were concerned

---

[15]*Patterns of Culture* (New York: Penguin Books, 1946).
[16]*Sex and Temperament in Three Primitive Societies* (New York: Dell Publishing Co., 1935), p. 213.

deCarlo in the Saturday Review.

with the immediate situation, and once they got relief, they were happy and optimistic. Jewish patients, in contrast, were anxious about the source of the pain and about possible side effects of pain-relieving drugs, as well as about the meaning of the pain in relation to their general health and the future of their families. Where Jewish patients tried, semi-consciously or otherwise, to provoke worry and concern on the part of others, Italians tried to provoke sympathy.

Most of the doctors, being "old American" or WASP types, found it easier to understand the reaction of "old American" patients, whose complaints were essentially reports defining the quality, location, and duration of pain, and who preferred to be left alone when they reacted emotionally. They appeared optimistic, confident that experts would tinker efficiently with the troublesome mechanism.

Inquiring into their childhoods, the investigators found that the parents of Jewish and Italian patients had been worried and overprotective, quick to respond sympathetically to crying and complaints, and reluctant to let their children take part in sports. Where the Jewish parents, however, were concerned with the symptomatic meaning of the child's aches and pains and looked on each deviation from normal behavior as a sign of illness, Italian parents expressed sympathy but not anxiety, and at the same time they often punished the child for not taking care of himself. Parents of "old American" patients, in contrast, had exhorted them not to be sissies, encouraged games and sports in spite of the risk of injury, and taught them to take immediate care of an injury or illness rather than crying and getting emotionally upset.[17]

[17]Mark Zborowski, "Cultural Components in Responses to Pain," *Journal of Social Issues* 8 (1953): 16–31; reprinted in Peter I. Rose, ed., *The Study of Society*, 2nd ed. (New York: Random House, 1970), pp. 161–72.

In America, parents have sole responsibility for their babies; in the Soviet Union babies are often cared for in a collective nursery.

In all the studies we have discussed here, the emphasis is on intimate interaction between parent and child or on general world view, values, and personality traits. In modern industrial societies, however, socialization is institutionalized, and shared by clearly identifiable and even specialized agencies. The structure and functioning of these agencies, and the ways in which they work together or fail to do so, are reflected in personality, as we shall see from a comparison of child-rearing patterns in the United States and the Soviet Union, with some data from other modern societies.

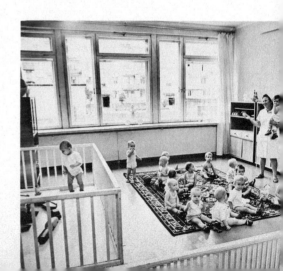

Socialization in Modern Societies:
American and Soviet Styles

In the United States, raising children is regarded as a private matter, and is left largely to the nuclear family and the informal pressures of the peer group; in the Soviet Union it is seen as a major responsibility of the society at large. In comparing these societies we ask two questions: What effect does a society's approach to upbringing have on individual personality? What are the consequences for that society? We base our discussion largely on an extensive empirical study by Urie Bronfenbrenner.

His observations in the U.S.S.R. and several other countries alerted him "to the impressive power—and even greater potential—of models, peers, and group forces in influencing the behavior and development of children."[18] One criterion for judging the worth of a society, he suggests, is the concern of one generation for the next. He is disturbed by the fact that most Americans leave the socialization of children after a certain age almost entirely to peer groups and the mass media, while parents, other adults, and older youths are largely removed from active participation in their lives. This, he believes, will result in increased alienation, indifference, antagonism, and violence among children of the middle class as well as the disadvantaged. Sixth-graders were found to spend twice as much time with peers as with parents. Peer-oriented children held rather negative views of themselves and the group and of their own future; they rated their parents lower on affection and discipline than did adult-oriented children. Between ages six and sixteen, American children spend an average of 22 hours a week watching television as compared to 14 in Britain. By the time the average American child is sixteen he has spent 12,000 to 15,000 hours in front of the TV set—15–20 solid months of 24 hours a day. Yet we know little about the effects of TV on personality.[19]

In sharp contrast to this laissez-faire approach, the Soviet Union makes proper socialization a duty of responsible citizens. A. S. Makarenko's *A Book for Parents* (the Soviet equivalent of Dr. Spock's book) declares that, "In handing over to you a certain measure of social authority, the Soviet state *demands* from you correct upbringing of future citizens," and that they *must* give their children parental love.[20]

[18]*Two Worlds of Childhood: U.S. and U.S.S.R.* (New York: Russell Sage Foundation, 1970), p. 1. With the assistance of John C. Condry, Jr.

[19]Social psychological experiments suggest, however, that people observing aggressive models, even on film, may act more aggressively, especially toward those they dislike. Albert Bandura, Dorothea Ross, and Sheila A. Ross, "Transmission of Aggression Through Imitation of Aggressive Models," *Journal of Abnormal and Social Psychology* 62 (1961): 575–82.

[20]Bronfenbrenner, *Two Worlds of Childhood*, p. 3. [Emphasis added]

Upbringing, says Bronfenbrenner, "is virtually a national hobby." Teen-age boys—complete strangers—would swoop up his 4-year old son on the street, hug him, swing him around. Strangers scold others for wearing their skirts too short or littering the street.

Emotional ties between parents and children are stronger in the Soviet Union and Germany than in the United States, as indicated by maternal protectiveness, overt display of physical affection, and the time adults spend in play and conversation with children. Obedience is stressed; withdrawal of love is the most common sanction for misbehavior.

The most distinctive feature of Soviet upbringing is the "children's collective," which is by no means an autonomous peer group, but one firmly guided by adults (some of whom, in nursery school and kindergarten, are actually called "upbringers.") For about 5% of Soviet children, the first collective is an infant nursery, and one child out of five between ages three and six is in a preschool. In the nurseries six to eight babies live in each raised playpen; there is one upbringer for every four children. She is more than a babysitter, as she provides fondling and other sensory stimulation. The collectives encourage self-reliance; by 18 months they expect complete toilet-training. Sharing, cooperation, and joint activities are encouraged from the start. Small children serve at the table, clean up, garden, care for animals.

The first day of school is a gala occasion, a national holiday when family and friends accompany children to school and present the teachers with flowers. Each classroom is a unit of the Communist youth organization for the particular age level. The teacher does not correct or discipline the individual child, but calls on his peers for criticism. Competition is not among individuals, but groups: first the "links" or rows in a classroom, then classes, schools, cities, and regions—and not only in academic achievement and sports, but also in shop work, service projects, housekeeping, personal grooming, and moral conduct.

> The overall status of each pupil is evaluated weekly by his peers, following standards and procedures taught by the upbringers. Since each child's status depends in part on the standing of the collective of which he is a member, it is to each pupil's enlightened self-interest to watch over his neighbor, encourage the other's good performance and behavior, and help him when he is in difficulty. In this system the children's collective becomes the agent of adult society and the major source of reward and punishment. The latter typically takes the form of group sanctions expressed through public criticism and, ultimately, the threat of exclusion from membership. The individual is taught to set the judgment of the group above his own and to subordinate his interests to those of the collective.[21]

21*Ibid.*, pp. 49–50.

Criticism of others in the group is regarded as a duty, not "tattling" as it is in our society. Adult organizations are also involved in upbringing; a shop, factory, or city agency may "adopt" a school, and its members give the pupils much of their free time. Similarly, a fourth grade may adopt a first grade in the same school, escort the children to and from school, play with them in the school yard, teach them games, read to them, and help with their schoolwork.

One consequence of this pattern of socialization is that Soviet children are much less willing to engage in antisocial conduct than are children in the United States, England, and West Germany. An American child is *more* likely to engage in misconduct if his classmates know of it; the opposite is true in the Soviet Union. Asked what they would do if they knew of another's misbehavior, 20% of a sample of Swiss children said they would do nothing, while only 1% of Soviet children gave that reply.

Assessing the consequences of this system, Bronfenbrenner cites standards of behavior among sixth-graders in England, Switzerland, the United States, and the Soviet Union, concluding that "Soviet youngsters placed greater emphasis on overt propriety, such as being clean, orderly, and well-mannered, but gave less weight . . . to telling the truth and seeking intellectual understanding."[22] Another observer credits the system with providing "a sense of identification and purpose that is so often lacking among youth in modern societies" and playing "a significant part in creating an able, skilled, highly educated population." But, he says, "It has also contributed to the intellectual and moral paralysis that was and is the legacy of Stalinism," and he adds that a number of young people are indifferent or even rebellious simply because the youth program is imposed from above and there are no alternatives.[23]

Bronfenbrenner sums up what Americans might learn from the Soviet system:

> The concern for the nutrition and health of infants and pregnant mothers, the heavy use of modeling through the large-scale involvement of older children and adults in work with younger age groups, the deliberate employment of group forces in reinforcing desired behaviors within the enduring social context of the collective, and the assignment of responsibilities even to the very young in the name of superordinate goals in the classroom, the school, and the community —all these qualify as examples *par excellence* of the strategies we have laid out as representing our most powerful resources for influencing the socialization process. . . . The principles that we in the West have investigated in—and largely confined to—the laboratory, the Russians have discovered and applied in practice on a national scale. . . .

[22]*Ibid.*, p. 81.
[23]Allen Kassof, *The Soviet Youth Program: Regimentation and Rebellion* (Cambridge: Harvard University Press, 1965), pp. 1–2, 174.

T.V. socializes American children with
cops-and-robbers, cowboys-and-Indians,
good guys-and-bad guys.

If the Russians have gone too far in subjecting the child and his peer
group to conformity to a single set of values imposed by the adult
society, perhaps we have reached the point of diminishing returns in
allowing excessive autonomy and in failing to utilize the constructive
potential of the peer group in developing social responsibility and
consideration for others.[24]

However you feel about Bronfenbrenner's conclusions, one
thing is clear from all studies of culture-and-personality and of comparative patterns of socialization: The process of becoming human,
which we described in Chapter 11 as the development of a self, is also
inevitably the process of becoming a member of a specific society and
learning its culture. The two aspects of socialization cannot be separated. As the baby learns to be human, he learns to be a *particular kind*
of human.

Continuing Socialization

In focusing on child development so far in this chapter, we do not mean
to imply that socialization is complete when a person reaches a certain

[24]Bronfenbrenner, *Two Worlds of Childhood*, pp. 151, 165–66. For other studies of
collective socialization, see discussions of Israeli *kibbutzim* in Bruno Bettelheim,
The Children of the Dream (New York: The Macmillan Company, 1969), and
Melford Spiro, *Children of the Kibbutz* (New York: Schocken Books, 1965). For a
critique of the former by Urie Bronfenbrenner, see "The Dream of the Kibbutz,"
Saturday Review (Sept. 20, 1969).

level of maturity. He may be considered "socialized" when his behavior enables him to fit into a group and interaction can proceed without serious hitches. But in a stricter sense, socialization is never finished. First, there is always some resistance to it: "Do I *have* to? Why?" Second, a person enters new statuses as he goes through the life cycle, and joins new groups and even new societies.

For several reasons the first 5 years are most important in forming personality: Growth and development are fastest during those years; the learning process is a sequential one, building on what has gone before—so it is much easier to learn something entirely new than to stamp out something and replace it. Basic values and motives are instilled in childhood; later socialization is more concerned with overt performance. If the values and motivations for an adult role are lacking, and a person is extremely resistant to socialization in a new role—say that of soldier—he may be excluded from it, or jailed, or relegated to some inconsequential status.

Assuming, then, that basic values and motivations have been learned in childhood, **adult socialization** includes learning new skills (mainly by combining old ones in new patterns, with perhaps some new material); getting to "know the score," to know what the real patterns are as compared to the ideals learned as a child; and resolving role conflicts, striking some sort of bargain, for example, between being a dedicated organization man and a good family man. Adult socialization is more specific than childhood learning, although in some instances socializing agencies must deal in general orientations as well: College fraternities, for example, may teach lower-middle class boys the norms and values of a higher social class. An adult has usually decided who are his really significant others, and virtually ignores people who do not matter, while an adolescent may try to please everyone. A person also tends to initiate action more frequently as he gets older.[25]

THE LIFE CYCLE: CONTINUITIES AND DISCONTINUITIES

As a person grows, matures, and ages, he must learn new roles and relationships. In some societies this process is fairly smooth; in others it may be jerky and traumatic, with sharp discontinuities. Ruth Benedict compared the way a boy becomes a man in American society to the way this happens in several Indian societies. In ours, "The child is sexless, the adult estimates his virility by his sexual activities; the child must be protected from the ugly facts of life, the adult must meet them without psychic catastrophe; the child must obey, the adult must

[25]Orville G. Brim, Jr., "Socialization in Later Life," in Orville G. Brim, Jr., and Stanton Wheeler, *Socialization After Childhood* (New York: John Wiley & Sons, 1966), pp. 18–33; reprinted in Edgar F. Borgatta, ed., *Social Psychology: Readings and Perspective* (Chicago: Rand McNally, 1969), pp. 238–48.

CHARLIE BROWN UNDER PSYCHOANALYSIS
A humor that hurts.

TIME, APRIL 9, 1965

command this obedience."[26] While an American child is expected to play and an adult to work, in American Indian societies the child is gradually entrusted with responsibilities he can handle. An American child may be spanked if he disobeys his father; a Crow Indian takes spanking as a sign of lack of love and interprets his child's disobedience as a sign that he will become a man. Socialization into adult sex roles, obviously, presents a somewhat different problem. Where Americans tend to instill a feeling that sex itself is wicked and dirty, the Dakota observe great modesty and privacy about sex, and thus the child does not learn anything that he will have to unlearn later, and a Zuñi child is impressed with the wickedness of premarital sex but not of sex in general.

Other tribal societies minimize the strain of discontinuity in the life cycle by a system of age-grading, with rites of passage to different age groups. Socialization into a new age status is made easier by the support of peers, by ritual and ceremony, and by the prestige of the new status.

Each stage in the life cycle alters the self-conception and may even change personality traits. Measuring married and unmarried women according to the California Personality Inventory, a social psychologist found that married people changed in such traits as self-acceptance and dominance, the more so the earlier they married.[27]

RESOCIALIZATION

A person may be socialized in one society and then through some turn of fate or choice move to another. This is the common case with immigrants, many of whom find themselves "marginal men," at

[26]"Continuities and Discontinuities in Cultural Conditioning," *Psychiatry* 1 (1938): 161–67; reprinted in Rose, *The Study of Society*, pp. 153–60.

[27]Borgatta, *Social Psychology*, p. 247.

home in neither culture. Dramatic instances of quite thorough resocial-ization are afforded by "white Indians" and by inmates of or recruits to "total institutions."

American children kidnapped and raised by Indians in the eighteenth and nineteenth centuries came to look like Indians in many ways, such as posture, walk, and bearing; to exhibit Indian traits (stamina, vigor, reserve, and resistance to extremes of discomfort) that had been believed to be hereditary; and above all to grow so accus-tomed to living in an Indian culture that they usually refused to rejoin the whites and felt uncomfortable in white men's houses and beds. They thought of themselves as Indians, and experienced the same kinds of dreams and visions as Indians. Comfortable with the values and sense of cohesion of Indian groups, they criticized the actions of whites to-ward them, such as their corruption by alcohol.[28]

An army recruit, a novice in a severely traditional order of nuns, a prisoner, or a mental patient sheds an old identity and, through a process that in all these cases is very much alike, takes on a new one. Erving Goffman has described the resocialization process in such "total institutions" as involving these elements: isolation from the out-side (perhaps by virtue of barbed wire, high walls, or locked doors); spending all one's time in the same place with the same people at work, play, and sleep; shedding of individual identity by giving up old clothes and possessions for uniforms or habits and standard equipment, and being called by first or last name, number, rank, or status ("sister" or "soldier"); a clean break with the past; and loss of freedom of action. A similar process accounts for the success of the Chinese Communists in "brainwashing" some American soldiers during the Korean War.[29]

Once a person has been thoroughly socialized into a very spe-cific role, it is hard for him to re-enter the society at large. Returning war veterans, for example, find it hard to tailor their language to their families, and to experience empathy and compassion once they have been encouraged to regard people as dehumanized things; they feel like strangers among their old friends.

Summary

Each of us is a unique personality, a dynamic, complex system whose growth is a process of creative becoming because he can interact with himself, reflecting and deciding between his perception and his chosen

---

[28]Erwin H. Ackerknecht, "White Indians," *Bulletin of the History of Medicine* 15 (1944): 15–35; reprinted in Thomas E. Lasswell, John H. Burma, and Sidney H. Aronson, eds., *Life in Society: Readings in Sociology*, rev. ed. (Glenview, Ill.: Scott, Foresman, 1970), pp. 99–107.

[29]Erving Goffman, *Asylums: Essays on the Social Situation of Mental Patients and Other Inmates* (New York: Doubleday & Company, Inc., 1961).

action. Our characteristic ways of perceiving, acting, and relating to others are often described in terms of traits and social types.

But we are also like some other men and like all other men. All members of the human species are born with essentially the same biological attributes, but even so there is great variation in reaction patterns, strength of drives and reflexes, temperament as affected by glandular balance, and potential intelligence. The rate of maturation and the development of potential intelligence depend on many experiences, including psychic and organic nutrition. Among these is the kind of nurturing one gets in infancy and early childhood, which affects his general orientation to life and to others, his health and survival, and the degree to which his potential intelligence is realized.

Studies of the ways in which culture shapes personality have related the most typical traits of members of a society to its general world view and core values, to its patterns of childrearing, and to its role definitions. A comparative study of American and Soviet patterns of socialization concludes that the Soviet system of children's collectives, with great interest shown by older youth and adults in the "upbringing" process, produces conformist personalities with a sense of purpose and belonging that is lacking in our own society. In the United States the autonomous age-segregated peer group and the mass media appear to produce persons who are more likely to feel alienated and engage in antisocial behavior. At the same time, our system leaves more room for intellectual curiosity and innovation.

Socialization is a lifelong process, but in general basic values and norms are learned in childhood, and more specific skills in adulthood. In some societies the transition to various stages of the life cycle and to new roles is jerky and traumatic; in others it either is a continuous, gradual process or is eased by such devices as age-grading and rites of passage. Resocialization into a new society or a total institution may make one a marginal man, at home in neither, or may change one's self-conception drastically.

In the final chapter of this discussion of *The Person in Culture and Society*, we consider other variations in the relationship of the person, culture, and society: differing orientations to norms, varying degrees of commitment and participation, and the possibilities of achieving personal autonomy.

QUESTIONS FOR FURTHER THOUGHT

1. Walt Whitman wrote, "I find no sweeter fat than sticks to my own bones . . . Nor do I understand who there can be more wonderful than myself." Do you think most people feel the same way? Why or why not?

2. In what ways do you think you are unique? Like some other people? Like all other people?

3. Listen for mention of social types and personality traits in conversation, and watch for them in TV programs, movies, and reading. How do they guide interaction? Do they block or promote appreciation of particular persons?

4. Some sociologists prefer to take the human organism as "given." To what extent is this a valid approach? In this book it is seen as one of the five interrelated systems we must consider in order to understand human behavior. Does this chapter imply reasons for the validity of this approach?

5. Infant nurturing appears to be important to the development of monkeys as well as of human beings. (See footnote, page 360). Are humans more likely to be able to overcome the effects of poor nurturing than other animals? How and why, or why not?

6. After each of these categories, list at least one trait that immediately occurs to you: Englishmen; Frenchmen; Swedes; Mexicans; Americans; Japanese; Spaniards; Scotsmen. Do you believe your answers indicate the validity of the concept of national character or basic personality type? To what extent are they a stereotype or "petrified expectation"?

7. How did you react to Bronfenbrenner's comparison of socialization patterns in the United States and the Soviet Union? What might each society learn from the other? Would any Soviet practices fit into American culture and social structure?

8. Have you experienced discontinuities in socialization? With what consequences for your personality? Have you ever undergone thorough resocialization? With what consequences?

The danger lies in what man thinks he is, for this may shape what he becomes.

RICHARD L. MEANS

By and large, Middletown believes in being, when in doubt, like other people.

ROBERT S. LYND and
HELEN MERRELL LYND

No one ever became thoroughly bad all at once.

JUVENAL

For, as without law there is no sin, without eyes there is no indecorum.

THOMAS HARDY

A "free" society is not "free." It is one in which there is a delicate balance between self-determined activity on the part of its citizens and activity conforming to standards set by the society.

EDWARD L. WALKER and
ROGER W. HEYNS

VARIATIONS IN THE QUALITY AND MEANING OF LIFE: CONFORMITY, DEVIANCE, AND AUTONOMY

W‌HAT IS THE GOOD LIFE? That question, always a concern of philosophers, has long been shunned as "unscientific" by positivist-empiricist sociologists. But social critic-philosopher, David Riesman, among others, considers it of paramount importance. "Each life," he insists, "is an emergency, which only happens once." He suggests that when daily life is not sufficiently interesting and challenging, many of us welcome such violent events as wars and fires, because they relieve our anxiety about "the quality and meaning of individual existence."[1]

As primary relationships decline and feelings of alienation increase, many of us are indeed anxious about the quality and meaning of our lives. Unlike men of past ages, the ideal or model against which we measure ourselves today is not a saint, hero, gentleman, knight, or mystic, but only "the well-adjusted man without problems, a very pale substitute."[2] We suffer feelings of emptiness, loneliness, and boredom. Rapid social change may be largely responsible for these feelings. As men go from farm to factory, village to city, old ties are rent. As they become cogs in large organizations, they must struggle to attain and preserve a strong sense of personal identity and worth. As science and technology accelerate production, they come to feel they must consume more and more material things as a measure of their own status. Many lead empty lives, marking time, filling it, even "killing" it as they await the arrival of death or Santa Claus.[3]

Why is this? Why, in modern societies especially, do many of us feel uncomfortable and unhappy, even though we have largely accepted the norms and values of our society and try to identify our personal goals with the opportunities it offers? Why do so many others of us reject these norms and values, seeking identity and self-esteem in ways the society labels "deviant"? Is it possible to be neither a re-

[1]David Riesman, in collaboration with Nathan Glazer and Reuel Denney, *The Lonely Crowd: A Study of the Changing American Character* (New York: Doubleday & Company, Inc., 1955), p. 338.

[2]Abraham H. Maslow, *Toward a Psychology of Being*, 2nd ed. (New York: Van Nostrand Reinhold, 1968).

[3]Eric Berne, *Games People Play* (New York: Grove Press, 1964), p. 184.

jecting deviant nor a blind conformist, but an autonomous and self-fulfilling person?

In this chapter we explore these great questions somewhat tentatively, considering conformity to and deviance from cultural norms, and some of the factors that are correlated with personal commitment and social participation. We conclude with a re-examination of the self-conception, especially as it effects the quality and meaning of life, and touch upon the possibilities for achieving autonomy, for fulfilling one's potential for humanness.

Conformity

Conformity, we may safely assume, is probably not an issue in many societies, such as those of Alor, New Guinea, and the Plains and Southwest Indians. Most people accept the idea that tradition is good. We might also assume that this is true in China, where, after decades of upheaval, most citizens probably accept the idea that the needs of the society as a whole are far more important than individual desires. In the United States we worry about internal divisions, and each candidate for the presidency in 1972 was anxious to prove that he was the one man who could get the nation back together. But did these aspirants have in mind the kind of consensus or conformity we see in small homogeneous societies and some modern states?

Probably not. Individual freedom is one of America's most sacred values. And we attack conformity from pulpit and press, stage and podium. However, as we saw in Chapter 4, every society depends on a considerable measure of conformity in order to function and survive—conformity to overt behavior patterns and to core values.

And indeed, most of us do conform to most of the rules most of the time. And all of us—including "conformists"—deviate from some of the rules some of the time, consciously or unconsciously, with or without a sense of guilt. Some people deviate from some of the rules most of the time, and their behavior may or may not be defined as a "social problem." But the power of internalized cultural norms and of social group pressures is so strong that no one—with the exception of a few extremely retarded or psychotic persons—deviates from most or all of the rules most or all of the time. For the individual, conformity may seem the way to ingratiate himself with others, to adjust and get along. It also frees him from much uncertainty and anxiety.

KINDS OF CONFORMITY

It appears that two main kinds of **conformity** draw the fire of social critics—unthinking, or even compulsive, adherence to conventional beliefs and behavior patterns, and yielding to group pressures against one's better judgment. The first form may be simply the "useful tyranny of the normal," the habitual acceptance of the language, food patterns, and other folkways of a culture; but it may also include the dogmatic belief that only one religion or economic system or political arrangement is moral—a conviction that is at the root of much conflict in the modern world. Conformity of this type depends largely on past influences; of the second type, on present pressures. Both are to some extent the inevitable results of the socialization process—of learning norms and values, and taking the role of the other. But carried to extremes, they stifle the constructive innovation that produces necessary social changes. "Where everyone thinks alike, no one thinks very much."[4]

A conventional conformist may be so thoroughly socialized that it never occurs to him to question the norms, which seem right and natural. He may repress contrary impulses, or sublimate them in approved kinds of activity. On the other hand, an acquiescent or compliant conformist may be aware of impulses to deviant behavior but not give in to them, for any of several reasons. (1) Through his process of self-interaction, he exercises self-control, knowing the cost of deviant behavior would be guilt, shame, loss of self-esteem. (2) He also wants to keep the approval of his significant others. But, say Judith Blake and Kingsley Davis, these two motives, although valid and powerful, have been assigned too much of the responsibility for conformity. (3) One may also fear punishment; he weighs the possible rewards of deviant behavior against ostracism, loss of his job, his citizenship, his freedom, or his life. (4) He may see no point in deviating from the straight and narrow if the rewards do not seem glamorous. (5) He may simply have no opportunity for deviant behavior despite fantasies and impulses toward it; there may be no alternatives in a constricting society, or he may be so weighed down with obligations that he has neither the time, money, nor energy for cutting loose![5]

If one or more of these five blocks to deviant behavior is lifted, and motives are strong enough, such behavior may occur. In a riot, for example, a person may see his significant others "trashing" and looting; he knows they can hardly disapprove of his doing so. In this example systems of formal punishment have broken down; there is reward for deviant behavior in the acquisition of goods and release of frustrations, and there is opportunity on all sides. Add weak internalized norms to these conditions and he may well join in. And yet a large majority of people in riot areas do not engage in such behavior, possibly because it does not fit their self-conceptions, norms, and values, and because they identify with a reference group such as a church or family that would not condone it.

[4]Norman Tallent, *Psychological Perspectives on the Person* (Princeton: D. Van Nostrand, 1967), p. 212.

[5]"Norms, Values, and Sanctions," in Robert E. L. Faris, ed., *Handbook of Modern Sociology* (Chicago: Rand McNally, 1964), pp. 456–84.

MISS PEACH by Mell Lazarus

Reprinted from the Detroit Free Press through the courtesy of Mell Lazarus and Publishers-Hall Syndicate. Copyright 1972, Field Enterprises.

FORMATION OF SOCIAL NORMS

To the cultural determinist, it seems the norms are simply "there": People internalize them in childhood and hence must always abide by them except in most unusual circumstances. But the norms themselves do not control anything. *People interpret and define and enforce norms as they interact in groups; and where no norms seem to apply, they create them.* A classic laboratory experiment conducted by social psychologist Muzafer Sherif illustrates the process of group formation of norms. As the basis of his experiment, Sherif used the "autokinetic effect"—the tendency to perceive a small stationary point of light in a dark room (or other dark space) as moving. Subjects were asked, first individually and then in groups, to judge how much and in what direction the light moved. Groups were also asked to form a judgment collectively without any of their members having been exposed to the situation previously, and then each member was asked to make individual judgments. Sherif arrived at several interesting conclusions.

1   "When individuals perceive movements which lack any other standard of comparison, *they subjectively establish a range of extent and a point (a standard or norm) within that range which is peculiar to the individual . . .* [and this] norm serves as a reference point with which each successive experienced movement is compared and judged to be short, long, or medium—with the range peculiar to the subject." This norm was found to persist during experiments on subsequent days.

2. When a number of individuals who have previously estab-
    lished norms regarding the perceived movement of the
    stationary light are brought together in an experimental
    situation, their ranges and norms tend to converge.

3. When individuals who have *not* previously established
    individual norms are brought together in a group, they es-
    tablish ranges and norms which converge more rapidly and
    more closely than do those in groups whose members first
    worked individually. Even if a leader emerges in such a
    situation and influences others in establishing a group
    norm, he will not be followed if he changes his norm after
    the group is settled.

4. "When a member of a group faces the same situation sub-
    sequently *alone*, after once the range and norm of his group
    have been established, he perceives the situation in terms
    of the range and norm that he brings from the group sit-
    uation."[6]

THE EFFECT OF GROUP PRESSURE

Another classic experiment tested the effect of group pressure
with a clear-cut stimulus rather than a vague illusory one. Solomon Asch
presented his subjects with an 8-inch line on a white card on a wall, and
about 40 inches away another 8-inch line with a somewhat longer line
on one side and a shorter one on the other. They were asked to choose
which of the three lines was the same length as the one on the first
card. A control group making independent judgments almost always
chose correctly. Then in an experimental group all but one of the subjects in each trial were confederates of the experimenter, and they had
been instructed to choose a wrong line, announce their choice publicly,
and react with expressions of disbelief and ridicule if the person who
was not in on the secret disagreed with them. The lone individuals in
the various trials found themselves contradicted time after time. In
half or more of the trials, one-third of them joined the majority in the
incorrect estimate. In the interviews that followed some of them said
they came to perceive the majority opinion as correct; most decided
their own perceptions must be wrong; still others felt they were right
and yet did not want to appear different from or inferior to the others.
Of the "independents," who insisted on the correct estimate, some were
confident of their own perceptions and withstood the group opposition
with vigor in spite of being sensitive to their opinion; others resisted
pressure on the principle that they had to stick to their individuality;
the third type felt considerable tension and doubt but felt they had

[6]*Social Interaction: Process and Products* (Chicago: Aldine Publishing Company,
1967), pp. 138–45.

Farris in The Saturday Review

*"Do you suppose they know something
we don't?"*

to perform the task as best they could. In a variation of the experiment, when one member of the majority was instructed to give the correct judgment, the subjects were much less likely to yield to majority opinion.[7]

Deviance

Deviant behavior is socially disapproved behavior that exceeds the limits of tolerance and, if discovered, is subject to negative sanctions.[8] It is regarded as immoral (prostitution and homosexuality, for example), dangerous to person and property (assault, robbery, embezzlement), disruptive to social interaction (mental illness), harmful to the deviant person himself and to his interpersonal relationships (drug addiction, alcoholism, suicide), or harmful to the society (treason, incitement to riot, conspiracy). It may be defined as sin, crime, error, or illness—and the same act may be defined differently at different times and in different societies. No act is *inherently* deviant, as we saw in our discussion of the morality of infanticide in Chapter 6. Under certain circumstances,

[7]Solomon E. Asch, "Studies of Independence and Conformity: A Minority of One Against a Unanimous Majority," *Psychological Monographs* 70, No. 9 (1956): 1–7. Another report of this experiment is reprinted in Lasswell, Burma, and Aronson, *Life in Society*, pp. 126–34.

[8]It should be noted that in a society such as ours, not all nonconforming behavior is disapproved, and not all disapproved behavior is sanctioned. We are concerned here with the behavior a society considers antisocial and/or self-destructive.

suicide may be defined as the only honorable course, and killing another man may be a duty rather than a crime.

MOTIVATIONS FOR DEVIANCE

Some who deviate do not want or intend to: A psychotic, mentally retarded, or brain-damaged person may not want to deviate, and nevertheless do so. A visitor to a strange society or subcultural group may deviate out of sheer ignorance of the norms. A person may not be able to live up to role expectations because of illness or lack of energy. On the other hand, a person may be perfectly conscious of the norms and deliberately flout them. A tiny fraction of motorcyclists, for example, belong to gangs that find their satisfactions in being "dedicated rowdies," "perhaps the only status in which they feel they can stand out as individuals."[9]

But the question of motivation of deviant behavior is too complex to fit a simple dichotomy into intentional and unintentional. People usually want to do the right thing, and take pleasure in doing so; they do not often deliberately decide to flout norms. Instead, they take risks, drift into deviance, acquire deviant status according to the discovery and definition of their deviance by others, finally incorporating the status into their self-conceptions. Some deviant behavior is so compulsive in a physiological sense that many modern societies define it as illness rather than deliberate deviance. Drug addicts and alcoholics, for example, have long since forfeited the "high" or pleasure the original indulgence afforded; now an unbearable craving has taken hold, and their chief desires are to avoid the pains of withdrawal and to achieve oblivion and so escape reality.

KINDS OF DEVIANCE

The degree of social disapproval attached to deviant behavior varies, as does the severity of the accompanying sanctions. Those with power to impose sanctions may identify the behavior as "just a prank," the normal mischief of young people who have to sow their wild oats. They may call it sick, unfair, dirty, disgusting, depraved, immoral, vicious, dangerous, criminal, insane, sinful. Authorities may cover it up, impart friendly counsel, and point out preferred alternatives. Or they may degrade the person and stigmatize him publicly, setting him apart with others similarly stigmatized, in jails, mental hospitals, reform schools, rehabilitation centers. Their definition of the act and the sanctions they impose may not be proportionate to the harm done society by the deviant behavior. For example, "white-collar crimes" such as

[9]Robert Shellow and Derek V. Roemer, "No Heaven for 'Hell's Angels,'" *Transaction* (July–Aug. 1966): 12–19.

income tax evasion, false advertising, adulteration of food and drugs, and price fixing are not generally considered as reprehensible as the overt and visible crimes of robbery and burglary, even though their consequences may be more far-reaching.

Deviant behavior may be an occasional, or even a unique, act, such as murder. Or it may be chronic, part of one's life style, as in cases of prostitution, drug addiction, alcoholism, and petty burglary. It may be secret or known. A "junkie," for example, must get his heroin by criminal means and try to avoid being caught in the act; a reputable physician can get morphine or other drugs through legitimate channels, and is not identified as criminal.

Deviant behavior may be engaged in on an individual basis or in a group. People acting alone are usually responsible for crimes of violence, check forgeries, alcoholism, and some kinds of sex offenses; the loner who kills a public figure with a rifle with telescopic sights, the psychotic who retreats from the world, the rapist, has no group support for his deviance. Group deviance may be subcultural: A person may be born into a gypsy band that makes its living by various confidence games; homosexuals and drug addicts band together; and juvenile gangs engage in violence or burglary. Group deviance may also be associational, part of the everyday business of getting things done in corporations, trade unions, armies, and even national governments. Price fixing, extortion by racketeers, graft and corruption in government contracts— all these kinds of deviance "follow from informal, clandestine, policy decisions of associations."[10] Deviant behavior may also be collective— part of mob excitement and a breakdown of social control, as in rioting. Over half of those arrested in the Detroit riot of 1967 had no previous police record. Finally, deviant behavior may be organized, as are the feudally-structured crime syndicates in urban America.

SOCIOLOGICAL PROPOSITIONS REGARDING DEVIANCE

Among numerous generalizations in the form of theories or empirical findings, let us touch upon a few sociological propositions about the sources of deviance and the process by which one becomes "a deviant."

The field theory of deviance.   Deviance cannot be explained in terms of individual traits or of social situations or structures alone. The inner tendencies or readiness to respond in certain ways must be there for the deviant behavior to occur, but so must the opportunities or the triggering external circumstances. Neither alone is sufficient. Other-

[10]Edwin M. Lemert, *Human Deviance, Social Problems, and Social Control* (Englewood Cliffs, N.J.: Prentice-Hall, Inc., 1967), p. 15.

wise, all persons with certain traits would engage in deviant behavior, as would all persons in situations encouraging deviance. "Among persons equally anxious, one may become delinquent, another neurotic or a drug addict, and another deeply religious, depending upon situational variation. Conversely, however, the same situation may precipitate neurosis in one, delinquency in another, and unusual effort in a third, because of different 'selector systems' within individuals."[11]

Deviant subcultures. Much deviance is associated with established or emergent subcultural influences. Some deviant behavior, because of its very nature, *must* be engaged in with others: The homosexual needs a partner, the drug addict needs a supplier, and both need protection against sanctions. They tend to band together with others with similar desires and habits, to feel they belong with them as against the "straight" world, to congregate in certain areas and hangouts, and to speak a special jargon—in short, to share a "way of life."

The role of the subculture in promoting and perpetuating deviance seems quite clear in these cases; it is less so in crime and delinquency. Is the high crime rate essentially a function of the subsociety of the urban slum in which lower-lower-classes live? Do they have a distinctive style of life and sense of belonging such as is implied by the concept of culture? Or do various kinds of gangs arise in response to such factors as mobility; presence or absence of the father; lack of formal social control agencies and of opportunities for success by legitimate means; and presence of opportunities for use of illegitimate means? These factors do not involve "shared patterns for behavior and shared understandings concerning the nature and meaning of things, ideas, feelings, and actions"—i.e., culture.

In general, we might say that a deviant subculture exists (1) when members of groups are socialized into patterns of deviance by those who already know the tricks of the trade and the use of facilities; (2) when they are subject to sanctions for refusing to obey the norms of the deviant group; (3) when they feel a stronger sense of belonging to the deviant group than to the larger society; and (4) when they turn to it for sympathy, understanding, and protection, and confine most of their meaningful interaction to it—when, in short, they share its values and norms, and feel a sense of belonging.

Criminologists Marvin E. Wolfgang and Franco Ferracuti, have studied "subcultures of violence" scattered throughout the world. These subcultural groups account for a very high proportion of assaultive crimes such as murder. (Only about 5% of all murders are premeditated, and a few more are committed by psychotics. But by far the largest share, according to Wolfgang and Ferracuti, arises out of a style of life geared to violent aggression.)

[11]J. Milton Yinger, *Toward a Field Theory of Behavior: Personality & Social Structure* (New York: McGraw-Hill Book Company, 1965), p. 278.

They found similar subcultures of violence in Colombia, Sardinia, a lower-class black district in Philadelphia, and in Albanova, an Italian district of 30,000 people near Naples with the highest rate of assaultive crime in Europe. All have similar values and norms and a life style that takes the form of "a culturally transmitted and shared willingness to express disdain, disgruntlement, and other hostile feelings in personal interaction by using physical force."[12] Because violence is the norm in these subcultures, its use arouses no feeling of guilt.

The people of Albanova, for example, accept a code of honor which demands that they kill to redeem an offense, and carry on ruthless vendettas. They ostracize the nonviolent person, whom they consider not quite a man (deviant by their own norms), and place such a ritualistic value on weapons that a godfather commonly gives his godson a gun at his christening. The Philadelphia study found that many acts that middle-class laws define as trivial are interpreted by lower-class males as derogations calling for violent reprisal: a jostle, for example, or a slur on one's race or mother or masculinity. Where knives and guns abound, and people are socialized to be ready to use them in attack or defense, crimes of violence will obviously be numerous.

Such established subcultures may be distinguished from *emergent* subcultures. Interacting in an anomic or normless setting, a group of boys, seeking satisfactions of various needs and sharing similar problems and feelings of alienation, tentatively explore and test one another's reactions to various possible actions. They may, as a result, settle on theft as a norm for action. This is not the same as being socialized into a subculture that already includes theft as an established way of reaching goals. If a norm of violence persists, and is transmitted to new recruits by a socialization process, then it becomes a subcultural source of deviant behavior. A number of studies show that of every ten offenses committed by juveniles, at least six, and possibly as many

[12]*The Subculture of Violence: Towards an Integrated Theory in Criminology* (London: Social Science Paperbacks, 1967), p. 152.

Spokesmen for the Gay Liberation Front (GLF).

as nine, occur in groups—usually small groups of two to four members, who in turn may belong to larger gangs.[13] "Popular thinking about delinquency and crime is quite correct in its emphasis on the role of 'evil companions' in this behavior."[14]

The process of becoming a "deviant." A deviant act by itself, or even a series of deviant acts, does not make a person a "deviant." To acquire that status, his behavior must be perceived and defined as deviant, the label or stigma of "deviant" must be applied to him, and he must incorporate this status into his self-conception. This is an interactional process, a sequence of events that may be interrupted at any point.

How does the deviant act itself occur in the first place? Edwin Lemert thinks it is rarely a matter of deliberate choice, as it has traditionally been held to be, or of savage animal impulses, or bad heredity, or simple lack of will power. He advances a theory that people drift into deviance. Persons "caught in a network of conflicting claims or values choose not deviant alternatives but rather behavioral solutions which carry risks of deviation."[15] In the flux and pluralism of modern society, many situations are loosely structured, and various groups make conflicting and shifting claims. It is hard to define situations and to foresee the consequences of various alternative acts. A young boy who runs with a gang is coaxed to join them in burglarizing a store; he may decide to take the risk of being caught rather than the risk of being ostracized by his companions. He is thinking not in terms of cultural goals, but in terms of group claims and pressures, and he lets chance decide the outcome. The further he drifts toward deviant behavior, the more alternative avenues he closes off. "Deviant actions act as social foreclosures which qualitatively change meanings and shift the scope of alternatives within which new choices can be made. . . . All of this makes me believe that most people drift into deviance by specific actions rather than by informed choices of social roles and statuses."[16]

The next step in the process is perception of the act as deviant by those in authority. Deviant acts may go unnoted: A falsified tax return may escape the auditor; the boys who burglarize a store may get away with it that time. But an act may also be seen without being perceived as deviant. If two boys are both arrested for driving cars without permission, one may get away with a warning (perhaps because his father's standing in the community causes the policeman or judge

---

[13]James F. Short, Jr., ed., *Gang Delinquency and Delinquent Subcultures* (New York: Harper & Row, 1968), p. 297.

[14]Marshall B. Clinard, *Sociology of Deviant Behavior*, 3rd ed. (New York: Holt, Rinehart & Winston, 1968), p. 229.

[15]Lemert, *Human Deviance*, p. 11.

[16]*Ibid.*, p. 51.

to perceive the act as "borrowing") while the other is perceived as a car thief.

Labeling is part of the next step, stigmatization. The social control apparatus of respectable society attaches some sign to the person notifying others that he is morally repugnant, dangerous, or not to be trusted. They degrade him in status by calling him a thief or crook, insane or perverted. They may even attach marks or brands such as a scarlet letter, a convict's uniform and number, a shapeless hospital robe. They curtail his freedom and close off alternatives. He may also experience hurtful rejections and humiliations in interpersonal contacts; these may extend to his family.[17]

Stigmatization advances the process of alienation. A person may feel he has been treated unfairly, that society has behaved tyrannically and brutally. He may come to regard other deviants as the only ones who understand him and treat him decently. Homosexuals, drug addicts, the physically handicapped, as well as delinquents and criminals, often have this feeling. To find some sense of status, of dignity and self-respect, they seek out their own kind.

Even the stigmatized and alienated may not think of themselves as truly deviant. In white-collar crime, especially, the stigma of being found guilty does not appear to weigh heavily; a tax evader or a corporation official found guilty of bribery or price fixing may think of himself as a lawbreaker at worst, but still considers himself a respectable citizen who happened to get caught—not a criminal. Those who do accept the stigma incorporate it into their self-conceptions; they assume deviant identities. The knowledge that one has become a "criminal" or a "known heroin addict" alters his self-image. Most career criminals think of themselves as criminals.[18]

Once the person defines himself as a deviant, accepts the status and role, he is likely to engage in further deviance. His identity and way of life become organized around the fact of his deviance, whether it is crime, delinquency, mental disorder, alcoholism, or drug addiction.

Like conforming people, the deviant tries to make out as best he can in the face of the limited alternatives now open to him. He seeks out those who will give him some emotional support (or, sometimes, he withdraws further from society). He learns more of the tricks of the trade. He adapts somehow, in some social role, perhaps a "leftover" role in a menial or part-time job with low status, or in a subcultural role in the underworld. He may no longer be afraid of conventional punishments: To the wino of Skid Row, jail once meant shame and disgrace; now he may seek to get in for the sake of warmth and food. He settles for such immediate satisfactions and rewards as are available.

[17]Erving Goffman, *Stigma: Notes on the Management of Spoiled Identity* (Englewood Cliffs, N.J.: Prentice-Hall, Inc., 1963).
[18]Clinard, *Sociology of Deviant Behavior*, p. 264.

DEVIANCE AND PUBLIC POLICY

The fact that deviance becomes a "way of life" is often trace-able, at least in part, to the expectations and actions of the society's agents of social control. Like the Puritans, we Americans do not have much faith in the possibility of reform or rehabilitation. Such phrases as "he is a thief" betray the attitude that thievery is an occupation or a deep-seated character trait. We publicize the deviant act, stigmatize and degrade the person who committed it, set him apart—often with others who will reinforce his conception of himself as deviant—and thus "lock" him into the role. We provide few if any return routes back to respectable society. The dramatic and publicized imprisonment of the convict and the traumatic commitment of the mentally disturbed to an institution (often by policemen) have no equally dramatic counterparts in returning to normal social interaction the man who has served his time or the patient who has recovered. A stigma is as difficult to erase as a brand on the forehead. People are apprehensive about the return of the deviant; thus they make it harder for him to act a normal role. This process is an example of the "self-fulfilling prophecy." We do not expect the "deviant" to reform, and so unconsciously ensure that he does not.

The importance of the social definition and policy regarding deviant behavior is particularly well illustrated in the kinds of behavior that Edwin M. Schur calls "crimes without victims"—abortion, homo-sexuality, and drug addiction.[19] Each involves a willing and private exchange of goods and services which are essentially harmless to oth-ers; but each is defined as a crime. Public policy affects the problem itself; instead of solving it, it may make it worse or create new prob-lems. The laws for defining and dealing with these crimes, Schur at-tempts to demonstrate, do not deter them. They are unenforceable because of the elements of privacy and mutual consent. On the con-trary, they set the stage for business enterprises that exploit the devi-ant, for police corruption, and, in the cases of drug addiction and homo-sexuality, for reliance on subcultural support, and for deviance as a way of life.

Sociological studies of deviant behavior and public policy have prompted such suggestions as the following: changes in laws concern-ing "crimes without victims" that would lessen the possibility of ex-ploitation and corruption; penal reforms that would lessen the likeli-hood of reinforcement of deviants in early stages of the process by those who have accepted deviance as a way of life; the use of group

[19]*Crimes Without Victims: Deviant Behavior and Public Policy: Abortion, Homo-sexuality, Drug Addiction* (Englewood Cliffs, N.J.: Prentice-Hall, Inc., 1965). Since Schur's book was written, some states have legalized abortion, and the general attitude toward homosexuality appears to be changing.

therapy to retrain the mental patient in social interaction; and far more fundamental suggestions regarding the eradication of slum conditions, socialization of children, and control of the power to stigmatize and degrade people accused of deviant behavior.[20]

Variations in Commitment and Participation

In discussing social cohesion (Chapter 8), we noted that some people are emotionally committed to and deeply involved in group interaction, while others feel isolated, segregated, alienated, or ineffective. Various kinds of reference groups encourage participation; people vary in their ability to interact satisfactorily with others, and some feel cut off from the mainstream of group interaction for various reasons.

REFERENCE GROUPS

Throughout the life cycle, groups of "significant others"—reference groups—are very important in encouraging socialization and effective participation. "A reference group is a group, collectivity, or person which the actor takes into account in some manner in the course of selecting a behavior from among a set of alternatives, or in making a judgment about a problematic issue. A reference group helps to orient the actor in a certain course, whether of action or attitude."[21]

Some of these groups are *normative*. Families, nations, and religious organizations, for example, may guide action by setting norms; one thinks of Mother, God, and Country, and may conform to their expectations or be spitefully deviant. Other reference groups are thought of in terms of *comparison*: One may judge the fairness or equity of his lot against such a group ("I complained that I had no shoes until I met a man who had no feet"); he may legitimate his actions by theirs ("Everyone cheats on his income tax"); he may set up a certain person or group as a "role model" from whom he can learn technical skills or artistic ways of behaving toward others (Benjamin Franklin read Plutarch's *Lives* with this in mind, and tried to pattern his literary style after the *Spectator*); finally, he may adjust his behavior to the perceived

[20]See, for example, Clinard, *Sociology of Deviant Behavior*; Schur, *Crimes Without Victims*; Eugene Talbot and Stuart C. Miller, "The Mental Hospital as a Sane Society," *Trans-action* (Sept.–Oct. 1965): 39–42; M. Brewster Smith, "The Revolution in Mental-Health Care—A 'Bold New Approach'?" *Trans-action* (April 1968): 19–23; Robert M. MacIver, *The Prevention and Control of Delinquency* (New York: Atherton, 1966); John Irwin, *The Felon* (Englewood Cliffs, N.J.: Prentice-Hall, Inc., 1970).

[21]Theodore D. Kemper, "Reference Groups, Socialization and Achievement," *American Sociological Review* 33 (1968): 31–45; reprinted in Borgatta, *Social Psychology*, pp. 297–312.

behavior of others, living up to the norms of a cooperative group or using a competitive group to trigger greater exertion.

A third type of reference group is an *audience*, one or more persons an individual feels he must attract and impress. The same group may serve all three purposes: A parent is a source of norms, may be a role model, and usually is an audience to his child. All three kinds of groups are necessary for performance to reach peak levels.[22]

INTERPERSONAL SKILLS

Good interpersonal relationships depend on sensitivity, understanding, and behavioral skills. Sensitivity implies empathy, or ability to take the role of the other; it involves listening and perceiving accurately and fully, being alert to cues, and encouraging expressions of ideas and feelings by others. The more self-insight a person has, the more empathy. Understanding implies ability to assess a situation accurately, to know "what's going on." Behavioral skill implies ability to communicate one's own feelings and ideas accurately (within the bounds dictated by empathy and understanding), and to act creatively according to the perceived cues and the defined situation in order to bring about the primary goal of a particular relationship, whether it is emotional satisfaction, confirmation of the self-conception, change or learning, or a particular task.

Some people seem to learn these capacities easily and naturally, perhaps in family or peer group interaction. Tomatsu Shibutani suggests that the games of the peer group train its members for successful interpersonal relationships in later life. "It is possible that lack of experience in the free give and take of peer groups, where mistakes are rudely corrected, blunts one's sensitivity to the interests of other people."[23]

Many people, however, feel they lack these qualities, and various movements for "sensitivity training" have sprung up in recent years. Unlike courses on how to "win friends and influence people," which teach manipulative tactics, these generally try to promote self-insight and empathy by focusing on the actions, feelings, and interactions of people in a group. Springing from the study of group dynamics, they have assumed two main patterns. *Encounter groups* stress expression of emotion, unity of mind and body, nonverbal communication, and the sense of intimacy and belonging. They demand honesty, openness, and cooperation, and emphasize full use of all the senses in the "here and now." *T-groups*, or training groups, are less emotional and more verbal. Most often they are used to improve relationships within organizations such as churches, business corporations, government

[22]*Ibid.*
[23]*Society and Personality* (Englewood Cliffs, N.J.: Prentice-Hall, Inc., 1961), p. 515.

agencies, and schools, so that participants come to "work things out together."

In both, people are helped to learn about their own motives, feelings, and strategies in dealing with others. By seeing how others react to them, they locate barriers to good interpersonal relationships. Ideally, participants learn not only to be good group members but also how to change and improve their social environments as well as themselves.

Psychiatrist Carl Rogers calls this "Human Potential Movement" the most significant social invention of this century. It is still in the experimental stage, however, and seems to attract a number of quacks out to exploit it for monetary gain. When well conducted, sensitivity training may be valuable for average but psychologically dulled people who want to experience life more intensely. But encounter groups make negative values of intelligence, rationality, and thoughtfulness, some charge, and demand conformity to their own norms of complete openness, denying members the right to be reserved about anything. The remorseless give-and-take of such groups is dangerous for severely disturbed people, who have been known to go off the deep end.[24]

ALIENATION

Anomie, we said in Chapter 8, is a lack of cultural unity or agreement on norms and values within an interacting group or society; it represents a loss of patterns in the mutual expectations for interaction. Alienation is a feeling that one is an alien, a stranger—to others, to his environment, and even to himself. Just as anomie is measured against cultural unity, alienation is measured against the ideal of personality integration. An integrated person feels at home in the world and at ease with others; he knows who he is and where he belongs, and has an adequate level of self-esteem. He feels he has some control over the course of his own life; he is willing to get involved and to participate in social interaction, feeling committed to the values and goals of his group and playing his roles responsibly, that is, according to normative expectations.

In urban society, however, millions of people are alienated. First, they are cut off from the natural world as a source of wonder and pleasure. (A teacher asked her class to be sure to watch the eclipse of the moon that night. "What channel?" inquired a youngster.) The alienated feel cut off from others. Perhaps they do not know the norms and therefore feel a lack of guidance in behavior; or else they reject the norms and values of the larger society; or they distrust the motives of

[24]See Bruce Maliver, "Encounter Groupers Up Against the Wall," *The New York Times Magazine* (Jan. 3, 1971): 4 ff.; and Jane Howard, *Please Touch: A Guided Tour of the Human Potential Movement* (New York: McGraw-Hill, 1970).

others, and feel that others regard them as things to be used for their own ends. They are often apathetic: The thirty-eight New Yorkers who heard or saw a screaming woman stabbed to death below their apartment windows said they did not go to her aid or even call the police because they did not want to "get involved." Alienation may also mean a sense of meaninglessness, a loss of goals and values, a feeling that one is alone and that no one cares or understands—as is true for many elderly people in our society. It may mean a feeling of helplessness, or even hopelessness, stemming from anxiety in a world that is too complex to be controlled. An alienated person thus "experiences the world passively, receptively, as the subject separated from the object."[25]

Alienation from the self means experiencing oneself as a depersonalized, dehumanized thing. The industrial worker, as Marx pointed out, is alienated from his product; his labor is a commodity like other commodities. He therefore loses his sense of dignity as a person. Alienation also means a sense of anonymity, of being nothing but a name on a driver's license or passport; a member of a statistical category; or "an atom whirled about with other atoms."[26]

Those who feel alienated do not necessarily deviate from cultural norms. They may, in fact, ward off anxiety by conforming compulsively. But most alienated people reject or feel rejected by the larger society, and do not abide by some of its norms. Whole groups, such as oppressed minorities, may feel alienated and not bound by the rules; deviant subcultural groups may have norms of their own. Self-defeating forms of deviance, such as alcoholism and drug addiction, are also an escape from anxiety. All deviants have one thing in common: "they feel cut off or have cut themselves off from the main stream of community life."[27]

Those who suffer from mental and emotional disturbances are more or less deeply alienated from themselves and others. Many of the subjective feelings of alienation are present in neuroses—feelings of helplessness, lack of identity, lack of guidance in behavior. Always there is anxiety, ranging from uneasiness to panic, and far out of proportion to any real threat. Neurotics may try to escape their anxieties by interpreting them as rational fears. The chronically worried and overprotective mother may point to the fact that children do get run over as a reason for keeping her 7-year-old confined to the yard. Or the neurotic may deny the existence of his anxiety, but it manifests itself in certain psychosomatic symptoms that he may interpret as signs of organic illness. He may try to drown his anxiety in drink or work or drugs or sleep or excessive sexual activity, or avoid all situations that

[25]Erich Fromm, *Marx's Concept of Man* (New York: Frederick Ungar Publishing Co., Inc., 1966), p. 44.

[26]Harvey Warren Zorbaugh, *The Gold Coast and the Slum* (Chicago: University of Chicago Press, 1929), p. 86.

[27]Eric Josephson and Mary Josephson, eds., *Man Alone: Alienation in Modern Society* (New York: Dell Publishing Co., Inc., 1962), p. 356.

Alienation.

arouse anxiety. In any case, he is not at ease in normal interaction; he is unhappy and perhaps ineffective as well.

While the neurotic is invariably anxious, the psychotic is invariably out of touch with reality, in greater or lesser degree. He perceives, feels, and interprets in deviant ways. "It appears that the mentally ill have always been regarded primarily as deviants."[28] Once regarded as witches, or as possessed by devils, the mentally ill are now considered sick. But, in comparison to the physically ill, they are still regarded with more apprehension, and there is less willingness to recognize them as ill and to welcome them back into normal social interaction when they recover. Mental illness still bears a strong stigma, which further alienates its victims from others.

Psychoses are usually divided into functional and organic types. Organic psychoses stem from impairments in the nervous system due to senility and hardening of the arteries of the brain, degeneration of the brain due to various diseases, and alcoholism. Functional psychoses have been loosely and somewhat unsatisfactorily classified as schizophrenia and manic-depressive psychoses, with paranoia sometimes regarded as a type of schizophrenia and sometimes as a distinct disorder.

The mentally ill person is unable to relate to others, communicate, take the role of the other, control himself, and test his conception of reality in interaction. The schizophrenic is the completely alienated person; he withdraws from others and from life in general, and considers himself a thing. His emotional and intellectual processes are not integrated. Most mental patients under forty suffer from this family of disorders. The manic-depressive lacks self-control. He experiences epi-

[28]John A. Clausen, "Mental Disorders," in Robert K. Merton and Robert A. Nisbet, eds., *Contemporary Social Problems* (New York: Harcourt, Brace & World, 1966), pp. 26–83.

sodes of manic elation alternating with longer periods of despair and depression in which he condemns himself.

Clues to the relationship between mental illness and socialization and the social structure have been sought by many sociologists and psychologists. It appears that schizophrenia is most common among those who are relatively isolated socially: farmers, unskilled laborers, rooming house residents. Plotting the different rates of hospitalized mental illness for various areas of Chicago, Robert E. L. Faris and H. Warren Dunham found that the rates were higher the nearer the patients had lived to the center of the city. The nearer one goes to the center of the city, the more heterogeneous and mobile the population, and the lower its socio-economic status; hence the less the sense of belonging.[29]

Manic-depressive psychoses occur more often among people with a strong need to live up to the expectations of others—professionally or socially prominent persons, or deeply religious ones. Joseph Eaton and Robert Weil found that the Hutterites, a close-knit and self-contained religious group that practices communal living, have, in contrast to other groups, far more mental illness of the manic-depressive than of the schizophrenic type. Besides cultivating the need to live up to the expectations of others, the Hutterites' religion teaches them to look to themselves rather than others for blame and guilt.[30]

Socialization—as Freudian psychologists emphasize—is at the root of many mental illnesses. We have already commented on the importance of nurturing attitudes of parents in infancy and early childhood. It appears that as children many schizophrenics were treated as things, as rigid units in a system rather than as persons in their own right; therefore they did not develop strong self-identities. Dunham found that some kinds of schizophrenics had not experienced intimate and informal peer group relationships, and therefore had been unable to form adequate self-conceptions.[31] All functional mental disorders, in fact, appear to stem from lack of satisfactory interpersonal relationships and faulty self-conceptions. Sociologists and psychologists continue to investigate the role of the balance of biological, infant-nurturing, and socio-cultural factors, as well as of the happenstances of interpersonal relationships, in bringing on neuroses and psychoses of various kinds.

Autonomy and Self-Actualization

Looked at in relation to norms, **autonomy** is a balance between conforming and nonconforming behavior, guided by rational, self-aware

[29]*Mental Disorders in Urban Areas* (Chicago: University of Chicago Press, 1939).

[30]Joseph W. Eaton and Robert J. Weil, *Culture and Mental Disorders* (New York: The Free Press, 1955).

[31]"The Social Personality of the Catatonic-Schizophrenic," *American Journal of Sociology*   49 (May 1944): 508–18.

choices. It implies awareness of norms, with a sense of freedom to decide whether or not to follow them in given situations. "Autonomy," says Mary Ellen Goodman, "is emphatically not a matter of either acceptance or rejection as a matter of principle—a process which has more in common with conformity. Autonomy rather reflects reasoned, judicious, flexible selectivity or uncoerced creativity and innovation."[32] Autonomous behavior may be measured against the "oversocialized, robotized, ethnocentric" behavior of the conformist, the alienated nonconformism of the dropout, and the angry rejection of the rebel.

Autonomy is independence, self-government, freedom, says the dictionary. An autonomous person may or may not be unconventional; he may or may not appear acquiescent; whatever he is, he has decided for himself. He is able, in Riesman's phrase, to "meet life flexibly, listening to the ancestor within and the friend without, but not bound to obey either."[33]

Autonomy is essential to the achievement of full humanness, to return to Maslow's self-actualization. A high degree of awareness distinguishes man from other animals, leading to despair as well as joy. Often as he sang the joy of living, Walt Whitman also wrote:

> I think I could turn and live with animals. . . .
> They do not sweat and whine about their condition,
> They do not lie awake in the dark and weep for their sins.

But neither can they fall in love, delight in sunsets, write poems, make jokes, and create music, or lighten the burden of their condition by talking with friends. They may achieve the full potential of dogness and giraffeness (and we marvel at them), but they have no alternatives. Man alone must make himself.

Determinist philosophies such as behaviorist psychology deny that man is free to make himself. Philosophies that see man as a self-actualizing being capable of fulfilling his potential for full humanness admit that he does not do this in a vacuum; he is shaped and limited in many ways. But within these limits he can think, reflect, appraise, choose, and decide, and forge his action out of these processes. Once he has achieved a self, a sense of identity with unity and continuity, he continues to make himself, largely by his own choices. To the extent that he can do so, he is free. He is not "swept along as a neutral and indifferent unit by the operation of a system."[34] The personality itself is a dynamic and complex system, and like all systems it has a degree of freedom; in fact, says William Kolb, "personality is the freest [system] of all."[35]

[32]*The Individual and Culture* (Homewood, Ill.: Richard D. Irwin, 1967), p. 219.

[33]David Riesman *et al.*, *Selected Essays from Individualism Reconsidered* (New York: Doubleday & Company, Inc., 1955), p. 9.

[34]Blumer, *Symbolic Interactionism*, p. 114.

[35]Kolb, "A Social Psychological Conception of Human Freedom."

One's degree of freedom depends on the extent to which he is aware of himself as the experiencing and acting "I" at this very moment. Not rebelliousness nor planlessness nor anarchy, freedom is rather "man's capacity to take a hand in his own development. It is our capacity to mold ourselves. Freedom is the other side of consciousness of self; if we were not able to be aware of ourselves, we would be pushed along by instinct or the automatic march of history, like bees or mastodons. . . . The less self-awareness a person has, the more he is unfree."[36]

Freedom, then, is essential to the achievement of autonomy and self-fulfillment. But what do these terms mean? **Full humanness**, said Maslow, is such a high level of health, maturation, and self-fulfillment that those who achieve it seem almost like a different breed of human beings. Far more than other people, they perceive reality clearly; accept themselves, nature, and others; are spontaneous and expressive; look outward at problems rather than inward to their own egos; appreciate with freshness and react with rich emotion; are creative, loving, given to privacy and meditation, and capable of satisfying friendships; and enjoy play that is both private, reverie-filled, and fantasy-rich and play that is sociable and even ceremonial.[37] They feel that they are members of the human species rather than of a narrow group, and accept people and the world in general with compassion and amusement.

Growth and peak experiences are the rewards of self-actualization. Growth in itself is exciting and rewarding, whether it fulfills a yearning or ambition to be a good doctor or violinist or carpenter; leads to a better understanding of oneself, the universe, and people in general; or, most important, simply makes one feel that he has become "a good human being." **Peak experiences** are moments of highest happiness that usually come without planning. Self-actualizing people see these unexpected experiences as among the ultimate goals of living, which enrich all the rest of life. Unselfish love and parenthood—or grandparenthood, insights (achieved intellectually, scientifically, mystically, or therapeutically), orgasm, a moving aesthetic experience, a creative moment, an athletic effort, or a sense of communion with nature—all these are examples of what Maslow called peak experiences.[38]

In previous chapters we have discussed various ways of judging

[36]Rollo May, *Man's Search for Himself* (New York: W. W. Norton, 1953), p. 138.

[37]Maslow, *Toward a Psychology of Being*, pp. 26 and 157; and Riesman, *The Lonely Crowd*, p. 328.

[38]We present Maslow's seminal ideas with the value judgment that perhaps "this is what life is all about," and with the further assumption that they can be studied by the methods of social science. If such studies have thus far been made to the satisfaction of sociologists, however, we are not aware of them. Compare Maslow's clinically-based descriptions of joy, for example, with a positivist-empiricist study of happiness in Norman M. Bradburn and David Caplowitz, *Reports on Happiness: A Pilot Study of Behavior Related to Mental Health* (Chicago: Aldine Publishing Company, 1965).

cultures and societies. Maslow insisted that "the main function of a healthy culture is the fostering of universal self-actualization."[39] To do so, a society must first assure its members of gratification of the more basic needs: safety, belongingness, love, respect, and self-esteem.

To what extent does modern society assure or deny these satisfactions? What opportunities does it afford for self-fulfillment? Do the sweeping social changes we associate with modernization threaten us with dehumanization or open up new ways of becoming more fully human? What do the urban trend, population growth, changes in the family, religion, and education mean to us as persons? Can we turn science and technology to human ends or have we created a soul-destroying Frankenstein? Must political systems grow ever more bureaucratized and impersonal, or can they be made instruments to serve human needs more adequately? As we go on to discuss social change and social institutions in the chapters that follow, let us keep in mind that, in terms of "the quality and meaning of individual existence," man is the measure of all things.

Summary

One way to approach the question of "the good life," or "the quality and meaning of individual existence," is to consider how a person fits or fails to fit into society, and to what extent this is related to his freedom and happiness. Studies of conformity, deviance, and autonomy may illuminate these problems.

Because most of us conform to most of the rules most of the time, the social order continues to exist. Much conformity is unreflecting, a matter of habitual subjection to "the useful tyranny of the normal." Some, however, represents a yielding to group pressures against one's better judgment. Laboratory experiments have demonstrated the function of such pressures in both the formation and enforcement of norms.

Deviant behavior is socially disapproved behavior that exceeds the limits of tolerance. It results from an interplay of individual motivations and social structures. Many kinds of deviance are associated with either established subcultures, such as the subculture of violence in Albanova and elsewhere, or with emergent subcultures typical of street gangs. A person becomes "a deviant" by drifting into and risking a deviant act, which may be perceived as such by those in authority; he may then be stigmatized, feel alienated, define himself as a deviant, and adopt deviance as a way of life. Public policy in American society provides few paths back to conventional society for most deviants.

Actions and decisions are often guided by reference groups,

[39]Ibid., p. 159.

which inculcate norms, afford standards of comparison, and serve as audiences. Participation in social interaction is facilitated and encouraged by skill in taking the roles of others, communication, self-insight, and understanding. Recent attempts to improve such skills are manifestations of the "Human Potential Movement." In various kinds of encounter or T-groups, people experience sensitivity training and learn about their own motives, feelings, and strategies in dealing with others.

The opposite of personality integration, which encourages commitment to and participation in groups, is alienation, the feeling of being an alien or stranger cut off from the mainstream of community life. Many people feel alienated from nature and from others—even from themselves. Their alienation may take various forms: feelings of normlessness or rejection of norms and values; apathy; distrust; a sense of meaninglessness and helplessness; a sense of being a thing rather than a human being. Many mental and emotional disturbances indicate severe alienation. The neurotic is extremely anxious as well; the psychotic is out of touch with reality. Functional mental illness appears to stem from faulty self-conceptions and lack of satisfactory interpersonal relationships.

Being capable of self-awareness and self-interaction, man is also capable of decisions and choices, and thus he is responsible in large measure for making himself. To the degree that he realizes his potential, he achieves full humanness or self-actualization. Self-actualizing people experience great satisfaction not only in the process of growth but also in the unexpected delights of peak experiences of many kinds. Among their traits are spontaneity; openness to experience; creativity; capacity to love unselfishly; playfulness; and compassionate, understanding, and even amused acceptance of themselves, of others, and of nature. One criterion for judging the worth of a socio-cultural system is the extent to which it allows its members to fulfill their potential humanness.

QUESTIONS FOR FURTHER THOUGHT

1. Why do you think Riesman says each life is an emergency? Would a Hindu agree with him?

2. What is your conception of "the good life"? How do you think you might achieve it?

3. Do you consider yourself a conformist, a nonconformist, a deviant, or an autonomous person? Do you have elements of all types?

4. Which of the five blocks to deviant behavior do you rec-
    ognize as operative in your own life? What kinds of devi-
    ant behavior might you engage in if they were lifted?

5. Watch for a natural situation in which a group creates
    norms. How does the process occur?

6. Watch for a situation in which group pressure results in
    conformity. Describe the interaction.

7. What is the significance for social interaction in general
    of Asch's experiment? Of the fact that subjects were much
    less likely to yield to majority opinion when even one
    member of the majority gave the correct judgment?

8. How does "the process of becoming a deviant" illustrate
    these concepts: definition of the situation, self-fulfilling
    prophecy, alienation?

9. In *Social Stratification and Deviant Behavior* (New York:
    Random House, 1970) John Hewitt concludes that lower-
    class people are more likely to be deviant than middle- and
    upper-class people because they are lower in self-esteem.
    Construct this as a hypothesis with an independent, a de-
    pendent, and an intervening variable.

10. What do you imagine society would be like if most of its
    members were characterized by autonomous behavior? Do
    you know any people you consider autonomous?

11. List the various kinds of reference groups to which you
    belong. Which are most important to your self-conception?

12. Do you consider yourself alienated? In what respects? Do
    you think alienation may be functional under some cir-
    cumstances? Why or why not?

13. Freedom has been defined in many ways. Do you feel free
    by the criteria of self-awareness and opportunity for self-
    fulfillment? What blocks exist to such freedom in your
    life? Are they part of "the human condition" in general,
    of your society in particular, of some status that places
    you at a disadvantage, or some personal misfortune?

14. What "peak experiences" do you recall? Were they usu-

ally, as Maslow says, unexpected and unplanned? What consequences did they have for your feeling about yourself? Did you, as many do, forget time and "lose yourself" in the moment? Or were you more intensely aware of yourself than usual?

15. Do you think such ideas as Maslow's and Riesman's can be studied systematically? By what methods?

Part Four

SOCIAL

AND

CULTURAL

CHANGE

People can stand only so much boredom and repetition, and only so much novelty and disorganization. If things are dull, they ask, "What's new?" If things are too much in flux, they sigh for "the good old days" and ask what the world is coming to. And in recent times, change has occurred so fast, in so many areas of culture and social structure, with so many repercussions, and over such broad areas of the world, that many of us feel disturbed and threatened.

Even today, however, there is a remarkable degree of stability and predictability in society and culture. If there were not, we could not speak of a social *order*; nor could we have a discipline of sociology, which is based on patterns and regularities. We should keep in mind, too, that sociology emerged in another period of disturbing change, when industrialization was beginning to transform a social order already altered by democratic revolutions, and the emergence of a class of poor factory workers resembled the invasion of an alien horde. Theorists like Marx, observers like de Tocqueville, and empiricists like Le Play and Booth were all concerned with these great changes and their consequences.

Within any social order, man's desire for novelty is to some extent fulfilled by patterns repeated over the days and years of a lifetime. As the sun or the clock marks off the times of sleeping and waking, working and playing, mealtimes and TV or radio programs; as the calendar page is turned for a new month or a new year; as seasons change, holidays recur, children are born, birthdays or puberty or manhood celebrated, marriages toasted, and parents mourned, there is a sense of both change and continuity.

But these cycles are not what we mean when we speak of social and cultural change. Rather we mean alterations in social structures and in norms or patterns of thought, feeling, and action: changes in knowledge, beliefs, and values; in technology and material culture; in the various institutional complexes such as the family, education, religion, govern-

402

ment, and the economy; in art and play; in systems of stratification and intergroup relationships; and in the conceptions people have of the world and of themselves. Many such changes seem to fill needs—to adapt man better to his own biological nature, his physical environment, and his group life. They are, therefore, welcomed as growth or progress. Other changes are mere substitutions for fairly superficial norms that do not deeply affect human life. Still others are felt to be social problems that disturb and threaten to destroy social organization.

Throughout history most people have apparently preferred the comfort of stability to the disturbance of change—not only disruptive, major change, but even minor changes such as those represented by new styles in art, music, literature, and dress. "May your children live in interesting times," ran an ancient Chinese curse. Such philosophers as Plato and Marx saw change as only a necessary way of creating a Utopia—a perfect, and therefore unchanging, social order.

But change is natural, inevitable, and universal. Those who sigh for a golden age of harmony and order, and presume it existed in some earlier time, are reminded that "Things ain't what they used to be—and they never wuz!" Whether we resist or welcome it, fear or encourage it, ignore it or try to guide it, change is a fact of life.

Perhaps what bothers people even more than the loss of accustomed ways is that the news of change is so often "bad news." Not only does too much change too fast in our era, but the process is accompanied by violence, noise, threats, and other phenomena that many people find repulsive. Wars, riots, and demonstrations are standard fare on the TV screens in our living rooms. Young people who reject their parents' values build a counterculture. Activists seek to change "the System" drastically, if not to wreck it entirely.

To many parents these things are closer to home than "the news." They do not merely read of hippies, pot, "the new morality," and "the New Left"; they feel they are being put through a crash course in social change by their own children—a course from which they can scarcely drop out, and which many fear they will flunk. A little more routine, convention, and even boredom would be welcome indeed!

In Chapter 14 we shall consider the sources, processes, and directions of social change. Our approach will be fairly general and theoretical, laying the basis for more specific and substantive considerations of change in all the rest of the book. In Chapter 15 we shall outline the "great transformation" from traditional to modern society. We shall consider signs of the emergence of a "post-industrial society," and ask what effect each of these types of social organization has on the quality and meaning of individual existence. As in all the rest of the book, we shall inevitably have to touch upon "social problems" and "social issues" that arise as consequences of the great transformation.

The nature, causes, and consequences of the worldwide urban trend are considered in Chapter 16. The population explosion and the impact of population growth, industrialization, and urbanization on the environment are our concerns in Chapter 17. In the final chapter of Part Four we consider social unrest and attempts to change the socio-cultural order through collective behavior and social movements.

In this part and the rest of the book it will become clear that the true challenges posed by change are not to be found in the superficial phenomena of beards, sit-ins, marches, demonstrations, and rebellions, but in the search for answers to the great questions about the future of mankind: Will man learn to live in cities as we know them, or will he develop some alternative pattern? Will he learn to live peaceably in multi-group societies and in an interdependent world? Will he master technology or be its captive? Will he survive, and will he prevail?

Change is not doom—it is the antithesis of
doom. Doom is to be found in the struggle
to resist change; salvation comes with understanding it.

PAUL BOHANNON

Anything one man can imagine, other men
can make real.

JULES VERNE

Loyalty to petrified opinion never yet broke
a chain or freed a human soul.

MARK TWAIN

Personality is a knife-edge pressed against
the future.

GEORGE SANTAYANA

The individual is the yeast in the cultural
brew, and every new element of culture can
be traced back ultimately to some individual's mind.

RALPH LINTON

PROCESSES
OF
SOCIAL
AND
CULTURAL
CHANGE

ANYONE WHO STUDIES SOCIAL CHANGE, or even tries to keep up with the news, sometimes feels depressed by the prophets of doom, exasperated with would-be anarchists, and helpless in the face of "runaway" technology and man's apparent inability to adapt his institutions to social change fast enough to avoid serious problems. Each of us sometimes feels tempted to forget the whole thing, and bury his head in the sand.

But a sociologist cannot succumb to this temptation. As Robert Lynd said, the social sciences are "man's working tool for continually rebuilding his culture." They are in themselves instruments of change. Even the most pessimistic social scientists keep on trying to make sense of the confusing turmoil of the current scene; and there are optimists who see glimmers of hope and believe a better social order is in the making. In any case, they keep trying to understand and explain, hoping that those elusive ends of scientific endeavor—prediction and control—may also be served by their efforts.

Among the questions to which they seek answers are these: What *is* social and cultural change? What directions and patterns does it assume? What are its sources or causes, its dynamics—what makes it possible and gives it impetus in one direction or another? What are the possibilities of guiding change?

What Is Social and Cultural Change?

Socio-cultural change includes significant alterations (1) in social organization: the size, formality or informality, kinds of relationships, and systems of statuses and roles that characterize groups, including whole societies; (2) in cultural definitions: the knowledge, beliefs, values, and norms that guide action, thought, and feeling; and (3) in the material products of socio-cultural action.[1]

[1]The adjective "significant" may seem to beg the question; let us say that changes are significant if they make a difference that is felt to be important by the people they affect.

Studies of social change range in scope from Theodore Newcomb's survey of the effects of college experience on the attitudes of Bennington graduates to analyses of the transformation of man's way of life through industrialization and urbanization. They focus on peaceful changes like the expansion of free education; violent changes like the effects of labor strikes or race riots; long-run trends like the shift from rural to urban living; and short-run ups and downs such as shifts in the conservatism or liberalism of the Supreme Court. In any case, a student of change specifies the unit that is being studied: what group, which attitudes, what values, what institution, what society, what pattern of behavior. He is concerned with the rate of change over a specified period of time, its degree, and its direction. He seeks its probable sources, and tries to assess its consequences thus far, and to anticipate further changes and consequences. There is as yet no generally accepted theory of the direction and sources of social change; we shall touch upon numerous conflicting explanations in this chapter.

Directions and Patterns of Change

Where are we headed? Are we "progressing" toward something better, or going downhill from a past golden age? Does every society follow the same general path over decades and centuries? How are different changes interrelated?

EVOLUTIONARY THEORIES

A century ago Darwin's theory of biological evolution inspired anthropologists to theorize that social arrangements and cultural forms are tested in a process of natural selection; if they prove adaptive and useful, they survive. According to this theory human history is a movement toward ever higher forms, from savagery through barbarism to civilization. Some evolutionists see man advancing along a steady, straight path; others think progress occurs in spurts followed by pauses; still others discern stages, either regular stairsteps or with some regressions. Dialectical theorists conceive of the course of history as an upward spiral; each stage of evolution contains its own weaknesses and contradictions, which must be resolved through conflict before the next stage can be reached. A reverse kind of evolutionary theory, called primitivism, says man is sliding from an original state of natural goodness into evil, retrogressing rather than progressing. Contemporary cultural evolutionists like Leslie White argue that culture is an independent force that evolves toward ever greater use of physical power sources and ever greater control of the environment.

Ralph Linton saw some valid elements in evolutionary theory. In general, he said, changes in culture have been directed toward "a better adjustment of the social organism to its environment," but there are exceptions: Nonfunctional elaboration of certain aspects of culture leads to degeneration, even to the point of danger to the society as a whole. Just as the Irish elk evolved enormous horns which endangered its survival, modern warfare indicates that "man is an ape with a brain too active for his own good."[2] Nonetheless, human history as a whole displays certain common, if not universal, sequences. Hunting-and-gathering appears to have preceded food-raising everywhere; agriculture and settled village life preceded cities. With some exceptions, stone tools preceded metal ones; and metals that could be worked cold preceded those that had to be smelted and forged.

The progress of science and technology, suggests one commentator, does indeed seem to follow a line moving up and forward; but the "history of man—what he decides to do with his life—is just as clearly a line that rises and dips and curves, moves forward an inch, retreats a yard, moves again. . . . There is a quantitative difference between Kitty Hawk and Apollo 8, but there is a *qualitative* difference between slavery and emancipation, between illiteracy and reading, between creativity and obedience, between free process and authoritarianism."[3]

CYCLICAL THEORIES

Cyclical theorists of social change insist that there is no long-run trend toward the perfection of man and society; rather civilizations rise and fall, or swing from one extreme to another, or experience shorter-range ups and downs. Pitirim Sorokin, for example, held that societies are oriented toward either "sensate" or "ideational" values, and that a certain amount of development in either direction is bound to be followed by its opposite. As the pendulum swings, there are periods when an "idealistic" mixture of both sensate and ideational values prevails. He detected this pattern in painting, literature, law, war, and revolution. Medieval Catholic art, for example, was thoroughly ideational or spiritual; during the Renaissance there was a glorious mixture of the ideational and the sensate; and modern art typifies sensate excess.[4] "Rise and Fall" theories of change compare societies to living organisms, which pass through an organic life cycle: They are born, grow, decay, and die. Change, then, leads to extinction, not perfection.

[2]*The Tree of Culture* (New York: Alfred A. Knopf, 1955), pp. 50–51.

[3]A. M. Rosenthal, "Level of Discourse Is a Key to Tone of Society's Future," *The New York Times* (Jan. 9, 1969). [Emphasis added.] Kitty Hawk was the scene of the first plane flight by the Wright brothers.

[4]*Social and Cultural Dynamics* (New York: American Book, 1937), vol. 1, chap. 4.

A popular enterprise is to compare modern American society with that of decadent Rome.

Insofar as we can see ups and downs or pendulum swings in man's social history, we are prevented from exaggerating the uniqueness of contemporary events and from expecting current trends to continue indefinitely. Perhaps this can save us from feeling that we are all "going to hell in a hand-basket." Political sociologist Seymour Martin Lipset lends perspective to the turmoil of the 1960s and 1970s, for example, by outlining several epochs in American history since 1918, each of which was marked by trends that some observers thought would go on for much longer than they did. After the First World War the country seemed ripe for a long right-wing period, indicated by anti-Semitic and anti-Catholic immigration laws, race riots (usually initiated by whites) in both Southern and Northern cities, strong repression of radicals, the rejection of the League of Nations, and the surge in the growth and influence of the Ku Klux Klan. But all these trends declined, and the thirties saw a great shift toward liberal attitudes, particularly in economics, as a result of the Depression. In the 1950s, McCarthyism indicated a swing back to the feeling of the 1920s; dissent and personal deviance were so lacking that social critics worried about the blandness and conformism of college students. And now, after a decade and more of activism, there are indications of a swing back to "privatism" with an emphasis on individual enjoyment rather than social action. "Culture styles, political trends, intellectual orientations have a tendency to be self-exhausting. As they move toward extremes they produce counter-reactions."[5]

SYSTEMS THEORY

Equilibrium or adaptation. As we saw in our discussion of the various systems models of society, some theorists hold that the functioning of every social system has equilibrium as its goal. Changes in one part of the system produce adaptations in other parts, restoring the balance of the social machine, the health of the social organism. Those who subscribe to the cybernetic model of society as a complex adaptive system see change as a positive element, contributing to the dynamics of systems in a way that keeps them from sliding into entropy.

Manifest and latent functions and consequences. Because a socio-cultural order is a complex, interdependent, even fragile system, you can never "do just one thing." Many planned changes have unexpected and unintended consequences, which may or may not be desirable.

Robert Merton has used the example of the urban political machine headed by a "boss" to illustrate the idea of the *manifest*

[5]"The Banality of Revolt," *Saturday Review* (July 18, 1970): 23 ff.

or intended consequences and the *latent* or unintended consequences of a social structure. It appeared obvious or "manifest" to most citizens that the boss created an organization in order to gain personal wealth and power, and that this entailed corruption in the form of graft, political appointments on bases other than merit, vote-buying, and even racketeering. But Merton asks us to consider the consequences of the phenomenon neutrally, without passing a moral judgment.

In our decentralized system of government, certain needs went unfulfilled until the boss set up an organization that met them. His machine served as a highly efficient go-between for public and private business; the boss and his henchmen "knew the ropes." It also served as a channel of social mobility for many men of low social and economic status, perhaps sons of immigrants who could not rise through the conventional channels of schooling and work but who could gain wealth and power as faithful precinct captains for the boss. The most important latent function of the machine, perhaps, was to humanize and personalize assistance to the poor, many of whom could not speak English and were at a loss to cope with the environment. The precinct captain was always available in time of need, to help a widow with a basket of food or coal, to find a job, to get a scholarship, to comfort the bereaved, to settle minor violations of the law. This network of personal relations paid off in votes. The grateful voter preferred such help to that of the impersonal welfare worker; the precinct captain did not pry or demand proof of eligibility, and he had "connections" in city hall and elsewhere that the welfare worker lacked.

Political machines demonstrated a striking ability to survive reform movements. Why? Because they filled these needs, and reformers either did not eliminate the needs or failed to provide other ways of meeting them. Says Merton, "To seek social change, without due recognition of the manifest and latent functions performed by the social organization undergoing change, is to indulge in social ritual rather than social engineering."[6]

The Aswan Dam in Egypt was hailed as a godsend that would prevent floods, provide irrigation and electricity, and add great stretches of arable land for feeding a rapidly increasing population. But the dam interferes with the annual floods that brought rich new silt to the farms along the Nile; this silt now builds up behind the dam. Silt-free water erodes the river banks. Snails carrying a dread disease multiply in the new irrigation ditches. The sardine crop, which fed on silt-borne nutrients carried out to sea, has vanished from the Eastern Mediterranean. These unexpected and undesirable consequences demonstrate how many variables must be considered in any far-reaching plan.

[6]*Social Theory and Social Structure*, p. 135. See pp. 114–36 for his discussion of manifest and latent functions. [These pages have been reprinted in *Readings in Sociology*, 4th ed., Edgar A. Schuler *et al.*, eds. (New York: Thomas Y. Crowell, 1971), pp. 28–35.]

Introduction of a new culture element may even be a primary factor in destroying an entire socio-cultural order and creating "an appallingly sudden and complete cultural disintegration and a demoralization of the individual." The Yir Yoront tribe of Australia had an Old Stone Age culture based on hunting, fishing, and gathering. Their sex, age, and kinship roles centered around the manufacture and use of stone axes: Men made them of stone acquired through a network of trading partners in other tribes; they were used, with permission, by women and children in certain kin relationships with their owners. Axes were thus associated with definite norms, values, and rituals. When steel axes became freely available to all, the whole system collapsed; people became apathetic, and any leisure time they gained was spent "in sleep, an art they had thoroughly mastered."[7]

Sources of Change

Why does change occur? What is there in the nature of man, society, and culture that allows, encourages, or demands change? And what is there about *modern* society and culture—and modern man—that produces so much rapid, extensive change that it appears to be an uncontrollable threat?

DETERMINISTIC VS. VOLUNTARISTIC THEORIES

What role does man himself play in social and cultural change? None at all, say **determinist theories** of various kinds; change proceeds according to blind forces over which man has no control. Such theories typically center around the determining force of culture itself or of some one aspect of culture and social structure such as technology, the economic system, or the class structure. **Voluntaristic theories,** in contrast, give man credit or blame for what happens in society. They see man as the active agent, "the yeast in the cultural brew."

Universal aspects of human nature, in one version of voluntaristic theory, are universal sources of change. Man, says Wilbert E. Moore, is a problem-solving animal, who sees the maladjustments of his culture and social structure as challenges, and works to invent new ways and to get them adopted: new gadgets, new techniques, new laws, new values, new patterns of social relationships.[8] He must also con-

[7]This brief account can only suggest the intricate system of meanings and relationships centering on the stone ax. See Lauriston Sharp, "Steel Axes for Stone Age Australians," in Edward H. Spicer, ed., *Human Problems in Technological Change* (New York: Russell Sage Foundation, 1952), case 5, pp. 69–90; reprinted in Schuler et al., *Readings in Sociology*, pp. 619–27.
[8]See *Social Change* (Englewood Cliffs, N.J.: Prentice-Hall, Inc., 1963).

tinually cope with the challenge of his physical environment and biological nature—with the danger of flood, drought, earthquake, and storm,
as well as with disease, accident, and the certainty of his own death.
The human animal also seeks novelty to relieve him of boredom. His
intelligence and curiosity, his restlessness and dissatisfaction, lead man
to discover new continents and explore the moon; to learn through accident and experiment that copper ore will melt; to notice that a mold
he names penicillin inhibits the growth of bacteria; to formulate new
laws that ensure some financial security for the aged.

There is always a margin of individuality and nonconformity
in personality, and some theorists attribute change to unique individuals
or groups rather than to the nature of *Homo sapiens*—to great men or
heroes; to ruling elites or ambitious conspirators; to planners, reformers, and revolutionaries; to skeptics and deviants. The course of history,
they say, is determined by the chance appearance of such people as
Napoleon and Lenin, Edison and Madame Curie, Jesus and Pope John
XXIII, Peter the Great and Kemal Ataturk, Gandhi and Stokely Car-
michael, Giotto and Picasso, Beethoven and the Beatles.

Others see more ordinary people as agents of change: a Peace
Corps worker who helps a village establish a pure water supply; a
Bob Dylan or Joan Baez who expresses discontents; a Congressman
who pushes for reform of welfare legislation; a teacher who encourages
(or fails to encourage) development of human potential; a parent who
teaches (or fails to teach) norms and values; a planner and policy-maker
who initiates change; and a social scientist who points out possible
alternatives and their probable consequences.

Kalman Silvert argues for the voluntaristic approach. He believes "our hearts and minds have been poisoned by determinisms that
make man the dependent variable in society."[9] Events happen because
men make them happen, whether consciously or not, through choice or
through custom, freshly applied rationality or rote response. The real
challenge to man, he insists, lies in discovering how much it is possible
at given times and places to submit to rational choice.

SOCIO-CULTURAL DRIFT

Man's minor decisions and individual actions, said William Graham Sumner, the author of *Folkways*, add up to broad general trends
called **socio-cultural drift**. He believed that this slow but sure accumulation of small changes in folkways and mores is the only effective type
of change. If man tries to initiate a change before its time has come,
the prevailing mores will sabotage his efforts; often the only result will
be social disorganization. Thus his theory has elements of both voluntarism and determinism.

[9]*Man's Power: A Biased Guide to Political Thought and Action* (New York: Viking
Press, 1970), p. 148.

Although he does not agree with Sumner that it is the only effective type of change, Norman F. Washburne agrees that socio-cultural drift is very important. Many individual actions and decisions converge in such a way as to bring about unplanned and unheralded changes in institutions, laws, administrative patterns, business practices.

> As people learn more, experiment, work out problems concerning their daily life, and as they communicate their ideas and methods to one another, major social changes take place with none of the reformer's zeal or the revolutionist's violence. It is probable that such socio-cultural drift accounts for much of the social change that occurs in America today and perhaps this form of change is the most important, [although] not the most dramatic, form that exists.[10]

SUCCESSION OF PERSONNEL

Man unwittingly plays a role in social change in other ways. In every society, the succession of personnel is a built-in source of change. Man is mortal; socialization is never perfect; and the uniqueness of personality results in varying performances of similar roles. Fertility and mortality rates vary from one generation to another, so that the number of people in a society and their distribution in various categories—age, social class, and occupational training, for example—may vary significantly from one generation to another. (The shortage of teachers for the products of the postwar baby boom has given way to a surplus as some of those products grew up to teach a proportionately smaller generation.)

Another aspect of the succession of personnel is the "circulation of elites." Those who control a society seldom replace themselves from their own "stock," but rather recruit new members from those in subordinate positions; people in these groups may also revolt and take over power.

Resistance to change is greatest among the older members of a society, but "to the young, unformed personalities all habits and ideas are equally new and all can be incorporated with ease."[11] One generation violently resists "drastic reforms" that may be commonplace to the next. A thousand young people were selected to attend the White House Conference on Youth in 1971, and their recommendations were distinctly "anti-Establishment," motivated, said the committee on ethics, "not by hatred, but by disappointment over and love for the unfulfilled potential of this nation."[12] This generation gap is not peculiar to our

---

[10]*Interpreting Social Change in America* (New York: Doubleday & Company, Inc., 1954), p. 21.

[11]Ralph Linton, *The Study of Man* (New York: Appleton-Century-Crofts, 1936), pp. 292–93.

[12]*The New York Times* (April 22, 1971).

times; for thousands of years parents have bewailed the fact that the younger generation is going to the dogs; the young have always condemned their parents as either utter incompetents or pious hypocrites. But the gap does appear to be especially pronounced in our time of incredibly rapid change and in itself makes further change possible.

CONFLICT AND CHANGE

As we saw in our discussion of social interaction, conflict is inevitable in any society, because of opposed interests or incompatible claims to scarce values such as money, incompatible beliefs and norms, and the existence of emotional urges that find release in conflict. Some see conflict as necessarily destructive; others as a creative source of change; still others as the only possible means of renewing a society. A political system that works well has institutionalized various means of resolving conflicts without violence, and bringing about peaceful change. "The clearest sign that a political system is working badly is an outburst of extreme action. Police killing looters or snipers killing police, mob violence and its accompaniments, are evidence that new powers and ideas exist that have no ready channels for expression."[13]

An entire social order may be destroyed by overwhelming conquest, as were Carthage, Tasmania, and a number of tribal societies; nuclear powers may destroy the world system. But social systems may also be destroyed by internal conflict as a result of polarization or fragmentation (based on opposed interests and values) so massive and so severe that the mechanisms for coping with conflict prove inadequate, and a destructive civil war occurs.[14]

MARXISM

Marxism is a single-factor theory with elements of evolution, conflict, voluntarism, and determinism. Marx was an evolutionist in the sense that he believed that society proceeds inevitably toward the utopia of perfect communism, even though the stages of progress are sudden revolutionary jumps emerging from the dialectical contradictions of each stage. He was a conflict theorist in that he saw the class struggle as the means by which each inevitable stage is brought about. He was a voluntarist in the sense that people must unite and work to bring about the downfall of their oppressors and achieve the next phase of development. And he was a determinist in the sense that these actions, voluntary though they may seem, occur only because each person is a member of a certain class and cannot help behaving accordingly;

[13]Silvert, *Man's Power*, p. 94.

[14]Robin M. Williams, Jr., *American Society: A Sociological Interpretation*, 3rd ed. (New York: Alfred A. Knopf, 1970), p. 587.

Handelsman in The Saturday Review

"A limited monarchy—what an interesting idea! Why didn't I think of that?"

even the exploiter is not to be blamed personally, for he is simply fulfilling his destined role.

Generally, however, we call Marx an *economic* determinist—a single-factor theorist—because he saw the economic factor as basic to change. All social arrangements and all cultural values and beliefs, he believed, stem from the mode of production, including (1) technology or *forces of production*, such as the peasant agriculture of feudalism or the large-scale factory of industrialism, and (2) an accompanying set of *relations of production*, a structure of statuses and roles such as the feudal estates or the capitalist and worker classes of industrial society. He distinguished five modes of production: primitive communism or tribalism, slavery, feudalism, capitalism, and socialism (which will be followed by the perfect society of communism). Each succeeding system is more productive than the one before and gives power and freedom to a wider class of people. Within each stage there is a gradual change, but it is quantitative, a matter of increasing productivity and piecemeal reforms. Man's relationship to property is not altered without revolution. In the slavery stage he *is* property; in feudalism, he is *tied to* property; in capitalism, he *seeks access to* property by renting out his time and labor; and under socialism, property is jointly owned by the society, and the institution of *private property is destroyed*. Marx, then, felt that change is built into the nature of a social structure in the tension and conflict between classes, and that it is directed toward a vague, wonderful, and presumably unchanging utopia.

World events in our century show how such beliefs can effect social change. Although Marx would hardly recognize many of the twists his ideas have been given to fit different circumstances, the Russian, Chinese, Cuban and Chilean revolutions reflect his influence, as do revolt and insurrection in many other settings.[15]

THE ROLE OF TECHNOLOGY

Technological determinists argue that changes in technology are the source of all other cultural and social changes (also a single-factor theory). William F. Ogburn traced direct connections between such phenomena as the invention of the automobile self-starter and the emancipation of women, for example; when it became easy for women to drive cars, they entered the business world, and this changed their role and the nature of family relationships. Technological changes call for adaptive changes in nonmaterial culture, which is inherently more conservative; these are often so slow in coming that a social problem or maladjustment Ogburn called "cultural lag" occurs.[16] Examples might be the population explosion brought about by the lowering of death rates through medical technology, which has not been accompanied by a decline in the birth rate in most countries; the decay of the inner city after the automobile contributed to suburban growth, which has not been followed by rational metropolitan government; and the pollution of air, water, and land by short-sighted use of chemicals and fossil fuels, which has not been ameliorated to any extent by a system of social-cost accounting[17] and effective legislation.

Technology is often cast as the villain of the modern melodrama. It is obvious that its growth has been rapid and to a large extent uncontrolled, its effects unanticipated; and that such social problems as pollution, traffic chaos, unemployment, the population explosion, and the threat of nuclear war appear to be largely consequences of technological change. But to condemn technology altogether is to forget that it also saves lives, makes deserts bloom, and lets us hear symphonies in our living rooms.

Although technological and economic factors cannot be accepted as prime movers in social change, says Robin Williams, they must be

[15]For an example of neo-Marxist interpretation in the United States, see Roderick Aya and Norman Miller, eds., *The New American Revolution* (New York: The Free Press, 1971).

[16]William F. Ogburn, *Social Change* (New York: Huebsch, 1922).

[17]Social-cost accounting allows for the side effects of industrial production, such as pollution, to be included in calculations, thus earmarking funds for their amelioration.

accorded an important place in any theory of change in modern societies. Technology doesn't cause socio-cultural change directly, but it does make change possible, as the automobile and telephone made suburbs possible.

> This does not mean that "material" factors become the source of change. Modern technology derives from a vast fund of knowledge and ideas, and from a particular set of beliefs, interests, and values. But it is *through* technology, applied primarily in the service of economic and political organizations, that these cultural elements become dynamic in the social system.[18]

The fact that ideas precede technological development is clear in many countries where the desire for economic development through industrialization precedes the reality. Technology is controlled through social organization; it is not "a kind of inanimate force. It rather consists of a body of practical knowledge and skills, a social product having social consequences only as utilized through the organized direction of human ingenuity."[19] And whether or not we blame many of our social problems on technology, we can hardly solve them without employing science and technology.

KNOWLEDGE, BELIEFS, AND VALUES

If we accept the theory that human decisions rather than blind forces provide the essential dynamics of change, then we must emphasize the role of knowledge, beliefs, and values in bringing about—or retarding—change. Kenneth Boulding sees learning as the primary source of the great transition from agricultural to industrial-urban and now to post-industrial civilization.[20] The value judgment that change—in a desired direction, of course—is "progress" has given great momentum to Western societies; so has the idea that man is in charge of his own destiny, which accompanied the Reformation and the secularization of culture. The idea that "God helps those who help themselves" gives impetus to change; traditionalism and fatalism retard it. In the face of other pressures for change, values "hold on most tenaciously. They stand as focal points of system identity and heavily defended strongholds against change. A social structure may withstand, without disintegrating, extensive change in its other components—people and artifacts, for example—so long as its values hold firm. When values go, when they are at last torn asunder, the total social edifice tends to

---

[18]*American Society*, p. 629.

[19]Moore, *Order and Change*, p. 34.

[20]*The Meaning of the Twentieth Century; The Great Transition* (New York: Harper & Row, 1964), p. 27.

crumble."[21] This is the basis for the idea that the growth of a counter-culture (Consciousness III, in Charles Reich's phrase in the popular book *The Greening of America*) is bringing about a revolution in the United States.[22] Chinese leaders "deeply believe that the moving force lies in the motivations and attitudes of men, and that external persuasion must be supported by the 'faith' of men."[23.]

Nonconformist religion and the rise of capitalism. The most famous argument for the theory that cultural beliefs and values can be instrumental in bringing about fundamental change was advanced by Max Weber. He asked, "Why did industrial capitalism [the dependent variable] arise in England and the Netherlands?" He theorized that the independent variable was the Protestant ethic. In order to build a factory system, people had to be motivated to save and invest rather than spend—"a form of insanity." Nonconformist Protestantism, especially Calvinism, provided this motivation. Many English and Flemish Protestants chose production as their calling, and to prove that they were predestined to be saved rather than damned, they lived hardworking, thrifty, ascetic lives, plowing their profits back into industry rather than spending them for enjoyment and display. Thus the Protestant ethic, a set of cultural beliefs and values, provided the impetus for economic development.

Moral crisis. Some theorists see a gap between society's ideals or core values and its real patterns as an important source of social change. When this strain appears especially disruptive, many members of the society feel a sense of moral crisis—of guilt and self-accusation. They identify the strain as a social problem, and seek to bring the real patterns into correspondence with the ideal. They may do so through dissent, protest, legislation, planning, reform, or revolution. A generation ago Gunnar Myrdal saw racial inequality and discrimination as producing such a crisis in the United States. Many see the Vietnam War and the extent of poverty in the United States as violations of our core values.

But awareness of a problem is not enough to produce change. It has been said that the *real* cultural lag in a society is that between knowledge of a problem and its solution.

> As soon as we learn that protein deficiency in infants creates mental retardation, we see the evil of existing poverty programs. Indeed, as soon as we learn that poverty can be practically eliminated, we see that to tolerate poverty is evil. But to feed protein to infants and

[21]Joseph A. Monane, *A Sociology of Human Systems* (New York: Appleton-Century-Crofts, 1967), p. 161.

[22]See Chapter 18, "Collective Behavior and Social Movements."

[23]William T. Liu, ed., *Chinese Society Under Communism: A Reader* (New York: John Wiley & Sons, Inc., 1967), p. 7.

pregnant mothers or to cure poverty require[s] a significant change in the cultural norms which now determine who gets income, for what reason, and how he uses it. Cherished beliefs are shattered.[24]

Anomie and alienation. Mutual trust and agreement on core values hold a society together; anomie and alienation indicate mutual distrust and estrangement among members of groups and among groups within a society. This climate fosters social change, especially through various forms of collective behavior, which is our concern in Chapter 18. Alienated persons are more likely than others to be aware of problems that call for change. Anomie in society is comparable to anarchy in government. It is not necessarily a "bad" state of affairs; it may lead to a better social order. It does, however, tend to disrupt the workings of a society, and to spread through the system.[25] If this loss of trust and commitment pervades a society, people lose faith and withdraw the energy and motivation that keep things going; the whole socio-cultural system may collapse.[26]

Merton sees anomie as the lack of fit between the chief values or goals of a society and the avenues or opportunities for achieving them. In American society, for example, material success is highly valued, and most of us accept the norms that prescribe hard work, education, and thrift as the means to its achievement. Many members of the lower class, however, find these avenues to success blocked, and they resort to such deviant means as crime and delinquency. Some escape from the race by retreating or dropping out; others get into a rut to lessen their anxiety.

But still another reaction is rebellion, an attempt to modify the social structure in such a way that the disadvantaged groups will find the avenues of opportunity opening up. The rebel is ambivalent about cultural goals and institutionalized means. He may accept the goals of the society but question the means for reaching them; he sees the "system" or social structure as barring access to satisfactions, especially for the lower classes (or women, or blacks). He seeks new norms and perhaps "higher" goals. The rebel may become a reformer or revolutionary by transferring his allegiance to a new group possessed of a new myth (a set of core beliefs and values), and rebellion may then pass into organized social action, seeking to develop and establish new norms and structures.[27]

[24]Carl H. Madden, "The Cost of a Livable Environment," *AIA Journal* (May 1971): 26–28.

[25]Yinger, *Toward A Field Theory of Behavior*, chap. 9, "Anomie and Alienation."

[26]Williams, *American Society*, p. 587.

[27]Robert Merton, *Social Theory and Social Structure*, chap. 6, "Social Structure and Anomie," pp. 185–214, and chap. 7, "Continuities in the Theory of Social Structure and Anomie," pp. 215–48. Note that rebellion may also be limited to small subgroups alienated from the rest of the community, like adolescent gangs or youth subcultures.

The role of intellectuals. If knowledge, beliefs, and values are prime sources of social change, then it follows that those whose chief role is to acquire knowledge and assess beliefs and values—the intellectuals—play a key role in social change. Writers, teachers, and thinkers who are "the keepers of the myths" help support the legitimacy of a social system in the minds of its members. By the same token, when they withdraw their support, the system is due for change. Crane Brinton sees "the desertion of the intellectuals" as the most reliable symptom of imminent revolution.[28] In the nineteenth century "the world's first self-proclaimed, alienated 'intelligentsia'" emerged in Russia, espousing various forms of anarchism, reacting against "both the repressive rule of the official bureaucracy and the irrational alternation between passivity and violence associated with the rural Russian masses. It meant both a group of people and a supra-personal force of scientific intelligence."[29] While Lenin thought they perverted the revolutionary movement (and Stalin killed them off, and Khrushchev was anti-intellectual), most historians agree that the intelligentsia paved the way for the Russian revolution by seriously questioning the legitimacy of the Czarist system. And it was not the rank-and-file American colonist or Frenchman who first questioned absolute monarchy, but the philosophers of the Enlightenment, such as Rousseau, Locke, and Montesquieu.

INVENTION AND THE COMPLEXITY OF THE CULTURE BASE

The more varied and complex, specialized and differentiated a socio-cultural system, the more likely it is to change, and to change rapidly. This principle is most obvious in connection with technological innovation. All innovators, except for some who make purely accidental discoveries, have only the existing "storehouse of knowledge" with which to work. Thomas Edison might have been a great man if he had lived 500 years earlier; but he certainly would not have invented the electric light or the phonograph, because the steps that laid the groundwork for these inventions would not have been taken. Leonardo da Vinci, for all his fascination with the idea of flight and the amazing draftsmanship of his models for flying machines, could never have succeeded in inventing the airplane. Such necessary preliminary inventions as the gasoline engine were still far in the future. Recognizing his debt to his predecessors, Isaac Newton said: "If I saw farther, 'twas because I stood on giant shoulders."

Given the proper stage of cultural development, someone is likely to come up with a combination of things and ideas that is hailed

[28]*The Anatomy of Revolution* (New York: Vintage Press, 1959).
[29]James H. Billington, "The Intellectuals," in Allen Kassof, ed., *Prospects for Soviet Society* (New York: Frederick A. Praeger, 1968), p. 453.

as a great discovery or invention. Ogburn lists 148 innovations that occurred almost simultaneously without the inventors being in communication.[30] Thus the old saying "Necessity is the mother of invention" would be closer to the truth if it were rephrased: "The existing culture is the mother of invention." Necessity is not enough; often men are conscious of a need long before they have the means for meeting it.

Because it rests on existing culture elements, change occurs much more rapidly in a complex culture than in a simple one. If there are ten thousand elements in a culture and they yield one invention, a culture with ten times that number will yield not ten, but far more; for as the number of elements increases, the number of possible combinations increases at a greater rate. Stuart Chase illustrates the speed of geometric progression with his story of the blacksmith who suggested that for each of the thirty-two nails needed to shoe his horse, the farmer should pay twice as much as for the previous nail. Since the price of the first was a mere penny, the farmer thought he was getting a bargain. But the total came to $42,946,672.95![31] Culture does not, of course, multiply quite that rapidly and predictably; it would be overwhelmingly complex if it did. As we shall see, there are many barriers that block acceptance of innovations and slow the rate of change. Furthermore, many innovations *replace* old ways of doing things; they are not mere additions. But the fact remains that a complex culture has a greater potential for change than does a simple one.

CULTURE CONTACT AND DIFFUSION

Culture in general could not grow without inventors and discoverers. But the great bulk of any rich and complex culture comes not from innovations within the society but from *diffusion*, the process by which culture traits and patterns spread from one society to another or from one group to another within a society.[32] The Tasmanians, when first visited by Europeans in the eighteenth century, had a Stone Age culture. Cut off from the rest of mankind about 20,000 years before, they had doubtless produced some minor inventions; but because the content of other cultures was not available to them, their own changed with glacial slowness.

Diffusion occurs through contact, whether face-to-face or not, between the members of different societies and groups. Travelers learn new ways; Marco Polo's Chinese cook introduced spaghetti to Italy, and

[30]William Fielding Ogburn, *Social Change*, pp. 90–102. Three others besides Galileo discovered sunspots; four men introduced the decimal point; two discovered oxygen; four invented the telegraph.

[31]Stuart Chase, *The Proper Study of Mankind* (New York: Harper & Row, 1956), p. 131.

[32]See pp. 129–131.

centuries later Italian immigrants brought it to America. Today's youth culture is a mélange of many influences, including British mod and American lower-class clothing, folk, black, and rock music, Oriental music and philosophy, and "hip" argot from the drug and jazz subcultures. All over the world, missionaries have introduced new moral codes, new religious beliefs, and new customs in dress, hygiene, and schooling. Commerce diffuses movies, soft drinks, chewing gum, clothes, utensils, and gadgets of all kinds to all the corners of the earth. Conquerors impose their own ways and sometimes adopt some patterns of the subordinate culture, as the Romans adopted much of Greek culture. Members of the Peace Corps and foreign aid organizations engage in planned diffusion of knowledge, skills, values, and norms.

Hundreds of thousands of inexpensive radios and an estimated 270,500,000 TV sets (in 1971) reach people all around the world. The increasing use of communications satellites may turn the world into what Marshall McLuhan calls "a global village" in which everyone knows the news almost as soon as it happens. Along with movies, these have created in the poor a desire for change, not only in our own society but all over the world. Man is imitative and envious as well as creative.

Acceptance of Change

In discussing the directions and sources of change, we have touched on some factors that lead man to accept or even seek change, as well as to resist it. Intelligence, curiosity, restlessness, imitativeness, envy, and desire for novelty lead men everywhere to seek change; and the succession of generations makes acceptance easier. Anomie, alienation, conflict, and a sense of moral crisis, a definition of change as progress, and the desertion of the intellectuals all create a climate receptive to change. Some societies, especially modern secular ones, value innovation in general.

Historical accidents, such as an Ice Age or the Black Plague, bring inevitable changes in their wake, and present man with challenging problems that can be met only by innovation. When crises occur, old gods and old ways, and even the wisdom of the elders of a traditional society, may be called into question, and innovations are more readily accepted than in stabler times. During the Great Depression, changes were made in the American economic system that would have seemed inconceivable 5 years earlier. During World War II the shortage of manpower opened previously masculine fields to women: they drove cabs, operated turret lathes, and even served in the military forces.

Selective accumulation. Regardless of the social climate, every society is only selectively accumulative, for several reasons. First, in varying degrees, all men value consistency and tend to accept only those innovations that are compatible with established norms, values, and beliefs. Moslem women, for example, will not adopt health practices that include examination by a male doctor. Second, the attitude toward the lending culture or the innovators in their own culture influences acceptance or rejection. Many Africans despise "Afro" hairdos because they define them as symbols of Americanism and imperialism. Others like them because they come from America, "the home of exciting and popular soul music."[33] Third, an innovation may or may not fill a gap in another culture. The cultivation of maize spread from the New World to Africa and Europe because there was a need for such a grain; but Orientals and Central Americans show little interest in potatoes because they already have a starchy food, rice. Some elements can, however, be added without displacing others. Puerto Ricans have found room for Santa Claus as well as the Three Kings in their Christmas festivities.

Fourth, the rationality and desirability of a change may be obvious, but the sheer inconvenience and irritation of the shift blocks change. Only now is the United States beginning the gradual and long-drawn-out process of changing from medieval weights and measures (pounds, gallons, acres, feet) to the simple and sensible metric system used in science and in most societies. Although the change may cost $11 billion, it is said it will save a fourth of the time school children now spend in learning arithmetic, and cut perhaps $705 million a year from the cost of schooling.[34] Our spelling is far from phonetic; and in the Space Age we struggle along with a calendar devised by ancient Egyptians, formalized in 45 B.C., and last altered in 1582. But which

[33]Stanley Meisler, "Afro Haircut 'Out' in Africa," *Detroit News* (Oct. 8, 1970).
[34]*The New York Times* (Dec. 13, 1970).

Education by T.V. in a small village
in Nigeria.

generation will take upon itself the burden of changing them to more rational systems?

Although the desirability of a change may seem self-evident, especially to outsiders, it may turn out that the old way served purposes other than its obvious one. In rural India, for example, open dung fires are used for cooking in rooms with no chimneys and few windows. The rooms are filled with choking smoke, which filters slowly through the thatched roofs. In an attempt to relieve the discomfort, as well as the respiratory and eye ailments that result from the smoke, the Community Development Programme made available at low cost a smokeless pottery stove with a chimney. It was found, however, that smoke keeps down the wood-boring white ants that destroy the roofs; villagers are reluctant to adopt the new stove that would force them to replace the roof more often. Similarly, in Iran, the smoke discourages malaria-carrying mosquitoes.[35]

Adaptation of innovations.   Only very simple elements can be adopted without some alteration to fit the culture: Thus the Guatemalan Indians adopted coffee from the Spanish-speaking residents, who in turn added the aboriginal tortillas to their own diet. Often only the *form* of a culture element is adopted, and it is given a different meaning. Thus the colorful masked dances of the Pueblo Indians are associated with fertility, rain, and good crops; the Navaho borrowed them and reinterpreted them as useful in healing disease. An old cultural element and a new one may be merged in a creative synthesis. Pagan religions often revolved around one great goddess who was the mother and guardian of life. With the diffusion of the Christian religion, her identity became merged with that of the Virgin Mary, and the local goddess became the local Madonna, still credited with many of the powers and traits of the original pagan goddess.

Social Problems and Social Change

Social change and social problems stand in a reciprocal relationship; each can be seen as both cause and effect of the other. Social problems arise when social changes make different groups aware of conflicting values and interests. And many social changes result from attempts to resolve social problems, whether through peaceful or violent means, through established channels or the phenomena of collective behavior.

What constitutes a **social problem**? (1) Deviant behavior perceived by significant numbers of people as a threat to or a violation of cultural norms and values (drug addiction, for example); (2) blockage or frustration of the personal goals of specific social categories of people within a social system (such as race discrimination); (3) threats to the

[35]George Foster, *Traditional Cultures and the Impact of Technological Change* (New York: Harper & Row, 1962), p. 81.

continued organization and stability of the system itself (such as violent protest or the population explosion); and (4) anything that threatens the quality of life, and life itself. The perception of a social problem varies; some define abortion as a social problem, while others see it as a solution of a personal problem and believe that anti-abortion laws constitute the real problem.[36] Some blame social problems on "evil" people, others on a "sick" or "evil" society; still others attribute them to a number of factors that make for maladjustment among members of a group or among groups within a larger system. Fatalists believe nothing can be done about them; activists believe something can and should be done, and feel called upon to try.

Sociologists take both theoretical and practical approaches to social problems. Many great sociologists have been motivated by "a deep and penetrating concern over the fundamental and immediate social problems of man."[37] Sociologists see problems as laboratories for developing and testing theories about social structure and social psychology. Durkheim in his study of suicide and Thomas and Znaniecki in their study of problems of adjustment faced by Polish immigrants to the United States related social problems to the larger social changes of industrialism, secularism, urbanism, and individualism, which have profound consequences for society and personality.[38] In a more directly "practical" vein, sociologists try to make clear what the costs and consequences of various problems are, as well as the costs and consequences of alternative policies for dealing with these problems. They may also recognize latent problems that might have serious consequences long before they become manifest, that is, recognized as problems by significant numbers of people.

> When the demographer Kingsley Davis, for example, identifies the social, economic, and cultural consequences of rapidly growing populations in diverse kinds of society, he in effect calls the advocates of alternative population policies to account for the results of one or another policy. They can no longer evade responsibility for the social consequences of policy by claiming these to be fundamentally unforeseeable. . . .[39]

[36]Robert K. Merton and Robert Nisbet list fifteen social problems in their text, *Contemporary Social Problems*, 3rd ed. (New York: Harcourt Brace Jovanovich, Inc., 1971): drug use, mental disorders, delinquency, organized crime, alcohol abuse, suicide, sexual deviance, population increase, race relations, family disorganization, work and automation, urban conflict, poverty, violence, and the youth revolution.

[37]Richard L. Means, *The Ethical Imperative* (Garden City, N.Y.: Doubleday, Anchor, 1970), p. 27.

[38]Emile Durkheim, *Suicide* (1897), J. A. Spaulding and G. Simpson, trans. (New York: The Free Press, 1951); and William I. Thomas and Florian Znaniecki, *The Polish Peasant in Europe and America* (Boston: Badger, 1920).

[39]Robert K. Merton, "Social Problems and Sociological Theory," in Merton and Nisbet, *Contemporary Social Problems*, p. 806.

Planning Social Change

Most societies still play a passive role in change, struggling to adapt to changes, such as technological innovations. But the idea of planning is gaining ground. **Planning** is "the more or less efficient and foresightful devising of means to reach specified goals."[40] It involves, therefore, choices of goals, predictions of likely or possible future states of affairs, and decisions on means.

Although private corporations plan many years ahead, only recently—and then only in piecemeal efforts—have Americans adopted planning in the public sector of national life. We have usually associated planning with rigid, totalitarian "Five-Year Plans" and believed in the inevitable goodness of spontaneous change as an essential part of the American Dream. At the opposite extreme is the policy of authoritarian intervention followed by Soviet central planners. Such planning involves little concern for the second-order consequences of means used to reach a goal. Thus in the early years of Soviet modernization, master plans were imposed from above with no effort to build consensus or to profit from feedback from the people. Such plans required large applications of power through coercion and control and invited massive resistance and alienation; the consequences were enormous waste of human, physical, and social resources, and great oppression and suffering.[41]

Somewhere in the middle are the British, who have long been known for handling problems by "muddling through." This does not mean they disdain planning, but rather that they are so keenly aware of the possible consequences of any predetermined course of action, of the complexity of social processes and social systems, and of the impossibility of precise prediction that they prefer to proceed with great sensitivity to feedback and are disposed to change tactics when this is indicated.[42]

Most planning thus far, says Alvin Toffler, has several shortcomings. It focuses on economic growth with technology as its primary tool; it is short-range (even 5 years is a very short time for real planning, and Americans tend to regard 1- and 2-year forecasts as "long-range" planning); it is controlled by bureaucrats, and hence is undemocratic. Furthermore, it is essentially deterministic: It assumes that the framework is given, and plans must be made within it. As a result,

[40]Bob Ross, "Is Planning a Revolution?" in Steven E. Deutsch and John Howard, eds., *Where It's At: Radical Perspectives in Sociology* (New York: Harper & Row, Publishers, 1970), p. 218.

[41]Warren Breed, *The Self-Guiding Society* (New York: The Free Press, 1971), p. 176.

[42]Raymond A. Bauer, ed., *Social Indicators* (Cambridge: The M.I.T. Press, 1966), p. 7.

things get more and more out of control, and people turn more and more to mysticism and nostalgia in their disillusionment with "planning."[43]

This inept, undemocratic, anti-human planning, Toffler argues, is not really planning at all. What we need is a new strategy, "social futurism," through which we can arrive at greater competence in managing change. And more and more social planners in various disciplines are "futurists" of some kind. What assumptions do they share? How do they propose to predict and shape the future?

ASSUMPTIONS OF SOCIAL PLANNERS

Those who accept the need for some sort of social planning in democratic societies assume, first of all, that peaceful change is to be preferred to violent change.

> Although revolution may in some circumstances be necessary, man's history shows that it is an extremely wasteful mode of change. Revolution destroys physical and social capital and leaves in its wake a large reservoir of wrongs and inequities that require generations to liquidate. Evolutionary social change can avoid these setbacks. It can steadily augment social justice and material well-being. It can yield progress without hiatus.[44]

Second, most planners are aware of the complexity of social systems and of the interdependence of all forms of life, and thus are concerned with the effects a change in one part of a system will have on other parts. Buckminster Fuller takes an especially broad view of these principles; he speaks of devising "an operating manual for Spaceship Earth."[45] In his view, human beings, resources, ideas, and possibilities constitute one complete environmental system. Modern planners cannot be egocentric or ethnocentric, or even anthropocentric (that is, focused on one's self, or group, or even all mankind); they must be *bio-centric*, conscious of all life or "universe." Fuller insists that we look first at problems in their largest context and then work down to their more detailed and particular aspects. Etzioni calls for "mixed scanning," the combination of a bird's-eye view of the whole scene with a zoom-lens camera that zeroes in on specific problems. The panoramic

[43]"The Strategy of Social Futurism," in Alvin Toffler, ed., *The Futurists* (New York: Random House, 1972), pp. 96–130; excerpted from *Future Shock* (New York: Random House, 1970), pp. 395–400.

[44]Neil H. Jacoby, "What Is a Social Problem?" *The Center Magazine* (July/Aug. 1971): 35–40.

[45]"Technology and the Human Environment," in Robert Disch, ed., *The Ecological Conscience: Values for Survival* (Englewood Cliffs, N.J.: Prentice Hall, Inc., 1970), pp. 174–80.

view takes in basic goals, fundamental decisions, and the whole pattern. Focusing on details allows "bit changes" in parts of the system, which when added up may help the whole system to work better.[46]

Third, planners assume that there are alternatives: "alternative theories of learning in the classroom; alternative environments to deter delinquent boys; . . . alternative patterns of industrial relations"—none of which necessarily disturb the status quo. Other planners are more radical—in the sense that they believe no problem can be solved without getting at its "root" causes. They propose that we think about basic alternatives in systems of social priorities, values, and distributions of power.[47]

A fourth assumption is that error is inherent in natural, physical, and social systems. The best-laid plans toward achievement of the most carefully chosen goals must continually be reviewed in terms of information, communication, or "feedback," and planners must be ready to change course when results are different from those desired or intended.

Finally, advocates of planning believe, above all, that things left to themselves generally do not get better. Man's own constitution and the societies he creates "are precarious, in the sense that their equilibrium, maintenance, and development require constant vigilance, attention, and work. . . . It requires work to keep the social system at peace and to prevent it from slipping down into arms races and mutually destructive violence."[48]

PREDICTION, ANTICIPATION, AND IMAGINATION OF CHANGE

If we subscribe to the theory that we can to some extent "invent the future" we must be guided by some ideas about that future. *Prediction* identifies the most probable future state of affairs; *anticipation* takes into account a broad range of *possible* outcomes, in order to keep open more options than does prediction alone. Prediction and anticipation combined with imagination and social philosophy—ideas of what the future *should* or *should not* be like—result in utopian visions and anti-utopian nightmares. All three aspects of social futurism play a role in guiding planning.

Prediction.   There are two main procedures for predicting the future (aside from such hoary means as crystal-gazing, horoscope-reading, and studying the entrails of chickens). One is projection of current trends into the future, assuming that they will go indefinitely. Many

[46]Breed, *The Self-Guiding Society*, pp. 104–11.

[47]Steven Deutsch, "Alternatives, Social Change, and the Future," in Deutsch and Howard, *Where It's At*, pp. 533–41.

[48]Boulding, *The Meaning of the Twentieth Century*, p. 145.

such projections concentrate almost entirely on technology, depicting marvels of transportation and communication, housekeeping, and even baby-producing. The prediction of social trends is trickier in some ways; population projections, for example, have often proven false. Trends do not necessarily continue; in the evolution of social systems, as in the evolution of plant and animal life, there are surprises. But Daniel Bell, chairman of the Commission on the Year 2000 of the American Academy of Arts and Sciences, insists that inventions and events are less predictable than social trends and the consequences of technological innovations. Hitler's enemies were confident that he could not last long if trade routes to Chile were blocked, cutting off nitrates for his war machine; then his scientists developed a synthetic product. In contrast, President Hoover's committee of scholars, which published *Recent Social Trends* in 1933, predicted with remarkable accuracy many of today's problems connected with race, education, poverty, and medical care. Lewis Mumford warned us over three decades ago what our cities would be like in the seventies if we did not seriously concern .ourselves with guiding their future.[49]

The other important method of prediction is based on identifying key patterns of culture and social structure. De Tocqueville, for example, delineated what he thought were the central features of American society, especially the trend toward economic and social equality, and constructed the pattern of the future "perhaps better than any individual before or since."[50] Similarly, contemporary social scientists may identify key features of a future society and, predict, from their knowledge of how things cohere in patterns, a number of other features that are likely to accompany them.

Anticipation. Simple prediction of the most probable state of affairs is not enough. We must also *anticipate* a broad range of possible outcomes so that we will be better able to deal with them in the event that they do occur.[51] Daniel Bell says we seek pre-vision "as much to 'halt' a future as to help it come into being, for the function of prediction is not, as often stated, to aid social control, but to widen the spheres of moral choice. Without that normative commitment, the social sciences become a mere technology rather than humanistic discipline."[52]

[49]Lewis Mumford, *The Culture of Cities* (New York: Harcourt Brace Jovanovich, Inc., 1938).

[50]Andrew Shonfield, "Thinking About the Future," *Encounter* (Feb. 1969); reprinted in *Current* (March 1969): 41–53.

[51]Bauer, *Social Indicators*, pp. 17–18.

[52]Daniel Bell, "Twelve Modes of Prediction—A Preliminary Sorting of Approaches in the Social Sciences," in Warren G. Bennis, Kenneth D. Benne, and Robert Chin, eds., *The Planning of Change*, 2nd ed. (New York: Holt, Rinehart & Winston, Inc., 1969), pp. 532–52.

The utopian imagination. Like social philosophy in general, utopian thinking has long been in disfavor among most sociologists; but more and more of those involved with the study of the future believe utopias (such as Skinner's *Walden Two* or Huxley's *Brave New World*) can perform a useful function. These normative pre-visions, whether idyllic dreams or appalling nightmares, open up new ranges of possibilities, and thus provide ideas for social change. Utopian thinking can be a corrective for a narrow positivism that "has no place for the potential, the purposeful, or the ideal."[53] Universal suffrage, the separation of governmental powers, and the basic features of the welfare state were first suggested in the mental experiments of utopian writers. Some contemporary thinkers assert that in science, religion, and political action "some form of utopia is antecedent to every important human adventure," and that "man cannot live as a full human being without utopian visions."[54]

In our rapidly changing, apparently uncontrolled society, with no one in charge, we need utopias more than ever. "A positive future-consciousness," insists Frederik L. Polak of the Netherlands, "is an absolutely indispensable antidote against the mind-poisoning negativism and threatening ideologies now undermining the foundations of Western culture. . . . Only images of the future which can depict a drastically changed but viable society can help to write the history of a better future."[55]

What kinds of visions of the future might perform such a service? First of all, they have to be broad in scope, taking in the world as an interdependent system (rather than focusing on isolated communities on mountaintops or islands or in hidden valleys). Second, they must consider the entire socio-cultural order, and not just the science fiction wonders of technology. "What would its family structure be like? Its economy, laws, religion, sexual practices, youth culture, music, art, its sense of time, its degree of differentiation, its psychological problems?"[56] By the same token, they must not repudiate modern science and technology, as many regressive utopias do. (Even *Walden Two* has an essentially agrarian and handicraft economy.) Traditionally utopias have depicted technology as a Frankenstein monster and predicted man would be enslaved by his own creations, such as robots and computers. Even utopias based on advanced technology do not take into account the complexity of society; their social and cultural relationships are fixed and oversimplified.

Third, social planners with democratic values reject many utopias as essentially totalitarian, based on some sort of control of individ-

---

[53]Lewis Mumford, "Utopia, the City, and the Machine," in Frank E. Manuel, ed., *Utopias and Utopian Thought* (Boston: Beacon Press, 1967), p. 3.

[54]Frank E. Manuel, "Introduction," in *ibid.*, p. xx.

[55]"Utopia and Cultural Renewal," in *ibid.*, p. 295.

[56]Toffler, *Future Shock*, p. 413.

ual behavior by an arbitrary means—by drugs (Aldous Huxley's *Island*), terror (George Orwell's *1984*), or by the behavioral engineering of benevolent despots (in *Walden Two*, children go about with tempting lollipops hung about their necks, and if they develop enough willpower not to lick them, they are rewarded, or "positively reinforced").

Fourth, the utopias we need must be collaboratively constructed. We need "utopia factories" in which social scientists work together "to hammer out among themselves a set of well-defined values on which they believe a truly super-industrial utopian society might be based." Then each member of the team might try to describe a part of the society, built on these values. "At this point, with the completion of detailed analysis, the project would move to the fiction stage. Novelists, filmmakers, science fiction writers and others, working closely with psychologists, could prepare creative works about the lives of individual characters in the imagined society."[57] To throw into sharp relief the possible alternatives, other groups could meanwhile be working on counter-utopias, one stressing materialist, success-oriented values; another sensual, hedonistic values; a third esthetic ones; a fourth individualism; a fifth collectivism. Ultimately, a series of "scenarios" could be presented to the public in books, films, plays, and TV programs to show them the pros and cons of each type of utopia, and some groups might experiment with the alternative patterns of living.

Does this seem far in the future, even for "futurists"? Something like it is being tried in Europe. Bertrand de Jouvenel sees the future as composed of a large set of alternatives, many of which should be presented to the public as viable possibilities (and are being presented on French television). A useful Utopian vision, he says, might start with a picture of the daily life of the average man, vividly depicted so that people can imagine and choose their future. For practical purposes, each such picture should begin with a man awakening and recovering "awareness of his surroundings. If he thinks gladly of his family and looks forward to the day's work he can be called happy."[58] Thus a practical utopia is not made up of robots, nor actors in a pastoral idyll, nor supermen, nor pacified and controlled creatures. Useful previsions take into account both social needs and individual fulfillment.

CHOICE OF GOALS

Such vivid depictions of possible futures can be especially useful in guiding the choice of goals. Every choice among alternatives inevitably closes off some other possible choices. One criterion of farsighted planning is to keep as many options open for the next generation as possible. This means that long-range plans cannot be too

---

[57]*Ibid.*

[58]"Utopia for Practical Purposes," in Manuel, *Utopias and Utopian Thought*, p. 233.

specific and detailed, and that they must be made with a keen sense of priorities and of consequences.

Insofar as visions of the future "widen the spheres of moral choice," they force the members of society, and especially those in charge of planning, to weigh priorities in determining their goals and to consider possible consequences of the means chosen for reaching those goals. In traditional utopias, the choices have already been made. In a set of alternative scenarios of the future, however, one is impressed with the importance of deciding on priorities and made aware of "the consequences of pursuing a lot of desirable things that happen to be incompatible with one another."[59] We are forced to think, for example, about "the central issue of the politics of this generation"—the conflict between our wishes as private consumers and our concern with getting the best out of what we use collectively. We also see how the means we choose to fulfill some desire may actually frustrate us in achieving it, just as people fleeing the city have turned the countryside into urban sprawl.[60]

Who shall decide on the goals? Not only systems engineers and professional planners or political decision-makers; they may not ask the right questions. They may have the "know-how" but not the "know-what," in Norbert Wiener's phrase.[61] They must be joined by humanists, artists, architects, and social scientists, who may form (and are forming, in various institutes) "unique coalitions of resources to serve man and society." What can humanists contribute to social planning?

> The aesthetic sensitivities the great humanist cultivates or makes us aware of, the perspectives of history he reveals, and the questions about the future he insists on asking, the 'vision of greatness' and the 'study of perfection' he brings before us, his search for the moral and the first-rate in living, the eternal questions he asks—all these activities help to create the conditions and the outlook which science requires to flourish and men require for fulfillment.[62]

SYSTEMS APPROACHES TO PLANNING

Much fruitful planning is based on the systems model of society. According to the *systems concept* (as we said in the Introduction and elsewhere), human social behavior occurs in a field of five sets of systems, all simultaneously present and interacting: the physical and biological environment, the human organism, the personality, cultural

[59]Shonfield, "Thinking About the Future."
[60]*Ibid.*
[61]*The Human Use of Human Beings: Cybernetics and Society* (New York: Avon, 1967), p. 254.
[62]James R. Killian, Jr., "Toward a Working Partnership of the Sciences and the Humanities," in Taylor Littleton, ed., *Approaching the Benign Environment* (London: Collier-Macmillan, Ltd., 1970), pp. 132–60.

systems, and social systems. Planning ideally takes all these into account, but typically stresses the social system as the most complex and adaptive of the five.

Social systems are not, however, *infinitely* adaptive; as we saw in Chapter 7, they operate under many constraints. Nonetheless, there is always some free play, some alternative possibilities.

Complexity, interdependence, and conflict. It is hard enough to establish a cause-and-effect relationship between two variables, and to distinguish clear-cut sequences of events. Looking into the future of a society involves many unknowns and many variables.

> The major difficulty in understanding social behavior is the great complexity of human beings, groups, and formal organizations, of the subsystems within them, and of the intricate clusters, constellations, and macrosystems into which they combine. Here one finds that a tremendous number of variables interacting simultaneously in many subtle ways produces . . . 'organized complexity.' . . . This organized complexity—difficult enough at the level of smaller social systems [families and villages, for example]—becomes still more formidable in the case of such territorial entities as cities, urban areas, and nation-states. These are complex aggregates of smaller systems, with varying degrees of cohesion and integration. Thus any effort to understand a national society requires that one deal with the interrelationships among different kinds of subsystems.[63]

Every social system and subsystem is open. It has entries and exits, as people are born, age, marry, and die, are accepted into or dismissed from different groups, are recruited or promoted, move across the face of the earth or up and down the social ladder. Each member is also a member of other systems and subsystems with different values and goals; he may, therefore, have divided loyalties and feel role conflicts. Each system exchanges goods, services, and information with other systems (inputs and outputs in the jargon of systems theory). Finally, each exerts varying degrees of influence on the others with which it is interrelated and interdependent.[64]

Because of differing values, interests, and loyalties, conflict is inevitable within and among social systems. It is "probably the greatest source of continuing change, [for] bargaining and negotiation are a way of life in social systems."[65] Conflict, strain, and disturbance are thus sources of dynamic adaptation.

[63]Bertram R. Gross, "The State of the Nation: Social Systems Accounting," in Bauer, *Social Indicators*, p. 171. Gross remarks that the only serious attempt to study the United States in this manner was made by Robin Williams in *American Society*.

[64]*Ibid.*, p. 175.

[65]*Ibid.*, pp. 176–77.

Information.   The essence of the systems concept is the exchange of information through communication among the parts of a system, with continuous feedback about the success or failure of goal-directed efforts. Adaptive systems (amoebas, persons, groups, societies) continually process information from within and outside the system in an attempt to adapt.

In planning social changes, how can such information be made relevant and useful? How do we know if things are getting better or worse?

Assessment of actual and proposed changes and their perceived or predicted consequences can be made through social systems accounting based on sets of social indicators, which serve as feedback, letting the society know how well or badly it is doing in attaining its social goals. A **social indicator** is defined as:

> a statistic of direct normative interest which facilitates concise, comprehensive and balanced judgments about the condition of major aspects of a society. It is in all cases a direct measure of welfare and is subject to the interpretation that, if it changes in the "right" direction, while other things remain equal, things have gotten better, or people are "better off." Thus statistics on the number of doctors or policemen could not be social indicators, whereas figures on health or crime rates could be.[66]

Social indicators, then, could allow comparisons of the state of affairs in different areas of concern, both over time and across societies and groups within a society. Let us take infant mortality as an example of how a social indicator might be used:

> This information must be broken down by geographic regions and by racial and ethnic patterns before it can be analyzed. From this base the factors needed to decrease the rate of infant mortality should be determined. These factors include, for example, improving prenatal care, expanding health insurance coverage, establishing more health facilities, and increasing the number of trained medical personnel.[67]

Wilbur J. Cohen, former Secretary of Health, Education, and Welfare, suggests that a "Social Report" comparable to the national Economic Report might use such indicators of change as infant mortality, expectancy of healthy life, persons 25 years and older who graduate from high school and from college, average weekly hours of work, labor force participation of women aged 35–64, percentage of population illiterate, percentage of population in poverty, income of lowest fifth of population, and percentage of Gross National Product spent

[66]U. S. Department of Health, Education, and Welfare, *Toward a Social Report,* with Introductory Commentary by Wilbur J. Cohen (Ann Arbor: University of Michigan Press, 1970), p. 97.

[67]*Ibid.*, p. x.

on health, education, and welfare. A Social Report, he says, would lessen uncertainty and fear by giving us "a firm grasp of where we have been, where we are, and where we are going. . . . It could also aid us in forging an intelligent policy of national growth and a balanced and coordinated program of economic and social development."[68] A Social Report would not be used for social control by government any more than the Economic Report is used to control industry and commerce. It would inform the public, highlight issues, and suggest courses of action. It will take many decades and the work of people from many disciplines throughout the world to work out the system of social accounting we need, especially in measuring qualitative aspects of life such as the democratic process, the freedom of individuals to develop their potentialities, equality of opportunity for people in various social categories, physical vigor, mental health, satisfaction, environmental beauty, and creativity and intellectual curiosity.[69]

Use of the computer.   Whether classical utopias were more concerned with saving men's souls or filling their stomachs, their primary concern was *people*. But computer-happy systems engineers, "the new Utopians," says one observer, are not oriented to human beings in their construction of large-scale industrial, military, and space systems; in fact, they keep trying to lessen human responsibility. They set their goals and means more according to what their equipment is capable of doing than according to "the full moral, intellectual, and even physical requirements of mankind."[70]

Computers need not, however, be limited to such a narrow compass. Just as computers guide astronauts to the moon, calculating a number of variables and correcting for errors that show up in feedback from instruments and the astronauts themselves, they can be employed in guiding society toward its goals. In fact, computers are, says Buckminster Fuller, an antidote to our overspecialization. "We got all specialized, with everybody minding his own business—and now nobody can mind everybody else's business in order to put things together. [But with computers] we can now take the universe apart and put it together again in preferred ways."[71] The use of computers for public planning is only beginning to be explored. Fuller has devised a World Game, teaching students, individually and in groups, to work out preliminary solutions for such world problems as food supply.[72] The

[68]*Ibid.*, p. xiii.

[69]*Ibid.*, p. xxxiv.

[70]Robert Boguslaw, *The New Utopians: A Study of System Design and Social Change* (Englewood Cliffs, N.J.: Prentice-Hall, Inc., 1965), p. 6.

[71]"Education for Comprehensivity," in Littleton, *Approaching the Benign Environment*, pp. 52, 92.

[72]See our discussion of Jay Forrester, *Urban Dynamics* (Cambridge: The M.I.T. Press, 1969), in Chapter 7. The model's complexity is indicated by the fact that one variable—arrival of the underemployed from outside the city—is regulated by 31 separate feedback influences.

Rand Institute is using computer-aided techniques to help New York City government with some of its day-to-day problems. The Club of Rome, an informal international association of about 70 persons of 25 nationalities, has undertaken a "Project on the Predicament of Mankind."

> Based on the work of Jay Forrester and other pioneers in Systems Dynamics, its formal, written model of the world . . . constitutes a preliminary attempt to improve our mental models of long-term global problems by combining the large amount of information that is already in human minds and in written records with the new information-processing tools that mankind's increasing knowledge has produced— the scientific method, systems analysis, and the modern computer. . . .
>
> To our knowledge it is the only formal model in existence that is truly global in scope, that has a time horizon longer than thirty years [as much as a century] and that includes important variables such as population, food production, and pollution, not as independent entities, but as dynamically interacting elements, as they are in the real world.[73]

The philosophy behind all efforts to plan and guide social change is summed up in *The Self-Guiding Society*:

> Harnessing societal energy is the societal equivalent of the physicists' harnessing of nuclear energy. Unleashed in an explosion, it becomes the most destructive force ever known. Released gradually and employed in men's service, it can change human life.[74]

Summary

Socio-cultural change includes significant alterations in social organization, cultural definitions, and material products of socio-cultural action.

There are various theories concerning the direction and pattern of change. Evolutionary theorists see man becoming ever better adjusted to his environment and gaining more control of sources of energy. Some consider human development to be progress, onward and upward; others think it takes place in stages of various kinds. A reverse evolutionary theory depicts mankind as regressing from a state of perfection. While cultural development is uneven, empirical observation shows that

[73]Donella H. Meadows, Dennis L. Meadows, Jørgen Randers, and William W. Behrens III, *The Limits to Growth: A Report for the Club of Rome's Project on the Predicament of Mankind* (New York: Universe Books; a Potomac Associates Book, 1972), pp. 21–22.

[74]Breed, *The Self-Guiding Society*, p. 7.

many aspects of it occur in the same sequence in different societies.

Cyclical theories are stated in terms of pendulum swings between extremes, the rise and fall of societies, and the short-term ups and downs of self-exhausting trends. Functional theory sees systems as adapting to change in an effort to restore equilibrium. Modern systems theory depicts change as a dynamic process arising out of conflict, strain, and complexity. Examples of the manifest and latent functions and consequences of various aspects of social structure and culture illustrate the complexity of systems.

The sources of change are also variously accounted for. Determinists say blind forces determine the course of change; voluntarists give man a great deal of credit for change. Some voluntarists see its source in universal human nature and the human condition: Man is a restless, curious, problem-solving animal faced with many challenges. Others find the motive force of change in such unique people as great heroes and villains; or in leaders who guide reform and revolution; or in all of us, who share responsibility for choices and decisions. The theory of socio-cultural drift attributes most change to the convergence of innumerable small actions or decisions, which create unplanned and unheralded trends. Man's mortality, his imperfect socialization, his different ways of performing the same role, and the plasticity of youth as compared with their elders also account for changes as one generation succeeds another.

Conflict, internal or external, may destroy a social system. Inevitable within systems, it is seen by some as a creative source of change, by others as the only possible means of change. An effective political system has institutionalized certain kinds of conflict to bring about peaceful change.

Marxism is essentially economic determinism, with elements of evolutionary, voluntaristic, and conflict theory. Technological determinism is even narrower, for it holds that changes in material culture are the source of all other cultural and social changes, and that cultural lag occurs when adaptive changes in nonmaterial culture come too slowly. Critics of this theory deny that technology is a blind force, pointing out that men's ideas and social organization control technology.

Knowledge, beliefs, and values powerfully influence the direction, rate, and consequences of change. Learning is a crucial element in the shift to industrial society. Values affect men's motivation to exert effort in one direction or another, to resist or promote change. If they perceive real patterns as extremely incompatible with ideal ones, they may feel a sense of moral crisis and try to resolve the difference. A state of anomie fosters social change; alienated people are likely to perceive social problems; extreme anomie and alienation endanger social cohesion. Intellectuals support or deny the legitimacy of a social system, and thus may help maintain the status quo or bring about reform or revolution.

The more complex the culture base, the more likely change is to occur through invention, and to proceed rapidly. Most elements in any rich and complex culture, however, have been introduced by the process of diffusion, as a result of contact with other cultures.

A number of factors make societies receptive to change—historical accidents and crises among them. But new culture traits are usually reinterpreted or otherwise adapted to fit the existing culture; they may also be rejected for various reasons such as lack of fit, vested interests, or the annoyance of enduring such an obviously rational change as a shift to the metric system.

Social change may create social problems, which in turn create a demand for further change. Social problems include deviant behavior, frustration of the goals of those in various social categories, threats to the survival of the social system, and threats to the life and well-being of a society's members.

Planning for guided change involves the choice of goals and means, as well as predictions, anticipations, and "utopian" visions of possible alternative futures, desirable or otherwise. Those who accept the need for planning in democratic societies assume that peaceful change is preferable to violent change; that social systems are complex and interdependent; that there are alternatives to the status quo; that error is inherent in the action of systems; and that things do not usually improve spontaneously. The question of how and by whom goals shall be chosen is crucial. One guiding principle is to keep as many options as possible open for the next generation; another is to allow wide participation in the choice of goals.

Those planners who think of a society as a complex adaptive system see information as essential, in the form of social systems accounting based on social indicators, both quantitative and qualitative. Computer analysis holds promise of handling the numerous variables involved in projecting trends into the future and predicting the consequences of alternative choices and decisions. Such planning may be seen as "harnessing societal energy."

In the next chapter we are concerned with a vast change that came about in Western nations with little or no planning, and is eagerly sought, and planned for in various ways, by the so-called underdeveloped nations—the great transformation of "modernization."

QUESTIONS FOR FURTHER THOUGHT

1. Can you think of any unintended but *desirable* consequences of a planned social change?

2. Do you think modern societies have more problems than traditional ones? Is this a matter of standards and perception?

3. Merton and Nisbet say that every social problem, though it may be predominantly one of deviant behavior or social disorganization, has aspects of both. Consider several of the social problems they list (see *Anomie and Alienation*) according to this generalization.

4. Referring back to Parsons' list of system needs, relate social problems to failure to meet various needs. (See Chapter 8.)

5. Discuss the imbalance of highway, rail, and air transportation in terms of American values, vested interests, consequences for other parts of the system, and possible solutions through systems analysis.

6. What do you think your life *will* be like in the year 2000? What do you *want* it to be like? What do you think you can do about it?

7. In terms of your values, what social indicators might be used to measure the quality of life?

8. Do you have a negative or positive attitude toward the use of computers in social analysis and planning? Examine the basis for it.

9. Do you believe that some gap between expectations and realities is good for both societies and individuals? Why or why not?

10. Howard Becker, in *Social Problems: A Modern Approach* (New York: John Wiley, 1966), divides social problems into the following categories: problems of the life cycle, problems of deviance, problems of community and nation, and world problems. Without consulting the text, think of several examples of each.

11. Another text [J. Alan Winter, Jerome Rabow, and Mark Chesler, eds., *Vital Problems for American Society: Meanings and Means* (New York: Random House, 1968)] relates our nation's problems to the values and goals set forth in the Preamble to the Constitution, and sees them as continuous and ever-challenging, rarely completely solved. Relate some problem such as poverty, race discrimination, or military power to this larger framework.

12. Why are people more likely to consider deviance a problem than social disorganization?

13. In some societies, prostitution is seen simply as an existing social arrangement, in others as a necessary evil. Why do Americans perceive it as a social problem?

14. Merton believes that a nonconforming minority may represent the interests and ultimate values of a society more effectively than the conforming majority (*Contemporary Social Problems*, p. 844). Do you agree or disagree? Why?

15. Many "social inventions" such as baby sitting and traffic laws are clearly adaptations to other changes. Give several examples, and relate them to the changes that called for them.

16. Robert Lekachman argues that if a need is not felt urgently enough, the tools for satisfying it will not be developed or used; he points to military technology as the prime example of a need that *was* felt to be urgent. What needs do you see that might be satisfied if policy-makers felt them to be truly urgent? [See "The Automation Report," *Commentary* 41, No. 5 (May 1966); reprinted in Robert Perrucci and Marc Pilisuk, eds., *The Triple Revolution: Social Problems in Depth* (Boston: Little, Brown, 1968), pp. 178–90.]

15

THE GREAT TRANS-FORMATION: MODERNIZATION

Men resemble their times more than they do their fathers.

ANCIENT ARABIC PROVERB

This is the age of development, the first challenge to stir all mankind, and no less than the awakening of man's first *universal* civilization. It is recreating every culture with a new and common mold, penetrating all parts of every continent, restructuring the patterns of all settlements, remaking the very means to sustain life, even transforming life purposes.

KENNETH R. SCHNEIDER

Now 75 and born before the automobile, radio, airplane or cinema, my memory spans humanity's transition from a myriad of vastly isolated, popularly illiterate communities and tribes . . . with only vague awareness of one another . . . [to] the beginning of an omni-integrated, freely intercirculating, omni-literate world society. I have seen humanity transformed!

BUCKMINSTER FULLER

A GENERATION YOUNGER THAN "BUCKY" FULLER, the senior author has also felt the impact of modernization. For a few years of the seven she spent in a two-room country school she got there by horse-drawn sleigh in winter, wagon in summer and fall. Bathed in a log-cabin Finnish sauna long before it became an international status symbol. Carried firewood and water to the house and read by kerosene lamps. Handcranked a wall phone and knew neighbors were probably listening on the party line. Fetched cows, fed chickens, churned butter, raked hay, pulled weeds, picked potato bugs. Knew where the trailing arbutus put forth its fragrant pink blossoms under the pine trees when the last snows melted in early May.

The Finnish immigrants in that community in the north woods of Minnesota were hunters and gatherers as well as farmers, and their children grew up not only on milk and potatoes but also on blueberries and venison (in and out of season). Nearly all the families belonged to the Farmers' Club and the Consumers' Co-operative Association, attended the Lutheran church, enjoyed community picnics and programs (often in two languages), and exchanged frequent visits during which parents talked over coffee while children played hide-and-seek among the haystacks and caught fireflies during the long summer twilight.

Though partly self-sufficient, these families had many ties to the larger society: Sears, Roebuck and Montgomery Ward catalogs, day-long Fourth of July celebrations in the nearby town, teachers who were often Jewish or Catholic rather than Finnish Lutheran, occasional work on the county roads, visits from the community development workers of Depression years—county agents who taught farmers about better seeds and methods, and home demonstration agents who taught house-wives about gardening and preserving food. And there was the radio, which brought Eddie Cantor and Fred Allen and President Roosevelt into our homes.

Only traces remain of that close-knit community. The old schoolhouse is gone, and children ride big yellow buses to large con-solidated schools. Trade is slow at the local Co-op; people think noth-ing of driving 20 miles or more to shop. Most of the barns and haylofts have been pulled down. Few of the second and third generation try to farm the fields their parents and grandparents cleared from the forest;

"No one had to walk more than two days to reach a polling place." (Elections in Papua New Guinea, 1972.)

most are office clerks, miners, storekeepers, schoolteachers, electronic engineers, soldiers, writers, ministers, nurses. Our old farmhouse (which now has electricity, running water, and a dial phone) serves as a summer cottage and fall hunting lodge for city visitors, who find the old sauna a rare treat and wish they could bottle the crystal-clear, pine-fragrant northern air.

This same story, with variations, is being repeated in many different settings all over the world. Traditional ways of life are crumbling everywhere. Every once in a while a small Stone Age tribe is discovered, usually in the Amazon basin or on a Pacific island. (The cave-dwelling Tasadays were discovered in the Philippines in 1971; three previously unknown tribes were found in the jungles of Papua New Guinea in 1972.) At the other extreme is the United States, which many observers believe is entering a new and revolutionary era comparable to the agricultural revolution of 10,000 years ago and the Industrial Revolution that began in Europe about 500 years ago; it is, they say, becoming the first "post-modern," "post-industrial," or "technetronic" society. But most tribes, communities, and nations are in a transitional stage somewhere along a continuum between the traditional folk way of life and the modern industrial urban society described in Chapter 8.

Our first concern in this chapter is the meaning of modernization—its definition and significance. We then analyze the closely interrelated changes that make up the modernization process in terms of the five systems in which human social behavior takes place—culture, social organization, personality, the human organism, and the ecosystem. What promise, we ask, does modernization hold for man and society? What problems does it bring? How does the process begin? How can it be accelerated and guided?

The Meaning of Modernization

Modernization is the transition from traditional folk society to urban industrial society. This transition (which does not always—or even often—take place smoothly and evenly) affects every institution, touches every community, is felt in every life. It changes the way people are distributed over the face of the earth, and the way they think of themselves and of their world.

Modernization is a comprehensive term, embracing many changes that tend to occur together. Its central feature is industrialization. With this, in spirals of cause-and-effect, go changes in government, the family, education, religion, and social organization; a shift from rural to urban living; and changes in knowledge, beliefs, values, self-conceptions, and ways of life.[1]

The great changes of modernization are closely intertwined. One appears to make another possible, or necessary, or desirable, or inevitable; and as the various changes proceed, they tend to reinforce one another and to accelerate together. For purposes of analysis, however, let us try to pick apart these interrelated changes in terms of the five systems mentioned above. Such analysis is essential to understanding, even though it is somewhat artificial. When we discuss cultural values, for example, how can we avoid touching upon changes in personality? Similarly, the growth of science and knowledge can hardly be discussed apart from the changes in technology that make the communication, storing, and retrieval of information swift and efficient.

[1] Like all ideal types, the models of folk and urban society represent "a conceptual recognition of a general tendency for certain formal characteristics of cultures to vary together." Societies all do seem to change from a traditional to a modern type, and the conception of the transition has proven to be "one of the most fruitful insights of sociology." Amitai Etzioni and Eva Etzioni, *Social Change*, citing Horace Miner, "The Folk-Urban Continuum," *American Sociological Review* 17 (Oct. 1952): 529–37.

Changes in Cultural Systems

During the modernization process, ways of thinking, doing, believing, and evaluating change enormously. The general tendency is toward uniformity of culture. Beliefs, values, and tastes come to be widely shared by people of different groups and categories because of popular education, mass literacy, travel, mobility, mass production, mass markets, the growth of centralized government, and society-wide mass communication and entertainment. Patterns of consumption and use of leisure time become increasingly standardized.[2]

SCIENCE AND KNOWLEDGE

One student of the future calls the growth of knowledge "the most basic and influential of all general social trends. . . . It does not depend upon any other social trend, though other trends may accelerate the growth of knowledge."[3] Beginning with the revival of Greek science in western Europe in the twelfth century, the growth of knowledge has now reached explosive proportions. Modern societies actively seek more knowledge, employing professionals in research, institutionalizing the process, and investing huge sums. Of about $25 billion spent on research and development in the United States in 1970, the federal government invested over $15 billion; about 30% was related to "defense" and about 13% to space exploration.[4] Computers allow us to organize and store this vast outpouring of data, and to process and retrieve it with incredible speed.

TECHNOLOGY

By **technology** we mean both the application of scientific knowledge to the production of goods and services, and the techniques and tools employed in their production—both "know-how" and "wherewithal." Technological advances in agricultural and industrial production, transportation, and communication—the continuing Industrial Revolution—are the most conspicuous feature of modernization.

One basis for this acceleration of productivity is the harnessing of ever more efficient and powerful sources of energy. A full-grown man produces only 1/20 of 1 horsepower in a working day of 8–12 hours; an entire primitive society can produce a total of perhaps 4

---

[2]Harold L. Wilensky, "Mass Society and Mass Culture," in Gerald D. Bell, ed., *Organizations and Human Behavior* (Englewood Cliffs, N.J.: Prentice-Hall, Inc., 1967), pp. 41–60.

[3]Burnham P. Beckwith, *The Next 500 Years* (Exposition-University Book, published by the World Future Society, 1968); quoted in *The Futurist* 2, No. 5 (Oct. 1968): 88.

[4]*The American Almanac* (1971), p. 519. Estimates.

horsepower per day. For most of recorded history, 99% of all productivity came from man's labor; the remaining 1% was generated by wind, water, and work animals. Not until about 200 years ago, when the steam engine was invented and applied to textile manufacturing, did the spectacular industrialization of western European nations begin. The generation of electricity and the invention of the internal combustion engine were also milestones in the "energy revolution." It was estimated that in 1960 only about 1/200 of 1% of all energy expended in production of goods and services in the United States came from human muscle. A decade later, the total horsepower of all mechanical engines and turbines was close to 19 billion, or about 94 horsepower per capita. Most of this energy comes from fossil fuels, such as coal, oil, and gas.[5] As a result, more goods have been produced during the past 100 years than in all previous human history.[6]

Solar and nuclear sources may eventually replace fossil fuels. Already man's ability to split the atom has created a revolution in weaponry: Nuclear physics has, in the words of James Agee, put into the hands of man "the fire and force of the sun itself."

The application of science, knowledge, and power to means of communication and transportation is an integral part of the Industrial Revolution. The evolution of speech allowed people to develop and communicate ideas in the here and now; writing enabled them to preserve thoughts and communicate at a distance in time and space. Printing made new levels of cultural complexity possible; the use of the printing press may be thought of as the first mass production. The electronic revolution allows us to transmit information and images ever farther and faster—beginning with the telegraph and telephone, then movies, radio, and television, and now communications satellites and the promise of many refinements in electronic communication. It also (like many advances based on transistors, lasers, and similar devices) "does more with less." A communications satellite, weighing ¼ of a ton, "outperforms 150,000 tons of transoceanic cables."[7] The mass media are so widely used in modern nations that we speak of "mass culture." Daniel Bell suggests that on the evening of March 7, 1955, a historic event occurred when nearly half of all Americans watched Mary Martin perform in *Peter Pan* before the TV cameras. "Never before in history had a single person been seen and heard by so many at the same time."[8] In 1972 there were 94 million TV sets in the United States.

[5]*Ibid.*, Table 773, p. 505. This was over six times the amount generated in 1940, and in per capita figures about five times as much. About 94% of this power is used in automotive vehicles.

[6]Cyril Edwin Black, "Change as a Condition of Modern Life," in Myron Weiner, ed., *Modernization: The Dynamics of Growth* (New York: Basic Books, Inc., 1966), p. 18.

[7]Buckminster Fuller, *Utopia or Oblivion*, p. 4.

[8]"Toward a Communal Society," *Life*: 115.

The communications revolution produces changes in spirals of cause-and-effect. Millions of poor people in remote corners of the world become aware of new possibilities as they read (if they are literate) and as they see movies, listen to radio, and increasingly watch TV. And nothing is more revolutionary than a road, which opens up isolated communities, allowing their members to travel to work or market and to see and buy new things, and bringing officials, businessmen, vote-seekers, and perhaps doctors and tourists into the community. As people become physically mobile, their image of the world changes, and they see a different possible future for themselves and their children. The automobile and bus, jet plane, and space capsule shake them from their traditional moorings, mentally as well as physically.

NORMS AND VALUES

Everyone has always wanted the things modernization promises —health, longevity, and material well-being. What is new in societies aspiring to modernity is the hope of achieving these goals largely by one's own efforts, and quickly. Extensive changes in values "are the most fundamental condition for economic transformation."[9] The most important of these are secularization and individualization.

Secularization, a shift from sacred to secular values, implies that received doctrines, dogmas, and traditions are opened to skeptical questioning, and that the attitude of reverence for traditional procedures, norms, beliefs, and associations is replaced by a rational-utilitarian attitude that permits them to be discarded or changed with relative ease. It embraces, then, a shift from custom to rationality, from fatalism to activism, from reverence for tradition to desire for progress and an acceptance of, even desire for, constant change and novelty.

In a traditional or sacred society, many statuses are compounded (adult-male-hunter-warrior, for example), and their accompanying roles are diffuse, applying to many situations. These roles are made up of prescriptive and prohibitive norms, which tend to channel and constrain behavior. Decisions are made not by considering alternatives, but ritualistically: That is how it has always been done. The natural environment is seen as a mystery to be feared, revered, and propitiated, or as an illusion to be ignored. Almost everything is imbued with sacred meaning; corn or bread is holy.

In modern society, statuses and roles are specific, applying to certain situations. While some norms are highly specific and prescriptive (occupational norms in particular), many are blurred and conflicting, subject to a wide latitude of interpretation and redefinition in interaction. The natural environment is seen as an orderly universe governed by laws that can be understood and forces that can be tamed or har-

[9]Wilbert E. Moore, *Social Change* (Englewood Cliffs, N.J.: Prentice-Hall, Inc., 1963), p. 93.

nessed; modern man strives to understand these laws and manipulate these forces. All industrial societies, no matter how they are organized, value science, rationality, technical knowledge and skill, efficiency, progress, modernity, education, mobility, work, and high productivity.

Individualization means that each person becomes identified as a responsible member of society in his own right rather than as a unit of a family or tribe. He therefore is accountable for his own actions; he must make his own effort and receives his own rewards. People are employed on the basis of ability rather than kinship or friendship. In much of the world this emphasis on individual achievement and reward has been accompanied—and fostered—by a "human rights revolution," a demand that everyone, regardless of such ascribed statuses as race, religion, nationality, sex, and even age, be given equal opportunity to participate in social, economic, and political affairs, to prove himself and realize his potential.

Changes in Social Systems

As societies modernize, political and economic units generally become larger; men and institutions more specialized; social contacts more numerous; the proportion of formal and impersonal relationships greater; the class system more fluid, open, and ambiguous. Control and administration become more centralized, formal, and rational—in short, bureaucratic; and the system as a whole grows more complex and its parts more interdependent.

CHANGE OF SCALE

Traditional societies are organized on a small scale and in a rural setting, typified by the nonliterate tribe, the medieval manor, and the peasant village. The ability to communicate at a distance and to cover ground swiftly makes it possible for modern societies to include large territories. During the transition, folk communities often crumble, the focus of loyalty and source of identity moving to the nation-state, based on "a civil order . . . in which all citizens, irrespective of kinship, status, or [local] territorial belonging, participate and share the same set of central institutions."[10] Most production (whether in market or command economies) is handled by huge corporations with nation-wide or world-wide markets.

Man's world grows even as it shrinks. Jet planes, radio, TV, movies, and newspapers make people more and more aware of all the

[10]S. N. Eisenstadt, *Modernization: Protest and Change* (Englewood Cliffs, N.J.: Prentice-Hall, Inc., 1966), p. 16.

other millions of human beings in the world. And in spite of all its divisions and discords, the world is increasingly a single system, with common value orientations, a common pool of knowledge and techniques, and so many interrelationships that events in one society often have repercussions in many others.

SPECIALIZATION, COMPLEXITY, AND INTERDEPENDENCE

In a traditional society, economic roles are relatively undifferentiated. Communities are largely self-sufficient, producing their own food, clothing, and shelter. In a modern society the roles of producer and distributor are distinct from that of consumer, and they are broken down into infinite specialties and narrowly defined. Fewer and fewer people work in primary production (farming, fishing, and forestry) as modernization proceeds; more and more take on specialized jobs in industry, and the proportion in service occupations and professions keeps growing. The demand for unskilled and semiskilled workers, which is high in the early stages of industrialization, falls during later stages. In highly industrialized societies, there is a rising demand for clerical and sales workers, scientists, engineers, and technicians, as well as for those in service occupations, such as finance, insurance, wholesale and retail distribution, transportation, utilities, entertainment, and the lodging and restaurant businesses.

Various institutional functions are embedded in the fabric of traditional society. It is hard to label one activity as wholly economic and another as wholly religious or political. Family life, religion, government, education, and the tasks of getting food, clothing, and shelter are all woven together and imbued with sacred meanings. In modern society, life is more segmented; its various aspects are put into separate compartments, so to speak. The economic aspect is quite distinct from others, and its rationality is at a maximum. Leisure and play are altogether distinct from work, which is set apart from the rest of life by the tyranny of the clock. The sacred is for the Sabbath and a few core values and group symbols. A number of agencies and associations with quite specific functions arise within the system. Some take over functions that once were performed by the family (such as education of children and care of the aged), and others connect and coordinate the various specialized parts of the complex system (government and market agencies, for example).

Specialized, complex systems are necessarily interdependent. In traditional societies families and communities may be almost entirely self-sufficient. But each member of a modern society depends on a multitude of others to supply his needs and wants through a system of exchange. More and more of the things that need to be done are undertaken through communal means, such as government or voluntary agencies.

CONTROL AND ADMINISTRATION

Neither a council of tribal elders, a town meeting, nor an omnipotent monarch can function in a modern setting. Large, complex, formal organizations, as we saw in Chapter 8, give rise to hierarchical organization; systems of authority based on consensus, rationality, and rules; centralized control; bureaucratic administration. Utilitarian controls—the hope of material rewards—predominate over normative and coercive controls, although these are still important in ensuring social cohesion.

SOCIAL STRATIFICATION

Status in small folk communities rests primarily on sex, age, and kinship; otherwise there may be little differentiation in wealth, power, and prestige. In larger premodern societies, status lines also depend on ascription and are clearly drawn in a rigid hierarchy. Everyone has his prescribed place and duty. The superior protects; the subordinate obeys. A modern society, in contrast, has a relatively open and mobile class structure in which status depends largely on achievement, on individual efforts to gain the education and skills an industrial society demands and rewards. The labor force of necessity is hierarchically organized, for industry needs both the manager and the managed; various skills are differentially valued and unequally rewarded. But advancement within this hierarchy is far more likely to reflect achievement than ascribed qualities.

SOCIAL RELATIONSHIPS

As the scale of social organization grows larger, as individual qualities take precedence over ascribed group memberships, and as rational and utilitarian values largely replace sacred traditional ones, the importance of family and community declines, and social relationships become increasingly impersonal, functional, and secondary.

The extended family is the cornerstone of a traditional society. Its members share the family income regardless of their contribution to it; productive workers provide for old, ill, disabled, and even lazy ones. Economists see this tradition as diluting the workers' incentive to work hard, save, and invest. If a member of modern society who advances shares the fruits of power and wealth with his relatives, it is labeled nepotism! Here the nuclear family of parents and children constitutes the extent of the breadwinner's responsibilities, and his incentives to work, save, and invest are therefore supposedly stronger. Where the extended family is strong, change tends to be slower, because the grand-parent generation is closely woven into the fabric of family life and teaches children the traditional ways. In modern society, the discontinuity of family life—the generation gap—is both cause and effect of rapid change.

Since the Neolithic era, most of the world's population has lived in small village communities, and many still do. Robert Redfield defined the classic community as having distinctive boundaries, being so small that its members perceive it as a unit; homogeneous and slow-changing, because its members share similar activities and states of mind; and self-sufficient, providing for most or all of its members' needs.[11] Such a form of human settlement and association has tremendous meaning for the person:

> When we speak of community we speak of a social organization wholly reflecting man as a social being. Community may be thought of as a social matrix with a comprehensibility, wholeness, and immediate relevance to the emotional realities of being human. For the person, community should present a sense of social identity, promote a sense of self-sufficiency, and therefore prompt greater personal integrity.[12]

Modernization typically brings about "an eclipse of community." As many functions once performed by family and local community are turned over to large formal organizations, individuals become more dependent on centralized authorities and impersonal agencies; loyalties to community, neighborhood, and relatives outside the immediate family fade.[13] People lose the middle range of human association "between the complete intimacy and protection of the family and the awesome anonymity and performance-governed behavior of the cosmopolitan society."[14] This means a loss of many primary contacts, of a sense of roots, of informal social controls, and of ease of understanding.

Yet, as we saw in Chapter 8, the need for intimate personal relationships is so strong that many kinds of groups emerge within the anonymity and formality of the larger society to fill this need. Work groups, office cliques, army buddies, fraternal societies, and voluntary associations of many kinds emerge or are organized. Some intimate relationships are commercialized, and constitute what has been called "pseudo-Gemeinschaft"; prostitution is an extreme example.

[11] *The Little Community* (Chicago: University of Chicago Press, 1955), p. 4.

[12] Kenneth R. Schneider, *Destiny of Change: How Relevant Is Man in the Age of Development?* (New York: Holt, Rinehart & Winston, Inc., 1968), p. 106.

[13] Maurice R. Stein, *The Eclipse of Community: An Interpretation of American Studies* (New York: Harper & Row, Publishers, 1960), p. 329.

[14] Schneider, *Destiny of Change*, p. 107.

IS MODERN SOCIETY MASS SOCIETY?

Do these changes in social interaction and social structure add up to a "mass society"? The answer depends on the definition used.

According to one point of view, a mass society is an aggregate of powerless, alienated, dehumanized cogs in a mechanized system created by the disruption of kinship and community ties, the mass media, and the division of labor. These detached, unorganized atoms form a mass audience, passively receiving common stimuli. Like the Roman mobs pacified by bread and circuses, they consume a vulgar, debased mass culture. Lacking a common faith or purpose, they are easily manipulated through the mass media, like puppets on strings; clever demagogues use them to pursue their own ends, to propagandize and inflame, as Hitler did in Germany.

Others say that modern society is mass society in the sense that the masses of ordinary people participate in social, economic, political, and cultural affairs. In premodern societies, the masses were denied any meaningful role; an elite controlled them. But even in modern authoritarian societies, the elite must take the people into consideration, and give them a sense of participation in the moral order. The critics of mass society, say proponents of this view, are not describing modern Western society; they are, rather, protesting against contemporary life by romantically glorifying a folk society that exists only in their dreams, and that was in fact narrow and constricting, and not necessarily united by a common faith or goal.

Modern society, furthermore, according to this more optimistic view, is pluralist as well as participant. It embraces many subsystems such as various racial, religious, and ethnic groups. In premodern communities people do not actively participate in a variety of voluntary associations. Is a nation atomized that has over 200,000 voluntary associations, such as clubs, lodges, pressure groups, and nationality groups, and has numerous neighborhood newspapers even in its largest cities? The pessimistic view of mass society does not take into account the adaptability and creativity of human beings, their irresistible tendency to create new social forms and cluster in cliques and other informal groups within such large formal organizations as armies, corporations, factories, and bureaucracies.[15]

[15]For discussions of the various viewpoints regarding this theme, one of the most controversial in modern sociology, see: Daniel Bell, "The U.S. as a Mass Society," in Alex Inkeles, ed., Readings on Modern Sociology (Englewood Cliffs, N.J.: Prentice-Hall, Inc., 1966), pp. 71–86; Edward Shils, "The Theory of Mass Society," Diogenes, No. 39 (Fall 1962), reprinted in David W. Minar and Scott Greer, eds., The Concept of Community: Readings with Interpretations (Chicago: Aldine Publishing Co., 1969), pp. 298–316; Breed, The Self-Guiding Society, pp. 158–60; and a strong dissent from Shils's viewpoint by Ernest van den Haag, "A Dissent from the Consensual Society," Daedalus (Spring 1960), reprinted in Paul Hollander, ed., American and Soviet Society: A Reader in Comparative Sociology and Perception (Englewood Cliffs, N.J.: Prentice-Hall, Inc., 1969), pp. 361–66.

Changes in Personality

Living in socio-cultural orders as different as the traditional and modern societies sketched above, members of *Homo sapiens* exhibit such varied personalities that we speak of different kinds of people. "Indeed, in the end, the idea of development requires the very transformation of the nature of man—a transformation that is both a *means* to the end of yet greater growth and at the same time one of the great *ends* itself of the development process."[16] In between traditional man and modern man is transitional man, who lives the modernization process in his own life and feels the ambivalences and paradoxes, the peculiar mixtures of freedom and loss, that occur with this wrenching social change; we shall discuss him in connection with the ways modernization comes about.

TRADITIONAL MAN

We can draw a profile of traditional man from what we have said about the traditional socio-cultural order. He follows a well-worn path marked out by his elders, and feels shame if he fails to conform. He feels merged with family and village; they give him his identity. When asked who he is, he says, "I am the son of my father." He is a fatalist, accepting things as they are. He cannot conceive of changing his status; he accepts it as given and sacred. He suffers "from a poverty of wants as well as from a poverty of ideas for satisfying them."[17] If he lives in a large premodern society rather than in a small tribe (which may be fairly equalitarian), he sees the community as dominated by an elite that pays little attention to the masses. He tends to be authoritarian: There is only one right way. He understands the members of his community because they are so much like him; but he cannot make the leap of putting himself in a very different pair of shoes. He cannot conceive of being someone else or living somewhere else.

This lack of empathy and imagination is documented by Daniel Lerner in his study of the Turkish village of Balgat. Interviewers asked what the nation's greatest problem was, and then what the respondent would do about it if he were President of Turkey. "Most responded by stolid silence—the traditional way of handling 'projective questions' which require people to imagine themselves or things to be different from what they really are." Some were shocked by the impropriety of the very question. " 'My God! How can you say such a thing?' gasped the shepherd. 'How can I . . . I cannot . . . a poor villager . . . master of the whole world.' "[18] To another question, "If you could not live in

16Alex Inkeles, "The Modernization of Man," in Weiner, *Modernization*, pp. 138–50.

17Irving Louis Horowitz, *Three Worlds of Development: The Theory and Practice of International Stratification* (New York: Oxford University Press, 1966), p. 300.

18Daniel Lerner, *The Passing of Traditional Society: Modernizing the Middle East* (New York: The Macmillan Company, 1958), "The Grocer and the Chief: A Parable," pp. 19–42.

Turkey, where would you want to live?" most villagers replied that they would not live anywhere else and could not imagine doing so; and several "wholly routinized" personalities, like the shepherd, replied that they would rather kill themselves. The village Chief "responded with the clear and confident voice of traditional man. 'Nowhere,' he said. 'I was born here, grew old here, and hope God will permit me to die here.' "[19]

MODERN MAN

A member of modern society is likely to be urban, literate, educated for a specialized occupation, mobile, and politically active, and to depend for many services and for aid in time of distress on impersonal and bureaucratic agencies. But "it is only when man has undergone a change in spirit—has acquired new ways of thinking, feeling, and acting—that we come to consider him truly modern."[20]

Modern man is flexible, adaptable, ready to accept new ideas and try new methods. He lives with change, choice, and decisions. He is oriented to the present and the future rather than to the past. He is rational and orderly; he believes in planning and organizing his life. His self-conception is based not on kinship and community, but on experience and achievement. Along with this goes a belief in "distributive justice," an idea that people should be rewarded according to their contribution, not their connections, special properties, or the whims of those in power.

Modern man has empathy and imagination. He can imagine himself in other statuses, situations, and places. The Grocer, in Lerner's Turkish village, was the only man who came up with ready answers to the projective question about what he would do if he were President of Turkey; he would, he said, make roads for the villagers to go to towns to see the world and not let them stay in their holes all their lives. And he could easily imagine himself in the United States, where he had heard there were opportunities for "even the simplest persons" to get rich.[21]

Modern man has faith in science and technology. He believes man can learn to dominate his environment, to control floods and prevent storms. He admires professional competence, craftsmanship, technical skill.[22] Optimistic, confident, and trusting, he believes he can rely on others to meet their obligations and responsibilities. He does not believe that everything is determined either by fate or by the peculiar qualities of particular men; he has confidence that the world is calcula-

[19]*Ibid.*

[20]Inkeles, "The Modernization of Man."

[21]Lerner, *The Passing of Traditional Society.*

[22]Kenneth Keniston, "Does Human Nature Change in a Technological Revolution?" *The New York Times* (Jan. 6, 1969), citing studies of astronauts.

ble, "a reasonably lawful world under human control."[23] It follows that he is activist, and believes that he can change things. Modern man, then, is a participant—in the market, the political forum, and other aspects of social life. He forms and expresses opinions on many matters which are not strictly his personal business; and he does not assume that everyone thinks alike, or even that his wife and children must agree with him. He is more aware of the dignity of individual human beings and more disposed to show respect for them than the typical traditional man.

This complex of attitudes and values, according to Alex Inkeles, is "intimately related to the individual's successful adjustment as a citizen of a modern industrial nation. They are qualities that we feel will contribute to making a man a more productive worker in his factory, a more effective citizen in his community, a more satisfied and satisfying husband and father in his home."[24]

Changes Involving the Human Organism

How does modernization affect man as a biological species? Each of us is not so very different in biological makeup from Cro-Magnon man. But as a species, we are far more numerous; from a few nomadic hunters *Homo sapiens* has grown to number almost 4 billion, and may reach 7 billion or so by the year 2000; we also live much longer. This demographic revolution is the subject of Chapter 17. *Homo sapiens* is at once more mobile and more crowded; his tendency to cluster into cities is such an important aspect of modernization that it will be discussed in the next chapter.

Other changes connected with the modernizing process may affect the biology of the species. Diet may improve; but more often it deteriorates as the balance of nutrients dictated by folk wisdom is replaced by refined foods; and resistance to disease declines. There is a strong cultural resistance in the United States to acceptance of natural foods in place of processed products, but it appears to be weakening.[25] Man's growing ability to tamper with the body through genetic manipulation may allow him to determine the sex of babies, program heredity, reproduce an individual from skin cells, change temperament through drugs, replace diseased organs, and lengthen life. His pollution of the environment through the use of fossil fuels, chemical fertilizers, and radioactive substances is increasingly suspected of damaging his health and that of unborn generations. This brings us to the last of our five systems.

[23]Inkeles, "The Modernization of Man."

[24]*Ibid.*

[25]Adelle Davis, *Let's Eat Right to Keep Fit* (New York: Harcourt Brace Jovanovich, 1970). Pages 243–52 document research on "primitive" diets as compared to modern American eating habits, and their consequences.

Changes in the Physical and Biological Environment

The massive changes of geologic eras and ice ages formed the essential topography of the earth, and man tampered little with it for most of prehistory and history. Canals, irrigation systems, pyramids, campsites, villages, and even early cities were mere scratches on the face of the planet. Although many early societies apparently lived in close harmony with nature, others cut too much forest and eroded the land, making deserts where fertile woods and fields had been; but neither their construction nor their destruction compares with the changes modern man has wrought.

Modern man thinks in terms of conquering or mastering nature. And through his technology he has adapted to many climates, largely conquered time and space, made 10 bushels of wheat grow where 1 grew before. He forecasts the weather ever more accurately over longer periods, and promises to control it more and more. But only now is he beginning to be aware that the conquest of nature may be not merely an empty victory but a defeat. Modern technology has affected and disturbed the balance of nature. Because this balance is reciprocally related to social and cultural systems, the human organism, and personality, it, too, must be taken into account when we consider the promise and problems of modernization. The "environmental problem" will be discussed in Chapter 17.

The Transition from Traditional to Modern Society

"I have seen humanity transformed!" says Buckminster Fuller. In about fifteen or twenty of the world's countries, most people enjoy economic standards of living beyond the dreams of any king who reigned before this century.

But much of humanity lags far behind, and is still struggling to achieve that transformation. The gap between the material bounty showered on members of affluent societies and the misery of the over-populated, underdeveloped[26] majority is enormous, and appears to be

[26]Thus far in the chapter we have avoided using the term "underdeveloped" because of negative connotations, preferring "modernizing" or "transitional." These, too, have their shortcomings. "Shifting terms to designate the same entity is a familiar practice in social science. The terms used to refer to backward nations are a notorious example. What used to be called savage societies came to be called primitive, then backward, then preliterate, then non-literate, then undeveloped or 'so-called underdeveloped' and now, in an optimistic reversion to evolutionary theory, the emerging or even expectant nations." David Matza, "The Disreputable Poor," in Neil J. Smelser and Seymour Martin Lipset, eds., *Social Structure and Mobility in Economic Development* (Chicago: Aldine Publishing Co., 1966), p. 310.

widening. The per capita share of the Gross National Product in 1968 was $4379 in the United States, $3315 in Sweden, $2997 in Canada, $1404 in Japan; but only $380 in Turkey, $170 in Bolivia, $96 in Indonesia, and $58 in Malawi, Africa.[27] Of the forty-two independent African countries, forty have annual per capita incomes of less than $300, and in eighteen of these it is less than $100. Of India's 550 million people, 70% are poor even by India's standards; the annual per capita income is under $80. There, 289 million people subsist on less than 18¢ each per day; 8 out of 10 suffer retarded growth due to faulty diet.[28] Two billion of the world's people have no electricity. With half of the world's people, Asia produces only a tenth of the total power.

This unevenness in modernization, this increasing inequality, is one of the greatest challenges facing the human race. In most of Asia, Africa, and Latin America, the need for modernization—especially for economic development—becomes ever more urgent because of the grim race between exploding populations and the ability to feed them. In contrast to Westerners, who worry about "runaway technology," they struggle for sheer survival and the beginnings of industrialization. Members of affluent societies, says Riesman, may have misgivings about the array of cans at the supermarket and the lack of meaning in life, but "we cannot bring ourselves to begrudge others the literacies and comforts that no longer wholly assuage us. Just as only an arrogant and heartless rich man can say to the poor man, 'Why do you want my job, with my troubles and taxes?' so very few Americans are likely to say to the Turks, 'Don't be like us.' "[29]

THE BEGINNINGS OF MODERNIZATION

"Modernity, [however,] does not automatically begin when tradition passes."[30] Where does it begin? Must people change first, adopting new attitudes and values? Or will appropriate changes in personalities be forthcoming when people are offered enough opportunities and incentives through the institutional structure? If we think again in terms of the five interrelated systems in which human behavior takes place, it is obvious that no biological mutation accounts for modernization, nor does any great change in the earth's physical nature. Healthy human beings in sufficient but not overwhelming numbers, and abundant natural resources such as fossil fuels, arable land, good water, access to transportation routes—all these obviously contribute to the speed of modernization and the ease with which it is achieved. But the health of

[27]*The American Almanac* (1971), p. 810.

[28]Data on Africa, *The New York Times* (Jan. 29, 1971); on India, *The New York Times* (Jan. 18, 1971).

[29]Introduction to Lerner, *The Passing of Traditional Society.*

[30]*Ibid.*, p. viii.

people and their use of resources depend on socio-cultural systems, including the values and knowledge of individual members.

THE MODERNIZATION OF MAN

The impulse to modernize comes from the awareness, discontent, and aspirations of many people. The achievement of modernization depends on effective leadership, entrepreneurship or risk-taking, and a change from a traditional to a participant society.

Transitional man. The first sign that a community or society will modernize is the appearance of men with new discontents and new desires, pried loose from their rocklike attachment to kin and birthplace, perhaps physically as well as psychologically. They are aware that things could be better, conscious of a gap between what they have and are and what others have and are. A typical response of an Egyptian youth to survey questions in 1962 was, "Why should I stay in my village? It's dreary, dark, and dirty. There is nothing to do in the village, no movies, no night clubs, no dancing! Anyway the land [where his father was begging him to stay] could not support both me and my brothers."[31]

Transitional man, then, "is miserable and, most importantly, is newly aware of his misery. To a greater or lesser degree, men of all nations have accepted the originally Western convictions that there is progress and that all men should share in it."[32] What Lerner observed of the Middle East applies to perhaps a hundred other countries: Traditional society is passing because relatively few people still want to live by its rules. And transitional man "blames his shortcomings, his failings, and his condition on society rather than on himself as in former times."[33]

A study of modernization in Indian villages confirmed the importance of empathy in transitional personalities. "Unless the villager can take the role of others how can he engage in anticipatory modernization? In three samples of respondents, the scores for empathy were positively and significantly correlated with the adoption of birth control and new agricultural practices."[34]

The expectations of transitional men are for the most part realistic and specific; they do not have utopian visions. Their "revolution of rising expectations" consists mainly of "a hope that their immediate,

[31]William McCord, "Portrait of Transitional Man," in Irving Louis Horowitz, ed., *The New Sociology* (New York: Oxford University Press, 1965), p. 429.

[32]*Ibid.* p. 441.

[33]Horowitz, *Three Worlds of Development*, p. 291.

[34]Charles P. Loomis and Lalit K. Sen, "Social Organization and Social Change," *Institut International de Sociologie,* 22nd Congress (Rome, Sept. 15–21, 1969).

limited economic needs can be satisfied, and a desire that their children may escape the compulsions of poverty."[35] Yet they do not believe they can realize even these hopes without a fundamental change in the social order.

The Grocer of Balgat, who displayed the empathy and imagination of modernizing man, was a prototype of transitional man. He was a misfit, unhappy in his village, frustrated by the fact that no one agreed with him, that in order to enjoy radio, movies, and free discussion, he had to escape to Ankara, which, although only 8 miles away, was inaccessible by road when he was interviewed. Transitional man's opinions and desires outrun his opportunities.

Entrepreneurs and leaders. Besides a large pool of people ready to modernize, a society must have entrepreneurs and leaders. "Ambitious and mobile men, if produced in sufficient quantity, can transform society."[36] Max Weber, as we saw in the last chapter, associated the beginnings of industrial capitalism with the ways in which nonconformist religion contributed to a spirit of enterprise.[37] Others believe that in the initial stages of industrialization most entrepreneurs come from among people who have experienced some loss of status in the traditional society, which looks down on business, and especially manufacturing, and encourages its elite to follow military, professional, and literary careers. Only commerce and industry are open to the group that has lost status or been denied respect, and some of its members take the risk of inaugurating new enterprises.[38]

In many instances, the first to adopt new ways—such as birth control and vaccination—are "live wire" and aggressive individuals, often regarded as deviants by their fellow villagers.[39] Thus the Grocer of Balgat, "with his 'city-dressed' ways, his 'eye at the higher places' and his visits to Ankara, provoked the Balgati to wrathful and indignant statements of the old code." He was disreputable, heterodox, and probably infidel, for he criticized the village and could imagine himself as President of Turkey and as a resident of America. Nonetheless they

[35]McCord, "Portrait of Transitional Man." He cites surveys in three Indian cities, which showed that people regarded the rise in food prices and unemployment as the most serious problems requiring government attention, and a study in Africa in which 98% mentioned poverty and hunger as their greatest fears and 60% expressed a fear that their children might have to steal or commit other crimes in order to live.

[36]Kahl, *The Measurement of Modernism*, p. 8.

[37]See *The Protestant Ethic and the Spirit of Capitalism*. This thesis has been questioned by some social scientists, who suggest that some other factor may have been responsible for both nonconformity in religion and the spirit of enterprise.

[38]Everett E. Hagen, *On the Theory of Social Change: How Economic Growth Begins* (Homewood, Ill.: Dorsey, 1962). Hagen traces the loss of status back several generations from the entrepreneurs and sees its effects in personality changes over the generations.

[39]Loomis and Sen, "Social Organization and Social Change."

asked his advice about trips to Ankara: what to do, where to go, what to buy, what price to ask for their products. And 4 years after the interviews, when Lerner went to Balgat and asked what people thought of the Grocer, now dead, one finally replied, "Ah, he was the cleverest of us all. We did not know it then, but he saw better than all what lay in the path ahead. We have none like this among us now. He was a prophet." There was now a bus service on the road to Ankara, and the Grocer had won out over shepherd and Chief. The Chief's sons had disappointed him by rejecting farming and war; they were now storekeepers. Many who had scoffed at the Grocer's neckties now had ties of their own, ready for some special occasion when they might venture to wear them.[40]

Although innovators are often despised as deviants, Loomis and Sen found that the most respected people in the three Indian villages they studied led in fields fertilized, vaccinations, and birth control. By sociometric tests, they identified these "influentials"—the best farmer, the most important person, and one regarded as an effective organizer of village programs. These, together with the village president, had adopted many more new practices than the villagers in general.[41]

Where does the impulse to modernization come from in the first place? How can it be implanted? Psychologists have isolated a kind of "mental virus," a **need for achievement** (called *n* Ach) which causes people to behave in a peculiarly energetic way. David C. McClelland and his associates conducted an experiment to see if this virus could be infectious. Previous research had established that businessmen already have some of this *n* Ach. About fifty-two businessmen from Kakinada, an Indian town of about 100,000, were invited to attend a 10-day self-development course designed to increase their *n* Ach and give them more insight into themselves and their work. They "learned how to think easily in terms of *n* Ach, to act in lifelike games like a person with high *n* Ach, to reconcile *n* Ach with their self-image and conflicting cultural values, to form a self-perpetuating interest group . . . that would keep the idea alive."[42] The conclusions of this and other such studies in India were that in a given 2-year period about one-third of businessmen would engage in unusual or innovative business activity— such as starting a new line of products, doing something that earned a large raise in salary, or taking a course in accounting. But in the group coached in *n* Ach, two-thirds showed such signs of unusual activity. They paid more attention to business, not for money but "because they were determined to do a better job, to make a better showing for themselves, for Kakinada, and for India . . . and get more satisfaction out

[40]Lerner, "The Grocer and the Chief: A Parable," *The Passing of Traditional Society.*

[41]"Social Organization and Social Change."

[42]"The Impulse to Modernization," in Weiner, *Modernization*, p. 31.

of life."[43] Some started innovating, several began to invest money differently; a few started entirely new enterprises. Not *n* Ach alone, but the desire to do something for the common good—a spirit of public service—accounted for these actions.

These impulses, says McClelland, did not result from opportunities, nor in any simple way from education or technological innovation. They have been found to be high in zealous, reformist religious groups —not only the English and Dutch Calvinists, but also the Parsis and Jains in India, the Jews in many countries, the Zen-oriented Samurai in Japan, and the overseas Indians in East Africa or Asia.

> What is characteristic of all these communities is an intense, religiously based feeling that they are *superior* to other people living around them and that in one sense or another they hold the key to salvation, perhaps not only for themselves but for all mankind. Thus the two psychological elements essential to economic success are there: the desire to prove oneself better than others and the need to promote the common good—at least of their minority group, which is often somewhat persecuted.

> Must we, then, encourage people to embrace rigid, doctrinaire, minority convictions so that they may feel superior and develop *n* Ach? Fortunately, science has provided us with an alternative that is less dangerous to the peace of the world and probably more effective. By direct training, we can apparently infect the people who need it with both *n* Ach and a sense of public responsibility [and thus] increase the strength of their own impulse to modernize.[44]

AGENTS OF CULTURAL CHANGE

Transitional men, as we have seen, acquire their new ideas through culture contact, which dissolves the "traditional wantlessness" of the poor. Because modernization began in Western countries, and spread, first to central and eastern Europe, and then the Middle East, and finally to the numerous colonies of the great powers, it is often called "Westernization," indicating the role of diffusion. European nations at one time ruled about a third of the world, including almost all of Africa. Colonial administrators prepared the ground for industrialization in several ways. They brought medical science and sanitation that raised life expectancy and improved health (and also resulted in a population explosion that hampers the process of development). They opened the gates to the industrial world by setting up plantations to produce raw materials such as rubber for industry and by importing things that showed the natives how Westerners lived. They often built

[43] *Ibid.* p. 32.
[44] *Ibid.* pp. 38–39.

Drawing by Chas. Addams; © 1971
The New Yorker Magazine, Inc.

*"I danced the best I could, but what the guy
really has is an iron deficiency."*

the roads, railroads, schools, power stations, and hospitals that are part of the social capital upon which further development must be based. And by their very denial of status to those they ruled, they awakened a spirit of enterprise in some of the population. Thus they aroused new wants and stimulated the desire for change. Today agents of planned change are sent from industrialized to underdeveloped countries: educators, technicians, consultants, in government and private agencies and numerous United Nations agencies.

The mass media play a role. Loomis and Sen found that those who rated highest in general knowledge (not necessarily literacy) and who most frequently saw movies and listened to the radio were also most likely to adopt new practices.

A system of formal education, however, appears to be even more important.

Education, especially in schools emphasizing the more modern type of curriculum, seems to be the most powerful factor in developing a population more modern in its attitudes and values. This effect depends in part on the direct instruction provided, but we assume as well that the school as a social organization serves as a model of rationality, of the importance of technical competence, of the rule of objective standards of performance, and of the principle of distributive justice reflected in the grading system. All these models can contribute to shaping young people in the image of modern man.[45]

Universities train managers, technicians, administrators, and other modernizing agents, and are connected with the universities of developed countries, thus providing a channel for the stimulation and guidance of change. The decade of the 1960s saw the establishment of numerous universities; in 1950 Africa between the Sahara and South Africa had no university; by 1965 three dozen had been founded. In Indian universities there is a shift away from classical studies toward science, engineering, and agriculture.[46]

INSTITUTIONS AND MODERNIZATION

The general shape of the institutional structure is extremely important in modernization. To modernize successfully, a society must be both stable and adaptable; it must be capable of internal transformation and accept the need for continual change. These conditions are most likely to be fulfilled where a centralized, large-scale, unified institutional framework already exists, and where within this framework the different institutional systems are relatively autonomous. China, for example, was extremely stable but not adaptable, and great upheavals were necessary before modernization could proceed. It "had a long tradition of centralization, and a degree of social, cultural, and political continuity probably unparalleled in the history of mankind. . . . Yet this great civilization was relatively unable to modernize itself from within" because the entire socio-cultural order was identified with the political order, and the system of social stratification was also bound in with the "monolithic political-religious center."[47] There were no independent sources of strength, cohesion, and identity within which reform could begin. In India, in contrast, the cultural and political orders were more or less dissociated. Such autonomy of the various cultural, social, and political institutions means that change can begin in one sphere without threatening the others all at once and calling for a complete transformation of the entire socio-cultural order.

Economic take-off.   Two essential economic changes are basic to industrialization: a shift from subsistence to commercial agriculture,

[45]Inkeles, "The Modernization of Man."

[46]Schneider, *Destiny of Change*, pp. 19–20.

[47]S. N. Eisenstadt, "Transformation of Social, Political, and Cultural Orders in Modernization," in S. N. Eisenstadt, ed., *Comparative Perspectives on Social Change* (Boston: Little, Brown, 1968), pp. 256–79.

and a great increase in savings and investment. Some farmers must convert to mechanized modern farming, feeding more people per man-hour of work; others must leave the land to work in factories. This process of displacement is often stressful and creates huge social problems. Like the craftsmen of France who threw their wooden shoes into the machinery that took away their jobs (thus suggesting the word "sabotage"), Indian farm workers displaced by tractors have demonstrated to show their distress. Cities all over the underdeveloped world are ringed with the slums of dispossessed migrants from rural areas.

Only by sacrificing present consumption (saving) at a sufficient rate—perhaps 10–20% of the national income—and investing in more productive equipment and tools (capital) does a society achieve "take-off" into sustained economic growth. This is extremely difficult in nations where most people live at the barest minimum of subsistence. It demands great sacrifice, voluntary or involuntary. In England and other countries that industrialized early, this saving was forced upon the workers through long hours and miserable wages for men, women, and children; they were denied immediate consumption of the fruits of their labors. Entrepreneurs also denied themselves; rather than indulging in conspicuous consumption (as did the later industrialists) they reinvested profits, and economic growth proceeded rapidly. In the Soviet Union, the repression and terror of a totalitarian regime were used to push rapid industrialization; production of consumer goods was minimal as compared to heavy industry. Even in today's more affluent society, a hidden "turnover tax" of about 44% of the price of consumer goods goes back to the Soviet government, thus draining off the purchasing power of wages in a less conspicuous way than through low wages and high income taxes.

Political institutions.   In their patterns of historical development, their stage of industrialization, and their forms of government, the nations of the earth are generally thought of as divided into three general categories. The First World—the West—includes the nations which evolved from feudalism into some form of capitalism, not through invasion or conquest but

> through the internal breakdown of the older landed classes, a general disintegration of agricultural societies, or through the initiative and creation of new life styles. The basic characteristic of the First World is that economic development was a consequence of the internal machinery of each nation and not the result of international planned agreement. [In both Europe and North America,] the formation of the parliamentary state system followed the bourgeois dominance over the forms of economic production. . . . The United States is the best example extant of the First World—of the highly mobile, commodity oriented, and ideologically egalitarian social system . . . the

most perfect representative of parliamentary democracy and capitalist economics. . . . [It is] the classic case of national development without a national plan.[48]

The Second World includes the Soviet Union and its bloc, in which a radical shift from feudalism to socialism occurred. Russian society was the first to engage in serious debate over the relationship between economic backwardness and political modernization, especially in the context of international relations. The decision was to mobilize and regiment the entire economy and demand the utmost sacrifice and effort from all workers. Marxist ideology had predicted the downfall of capitalism through increasing depressions and the worsening condition of the proletariat, who would unite and throw off their chains, but capitalist nations were prospering. Lenin revised Marxism to account for this, advancing the notion of capitalist imperialism, in which exploitation of backward nations postponed the inevitable downfall of capitalism. And Stalin proclaimed the doctrine of "socialism in one country," which had to take precedence over world revolution. The rigid ideology that guided Soviet modernization resulted in an emphasis on heavy industry rather than consumer goods; on size, even gigantism, rather than quality; and on planning from above with little feedback from below. Today, however, there is a great deal of experimentation within the Soviet Union itself as well as in other communist nations.

The Third World is "a social universe in limbo and outside the power dyad of East and West." Much of it was colonized until World War II. The Third World today is "thoroughly dedicated to becoming industrialized [and is] a self-defined and self-conscious association of nation-states." China has recently emerged as a marginal member of the Third World bloc; it resembles that sector in its organizational and economic problems, but its ideological stance is very different. Neither the First nor Second World has captured the imagination of the Third World. "The 'mix' in the Third World is ostensibly between *degrees of* (rather than *choices between*) capitalism and socialism at the economic level, and libertarianism and totalitarianism politically."[49] Yet they are not truly independent; they receive aid from the advanced nations, who have the power to set market prices paid for Third World raw materials and prices of goods imported by these nations, and to control the international trade and money markets. And while their formal systems of government are nearly always parliamentary and democratic, their real systems are almost without exception authoritarian.

The nations of the Third World are different not only from advanced industrial nations with capitalist or market economies and parliamentary governments, and from nations with command economies and totalitarian governments, but also from a Fourth World of "un-

[48]Horowitz, *Three Worlds of Development*, pp. 6–7.
[49]*Ibid.*, p. 3.

development" rather than underdevelopment, of tribal societies unconscious of alternative ways of life.

> The Third World nations have a concept of emergence and charac-
> terize themselves as being developed socially and culturally, and of
> being *under*developed economically and technically. This gulf between
> *un*development and *under*development is thus central in relation to
> the definition of the Third World. We are dealing with mature peo-
> ples and backward economies.[50]

The Unevenness of Modernization

Quite aside from the tremendous and growing gap between the industrial, exporting, affluent nations and the underdeveloped nations of the
world, modernization is an uneven process. Social change "moves ahead
by a complicated leapfrog process, creating recurrent crises of adjustment. The first paradox of development, then, is that a developing society must change in all ways at once, but cannot conceivably plan such
a regular, co-ordinated pattern of growth. A certain amount of social
unrest is invariably created."[51]

The unevenness of modernization is apparent in the different
rates of change in various aspects of the socio-cultural order, and in
interruptions and discontinuities of various kinds. Neither continents
nor nations as wholes develop, but geographic areas within them develop at different rates. Northern Italy, around Milan, for example, is
highly industrial; southern Italy is backward, and many of its people
migrate north and experience all the problems of immigrants. Almost
invariably, agricultural productivity lags behind industrial productivity,
and the peasants suffer most from the transition. This is especially apparent in the highly industrialized Soviet Union, with its backward
agriculture. In 1960, there were 160 farm laborers to 100 factory workers; and while the population living on farms dropped nearly 18%
between 1913 and 1961, the actual numbers of farm workers continue
to increase.[52]

As an example of the "leapfrog" process of development, Smelser points out that as soon as most colonial nations attained independence, they established some form of universal suffrage; this created a
crisis in education, because a mass electorate, it is assumed, must be
literate and informed in order to vote. But a mass education system cannot be established without a developing economy, both to support its
cost and to employ its graduates.[53]

---

[50]*Ibid.*, p. 19.

[51]Neil J. Smelser, "The Modernization of Social Relations," in Weiner, *Modernization*, pp. 110–21.

[52]Horowitz, *Three Worlds of Development*, p. 145.

[53]"The Modernization of Social Relations."

UNEVENNESS OF PERSONALITY CHANGE

Societies in transition obviously have personalities that fit both traditional and modern patterns, as well as transitional men who are mixtures of both types. But we also find some "modern" traits in societies that fit the model of folk society very closely: Guatemalan Indians, for example, are market-oriented.[54] On the other hand, there are not only vestiges of traditionalism in modern societies, but strong survivals. Sacred values may adhere to economic and political systems. Faith in science and knowledge may not be general: Surveys of Americans after the first moon landing found many skeptical of the feat; some insisted it had been staged in the Arizona desert. Some members of modern societies are as authoritarian as any tribesman; and many are fatalist, nonparticipant, lacking in empathy, mistrustful, and unwilling to respect all human beings regardless of social category. Some fear change, look to the past, and have reactionary opinions—especially those whose ways of life, skills, and values have become obsolete or are being severely challenged.

An empirical study of values in two modernizing societies by Joseph Kahl, and a broad-ranging theoretical analysis of the "characterological revolution" by David Riesman are both concerned with the unevenness of change. Kahl and his associates found that modernism tends to vary with social class and urbanism. To find out how a peasant learns to think and act like a factory worker or the son of a small-town storekeeper learns to be a big-city accountant, they conducted more than 600 interviews in Brazil and over 700 in Mexico, concentrating on values concerning work and career. Kahl's operational definition of one modern trait—activism—illustrates his approach: Respondents were asked to agree or disagree (very much or a little) with the statement "Making plans only brings unhappiness, because the plans are hard to fulfill." They concluded that the larger the city of residence and the higher the social class of a respondent, the more "modern" his values: That is, he was more activist and individualistic; interested in success in a career even at the expense of other rewards such as time for recreation; less inclined to refuse an opportunity that took him away from his parents; and more inclined to believe that he could change his own status and influence public policy.[55]

In *The Lonely Crowd: A Study of the Changing American Character*, David Riesman and his associates outlined personality changes that they believe go along with modernization. They distinguished three kinds of conformity: tradition-direction, inner-direction, and other-direction. **Tradition-directed** persons, as we saw, characterize premodern societies; when they stray from the well-worn path marked out by their elders, they feel shame, and are punished by external sanc-

---

[54]Sol Tax, *Penny Capitalism* (Chicago: University of Chicago Press, 1953).
[55]*The Measurement of Modernism.*

tions. In contrast, an inner-directed person (typified by the entrepreneurs of the early Industrial Revolution) follows a firm and clear set of principles or internalized norms and values built into him by his elders; it serves as a sort of "gyroscope" set spinning by home, church, and school, guiding his behavior throughout life, even under the changing conditions of a dynamic society. When he violates these implanted principles he is punished by feelings of guilt.

Increasingly characteristic of modern society, and especially of the middle class, is the other-directed person. He is motivated by a desire to adjust to peer-group expectations, to catch in his "radarscope" the signals that others are sending out and to act according to them. Instead of shame or guilt, he feels a diffuse anxiety lest he fail to perceive these expectations correctly and conform to them. He harbors an insatiable need for approval. His goals may shift at times; but the process of striving to be liked and of paying close attention to others' reactions goes on throughout his life.

There is a "characterological struggle" within a changing society among the different personality types as one gains ascendancy over the others; this struggle also occurs on a world-wide scale. Transitional men like the Grocer are marginal to their traditional communities; but as modernization proceeds, they win out over shepherd and Chief, and are belatedly recognized as prophets of change. A struggle between inner- and other-directed people characterizes recent American social history. The inner-directed person, who possesses a relatively inflexible standard for judging success and morality and is buttressed by steady internalized values and a personal sense of discipline, may feel resentful when his formulas no longer work, when standards seem to shift with situations, and when the people who succeed are the flexible ones, who appear unprincipled to him. Other-directed people in turn see his ambition for an individualistic career as outmoded; they wish only to be slightly or marginally different from others, to be cooperative, adjusted, and popular. The ambitious inner-directed person feels guilty when he fails; the other-directed person feels guilty when he succeeds too well![56]

Is There an End-Product of the Modernization Process?

The concept of the polar types of traditional and modern societies may imply that modernization is inevitable, that there is a certain end-product, and that all modernizing societies must converge toward great similarity in their socio-cultural orders. Is this the case?

IS MODERNIZATION INEVITABLE?

Modernization has been called an inexorable trend, irresistible and all-embracing. But it is not inevitably successful. The population

[56]Riesman, in collaboration with Nathan Glazer and Reuel Denney (New York: Doubleday, 1953).

explosion, international rivalries, and other obstacles may prevent its realization. Another obstacle, insists Kenneth Schneider, is the lack of excitement in purely economic motivations, which are expressed in such impersonal terms as economic growth models, high finance, bureaucratic organization, and technical specialization, as well as in the material rewards of industrialization.

> Given a universal taste for money, can we still expect traditional peoples to quickly shake off the security of community, the comfort of old beliefs, the web of family welfare, the peace of the rural village life, and the simple familiarity of one's locality for the uncertain rewards of a laborer's day wage, a submission to imposed performance and working hours, the bewildering pecuniary relationships among unknown persons, and the social formlessness of cities? . . . [Impersonal appeals to economic motives] do not arouse the excitement that all men should have while creating a new civilization: the excitement that arises when personality is intimately a part of a cultural adventure; when it directly builds and shares something that is much larger than the individual; when it links the past and the future with the present role of the individual; when it bears upon and relates friends, family, community, the young and the aged, the high and the humble, all in a highly personal way.[57]

Successful industrialization, however, need not destroy the traditional order, says Manning Nash, who studied the Guatemalan town of Cantel, the site of Central America's largest textile mill. Over three generations of trial-and-error adaptation, the people have kept their social integrity and cultural distinctiveness. "A people still speaking Quiché, the women yet in costume, the world view of spirits and saints largely intact, have learned how to coexist with a factory regime." Nash suggests that industrialization need not be—as it often seems to be—"the beginning of a drastic chain of social and cultural change which may some day transform the peasants and primitives of the world into one gray mass of proletarians and level their distinctive and valuable ways of life into one or another pale copy of Western life." Nor need the process involve social disorganization. One reason for the success of the Cantel experience is that its people rather than a central government are the agents and adherents of the new ways, and the factory came to them; they did not leave their town for the city.

> Cantel indicates that many areas of traditional life can flourish on a new level in the process of industrialization, and that the release of human energy and creative ability in a process of social change can devise solutions to problems of social life—solutions not prefigured in our theory or achieved in other instances of similar change. . . . Cantel teaches the general lesson that the human tolls in industriali-

[57]*Destiny of Change*, pp. 18, 16.

zation are not built into the process itself. They are the result of an image of man in social change which delineates him as the passive agent mechanically responding to immutable forces, or as the pawn in a political chess game, or as the expendable material in an economic vision. The questions we must ask of the process of industrialization cannot be phrased apart from the ineluctable fact that man makes himself, or he is not made at all.[58]

DO MODERNIZING SOCIETIES CONVERGE TOWARD SIMILARITY?

Cantel, however, is only one community in a still underdeveloped society. Many observers have suggested that all modernizing societies become increasingly alike, converging toward a common pattern, "toward a nonexperimental hardfastness and the acceptance of a single [economic] measure of worth."[59] They perceive increasing similarities between Soviet and American society; some say each is borrowing the best features of the other, such as more planning in the United States and more use of the market system in the Soviet Union; others that they are tending toward the worst, the Soviet Union adopting American popular culture, obsession with cars, and perhaps advertising and even pornography, while the U.S. learns and uses more efficient means of suppressing freedom of thought, expression, and political organization. More realistically, some convergence theorists maintain that industrialization and other aspects of modernization inevitably shape every society in a similar mold. Giant corporations, bureaucratic structures, urban congestion, the eclipse of family and community, dehumanization and alienation—these will occur, they say, regardless of ideologies and political systems.[60]

Other sociologists grant that many features of industrial societies conform to a very similar pattern, and that "there are inherent limits to the kinds of societies that are compatible with the industrial mode."[61] But these limits are very broad, and it is provincial to regard "the Western pattern of industrialism as a mean toward which all modern societies eventually evolve."[62] French sociologist Raymond Aron puts it this way:

[58]"Machine Age Maya: The Industrialization of a Guatemalan Community," *The American Anthropologist* (Memoir No. 87) 60, No. 2, Pt. 2 (April 1958).

[59]Schneider, *Destiny of Change*, p. 21.

[60]See readings in Part 7, "Are the Two Societies Becoming Alike?" in Paul Hollander, ed., *American and Soviet Society: A Reader in Comparative Sociology and Perception* (Englewood Cliffs, N.J.: Prentice-Hall, Inc., 1969), pp. 557–89.

[61]Allen Kassof, ed., *Prospects for Soviet Society* (New York: Frederick A. Praeger, 1968), p. 505.

[62]*Ibid.*, p. 506.

Only a technological interpretation of history would allow us to assert that all societies that use atomic energy and computers are the same. It is absurd to state as a foregone conclusion that what they have in common is more important than the differences between them.[63]

IS THERE AN END-PRODUCT?

The concept of polar types may seem to imply that there is a point at which the members of a developing society may look about them and say, "There! We did it! Now we are a modern society!" But continual change is even more characteristic of advanced industrial societies than of modernizing underdeveloped societies. Many observers say the United States is the first society to enter a post-industrial stage. How does it differ from the model of urban industrial society?

Where traditional society relied on muscle power and industrial society on mechanical power, post-industrial society relies on brain power multiplied by electronic means, such as computers. Capital and business enterprise are rapidly being replaced by scientific knowledge as the chief generator of wealth. This is especially apparent in the largest American ventures—aerospace, communications, and military development. The university "becomes an intensely involved think-tank, the source of much sustained political planning and social innovation and no longer a withdrawn ivory tower."[64]

Just as in the early phases of industrialization, many roles become obsolete. There is less demand for unskilled labor and even for specialized technicians; knowledge changes so fast that an experienced worker or even a professional may find himself superseded by a recent graduate. Lower white-collar employees and middle management will be unable to compete with the speed, accuracy, and dependability of computers. There will be a three-class occupational structure of professionals, technicians, and service workers.[65]

Bureaucracy as we know it may disappear. When necessary, executives will call upon the diverse professional skills of relative strangers who will work on a specific problem. Children will not be taught the skills of simple recall and repetitive dexterity demanded of bureaucratic clerks, but will be educated for an unknown future; they must learn how to think, how to find out, and how to create new knowledge. Already there are organizations, such as consultant and research firms, that produce, process, and apply knowledge. Their rapid rise is seen as part of the promise that a society can guide its own future course, and

[63] *The Industrial Society: Three Essays on Ideology and Development* (New York: Simon and Schuster, 1967), p. 96.

[64] *The New York Times* (Jan. 6, 1969).

[65] Robert Perrucci and Marc Pilisuk, eds., *The Triple Revolution: Social Problems in Depth* (Boston: Little, Brown, 1968), p. 173.

a recognition that once a society is committed to change, it cannot retreat.

Summary

Modernization, the transition from traditional folk society to modern urban society, includes many changes that tend to occur together, the chief of which is industrialization.

A vast increase in science and knowledge and its application to the production of goods and services, including transportation and communication, have created a great abundance of goods in fifteen or twenty countries. Modernization includes other cultural changes: secularization of values, with an emphasis on science, rationality, skill, work, progress, and education; and individualization, which means that each person is judged by his achievement.

Social organization changes. Political and economic units grow larger; roles become more specialized, and complexity and interdependence increase. Bureaucratic organization and utilitarian controls dominate. The class system becomes relatively open and mobile. The extended family declines in importance, and the feeling of identity with the local community diminishes. Some observers think these changes add up to a mass society in the sense of dehumanized units in a regimented and homogenized system; others say mass society means more participation in social, political, and economic and cultural affairs by larger masses of people.

Traditional man is typically identified with family and community; he is fatalistic, authoritarian, and lacking in empathy and imagination. Modern man is not only urban, literate, educated for a specialized occupation, participant, and dependent on large centralized formal agencies for many services, but also activist, adaptable, oriented to change and decisions, rational and organized, optimistic, confident, and trusting. He has faith in science and technology, and feels empathy for others. His self-conception is based more on achievement and experience than on ascribed status.

The human organism has not changed basically since Cro-Magnon man; but the number of human beings increases explosively, as does their tendency to cluster in cities. Man's organic make-up may be affected for better or worse by his diet as modernization proceeds. Science and knowledge are enabling him to tamper with mind and body, even to change heredity and reproduction. The wastes of industrialization and modern living pollute his environment and thus damage his health, for they disturb the balance of nature.

The gap between affluent developed societies and underdeveloped ones is growing, and this inequality may be the most serious challenge to the human race. Underdeveloped nations are full of "transitional men," newly aware of their poverty and inclined to blame the social order rather than themselves for their difficulties. Many feel empathy and can imagine better things; but their aspirations tend to be quite realistic and limited rather than utopian. They are willing and eager to modernize; but their societies must also have entrepreneurs or risk-takers and leaders willing to innovate. Leaders in the transition may be deviants, looked down on by their fellows; or they may be influential members of the community. Often they have a high need for achievement, and this can be implanted and increased by training. Entrepreneurs frequently come from minority groups that feel superior even though they may be looked down upon by others.

Modernization of underdeveloped nations today is often called Westernization, for it occurs largely through diffusion. In many countries colonial administrators laid the groundwork; agents of planned change financed by advanced countries continue the process. Mass media, schools, and especially universities promote modernization.

Where institutions have some autonomy within a stable system, they are more adaptable than institutions that are closely connected with the political or religious order. Two economic changes are fundamental to modernization: a shift from subsistence to commercial agriculture, and a saving and reinvestment of perhaps 10–20% of the national income. This has almost invariably meant great sacrifice on the part of the poor.

The nations of the earth are often thought of as divided into three general categories according to their patterns of historical development, their stage of industrialization, and their forms of government. The West, or the First World, includes advanced industrialized nations that went from feudalism to capitalism and have some form of parliamentary democracy. The East, or Second World, is also advanced industrially, but went from feudalism to socialism, and tends to be authoritarian and even totalitarian. The Third World has gone from colonialism to nationhood largely since the Second World War, desires industrialization, and is not committed to the ideologies and systems of either of the other worlds, but tends toward a mixture of capitalism and socialism, and of parliamentary forms and actual authoritarianism.

The process of modernization is uneven not only among nations but also within nations. This unevenness appears in geographic areas, in various sectors such as agriculture, consumer goods, and heavy industry, and in the need for education before development can proceed very far, at the same time that schools must be financed by the developing economy. Nor is the transition from traditional to modern personalities uniformly smooth and successful; many people in modern societies display traditionalist traits. An empirical study in Brazil and Mexico found modern values highly correlated with social class and urban residence. A theoretical survey of "the changing American character" suggests that as a society modernizes, other-directed people concerned with the opinions and approval of others win out over inner-directed people guided by firmly implanted norms and values. Where the tradition-directed people of a premodern society feel shame if they fail to conform and inner-directed people feel guilt, other-directed people are subject to anxiety.

Although in general, modernization is an irreversible trend, its success in achieving the goals of abundance, health, and longevity is not inevitable. Other values may deter people from pursuing economic ones; and international unrest and the population explosion are also obstacles. But there is some evidence that industrialization can be achieved without destroying the traditional order and that there are a number of alternative paths to successful modernization besides the ones exemplified by the United States and the Soviet Union. Although industrial societies have many features in common, there are also many differences that persist, and convergence toward almost identical sociocultural orders may be unnecessary, undesirable, and even unlikely.

Modernization, in fact, has no end-product. To embark on the modernization process is to accept the fact of continual change. The United States is considered by many to be entering a "post-industrial" stage in which knowledge and electronics will multiply wealth, teams of experts rather than bureaucrats will solve problems and set policy, and children must be educated for an unknown future.

In the next chapter we turn to a world-wide aspect of modernization: the urban trend.

QUESTIONS FOR FURTHER THOUGHT

1. Have you observed modernization in the course of your own life? Have you moved or migrated? For what reasons? Interview parents, grandparents, or other elders on their experience of modernization.

2. Looking over the outline of the text, account for the placement of this chapter.

3. Do you know any completely "traditional" men? "Transitional" men? "Modern" men? (Or women, of course!) Write a character sketch of someone you know well, in terms of the different personality traits of these types. Construct a hypothesis connecting these traits with varia-

bles of census data and variables involved in the modernization process.

4. Do you belong to a community in the territorial sense? In a social-psychological sense?

5. To which view of mass society do you subscribe? Why?

6. What do you consider the nation's greatest problem? What would you do about it if you were President? If you could not live in this country, where would you want to live? After answering these questions, put them to several people. Do they respond like traditional or modern man? What may account for their responses?

7. The belief that the American diet is highly nutritious and well balanced is almost a sacred cultural norm. Do you share it? If so, how do you react to the phrases "health food" and "organic gardening"? If not, how do you account for the strength of this belief?

8. Do you consider yourself tradition-directed, inner-directed, or other-directed? Are you most likely to feel shame, guilt, or anxiety about violating norms? Apply these questions (operationally defined) to your parents and grandparents. Do you perceive a generational difference?

9. Soviet economists reject the convergence theory. Speculate about probable reasons. (You might check your ideas with those in the Hollander reference.)

10. What occupational plans do you have? Is your planned role likely to fit into a post-industrial society?

11. China appears to be trying very hard to avoid a high degree of specialization, demanding that students, office workers, and the military spend some time in farm and factory work. Do you think this approach to modernization can continue as development proceeds?

12. Raymond Aron does not agree that there is a break between industrial and "post-industrial" society, insisting that the shift to knowledge and electronics is a normal

development in the use of science and technology. He believes the concept of a post-industrial society smacks of technological determinism. Do you agree? Would the greater productivity and leisure of post-industrialism change culture and social structure in ways as fundamental as the effects of the industrial revolution?

16

We cannot all live in cities, yet nearly all seem determined to do so.

HORACE GREELEY

Stadtluft macht frei (City air makes free).

MEDIEVAL GERMAN SAYING

History is mainly the account of what happened in the cities.

JAMES MICHENER
The Quality of Life

Pueblo chico, infierno grande (A small village is a great hell).

SPANISH PROVERB

All big cities of mankind are sliding into chaos.

CONSTANTINOS DOXIADIS

CITIES
AND
MODERNIZATION

THE COMPLEXES OF BUILDINGS, STREETS, AND PEOPLE we call cities are bustling centers of work, trade, learning, politics, art, fashion, and fun. To some "the city" spells "civilization"; to others the word "urban" is always followed by "crisis" or "problems." Samuel Johnson, who enjoyed the urbane conversation of London coffeehouses, thought that only in cities could men be truly civilized: To be tired of London was to be tired of life. Oliver Goldsmith, seeing the deserted villages and the smoky factory towns of the early Industrial Revolution, bewailed the loss of "a bold peasantry, their country's pride," and vilified cities as places "where wealth accumulates, and men decay." "God made the country and man made the town" wrote William Cowper; Oliver Wendell Holmes retorted, "God made the cavern, and man made the house."

Americans, who crowd more and more into metropolitan areas, are especially ambivalent about cities. They tend to see rural life as normal and moral, city life as corrupting and unnatural. This may be a heritage from Old Testament days, when Hebrew prophets glorified pastoral life and called down the wrath of God on Babylon and Sodom and Gomorrah. Perhaps because of the Puritan interpretation of this heritage, and perhaps because American cities were haphazardly and often hurriedly built, as frontiersmen and peasant immigrants pushed West, they never acquired the urbanity and sophistication of the old cities of Europe. They burgeoned unplanned, with commercial and industrial convenience, private interest, and happenstance their only guides.

Early urban sociologists reflected our cultural bias against cities. During the decades when immigrants poured into city ghettos, factories mushroomed, and the Depression revealed many weaknesses in the socio-cultural order, they tended to emphasize urban disorganization. In recent years, however, sociologists increasingly see the urban community as "a highly intricate social as well as economic and cultural organization," which includes all the simpler elements of rural society, such as primary groups, as well as some new forms that emerge in the new setting.[1]

[1]Ernest W. Burgess and Donald J. Bogue, *Urban Sociology* (Chicago: The University of Chicago Press, 1967), p. 115.

Can we generalize about something as varied as cities and city-dwellers? What can we say that applies equally to Viennese opera-goers, Harlem hustlers, San Francisco gourmets, Parisian boulevardiers, and Chicago grain merchants? What do planned cities such as Columbia, Maryland, and the Helsinki suburb of Tapiola have in common with each other and with New Orleans, São Paulo, Calcutta, and Tokyo? When cities differ so much from one another, and when each city has so many diverse aspects, can we discern any patterns and regularities, or are we condemned to grope for partial understanding, like the blind men touching different parts of the elephant?

In this chapter we ask, first, What constitutes a city, and what is urbanization? We then trace the history of the urban revolution, emphasizing the speed and degree of recent changes, and their different manifestations in cities, suburbs, metropolitan areas, and urban regions. We consider how this trend differs in various societies, how it is related to industrialization and to modernization in general and by what processes cities assume their characteristic patterns.

We then ask, Is urbanism a distinct way of life, or are there many different ways of urban life? Is the city as such responsible for the life style or styles we find there?

In the final sections of the chapter we consider the role of cities in newly developing societies. What place does rural life have in today's world? What alternative futures may we envision for cities, and how might these come about? Finally, what problems—and what promises—do cities hold for mankind?

What Is a City?

We can define cities in several ways. The most neutral definition is *demographic*[2] and concerns the distribution of people in space: A **city** is a relatively dense concentration of people settled in a relatively small geographic area. (Usually it is taken for granted that these people are engaged, for the most part, in nonagricultural pursuits.) By *legal* definition, a city is a named place, incorporated or chartered by a higher political authority; it is bounded by clearly marked "city limits." The *census* definition varies from time to time and from country to country. In the United States, for example, 2,500 people in a city, village, or town, whether incorporated or not, comprise a city. In Denmark, Sweden, and Finland, 200 people constitute a city; in Venezuela, 1,000; in Ghana, 5,000; in Japan, 30,000. India's definition is more complex: A city consists of 10,000 people or more, with a density of over 1,000 to the square mile, and with at least 75% of its adult males engaged in nonagricultural pursuits.

[2]*Demography* is the study of the size, composition, and distribution of population, and of changes in these factors.

The *social* definition of a city includes features of culture and social organization: heterogeneity, specialization, interdependence, mobility, and an "urban way of life" that is assumed to result from these factors and to have certain consequences for the social relationships and personalities of city-dwellers. This definition is usually associated with industrialization and other aspects of modernization; culture and social structure are quite different in pre-industrial cities, where home and work-place are less likely to be separated than in a modern city. Urban sociologists sometimes set a minimum figure for cities, say 20,000; in smaller aggregates, they believe, the characteristic features of urban life are not as apparent as in larger ones. The standard criterion for a "large city" is 100,000.[3]

What Is Urbanization?

The definition of urbanization, like that of a city, may be primarily demographic or primarily social. In the demographic sense, **urbanization** refers to *where* people live, to a degree or a trend—to "the proportion of the total population concentrated in urban settlements, or else to a rise in this proportion."[4] It is not the same thing as the growth of cities as such, for if they grow at the same rate as the rural population, no change in rural–urban proportions would occur. Nor is it the same as the population density of a whole society. Argentina has a low density and a relatively high degree of urbanization, whereas India, a land of numerous peasant villages as well as huge cities, has a high density and a relatively low degree of urbanization.

In the social sense, urbanization refers to *how* people live, to their occupations, behavior patterns, and social relationships. An enduring sociological concern is the extent to which these two aspects of urbanization are related—the consequences *where* people live have for *how* they live. The urban sociologist asks: Is there something inherent in the crowding together of large numbers of people in a relatively small space that makes their social life, their personalities, their beliefs and values, and their health and happiness different in significant ways from

[3]Gerald Breese, *Urbanization in Newly Developing Countries* (Englewood Cliffs, N.J.: Prentice-Hall, Inc., 1966), p. 11. International Urban Research, an American research team, worked out a definition of a large city that would permit precise international comparisons of the degree and rate of urbanization: "an urban unit containing a population of at least 100,000 people, being an area embracing a central city or cities, plus adjacent areas with an economic relationship with that city and with 65% or more of their economically-active populations engaged in non-agricultural activities." [Peter Hall, *The World Cities* (New York: McGraw-Hill Book Company, 1966), p. 19.]

[4]Kingsley Davis, "The Urbanization of the Human Population," in Sylvia Fleis Fava, ed., *Urbanism in World Perspective: A Reader* (New York: Thomas Y. Crowell, 1968), pp. 32–45; reprinted from *Scientific American* (Sept. 1965): 41–53.

those of people who live in isolated farmsteads, peasant or tribal villages, and small towns? Or are both the benefits and the problems of urban living due not to this crowding but to the other trends we associate with modernization, such as industrialization, secularization, and bureaucracy?

The Urban Revolution

We speak of urbanization as a revolution because it has proceeded so very rapidly since 1800, and because of its effect on culture, society, and personality. Although there can be cities without industry, and industrialization without great cities, the two tend to go together. The mechanization of agriculture pushes people off the land; the hope of jobs, schooling, freedom from primary group controls, and excitement pulls them to the city.

EARLY CITIES

About 10,000 years ago, when men first learned to cultivate crops and began to store grain, they congregated in Neolithic villages.[5] Urban centers, with administrative buildings, food storage systems, and written symbols for calculating and recording business transactions, emerged in the Fertile Crescent of Southwest Asia—in Mesopotamia, Iran, and the Indus Valley of Pakistan—as early as 3900 B.C., and there is no doubt that by 2300 B.C. true cities existed. The cities of Mexico discovered by the Spanish conquistadores in the 1500s had emerged as early as 100 B.C. In both regions, cities were integrated not on the basis of kinship or other ascriptive relationships, but as states or "polities." At first theocracies governed by priests, cities became militaristic as the urge to expand their territories increased.[6]

Cities wrested the food they needed from nearby peasants through coercion or taxation, or through trade for city-made goods and supplies from other regions. Besides being warehouses for such wealth as grain, cities were centers of distribution, of exchange with other cities, and of crafts. They were linked to one another by transportation networks, to the country by symbiosis.[7] The city was thus a means, sometimes a tyrannical one from the peasants' point of view, of accu-

[5]Recent excavations in Thailand indicate that the agricultural revolution may have begun 5,000 years earlier in Southeast Asia. [Wilhelm G. Solheim II, "An Earlier Agricultural Revolution," *Scientific American* (April 1972): p. 34.]

[6]Robert McC. Adams, "The Evolution of Urban Society: Early Mesopotamia and Mexico," in Fava, *Urbanism in World Perspective*, pp. 98–115.

[7]Norton Ginsburg, "The City and Modernization," in Myron Weiner, ed., *Modernization: The Dynamics of Growth* (New York: Basic Books, 1966), pp. 122–37.

mulating and organizing capital for such projects as large-scale irrigation, water conservation, and flood control, which made greater productivity possible.

But no society was really *urbanized* until modern times. The
city of Rome may have had a million people at its height, but nine out
of ten citizens of the empire lived in peasant villages. After its decline
and fall, social organization reverted to small communities such as
feudal manors. In the Middle Ages such European ports as Venice and
Bremen grew into city-states through commerce. It was in cities such
as these that the urban revolution began.

WORLD URBANIZATION

Not until the complex of trends we call modernization got under
way, however, did urbanization gain momentum. Since 1800, when only
about 3% of the world's people lived in settlements of 5000 or more,
the trend away from the farm has accelerated with hardly any setbacks.
Now about a third of the world's people are urban. In 1970 more than
a quarter of the world's people lived in cities of 20,000 or more. In what
the United Nations demographers call "the more developed regions,"
two out of three people live in cities (by census definitions); in the "less
developed" regions, one out of four. They predict that by the end of
the century there will be 3 billion city-dwellers.[8]

While population has grown enormously during this period,
urbanization has proceeded even faster. World population grew 29%
between 1800 and 1850, but the number living in cities of over 100,000
people grew 76%. From 1900 to 1950, population grew 49%, large
cities, 254%.

A striking feature of this trend is the emergence of really enormous cities. Twelve per cent of mankind is clustered in 141 metropolitan areas of a million or more people.[9] Among these are "the World
Cities," which are not only great centers of population, but dominant
centers of national and international political power, trade, transportation, banking and finance, professional talent and learning, art and entertainment, libraries and museums, publishing and communication,
riches and luxury. Prominent among them are London, Paris, New York,
Tokyo, Moscow, the Rhine–Ruhr area of Germany, and the Randstand
complex of the Netherlands.[10]

Gist and Fava distinguish three levels of urbanization according
to the proportion of population living in large cities (of 100,000 or
more). (*1*) Countries with more than 20% in large cities include three

[8]*The World Population Situation in 1970.* United Nations, Department of Social and
Economic Affairs, Population Studies, No. 49, 1971.

[9]Jorge Arango, *The Urbanization of the Earth* (Boston: Beacon Press, 1970), p. 9.

[10]Peter Hall, *The World Cities.*

levels of modernization: (*a*) The established urban–industrial countries, which were highly industrialized by the end of the nineteenth century, including England and northwestern Europe and the countries that drew most of their colonists from these areas—the United States, New Zealand, and Australia. These tend to have the highest levels of urbanization. A third or more of the people in England and Wales, West Germany, and the Netherlands live in large cities. (*b*) The newly industrial countries that have achieved significant levels of modernization in the present century: Spain, Italy, Hungary, Poland, the Soviet Union, and Japan. (*c*) The "overurbanized" countries where industrialization lags far behind urbanization. In Venezuela, Argentina, and Uruguay, for example, over 30% of the population lives in large cities in spite of relatively low levels of industrialization; in Mexico, Costa Rica, Cuba, Jamaica, Colombia, Egypt, Syria, Lebanon, and Korea, between 20 and 30%. (2) Countries with between 10 and 20% in large cities typically have low levels of industrialization; they include many countries of Latin America, the Near East, the rim of South and Southeast Asia, northern Africa, and a few European countries. (3) Finally, the least urbanized nations, with less than 10% in large cities, are also the least industrialized and Westernized. Asia, except for Japan, and Africa are most highly represented in this category. Only about 8% of the population in India and China live in large cities. Albania and Yugoslavia in Europe, and the Guianas in the Western Hemisphere, are also minimally urbanized.[11]

URBANIZATION IN THE UNITED STATES

Once a large expanse of farmland and wilderness punctuated here and there by cities, the United States today presents a picture of numerous sprawling metropolitan areas linked by heavily settled corridors, and vast open stretches, especially in the Midwestern plains, where many small towns are almost deserted. But it also includes a number of thriving small towns and cities. Several trends have produced this pattern.

First of all, industrialization has drawn rural people to cities. The shift from farm to city, which is what we usually mean by demographic urbanization, was as great in volume—about 40 million people —as the flood of immigrants that came to the United States between 1820 and 1960; and it occurred in a much shorter period, from 1920 to 1970. The sixties were especially dramatic: The number living on farms dropped from 15 million to 10 million! Half a century ago, the American population was almost evenly divided between city and farm.

[11]Noel P. Gist and Sylvia Fleis Fava, *Urban Society*, 5th ed. (New York: Thomas Y. Crowell Company, 1964), pp. 58–61.

AUDIO NOSTALGIA

- A DOG BARKING IN THE DISTANCE
- MOURNFUL WHISTLE OF A FREIGHT TRAIN
- A STREETCAR RUMBLING THROUGH THE NIGHT
- GULLS ON A DESERTED SHORE

25¢

Drawing by H. Martin; © 1970
The New Yorker Magazine, Inc.

In 1970 three out of four Americans were urban, and most of the rural inhabitants were "rural non-farm."

Urbanization embraces several other trends: metropolitanization, suburbanization, and the emergence of urban regions. Metropolitan areas include a number of cities and urban fringe areas that form a social and economic community (but seldom a political one). According to the official definition, a Standard Metropolitan Statistical Area (SMSA) includes at least one city of 50,000 or more inhabitants, and adjacent counties that are urban in character and economically and socially integrated with the central city-county. There are now 243 such SMSAs in the United States, and seven out of ten Americans live in them. The number of SMSAs with over a million people rose from 24 in 1960 to 33 in 1970.

The metropolis is not simply a traditional city grown larger. It is a new and complex urban form. Most metropolitan areas consist of a "downtown" commercial business district; a ghettoized "inner city"; satellite towns and suburbs, some predominantly residential, some largely commercial and industrial; and unincorporated "urban sprawl" spreading out along highways.

Suburbanization is inseparable from metropolitanization. During the 1960s, 14 million whites and 800,000 blacks moved to the suburbs. Most central cities lost population, including thirteen of the twenty-five largest central cities; St. Louis declined 19%, Cleveland, 15.6%. In 1970, suburbanites became the largest sector of the population, more than 71 million, exceeding by far the 59 million in central cities and edging ahead of the 71 million in smaller cities and rural areas.

The urban trend is now proceeding to the urban region, an area of one million people or more comprised of a continuous zone of metropolitan areas and intervening counties within which one is never far from a city. . . . An urban region is not a single "supercity"; it is a regional constellation of urban centers and their hinterland. . . . Even in the largest urban region, running along the Atlantic coast from Maine to Virginia, and westward past Chicago, it is estimated that only one-fifth of the area is currently in urban use.

The total land area encompassed by urban regions is estimated to double in the period 1960 to 1980, while the number of such areas is expected to increase from 16 to at least 23. By 2000, urban regions will occupy one-sixth of the continental United States land area, and contain five-sixths of our nation's people.

If our national population distributes itself according to these projections, 54% of all Americans will be living in the two largest urban regions. The metropolitan belt stretching along the Atlantic seaboard and westward past Chicago would contain 41% of our total population. Another 13% would be in the California region lying between San Francisco and San Diego.[12]

Some urban areas are extremely crowded. In the central cities of the United States, the average density is 8000 people per square mile. At the density rate of some sections of Harlem, the whole population of the country could fit into three of New York City's five boroughs.

But in metropolitan areas as a whole, density is declining. In 1920, it was 6580 per square mile; in 1960, 4230; by 2000, it is predicted, it should be only 3720. (These figures average inner-city ghettos and working-class neighborhoods as well as spacious suburbs.) Much of the United States is sparsely settled, and a very large number of Americans live in towns of less than 50,000.

The accepted minimum measure of an urban environment is a population density of 1,000 or more per square mile; the measure of suburbanization is a population density of 500 per square mile. Seventeen states do not have even one county—not a single county—with a population density of 500 per square mile. . . . In short, what is developing in the United States is the spread of a relatively low-density population engaged in urban economic pursuits; many of these American-style city-dwellers actually live on plots of land that would look large to a Chinese or Indian farmer.[13]

[12]*Population and the American Future: The Report of the Commission on Population Growth and the American Future* (New York: New American Library, 1972), pp. 40–42.

[13]Daniel J. Elazar, "Are We a Nation of Cities?" *The Public Interest* (Summer 1966); reprinted in *Current* (Dec. 1966): 15–21.

Even within the orbit of the metropolis, Americans tend to cling to many features of small-town living.

The Ecology of American Cities

Why and how have American settlements assumed these patterns? Sociologists have attempted to answer that question in terms of "ecological processes." Ecology, as used in biology, refers to the way plants and animals are distributed over a given area, and to their interdependence. Human ecology is concerned with the distribution of various functions, groups, and kinds of buildings within a given area, and the processes involved in that distribution. Urban ecological processes—the steps by which a city grows and changes—are related to technological change, physical mobility, the degree of freedom of choice of various groups, competition for space and desirable locations, economic advantage, and such values as traditional attachment to a certain place.

Concentration refers to the drawing of population into given areas of varying degrees of density; it is often highest at the center of a city, and is affected by access to transportation and by variations in economic capacity to choose a place to live or do business. Centralization is the drawing together of institutions and activities, the assembling of people to work rather than to reside in a given area. Some highly centralized areas may show a low density in census statistics, which are based on dwelling rather than working place. The downtown or central business district is usually the area of greatest centralization; executives and white-collar workers alike commute from the outer city and the suburbs. Sub-centers scattered through every metropolitan area, often at important intersections, result from the same process. This clustering of activities in outlying sections is also evidence of decentralization, for it indicates the spread of activities and dwelling places farther and farther out from the center of the city. Suburbanization, one aspect of decentralization, is made possible, like urbanization itself, by technological change. The automobile, delivery truck, telephone, freeway, and some surviving commuter trains, as well as the shorter work day and work week, make it possible for home and work-place to be many miles apart. (Still four out of five commuters spend less than half an hour getting to work.) Regional shopping centers, which have mushroomed in the last two decades, make it unnecessary for suburbanites to "go downtown," and decentralized industries and businesses have brought more and more jobs to the suburbs.

Specialization refers to the clustering of particular types of institutions and activities in "bright lights" districts, wholesale areas, civic and "cultural" centers, financial districts, planned industrial areas, and professional or office buildings. Routinization is the regular movement of people from home to work, and of goods from point of origin to point of use, in patterns that recur daily, weekly, seasonally, or even annually.[14]

Of special interest to sociologists are the processes by which "birds of a feather flock together"—segregation, invasion, and succession. **Segregation** is sometimes used synonymously with specialization to refer to functions of different areas. More often we think of it as the drawing together of similar types of people. Whether they want to because of similar background or are compelled to by prejudice and poverty, individuals tend to gravitate to areas where they can compete most effectively and where others of similar race, culture, economic status, and point of view dwell. The "ghetto" (once the Jewish immigrant neighborhood, now largely black), Little Italy, Chinatown, "Nob Hill," the "Main Line," and the "wrong side of the tracks"—known by different names in different cities—are all results of segregation.

The clusters of similar people, institutions, and interests resulting from segregation and specialization are called **natural areas** because they are the spontaneous, unplanned results of social and economic forces. Each natural area is somewhat of a unit, with a relatively homogeneous population, perhaps its own peculiar traditions, customs, conventions, standards of decency and propriety, and often a language of its own. Each large city has its hobohemia, its Bowery or Skid Row, its Greenwich Village or Latin Quarter, where flock the unconventional or eccentric; its cultural and racial colonies; its ultra-smart residential area; and its dingy world of furnished rooms.

But these areas are not static. Areas change through the process of **invasion**, the penetration of a segregated area by an institutional function or population group different from the one already there. In a rapidly growing city, the commercial and industrial districts invade residential areas. One racial or cultural group invades an area occupied by another, or an economically inferior but otherwise similar group may invade an upper-class area, as in the rooming-house districts that once were rows of dignified brick and brownstone residences. Invasion may be resisted, even to the extent of mob behavior. In other cases, invasion is successful and rapid, as in Harlem in the 1920s. When an invasion is successful and the new type of institution or population is established in the area, we say **succession** has taken place. One section of Chicago was successively inhabited by Czechs, Jews, Italians, and blacks.

The way buildings, people, and activities are sorted out into areas and patterns in our society is, because of our cultural aversion to planning, largely haphazard—the result of many uncoordinated decisions. One very important decision reflects the power, physical and political, of the automobile. The Interstate Highway System, the largest

[14]Breese, *Urbanization in Newly Developing Countries*, p. 114. Breese points out that specialization is greatest in Western cities; elsewhere there is more mixing of various land uses.

488 SOCIAL AND CULTURAL CHANGE

public works project in modern history, was originally intended to serve interstate traffic and connect the most densely settled areas of the country. Like the Aswan Dam, this project has had unforeseen and largely undesired consequences:

> . . . the Interstate Highway System has diverted traffic from other surface modes of transportation, dumped car traffic into unprepared central cities, caused the building of 5,600 miles of urban freeways, spurred the suburban migration of business and shopping, taken freeway land off central city tax rolls, created windfall gains for suburban landholders near intersections, and through the trust fund financing has allowed auto transport to feed on itself by piling up capital restricted only to further highway building. The result is that in many cities people must rely on personal transportation to get to work. Yet by 1960 House and Senate District Committees in Washington concluded: "Any attempt to meet the area's transportation needs by highway and private automobiles alone will wreck the city."
>
> The Interstate Highway System was a primary policy decision of Congress which literally has changed the urban structure of the entire nation and has resulted in [many] of the present problems of cities.[15]

As industry moves to the suburbs, the number of blue-collar jobs in the inner city declines. Housing in the suburbs is scarce and expensive; public transportation from city to suburb poor. Welfare rolls in the cities grow. In spite of the fact that the poor spend proportionately more on rent than those with higher incomes, a large number of slumlords abandon their properties every year—first psychologically, then fiscally, and finally physically. There are over 100,000 burned-out, desolate, abandoned buildings in New York City, and 25,000 in Philadelphia; many were built for the immigrants of 75 to 100 years ago.

While we cannot blame the decay of inner cities on the highway system alone, we can with some justification point to the lack of planning. Had highway advocates considered the long-range effect of their project on the economy and social structure of the cities they sought to connect, they might have proceeded differently—devoting some of their funds to mass transit and urban renewal.

Urbanism as a Way of Life

Still concentrating mainly on cities in Western industrial countries, and especially the United States, we turn now from where people live to how they live. Is there something inherent in the settlement patterns

[15]Carl H. Madden, "The Cost of a Livable Environment," AIA Journal (May 1971): 26–30.

of cities and their various areas that produces a distinctive "urban way of life"?

WIRTH'S THESIS

Writing in the 1930s, Louis Wirth answered in the affirmative.[16] He began by postulating that "the larger, the more densely populated, and the more heterogeneous a community, the more accentuated the characteristics associated with urbanism will be."

These characteristics are essentially those we outlined in discussing modern industrial society. Wirth saw heterogeneity as a natural result of numbers and density, which produce cultural and occupational specialization in the city just as they lead to differentiation among flora and fauna. Ecological processes produce a "mosaic of social worlds in which the transition from one to another is abrupt." Being highly specialized, city-dwellers are also extremely *inter*dependent; they are less dependent than rural people on particular persons, but more dependent on numerous people in specialized roles. They know one another not as whole persons, but in these fragmented roles; in other words, secondary relationships predominate over primary ones. In the crowded city, thus, "our physical contacts are close but our social contacts are distant. The urban world puts a premium on visual recognition. We see the uniform which denotes the role of the functionaries and are oblivious to the personal eccentricities that are hidden behind the uniform."

Living and working so close together without sentimental or emotional ties fosters in city-dwellers "a spirit of competition, aggrandizement, and mutual exploitation." People are connected by financial interest; virtually no human need remains unexploited. Tradition and primary relationships are not sufficient social controls; the city relies on formal controls—symbolized by the clock and the traffic signal— to prevent disorder. The individual feels powerless; to get anything done, he must join various groups, each of which involves only a segment of his personality. There is an "enormous multiplication of voluntary organizations directed toward as great a variety of objectives as there are human needs and interests." But turnover is rapid in these groups and no single one has his undivided allegiance; he is rarely even a true neighbor. He has little opportunity to conceive of the city as a whole or to comprehend his place in the total scheme.

As a result of all these factors, the city-dweller develops characteristic personality traits and attitudes. Seeing so many different modes of life and kinds of people living elbow to elbow, he tends to adopt a relativistic perspective, to become secularized. Reserve and in-

[16]"Urbanism as a Way of Life," *American Journal of Sociology* 44 (July 1938): 3–24; reprinted in Fava, *Urbanism in World Perspective*, pp. 46–53. All citations in this section refer to this article.

difference immunize him against the personal claims and expectations of others. Free of intimate ties, he also lacks a strong sense of integration or participation: The city is characterized by anomie. In the midst of crowds, he tends to feel lonely, to sense friction and irritation, personal frustration and nervous tension, "accentuated by the rapid tempo and the complicated technology under which life in dense areas must be lived." Because of the mobility and diversity in the city, he tends to accept instability and insecurity in the world at large as a norm, and to be sophisticated and cosmopolitan. But because he spreads his allegiance thin and acts in segmental roles, his personal integrity is constantly threatened, and he is vulnerable to manipulation through the mass media.

For all these reasons, said Wirth, we can expect the incidence of "personal disorganization, mental breakdown, suicide, delinquency, crime, corruption, and disorder" to be higher in cities than in rural communities; and indices confirm this hypothesis.

As Wirth himself recognized, his thinking was probably both time-bound and culture-bound. The cities he saw in the 1930s were shaped by the task of assimilating immigrants, the recency of the shift from rural to urban living, and the Depression. Wirth saw that "the direction of the ongoing changes in urbanism will for good or ill transform not only the city but the world," and urged others to test and revise his theories through further analysis and empirical research.

URBANISM AS MANY WAYS OF LIFE

Taking up Wirth's challenge, other sociologists have begun to feel that size, heterogeneity, and density have different meanings in the modern metropolis, in such stable non-Western pre-industrial cities as those of the Yoruba in Africa, and in the exploding cities of underdeveloped nations. Wirth's thesis applies particularly to the American industrial city, and especially to what we call the inner city; we cannot apply it to the entire urban area.

First we must distinguish the main urban areas. The "inner city" refers to slums that typically surround the central business district of American industrial cities. The outer city includes stable residential areas of working-class and middle-class people. The suburbs are "the latest and most modern ring of the outer city, distinguished from it only by yet lower densities, and by the often irrelevant fact of the ring's location outside the city limits."[17]

In today's highly affluent, mobile society, says Herbert Gans,

[17]Herbert J. Gans, "Urbanism and Suburbanism as Ways of Life: A Re-evaluation of Definitions," in Arnold Rose, ed., *Human Behavior and Social Processes* (Boston: Houghton Mifflin Company, 1962), pp. 625–48; reprinted in Fava, *Urbanism in World Perspective*, pp. 63–81.

residential location has less impact on social life than do other factors such as social class and the stage of the life cycle in which the residents of a given area find themselves. There is not yet enough evidence to prove or disprove that number, density, and heterogeneity have the social consequences Wirth saw. Furthermore, even if a causal connection could be demonstrated by empirical research, many city-dwellers are protected against these consequences by "social structures and cultural patterns which they either brought to the city, or developed by living in it."[18]

It is true, says Gans, that many people in the inner city fit Wirth's picture of isolated individuals torn from accustomed social moorings and unable to develop new ones, and therefore prey to social anarchy. But many do not. "Economic condition, cultural characteristics, life-cycle stages, and residential instability explain ways of life more satisfactorily than number, density, or heterogeneity." Five main types of people live in the inner city: (1) Cosmopolites such as students, artists, writers, musicians, entertainers, and other intellectuals and professionals, who *choose* to live there because they want to be near "cultural" facilities. (2) Unmarried people and childless couples who may move later, but meanwhile prefer to be near the heart of things. (3) "Ethnic villagers" who live much as they did in the peasant villages of Europe, Mexico, or Puerto Rico, with strong kinship and other primary group ties, weak ties to formal organizations, and suspicion of everything and everyone outside their neighborhood. They live in the inner city partly by choice, partly from necessity. (4) The deprived, who have no choice, including the very poor, the emotionally disturbed or otherwise handicapped, broken families, and many nonwhites. (5) The trapped and downwardly mobile who cannot afford to move despite invasion by groups they may be prejudiced against; often these are old people on small pensions.

In spite of crowding, these groups are isolated from one another. Cosmopolites feel detached because of their subculture, the unmarried and childless because they plan to move on; neither are particularly interested in the welfare of the other residents of the inner city. The deprived and trapped clearly suffer the undesirable consequences of city living as Wirth saw them; but Gans believes they result from residential instability rather than sheer numbers, density, or heterogeneity.

Despite various myths about suburbia, Gans does not see very much difference between the outer city and the suburbs. In both, fairly homogeneous neighborhoods, made up largely of families in the child-raising years, develop. In the outer city people become segregated into distinct neighborhoods on the basis of "place and nature of work, income, racial and ethnic characteristics, social status, custom, habit, taste,

[18]*Ibid.*

Drawing by W. Miller; © 1971
The New Yorker Magazine, Inc.

"Good morning, Cross Bronx Expressway."

preference, and prejudice"[19]—a process Wirth believed applied to the city as a whole. Gans sees the outer city not as anonymous and impersonal but as "quasi-primary" by virtue of its separation into fairly homogeneous neighborhoods. An Italian or Polish working-class neighborhood, for example, is very much like a small town. It tends to break up, says one social anthropologist, when residents become upwardly mobile—a greater change than a simple transition from a rural setting to this type of urban neighborhood.[20]

Gans' studies of suburbia led him to question many popular images. It is often assumed that the move from city to suburb plunges one into a new way of life that changes behavior and personality, imposes conformity and other-direction, and "is socially, culturally, and emotionally destructive."[21] He lived as a participant-observer in Levittown, New Jersey, for the first two years of its existence, "to find out

[19]Wirth, "Urbanism as a Way of Life."

[20]Joel M. Halpern, *The Changing Village Community* (Englewood Cliffs, N.J.: Prentice-Hall, Inc., 1967), p. 39.

[21]Gans, *The Levittowners: Ways of Life and Politics in a New Suburban Community* (New York: Pantheon Books, 1967), p. 153.

how a new community comes into being, how people change when they leave the city, and how they live and politic in suburbia."[22] Like outer-city neighborhoods, suburban neighborhoods exhibit a quasi-primary way of life; but this is not due to peculiarly suburban pressures for conformity and sociability. The new suburbanites came, he found, to seek compatible neighbors, and they engage in more "neighboring" than formerly because they are similar, and friendly. They need one another; the first criterion of a good neighbor is readiness to provide mutual aid. Residential location does have consequences for roles and relationships; but people do not *live* in cities, small towns, or suburbs, but rather in small areas, such as blocks. Some features of the quasi-primary way of life in both outer city and suburb, therefore, evolve from the fact that families in their child-rearing years happen to occupy adjacent dwellings.

But are suburbanites, as some charge, so homogeneous and conformist that they cannot be autonomous individuals or share deep relationships? Gans believes they rarely conform passively or bow to pressure. They conform when they think it does not really matter or threaten their individuality, but will make for friendly relations and perhaps allow them to share useful ideas. "Indeed, given the random way in which Levittowners become neighbors, it is amazing that neighbor relations were so friendly and tolerant of individual differences."[23]

Like Wirth, he suggests the need for further research based on the hypothesis that the greater the freedom of choice as to place of residence, the more important such characteristics as class and stage in the life cycle are in understanding behavior. After discovering these characteristics and holding them constant, then the sociologist can go on to find out what aspects of culture, social organization, and personality may be attributable to the settlement pattern itself.

The City in Newly Developing Countries

Thus far we have been concerned almost exclusively with American cities, with some side glances at the classic cities of Europe, where people have evolved a truly urbane way of life over the centuries. What of cities in newly developing countries? How is urbanization in these countries related to industrialization? What ecological patterns do their cities assume? What does empirical observation in such cities demonstrate about urbanism as a way of life?

THE GROWTH OF CITIES

The acceleration of the urban trend in recent decades has been most startling in the Third World. While the *proportion* of the popula-

[22]*Ibid.*, p. v.
[23]*Ibid.*, p. 180.

tion living in cities is low in many underdeveloped countries, their populations are so enormous that they have millions of city-dwellers. Some are overurbanized: Because industrialization lags far behind urbanization, millions of migrants from rural areas are unemployed or underemployed, and the high urban birth rate swells the potential labor force.

In India and China, as we saw, only about 8% of the population lives in cities of 100,000 or more. Yet because of their huge populations, about 35% of all the people in the world in such large cities are Asians, and it is very likely that by 1975 Asians will constitute nearly half of such city-dwellers. Between 1900 and 1950, Asia experienced a gain of 444% in the proportion living in large cities; Africa, 629%. United Nations experts predict that by the end of the 1970s the poor countries of Asia, Africa, and Latin America will have 360 cities of at least half a million; Bombay and Calcutta may reach 20 or 30 million each. U Thant has called them "exploding cities in unexploding economies."

While the population of Latin America grows about 3% a year, its urban population grows between 5 and 7% a year. From 1955 to 1970 its urban population increased by 50%, and some predict that it will double between 1970 and 1985, adding 100 million city-dwellers. Latin America is now about half urban; by 1980 it may be 60 to 65% urban. Mexico City adds 350,000 people a year; if this rate continues, the 1970 population of 8 million would double in 20 years. São Paulo, Brazil, had 800,000 people in 1940 and expects 13 million by 1990.[24]

Many of the large cities in developing countries, particularly in Latin America, are "primate cities," overwhelmingly larger than the next largest cities, and overwhelmingly dominant. Most national functions are concentrated in these cities. They are the centers of political and economic power, of administration and commerce, the chief point of contact with the outside world. Such cities tend to be parasitic, exploiting a backward countryside rather than promoting development; many are located for import and export rather than for industry. They attract foreign political representatives, travelers, and tradesmen, and often erect imposing public structures to impress visitors. They serve as diffusion points for social change, and are a magnet for rural migrants, with or without marketable skills and talents.[25]

URBAN ECOLOGY IN THE THIRD WORLD

The pattern of urban settlement in most newly developing countries is very different from that of an American industrial city.

[24]James Nelson Goodsell, "Latin Americans Flock to Cities," *Christian Science Monitor* (Dec. 31, 1970).

[25]Irving Louis Horowitz, *Three Worlds of Development: The Theory and Practice of International Stratification* (New York: Oxford University Press, 1966), pp. 34–35; and Breese, *Urbanization in Newly Developing Countries*, pp. 40–43.

"Just as modern metropolitanism seems to represent *a social and economic community composed of many politically defined cities*, the form of urbanism on view in backward areas (and even in some Western cities) may consist of *politically defined cities composed of many social and economic communities*."[26] And where many American metropolitan areas include a decaying central city, largely black, surrounded by more affluent, largely white suburbs, the picture of a burgeoning Latin American or Asian city is often that of an older established commercial–administrative city surrounded by a densely settled ring of shanty towns. There is also usually a "Western" area including suburbs, new central business district developments, and possibly new planned industrial districts.[27]

Because industrialization lags so far behind urbanization in many of these countries, the squatter areas on the city's fringe are miserably poor. Large families crowd into tiny shacks, often made of scraps of tin cans, old gasoline drums, tar paper, cartons, sheets of zinc, and palm or cane thatch. According to the Organization of American States, half of Latin America's city-dwellers live *below* subsistence level. Besides living in these shanty towns—the aptly named *Villas Miseria* of Buenos Aires, the mud huts in which a third of Lima's people live, the "bustees" of Indian cities—squatters also occupy vacant spaces within the cities, even in swamps and sewers. They carry on many of their activities, often marginal economic services such as shoe shining or barbering, on the street. In Calcutta—one of the largest cities in the world—300,000 people have nowhere to *sleep* but the street.

URBAN WAYS OF LIFE IN NEWLY DEVELOPING COUNTRIES

The thesis that size, density, and heterogeneity result in a distinct urban way of life has been tested in both long-established traditional cities and newly exploding cities of the Third World.

Yoruba cities.   The Yoruba of Western Nigeria have traditionally lived in large, densely settled cities, a fact that "cannot be explained in terms of industrialization, acculturation, or the development of colonial administrative headquarters, ports, and mining centers [but] existed . . . before the first penetration of their area by Europeans."[28] The cities were centers of trade and warfare, and some were political capitals. Farming, specialized crafts, and trade were the bases of their economy;

[26]Leo F. Schnore and Eric E. Lampard, "Social Science and the City: A Survey of Research Needs," in Leo F. Schnore, ed., *Social Science and the City: A Survey of Urban Research* (New York: Frederick A. Praeger, 1968), p. 30.

[27]Breese, *Urbanization in Newly Developing Countries*, p. 116.

[28]William Bascom, "The Urban African and His World," in Fava, *Urbanism in World Perspective*, pp. 81–93; reprinted from *Cahiers D'Etudes Africaines* (1963).

they had money, large markets, and middlemen. Although not an industrialized people, Yoruba city-dwellers were interdependent. But they
were ethnically homogeneous; their heterogeneity was limited to craft
specialization, social stratification, and socio-political segmentation into
wards, political precincts, and tribal lineages. Because of the market
economy, many contacts were secondary. Yoruba city-dwellers ridiculed
the unsophisticated "bush" dwellers. The anomie Wirth suggested as
part of the urban way of life does not exist among the established urbanites of the Yoruba; rather, it is apparent as a form of culture shock
among recent migrants.

Heterogeneity, then, is not essential to the definition of a city.
William Bascom suggests that cities should be defined strictly in terms
of demographic factors (size, density, and permanence) in order to facilitate cross-cultural studies. He suggests that cultural and social factors
such as acculturation, Europeanization, detribalization, cosmopolitanism, and other types of social heterogeneity, the economic or technological factors of specialization and industrialization, and political factors
such as city government should each be considered separately to determine whether they are necessary to city growth or are the results of
urban life, and whether they pertain to all cities.

Exploding cities.   In cities that attract thousands of migrants a
year, ways of life differ enormously in the various areas. In the old
cities and Western areas, traditional upper- and middle-class life styles
exist side by side with Western ways, and often mingle. Many squatters, however, are in the city but not of it. They identify more closely
with their native villages or with such socio-cultural groupings as caste,
tribe, race, or religion than with the city.[29] Exploding population has
pushed them off the land; inheritance has fragmented holdings; mechanization has made it more economical to consolidate farms and dismiss laborers; perhaps the government has collectivized or expropriated
their land; they may be refugees of international conflict. The push of
hardship and the pull of urban possibilities (jobs, welfare, schools, freedom) combine to bring them to the city. Perhaps they already have relatives or fellow villagers there. But there is little or no employment for
them, not only because economic development lags but also because
they lack the skills, and sometimes even the language, for competing
in the city, and they may be unused to a cash economy. They have the
bare necessities for survival, and often not even those. Their culture is
primarily a culture of poverty rather than a distinctively urban way of
life.[30]

Halpern refers to this phenomenon as the "peasantization of
the cities." In Yugoslavian cities, rural migrants build new houses iden-

[29]Noel G. Gist, "Urbanism in India," in Fava, *Urbanism in World Perspective*, pp.
22–32.

[30]See Chapter 9, pp. 250–251.

tical to those they left behind, with a garden, a chicken coop, and, de-spite city ordinances, a pig or two. For at least a couple of generations, they retain ties to their villages. If they live in modern apartment build-ings, they create maintenance problems, being unfamiliar with plumb-ing and central heating.[31] Like immigrants from other countries to the United States, rural migrants the world over often suffer discrimination and ridicule. They, much more than the established residents, feel the stress of urban anomie. Rural migrants to Helsinki, for example, were found to have more personality problems than either natives of Helsinki or the rural population. In Poland, recent migrants showed slackening social control and poor work morale. "Hillbillies" in Chicago, similarly, had high rates of absenteeism, worked at their own pace, and had differ-ent mores and sanitation customs from older Chicagoans.[32]

The shock of the change to urban living, however, may be cushioned by communities within the city. In Mexico, for example, one finds an urban peasantry even in the capital city of 8 million people. The family structure, diet, dress, and religious and other belief sys-tems of those who have lived there 30 years or more are the same as those of recent arrivals from the same village. Living together in neigh-borhoods or *vecindades*, each one centered on a common courtyard, they are villagers in metropolis.

Rural Life in an Urbanizing World

The urban revolution we have been describing began on the farm, and its brushfire speed is due in large part to the application of technology to agriculture.

> To understand how food supply has changed from primitive times to the present is to recognize that when man depended upon hunting it required eight square miles to support one person. When he combined hunting with foraging, the area required to support one person was reduced from eight to one square mile. The development of the use of the hoe to cultivate land made it possible for one square mile to support three people, and the tremendous advance associated with the use of the plow made it possible for 750 people to be supported on one square mile of land surface. Modern agriculture, with its use of power, makes it possible, on the average, for one square mile to support 2000 people.[33]

This rural revolution is especially advanced in the United States. In 1920 nearly 32 million people, about 30% of the population, lived

[31]Halpern, *The Changing Village Community*, pp. 34–35.

[32]Gist and Fava, *Urban Society*, pp. 466–68.

[33]J. A. Shellenberger, "The 'Green Revolution' Revisited," *Current* (Sept. 1969): 37–41.

on 6.5 million farms, averaging 147 acres. In 1950, 23 million people, 15.3%, lived on 5.6 million farms, averaging 213 acres. The decline of the next two decades was even more dramatic, as cities burgeoned and agriculture became ever more commercialized. By 1970, only about 10 million people, or 5% of the population, lived on fewer than 3 million farms, averaging 387 acres. But not all those living on farms work in farming. The agricultural labor force, which includes unpaid family members who work at least 15 hours a week, numbered nearly 10 million in 1950; by 1970 only a little over 3.5 million, or 4.5% of the labor force, were farm workers.

The traditional American farm is still a one-family enterprise; two out of three farms are "small, part-time, residential, or hobby farms." But the other 1 million farms produce nearly all of the farm products marketed.[34] Dairy farms in the "milk sheds" of large cities, assembly-line chicken farms, huge specialized fruit and vegetable farms with acres upon acres of strawberries, or lettuce, or onions, or potatoes —these are "agri-businesses," factories without chimneys. Where the average farm worker supported twelve people in 1940, he now supports fifty-one.[35] This means a huge investment in equipment, fertilizer, and other supplies. Similar trends occur in other heavily industrialized countries. As Japan's economy boomed in the 1960s, the proportion of agricultural workers declined from 31 to 16.3% of the labor force.

But modern agricultural technology has not reached much of the world, and about 60% of the world's workers are still in agriculture.[36] According to Community Development experts in the United Nations, there are from 3 to 5 million rural communities, ranging from nomadic tribes to densely settled agricultural villages of several thousand. About 80% of the populations of the less developed countries live in such communities. Productivity remains low. In Peru nearly a third of farm units are cultivated without even the aid of draft animals; in upland Guatemala, there is one animal-drawn plow per 1000 farms. Few countries have achieved even a fifth of American productivity; in India, output per farm worker is a *fiftieth* that of the United States.[37] Although two out of three Chinese work on farms, they produce less than a third of the national product.[38]

Yet, as we have seen, the urban trend appears to be inexorable and irreversible. What does this mean for traditional rural life? "It is possible," says Joel Halpern, "to conceive of the export of trained tech-

[34]John A. Schnittker, "The Farmer in the Till," *The Atlantic* (Aug. 1969); reprinted in *Current* (Sept. 1969): 32–37.

[35]Earl L. Butz, Secretary of Agriculture, "The Farmer as the Good Guy," *The New York Times* (April 15, 1972): L 31. The figure in 1951 was 16; in 1960, 28.

[36]*The New York Times* (Dec. 22, 1970).

[37]Yujiro Hayami and V. W. Ruttan, "Agricultural Productivity Differences Among Countries," *The American Economic Review* (Dec. 1970).

[38]W. Klatt, "A Review of China's Economy in 1970," *The China Quarterly* (July–Sept. 1970): 115.

Hoe agriculture in the South Pacific.

nicians, skills, and products to the villages and the incorporation of rural people into town life as resulting in the simultaneous peasantization of the cities and the urbanization of villages. . . . In the process cities are modified but rural society is transformed."[39]

This modification and transformation mean, first of all, the elimination of great differences between rural and urban modes of life. It is during the height of the transition from rural to urban living that people are most conscious of these differences. In the late 1800s and

[39]*The Changing Village Community*, pp. 2, 125.

A modern agri-business.

early 1900s in the United States, for example, rural–urban political conflicts were intense, and people thought in terms of such stereotypes as "rubes" or "hayseeds" and "city slickers." Now the boundary between rural and urban is diffuse and unclear—socially, culturally, and geographically. Many people of many kinds live on urban fringes classified as rural areas; there are upper-class and working-class suburban fringes, magnificent estates next to shacks, country clubs near garbage dumps and farms. "In short, the fringe is a complex labyrinth of human relations, ideologies, and patterns of land use."[40]

Aside from this blurring of distinctions, farmers are increasingly like city-dwellers. The farmer listens to stock market reports before he sells his wheat; his wife buys store bread and prepared cereals. His children see the same movies, watch the same TV shows, buy the same records, wear the same kind of clothes, read the same comics, magazines, and schoolbooks as their city cousins. His wife uses the same appliances and furnishings as the urban housewife, and shops at the same kind of shopping center.

In many countries, however, distinctions are still sharp, and strains created by the transition are readily apparent. The older generation may cling to traditional ways, while the young look down on agriculture as a low-status occupation. "How are you going to keep them down on the farm?" In the Soviet Union, a wide gap between rural and urban ways of living persists; recreation, schooling, communications, and consumer goods are all vastly inferior in rural areas. Some collective farms have tried to stem the exodus of youth to cities by establishing a ritual inducting youths into formal membership at age sixteen, and even having them swear an oath of allegiance, hoping that this will instill a sense of loyalty.[41] China is trying to integrate the cities and the countryside by emphasizing rural industrial development and urging city-based factories to engage in agriculture.[42]

The transition to commercial agriculture means that thousands, even millions, of "displaced persons" must somehow be taken care of. During the earliest stages of English modernization, between the thirteenth and sixteenth centuries, agriculture was transformed from subsistence to commercial farming. The Black Death (bubonic plague) contributed to this change by killing about a quarter of the population of Europe in the fourteenth century, including from 30 to 50% of the peasants in England. Prices of agricultural products fell because of the sudden drop in population. Because prices were low and labor scarce, landowners looked for new ways to use the land.

One of these uses was sheep-farming. The weavers of Flanders

---

[40]Lee Taylor and Arthur R. Jones, Jr., *Rural Life and Urbanized Society* (New York: Oxford University Press, 1964), p. 107.

[41]*The New York Times* (Jan. 15, 1969).

[42]*China! Inside the People's Republic*, by the Committee of Concerned Asian Scholars (New York: Bantam Books, 1972), p. 106.

needed wool; their old sources of supply on the continent of Europe were cut off by the ravages of long-drawn-out religious wars and the wolves that prowled the desolate countryside. English landowners therefore enclosed untilled land, waste land, and the commons on which the peasants had for centuries been allowed to graze their livestock. They stocked some of the enclosed land with sheep and, as they prospered, were able to experiment with new and improved agricultural techniques. The poorer peasants suffered from the enclosures, having no place to graze their livestock, and many of them fled to town. There they constituted a labor pool upon which the new factory-owners could draw.

The same process is occurring in underdeveloped lands, but its problems are aggravated by the population explosion. The "Green Revolution," which improves agricultural yields with better seeds, fertilizers, insecticides, and machinery, displaces subsistence farmers and many laborers. As Pakistani landowners buy tractors, they dismiss their tenant farmers, who farmed perhaps 10 acres with hoes and bullock-drawn plows. It has been estimated that mechanization reduces labor requirements from about eight persons per 100 acres to four; with each worker supporting a family of five, about 4 million will be displaced by 1985 if mechanization continues. And government policy aids those who buy tractors rather than those who are displaced by them; it supports wheat prices and keeps taxes low.[43] Like black farm workers displaced by cotton picking machines, like Brazilians who see more hope in the miserable *favelas* clinging to Rio's hillsides than a plot of land in the country, they may find no jobs in the city. The cards may be stacked against them because they have less schooling, different customs, and perhaps are of a different racial background than the city-dwellers. But their individual characteristics are not as crucial to their assimilation as the features of social organization that facilitate or impede their urbanization in the social sense. The city's "gatekeepers," official and unofficial—social workers, hospital and clinic personnel, landlords, police and court officials, even storekeepers and bartenders—have decision-making and counseling power that either furthers or thwarts integration into the community.[44]

In most cases these migrants "can't go home again," physically or psychologically. The "old homestead" is disappearing in all highly mobile industrializing societies. The once autonomous rural village has lost much of its social and cultural integrity; even for those who remain, "the local standards set by family, neighborhood, and community become less meaningful in terms of potential reward, and they lack the

[43]"Pakistani Landless and Jobless Increased by Green Revolution," *The New York Times* (Nov. 1, 1970).

[44]Lyle W. Shannon and Magdaline Shannon, "The Assimilation of Migrants to Cities: Anthropological and Sociological Contributions," in Schnore, *Social Science and the City*, pp. 49–75.

coercive power they once had."[45] When farmers need tractors, gasoline, fertilizers, schools, and hospitals, they are tied to the larger society as peasants are not; the nation-state demands their loyalty if it is to bring them modern facilities.

Many of us, perhaps, tend to romanticize farming as a way of life, just as we mourn the mythical "noble savage." In many ways it was not at all idyllic; it was often very difficult and constricting, as reflected in the Spanish saying that "A small village is a great hell," where everyone knows everyone else's business. "But it was a way of life, and it was cherished by most of those who knew it. . . . It is striking to see how much public and private effort is put into the promotion of change and how little into constructive channeling of the sweeping effects of change. The disappearance of the rural way of life was actually a painful expulsion of a part of society out the back door, not only because abandonment of farms was and is not the choice of most rural people but also because there are no [or few] programs to rectify economic hardship or to assist in occupational and social readjustment."[46]

The Future of Cities

Touting his automobile, which had so much to do with creating the modern city, Henry Ford once said, "We shall solve the city problem by leaving the city." Sociologist C. Wright Mills asked, "What should be done with this wonderful monstrosity? Break it all up into scattered units, combining residence and work? Refurbish it as it stands? Or, after evacuation, dynamite it?"[47]

ARE CITIES OBSOLETE?

Some predict that the city as we know it will die because it is no longer necessary. Futurist Arthur Clarke, who wrote the science-fiction film "2001: A Space Odyssey," says that by the end of the 1970s, thanks to advances in electronic communications, executives will have in their homes a general-purpose communications console comprising a TV screen, a TV camera, a microphone, a computer keyboard and readout device, and will be able to get in touch with anyone who has a similar system. They will not have to travel on business; they will communicate rather than commute. After 10,000 years the agricultural age is coming to a close, and much land can revert to wilderness, to dwell-

[45]Halpern, *The Changing Village Community*, p. 124.

[46]Kenneth R. Schneider, *Destiny of Change: How Relevant Is Man in the Age of Development?* (New York: Holt, Rinehart & Winston, Inc., 1968), p. 31.

[47]"The Big City: Private Troubles and Public Issues," in Irving Louis Horowitz, ed., *Power, Politics, and People* (New York: Oxford University Press, 1963), p. 395.

Tapiola, a suburb of Helsinki, Finland.

ings with far more space around them, and to recreation. It is already very easy to decentralize industry, but the central business district is, under the present system, necessary for administrative offices. Peter Hall sees the growth of white-collar occupations of all kinds as the most important single explanation for the growth of world cities since 1850. If we grant this premise, new means of handling white-collar and executive work will eliminate the need for the central business district.[48]

Those who identify cities with civilization, however, insist that we need them. Although we can dispense with the city in a technical sense, still many believe it is one of the world's finest inventions and has always represented the best of civilization.[49] Economist Carl Madden believes that our system of metropolitan communities represents enormous economies of organization developed over three and a half centuries, and "the centering of government, intellectual and artistic leadership, business and industry, communications, finance, health care and the rest in cities remains the subtle but profound economy and spur to achievement borne out by the whole history of civilization. People who have in recent decades been voting with their feet to escape the city can only run so far. And the bulk of the country's physical assets now domiciled in cities cannot be allowed to rot in discard. . . . The duplication of utilities that suburbanizing the whole population would involve comes only at astronomical real cost."[50]

What new forms might we envision for cities, and how can we achieve them? Some planned cities actually exist; others are still on paper. The Scandinavian countries exhibited unusual foresight, buying up large tracts of open land decades ago. Stockholm has extended its subway system to four or five satellite cities. Helsinki's suburb of Tapiola is half park, and has a density of only twenty-eight people per acre. It was built by the Finnish Housing Foundation, a nonprofit organization founded by the Family Welfare League and five other asso-

[48]*The World Cities*, p. 27.

[49]James Michener, *The Quality of Life* (Greenwich, Conn.: Fawcett Publications, 1970), p. 22.

[50]"The Cost of a Livable Environment."

ciations. Its directors had to supervise construction engineers, who, like their counterparts elsewhere, find it easier to bulldoze trees than to work around them. Tapiola includes different kinds of dwellings at different prices, some industry, easy access to recreational and cultural facilities, and proximity to a freeway that takes residents to the capital in 20 minutes.

Columbia, Maryland, covers 22 square miles and includes eight villages with a wide price range in housing. Each village has four to six residential neighborhoods and a downtown area. Hundreds of acres of open land remain, to be kept inviolate for relief from the city.

Urban planners advocate everything from great dispersion of dwellings and facilities to their concentration in several levels; one even goes so far as to put his envisioned multilevel city under a dome to protect it from the elements.[51] Athelstan Spilhaus stresses the need for "more human services if we are to remain human . . . When we talk about building a city, we think too much of the housing and often too little of the services to the people. . . . I dream of cities where the dwelling units are simple and adequate, but the services in education, sanitation, health, recreation, art, music, and all other forms of culture are systematized and magnificent. . . . Such cities must be large enough to afford social and intellectual variety, yet not so large that people cannot also see nature and regain individuality in open country."[52]

Not all cities need conform to the same pattern or fulfill the same functions. We might have cities that are primarily for ceremonial public celebrations and rituals, university cities, scientific cities for research and development, festival or arts cities such as Salzburg and Venice, recreational cities like Las Vegas, convention and conference cities, communications cities, museum cities such as Florence, Athens, and Williamsburg, and industrial and political and commercial cities such as now dominate our urban culture. We might even have cities that are strictly experimental, for trying out new life styles and patterns of social relationships.[53]

Meanwhile, how can we live with cities as they are now and as they seem destined to become in the foreseeable future? In the underdeveloped nations, the enormous problems of the population explosion and the need for economic development are inseparable from any successful solution to the problem of the millions of migrants living at or below subsistence level. In many European nations, long-range plans for "new towns" and reconstruction or preservation of existing ones are administered by the central government. In the United States, the "urban crisis" threatens to get much worse before it is resolved, for

[51]Paolo Solari, who calls his idea "arcology."

[52]A. F. Spilhaus, "One Man's Vision of the City of Tomorrow," *The New York Times* (Jan 6, 1969).

[53]Athelstan Spilhaus, "The Experimental City," *Daedalus* (Fall 1967); reprinted in *Current* (Jan. 1968).

several reasons: the race problem, our transportation system and policy, the political fragmentation of metropolitan areas, and above all our attitudes and values toward planning and toward cities themselves.

In the sixty-five metropolitan areas with more than 500,000 people, blacks form an increasingly large percentage of the central cities as whites move to the suburbs. In 1969 only about one white family in four lived in central cities of metropolitan areas, while more than half the nation's black families lived in such areas. In 1960 Washington, D.C. was the only city with a black majority; since then Newark, Gary, and Atlanta have also shifted to black majorities. Seven other central cities are more than 40% black—Baltimore, New Orleans, Detroit, Wilmington, Birmingham, Richmond, and St. Louis. Being generally poorer than whites, the black populations provide a smaller tax base for city government, and present more problems of welfare and social disorganization.

The area of city government is a conspicuous example of a cultural lag, in which antiquated arrangements persist in the face of obvious needs for change. Overlapping jurisdictions are headed by people jealous of their power and vested interests. The whites who flee to the suburbs do not want regional government (that is, one government for the entire metropolitan region); neither do blacks gaining political power for the first time. As a result we have such phenomena as Greater Chicago, with 1113 different and often competing local authorities; the Philadelphia metropolitan area, with 876 separate municipal governments; and Detroit, with 88 cities, 43 townships, and 3 counties.

The Minneapolis–St. Paul metropolitan area is a pioneer in regional government. In 1967 the state legislature created the Metropolitan Council, to coordinate the overall social, physical, and economic development of a 300-square-mile area with 320 separate but overlapping governmental units. It has taxing power and is in charge of such things as environment and growth patterns, leaving such institutions as schools and social services to decentralized power.

Our cultural aversion to planning, however, means that such experiments are unusual. We have preferred piecemeal renovation and "urban renewal," adding a highway or office building here, clearing slums there, lengthening subway systems. Often elderly people on pensions and disadvantaged minorities are removed from their homes with no provision for new ones; one plan in San Francisco, for example, called for the destruction of 4000 housing units, and the construction of less than 300 in the same area. High-rise housing projects for low-income groups or welfare families are other examples of bad planning, with disastrous unforeseen consequences. When people live on streets in one- or two-family houses, they exercise social controls, watching their neighbors and preventing some delinquent acts; but in a high-rise apartment building muggings, robberies, and other assaults go undetected. And without control of crime, the city may be truly doomed.

As we saw in our discussion of guided social change, there is no one answer to the problems of the city; attempts at systems analysis show how incredibly complex the interrelationships of variables are. Urban problems are ongoing or open-ended problems; if we hope to solve them in any degree, we are going to have to continue working at them indefinitely. But will we do so?

Perhaps Americans do not really care about cities. The myth of pastoral America persists even as the reality vanishes. Most Americans do not value sophistication, urbanity, and cosmopolitanism. Only 14% want to live in large cities or suburbs, and 22% in medium-sized cities or suburbs, while 30% would prefer a small town or city and 34% would like to live in open country.[54] "The American urban place is a noncity because Americans wish it to be just that."[55] Not caring for the city, they are abandoning it to the powerless who have no choice but to live there.

Summary

Attitudes toward cities differ almost as greatly as cities themselves. Urban sociologists have often reflected the conditions of their times and the biases of their cultures, particularly in studies of the relationship between demographic patterns of settlement and culture, social structure, and personality—the relationship between where people live and how they live.

Census definitions of cities vary so greatly that many sociologists have adopted a figure of 20,000 as the arbitrary minimum for a city, and 100,000 as constituting a large city. They distinguish between demographic urbanization, the proportion living in urban areas, or an increase in that proportion, and social urbanization, the adoption of an urban way of life.

Although cities date back nearly 6000 years, the great shift to urban living came with industrialization, and has been especially marked since 1950. In 1970 more than a quarter of the people in the world lived in cities of 20,000 or more, and 10% in cities of half a million people or more. In general, the more highly industrialized a country, the more highly urbanized; but some pre-industrial countries are overurbanized, with numerous migrants from rural areas living below subsistence levels in the squatter areas of large cities.

Forty million Americans left farms for cities between 1920 and 1970. Metropolitan areas, especially their suburbs, have grown fastest

[54]National Public Opinion Survey conducted in 1971 for the Commission on Population Growth and the American Future. *Population and the American Future*, p. 36.

[55]Elazar, "Are We a Nation of Cities?"

of all; suburbs now contain more people than rural areas, small towns, or central cities. Urban density drops as suburbanization proceeds. Urban regions, constellations of urban centers and their hinterlands, will probably contain five out of six Americans by the year 2000.

Ecological processes, the steps by which a city grows and changes, include concentration of population, centralization of activities, decentralization of both people and activities, specialization, routinization, segregation, invasion, and succession. The resultant patterns of land use reflect transportation technology and policy, the competition of different groups for space and desirable locations, relative economic advantage and other factors that affect freedom of choice, and such values as sentimental attraction to a certain place or interest in certain kinds of activities.

Louis Wirth defined the city as "a relatively large, dense, and permanent settlement of socially heterogeneous individuals," and postulated that these conditions result in a distinctive urban way of life. This includes features of social organization: specialization, interdependence, a predominance of secondary relationships, an emphasis on financial gain, and the emergence of formal controls and numerous voluntary associations. Urbanization also results in certain personality traits: relativism, reserve, indifference, lack of a strong sense of integration in the community, loneliness, irritability, sophistication, cosmopolitanism, and vulnerability to manipulation by the mass media. These aspects of social organization and personality have serious consequences such as a higher rate of personal and social disorganization and delinquency than in rural areas.

Other sociologists have tested this thesis and found it only partly valid, being time-bound and culture-bound. Herbert Gans finds that urbanism is many ways of life, and that it is more closely related to class and to stage in the life cycle than to place of residence. The suburb and the outer city are made up of family neighborhoods; the traits and problems Wirth discerned apply most closely to the inner city, and especially to those who have no choice but to live there or who are not established residents but recent rural migrants. In many cities in newly developing countries, migrants avoid culture shock by clustering with others from their former communities, and continuing their ways as much as possible; this results in "peasantization" of cities.

The urban revolution is also a rural revolution. Cities began when a surplus of food became available, and they grow most swiftly and successfully where agriculture is most commercialized and mechanized. Agricultural workers constitute only about 4.5% of the labor force in the United States, about 16% in Japan. But in the world as a whole, six out of ten workers are still agricultural, and in many countries, productivity is very low. Nonetheless, the urban trend continues, and rural villages lose autonomy as the need for industrial products—gasoline, tractors, fertilizers, medicines—ties them to the larger society, and teachers and other social change agents help prepare their children for a different way of life.

Some predict cities will soon be made obsolete by new communication and transportation technology. Others see them as essential centers of civilization. A few planned cities serve as models for possible future "new towns." But in most of the Third World, the pressing problems of the population explosion and the urgency of achieving economic development make such plans seem visionary. In our own country, the cultural bias against both the city itself and planning in general may explain why we fail to come to grips with "the urban crisis" and are perhaps abandoning cities to those who have no choice but to live there.

In the next chapter we consider a closely related topic—the population explosion—and examine the impact of modernization, urbanization, and population growth on the natural environment.

QUESTIONS FOR FURTHER THOUGHT

1. Where do you live? Where do your parents and grandparents live, and where did they grow up? Does your family history reflect the urban trend? Suburbanization? What were the motives involved in moving or not moving?

2. Would you prefer to live somewhere else? Is your preference general or specific? How do you account for it: cultural interests, personality traits, stage of the life cycle, socio-economic level, other factors?

3. Do you believe you, personally, *need* cities? What do they have to offer you that other patterns of settlement do not?

4. What do you consider the optimum size of a city? Why?

5. How close do you want to live to members of your family? Friends? Neighbors? Strangers? Theaters, museums, concert halls, movies, stadiums, marinas, camp grounds, parks?

6. Is density in itself a disease? Experiments with rats show that their adrenal glands grow bigger when they are crowded, and they exhibit fear and fury; and "crammed cats go through a 'Fascist' transformation, with a 'despot' at the top, 'pariahs' at the bottom, and a general malaise in the community." [Gus Tyler, "Can Anyone Run a City? *Saturday Review* (Nov. 8, 1969): 22.] Do you believe the same is true of human beings?

7. City planner Constantinos Doxiadis observes that we sleep 8 hours, work 8 hours, and spend 2 hours washing, dressing and eating; the 6 that remain are the difference between the civilized man and the animal, and commuting may often cut that by half. Relate this idea to urbanism and suburbanism as ways of life. Do you think rural life is intrinsically more civilized?

8. Distinguish between the physical and social problems of cities, and pose several hypotheses on the relationships between the two types of problems. (E.g., crowding and crime.)

9. Some Americans have declared they prefer pollution and crime to planning. Do you share this value judgment? Why or why not? If not, who do you think should be in charge of planning?

10. Aristotle defined a good city as one where a man could feel happy and safe. Do you agree? What other conditions, in your opinion, would be necessary to fulfill these two?

11. Historian J. H. Plumb wrote a scathing description of Detroit as "a desert of broken concrete," and asked why leading families do not take pride in American cities, as the Medici did in Florence. A couple of years later Henry Ford II announced plans for a complex of buildings and parks on the riverfront. Speculate about the possible connection in terms of the role of values, beliefs, and self-conceptions in bringing about social change.

12. Our discussion of ecological processes was confined to cities. Apply them to a larger area—perhaps a nation—including the processes that bring about the rural revolution.

13. Urban sociologist Mel Ravitz, long a Detroit City Councilman, insists that "the problems of the city are those of the whole society," and that the future of man is at stake in the urban crisis. Discuss. [See "The Crisis in Our Cities: An Action Perspective," in Leonard Gordon, ed., A City in Racial Crisis [Dubuque, Iowa: William C. Brown Company, Publishers, 1971], pp. 152–62.

17

It took 1700 years for the population of the planet to increase by a quarter billion; an equal increase took place in the years between 1965 and 1970.

SALIM LONE

Through the animal and vegetable kingdom Nature has scattered the seeds of life abroad with the most profuse and liberal hand; but has been comparatively sparing in the room and the nourishment necessary to rear them.

THOMAS R. MALTHUS, 1798

it wont be long now it wont be long till earth is barren as the moon and sapless as a mumbled bone
dear boss i relay this information without any fear that humanity will take warning and reform signed archy.

DON MARQUIS, 1935

Most people are *on* the world, not in it— have no conscious sympathy or relationship to anything about them—undiffused, separate, and rigidly alone.

JOHN MUIR, c. 1880

What is the use of a house if you haven't got a tolerable planet to put it on?

HENRY DAVID THOREAU, 1860
letter to a friend

Growth for growth's sake is the philosophy of the cancer cell.

ZERO POPULATION GROWTH

POPULATION AND THE ENVIRONMENT

SPACESHIP EARTH IS IN GRAVE DANGER. The number of passengers grows faster every decade. Its resources of space, soil, water, and minerals are finite. Its atmosphere is fragile. Its first-class passengers, seeking to conquer nature rather than to live in harmony with it, have squandered and despoiled it. The steerage passengers have been given enough crumbs from the first-class table to survive longer and multiply; more and more are born and survive to live in misery.

Although some farsighted people warned of this long ago—conservationists like John Muir, romantic poets like Wordsworth, philosophers like Thoreau, and the gloomy English clergyman-demographer Malthus—only in recent years have great numbers of people all over the world become aware of the urgency of the problem, which involves nothing less than survival. It is a complex problem, involving all the five systems in which human social behavior takes place—culture, social organization, personality, the human organism, and the ecosystem. Our emphasis in this chapter will be on the human organism in terms of population, and on the ecosystem in relation to population pressures and other aspects of man's social behavior. What do demographers and ecologists tell us about the future of mankind? What do sociologists and others offer in the way of possible solutions?

Demography

The word "demography" comes from the Greek words *demos* (people or populace) and *graphy* (a branch of learning descriptively treated). Demography is the science concerned with describing human populations: their size, composition, and distribution in a given area, and the processes of change through fertility, mortality, and migration. Formal demography is quantitative and statistical; social demography, or general population study, is concerned with interpreting these statistics in terms of causes and consequences, and is therefore basically a social science.

Our focus in this chapter will be primarily on size and growth,

511

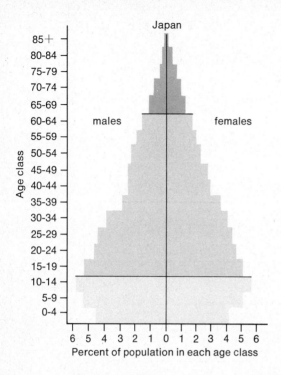

Japan

males   females

Age class

Percent of population in each age class

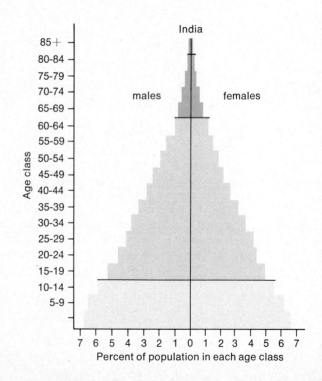

India

males   females

Age class

Percent of population in each age class

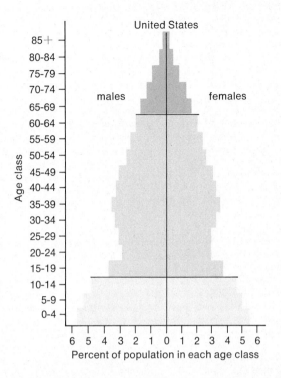

United States

males   females

Age class

85+
80-84
75-79
70-74
65-69
60-64
55-59
50-54
45-49
40-44
35-39
30-34
25-29
20-24
15-19
10-14
5-9
0-4

6 5 4 3 2 1 0 1 2 3 4 5 6

Percent of population in each age class

and their consequences. The composition of a population, however, also has important social consequences. The age-sex "pyramid" may take different shapes. If it is broad at the bottom and narrows off near the top, (as in Egypt, where 42% are under age 15), it is a young population, with relatively few people in the productive ages who bear a heavy burden of supporting dependents. If there are few males about age 20–25 as compared to females age 15–20, there is a "marriage squeeze," for men generally marry girls a few years younger than they, and many girls will be husbandless. If, as happened in the United States, there is a short-lived "baby boom" followed by a decline in births, many who were born during the boom and decided to be teachers will not find jobs, as the smaller "cohorts" born a few years later will require fewer teachers. The ethnic and racial compositions of populations, as we saw in Chapter 10, as well as socio-economic status and education, also have tremendous consequences for social relationships, personality, and institutions. So does population distribution—our emphasis in the chapter on cities.

Another basic demographic concept is fertility, the amount of reproduction actually achieved (which is distinguished from fecundity, or reproductive capacity). The fertility rate is the number of births per 1000 women of reproductive age, usually limited to 15–45. Demographers also calculate specific fertility rates for age groups, such as 20–24, and 25–29. The **birth rate**, however, is indicated in terms of the population as a whole: so many live births per 1000 population.[1] (This is often called the gross or crude birth rate). Death rates may be similarly calculated for the population as a whole, for each sex, or for age, ethnic, and other groups. The **rate of natural increase** of a population is the difference between the crude birth rate and the crude death rate. Thus the world's crude death rate of 14, subtracted from its crude birth rate of 34, gives us a natural increase of 20 per 1000. This is usually converted into a percentage or annual **growth rate**, in this case 2%. The population of any one country may also fluctuate because of migration; thus the rate of natural increase for the United States was 0.8% in 1970, but immigration brought total population increase to 1%.[2]

"Demographic facts have much to do with a person's chances of finding a mate, or even getting a date, choosing a career, getting a job, staying alive, and almost anything concerning day-to-day existence."[3] They affect the market for high chairs, wedding gowns, sofas, and coffins, and the political orientation of a society. In this chapter, however, we are concerned primarily with the overwhelming demographic fact of the "population explosion" and its consequences for the human race. To anticipate our more detailed discussion of population trends, every 24 hours 180,000 people are added to the world. This addition is more critical—in the short run, at least—in some areas than in others, but everywhere "it affects international relations, economic development, and eventually the quality of life which can be lived in a rapidly unifying world."[4]

The Growth of the Human Population

". . . All that tread /the globe," said the poet, "are but a handful to the tribes/ That slumber in its bosom."[5] If we date the appearance of *Homo sapiens* at 600,000 years ago, a reasonable guess is that 77 billion members of the species have walked the earth, only about 12 billion of them before 6000 B.C. If we accept a date a million years earlier, then there have been 96 billion humans, 32 billion of whom lived before 6000 B.C.

[1] No known society has a birth rate that reaches the upper limits of human fecundity, estimated at about 70 per 1000, or about twice the world's present crude birth rate. [Shirley Foster-Hartley, *Population: Quantity vs. Quality* (Englewood Cliffs, N.J.: Prentice-Hall, Inc., 1972), p. 40.]

[2] *Ibid.*, pp. 32–33.

[3] Samuel C. Newman, "The Teaching of Population by Sociologists," *Sociological FOCUS: On Population* 4, No. 1 (Fall 1970): 7–19. [Note that not all demographers are sociologists (and vice versa).]

[4] Louise B. Young, ed., *Population in Perspective* (New York: Oxford University Press, 1968), p. v. For a clear discussion of demography see Edward G. Stockwell, *Population and People* (Chicago: Quadrangle, 1968), "Introduction."

[5] William Cullen Bryant, "Thanatopsis."

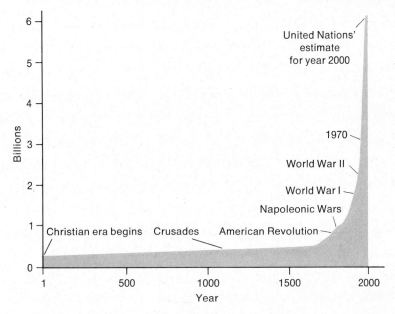

Joan Forbes in *The Christian Science Monitor*, March 18, 1968. Reprinted by permission from The Christian Science Monitor © 1968 The Christian Science Publishing Society. All rights reserved.

Today's 3.6 billion inhabitants of the globe, then, are perhaps 4% of all who have ever lived.[6]

THE POPULATION EXPLOSION

The human population grew very slowly for many thousands of years. Perhaps 5 to 10 million people existed at the beginning of the agricultural era, and somewhere between 200 and 400 million at the time of Christ. Not until 1650 A.D. did the world's population reach half a billion. Even a very low rate of annual increase could have given us today's huge population, but there were numerous setbacks such as wars, epidemics (including plagues), slave raids, and famines. During relatively stable periods, birth rates of at least 35 per 1000 and probably as high as 40 to 50 soon replaced the losses.[7]

As long as death rates remained high, the growth rate of the population stayed low; up to 1750 it probably averaged considerably less than 0.1% a year; from 1750 to 1900, about 0.5%; from 1900 to

[6]Robert C. Cook, ed., "How Many People Have Ever Lived on Earth?" *Population Bulletin*, Population Reference Bureau, 18, No. 1 (Feb. 1962).

[7]*The World Population Situation in 1970*. United Nations Department of Social and Economic Affairs, Population Studies, No. 49 (1971): 6.

1950, about 1%; and at present about 2%. This does not at first glance seem very high. But "if the human race had begun with a single couple at the time of Christ, and had grown steadily at 2 per cent per year since then, there would now be 20 million people for every person alive on the earth today! That would be the equivalent of 100 people per square foot of the earth's surface."[8]

Because of this accelerated growth rate, the **doubling time** of the world's population has become shorter and shorter. It took 200 years, from 1650 to 1850, to double from a half billion to 1 billion. The next billion was added in 75 years. Each half billion has come faster: By 1950 another half billion had been added, and the sixth half billion, bringing the total to 3 billion, was achieved by 1961. Only 7 years later, another half billion had been added. If present trends continue, the world population will double to over 7 billion shortly after the turn of the century. "A child born today, living 70 years, would experience a quadrupling of world population in his lifetime."[9] United Nations demographers predict that the 1970s may show the highest rate of growth in history.[10]

THE THEORY OF THE "DEMOGRAPHIC TRANSITION"

When only enough people are born to replace those who die, the population is stable; the society has **zero population growth.** For many thousands of years death rates were so high that birth rates also had to be high if the population was to be replenished and to grow at all. When death rates decline, there is for a time a "demographic gap" between high birth rates and low death rates, during which population grows rapidly; then birth rates begin to follow death rates downward. The shift from a balance of high birth and death rates, through a period of growth as declining death rates create an imbalance between fertility and mortality, to a new balance of low birth and death rates, is called the **demographic transition.** Rapid population growth ends when this transition is complete.

Death rates decline because of five factors: (1) increased production and an improved level of living; (2) the emergence of a stable government over larger areas, with better distribution of goods and services; (3) environmental sanitation; (4) improved personal hygiene; and (5) modern medicine and public programs.[11] In 1650, when the first dramatic rise in population began, the death rate was about 40

---

[8]Hartley, *Population*, p. 4, citing calculations by the Population Council, 1965.

[9]*Ibid.*, p. 33.

[10]*The World Population Situation in 1970*, p. 46.

[11]Philip M. Hauser, ed., *The Population Dilemma,* for the American Assembly of Columbia University, 2nd ed. (Englewood Cliffs, N.J.: Prentice-Hall, Inc., 1969).

per 1000 population per year. The first two factors caused the population to double during the following 200 years. These factors have accounted for perhaps a third of the population increase since 1650. All five factors have been responsible for growth since 1850; but the fifth—medicine and public health—is the chief cause of the population explosion since World War II.

The theorists who popularized the concept of the demographic transition emphasized that economic development, industrialization, and urbanization caused not only the initial decline in mortality but also a decline in fertility in the early twentieth century. And indeed at about the time of World War II, low birth rates in Western industrialized nations appeared to bear out the theory. But after the war, fertility rose sharply, especially in the United States, even though affluence, urbanization, and industrialization increased greatly. Those who saw economic development as *the* solution to the population explosion were forced to reexamine their assumptions. The death rate in what UN experts call "the more developed nations" is now generally below 10, with a life expectancy at birth of about 70 years. But the birth rate is about 18. Thus even industrialized societies have not completed the demographic transition, and will grow in population at an annual rate of at least 1% during the 1970s.[12]

POPULATION GROWTH IN PRE-INDUSTRIAL SOCIETIES

The most spectacular growth in population, however, is occurring in "less developed" regions. Two out of three of Earth's inhabitants now live in underdeveloped areas. By the end of the century, at present growth rates, 77% will live in such areas. There will be at least 4 billion Asians, half a billion Africans, and 600 million Latin Americans.[13] The main reason for this is that since World War II the more developed nations have exported "death control" with great success. Although living standards have not risen (and in many cases have fallen because of increased population pressure on resources), death rates have fallen dramatically because of such modern public health measures as vaccines, antibiotics, and insecticides. In the first postwar decade, for example, the World Health Organization helped cut the death rate in Ceylon from 20.3 to 11; the use of DDT cut the death rate from malaria alone by 70%. In just one year, 1946, the death rate fell 34%.[14]

[12]*The World Population Situation in 1970*, p. 18.

[13]Georg Borgstrom, *Too Many: A Study of Earth's Biological Limitations* (London: Macmillan, 1969), p. 318.

[14]Although this drop in the death rate is the main cause of the population explosion, health measures have also increased fecundity (reproductive capacity) by reducing sterility due to venereal disease, improving general health, lengthening life spans, and lowering the age of puberty. The result has been a slight rise in fertility, or actual production of offspring. Hartley, *Population*, p. 41.

But birth rates have not followed death rates downward.[15] They average about 40 in the less developed regions, and in some areas are as high as 50–54. At a 2% increase per year, population doubles in 32 years; current growth rates in "less developed regions" are 2.7%. Countries with especially high rates of growth include Mexico and Pakistan, with 3.2%, and Costa Rica, which had 4.3% in 1966 (meaning a doubling time of only 17 years). Such high growth rates may temporarily result in lower death rates than in industrialized nations, because of the high proportion of young people. The young also provide the TNT for further population explosions. For the crucial effect of high birth rates combined with low death rates is that more girl children survive to bear children of their own, and their daughters in turn live to childbearing age.

PREDICTIONS OF POPULATION TRENDS

How do demographers arrive at predictions? Largely through "projection"—assuming that present trends will continue. They also take into account the age composition of the population, particularly the number of females of childbearing age likely to be in the population over any given period. But projections are risky. One must ask *why* the current trend exists, and why it might continue or be slowed down or reversed. Suppose, for example, that we projected recent trends in the granting of Ph.D.s into the future; the logical prediction would be that in a few decades every man, woman, and child would have the degree.[16] The wavelike ups and downs in birth rates in industrialized nations also warn us to beware of expecting short-run trends to continue indefinitely.

Many projections of world population trends read like horror stories, predicting "standing room only" in a few generations. *At present growth rates* there would be nearly 14 billion people on earth by 2050 A.D., averaging 265 per square mile as compared to an estimated density of 74 in 1975. Some predict 30 billion 100 years from now. But, they add, if man does not intervene drastically to prevent this nightmare from becoming a reality, the death rate will climb again because of hunger, disease, and war.

Others are more optimistic. Donald Bogue insists that fertility control programs are beginning to pay off, that the pace of population growth began to slacken in about 1965 and will continue to decline with

---

[15]UN experts report the world birth rate as 33.8 per year between 1965–70; it was 18.6 in the "more developed" and 40.6 in the "less developed" regions. In North America and Europe, and Japan, it was between 17.5 and 19.4; in Africa, 46.8; in Central America, 45; in South Asia, 44.3; and in Latin America as a whole, 38.4. *The World Population Situation in 1970*, p. 18.

[16]Wilbur Zelinsky, "How Much is Enough? The Implications of Further Population Growth in the United States," *Journal of General Education* 20, No. 1 (April 1968): 46–73.

each passing year as such programs take increasing effect. He expects zero or near zero population growth rates (ZPG), to be reached by the end of the century. "It is quite reasonable to assume," he insists, "that *the world population crisis is a phenomenon of the 20th century, and will be largely if not entirely a matter of history when humanity moves into the 21st century.*"[17] He attributes this prospect to changed public attitudes; aroused political leadership; accelerated professional and re-search activity; a slackening in death control as the more easily prevent-able diseases decline and solutions for other health problems remain difficult or unknown; social-psychological motivation and communica-tion about fertility control; and improved contraceptive methods.

While few demographers share Bogue's optimism, there is some indication of a decline in fertility. Views on ideal family size have been found to be accurate predictors of long-term trends in the birth rate; and Americans apparently want smaller families than formerly. If each woman had 2.1 children, ZPG would eventually be achieved. Married women age 18 to 24 surveyed in 1967 expected to have 2.9 babies; a similar group in 1971, 2.4. In 1967, only 44% wanted 2 or less; in 1971, 62%. According to the Gallup Poll, in 1945 nearly 50% of the Amer-ican adults polled favored families of 4 or more children (and the fol-lowing years saw the baby boom); 40% in 1967, and only 23% in 1971. The younger adults tend to be more strongly in favor of small families.[18]

A number of countries show a decline in birth rates in recent years, whether or not they permit abortion (which is the chief means, legal or illegal, of fertility control around the world). The change in Costa Rica may be particularly significant because of its traditionally high birth rate and its great pride in it: From 45 in 1938 and 49.2 in 1953, the rate declined to 43 in 1965 and 33.9 in 1969.[19] (It is still twice the rate of "more developed" nations.)

Sharply differing with Bogue's view is Paul Ehrlich, author of *The Population Bomb*, among other books. There is no reason for com-placency, he insists, in short-term indications of a decline in fertility. The future mothers of a far greater population are already born, which means that even at low growth rates stability would not be achieved for many decades. Even if it were reached immediately, it would take until 2037 for the United States to complete the demographic transi-tion.[20] By 1975 there will be 5.5 million more people of prime child-bearing ages (20 to 29) than there were in 1970, and 5.5 million more in 1985 than in 1975.

---

[17]"The End of the Population Explosion," *The Public Interest* (Spring 1967); re-printed in *Current* (July 1967): 61–64. See also his *Principles of Demography* (New York: John Wiley, 1969).

[18]*The New York Times* (Feb. 17, 1972).

[19]*Information Please Almanac* (1972), p. 636.

[20]*The New York Times* (Jan. 14, 1971), quoting Conrad Taueber, chief demographer of the Census Bureau.

Even if the reproductive rate drops to the replacement level by 1980, the population of the United States will level off at more than 300 million in 2045. If we should not reach the replacement level until the year 2000, population growth will stop in 2065, with a final population size of more than 350 million people.[21]

Many demographers admittedly *prefer* to sound the alarm, because awareness of the consequences of high birth rates may in itself help prevent them from continuing!

In making projections, demographers often base their calculations on several rates of population growth. UN experts make high, medium, and low projections; but recent "high" projections have proved consistently low as the projected dates were reached. In 1958, for example, they predicted that by 1980 Africa would have 333 million people; that figure was reached in 1969—in half the time. Using the medium variant, based on the assumption that growth will continue at 2% until about 1985 and gradually decline thereafter, they predict a world population of nearly 6.5 billion in the year 2000[22]; many other demographers consider this an underestimate.

Similarly, the President's Commission on Population Growth and the American Future made two different sets of projections:

> If families in the United States have only two children on the average and immigration continues at current rates, our population would grow to 271 million by the end of the century. If, however, families should have an average of three children, the population would reach 322 million by the year 2000. One hundred years from now, the 2-child family would result in a population of about 350 million persons, whereas the 3-child family would produce a total of nearly a billion. Thus, a difference of only one extra child per family would result in an additional 51 million people over the next three decades, and if extended over a century, an additional two-thirds of a billion people.[23]

Even if we are inclined to accept the more optimistic projections, the size of the existing population, and the fact that so many future mothers are already alive, puts a stable population far in the

[21]Paul R. Ehrlich and John P. Holdren, "Deceptive Birth Rates," *Saturday Review* (Oct. 3, 1970): 58.

[22]*The World Population Situation in 1970*, p. 45.

[23]*Population and the American Future: The Report of the Commission on Population Growth and the American Future* (New York: New American Library, 1972), pp. 19–20. Note that Census Bureau projections result in a figure of 300 million for the year 2000, based on the assumption that women beginning childbearing after July 1, 1969, will, on the average, bear 2.78 children during their lifetime, and that for the rest childbearing will remain the same as in 1966. [*Information Please Almanac* (1972), p. 617.]

future even for the United States. The addition of many more millions to our society and more billions to the world is a certainty (always, of course, barring *other* catastrophes). We turn now to the implications of this fact.

Consequences of Population Growth

The consequences of demographic trends are complex. Here let us consider, first, what happens when mortality declines in a society; second, the impact of the current population explosion on society, culture, and personality.

David M. Heer outlines six changes that appear to follow a drop in the death rate, warning that much of what he suggests is speculative and should be investigated. Pointing out how often American families were broken by death—and using the experiences of Presidents Washington, Jefferson, and Lincoln as examples—he notes that "Contemporary citizens of developed nations rarely encounter death, except among the aged."[24] The institutions of mourning have consequently declined; norms of behavior for the bereaved and their friends are no longer clear, rituals are lacking, and people tend to act as if the death had not occurred, which may hinder the process of emotional healing. Religion has shifted from an other-worldly to a this-worldly emphasis; general concern with immortality has declined. Families are smaller and more independent of relatives, more mobile, more isolated from the larger kin group. In societies where mortality is high, arranged marriages are common, and possibly interpersonal ties, such as those between parents and young children, are less intense, as if parents feared becoming too attached; in low-mortality societies, in contrast, marriage is typically by free choice, emotional ties are intense, and since it is likely that the couple have many years ahead of them, there is also pressure for easier divorce. Members of high-mortality societies may tend to discount the future and enjoy the present, and be reluctant to make sacrifices for their children's education or to give up present enjoyment for other future goals, which death may prevent. Finally, when the death rate drops, people tend to decide in favor of fewer children, because they realize that there is more likelihood that those they have will grow to maturity—and also for another complex of reasons associated with modernization, which we shall consider later in the chapter.

Growth in sheer number of members in a society has historically been associated with power, success, and security. But for most societies, and certainly for the world as a whole, the current population explosion is a cause for great concern and alarm. Even an optimist like

[24]*Society and Population* (Englewood Cliffs, N.J.: Prentice-Hall, Inc., 1968), p. 43.

Bogue foresees some years of "acute crisis" immediately ahead for India, China, the Philippines, Indonesia, Pakistan, Mexico, Brazil, Egypt, and other nations. Unless international emergency measures are taken, there will probably be severe famines in some areas. Others, notably Ehrlich, call the "population bomb" a threat to world peace and order, a barrier to economic development, a menace to the quality of life, and even a danger to the survival of man and of all life on the planet.

The unequal distribution of the good things of life and the absolute deprivation of millions create misery and unrest. In spite of "the Green Revolution" which developed new and higher-yielding grains, "the limits of human capability to produce food by conventional means have very nearly been reached. Problems of supply and distribution already have resulted in roughly half of humanity being undernourished or malnourished. Some 10–20 million people are starving to death annually now. . . . There is reason to believe that population growth increases the probability of a lethal worldwide plague and of a thermonuclear war."[25]

A growing population demands resources that might be invested in economic development, and may consume any increase in production, making modernization impossible. In many underdeveloped countries, 40–45% of the people are under age 15, as compared to a maximum of 25–30% in industrialized nations. This means that each person in the productive ages has many others to support. Typically he is a peasant with a small patch of land. Where the economy is not expanding, food production may not keep pace with population growth, and the level of living often falls. Rapid rates of growth occurred between 1960 and 1970 in such countries as India, Pakistan, Mexico, Indonesia, and Brazil —countries which were already struggling with problems of economic development, and in 15 years added 40–60% more people. Not only food, but housing, schools, roads, medical facilities, and jobs must be provided for all these new passengers on Spaceship Earth if they are to participate in society and fulfill their potential in any measure.

Overpopulation is a menace to the quality of life in a number of ways: Overcrowding and pressure on facilities for housing, recreation, and medical care, even in the United States, are apparent in traffic jams, camping trailers packed like sardines in national parks, the rising cost of hospitalization. Peace, privacy, dignity, esthetic surroundings, and quiet are ever harder to come by. In a huge population it appears to be very hard to retain an emphasis on the value of each individual. Increasingly we see life becoming computerized, regulated, restricted, licensed, and dehumanized, and we hear people complaining that they are treated as mere numbers. They lose, or cannot attain, feelings of worth, dignity, and creativity. They are also apathetic toward others, as is apparent in the attitude of city-dwellers around the world

[25]Paul R. Ehrlich and Anne H. Ehrlich, *Population, Resources, Environment: Issues in Human Ecology* (San Francisco: W. H. Freeman, 1970), pp. 321–22.

to the dying beggar in the street or the girl being stabbed while neighbors fail to call the police.[26] Crime rates appear, in many societies, to be correlated with high population density.

Finally, the danger of hunger, the menace to the quality of life, and the threat to human survival are all made more acute by the failure of mankind to live as part of "nature." In order to appreciate the magnitude of this problem, we must examine the concepts of ecology.

Ecology and Ecosystems

Ecology, a new science (about 40 years old), is the study of all forms of life and their natural settings, and of their interdependence. The *ecosphere* or environment is the thin shell around the globe on which life depends. In the *lithosphere* or earth's crust are rocks, which wear so slowly that it takes 500 years to build 1 inch of good topsoil. In it also lie the fossil fuels that man exploits for energy, and the minerals he uses in other ways.

The zone of living things is the *biosphere*, the thin, fragile, and exquisitely complex portion of the earth's crust and atmosphere that supports life. On land, it extends as deep underground as the roots of trees, as high (370 feet) as the top of the tallest redwood and as far up mountain slopes as life can exist. It includes the hydrosphere, the seven-tenths of earth's surface covered by oceans, where marine life teems in the upper 500 feet, and in some forms exists right down to the ocean floor. Ocean currents and evaporation are essential to life on land. The biosphere also includes the atmosphere, the vital blanket of gases essential to life. About two-thirds of its mass is the troposphere, extending about 7 miles above earth, where weather is born, clouds move, and jets fly. Still higher is the stratosphere, extending about 25 miles above the earth. Then the atmosphere thins out further, and beyond it is the "emptiness" of space, shot through with cosmic rays from which the atmosphere protects us—empty except for a dead moon, a life-giving sun, and mysterious planets and faraway solar systems.

Within the biosphere exist any number of ecosystems. Each ecosystem is the sum total of living and nonliving elements that support a chain of life within a given area (and this may be as large as the global system or as small as a pond). The chain of life has four primary links: (1) Nonliving matter such as sunlight, water, oxygen, carbon dioxide, and the organic compounds and other nutrients necessary for the growth of plants; (2) plant organisms (as tiny as the microscopic phytoplankton in water, such as algae, and as huge as redwood trees) which use sunlight, carbon dioxide, and water through the process of

[26]See Robert Rienow and Leona Train Rienow, *Moment in the Sun* (New York: Dial, 1970).

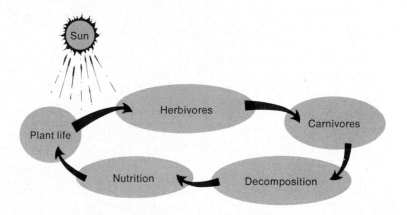

photosynthesis to produce carbohydrates; (3) consumers, higher organisms that feed on plants, or on animals that have fed on plants, or on animals that have fed on other animals; and (4) decomposers, including insects, bacteria, and fungi, that break down dead vegetable and animal matter and return their chemical compounds to the ecosystem so they can be used again by growing plants. Thus matter cycles through the ecosystem and is used again and again.

All living things, including man, depend on the cyclical processes in this chain of life. While green plants are converting carbon dioxide into food, fiber, and fuel, they are also producing oxygen (there is *no* other source) and converting inorganic nitrogen into the protein animals need. Animals in turn generate the chemicals plants need, and microrganisms break them down. Whether men are vegetarians or meat-eaters, "the human brain, so frail, so perishable, so full of inexhaustible dreams and hungers, burns by the power of the leaf."[27]

The global ecosystem is closed, finite, and complex. In a closed system everything counts; there is no "away." Nothing is ever "consumed." If you put 20 gallons of gasoline weighing about 240 pounds into your car and drive about 300 miles you burn it up; the tank is empty. But the gas is still in the ecosystem—now in the air, as 240 pounds of carbon dioxide, carbon monoxide, nitrogen oxide, carbon and other gases, and particles of "solid" matter.[28] Being finite, the ecosystem can take only so much; being complex, it is subject to the interplay of a multitude of variables. And modern man has added to this complexity and interfered with its balance so drastically that many people

[27]Loren Eiseley, *The Unexpected Universe* (New York: Harcourt Brace Jovanovich, Inc., 1969).

[28]Harold W. Sims, Jr., "Can Man Overcome the Noah Complex?" *The Florida Naturalist* 44, No. 4A (Nov.–Dec. 1971): 1–2 ff.

consider the "environmental problem" the one overarching concern of mankind, a concern that cannot be divorced from many others—least of all from the population explosion.

Why do we consider these principles in a sociology text? Because the ecosphere is one of the five systems in which social behavior takes place, and is closely interrelated with the others.

> The environment makes up a huge, enormously complex living machine—the ecosphere—and on the integrity and proper functioning of that machine depends every human activity, including technology. . . . This machine is our biological capital, the basic apparatus on which our total productivity depends. If we destroy it, our most advanced technology will come to naught, and any economic or political system which depends on it will founder. Yet the major threat to the integrity of this biological capital is technology itself.[29]

Ecology has been called "the subversive science" because it raises fundamental and disturbing questions about cultural goals, values, and norms, social organization, freedom, and the use and control of power. It is the systems science above all others, for it must take into account a multitude of delicately balanced variables. It is also an interdisciplinary science, for although in its narrower or "pure" sense it deals primarily with biology, chemistry, and physics, in its broader sense it employs the insights and findings of social science, psychology, engineering, and the humanities. Because in this sense it involves a definition of the universe, the earth, and man's role, ecology has an element of religion. And the movement to act upon its findings is in large part a crusade, with salvation as its goal.

Man, Modernization, and the Environment

Anthropologist Loren Eiseley compares the human population to a malignant fungus growth. Men are aggressive "earth-eaters," out of balance with the natural world.[30] This imbalance between the human race and the rest of nature has four chief aspects: (1) the exploitation of natural resources; (2) the latent consequences of modernization, especially economic development and urbanization; (3) the "demographic overload" of advanced industrial societies; and (4) the multiplier effects of population growth itself.

[29]Barry Commoner, "Salvation: It's Possible," *The Progressive*, special issue on The Crisis of Survival (April 1970): 12–18.
[30]*The Invisible Pyramid* (New York: Scribner's, 1970).

EXPLOITATION OF NATURAL RESOURCES

Man's zeal to conquer nature rather than to understand it and live in harmony with it is most apparent in the ruins of magnificent forests. Through carelessness, profiteering, ignorance, and the battle to provide for his family, man—especially American pioneers and robber barons—cut down the woods, and are still paying for it in loss of water reserves, erosion of soils, and ugliness, as well as in loss of the oxygen that only growing green things contribute to the biosphere.

Mineral resources are vanishing, and poorer grades of fossil fuels are now being exploited, often at great expense in pollution of the air, water, and landscape, as in the strip mines of Appalachia. Europe is depleting its ground water reserves at three times the replacement rate; the United States at twice the rate. Tokyo is slowly sinking into the sea; some parts have sunk 6 feet since World War II, mostly because industries pump water from underground reserves.

LATENT CONSEQUENCES OF MODERNIZATION

The exploitation of natural resources is an obvious consequence of industrialization, and has long been a subject of concern. Only recently, however, have such latent consequences as pollution, with its many ill effects, and the disturbances of the ecosystem created by dams, paving, and large-scale agriculture become alarmingly apparent. On certain days smog alerts in Los Angeles indicate that children are not to jump, run, or engage in athletics. DDT is found in mother's milk in higher concentration than in cow's milk. It is also found in Antarctic penguins, thousands of miles from any place where it is sprayed. Automobiles spew 95 million tons of noxious gases and chemicals into the air of the United States each year, nearly half of all air pollution. Industrial wastes, sewage, and detergents kill organisms in lakes and rivers; Lake Erie has been officially pronounced dead, and many rivers and lakes are choking to death. Solid wastes pile up. Highways and buildings eat away at land that could be used to grow plants that would provide more oxygen and more beauty. Emphysema, a lung disease, is the fastest growing cause of death in the United States. Noise pollution not only affects adult nerves but may even damage unborn babies. Dr. Paul Kotin, director of the National Institute of Environmental Health Sciences, estimates that a tenth of the nation's $70 billion a year for health services goes for treating illnesses resulting from environmental pollution; and Americans lose another $28 billion through missed wages and the cost of compensation and rehabilitation resulting from such illnesses.[31]

[31]*The New York Times* (Oct. 7, 1970). Lake Baikal in the Soviet Union is also heavily polluted.

The agricultural revolution, with its shift to large-scale farming with machinery, fertilizers, and insecticides, is responsible for much pollution. Nitrogen and DDT run off the land and into the waters; species of birds become extinct; some foods are dangerous. Exporting American agricultural know-how to underdeveloped countries has sometimes backfired by disturbing the ecological balance. In 1949, for example, American development interests promoted the widespread use of insecticides in the Cañete Valley of Peru to raise cotton yields. "Seven years later, the cotton crop had gone down 50 per cent and species of destructive insects had doubled. . . . [Later] the insecticide program was dropped in favor of biological control, which has been successful."[32]

"There is simply not enough air and water on the earth to absorb current man-made wastes without effect." Furthermore, nuclear testing results in the presence of Strontium-90 in the bones of every young person growing up since it began, and it "will be carried in the bodies of several future generations."[33]

DEMOGRAPHIC OVERLOAD

The "first-class passengers" on Spaceship Earth account for most of its environmental problems, and represent a "demographic load" out of proportion to their numbers. Only 6% of the earth's people, Americans consume 40% or more of the natural resources and produce 50% of industrial pollution. In these terms, the United States is one of the most *overpopulated* nations of the world.

> The average American uses more electric power than fifty-five Asians or Africans. The generation of electric power is a prime producer of pollution. A single American accounts for more detergents, pesticides, radioactive substances, fertilizers, fungicides, and defoliants in the rivers and oceans than are produced by a thousand people in Indonesia—a nation that is generally cited as a prime example of human overcrowding. One American is responsible for putting more carbon monoxide and benzopyrene in the air than 200 Pakistanis or Indians. One American consumes three times more food than the average person who comes from places that account for two-thirds of the world's population. The average American is responsible for 2,500 pounds of waste per year—many times the world average. If abandoned refrigerators, automobiles, and other bulky objects were included, the figure would be astronomically higher.

[32]Robert Kahn, *The Christian Science Monitor* (Dec. 19, 1968); reprinted in *Current* (Feb. 1969): 41–45.

[33]Barry Commoner, *Science and Survival* (New York: Viking, 1966); excerpts reprinted in *Population Bulletin* 23, No. 5 (Dec. 1967).

The United States . . . accounts for almost 30 per cent of poisons being dumped into sky and the seas. The notion, therefore that Americans are less of a drain on the Earth than Chinese or Indians, because there are so many fewer of us, is an absurdity and a dangerous one.[34]

Herman Miller of the Census Bureau predicts a jump in average family income in constant purchasing power from $9,800 in 1968 to $21,000 in the year 2000. These gains in affluence will be a far greater threat to the quality of life than increased population by itself. About two-thirds of the potential increase in pollution and pressure on resources "would take place even if our population stopped growing tomorrow but continued to increase its income and to spend its money in the same old way."[35]

THE MULTIPLIER EFFECT OF POPULATION GROWTH

According to Philip Hauser, even if the population were stabilized, pollution could continue to rise through increased consumption per capita or the relaxation of efforts to cope with it; and conversely, even if population continued to increase, pollution might be decreased by reallocating resources. "In the long run, however, as population densities approach saturation points in respect of the population-carrying capacity of the earth, pollution as well as the exhaustion of essential non-renewable resources would constitute a serious threat to the survival of mankind."[36]

The President's Commission on Population Growth and the American Future summed it up this way:

What are commonly referred to as population problems can be viewed more profitably as environmental, economic, political and social problems that are aggravated by population growth and density. The closest thing to a "population problem" in the pure sense is the speculation that increases in the sheer density of numbers have undesirable effects on social behavior. We regard population growth, however, as an intensifier or multiplier of many problems impairing the quality of life in the United States.[37]

Whatever the cause, it appears to be a lost one without some form of population control. We turn next to the highly controversial questions

[34]Norman Cousins, "Affluence and Effluence," *Saturday Review* (May 2, 1970): 53.
[35]*The New York Times* (Feb. 19, 1971).
[36]"On Population Problems and Population Policy," *Sociological FOCUS: On Population* 4, No. 1 (Fall 1970): 63–78.
[37]Interim Report (Mar. 16, 1971).

of how population growth and pollution can be controlled—two fields where conflicts of values and interests often generate more heat than light, exactly what the biosphere does not need!

Approaches to the Problems of Population and Pollution

It is generally agreed that if man is to survive, he must eventually achieve stability in population and learn to live without destroying his environment. Some feel we have only a short period of grace before we will be beyond salvation—perhaps 5 years, or a generation, or possibly a century. Both goals require a new attitude of responsibility for the welfare of future generations and an abandonment of the idea that More and Bigger = Better.

It is also agreed that these problems are so complex and so interrelated that they must be attacked from many angles, and on the international as well as national and local levels. But the specific means to these goals excite a great deal of controversy. Some condemn science and technology as the villains that brought about the current crisis; others insist that the problems cannot be solved without using them wisely. Some insist that all measures be strictly voluntary and based on education; others urge government and institutional pressures of various kinds.

POPULATION CONTROL

Four solutions to the problem of population pressure are theoretically possible: an increase in the death rate, migration from over-populated to underpopulated areas, a rise in food production sufficient to take care of the increase in population, and a decrease in the birth rate.

The first two "solutions" evade the problem. No one favors an increase in the death rate, although some demographers feel death control without birth control is immoral. Yet, as we have seen, such an increase may occur in spite of—and even because of—man's scientific and technological knowledge. Migration merely shifts the problem in space and postpones the final reckoning in time. True, it did help to save Europe from starvation during its own population explosion in the eighteenth and nineteenth centuries. (In England alone the population increased from 9 to 35 million between 1800 and 1900, even though many migrated. More than 60 million Europeans left for new continents between 1800 and 1924.) But there are no new Americas to populate, and even Australia is reconsidering her encouragement of immigration.

Fantastic science-fiction schemes for shooting people (and garbage) to other planets are logistically ridiculous. We must settle for solving our problems where we are.

The only real solutions to the pressure of population growth are, then, an increase in food production—part of economic development—and a decline in the birth rate. Most demographers feel that one cannot work without the other.

The most influential student of population the world has ever known was pessimistic about both measures. Thomas Malthus, an English clergyman, published his famous *Essay on Population* in 1798. Population, he said, depends on the means of subsistence but will always tend to outrun the means of subsistence. Because of man's strong sexual drive, population when unchecked has a tendency to double every 25 years; it increases in geometrical ratio—1, 2, 4, 8, 16, and so on. Food supplies, however, because of the "niggardliness of nature," increase only in arithmetical progression, as 1, 2, 3, 4, 5, and so on.[38] Only vice, misery, poverty, famine, disease, and war keep population within bounds. In his later editions Malthus added to these "positive checks" the idea of "preventive checks," and thus was able to "soften some of the harshest conclusions." Among these preventive checks were late marriage, celibacy, continence, and moral restraint. Although he did not have much faith in man's ability to exercise these controls, he disapproved of contraception (which "neo-Malthusians" advocate as the only ultimate solution). Thus in his view there was little to look forward to but growing populations ever subject to the evils of the positive checks. Even humanitarian efforts to help poor and starving people backfire, according to "the Malthusian dilemma"; they only result in increases in population and reduce them to a worse state of misery than before.

And in some ways economic development as it has been promoted thus far had indeed made the problem worse in the long run, both in advanced industrial societies and in those to whom these societies send "foreign aid." The miracles wrought by commercial agriculture lose much of their luster when weighed against the pollution of air and water by machinery, fertilizers, and pesticides, and the paradox of subsidies for *not* producing in a hungry world. Foreign aid is often extended on "the American plan," with little or no regard for a tropical environment or a Latin, African, or Oriental culture. The general attitude has been that everything a peasant in an underdeveloped country has been doing is wrong and must be changed.

Like our exportation of "death control," our exports of food have kept many citizens of underdeveloped nations alive, in misery, to produce more children to live in misery. No humanitarian would deny people food, but agriculturist Georg Borgstrom believes that equal dis-

[38]These ratios have not proved to be true.

tribution of all available food would only make hunger universal.[39] He questions the morality of trade patterns in which affluent nations, high consumers of fat and protein, import these materials from starving nations. "Is it reasonable that tropical Africa, so critically short of both fat and protein, is parting with a quantity of protein in the form of peanuts, consisting of one-third of its production, to feed the dairy cattle and poultry of western Europe and to bolster the fat intake of Europeans?"[40]

How can a decline in the birth rate be achieved? Ireland offers a classic example of the Malthusian principles, including the adoption of preventive checks. It also emphasizes the role of social institutions in the control of reproduction.

> The Irish learned the Malthusian lesson the hard way. In 1700 they had a population of about two million. They were living in misery on small grains. Then someone introduced the potato, which was a great technical improvement, enabling a larger amount of food to be grown per acre, and indeed per man, than before. For a while the standard of life of the Irish improved, infant mortality declined, and there was a great increase in population. By 1846 there were eight million people living in misery on potatoes. Hardly any better example of the utterly dismal theorem can be found. Then came the failure in the potato crop and the great famine. Two million people died of starvation. Two million emigrated and the four million who remained had learned a lesson. The population of Ireland has increased very little in over a hundred years, partly as a result of emigration, but more as a result of limitation of births. In this case the limitation was achieved through late marriages and the imposition of a strongly puritan ethic upon the young people which seems to have the effect of strongly limiting the number of children born out of wedlock. It is striking that one of the most successful examples of population control should have taken place in a Roman Catholic country, one, however, in which Catholicism takes an unusually puritanical form.[41]

But in much of the world no such limitations are the norm. In the scale of human values, birth and death are at opposite poles. Death is feared, and death control accepted eagerly. Birth has a positive value; it is a blessed event; increase and growth are good. Because high death rates long made it necessary for man to "be fruitful and multiply and replenish the earth," high fertility has been valued by most human societies and encouraged by religion, government, and other institutions. Children have also been a form of social security and of cheap labor. They have been "proof" of a man's virility and a woman's fertility, a

[39]*Too Many*, p. 323.

[40]*Ibid.*, p. 328.

[41]Kenneth E. Boulding, *The Meaning of the 20th Century: The Great Transition* (New York: Harper & Row, 1964), pp. 129–30.

fulfillment regarded as natural and desirable, and even, in some societies, the only means of achieving full adult status. Many couples "keep trying" until they have at least one child of each sex; sons are especially valued in most societies. The predicted ability to predetermine sex of children, therefore, may contribute to reducing fertility. But informal group pressures persist: "What? You've been married two years and no sign of a child?" "Your daughter is three; doesn't she need a little brother?"

How can these values be changed, so that people want fewer children? Modernization seems to bring with it a desire for smaller families, even before industrialization and urbanization occur. Literacy and mass education in Finland and Hungary as well as England and Wales apparently contributed to a decline in fertility that began in the 1880s.[42] As infant mortality falls, as public agencies provide help in time of need, and as kinship ties decline in importance, many couples want fewer children, and may take advantage of available means of preventing births. As the status of women rises, they find fulfillment in fields formerly closed to them; often they postpone marriage and decide to have no children or only one or two.

But as the example of the United States demonstrates, modernization is not enough. A positive program aimed at reducing fertility is advocated in more and more countries. Generally, it takes the form of "family planning," of making it possible for couples to have no more children than they want. If this goal were achieved, births would decline somewhat even in the United States. A national fertility study conducted in 1970 by the Office of Population Research at Princeton University found that 44% of all births to currently married women between 1966 and 1970 were unplanned. Only 1% of first births were unwanted, but nearly two-thirds of all sixth or higher-order births were. This implies that 2.65 million births would not have occurred during those years if the couples had had access to perfect fertility control. Many of these children, of course, were nurtured and cherished once they were on the scene; but according to the parents, 15% were *never* wanted.[43]

Unwanted births are most common among those with the least education and income; women with no high school education reported that 31% of their births were unwanted at the time of conception, as compared to 7% for college graduates. The Commission on Population Growth declares that if minority groups, such as blacks, had access to various means of fertility control, as well as to the education and income so closely connected with that access, their birth rate would be

[42]Ronald Freedman, "Norms for Family Size in Underdeveloped Areas," *Proceedings of the Royal Society* 159 (1963): 220–45; reprinted in David M. Heer, ed., *Readings in Population* (Englewood Cliffs, N.J.: Prentice-Hall, Inc., 1968), pp. 157–80.

[43]*Population and the American Future*, pp. 163–64.

about the same as that of the majority white population.[44] Some black leaders, however, suspect that programs of fertility control aimed at the poor are a pretext for "race genocide."

The chief shortcoming of the "family planning" approach is that it is individualistic, and people do not make decisions about having children in the light of national and international problems and needs. They continue to want more than the number necessary for ZPG to be attained. Family planning programs, says Kingsley Davis, sanctify the idea that every woman should have the number of children she wants, instead of asking why women desire so many children and how this desire can be influenced. Institutional and cultural changes must be added to medical and educational approaches. "Changes basic enough to affect motivation for having children would be changes in the structure of the family, in the position of women, and in the sexual mores."[45]

Such changes apparently are taking place in China, where Marxist theory long barred fertility control because of its dictum that capitalism was the real problem, and that under communism any number of people could be supported. With a density of about 305 people per square mile, the Chinese have adopted a comprehensive program aimed at changing not only attitudes but also the social structure. The commune rather than the family now provides security in illness and old age. Birth control is free, sterilization is cheap, and abortion easily available. A propaganda campaign urges late marriage and small families. Although equality of the sexes has not been achieved to the satisfaction of many women, it has proceeded far enough so that they find fulfillment in many ways other than bearing and raising children. It is reported that in Peking the birth rate is down to about 6 or 7 per 1000 and the growth rate is 0.1%, the lowest in the world. In the province as a whole, the birth rate is 17. The success of the program demonstrates the interrelated influence of changes in social structure and in beliefs, knowledge, and values.[46]

Among measures suggested for motivating people to have smaller families are an upgrading of the status of women, so they can find fulfillment in other forms of endeavor; a revision of tax laws that now favor married couples and large families; rewards for accepting sterilization and for having zero, one, or two children (old age security for such people in underdeveloped nations, for example); rewards for late marriage and fines for early marriage. One proposal is the licensing

[44]*Ibid.* Black women reported 61% unplanned pregnancies as compared to 42% for whites.

[45]"Population Policy: Will Current Programs Succeed?" *Science* (Nov. 10, 1967); reprinted as "Can Family Planning Do It?" in *Current* (Jan. 1968): 50–64.

[46]Jaime Zipper, "China: Family Planning Was Introduced into China to Guard Against Catastrophe," *The New York Times* (April 30, 1972), Section 12, supplement, "Population: The U.S. Problem; the World Crisis." It was estimated that the birth rate fell from 43 in 1949 to 32 in 1970, the death rate from 32 to 17. [*The New York Times* (Jan. 5, 1971).]

of births. Each girl would be given a license entitling her to have, say, 2.11 children; she could have one and sell the rest of her license to someone else, or have three or more by buying the privilege from someone else. Some proposals step beyond currently acceptable mores—putting an antifertility drug in the water supply, for example.

The main thrust of any program is not only to control the quantity of population, but to preserve, and if possible enhance, the quality of life for all. Any program for population control, therefore, must contribute to the solution of the environmental problem.

SAVING THE ENVIRONMENT

Like the problem of overpopulation, that of pollution can be solved only through a change in individual and collective goals and values, and in the system of rewards and punishments. Both are extremely urgent and both must be based on sound research.

More and more people are aware of the problem of pollution, and some have developed "the ecological conscience"—the moral discovery "of man's true place as a dependent member of the biotic community"; an attitude of reverence for life; a feeling of love and respect for the environment, rather than of separation from and dominion over it. The powerful value of materialism, so long dominant, is outweighed by this basic principle of the ecological conscience: "A thing is right when it tends to preserve the integrity, stability, and beauty of the biotic community. It is wrong when it tends otherwise."[47]

The Latin American shopper who goes to market with her basket and fills it with unwrapped fruit and with meat wrapped in banana leaves, and the Asian farmer using night soil to fertilize his land, is, according to the ecological conscience, more in harmony with nature than the American who loads her supermarket basket with processed and packaged foods raised on inorganically fertilized soil, sprayed with insecticides, and loaded with preservatives and other artificial additives. The ecological conscience brings about changes in the life style—ways of using less electricity, gasoline, paper, water, fewer pollutants, fewer calories; it may include recycling glass, metal, and paper.[48]

Collective goals and priorities must also be changed if a society is to live according to the ecological conscience. Most ecologists question the long-sacred goal of economic growth, in advanced countries, and insist that a "high standard of living" inevitably leads to a low

[47]Thomas Merton, "The Wild Places," in Irving Louis Horowitz, ed., *The Troubled Conscience: American Social Issues* (Santa Barbara: Center for the Study of Democratic Institutions, 1971), p. 363. (A publication of the Center for the Study of Democratic Institutions.)

[48]See Garrett De Bell, ed., *The Environmental Handbook: Prepared for the First Environmental Teach-In* (New York: Ballantine/Friends of the Earth, 1970), section on "Eco-Tactics."

quality of life.[49] They suggest that corporations should be given incentives for preventing or cleaning up pollution through taxes and other legislation, strongly enforced; that the system of rewarding those who use up resources like oil (through depletion allowances, for example) should be reversed; and that the social costs of production, such as pollution, should be charged to their source rather than to the public in general, which, in most societies, means they are "nobody's business." Mass transit rather than private automobiles should be promoted; consumers of large amounts of electricity should be charged at a higher rather than a lower rate. Above all, no technological innovation should be allowed without prior assessment of probable consequences.

Such assessment means prognosis rather than mere prediction.

> There is a very important difference. Prediction is based on the projection of trends. Experts plan for the trends and thus confirm them. They regard warnings as instructions. . . . Prognosis is something else again. An intelligent doctor, having diagnosed the symptoms and examined the patient's condition, does not say (except in soap operas): "You have six months to live." He says: "Frankly, your condition is serious. Unless you do so-and-so, and unless I do so-and-so, it is bound to deteriorate." The operative phrase is "do so-and-so." One does not have to plan *for* trends; if they are socially undesirable our duty is to plan *away* from them, and treat the symptoms before they become malignant.[50]

Both the population explosion and environmental deterioration, then, call for faith in man's power to effect social change.

Summary

In this chapter we have emphasized two of the five systems in which human social behavior occurs—the human organism (in terms of demography) and the environment (in terms of ecology).

Demography, the science of human populations, is concerned with their size, composition, and distribution, and their change through fertility, mortality, and migration. Our focus is on the population explosion that began in 1650, accelerated rapidly as modernization proceeded, and, through diffusion of "death control," has been most rapid since World War II in less developed societies. The drop in birth rates that occurred in industrialized nations before World War II led to the

[49]William Murdoch and Joseph Connell, "All About Ecology," in Horowitz, *The Troubled Conscience*, p. 323.

[50]Lord Ritchie-Calder, "Polluting the Environment," in Horowitz, *The Troubled Conscience*, pp. 327–29.

theory of a "demographic transition" to a stable population; but no country has yet completed this transition. The more developed countries grow at about 1% a year, the less developed at 2.7%. High birth rates combined with low death rates mean that increasing numbers of girls survive to the childbearing years, and give birth to more potential mothers.

Demographers arrive at predictions of population growth largely through projection of current trends, taking other factors into account. Optimists like Donald Bogue believe fertility is declining so rapidly that zero population growth rates may be reached by the year 2000. Most demographers, however, take sharp issue with him, pointing out that enormous numbers of future mothers already exist, that they will probably have more children than needed for replacement, and that most population projections in the past have been too low.

The President's Commission on Population Growth and the American Future sees a U.S. population of 271 million by the year 2000 if families have an average of 2 children, 322 million if they have 3.

Even optimistic demographers foresee years of acute crises and even famine. Overpopulation also blocks economic development, erodes the quality of life, and threatens human survival.

Ecology is the study of all forms of life and their natural settings, and of their interdependence. The global ecosystem is finite, closed, fragile, and almost infinitely complex. All living things—including man—depend on the cycling of matter through a chain of life in a closed system. Ecology is an interdisciplinary, systems science; it raises fundamental questions about the universe and man's role in it.

The imbalance of man and the rest of nature has four chief aspects: the exploitation of natural resources; the latent consequences (such as pollution) of modernization, and especially of economic development; the demographic overload of affluent societies; and the multiplier effects of population growth.

The interrelated problems of population growth and environmental deterioration are extremely pressing and closely interrelated. Both demand changes in values and goals, in collective priorities, in social structure, and in norms and sanctions.

Population control cannot be morally and ethically achieved through an increase in the death rate, or the other Malthusian "positive checks." Migration is no longer a solution. Economic development is hampered by the problem itself. Therefore, prevention of birth is the only answer. Thus far most policies have taken the "family planning" approach, making information about contraception available to those who want no more children. But individual values and social pressures, as well as current laws and tax systems, work toward more children than are needed for replacement of population. Kingsley Davis believes that only through changes in the social structure, the role of women, and the sexual mores will population growth be checked.

Saving the environment depends on learning the ecological conscience, which involves changes in values and life styles. It also demands a system of rewards for acts that prevent or counteract pollution and punishments for those that increase it. It depends ultimately on faith in man's power to change things, to turn trends around when he is made sufficiently aware of the urgency of doing so.

In the next chapter we deal with this same faith, as it is expressed, consciously or unconsciously, in collective behavior and social movements.

QUESTIONS FOR FURTHER THOUGHT

1. Relate this chapter to Chapter 14, "Processes of Social and Cultural Change." What principles and concepts are involved in the emergence and perception of the problems considered here? (Blind, deterministic forces, socio-cultural drift, voluntarism, the role of individuals such as Rachel Carson, the importance of knowledge, beliefs, and values, etc.?)

2. In a stable United States population, the average age would be almost 10 years higher than now, about 37, and there would be as many people over 60 as under 15. What would be the consequences for social institutions such as government? For values?

3. What do you consider the optimum (most desirable) size for the United States population? For the world? Why?

4. It has been suggested that the most obvious place to begin a strong birth control campaign is the American middle-class suburb. Discuss. Despite his drain on resources, do you think the average American contributes more to society than the average Indian or African? Discuss.

5. What would the United States have to do to get ready for 300 million population by 2000 A.D.?

6. How many children do you want? For what reasons? What external pressures to have (or not have) children have you been subject to? With what effect?

7. Community leaders succeeded in cleaning up San Diego Bay and the waters around Seattle. Is any such collective action occurring in your community? If not, why not?

8. Do you have the ecological conscience? If so, how did you acquire it? What effect has it had on your life style?

9. Population trends, says one demographer, are both "socially determined and socially determining." Discuss.

10. What rights do you believe "owning" land gives one?

11. Zelinsky asks us to imagine a world in which the process of aging has been slowed considerably or fully arrested. "The demography of a world in which people can die of little else but accidents, suicide, or boredom staggers the imagination; after an initial stage of confusion and agony, the strictest sort of controls would probably have to be imposed over entry into or exit from human existence, with licenses for births issued very sparingly." Does the prospect appeal to you? Why or why not?

12. Paul Ehrlich recognizes the fears of some blacks that fertility control would decrease their power; but he insists that smaller families would mean more "black power." Discuss in terms of life chances and the quality of life.

13. Japan has a density of 1083 people per square mile; India, 655; the United States, 85. Why, then, do we speak of the American population problem? How does it compare with those of Japan and India?

14. Carp live in the polluted depths of Lake Erie. Could man also adapt to a polluted environment? With what consequences for society, culture, and personality?

The trend toward equality is the most inexorable force in all of history.

ALEXIS DE TOCQUEVILLE

A society keeps from exploding itself by changing, and generally it is the young who prompt that change.

HARVEY WASSERMAN

Those who make peaceful revolution impossible will make violent revolution inevitable.

JOHN F. KENNEDY

Will it be answered that we [feminists] are factious, discontented spirits, striving to disturb the public order, and tear up the old fastnesses of society? So it was said of Jesus Christ. . . . So it was said of our forefathers. . . . So it has been said of every reform.

FRANCES D. GAGE, 1851

The major advances in civilization are processes which all but wreck the societies in which they occur.

ALFRED NORTH WHITEHEAD

Violence is as American as cherry pie.

H. RAP BROWN

COLLECTIVE BEHAVIOR AND SOCIAL MOVEMENTS

A PERUVIAN CROWD FLEES A SOCCER STADIUM IN PANIC, crushing dozens of people to death. All over the United States, teach-ins are held on Earth Day to discuss pollution. Welfare mothers sit-in for day-care centers. Suburbanites march to protest school busing. On college campuses around the world, students hurl rocks, Molotov cocktails, and epithets; policemen respond with tear gas and bullets. In many living rooms, small groups of women meet regularly to raise their "consciousness of oppression." Parents go to court to have their daughters admitted to the Little League. Ghetto mobs smash windows, burn buildings, loot stores. Thousands experiment with communal living. Hundreds of thousands march on the White House to protest the Indochina war. Millions learn of these and other events from the papers and the news on TV, discuss them, form opinions, debate.

What do all these phenomena have in common? They are not part of the established culture and social structure; they are not normal, routine occurrences; they run counter to established norms or are undefined by existing norms. They are instances of **collective behavior**, "large group activity that comes into being and develops along lines that are not laid out by pre-established social definitions [and arises to meet] undefined and unstructured situations."[1]

We can conceive of human behavior as forming a continuum from the unrelated behavior of individuals at one extreme to organized group behavior regulated by traditions and rules at the other. Collective behavior falls between the two. At the end nearer individual behavior we might place panic behavior. Near the other extreme, and often merging into it, are social movements, for, compared with other forms of collective behavior, **social movements** are comparatively stable and organized, and persist over time; they are collective actions directed toward the achievement or obstruction of change in some aspect or aspects of the socio-cultural order. Collective behavior comprises, then, both brief and spasmodic behavior and long-lasting, organized behavior.

[1]Herbert Blumer, "Collective Behavior," in J. B. Gittler, ed., *Review of Sociology* (New York: John Wiley, 1957), p. 130. Blumer is recognized as having constructed the landmark outline of the field of collective behavior. The sections on Elementary Collective Behavior and Groupings follow his conceptual scheme closely.

In this chapter we examine, first, the elementary forms of collective behavior apparent in the action of such groups as crowds. Besides discussing the nature of crowds, we inquire into the "mass" and the "public." How are such groupings related to social change and social movements? What kinds of collective actions for social change and protest can we identify? How do social movements arise, gain momentum, and acquire leaders, followers, and ideologies? What tactics and strategies do they use? What functions and consequences do they have for society and personality? In considering these questions we draw upon such current movements as Women's Liberation, various facets of the youth movement, and black protest.

Elementary Collective Behavior

As we saw in our discussion of symbolic interaction, we do not ordinarily respond directly to other people; we first interpret one another's actions or remarks and then act on the basis of our interpretation. Herbert Blumer distinguishes this interpretative interaction from **circular reaction**, in which persons reflect (rather than interpret) one another's states of feeling and in so doing intensify this feeling. It is this kind of interaction that builds up restlessness, fear, and excitement in a herd of cattle and results in a stampede.

When many individuals are restless—that is, discontented, frustrated, insecure, and perhaps alienated and lonely—and engage in circular reaction, we may speak of a condition of **social unrest**. It typically arises when there are significant changes in the lives of a number of people who have something in common and become sensitized to that fact—women, workers, blacks, students. Social unrest may be confined to a small area, or spread through a large population; it may be vague and mild, or intense and acute. It involves a strong urge to act, but no specific goals. It results in random, aimless, excited behavior, mingled with apprehension and a readiness to accept rumors uncritically and to follow suggestions readily.

This aimless, random behavior, or **milling**, is the circular reaction of people in physical proximity. During the process they become more sensitized and responsive to one another; they develop rapport. They focus on one another, ignoring outside stimuli, and become ready to respond to one another "quickly, directly, and unwittingly."[2] A more intense form of milling is *collective excitement* which compels attention and becomes contagious; it arouses people emotionally and

[2]Blumer, "Collective Behavior," in Alfred McClung Lee, ed., *Principles of Sociology*, 2nd ed. (New York: Barnes and Noble, 1951); reprinted in abridged form in Robert R. Evans, ed., *Readings in Collective Behavior* (Chicago: Rand McNally, 1969), pp. 65–88.

releases them from many controls by established norms. When collective excitement is intense and widespread, **social contagion** is very likely —"the relatively rapid, unwitting, and nonrational dissemination of a mood, impulse, or form of conduct," which is especially apparent in panics, war hysteria, crazes, manias, and fads.[3] This social contagion attracts and infects many who may have begun as mere observers.

Social unrest, then, is a sign that the routines of living have been disrupted, and people are receptive to new forms. Not only panic and riots, but also social movements of many kinds, religious cults, and revolutions emerge out of social unrest.

Elementary Collective Groupings

Blumer distinguishes four kinds of collective groupings which he calls elementary because—in the ideal-typical case—they arise spontaneously and act outside of set cultural patterns: the acting crowd, the expressive crowd, the mass, and the public. Each emerges under a special set of conditions.

THE ACTING CROWD

A **crowd** is a temporary grouping of a large number of people who are conscious of one another's physical presence or nearness, engage in relatively spontaneous or uncontrolled interaction, and lack an organized structure with a division of labor and system of statuses. The casual grouping of people watching a construction project is potentially a crowd, but it is not likely to engage in any interaction beyond the exchange of amused comments and glances. It is a simple aggregate, not a collectivity. Some crowds are so conventionalized that they do not engage in truly collective behavior: The stadium full of people watching the Rose Bowl game have a common focus of attention, but they have scarcely any unity and they behave in established and regularized ways.

Most studies of crowd behavior are concerned with *acting* crowds, that are aggressively directed toward a specific aim: to storm the Bastille, to lynch an alleged rapist. Verbal milling—rumor—may have caused them to gather, and it may also have been planned to some extent. In any case, they gather (or begin to engage in collective behavior) when an exciting event or goal catches their attention. They start milling: They move around and talk to one another, conveying their excitement and creating rapport. In the process they arrive at a common focus of attention, which may or may not be the original stimulus, but which gives them an objective. Being suggestible to others in the crowd

[3]*Ibid.* Note that milling may also occur by verbal communication such as the spread of rumor among people who are not in physical contact.

Rioters form an acting crowd.

(but ignoring authorities who may try to break them up), they readily respond to leaders who urge action.

This action may be strange, shocking, and frightening, because the crowd as an emergent social system has no culture and hence no morals; it acts on impulse, for its members do not pause to interpret stimuli as they do in ordinary interaction.

Dissenting from this model of the acting crowd, Carl J. Couch insists that the crowd is a distinctive social system, to be sure, but no more pathological and bizarre than many others. It is often less destructive than the social agents that try to control it; it is not really irrational if other means of achieving its goal have failed and crowd action promises to be effective; it is no more emotional than those it acts against; and its members are less subject to control not because they are mentally disturbed but because they are lost in the anonymity of the crowd where institutionalized sanctions are less effective.[4] Crowd behavior is not entirely discontinuous with conventional behavior; typically participants justify their behavior in terms of some existing social norm or value, perhaps one they feel has not been observed by the authorities.[5]

THE EXPRESSIVE CROWD

Where an acting crowd focuses outward on one objective (often political) and acts to reach it, an *expressive crowd* has no such goal; each member engages in expressive actions—uninhibited physical movements, laughing, shouting, weeping, dancing—and experiences a release of tensions. This behavior often assumes a rhythm; the expressive crowd is often a "dancing crowd." Cults, sects, and primitive religions often originate in expressive crowd behavior. Because the experience brings emotional catharsis and joy, and because each person feels the support of others with whom he is in rapport, it may seem to him that

[4]"Collective Behavior: An Examination of Some Stereotypes," *Social Problems* 15 (1968): 310–322; reprinted in Evans, *Readings in Collective Behavior*, pp. 105–19.
[5]Ralph H. Turner, "Collective Behavior," in Robert E. L. Faris, *Handbook of Modern Sociology* (Chicago: Rand McNally, 1964), pp. 382–425.

he is possessed mysteriously by some outside power. The crowd may project this feeling onto a person or object that they invest with sacredness—a snake, a song, a prophet—and strive to repeat the ecstatic experience through religious ritual.

THE MASS

A **mass** is a large number of people who react to a common stimulus but seek individual goals and make individual choices and decisions. They may be physically close, as in a gold rush, but every man is out for himself. More typical of modern society is the dispersed, anonymous *mass audience* or *mass market*. The "mass media" of modern society—books, newspapers, magazines, radio, television, and movies—reach huge audiences whose members are not in communication with one another and do not interact; but by conveying a common body of images and understandings, the media help create a readiness to interact in other forms of collective behavior. The mass as consumers are persuaded to buy standardized and mass-produced products advertised in these media.

Although the people who make up a mass come from many diverse groups and are physically separate, they have a common focus of interest. Each responds, however, with detached anonymity; each seeks to answer his own needs. He accepts or rejects a new toothpaste, a political party platform or candidate, a fashion, a philosophy, or a creed. When many such selections converge, the mass makes or breaks a politician or manufacturer.

THE PUBLIC AND PUBLIC OPINION

The type of collectivity known as a public is especially important in modern democratic societies. A **public** is a vaguely defined number of people who for a time confront an issue, disagree on how to

The Woodstock Festival, an expressive crowd.

resolve it, and discuss it. (It is not to be confused with a *following*, made up of the fans of some hero such as a singer or movie star.)

A public is not fixed and permanent: It emerges with an issue and dissolves when the issue fades from the scene. It is not a group, for it has no norms or rules to dictate the answer to the issue, no fixed set of social relationships, and no feeling of common identity; a person enters and leaves it freely. Unlike the mass, it interacts; unlike the crowd, it engages in *interpretative* interaction. Its members, in contrast to those in a crowd, are self-conscious and critical. There is some emphasis on fact and reason, even though the propaganda of interest groups exerts pressures toward irrationality.

The public, through discussion and argument, strives to arrive at **public opinion**—a collective opinion or decision on the issue around which the public has formed. Although it is not unanimous or even necessarily the will of the majority, public opinion is nonetheless a collective product. The very fact of controversy exerts some pressure toward rationality. "A given public opinion is likely to be anywhere between a highly emotional and prejudiced point of view and a highly intelligent and thoughtful opinion. . . . Perhaps it would be accurate to say that public opinion is rational, but need not be intelligent."[6]

A true public depends on freedom of association, of speech, and of the press. If these freedoms are missing, what might have been a public becomes an audience. The Soviet leaders have arranged to give their citizens a feeling that they are members of publics by arranging numerous small local "discussion groups." The right solutions to the problems to be discussed are, however, specified in advance and strong pressure is exerted against any "incorrect" thinking. And communication and participation at this level have little effect on what goes on at the top level. True public opinion, in contrast, affects policies; it is communicated to the decision-makers and influences their decisions.[7]

Collective Behavior and Social Change

Today we see protest and attacks on the Establishment all around the world, even, to some degree, in Communist-ruled states. Why is this? We may seek the sources of unrest in (1) the modernization process itself, (2) the continuing demand for freedom and equality, (3) demographic changes, (4) the loss of firm identity and a feeling of belonging, and (5) such technological innovations as the mass media and swift transportation. To these must be added (6) a growing aware-

[6]Blumer, "Collective Behavior," p. 83.

[7]Blumer lists other elementary collective groupings: "the panic, the stampede, the strike, the riot, the 'popular justice' vigilante committee, the procession, the cult, the mutiny, and the revolt. Most of these groupings represent variations of the crowd; each of them operates through the primitive mechanisms of collective behavior." *Ibid.*

ness of the magnitude of social problems and a loss of faith in the power and determination of established authorities to solve these problems, and (7) the fact that in a democracy dissent is recognized and even institutionalized to some extent as a way of evaluating and revitalizing the social order.

MODERNIZATION AND UNREST

Modernization creates unrest by bringing together in cities and industries many people of differing interests and values, and by breaking up old traditions. Centralizing governments and industrializing economies transgress the old boundaries of traditional communities and the power of local authorities. Aggressive modernizers are like colonizers. Contact with them "creates hope, ambition, and rising expectations, ending the fatalism characteristic of traditional societies. Simultaneously, it creates a new consciousness of group identity and destroys old group life, generates a desire for group power, and weakens the group's traditional power base."[8]

The unevenness of the process also creates unrest. Uprooted peasants and farmers may have nowhere to go except city slums, no jobs ready for them in industry. Education may create too many professionals and not enough technicians. Universal suffrage may be granted before a populace knows what to do with it. Jobs become obsolete and people feel useless and unwanted. Small wonder, then, that "a spectacular abundance of social movements marks the society whose traditions have been shaken by industrial urbanism and whose structure is scarred by cleavages between diverse groups."[9]

THE DEMAND FOR FREEDOM AND EQUALITY

The "human rights revolution" that began with the Enlightenment philosophers and the American and French Revolutions continues to inspire demands for freedom and equality. This unfinished revolution is a quantitative one, promising economic, social, and political rights for all. Groups that feel excluded become increasingly aware and vociferous, even when they have made absolute gains. "Relative deprivation" may seem worse than the absolute deprivation of the past.

Blacks, students, and women, for example, all feel they lack control over their own lives, and are demanding not only pure and simple equality, but greater democracy, more participation in political

[8]Richard E. Rubenstein, "Rebels in Eden: The Structure of Mass Political Violence in America," in Roderick Aya and Norman Miller, eds., *The New American Revolution* (New York: The Free Press, 1971), pp. 97–142.

[9]C. Wendell King, *Social Movements in the United States* (New York: Random House, 1956), p. 13.

and economic decisions that affect them, and more responsiveness from those in power. They also want autonomy, the freedom to choose how they will live and to be what they choose to be.

DEMOGRAPHIC CHANGES

Changes in the composition and distribution of population may contribute to unrest. The recent upsurge of Women's Liberation may be accounted for in part by demographic changes such as longer life expectancy and smaller families, which leave a woman with many years to fill after her children are old enough to fend for themselves. Similarly, the world-wide wave of student protests may be accounted for in part by such changes. There is not a larger *proportion* of young people in modern societies; traditional ones, with their low life expectancies, have comparatively more young people. But the sheer numbers of young people, the prolongation of youth, and their concentration in college communities all contribute to unrest and collective behavior. United Nations sociologists say that in 1969 there were 750 million persons in the twelve to twenty-five age group, and predict that there will be 1 billion by 1980. In the United States, colleges are used as "warehouses for the temporary storage of a population [our post-industrial society] knows not what else to do with."[10] There is no place for youth in the mainstream of full social participation; they are kept waiting in the wings. Some must stay on campus for years because of the rigid requirements of their professional and technical specialties. Being concentrated in a community of their peers, with easy communication, they tend to develop solidarity of sentiments and their own subcultural style of life. Another example of the influence of population composition and distribution is the massive migration of rural blacks to the slums of Northern cities, which contributed to social unrest.

ALIENATION: LOSS OF IDENTITY
AND COMMUNITY

"Conditions inherent in the structure of modern society result in the alienation of industrial man."[11] Modernization creates urban societies of mobile persons who often feel anonymous and dehumanized because they are treated as things rather than as unique and valuable persons. They lose their sense of belonging, of rootedness in a certain group, a certain community, a certain place. Modernization changes place into space. "A place," says Orrin Klapp, "is a space with a sense

[10]Bennett M. Berger, "The New Stage of American Man—Almost Endless Adolescence," *The New York Times Magazine* (Nov. 2, 1969).

[11]William A. Faunce, *Problems of an Industrial Society* (New York: McGraw-Hill, 1968), p. 2.

of locality and identity. It is a recognized territory of symbols: my old neighborhood, Plymouth Rock, Canterbury Cathedral where Becket was murdered. . . . As America becomes one vast suburbia, high-rise center, and parking lot, it will cease to be a place and become a modernized space."[12]

While the mobile and uprooted are freer in many ways than the stable members of traditional societies, they also suffer problems of identity. As they move from one community, job, church, class, subculture, association, and even family, to another, they have to make rapid adjustments. Is this, asks Klapp, a road to richer identity and more freedom, "or merely a wallet full of membership cards that don't mean anything? A crucial point seems to be reached when people enter statuses at a faster rate than they can grow the loyalties, self images, character, habits, and life styles that go with them."[13]

Another identity problem is felt by those attracted to the Women's Liberation movement; they feel they never have been allowed to have an identity of their own. Their "maiden" names are their father's; their "married" names are their husband's.

A feeling of powerlessness is conspicuous in alienated people such as ghetto-dwellers, who typically have low levels of social participation, not only in voluntary associations but in informal friendships. Others feel powerless for lack of opportunity, finding their efforts blocked at every turn. They wonder if anything they do matters, if they really "count." Students feel their lives are preprogrammed by bureaucratic organizations. And Klapp insists there is a lack of *meaning* in modern life: that it is boring and empty, emotionally impoverished.[14]

Feelings of loss of identity and community, of entrapment, isolation, powerlessness, and meaninglessness, then, contribute to social unrest. Add to this the feeling of injured dignity and pride that many suffer because of prejudice and discrimination, and we see the alienated, deprived, and excluded as tinderboxes ready for a spark.

MODERN TECHNOLOGY AND SOCIAL UNREST

Mass communication and swift transportation contribute to unrest, to unity in groups that find common ground, and to polarization. Much of the student protest around the world may be attributed to social contagion through mass media, which leads not only to similar complaints but also to similar protest tactics. At the same time, the more flamboyant and extremist elements of each movement, being the most "newsworthy," get the major share of attention. This tends to create a reaction: Women's Lib advocates may all be labeled "bra-burners"; blacks may all be identified with armed militants; students are stereo-

[12]*Collective Search for Identity* (New York: Holt, Rinehart & Winston, 1968), p. 28.
[13]*Ibid*, p. 17.
[14]*Ibid*.

typed as dirty, disrespectful, and obscene. Yet all the marches, demonstrations, and sit-ins of blacks and war protestors might have had far less effect on policy had it not been for their dramatization in almost every living room in the United States.

AWARENESS OF SOCIAL PROBLEMS AND THE CRISIS OF AUTHORITY

The word "unrest" suggests irrationality, vagueness, and maladjustment of personality. But social unrest may result from rational recognition of social conditions that call for change. When awareness is combined with a loss of faith in the power and willingness of those in authority to cope with problems (war, pollution, starvation), the stage is set for collective behavior and social movements that do more than appeal to reason and work through established channels. When those in power are perceived as arbitrary, inept, and ineffective—or even lacking in self-confidence—there is a crisis of authority. An administration, therefore, "has to be sensitive to what people want before they break the rules. [Otherwise] the awkward issues are postponed; the grievances accumulate; and we stumble from crisis to crisis, never acting until the strike notices have been posted and people's blood is up. We never tackle a frontier dispute until there is shooting; a labor demand until the garbage is piled high in the streets; and the restlessness of the young until they invade the president's office."[15] Under these circumstances, protest often becomes loud, desperate, and even violent.

DISSENT AND DEMOCRACY

Social movements, says Wm. Bruce Cameron, are most common in "a democracy with easy communication in a state of unrest. It is in a democracy that men are most likely to look to themselves as the source of power for social change."[16] Dissent has a special role in a democracy. Speaking of protest, scientist-philosopher J. B. Bronowski reminded his hearers:

> You are a republic today because your forefathers were impatient of social wrongs, what they called "a long train of abuses and usurpations," and revolted against them in 1776. This country was made by political dissenters and, even before that, by religious dissenters. . . .

[15]J. B. Bronowski, "Protest—Past and Present," *The American Scholar* (Autumn 1969).

[16]*Modern Social Movements: A Sociological Outline* (New York: Random House, 1966), p. 11.

Progress by dissent then is characteristic of human societies. It has been responsible for the growth and success of democracy in the last four hundred years, and the decline and failure of absolute forms of government. For the crucial feature of democracy is not simply that the majority rules, but that the minority is free to persuade people to come over to its side and make a new majority. Of course, the minority is abused at first—Socrates was, and so was Charles Darwin. But the strength of democracy is that the dissident minority is not silenced; on the contrary, it is the business of the minority to convert the majority; and this is how a democratic society invigorates and renews itself in change as no totalitarian society can.[17]

Collective Protest: The Ghetto Riot

Everything from a mob riot to Common Cause, which fills mail boxes with reasoned appeals for support on stationery bordered with a long list of prominent names, may be considered a collective action for social change and protest. And in between the sporadic violence of uncontrolled mobs and the respectable organization of reform movements are many kinds and combinations of episodic protest and organized action. Before inquiring into the more structured collective actions known as social movements, let us consider riots in general and the pattern of the ghetto riots of recent years in particular.

THE NATURE OF RIOTS

A riot is an outwardly hostile, illegitimate, and aggressive action by an acting crowd; it is relatively spontaneous and temporary. Unlike rebellion and insurrection, it usually does not aim to overthrow the government. The "riots" of vacationing college students on ocean beaches are more expressive than aggressive, and although they may include senseless violence and destruction participants are not protesting anything much but boredom. The riots that concern us here are, as Martin Luther King, Jr., said, "the language of those to whom no one listens."

In feudal Europe acting crowds often engaged in food riots, demanding more efficient distribution of food at a lower price, and reminding rulers of their duties. In the early period of industrialization, mobs of displaced workers wrecked agricultural and industrial machinery. During the eighteenth and nineteenth centuries, until the rise and subsequent institutionalization of the labor movement, workers engaged

17"Protest—Past and Present."

in "collective bargaining by riot," and powerless groups, such as prisoners, still do.

Riots are also common—almost part of the expected pattern—in developing nations where, although the government may be democratic, literacy is low, communication is poor, and the organizational skills for economic development and social reform are lacking. Riots involving race and religion appear, on the whole, to be bloodier than those that center on economic and political conditions: Witness those between Catholics and Protestants in Northern Ireland, Hindus and Muslims in India, and blacks and whites in the United States.

AMERICAN RACE RIOTS

The ghetto riots of recent years were different from earlier "race" riots. Between 1900 and 1960 there were twenty-three race riots and many lynchings. During the first few decades of the century the riots were essentially pogroms in which whites invaded black districts, bent on destruction and injury.[18] Later riots were pitched battles between whites and blacks, often under the trying conditions of wartime; the Detroit riot of 1943 is one example.[19] The riots of the 1960s—over 409 in number—reached a peak in the long hot summer of 1967, when 4 days of destruction in Detroit resulted in at least forty-three deaths by gunfire. Unlike earlier riots, these were directed by ghetto blacks, both aggressively and expressively, against property in their own neighborhoods. They had a carnival atmosphere in which blacks (and whites as well) looted stores; Lee Rainwater considers this "a direct reflection of the expressive emphasis in all group activity among Negroes, whether it be church participation, the blues, a rock and roll concert, or street corner banter."[20] But there was also a nightmare atmosphere of terror as buildings burned and guns were fired in both provocation and repression.

CAUSAL FACTORS

The Kerner Commission on Civil Disorders blamed ghetto riots on discrimination and inequality. Although blacks have made absolute

[18]See Walter White, *A Man Called White* (New York: Viking, 1948); excerpt "Atlanta 1906: Walter White Discovers His Identity," reprinted in Richard P. Sherman, ed., *The Negro and the City* (Englewood Cliffs, N.J.: Prentice-Hall, Inc., 1970), pp. 121–26.

[19]Joseph Boskin, *Urban Racial Violence in the Twentieth Century* (Beverly Hills: Glencoe Press, 1969).

[20]"Open Letter on White Justice and the Riots (1967)" *Trans-Action* (Sept. 1967); reprinted in Joseph R. Gusfield, ed., *Protest, Reform and Revolt: A Reader in Social Movements* (New York: John Wiley, 1970), pp. 214–25.

gains in status, many gains elude ghetto blacks, who feel both absolute and relative deprivation. Ghetto residents perceive the legitimate channels of change as closed to them. They have little confidence in elected officials or civil rights organizations. They are hostile to the agents of social control, symbolized by the police. In this atmosphere of threat, distrust, and fear, rumors of an impending riot constitute verbal milling, sensitizing people to the possibility of a riot and even arousing some hope that a riot would force improvements.[21] Add to this a warm summer night in a crowded neighborhood, with many people out on the street, and almost any small incident symbolizing their grievances may set off a riot.

THE COURSE OF A RIOT

Like all collective behavior, riots are unpredictable. But such studies as that of the Kerner Commission have established a few generalizations. The precipitating incident may be an arrest, or fury over some event such as the assassination of Martin Luther King, Jr. First there is a small active core of participants with a relatively passive audience. The forming crowd engages in milling, clustering around several impromptu leaders who help define the situation and "keynote" it, making various suggestions for action. The focus of action shifts according to how the police respond. The situation may get out of control swiftly; as members of the crowd perceive that deviant acts go unpunished, they begin to act on the complaints and grievances that circulated during the milling period. New norms emerge, such as "Burn out the white businessmen who exploit us, but spare 'soul brothers.'"

There is a sense of group solidarity, but little organization. People come out of different motives and engage in somewhat different kinds of actions. Some want to act out their grievances. Some come out of sheer curiosity. Some are drawn to the scene as they pass by and see the throng. Others may be agitators or instigators who hope to exploit the situation for revolutionary ends. Still others use it for their own ends, perhaps picking up a TV set. Then there are the agents of social control who try to "cool it" or repress the action—city officials, police, church, civic, and local leaders.

The first direct aggressive action is often throwing rocks and bottles at police and at stores, smashing windows; these early actions are typically carried out in small groups of five to twenty young men in their teens and early twenties. Looting and burning follow. The larger the riot gets, the easier it seems to participate, as deviance goes unpunished except sporadically. Finally, after hours of rioting, tired,

---

[21]James R. Hundley, Jr., "The Dynamics of Recent Ghetto Riots," *Detroit Journal of Urban Law* 45 (1968): 627–39; slightly revised version reprinted in Evans, *Readings in Collective Behavior*, pp. 480–92.

frightened men in uniform, perhaps the National Guard, get trigger-happy, and violence comes to a deadly peak. Reports and rumors of sniping add to the terror. Finally, rioting ends, having lasted as long as 4 or 5 days.

PROFILE OF A RIOTER

By no means are all the rioters "young hoodlums." More than half of those arrested in the Watts riot of 1965 were over twenty-five; 40% were over thirty. Two-thirds of those arrested were employed. The Kerner Report describes the typical rioter in 1967 as an unmarried black male between the ages of fifteen and twenty-four, a life-long resident of the city, of about the same economic status as nonpartici-pants. He had not usually finished high school but had attended for a time, and thus was better educated than the average ghetto-dweller. He was doing unskilled or menial work, and was often unemployed or worked part-time. He felt strongly that he deserved a better job but that he was discriminated against. He took great pride in his race and was extremely hostile to whites and also to middle-class blacks. "He is substantially better informed about politics than Negroes who were not involved in the riots. He is more likely to be actively engaged in civil rights efforts, but is extremely distrustful of the political system and of political leaders."[22]

CONSEQUENCES OF RIOTS

What do riots accomplish, if anything? Death and destruction, which hit the ghetto-dwellers themselves hardest, are measurable enough. What about social change?

Riots in general may invite brutal repression; or they may be tolerated, and serve merely to dissipate the energies of the angry or divert them to a scapegoat. They may also bring about change, directly or indirectly. Student riots in the 1960s helped topple several govern-ments (in Indonesia, for example); but such direct consequences are unusual. Most contributions to social change are indirect.

Riots are, in essence, a bargaining device used by powerless groups—a way of saying "Listen to me!" They may make those in power more aware of problems, or, if they have been aware but neglect-ful, pressure them into action. They heighten group consciousness and solidarity. They may serve as catalysts for more organized efforts at protest and reform. They may be the prelude to broader, more revolu-tionary social movements: Riots preceded the American, French, and Russian revolutions. They give rise to new groups, new leaders, new heroes and martyrs.

[22]*Report of the National Advisory Commission on Civil Disorders* (Washington, D.C.: U.S. Government Printing Office, 1968).

The most apparent consequences of the riots in recent years, however, have been polarization and heightened conflict. Attempts at control by uniformed authorities confirm the ghetto's estimate of white justice. Ghetto violence in turn confirms many whites in their prejudices. Extremists on both sides may see arming in "self-defense" as the only possible measure in anticipation of further violence. Some fear that the ghetto riots of the 1960s may give way to two armed camps engaged in terror and counter-terror, like the Black Panthers and the police.[23]

The Study of Social Movements

A social movement is "a collectivity acting with some continuity to promote a change or resist a change in the society or group of which it is a part."[24] Unlike a riot, it is not an outburst, but a continuing effort. Its members agree as to what is wrong with the social order, what should replace it, and how the change might be brought about. A social movement usually transcends local boundaries. Whether or not they formally "join" an organization, pay dues, and carry cards, members feel a sense of belonging and participation.

There are many possible approaches to the study of social movements. Psychologists are especially interested in the personalities of leaders and followers of various kinds of movements. Political scientists study them as a source of reform, a check on power, the incipient stage of new political parties. Anthropologists see them in relation to culture conflicts, often produced by contact between modern and traditional societies.[25] Historians and journalists are especially interested in revolutions and in utopian experiments. "Certainly one attraction in studying social movements is to marvel at the peculiar ideologies and forms of behavior some men can devise."[26]

Sociologists are especially interested in the relationship of social movements to social change (both as cause and effect), to demographic

[23]Sherman, *The Negro and the City*, chap. 6, "Urban Violence"; Boskin, *Urban Racial Violence*; J. Paul Mitchell, ed., *Race Riots in Black and White* (Englewood Cliffs, N.J.: Prentice-Hall, Inc., 1970); Gary T. Marx, "Riots," *Encyclopedia Britannica*, reprinted in Peter I. Rose, ed., *The Study of Society: An Integrated Anthology*, 2nd ed. (New York: Random House, 1970), pp. 906–14; Leonard Gordon, *A City in Racial Crisis: The Case of Detroit Pre- and Post- the 1967 Riot* (Wm. C. Brown Company Publishers, 1971); Bob Clark, "Nightmare Journey," *Ebony* (Oct. 1967): 121–30, and Sol Stern, "The Call of the Black Panthers," *The New York Times* (Aug. 6, 1967), both reprinted in Freeman and Kurtz, *America's Troubles: A Casebook in Social Conflict* (Englewood Cliffs, N.J.: Prentice-Hall, Inc., 1969).

[24]Ralph H. Turner and Lewis M. Killian, *Collective Behavior*, 2nd ed. (Englewood Cliffs, N.J.: Prentice-Hall, Inc., 1972), p. 246.

[25]See page 560 for a description of the Melanesian "cargo cult."

[26]Cameron, *Modern Social Movements*, p. 173.

and ecological variables, and to social institutions. They study the various kinds of movements, their careers, their strategies and tactics. How, they ask, is one movement related to others, to the less organized phenomena of collective behavior, and to the status quo? What consequences does it have for its members, for specific social institutions, and for the society as a whole?

Such study is especially urgent in our time, for, as the President's Commission on Campus Unrest declared in September 1970, American society is undergoing a crisis of violence and a crisis of understanding greater than at any time since the Civil War, and Americans are in danger of losing their common values because of their growing intolerance of opposition and of diversity.

Kinds of Social Movements

Although all social movements are "collective actions to establish a new order of life," in Blumer's comprehensive definition, they exhibit great variety. Some are oriented toward action, others to expressiveness. Some have broad, sweeping goals, others narrow and specific ones; some, immediate goals, others long-range ones. Some are diffuse and uncoordinated; others clear-cut and well organized. Some are pluralistic, made up of a number of groups with the same general goal but differing ideas of specific ends and means; others are monolithic, consisting of one large strong organization.

RELATION TO THE STATUS QUO

Perhaps the most common way of classifying social movements is according to their orientation to the status quo. **Reactionary** social movements reject the status quo (in whole or in part) because old values and goals have been abandoned. They hark back to the good old days and seek to restore a presumably superior way of life, a grand and glorious heritage. (To the John Birch Society, it is "the American Way of Life" as they define it; to the Ku Klux Klan, the restoration of white supremacy.) **Conservative** movements (often taking the form of factions in the major political parties) aim to keep things as they are, to save or conserve, to maintain the status quo. Their goals have for some time been those of the society in general, and they resist changes that threaten those goals.

Reform or revisionary movements work for partial change within the system—changes in specific norms, beliefs, values, or relationships. They seek to promote or defeat laws about abortion or homosexuality or school segregation; to clean up a city's government; to meet the needs of retarded children. They do not threaten the existing structure. **Revolutionary** movements, in contrast, reject the total social order as inadequate or evil and aim to replace it with something different. ("Liberals" are usually reformers; "radicals" may be either reactionaries or revolutionaries.) History is replete with such movements, including the political revolutions of America, France, Russia, Cuba, and China; and contemporary ones also abound.[27] **Separatist or withdrawal** movements consider the status quo hopeless and seek only to escape it by setting up their own socio-cultural order, as do secessionist blacks, as did the Mormons who migrated to Utah, and as do many sects and secret societies, as well as the diffuse groups in modern societies who are building an alternative society with a counterculture. Finally, **expressive** movements, such as some dancing sects, provide emotional release from the tensions and pressures generated by the status quo as it affects different groups.

The modern era has been characterized by mass movements that seek revolutionary change. Communism, like Nazism, promises total social change and demands total allegiance. Mass movements arise out of serious social disorganization, such as that of Germany after World War I and China after years of foreign domination, civil strife, and war with Japan. Their leaders are convinced that they hold the key to the future. When a revolutionary movement gains control of the society, it typically uses totalitarian methods to maintain control. Often it directs the attention of the people toward external expansion, war, and "enemies" to heighten the feeling of unity and of the urgency of building a new order. This was true of the Stalin era in the Soviet Union as well as of Hitler's Germany and Castro's Cuba, and only now is the People's Republic of China showing signs of relaxing this stance. Its leaders are keenly aware that coercion and fear have limits in motivating people; they depend largely on persuasion, including the use of inspirational "thoughts of Mao."

GENERAL AND SPECIFIC MOVEMENTS

The Back-to-Africa Movement of Marcus Garvey had a definite goal and a definite leader; it was a specific organization. Today's black protest movement embraces many groups and styles, including episodic protest such as ghetto riots, marches on Washington, organizations that

[27]The concept of revolution assumes many forms. It is generally distinguished from insurrection or revolt that merely seeks to replace one ruling elite with another; often it is limited to sudden and violent changes in the political structure. In previous chapters we have used it to refer to sweeping changes in the social order over long periods of time, such as the democratic revolution and the Industrial Revolution. In this sense, a revolution is a fundamental change in many aspects of a socio-cultural order—culture, social structure, and the distribution of wealth, power, and prestige. But it does not always come about through a concerted social movement with a definite goal; industrialization, for example, did not.

seek legal reforms for civil rights, black militant organizations, separatist movements, and political organizations. Similarly, the Women's Liberation movement has no monolithic organization, but is a coalition of many groups as small as those meeting weekly in someone's living room and as large as National Organization for Women; it also includes many different points of view on goals and tactics. The "student protest movement," too, is a general one, held together not by organization but by similar beliefs about war, racism, poverty, the role of the university, and a new life style. "Withdrawal, protest, reform, insurrection, and even revolution may co-exist among partisans of a movement, as separate organizations, events, or 'wings.' "[28]

REBELLION AND PROTEST VS. EDUCATION

Some social movements consist mostly of protest in its various forms; they seem to lack a program; they have "no place to go." Klapp thinks the contagious ghetto violence of the 1960s, New Left activism, radical right extremism, the countercultural rebellion, and the drug-oriented dropout movement have this in common. They all are characterized by protest against the status quo (the "Establishment" to those on the left, an ideologically corrupt welfare state to those on the right); against "progress" (which is seen as leading to all-powerful bureaucracies or to socialism); against the effort to attain affluence, except in the ghetto. "All, frustrated, seem to turn to irrational directions, and seem more concerned with style, slogans, and emotional outlet than with practical progress."[29]

Kenneth Boulding suggests that

> We might perhaps distinguish between protest movements and educational movements, the one designed to crystallize a change for which it is ready, the other to push the society toward a change for which it is not ready. The techniques of these two movements may be very different. A protest movement needs to be shrill, obstreperous, undignified, and careless of the pattern of existing legitimacy which it is seeking to destroy in the interest of a new pattern which is waiting to emerge. Educational movements have to be low-keyed, respectful of existing legitimacies, and tying into them wherever possible, and chary of arousing counterprotest. A good example of this in race relations is the work of the NAACP, which unquestionably laid the groundwork for the recent protest movement in civil rights. . . . The movement for social security in this country is an interesting example of one in which the educational process dominates it almost completely, and where the role of protest is almost negligible.[30]

[28]Joseph R. Gusfield, ed., *Protest, Reform, and Revolt: A Reader in Social Movements* (New York: John Wiley, 1970), p. 87.

[29]*Collective Search for Identity*, p. 57.

[30]"Reflections on Protest," *Social Education*   30, No. 1 (Jan. 1966): 28–29, 33.

Harper's Magazine, June, 1966.

*"In protest against everything, that's
what it's in protest against!"*

MILLENNIAL MOVEMENTS

Millennial movements believe the end of the world—at least as we know it—is at hand. They are based on a "future-oriented religious ideology," which rejects the present as "totally evil and abysmally corrupt" and looks forward to a time when "the world will be inhabited by a humanity liberated from all the limitations of human existence, redeemed from pain and transience, from fallibility and sin, thus becoming at once perfectly good and perfectly happy. The world will be utterly, completely, and irrevocably changed. Radical millenarian movements regard the millennium as imminent and live in tense expectation and preparation for it."[31] Adherents of some such movements expect the millennium to arrive suddenly and miraculously, with no preparatory struggle; others believe it will be born out of "unprecedented cataclysms, disastrous upheavals, and bloody calamities." Members gather, watch for signs, and purify themselves with rituals. In some movements, the follower must be active and responsible: "Every minute and every deed count and everything must be sacrificed to the cause." Most such movements are also **messianic**, that is, "redemption is brought about by a messiah who mediates between the divine and the human."

[31]Yonina Talmon, "The Millennial Dream," *The European Journal of Sociology* 2 (1962): 130–44; reprinted in Gusfield, *Protest, Reform, and Revolt*, pp. 436–52. Quotations in this paragraph and the next are from this source.

Fundamentalist Christians who await the Second Coming of Jesus, and millenarians who believe a sleeping monarch will be brought back to life, are examples.

Millenarianism is essentially a religion of the deprived, of oppressed peasants and desperately poor city-dwellers. It appears after calamitous wars, plagues, and famines when despair is "coupled with political helplessness." Being revolutionary, and often calling on its believers to prepare actively for the event, and even to revolt, it is "a very potent agent of change." It may be the forerunner of political action; if a millenarian sect is frequently proven wrong in its prediction of the end of the world, its disillusioned members may turn to political action.

The "cargo cult" of Melanesia is a crude and extreme form of millenarian movement. It emerged after contact with white men, whose array of goods or "cargo" seemed beyond the reach of dark-skinned islanders. Not understanding the economic system of Western man, they ascribed his affluence to magical rituals which he selfishly kept secret. Trying to discover his secrets, they experimented with contraptions of tin cans and string that resembled radios and telephones, and made "refrigerators" of packing boxes to be ready for the magical appearance of canned foods and beer. They cleared spaces in the jungle for fleets of airplanes loaded with goods; one group abandoned all its usual rice-growing and pig-raising to make a landing field on a mountaintop for 400 Boeing 707s. Another raised money to bring Lyndon Johnson to rule them in place of the Australians. Many believe that the arrival of the cargo will usher in the millennium of peace and happiness, free them from bondage to alien domination, and banish all human ills.[32]

CRUSADING MOVEMENTS

> A crusade is a type of movement that rises above ordinary life because it requires one to leave business-as-usual and commit himself earnestly to something he believes in deeply. [It] carries both a cross and a sword. The sword signifies attack on wrong, defense of right, and cutting the bonds of ordinary concern. The cross signifies commitment to higher ideals, mystiques—indeed, every crusade has a cultic aspect, whatever its practical goals, because it needs and uses ritual and achieves redemption of identity along with its practical work.[33]

A crusade differs from ordinary movements in its militance, its righteousness, its image of evil, and its sense of uphill struggle; any mem-

[32]See Robert Trumbull, "No One Had to Walk More Than Two Days to Reach a Polling Place," *The New York Times Magazine* (May 7, 1972): 32 ff., for an account of the consequences of this cult for the traditional order and its possible consequences now that Papua New Guinea is on the threshold of self-government.

[33]Klapp, *Collective Search for Identity*, p. 257.

ber can be a hero. Carrie Nation's hatchet and Don Quixote's lance are crusading symbols. The commitment of members ranges from zeal to fanaticism. Because a crusade rejects compromise, it may be a threat to democracy; absolute morality may lead to authoritarianism.

A John Birch Society meeting is like a church service for the faithful, who "come away confirmed and uplifted, feeling that life has more significance." The crusader role confers a feeling of "rightness" and power; it gives one a new self. Civil rights crusaders who went to Mississippi in the dangerous summer of 1964 had to break with the routines and obligations of normal life and start a new life, with a sense of courage and purpose.[34]

The Career of Social Movements

Not all unrest and protest is channeled into social movements, and not all social movements become highly organized and focused. "A movement has to be constructed and has to carve out a career in what is practically always an opposed, resistant, or at least indifferent world."[35] Values and norms emerge, are formulated, revised, and reformulated. Goals are defined and narrowed, tactics decided upon and changed as

[34]*Ibid.*, chap. 8, "Crusades."
[35]Blumer, "Collective Behavior."

Feminist protest.

the situation or new leadership may determine. Different types of leaders are prominent at different stages and in different kinds of movements; followers have varying motives for joining, and varying degrees of commitment. Some movements finally become institutionalized as an accepted part of the socio-cultural order.

EMERGENCE

Some movements emerge from crowds, others from publics. A crowd tends to develop a uniform course of action and to impose it on its members, while a public considers different positions before determining a course of action. A crowd gives birth to a social movement if it develops an enduring sense of group identity and adopts a plan of action that can be carried out only through sustained activity. Crowd activity may continue to be an aspect of the movement. A social movement emerges from a public if its members not only interact and discover common ground, but also decide to organize in order to promote their views more effectively.

Movements may also emerge from other movements. Many of the early activists in Women's Liberation were involved in the civil rights and antiwar movements (just as suffragettes were first abolitionists). When they found they were treated not as equals, but as envelope-stuffers and coffee-fetchers, they began to communicate their resentment to one another. Similarly, the student protest movement emerged out of the civil rights movement; the leaders of the Free Speech movement at Berkeley in 1964 had spent the summer trying to register black voters in Mississippi.

A vague sense of oppression must be defined, the oppressors identified, the resentment justified, and the means for overcoming it outlined. Several books that appeared during the sixties and early seventies performed these functions for Women's Liberation. The first was Betty Friedan's *The Feminine Mystique*, followed by Kate Millett's *Sexual Politics*, and Robin Morgan's anthology, *Sisterhood Is Powerful*.[36] Among various definitions of the situation is the Redstockings Manifesto:

> Women are an oppressed class. Our oppression is total, affecting every facet of our lives. We are exploited as sex objects, breeders, domestic servants, and cheap labor. We are considered inferior beings, whose only purpose is to enhance men's lives. Our humanity is denied. . . .
>
> We identify the agents of our oppression as men. Male supremacy is the oldest, most basic form of oppression.[37]

[36]*The Feminine Mystique* (New York: Dell, 1963); *Sexual Politics* (New York: New American Library, 1969); *Sisterhood Is Powerful: An Anthology of Writings from the Women's Liberation Movement* (New York: Random House, Vintage Books, 1970).

[37]Morgan, *Sisterhood Is Powerful*, pp. 533–34.

Other less sweeping definitions of the situation deal with job discrimination, the lack of choice and opportunity in careers, the constricting nature of conventional sex roles—male as well as female—and the waste of energy and talent involved.

During the incipient phase, a movement may be formless and confused. Despite unrest and enthusiasm, tactics may be crude or unformulated, aims undefined or very general; the danger of the movement's early demise because of disagreements, lack of experience, and scant resources is great. The success of a social movement in "getting off the ground" often depends on its leadership.

STAGES OF ORGANIZATION AND KINDS OF LEADERS

"It is the emergence of an organized structure that turns a sporadic demonstration, an angry crowd, or an aggregate of individual dissidents into collective action of significance for social change."[38] This involves a division of labor and a division of authority—the emergence of a structured system of leaders and followers.

The emergence of a new social movement is often symbolized in the person of a charismatic leader, whose power over his followers is based on the force of his personality rather than on traditional right or legal sanction. A charismatic leader is typically bold, impulsive, and dramatic—a symbol of the values of the new movement. Charisma is an aura, difficult to define, shared by saints and demagogues. Jesus and Martin Luther King, Jr., had charisma; so did Hitler. A charismatic leader is both agitator and prophet. He inspires confidence and loyalty, and builds morale by communicating his conviction that the purposes of the movement are absolutely right, his faith that its goal will ultimately be attained, and his belief that the movement is charged with a sacred mission. He may seem impractical, idealistic, or even fanatical to outsiders, but to his followers he is a hero. Martyrdom, the ultimate heroism, makes abandonment of the movement a betrayal.[39]

A charismatic leader has a band of faithful lieutenants or disciples, who try to gain followers by conversion, agitation, and promises. Some are fanatical "true believers"; their sense of mission is strong. Robin Morgan, for example, declares, "More and more, I begin to think of a worldwide Women's Revolution as the only hope for life on the planet."[40] Huey Newton of the Black Panthers is quoted as saying he would rather give up his life than his principles. Such people are also hard-core activists as compared to the rank-and-file members and the fellow travelers and sympathizers on the fringes of the movement.

One task of leaders is to build unity and continuity into a movement. "Many movements are composed of diverse segments, each with

[38]Gusfield, *Protest, Reform, and Revolt,* p. 453.
[39]Killian, "Social Movements," in Faris, *Handbook of Modern Sociology.*
[40]*Sisterhood Is Powerful,* p. xxxv.

its own structure, loosely united only by their allegiance to the central, explicit values and by the tendency of outsiders to view them as parts of a single whole. Yet there is a strain toward centralization in any movement, and lack of a unified structure can be a source of weakness."[41] Different segments compete for members and dispute goals and tactics.

Whether it is one large organization or a loose coalition, an organized movement is headed by a legal–administrative leader (who may also be the founder or charismatic leader). This kind of leader is more tolerant of compromise than the inspiring, single-minded charismatic leader; he must be practical to oversee the details of organization, recruitment, strategy, financing, and discipline. An organized social movement has a division of labor and a structure of authority—a name, a headquarters, perhaps local units, and a constitution. Examples are Planned Parenthood, Project Hope, and the NAACP.

A third kind of leader is the intellectual leader who formulates the movement's *ideology*, a set of ideas about how things came to be as bad as they are, how they can be changed, and why it is right to work for change through the particular movement. One of the chief tasks of leaders is to build *esprit de corps*, a sense of identification with the movement. "We" are the heroes; "they" are the villains. Members may take oaths, promising to fulfill duties and obligations, and recite creeds —capsule statements of the ideology—and thus acknowledge that they share the accepted beliefs. The unity of a movement may also be promoted with identifying symbols such as costumes, badges, secret handshakes, certain words and phrases. Ritual and ceremony exert a powerful influence. Discipline is enforced by a system of rewards and punishments. Informal fellowship may be encouraged as a way of building a sense of belonging. The Women's Liberation movement, still a diffuse and pluralistic one, is based on small groups of women who meet for "consciousness raising." Over a century ago, Lucy Stone proclaimed this tactic for gaining commitment to the feminist movement: "In education, in marriage, in everything, disappointment is the lot of woman. It shall be the business of my life to deepen this disappointment in every woman's heart until she bows down to it no longer."

Social movements, once organized, tend to become ends in themselves; their administrative leaders, in particular, come to have a vested interest in their continuance. The March of Dimes, established to combat infantile paralysis, did not dissolve when this goal was reached; it redefined its purpose to include the battle against birth defects.

INSTITUTIONALIZATION

A movement to promote social change may fade away for various reasons. It may have its teeth pulled when its goals become official policy, as happened to the Townsend movement of the 1930s, when

[41]Killian, "Social Movements."

social security legislation provided its goal of old-age pensions. Or it may become part of "the Establishment" itself, as the organized labor movement has done. Unions have long been the recognized agents for bargaining with management over wages, benefits, and conditions of work. Dissident sects may grow into organized, respectable churches. A revolutionary movement may topple the government and take over the seats of power; the Communist revolutions in Russia and China have been institutionalized.

Strategies and Tactics of Social Movements

A strategy is the general program for reaching the goals of a movement; tactics are the specific techniques and activities used to gain new members or attain goals. The NAACP, for example, adopted a legalistic strategy, using the tactics of negotiation, voting, educational training, and bringing test cases of civil rights violations into the courts. Strategies and tactics vary with the clearness, specificity, and nature of the movement's goals; its diffuseness or centralization; its orientation to the status quo; the nature of its leadership; and the stage of its career. In the earliest stages, they may be oriented more toward creating unrest among potential followers than toward attacking "wrongs."

Strategies and tactics may be legal or illegal, violent or nonviolent. Some movements adopt the strategy of *societal manipulation*, to reach their goals regardless of the extent of popular support; they may resort to military revolt or economic boycott, or they may use legislative, judicial, or executive authority in support of unpopular "rights." Others depend primarily on *personal transformation*, seeking success through widespread conversion of individuals to the beliefs and practices of the movement; examples are proselytizing religious movements and reform movements requiring popular support.[42]

Mass movements depend more on crowd behavior than on the democratic exchange of ideas in publics. The Chinese, for example, enforce decisions by assembling and manipulating crowds.

> A mass meeting may serve any ulterior purpose, such as popularizing the idea in the Marriage Law by utilizing the striking effect of an "unusual" issue or incident, for instance, the tragic death of a person on account of family conflict; for any unusual issue switches the attention of the audience from their routinized daily behavior and thought and focuses it on the issue which is magnified and dramatized for emotional effect. In the mass meeting the emotions of an unruly crowd are unleashed to throw the routinized thought and behavior further out of balance, to release institutionally inhibited feel-

---

[42]Lewis M. Killian, "Social Movements," in Faris, *Handbook of Modern Sociology,* pp. 426–55.

ings, to heighten the sense of popular justice by circular reaction induced by slogan-shouting, yelling, and repetitive speeches and stories, and finally to pass an unconventional resolution to settle an "unusual" issue. Immediately after passing the resolution as a "popular demand" comes the moralization of the lesson, which is the real aim of the whole show. Still reeling from the·high emotional tension generated, the audience is induced to accept not only the solution to the issue but also the moral lesson as interpreted by the masters of the show, the chairman, and the directors of the mass meeting. Thus a new rule is set up to govern an aspect of social life that used to be governed by a very different rule, and the formerly inviolate traditional pattern is broken.[43]

In democracies with free speech and tolerance of dissent, reform movements find political strategies effective. They try to influence public opinion, put pressure on legislators, and are willing to compromise and give-and-take. Ralph Nader exemplifies the crusading reformer, who unearths evidence of wrongs, publicizes them, and influences public opinion and legislation. But when goals are not clear, strategies may shift between constructive activism and nihilistic violence. Tom Hayden of the New Left, challenged to define its goals, retorted, "First we'll make the revolution—then we'll find out what for."

TACTICS OF PROTEST MOVEMENTS

The President's Commission on Campus Unrest distinguished between orderly and disorderly protest. It defined *orderly protest* as "peaceful manifestation of dissent, such as holding meetings, picketing, vigils, demonstrations, and marches—all of which are protected by the First Amendment." *Disorderly protest* includes disruptive tactics, which interfere with normal activity; violence, which involves physical injury to people and the willful destruction of property by vandalism, burning, and bombing; and terrorism, which involves the careful planning and deliberate use of violence in a systematic way to create an atmosphere of fear, in order to promote revolutionary change.

Protest movements with diffuse objectives often use demonstrations and marches. While any demonstration helps to build esprit de corps, an effective demonstration must be closely related to the object of protest. The black students who sat at a dime store lunch counter in Greensboro, North Carolina, where only whites were served, and refused to move until they were served or carried away, made a specific point. So did the Montgomery bus boycott. Such nonviolent protests do not deny the humanity of the adversary, but dramatize one of his injustices.

[43]C. K. Yang, *Chinese Communist Society: The Family and the Village* (Cambridge: M.I.T. Press, 1959), p. 204.

Women's Liberationists have used expressive symbolism spiced with humor. Posters calling for a strike used the slogan "Don't Iron While the Strike Is Hot." Women journalists in New Orleans ran pictures of the groom in wedding announcements. Women in the Netherlands placed pink ribbons across the doors of men's public urinals, protesting the lack of such conveniences for women.

Nonviolence and civil disobedience. Such tactics as sit-ins are sometimes defined as "disorderly protest" because they disrupt normal routine. They have, however, been highly effective in dramatizing injustice and changing public policy. Nonviolence, or passive resistance, is associated with the concept of civil disobedience, the deliberate breaking of some law or ordinance on moral grounds. Civil disobedience does not repudiate an entire system; rather it denies the legitimacy of certain laws, policies, or specific practices. This denial is based on a conviction that core values are being violated. Often its adherents declare themselves more deeply committed to the ideals of the system (American democracy, for example) than those who conform passively and obey without question. Herbert Kelman insists

> Democratic processes become meaningless and corrupt if citizens never challenge official policies in terms of their consistency with basic societal and human values, if they never consider civil disobedience as an option of last resort. In a healthy democratic society, there is a time to obey and a time to disobey, a time to say yes and a time to say no, a time to speak in words and a time to speak in actions.[44]

Those who engage in civil disobedience ideally adhere to nonviolence, are ready to accept legal punishment, and keep as close a connection as possible between the action and the object of protest. Like its leading proponents, Gandhi and Martin Luther King, Jr., they refuse to use violence themselves and are willing to give themselves to the violence of their opponents (perhaps the formal agents of social control) in order to display a superior moral force. Gandhi simply crossed his legs and refused to move; civil rights and antiwar protesters stood their ground and, when arrested, went limp and had to be dragged away.

Disruption and violence. Quasi-violent or disruptive tactics may dramatize a movement, but they may also provoke a strong backlash, especially when they have no obvious connection with the object of protest. In 1912–1914 women suffragists used disruptive methods as well as passive resistance and violence. One day in London women produced hammers, sticks, and stones from their muffs and bags, and for

[44]*A Time to Speak: On Human Values and Social Research* (San Francisco: Jossey-Bass, 1968); an excerpt, "The Relevance of Non-violent Action," appears in Schuler *et al., Readings in Sociology,* 4th ed. (New York: Crowell, 1971), pp. 253–67.

15 or 20 minutes broke store windows on main streets. They slashed upholstery in railroad cars, poured jam down mailboxes, cut phone wires, planted homemade bombs, turned in false fire alarms, and set fires. They taunted and spat on policemen. The tactics of Weathermen were anticipated by their grandmothers.

A small minority in the student and black protest movements is attracted to violence and terrorism, quoting with approval Mao's dictum that "Political power grows out of the barrel of a gun," and citing Franz Fanon's argument in *The Wretched of the Earth* that violence is useful, therapeutic, and indispensable. They condemn any compromise, any work within "the system" which they consider totally corrupt.

Americans generally subscribe to a myth that all our progress has come about peacefully, through reform and wise legislation. A study of history reveals, however, that the present cycle of violence and terrorism is about the seventh such cycle since Shays' Rebellion in 1786; there have been violent urban, agrarian, and racial-religious-ethnic disorders.[45] Furthermore, Americans tend to put a great deal of faith in the use of force to solve problems; if it fails, they escalate.[46]

Timely reform and peaceful protest drain away the urge toward violence. Repression controls it only temporarily. "In any social system, —whether a nation, a conquered country, a gang, a prison, or a family," says William J. Goode, "violence breeds violence. If you use violence to control people, they will hate you and use it themselves when they get the chance. . . . All social order and obedience to authority rests basically on people's belief that the system is fundamentally decent, fair, honorable, and protective to its members."[47] People deprived of autonomy and dignity are more inclined to harm others.

The Youth Movement

The diffuse, widespread "youth movement" in its varied aspects illustrates many of the concepts and principles we have discussed. The student protest movement, the hippie movement, and communal experiments are overlapping manifestations of a cultural revolution, mostly among the young—a revolution in life styles, including folkways, mores, patterns of human relationships, and above all values. Its members are mostly children of affluent middle-class parents, but in many cases they are not rebelling against the parents themselves.

[45]Richard Maxwell Brown, *American Violence* (Englewood Cliffs, N.J.: Prentice-Hall, Inc., 1970).

[46]Stringfellow Barr, "Violence and the Home of the Brave," in Irving Louis Horowitz, ed., *The Troubled Conscience: American Social Issues* (Santa Barbara: Center for the Study of Democratic Institutions, 1971), p. 6.

[47]*The New York Times* (Sept. 20, 1971), commenting on the Attica prison riot.

In a sample survey of activist students Richard Flacks found that they rebel out of deep discontent over the differences they see between the values they learned from parents and peers and the values represented by the authority and occupational structure of the larger society. "Whereas nonactivists and their parents tend to express conventional orientations toward achievement, material success, sexual morality and religion, the activists *and their parents* tend to place greater stress on involvement in intellectual and esthetic pursuits, humanitarian concerns, opportunity for self-expression."[48]

They are rebelling, then, against the general preoccupation with economic growth, maximum production, acquisition of material symbols of success, and conformity to "dehumanizing" institutions that have failed to solve the problems of war, racism, and starvation and have made people insensitive to one another. This rebellion manifests itself in activism ranging from orderly protest against specific policies to revolutionary terrorism among a minority, expressive and withdrawal movements, and experiments with communal living and other life styles.

In general these last two manifestations of the movement share a concern with the quality of life, with creativeness and fulfillment, joyful and zestful living. Affluence and the prolongation of youth provide them with the opportunity to explore and experiment, criticize and protest, without risking too much. They believe they are seeking and expressing "higher" values than the conventional ones, especially personal integrity and freedom, and a sense of identity and community (the spirit of the "Woodstock Nation"). They stress a balance of "doing your own thing" and helpfulness, sharing, and fairness, with collective decision-making (sometimes called "participatory democracy"). There is a strong expressive-religious element, seen not only in such wings of the movement as the "Jesus People" but in interest in astrology, mysticism, and the occult, and in meditation and spiritual search. Protest against the fragmentation of modern life is expressed in an interest in "wholeness," from whole grains to whole personalities. Rebellion against the domination of society by huge corporations and by the idea of technological progress is evidenced by the popularity of back-to-the-land movements and voluntary poverty; the best-selling *Whole Earth Catalog* promotes self-sufficiency by listing tools, devices, and sources of information about "doing it yourself." There is a great reverence for nature and for life, and the youth movement has in a sense adopted the ecological conscience as its central ethic.

The hippie "tribe" as an experiment in human relationships has been followed by a new wave of communal groups reminiscent in some ways of those that flourished—and failed—in great numbers a hundred years ago. Urban and rural communes include more and more adults.

48"The Liberated Generation: An Exploration of the Roots of Student Protest," *Journal of Social Issues* 23, No. 3 (1967): 52–75; reprinted in Rose, *The Study of Society*, pp. 939–56. [Emphasis added.]

It was estimated that in 1971 there were 3000 communes; *The New York Times* found 2000 in thirty-four states. They include a number of types, and some combine elements of more than one type: agricultural, back-to-nature, crafts, spiritual/mystical (like the Hare Krishna communes), denominational, church-sponsored but nondenominational, political-action (often revolutionary), community service (with members from the "helping professions" such as teaching and social work), art, teaching, homosexual, personal growth-centered, mobile or gypsy communes (financed by putting on shows, especially on college campuses), and street or neighborhood communes. Members of a commune share their money, work, space, ideas, and goals. Some hold "straight" jobs; many have small crafts industries; others work in underground newspapers or run consumer cooperatives or "food conspiracies." They have "free" churches, universities, schools, clinics. They are, in short,

> trying to create a new style of life halfway between dropping out and dropping in, a sort of Culture in Limbo that remains concerned with the system but is not part of it. . . . Something is happening here. It's very tentative, and very fluid, but quite real. . . . People really are beginning to build a community based on cooperation, not competition, on serving others rather than oneself. That could be a hell of a lot more revolutionary than smashing windows on Telegraph Avenue.[49]

The youth movement may be seen as a subsociety with a subculture, often called a **counterculture** because it is "so radically disaffiliated from the mainstream assumptions of our society that it scarcely looks to many like a culture at all, but takes on the alarming appearance of a barbaric intrusion."[50] The appearance of many young people is "a symbolic protest against the social order," a style rebellion that "asserts another way of life. It claims the right to be something that convention has heretofore said one has no right to be." Many dress in faded blue jeans, ragged tennis shoes, sandals, or bare feet, scraggly beards and long hair, and dark glasses, announcing "indifference and escape from prevailing norms . . . expressed by calculated uncouthness —the style of the castaway, beachcomber, drifter, vagrant, outcast. [It] says essentially, 'Let me live my own life, you square!' "[51] Many also

---

[49]Steven V. Roberts, "Halfway Between Dropping Out and Dropping In," *The New York Times Magazine* (Sept. 12, 1971): 44–70. See also Herbert A. Otto, "Communes: The Alternative Life-Style," *Saturday Review* (April 24, 1971): 16 ff.

[50]Theodore Roszak, *The Making of a Counter Culture: Reflections on the Technocratic Society and Its Youthful Opposition* (Garden City, N.Y.: Doubleday, 1969), p. 42.

[51]Klapp, *Collective Search for Identity*, pp. 88–95. He distinguishes other forms of style rebellion: Puritanism (the Amish and Black Muslims, for example); dandyism (London mods); mockery (by those who have to stay within the system), and barbarism (motorcycle gangs).

look like pioneers or Indians, or as if they had raided Grandmother's attic. Variety is very much a part of their experimental life style.

Many adults dismiss these phenomena as a passing phase that will be abandoned as the various young people marry and bring up children and settle into respectable jobs. Others take the cultural revolution more seriously. Fred Davis sees in the hippie subculture, for example, some indications of what life may be like in the future, when automation produces an abundance of material goods and leisure. He believes

> The flower children are already rehearsing *in vivo* a number of possible cultural solutions to central life problems posed by the emerging society of the future [such as] compulsive consumption, passive spectatorship, and . . . the time-scale of experience. . . . In phrases redolent of nearly all utopian thought of the past, [they] proclaim that happiness and a meaningful life are not to be found in things, but in the cultivation of the self and by an intensive exploration of inner sensibilities with like-minded others.[52]

For passive spectatorship and virtuoso standards of performance they substitute a belief that everyone can find expressive fulfillment in the moment, and they demonstrate this idea in folk-rock dancing, self-made music, poetry, painting, and other arts and crafts, and even in their bizarre dress. Where Western culture stresses future orientation, and acts acquire meaning from their relevance to success, salvation, career achievement, or a better social order—all to be realized in the future— the hippies shift their time perspective "from what will be to what *is*, from future promise to present fulfillment, from the mundane discounting of present feeling and mood to a sharpened awareness of their contours and their possibilities for instant alteration [and] a lust to extract from the living moment its full sensory and emotional potential." But while the culture has not taught them how to experience intense joy, it *has* taught them that a pill or a drink takes care of depression, aches and pains, insomnia, or whatever—so many have turned to drugs for a chemical boost (and sometimes escaped permanently from the reality of time perspectives!).[53]

The cultural revolution has some elements of the bohemianism of the 1920s (and long before) and of the beatnik dropout movement

---

[52]Fred Davis, "Focus on the Flower Children: Why All of Us May Be Hippies Someday," *Trans-Action* (Dec. 1967): 10–18.

[53]*Ibid.* A bestselling book, Charles Reich's *The Greening of America* (New York: Random House, Bantam Books, 1970), expressed the view that this cultural revolution will transform the social order, with political revolution as its last act. Jean-Francois Revel also believes that cultural revolution is essential to the transformation of political and economic institutions and the social structure in general, and that such a revolution is taking place in the United States, the only country where it has a chance of succeeding. [*Without Marx or Jesus; The New American Revolution Has Begun* (Garden City, N.Y.: Doubleday, 1971).]

of the 1950s. It is, however, much broader in scope, includes greater numbers of people in many more countries, touches upon more institutions, and involves more experimentation with various alternatives. Until recently, says Kenneth Keniston,

> the humanistic vision of human fulfillment and the romantic vision of an expressive, imaginative and passionate life were taken seriously only by small aristocratic or Bohemian groups. . . . They are today taken seriously as real goals by millions of students in many nations. . . . What the advanced nations have done is to create their own critics on a mass basis—that is, to create an ever-larger group of young people who take the highest values of their societies as their own, who internalize them and identify them with their own best selves, and who are willing to struggle to implement them. At the same time, the extension of youth has lessened the personal risk of dissent.[54]

Functions and Consequences of Collective Behavior and Social Movements

Collective behavior and social movements contribute to both the stability and the flexibility of a social order. To the extent that they act as safety valves for discontent, provide expression and reaffirmation of core values, and lead to solutions of problems, they prevent wholesale disruption. To the extent that they lead to new values, norms, and social structures, they contribute to change.

Even the spontaneous, unplanned episodes of riots may lead to change, by calling attention to specific actions of those in authority and creating awareness of dangerous unrest. Young civil rights activists and peace marchers stirred Americans out of apathy, and their impact on public opinion and national policy has been considerable. Some movements achieve their aims and either dissolve or become institutionalized. Others are apparent failures, but they pave the way for later and more successful movements.

Social movements such as the current cultural revolution force people to examine how they live and how they should live, to weigh their values and goals, and to become aware of alternatives. They give people a sense of power to influence authorities, or at least to control to some extent the way they will spend their own lives. The fact that movements are so numerous and episodes of collective behavior so frequent is disturbing to some. To others, it offers the solution to alienation, to loss of identity and community, out of which many movements are born. It gives them a sense of participating in the birth of a new and better socio-cultural order.

[54]"You Have to Grow Up in Scarsdale to Know How Bad Things Really Are," *The New York Times Magazine* (April 27, 1969); reprinted as "The Student Revolution" in Schuler *et al.*, *Readings in Sociology*, pp. 548–58.

Summary

Collective behavior is large-group activity that is not defined by established norms and occurs in unstructured situations. Social movements are collective actions directed toward achieving or obstructing some change in the socio-cultural order.

Circular reaction is an elementary form of collective behavior, distinguished from interpretative behavior by the fact that people do not pause to interpret stimuli and delay reaction, but reflect one another's state of feeling and intensify it. When many restless individuals engage in circular reaction, a state of social unrest exists, involving a strong urge to act, but no specific goals. It results in milling, either physical or verbal (rumor), which leads to collective excitement. If sufficiently intense and widespread, this in turn produces social contagion, the rapid and nonrational spread of a mood, impulse, or form of conduct.

These mechanisms are especially evident in crowd behavior. Acting crowds are aggressively directed toward a specific aim; expressive crowds engage in tension-releasing behavior, and may lead to the formation of religious organizations.

A mass is a large number of people who react to a common stimulus as separate, anonymous individuals, and make choices and decisions for individual reasons. The mass media create a set of common images and understandings that help create a readiness to interact in other forms of collective behavior.

A public forms around an issue and debates it, arriving at public opinion, which is based to some extent on fact and reason; true publics can form only where there is freedom of speech, of the press, and of association.

Much social unrest and collective behavior may be attributed to the dislocations inherent in the process of modernization, which uproots people from traditional communities and cultures and brings many diverse groups together. The continuing demand for freedom and equality, changes in the composition and distribution of population, alienation due to loss of identity and community, the ease of communication and transportation, awareness of social problems, and a crisis of authority—all these contribute to the frequency of collective behavior episodes and the number of social movements. They are especially apparent in democracies, where men see themselves as capable of changing things.

A riot is a relatively spontaneous and temporary outburst of hostile, illegitimate, and aggressive action by an acting crowd. Earlier in our history, riots were often pogroms directed against minority groups such as blacks; later they were pitched battles between blacks and whites; more recently they have been protest riots within ghettos. Powerless frustrated people who see other channels of protest and change as closed to them are likely to participate in riot behavior.

Social movements exhibit great variety in goals, means, and organization. In relation to the status quo they may be reactionary, conservative, reformist, revolutionary, separatist, or expressive. They may have specific goals and clear-cut organizations, or be general and diffuse, embracing many groups and different beliefs and tactics. Protest movements are designed to push a society toward a change for which it is ready, educational ones to make it more willing to accept change.

Millennial movements look forward to a cataclysmic end of the world and a new and perfect world that will replace it, often heralded by the appearance of a messiah. Crusading movements are militant and righteous and require deep commitment, allowing no compromise.

Social movements may or may not complete a career from emergence out of social unrest, through clear-cut organization, to institutionalization within the social order. A movement may be founded by a charismatic leader who symbolizes its values and goals and attracts loyal disciples and followers. Intellectual leaders formulate an ideology that defines the situation and explains and justifies the new goals and values. As a movement grows, a division of labor and a structure of authority are necessary, and an administrative leader takes charge of practical details. Finally a movement may be institutionalized—accepted as the right and proper institution for performing some legitimate function.

The strategies or general programs may be oriented toward societal manipulation regardless of popular support, or to personal conversion (an attempt to win support). Tactics include political pressure, expressive symbolism, protest demonstrations and marches, constructive activism, education, passive resistance, disruption, violence, and terrorism. Nonviolent passive resistance is the technique of many who advocate civil disobedience as a last resort. Violence invites violent repression and provokes a backlash.

The youth movement is a diffuse one, embracing action, expressiveness, and withdrawal. Its experimentation with new life styles such as communal living has created a cultural revolution. The counterculture, with its emphasis on an expressive life style, a return to nature, a greater sensitivity to others, and a spiritual search, may be seen as an experimental forerunner of new ways of living suitable to a postindustrial society.

Collective behavior and social movements contribute to both flexibility and stability. Movements may stir the public conscience, prod authorities into action, and force people to examine how they live and how they should live or might live—to reexamine their norms, beliefs, and values. They create awareness of alternatives, and give their participants a sense of identity and power, of a role in building a new and better social order.

QUESTIONS FOR FURTHER THOUGHT

1. In what kinds of collective behavior have you participated? With what motives? With what effects on you?

2. To what social movements do you belong? Why do you consider yourself a member? What are your motives for participating?

3. Distinguish between a social trend and a social movement.

4. Do you, as a student, feel discriminated against? If so, in what ways? To what do you attribute this behavior? How do you react?

5. Riots and other protests are often attributed to conspiracies and outside agitators. Assuming that they may be part of the scene, is their presence a necessary condition of protest? Is it a sufficient explanation? Discuss.

6. Analyze several current popular songs for protest themes. Do they carry a message regarding goals or methods of social change?

7. There are few hippies among blacks. How do you account for this?

8. A social movement itself may be an issue around which a public forms. Look through a few newspapers and magazines and talk to several people to get a feeling of the formation of public opinion around a particular movement. Do its goals or its tactics stimulate more controversy?

9. To your knowledge, has any leader of a current social movement combined charismatic, ideological, and administrative leadership? Any two kinds?

10. In recent or current political campaigns and elections, study the effect of the lowered voting age on (1) the sense of participation and power to change things; (2) actual participation; (3) the kind of candidates nominated and elected; and (4) the issues and tactics of the campaign.

11. One critic of the hippie movement pointed out several paradoxes, including the stress on "doing one's own thing" along with intolerance for the values of those in "straight" society. [Hans Toch, "Last Word on the Hippies," *The Nation* (Dec. 4, 1967): 582 ff.] Possibly every social movement is intolerant of opposing values. Discuss.

Part Five

SOCIAL INSTITUTIONS IN A CHANGING WORLD

In Part Four we examined the main changes of our time, the processes by which they occur, and the problems they bring. In Part Five we shall look first at the impact of these changes on three fundamental institutions —the family, religion, and education.

An institution in the general sense is an abstraction, a complex of norms or behavior patterns, understandings, and material objects, embodied in a social structure—a web of social relationships made up of interrelated statuses and roles. Each general institution is manifested in myriad groups and associations: families of many kinds, churches and sects, schools and universities.

The chief institutions of a society provide for the survival and adequate biological functioning of its members, for the birth and socialization of new members, for the production and distribution of goods and services, for the maintenance of order within the group and the protection of the group from outsiders, and for the motivation of members through a system of beliefs, values, and goals that defines the purpose and meaning of life.

In meeting these needs, institutions also channel human actions into patterned grooves, for they embody both the cultural script and the structural casting of social actors. They present a limited number of alternatives and bar other options so thoroughly that the available patterns seem to most people to be the only right and proper ones. In our time of rapid social change, however, many see each institution as open to question, experiment, and innovation.

In Chapter 19 we examine the family, religion, and education, the main institutions through which a baby becomes a human being. In asking, What *is* the family? religion? education? we shall see that the more we know about these institutions all over the world the harder it becomes to arrive at a precise definition that applies universally. Even the functions of each institution are not clear-cut. Yet everywhere there is some form of each institution, and everywhere they answer some basic need. Upon these foundations are built many varied structures, which change—not always fast enough to fulfill new needs—as circumstances change.

The final chapter is the most explicitly value-laden of the book. Building on many concepts and propositions presented throughout the book, it examines prospects for human survival and freedom. Its major premise is that the seemingly insurmountable problems of mankind demand that everyone work together, as individuals, in communities and nations, and above all as members of the human race, passengers together on the fragile Spaceship Earth. Global cooperation can occur only through some kind of international community. We examine economic and political trends indicating that such a community is emerging. The specter of nuclear warfare is the great obstacle to such a community, because of the institutionalization of war in nation-states, but at the same time it is a most compelling reason for a world order. As Albert Camus observed, atomic warfare has given us back our freedom of choice because it makes the future meaningless; "we have nothing to lose" by trying to build world order—"except everything."

If there is no natural law making the family universal, how can we explain why it is found practically everywhere?

CLAUDE LÉVI-STRAUSS

I see the world revolution in family patterns as part of a still more important revolution that is sweeping the world in our time, the aspiration on the part of billions of people to have the right for the first time *to choose* for themselves.

WILLIAM J. GOODE

The search for significance, the formulation of new meanings for the words God and Man, may be the most worthwhile pursuit in the age of anxiety and alienation.

RENÉ DUBOS

Education . . . is reaching out to embrace the whole society and the entire life-span of the individual. . . . It must no longer be thought of as preparation for life, but as a dimension of life, characterized by continual acquisition of knowledge and ceaseless re-examination of ideas.

RENÉ MAHEU

The problem of human learning is fundamental to the solution of all social problems.

KENNETH BOULDING

FAMILY, RELIGION, AND EDUCATION

19

To THE AVERAGE AMERICAN the title of this chapter probably conjures up a Christmas-card steepled church, a Norman Rockwell painting of a rosy-cheeked family around a Thanksgiving dinner table, and a classroom full of earnest students bent over their assignments while a spinsterish teacher writes on a blackboard.

Sociologists must be very careful, however, to distinguish between the institutions of family, religion, and education, which are found in every culture, and their various manifestations in different cultures. Our emotional involvement, especially in the family and religion, is so deep that we sometimes resist, consciously or unconsciously, any attempt to look at them objectively. But the ferment, unrest, and change in the relationships of the sexes and generations, in ways of thinking about man in the universe, and in all that concerns teaching and learning—these demand a dispassionate appraisal such as the social sciences offer.

What, sociologists ask, is "the family"? Religion? Education? How does each institution vary in form and function in different sociocultural contexts—not only in different societies, but in different classes and ethnic subsocieties in such multi-group societies as our own? What consequences does modernization have for each institution? What new directions are being taken during this time of ferment and change, and with what prospects for the future? In this chapter we can touch upon only a few of the sociological theories and studies concerned with these questions.

What Is the Family?

The family is so familiar to us, and most of us regard it as so secret, private, and sacred, that we tend to idealize it and regard any deviations from our ideal as wrong. Many Americans believe in the model of a father, mother, and children, living together in a single house, in affection, respect, and privacy, as the ideal to which everyone should build. They ask not why do the Browns stay together year after year, but why did the Joneses get a divorce? Not why do so many women accept an inferior status, but why are so many protesting? Not what are the dangers to children of being isolated with one woman all day long, but why do some women trust their young children to others and take jobs outside the home? Arlene and Jerome Skolnick suggest that sociologists must recognize that they, too, are bound in large part by the mystique surrounding the family, but must attempt "to make the familiar seem strange," to question conventional assumptions about the small family unit, sex differences, and human nature.[1]

In that spirit even the definition of the family becomes an exercise in caution and precision. For almost every generalization we make about its structure and its functions, we find some exception in some culture, if only a small group such as the Kaingang tribe of Brazil or the Nayar caste of India.[2] No general definition fits *all* the data; what we call "universal" may be only nearly so.

Let us begin with the obvious fact that babies are born and must be cared for. Each society has some durable kinship units that provide for infant care and childrearing. Each has some way of defining every person's relationship to many others—a set of norms outlining a kinship structure, with reciprocal statuses and roles, rights and obligations, according to age and sex, and biological and sexual relationships. Kinship includes the tie between progenitors and descendants (parents and children, grandchildren, etc.) and the tie of common descent (brothers and sisters, cousins, and so on). But in some societies the kinship structure is not entirely dependent on biological relationships; the Trobrianders, for example, do not understand the father's role in producing children, yet they view the father as kin; in other societies the biological father is not part of the kinship structure at all. *Social* definitions, then, determine who is kin. The kinship tie involves special rights of possession, and is generally the closest bond in a society, closer than friendship.[3] "Blood is thicker than water," as the saying goes.

Within the kinship structure exists a family system defined by cultural norms regarding mate selection, number of spouses, and so on. We can also think of the family as a concrete group—but we cannot

---

[1]*Family in Transition: Rethinking Marriage, Sexuality, Child Rearing, and Family Organization* (Boston: Little, Brown, 1971), p. vii.

[2]The nomadic Kaingang numbered only 106 when Jules Henry studied them in 1932; their units of social structure shifted with shifting sexual interests; unions were informal, almost accidental; children belonged to parents much as pets do; yet the father's family was held responsible for children if he died. The Nayar were an Indian warrior caste; family life centered around women because the men were away a great deal. See David A. Schulz, *The Changing Family: Its Function and Future* (Englewood Cliffs, N.J.: Prentice-Hall, Inc., 1972), chap. 2, "Do All of Us Live in Families?"

[3]Ira L. Reiss, *The Family System in America* (New York: Holt, Rinehart & Winston, 1971), p. 19. Reiss points out one of the reasons that we must be careful to take exceptions into consideration—they are so few! "No other human institution shows as much similarity in various cultural settings as does the family" (p. 10).

say "father, mother, and children," for there are other kinds of family groups. The basic definition of a **family**, says David Schulz, is "that group which legitimizes the birth of a child" and institutionalizes the social role of the father (who is not necessarily the biological progenitor) in some way. This definition may apply to a wide variety of concrete types.[4] *Almost* universally the family group also regulates sexual relationships and socializes children.

Marriage is the established procedure for founding a family, and is usually symbolized by a ceremony. It "most characteristically functions in the sexual realm . . . to license parenthood and legitimize children."[5] It typically (though again not invariably) involves the expectation of common residence, economic cooperation, and reproduction.[6] The marriage contract differs from ordinary contracts in that with his marriage each person takes on a new status and assumes *broad* obligations (rather than duties in some limited aspect of life). In the United States, the legal system "reflects the moral consensus of the society that fulfillment of marriage and kinship obligations is very important."[7]

NUCLEAR, POLYGAMOUS, AND EXTENDED FAMILIES

A **nuclear family** consists of a husband-father, a wife-mother, and one or more offspring-siblings. It may be conceived of as including several dyads: husband-wife, mother-offspring, father-offspring, and perhaps sibling-sibling. The nuclear family is found almost everywhere because it is the simplest way of joining the sexual dyad and the maternal dyad, both of which are essential to conceiving and raising children. But this does not mean, insists Richard Adams, "that the nuclear family is an indispensable, basic, stable, family type, and that its absence must therefore represent a breakdown." Women-headed households based on the maternal dyad, if we accept this view, are neither abnormal nor disorganized but "alternative or secondary norms."[8]

[4]Schulz, *The Changing Family*, p. 37.

[5]*Ibid.*, p. 64. Marriage is not universally the institution to regulate sexual behavior; many societies prescribe coitus outside of marriage. But "no society prescribes *conception* outside of marriage. Some, such as those of the Caribbean, accept such an event as a second best alternative when marriage is difficult to negotiate or maintain."

[6]Gerald R. Leslie, *The Family in Social Context* (New York: Oxford University Press, 1967), p. 27.

[7]Robin M. Williams, Jr., *American Society: A Sociological Interpretation*, 3rd ed. (New York: Alfred A. Knopf, 1970), p. 54.

[8]"An Inquiry into the Nature of the Family," in Gertrude E. Dole and Robert L. Carneiro, eds., *Essays in the Science of Culture* (New York: Crowell, 1960), pp. 35–49; reprinted in Skolnick and Skolnick, *The Family in Transition*, pp. 72–82.

A **polygamous family** consists of a single husband-father and several wife-mothers, in which case it is polygynous, or of a single wife-mother and several husband-fathers (polyandrous). Like the nuclear family it includes only two generations, parents and offspring.

When other kin and other generations are included in the family system we speak of an **extended family**. The stress is on kinship rather than marriage, on *consanguineal* rather than *conjugal* ties. The simplest kind of extended family consists of three generations living together: husband and wife, children, and a grandmother, for example. But traditional extended families typically consist of joint households in which the conjugal families are subordinate to the large group. There is close cooperation in work and economic dealings.

The typical independent American nuclear family is a conjugal family. In a conjugal system, the man's primary duties are to his wife and children; he leaves his parents to care for his own nuclear family. Because conjugal families include only two generations, they are transitory; as parents die and children marry, the unit disintegrates and new ones are formed. In such a system, each person belongs first to a "family of orientation," into which he is born and in which he is socialized, and then may form his own "family of procreation." Descent is reckoned bilaterally or bilineally; that is, the father's and mother's ancestors are regarded as equally important. It is rarely reckoned very far back, however, and ancestral ties are nebulous, as are ties with uncles, aunts, and cousins. Residence is *neolocal*; that is, the newly married couple leaves both sets of parents and establishes a new residence, perhaps at a great distance. In a conjugal system, there is considerable latitude in the performance of family roles.

Consanguine systems stress the ties of parents and children, brothers and sisters, rather than husband and wife. In a consanguine extended family one spouse, usually the wife, is considered "an outsider whose wishes and needs must be subordinated to the continuity and welfare of the extended kin group."[9] Descent is traced either through the mother's line or the father's (*unilineal* descent), but rarely through both (*bilineally*). (Even more rarely children are assigned alternately to the father's and mother's lines.) The continuity of the line generation after generation is considered all-important. In patrilineal families (with paternal rules of descent), the wife usually moves into the husband's household; in matrilineal ones, residence may be either patrilocal or matrilocal (with the parents of husband or wife).

Members of a consanguine family are expected to play their roles in the traditional manner: Individualism is discouraged; the family comes first. The extended family affords its members a great sense of security, even though it is also constricting. It is not dissolved by divorce, desertion, or even death; a child has many people besides his own parents and siblings to turn to in crises great and small.

[9]Leslie, *The Family in Social Context*, p. 35.

ENDOGAMY AND EXOGAMY

The family institution of every society includes norms that prescribe whom a person may or may not marry, and some have norms prescribing whom he *must* marry—a mother's brother's daughter, for example. Endogamy demands marriage *within* a certain group, which is usually determined by such criteria as residence, nationality, class, race, or religion. Exogamy means that a person must marry *outside* a certain group; he must choose a mate from some other clan in his tribe, for example.

Incest avoidance (the incest taboo) is the most nearly universal social custom; in fact, some anthropologists consider it the basis of all social organization. With rarest exceptions, sexual relationships and marriages are prohibited between brothers and sisters, parents and children; and in many societies the taboo extends to numerous other relationships as well. As a consequence, families are mutually interdependent; they must exchange children to found new families in order to perpetuate society. The incest taboo thus promotes social cohesion by creating a complex network of marital ties among different groups in a society.

Socio-Cultural Variations in the Family

The major rules governing kinship and marriage are interrelated so that change in any rule—of marriage, descent, residence, division of authority and obligations, and inheritance—is likely to result in changes in the others. There is not, therefore, an infinite variety of patterns of family structure and norms of family functioning. Nonetheless, sociologists have found a number of variations not only from one society to another and from one historical period to another, but also from one social class and ethnic subsociety to another.

FAMILY FORMS AND FUNCTIONS IN TRADITIONAL AND MODERN SOCIETIES

According to Gerald Leslie about one-fourth of all societies, including some non-industrial ones such as Eskimo societies, have the nuclear conjugal family only; another fourth have polygamous but not extended families; and about one-half have some form of extended family. The extended family predominates in pastoral and agricultural economies. "Most societies in the world today have unilineal descent systems, extended families, and male domination."[10]

[10]*Ibid.*, p. 69.

Whether it is conjugal-nuclear or consanguineal-extended, the family in traditional society performs many functions besides the almost universal ones of sexual regulation, reproduction, socialization, and assignment of status to the newborn. It is a unit of economic production; it exerts social control and provides economic and emotional security; it is an important unit for religious observance and for training in skills. With modernization, the family loses many of these functions. It is still the main unit of consumption, but production goes on largely outside the home. Religion and education are considered the province of separate institutions; government is expected to provide for the aged and disabled. At the same time, the expressive–emotional function becomes extremely important in deciding the choice of a mate and in guiding family interaction.

Talcott Parsons believes this change to the isolated nuclear family charged with providing psychological security and response is ideally suited to the needs of modern societies. As a society industrializes, its institutions undergo differentiation; units that formerly had several functions find they must concentrate on the one or two they perform best, because other, more specialized units have taken over some of their former functions and can perform them better. The loss of economic production in the home leaves the family free to concentrate on the socialization of children and on mutual affection and emotional support. And the occupational system is better off. The family is physically mobile, so it can go where jobs are available; the head of the family is not tied to the status ascribed by the extended family, so he is motivated to achieve for himself and his wife and children. When children grow up, they are free to leave home for the world of work; and if a wife is a drag on his occupational advancement, a man is free to find a more satisfactory partner. Romantic love, too, is functional, for it motivates people to choose mates, marry, and thus contribute to society, even though the family can no longer exert pressure on them to marry for the sake of family continuity, much less choose mates for their children. Even the youth culture of today performs a valuable function. The family, which keeps the child emotionally dependent in the early years, suddenly cuts back on emotional support at adolescence to impress on him that he must fend for himself eventually; in his peer group he finds emotional support.[11]

This optimistic functional view of the modern nuclear family has been questioned and qualified. First of all, a woman "liberated" from the extended family finds her domestic burdens greater rather than less. "If there is a peculiar fit between industrial work and the conjugal family, there is a peculiar lack of fit between domestic work and the conjugal family: any kind of economic analysis would suggest

[11]Hyman Rodman, "Talcott Parsons' View of the Changing American Family," in Hyman Rodman, ed., *Marriage, Family, and Society: A Reader* (New York: Random House, 1965), pp. 262–83.

that such tasks as child care, meal preparation, and clothes washing make more sense as communal work than as the reduplicated tasks of isolated individuals."[12] Second, children are more vulnerable to the power of parents alone, and parents (especially mothers) often more resentful and hostile because they are burdened with their constant care. Students of the "battered-child syndrome" in the United States found that parents who treated children under three so brutally that hospitals, doctors, or police became involved were a rather random cross section of the population, deviant only in degree of violence. "The amount of yelling, scolding, slapping, punching, hitting, and yanking acted out by parents on very small children is shocking. Hence, we have felt that in dealing with the abused child we are not observing an isolated, unique phenomenon, but only the extreme form of what we would call a pattern or style of child rearing quite prevalent in our culture."[13]

Third, the high rate of divorce—3.5 per 1000 population in the United States in 1970 as compared to a marriage rate of 10.7 per 1000 —indicates that the nuclear family is a brittle institution. It carries perhaps too great a burden in being made the chief source of happiness, the chief refuge from the pressures of the world of work.[14] "In a complex social system where well-rehearsed actors are mostly playing bit parts, the family provides a drama with all starring roles. Far from disappearing for loss of functions, the modern family is called upon to perform one of the most crucial functions for human personality formation and reinforcement, and some families collapse under the strain."[15] Yet even those whose marriages collapse usually try again, indicating that there is strong faith in the power of marriage and the family to provide psychological satisfactions.

Another qualification to the thesis that modernization reduces the family to an isolated nuclear unit is that there are still "modified extended families" in many industrial societies, including our own.

Marvin Sussman and others have demonstrated that the American family is not so "isolated" as some studies have suggested. Sussman studied the relationships of 95 middle-class white Protestant cou-

[12]Skolnick and Skolnick, *The Family in Transition*, p. 19.

[13]B. F. Steele and C. B. Pollock, "A Psychiatric Study of Parents Who Abuse Infants and Small Children," in R. E. Helfer and C. H. Kempe, eds., *The Battered Child* (Chicago: University of Chicago Press, 1968), p. 104. Parental brutality is a leading cause of infant death, and one reason why 18 other countries have lower rates of infant mortality.

[14]Note that some traditional societies have far higher rates of divorce, but with minor consequences for those involved. The Hopi, for example, a matrilineal society with extended families, places so many obligations on a man besides those to wife and children that he often leaves them because of role conflict; but this is not viewed as pathological, and the mother's brother assumes care of the children.

[15]Wilbert E. Moore, *Order and Change: Essays in Comparative Sociology* (New York: John Wiley, 1967), p. 280.

ples and their 195 married children living away from home. This and other studies indicate that there exists a very active "network of mutual aid," which includes financial support or aid (direct or indirect), emotional support, visiting, babysitting, help with household tasks and repairs, and help during illness or after childbirth. One norm of this arrangement is an unspoken understanding that parents do not interfere or criticize; Grandma becomes adept at biting her tongue. This adjustment is easiest if the son-in-law or daughter-in-law is of similar background; alienation from parents is far more frequent in interethnic marriages, for example.[16]

This "modified extended family" does not interfere with the demands of an industrial economy for social and physical mobility. It is actually easier to maintain such family ties now than it was a generation or two ago; long-distance calls are cheaper and faster, planes more frequent and more reliable, highways and automobiles better. Children appear to value the sense of emotional support that an extended family affords, just as grandparents like to feel included in the affections of the younger generation.

There are also cliques or networks of unrelated nuclear families, often living in the same neighborhood, who routinely extend mutual aid and feel they can depend on one another in times of crisis.

VARIATIONS IN FORM AND FUNCTION BY SUBCULTURAL GROUPS

Numerous studies have demonstrated social class differences in the form and function of the family, in definitions of sex roles, in child-rearing practices, and in stability. To mention a few:

Mirra Komarovsky in a study of "blue-collar marriages" found that working-class couples accept the traditional division of masculine and feminine tasks while many middle-class couples are troubled by ambiguity in sex roles, and that they are far more sure of how they should bring up children than are self-conscious, anxious middle-class parents. Yet despite their moral certainties they are typically less satisfied with marriage and less happy with life in general than the better-educated middle-class couples. They do not include friendship and companionship between spouses in their conception of marriage; and if they move away from the network of relatives and are thrown on their own, the wife particularly feels trapped and isolated.[17]

[16]Marvin B. Sussman, "The Help Pattern in the Middle-Class Family," *American Sociological Review* 15 (Feb. 1953): 22–23; "The Isolated Nuclear Family: Fact or Fiction," *Social Problems* 6 (Spring 1959): 333–40; and "Family Continuity: Selective Factors Which Affect Relationships Between Families at Generational Levels," *Marriage and Family Living* 16 (May 1954): 113–18.

[17]"Blue-Collar Marriages and Families," in Louise Kapp Howe, ed., *The White Majority* (New York: Random House, Vintage Books, 1970), pp. 35–44.

William J. Goode found that rate of divorce is negatively related to occupational level, income, and education. That is, families in the lower classes are less stable because of the effects of other institutions.[18]

Mother-centered families—incomplete nuclear families with the father absent—are most frequent among urban lower-class blacks in the United States and among the lower classes in many Latin American and Caribbean countries, and are often found among urban lower-class whites in the United States as well. Although 47% of black American families with incomes under $3000 are headed by females, so are 38% of such white families. What explanation do sociologists offer? Migration to cities breaks many extended family ties. Unemployed or marginally employed lower-class males are less able to perform instrumental functions; they are, in fact, less likely to find work than their wives. Moreover, lower-class fathers who do work often do not earn enough to support their families. If they leave the household the mother can get child-support. "Since the mother-child tie is stronger than the father-child bond, it is the biologically given, the mother-child dyad, that survives while the marital tie has little payoff for either spouse and is correspondingly fragile."[19]

Finally, a number of studies show that certain ethnic subsocieties are characterized by extensive kinship networks: Italian-Americans, Jews of Eastern European background, Appalachian Protestant whites, for example. Such networks are also characteristic of the upper class.[20]

The Changing Family

There is, then, no one family type we can call *the* modern type, the natural type, the universal type, or even the ideal type. What can we say with any confidence, then, about the future of the family?

Articles denying that there is a sexual revolution, a generation gap, or a threat to the conventional nuclear family as typified in the suburban middle class are as numerous (both in professional journals and popular books) as those that herald a bright new age or cry doom and disorganization. But recalling Sumner's dictum that once mores are openly questioned they are no longer mores, the very fact that peo-

---

[18]"Marital Satisfaction and Instability," in Reinhard Bendix and Seymour Martin Lipset, eds., *Class, Status, and Power: Social Stratification in Comparative Perspective*, 2nd ed. (New York: Free Press, 1966), pp. 381–83.

[19]Robert F. Winch and Rae Lesser Blumberg, "Societal Complexity and Familial Organization," in Skolnick and Skolnick, *Family in Transition*, p. 142.

[20]Milton Gordon, *Assimilation in American Life* (New York: Oxford University Press, 1954), and G. William Domhoff, *Who Rules America?* (Englewood Cliffs, N.J.: Prentice-Hall, Inc., 1967).

ple are aware of alternatives is a profound change. Except among working-class couples, people no longer can play traditional roles in traditional ways, "as the unquestioned and inevitable progression of life's stages. Rather, each step of the way involves a conscious choice among competing values. . . . [A girl who wants to follow a highly traditional life style] has to justify, if only to herself, a defense of her motives and behavior to counter the arguments of 'the other side.' The burden of proof has shifted from those who would depart from the conventional and has come to be shared by those who would maintain the status quo."[21]

CHANGING DEFINITIONS OF REPRODUCTION AND PARENTHOOD

The population explosion and effective contraception have changed the value of the reproductive function of the family. Parenthood is increasingly voluntary. Loosening of taboos on sex relations outside of marriage (and on the portrayal of sex in the mass media) has also contributed to a change in the once close association of the sex act with the possibility, the probability, and the hope or fear of pregnancy. A number of groups advocate free birth control, legalized abortion, zero population growth, and the definition of parenthood as a privilege involving a very serious decision and perhaps requiring a license, rather than as a right or a natural happenstance.

CHANGING DEFINITIONS OF SEX ROLES AND HUSBAND–WIFE RELATIONSHIPS

The fact that women live longer and have fewer children than before has contributed to a fundamental redefinition both of their status and of husband–wife relationships. The "empty nest" period between the departure of the last child and the death of one spouse has increased to an average of 16 years, and is now over one-third of the average 45-year marriage. The average period from marriage to the birth of the last child has decreased from 11 years for women born in the 1880s to about 9 years for those born in the 1930s.[22] With an average life expectancy of 74, 7.2 years more than her husband's, a woman has many years to fill with other activities than childrearing and housekeeping.

One consequence is a great increase in the number of women employed outside the home. In 1970 more than 36% of the gainfully employed working population over age 10 consisted of females. They earn, however, only about 60% of male income; they are greatly under-

[21]Skolnick and Skolnick, *Family in Transition,* pp. 4–5.
[22]*The New York Times Encyclopedic Almanac* (1971), p. 376.

represented in professional, academic, and political positions; they are discouraged from taking graduate degrees or entering traditionally masculine fields (especially, we must emphasize, in the United States as compared to many other societies).[23] Laws, hiring and wage policies, and public opinion appear to be reducing these discriminatory practices.

But traditional definitions of division of labor in the home, and of proper patterns of interaction between husband and wife, are more resistant to change. Working wives still find themselves doing all or almost all the housework. A survey by General Electric showed that working wives spent 39 hours a week on domestic tasks as well as their 40 hours a week on "the job." Even young couples committed to an equalitarian ideology often find it difficult to share domestic tasks. Sandra and Gerald Bem point out that if a young black man and a young white man were roommates, the division of chores and errands would be decided

> by preference, agreement, flipping a coin, given to hired help, or—as is frequently the case—left undone. A young white man would never assume that his black roommate would do all the chores. . . . But change this hypothetical black roommate to a female marriage partner and somehow the student's conscience goes to sleep. At most it is quickly tranquilized by the thought that "she is happiest when she is ironing for her loved one." Such is the power of a nonconscious ideology.
>
> Of course, it may well be that she *is* happiest when she is ironing for her loved one.
>
> Such, indeed, is the power of a nonconscious ideology![24]

Not only has the possession of a uterus been regarded as a unique qualification for doing domestic chores; it has also long meant a much more rigid set of sexual mores than that applied to men, and the assignment of status by virtue of relationship to some male, usually father or husband. Women are increasingly rebelling against the nonconscious ideology that they need men for identity. Both sexes will be

[23]In the Soviet Union, 75% of physicians are women; in Britain, 16%; in the U.S., 7%. In Denmark nearly half the lawyers are women; in Germany, one-third; in the U.S., 3%. Nearly half the university instructors in the Soviet Union are women; in the U.S., 9%, and in the major academic fields, 1 to 2%. Nearly a third of Soviet engineers and scientists are women; in the U.S. women are 9% of the scientists, 1% of the engineers. [Susan Jacoby, "Women in Russia," *The New Republic* (April 4/11, 1970), and Elizabeth Duncan Koontz, "Women as a Minority Group," in Mary Lou Thompson, ed., *Voices of the New Feminism* (Boston: Beacon, 1970), p. 128.]

[24]"Case Study of a Nonconscious Ideology: Training the Woman to Know Her Place," in Daryl J. Bem, *Beliefs, Attitudes, and Human Affairs* (Belmont, Calif.: Brooks/Cole, 1970), p. 99.

better able to fulfill their human potential, say feminists, when they are freed from the constrictions of traditional sex roles. Men need not feel they must be aggressive and insensitive (traditional masculine traits); women need not feel their attractiveness to men is the only criterion for success as a woman—or a human being.

When life expectancy was shorter and the family was a unit of economic production needing children as helpers and inheritors, and when the extended family network provided emotional support and security regardless of the personal relationships of a married pair, 20-year-olds could take marriage vows "until death do us part" without reservations. Now the possibility of having to live in double harness for 50 years or more is less attractive. The fact that divorce has lost much of its stigma makes lifelong married happiness a romantic dream, an ideal that is often not fulfilled. Some social scientists and others concerned with family relationships advocate a sort of "two-step" marriage, in which the couple lives together for a specified period without having children, to be more sure of their mutual compatibility, and then possibly takes a far more serious step, entering into a more permanent arrangement, probably with the idea of having children.

CHILDREARING PATTERNS
AND FAMILY STRUCTURE

The nuclear conjugal family is often held to be the ideal agent for socializing young children. But increasing recognition of the fact that not all parents are loving, nurturing parents, combined with the increasing number of working mothers, has led to a reexamination of child care patterns and to proposals for such innovations as day-care centers, communes, and part-time jobs for both husband and wife so that each can take a turn at child care and domestic chores.

"Maternal deprivation" has been held, especially by psychoanalytic childrearing specialists, to be uniformly threatening to children. Recent research, however, "has emphasized the need for environmental stimulation as well as loving care and has shown that even within the confines of an institution, infants' development can be normalized and even accelerated by providing them with interesting sights and playthings."[25] Day-care centers, supervised playgrounds, and similar institutions could relieve the strain for both parents and children, and enrich the cultural environment of many whose parents provide them with little stimulation.

Experiments in communal living sometimes include children who are regarded as belonging to the whole group and therefore are

[25]Skolnick and Skolnick, citing B. L. White, "An Experimental Approach to the Effects of Experience on Early Human Behavior," in J. P. Hill, ed., *Minnesota Symposium of Child Psychology*, vol. 1 (Minneapolis: University of Minnesota Press 1967), pp. 201–26.

free of the concentrated emotion, whether "smother-love" or hostility, that may affect them in an isolated family. The obsessive love and the parental power that characterize many nuclear families are neither natural nor universal. During the Middle Ages, says demographic historian Philippe Aries, such families did not exist; people lived "on top of one another" in all-purpose rooms where they ate, slept, danced, worked, and received visitors. Privacy, the idea of childhood as a distinct stage of life, and the idea of a separate inviolable nuclear family are relatively recent inventions in Western civilization.[26]

THE LIFE CYCLE AND RELATIONS BETWEEN GENERATIONS

The generations are barred from close interaction and understanding not only by the isolation of many conjugal families, but also by changing definitions of stages in the life cycle. Until after the Middle Ages, those lucky enough to survive the many hazards of infancy emerged as miniature adults at age six or seven. With the Industrial Revolution, the need for education increased; by the present century children were kept in high school if possible; thus emerged a new stage, adolescence. Today "youth" often continues into the twenties or even the thirties. At the same time, older people find it harder to find new jobs if they are fired; with mandatory retirement at about age sixty-two, they have years left to fill. In our rapidly changing society, each generation finds life different. The older generation has less and less control and influence over youth, partly because it cannot or does not keep up with the new trends, partly because it is isolated from them. In fact, Margaret Mead suggests that today the young are in a position to teach their elders—a reversal of the traditional roles of the generations.[27]

The Family in Post-Industrial Societies

Do these trends mean that the family has no future? Or only that it will take various forms in an attempt to serve the needs of men, women, and children as human beings searching for dignity and emotional security?

Most sociologists believe the family is tenacious and enduring, providing satisfactions and fulfilling certain functions as no other institution can. Men and women will go on falling in love, having children,

[26]*Centuries of Childhood* (New York: Random House, Vintage Books, 1962).
[27]*Culture and Commitment: A Study of the Generation Gap* (New York: D
   day, 1970).

Extended, nuclear, and communal families.

and guiding those children's first steps. The fact that many families do not fit the ideal type of the stable conjugal family does not mean that they cannot be made viable units in our social structure. Probably peer groups will gain importance; the burden of child care and domestic chores may be distributed more evenly.

> The functional problem of the family today is the re-creation of extended family relationships without kinship. It is virtually impossible to restore irrational ties of blood when the traditional social and economic conditions that made them meaningful no longer exist. Besides, it would be undesirable to do so. As Goode so eloquently argued, the conjugal family stands for equality, individuality, and freedom. The problem is one of maintaining these values while re-creating the kind of social solidarity that exists in the extended family, or the medieval village described by Aries. Two groups in our society have already begun to build this form of solidarity: the old and the young. The old in their retirement villages and the young in their crash pads and communes have much in common. The fact that one group has had this form of life thrust upon it, while the other has chosen it, should not obscure the similarities between them. They are both living out post-industrial, post-Protestant ethic, post-nuclear family lives during a time of social and technological transition.
>
> If there is anything to be said with some degree of assurance, it is that the future will probably see family arrangements at least as varied and colorful as those at present.[28]

[28]Skolnick and Skolnick, *Family in Transition*, pp. 29–30.

What Is Religion?

In a very general sense, religion is the social institution—the complex of norms—that deals with *sacred* things, things that lie beyond man's knowledge and control. Sacredness exists in the mind of the believer and can be ascribed to almost any object or idea; it is *transcendental*, that is, it transcends or goes beyond the empirical–technical realm of action, the profane and mundane world of observable and manipulable everyday reality. Like all of culture, says Peter Berger, religion is "an enterprise of world building"; but it occupies a distinctive place in the general culture, for it is "the audacious attempt to conceive of the entire universe as humanly significant [and] locates the individual's life in an all-embracing fabric of meanings that, by its very nature, transcends that life." It protects him from anomie or normlessness, constructing a "sheltering canopy" that makes the terror of death less overwhelming, suffering less painful, injustice more tolerable. Religion establishes a sacred cosmos which "is confronted by man as an immensely powerful reality other than himself. Yet this reality addresses itself to him and locates his life in an ultimately meaningful order."[29]

A complex of norms, religion includes patterns of thought, action, and feelings. Like other institutions, it may be embodied in a "seamless web," a total fabric of life (as in some folk and premodern societies); or it may be "institutionalized," that is, normalized and stabilized as an accepted and recognized way of doing something, of meeting some recurrent need. Like other institutions, it has certain consequences and fulfills certain functions for society and the individual.

Religion must be distinguished from another nearly universal phenomenon, *magic*, with which it may be, and often is, intermingled (as in propitiatory prayers). Like religion, magic involves the idea of a "beyond"—of something that transcends empirical reality—and the idea that man can establish some kind of contact with transcendental or supra-empirical forces. In addition, magic offers ways of *manipulating* these forces through ritual, in order to bring about changes in empirical reality (as Melanesians of cargo cults try to reproduce the white man's "magic" to hasten the arrival of planes laden with goods). Such manipulation is commonly found where an enterprise involves danger or uncertainty. Malinowski noted that the Trobriand Islanders used no magical rituals when fishing in the lagoon, where conditions were safe and results quite predictable, but they employed such rituals in deep-sea fishing, which was risky. They performed magical rites to prevent death in childbirth, and religious rites to celebrate the birth.[30]

[29]*The Sacred Canopy: Elements of a Sociological Theory of Religion* (Garden City, N.Y.: Doubleday, 1967), pp. 28, 54–55, 100.

[30]Bronislaw Malinowski, *Magic, Science, and Religion* (Garden City, N.Y.: Doubleday, Anchor Books, 1948), pp. 28–38.

In studying religion, sociologists are not concerned with the truth or falsity of religious beliefs. Beliefs about ultimate reality are always matters of faith, "the substance of things hoped for, the evidence of things not seen" (Heb. 11:1): These are the realm of theological dispute. Sociologists *are* concerned with the relationships between religion and other aspects of culture and social organization, and with the social processes through which beliefs and practices arise, develop, and perhaps become institutionalized and embodied in an organization. They ask such questions as: Why is religion universal, or nearly so? What *is* religion, and how does it vary in form and content from one social context to another? By what process does religion become institutionalized? What is the impact of modernization on religion? What functions does religion serve for society and the individual—or, put more empirically, what consequences does it have? What trends, innovations, and movements are in process today, and what is the future of religion?

The Origins of Religion

Speculation about the origins of religion is a fascinating exercise, but must remain largely that—speculation, based on empathy, introspection, and some anthropological and historical data. Most such speculation centers on "the human condition"—features built into the nature and quality of life for all men everywhere and always.

Life is full of puzzles—dreams, accidents, birth, death, plagues, earthquakes, eclipses, famines. Man cannot stand meaninglessness: He seeks some explanation of the pattern of bane and blessing. Neither can he stand loneliness, but his relationships with others involve power and coercion, love and loss. Inevitably they involve trust, which is the basis of social order, and therefore must be defined by moral obligations. Man needs some system of meanings to evaluate actions, and this ethical system is nearly always, though not inevitably, bound up with and supported by religion. To live with joy and zest, man must be vulnerable—open to bereavement as well as love, to disappointment as well as success. In explaining the good and the bad, religion shields him in this vulnerability.

Man is always uncertain about tomorrow: When Costa Ricans mention a plan or hope, even something as ordinary as "I'll see you tonight," they almost always add, "*si Dios quiere*" (God willing). Man is also powerless to affect and control all the conditions of his life: Modern man's confidence that he could do so through science and technology has been dashed by the threat of nuclear war. Finally, man is frustrated, deprived, and disappointed by the unequal distribution of the good things of life.

The myth system of a society, and especially its religion or religions, provides human life with a sense of meaning—of aim, purpose, and design. It provides a view of the world and of man's role in that world. It answers the questions to which Omar Khayyám believed no answer existed:

> Into this Universe, and Why not knowing,
> Nor Whence, like Water willy-nilly flowing,
> And out of it, as Wind along the Waste,
> We know not Whither, willy-nilly blowing.

Variations in Form, Content, and Expression

Because they are rooted in the human condition, religions around the world have much in common. But religion is limited only by man's capacity to imagine, both within and beyond the bounds of his culture: the range of religious beliefs, practices, and experiences is enormous.

RELIGIOUS BELIEFS

Beliefs are the intellectual or cognitive aspect of religion, expressed in the dramatic assertions of myths; the poetry, proverbs, preaching, and prophecies of scriptures; and the distilled theology of dogmas, doctrines, and creeds. They provide the answers to empirically unanswerable questions: Is there a God? The theist answers "Yes," the humanist, "No." How many gods? "One," say the scriptures of monotheistic religions such as Judaism, Christianity, and Islam; "Many," say the polytheistic myths of Buddhism and animism. Where is He, or where are they? In Heaven, all around us, in ourselves, on Mount Olympus, perhaps disguised as a beggar or walking with us in a garden. Men tend to conceive of their gods as very much like them—perhaps physically, perhaps only in personality traits; they *anthropomorphize* them. The Greeks attributed jealousy, lust, vengefulness, and other human failings, as well as wisdom, courage, and chastity, to their gods. The traits of a deity reflect the values of a culture: The Eskimos, who live from hunting and fishing, worship a sea goddess who usually appears as a seal; the militaristic Aztecs, Romans, and Norsemen had gods of war; agrarian cultures have gods of fertility. As the Jews' social life changed, their conception of God changed: When they were a divided and nomadic people in constant danger from all sides, *El* was a spirit who ensured success in battle. Settled in Canaan, the dominant tribes established the superiority of *Jahweh* (whose name was too sacred to be mentioned) over minor tribal spirits. Gradually they came to believe there was only one god for good Jews, *Jehovah.* "Then, in their struggle to maintain themselves in an area that was a crossroads of the ancient world, the Jews gained heart by picturing themselves as guardians of God—*the* God to whom all men should bow down."[31]

The belief system also defines the relationship of deities to mankind: Gods may be vindictive and punishing, loving and nurturing, capricious and demanding. The power and will of God or the gods impart blessings and sorrow. Why did my child die? It was the will of God; what God does is well done. I displeased the gods. Why did we have a good harvest? God is good. We pleased the gods. It seems that without such explanations many people cannot live happily or even sanely.

Religions define the meaning of human life in various ways: Man is a mere speck of dust in a great cosmos, whether that cosmos is highly structured or without time, shape, meaning, or direction. His life is a reflection or counterpart of an other-worldly existence; heaven is like earth, except that it is better, more spiritualized. This life is a mere prelude to another and higher existence, a preliminary period during which the soul undergoes tests of virtue, and is ultimately judged and punished or rewarded, either on a Day of Judgment or in successive incarnations; it either achieves perfection in heaven or is condemned to hell; or it is absorbed into a timeless eternity, losing its personality and humanity along with all its sins and defects, its fleshly desires and sufferings.

Eschatological religions (such as Christianity) are concerned with "last things" such as death, judgment, and a future life in eternal glory or damnation. Some religions are also concerned with death and judgment, but lack the idea of heaven or hell; still others have no conception of a judgment in after-life.

A special aspect of belief systems is what Max Weber called theodicy, the doctrine that justifies man's present status and reconciles his image of what *ought to be* with what *is.* Why does one man work hard and get nowhere? Why did my child die and his survive?[32] Theodicy answers such questions and thus gives meaning to inequality, suffering, and injustice. Weber saw the theodicy of *dominance* as appropriate to an elite (e.g., the Brahmin caste's justification of their status through the Hindu religion). A theodicy of *mobility* fits the middle classes in transitional and modern societies; they are bent on economic gain and see rationality as a break with the past and a means to personal advancement. (Weber elaborated on this theodicy in *The Protestant Ethic and the Spirit of Capitalism.*) Finally, a theodicy of *escape* is

---

[31]Thomas Ford Hoult, *The Sociology of Religion* (New York: Dryden Press, 1958), pp. 23–25.

[32]*Theodicy:* a vindication of the divine attributes, particularly holiness and justice, in establishing or allowing the existence of physical and moral evil. (*Random House Dictionary,* p. 1471).

appropriate to the poor and oppressed and outcast. Religion may promise escape through action in this world, bringing about radical social
change (as in secular doctrines such as Marxism). More often escape to
a better world after death is promised to those who keep the faith.
(Millennial social movements center around such theodicies.) Theodicy,
then, may be correlated with social class status and political ideology.
The religion of the oppressed may be revolutionary. The religion of the
elite may serve to preserve and justify the status quo; the Church of
England has been dubbed "the Conservative Party at Prayer."

RELIGIOUS PRACTICE

Religious beliefs are overtly expressed in a variety of practices,
including private or family devotions and prayers. In Western civilization we usually think in terms of *collective* religious practices centering
around churches and temples. The main element of collective worship
is ritual, the dramatization of men's relationships with the sacred in
speech, gesture, song, sacramental meals, and sacrifice. Rituals serve to
mark life crises, to celebrate and sanctify birth, puberty, and marriage;
to reassert religious identity and group bonds; to reiterate the group's
definition of death, perhaps as passage to a better life. The myths and
mysteries of a faith are reenacted in the dramas of the mass, Passover,
the crucifixion. Participation in a common ritual may strengthen belief
through social contagion, providing a strong sense of rightness and
consensual validation.

Although religious belief and its consequences for behavior in
everyday life are not necessarily reflected in church membership and
attendance, these do serve as rough indicators.[33] Americans are particularly concerned with religious identity. "Indeed, . . . an American
cannot be simply an atheist; he must be a Catholic atheist, a Protestant
atheist, or a Jewish atheist."[34]

Church membership, like membership in voluntary associations in general, is roughly correlated with social class, although "one
cannot help wondering whether high-status church membership is frequently a matter of form rather than substance."[35] Nearly one-fourth
of Christian Scientists, Episcopalians, and Congregationalists are upper
class, fewer than half are lower class; at the other end, fewer than one-
tenth of Roman Catholics, Baptists, and Mormons are from the upper

[33]See N. J. Demerath, III, and Phillip E. Hammond, *Religion in Social Context: Tradition and Transition* (New York: Random House, 1969), chap. 4, "Assessing
Individual Religiosity"; and N. J. Demerath, III, *Social Class in American Protestantism* (Chicago: Rand McNally, 1965), pp. 1–25, for discussions of the pitfalls
of these indicators.

[34]Demerath and Hammond, *Religion in Social Context*, p. 131.

[35]*Ibid.*, p. 121.

class, and roughly two-thirds are from the lower class. But these relative rankings are not absolute categorizations. "Baptists may be *relatively* lower class, but they claim their Rockefellers as well."[36] Furthermore, lower-class Episcopalians may be more religiously involved and committed than upper-class members; and upper-class Baptists may control their predominantly lower-class churches.

Perhaps a more revealing study of the relationship between religious affiliation and social class is a comparison along the lines of formalism vs. emotionalism. Studying 40 black churches in Chicago, V. E. Daniel used five criteria—emotional demonstration, thought content of sermons, prayers, hymns, and the use of liturgy—to identify four basic religious types, and then showed the relationship between class status and preference for these types. Ecstatic sects or cults, in which worship often took the form of a dancing crowd, were almost solidly lower class. Semi-demonstrative groups, in which the congregation assented to the preacher's points with spontaneous "Amens," were lower-middle class. The upper-middle class preferred deliberative or sermon-centered rituals, while the upper class preferred liturgical denominations, with a very formal, traditional ritual.[37]

RELIGIOUS EXPERIENCE

Besides culturally patterned beliefs and practices, religion has a third dimension—individual subjective experience or emotion, ranging from a mild feeling of goodness and rightness for having attended church to an ecstatic sense of mystical communion with the divine such as St. Teresa of Avila felt. Obviously this dimension is extremely difficult to analyze and measure.

Charles Glock calls the "experiential" dimension of religion "all those feelings, perceptions, and sensations which are experienced by an actor or defined by a religious group or a society as involving some connection, however slight, with a divine essence, i.e., with God, with ultimate reality, with transcendental authority. It is, in effect, spirituality—emotional experience defined as religious which in its extreme forms would be represented by conversion, the visitation of the Holy Spirit, mysticism."[38] Even the most intense mystical experiences are culturally conditioned. One cannot see a vision for which the culture

[36]Demerath, *Social Class in American Protestantism.*

[37]"Ritual and Stratification in Chicago Negro Churches," *American Sociological Review*   7 (June 1942): 352–61.

[38]*Religion and the Face of America* (Berkeley: University of California Press, 1958), pp. 25–42; reprinted in Norman Birnbaum and Gertrude Lenzer, eds., *Sociology and Religion: A Book of Readings* (Englewood Cliffs, N.J.: Prentice-Hall, Inc., 1969), pp. 397–410.

has not prepared him. Indian youths fasted and prayed in isolation until they saw some animal that became their totem; Bernadette saw the Virgin because she was raised a Catholic; Asians experience yogic trances.

What is a genuinely religious experience? Joachim Wach says it must meet four criteria: It is a response not to any single or finite phenomenon but to ultimate reality, something that undergirds and conditions our entire world of experience. It involves our total being, not only our mind, will, or emotions. It is, at least potentially, the most intense experience of which man is capable, for it can win out over all other loyalties, being a matter of profound concern and utter serious- ness. Finally, it involves a commitment impelling a person to action (thus distinguishing it from an intense esthetic experience and joining it to the moral sphere).[39]

Gerhard Lenski defines four ways of expressing religious com- mitment. Two are behavioral and thus lend themselves to measurement: associational involvement (attendance at church) and communal in- volvement (whether one's spouse and close friends are members of one's socio-religious group). The other two are more strictly mental: doctrinal orthodoxy or assent to the traditional beliefs of one's church, and devotionalism, the frequency of private prayer, scripture reading, or communion with God. We shall return to the latter distinction when we consider the consequences of religion for individual behavior.[40]

The Institutionalization of Religion

Like all cultural norms, religious ones are more or less institutionalized —that is, formalized, stabilized, and socially recognized as the right and proper way to do something. In small folk societies so much of the cul- ture is imbued with sacredness that we find religious ritual in the family and work group; food may be holy, the head of every household a priest.

SPECIALIZATION, ORGANIZATION, AND BUREAUCRATIZATION

As societies grow, religious roles become more specialized; a hierarchy and bureaucracy develop. First, a shaman who is thought to have special knowledge of and connections with the sacred performs religious rituals. As the society grows the need for shamen increases;

[39]*Types of Religious Experience, Christian and Non-Christian* (Chicago: University of Chicago Press, 1951), pp. 32–33.
[40]*The Religious Factor* (Garden City, N.Y.: Doubleday, 1961).

gradually a priest class emerges, and with it an established church. Historically the established churches of the West have struggled for power with the temporal rulers; it took centuries of bloody wars and persecutions to establish the separation of church and state, a process still not complete in some societies. In many Asian religions, in particular, institutionalization has not gone to the lengths it has in Western society; almost every Thai man is a Buddhist priest at one time or another, for example, and worship is less structured than in Western churches.

CHURCH AND SECT

A process that has fascinated a number of scholars is the dialectical interplay between church and sect, between large established denominations that compromise with "the world" and dissident groups that find this compromise morally repugnant and break off to form a "purer" group of their own. Christianity itself provides many classic instances of this process, from its very beginnings. Jesus, the charismatic leader, gathered a band of disciples to protest corruption in the temples, and he drew to him the poor and outcast and dispossessed. They formed a dissident sect, persecuted as such sects are likely to be.

Once Christianity became the established, powerful religion of Europe and the Americas, it in turn gave rise to sects. An other-worldly religion, Christianity doesn't fit political and economic realities. In compromising with the world, the church accepted the domination of middle- and upper-class values and interests, softening or playing down its other-worldliness and its message of equality and social justice. Members of the lower classes felt ignored or neglected, sold out and betrayed. Often they gathered around an inspiring personality who promised salvation and escape through a return to the purity of true Christian principles. Some sects have seceded from the church entirely; others have reformed it and been absorbed; still others have been incorporated as quasi-autonomous bodies, such as orders of monks.

Where a church has a hierarchy of authority, a sect is a band of brothers, with a nonbureaucratic organizational structure. Where a church has a ritualized worship service, a sect engages in spontaneous worship with group participation. Where a church has a flexible doctrine that evolves as it is reinterpreted and argued, a sect insists on doctrinal purity (not necessarily conservative or fundamentalist). Where a church tends to prescribe a system of relative ethics that recognizes possible conflicts and allows compromise, a sect has a total ideology of life and ethics that brooks no compromise and claims control over its members' most mundane activities (food, dress, and recreation, for example). Where a church accommodates to the secular society and seeks to work within it, a sect is either aloof from society or antagonistic toward it. Where the church draws its clergy from seminaries and divinity schools, the sect has a ministry of laymen with no professional pedigree. Where the church professes to have its doors open to all, it is actually dominated by the middle and upper classes, numerically and in terms of power; but the sect has exclusive standards of membership and may demand a "rebirth" or conversion of its recruits, who come mostly from the poor and powerless classes.

Secessionist sects may dissolve when the charismatic founder dies; but if they have already built up a strong body of belief and practice they may survive, and develop in one of several directions. (1) They may grow into a church, as did Christianity, with a professional priesthood, a more evangelistic recruitment procedure, a higher social class membership, a hierarchical structure, and a formal ritual. "Conversionist" sects, oriented to individual salvation, are most likely to become full-fledged churches; the Pentecostals and the Salvation Army, for example. "Gnostic" sects, which accept the prevailing goals of the society, but seek new means to reach them, are also likely to grow into churches; Christian Science, which is unusual in that its membership comes largely from the middle class, is one example. (2) But those which brook no compromise with society and urge severe changes in it become not churches but institutionalized sects; examples are "radical adventists" such as Jehovah's Witnesses (who predict and prepare for a sudden and drastic change in the world, with an apocalyptic upheaval preceding the millennium) and "introversionist" groups such as the Quakers and some Holiness sects (who reject societal goals and posit new ones that call upon different inner resources from individuals).[41] (3) Some sects, like the Amish and Hutterites, remain geographically and socially isolated, neither compromising with nor seeking to change the world. (4) The Mormons are a special instance of a sect that became a distinct subsociety or "people": "a specifically religious organization as the institutional core of a more diffuse social entity with its own history, its own traditions, its conviction of peculiarity, and even its native territory or homeland"—plus a sense of mission.[42]

SECTS, MYSTICS, AND REVITALIZATION

Like sectarianism, mysticism is a protest against the formality of an institutionalized church. It emphasizes purely personal and inward experience,

> the contemplative search for and achievement of the religious experience outside the established religious forms. It sees itself as the

---

[41]Based on a summary of voluminous literature on the church-sect scheme in Demerath and Hammond, *Religion in Social Context*, pp. 69–77, 157–63.

[42]Thomas F. O'Dea, *The Sociology of Religion* (Englewood Cliffs, N.J.: Prentice-Hall, Inc., 1966), pp. 66–71.

achievement of a relationship with the beyond, the ultimate, the One
—with God—by rising above all forms of the world—both those of
the natural and societal environment and those of formalized cult as
well. The mystic response is found in all the world religions: in
Christianity, Judaism, Hinduism, Buddhism, and even in Islam.[43]

Both sects and mystics, like social protest movements, contribute to the vitality of institutions by forcing reexamination of their values and premises, their patterns of behavior and social relationships.
Sects challenge abuses within a church that they see as violating its
original values; mystics remind us of the essentially private nature of
the religious experience—which may be encouraged or communicated
in collective rituals, but may also be considered deviant if carried to
extremes.

Religion and Modernization

Diffuse, pervasive tribal religions, the established state religions of
premodern societies, and churches in modern and post-industrial societies all experience the consequences of modernizing processes. First, as
a society becomes larger in scope, competing beliefs are incorporated
into the same socio-cultural order with varying degrees of success; that
is, religious pluralism appears, resulting sometimes in cooperation and
compromise, other times in hostility and conflict. Second, secularization
affects religious belief and practice. Third, there is some tendency, especially apparent in American society, toward the homogenization of
religious belief and practice under an overarching "civil religion."
Fourth, like other institutions, religion becomes less diffuse and more
specific in organization and function—more compartmentalized.

RELIGIOUS PLURALISM

A common religion is an effective source of social cohesion,
providing as it does a strong set of common values. The Reformation
and the rise of nation-states led finally—after bloody wars—to acceptance of the idea that various religions can coexist within a society. But
in a pluralistic society, says Berger, the classical task of religion can
no longer be fulfilled: "that of constructing a common world within
which all of social life receives ultimate meaning binding on everybody."[44] Instead, we have subworlds, fragmented universes of meaning
perhaps no larger than the nuclear family, perhaps as large as a church.

[43]*Ibid.*, pp. 70–71.
[44]Berger, *The Sacred Canopy*, p. 132.

Conflict and animosity are likely in a pluralist society where salvationist or missionary orientations predominate in the various churches, as in Christianity and Islam. In Asian society, in contrast, numerous religions coexist; in fact a person may follow more than one with no conflict. But as a result of the other trends—secularization, compartmentalization, and homogenization—religious pluralism may take on the character of a competitive market in which people are asked to name a "religious preference," which is essentially private, and, even if it involves church membership, can be changed (especially from one Protestant denomination to another) with little soul-searching.

Some see this kind of pluralism and competition as contributing to the vitality of religion as an institution. In countries where several faiths compete for allegiance, religion becomes a way of defining one's identity, and religious interest remains high. Holland, Ireland, Switzerland, Canada, and the United States are examples. Although the church attendance boom of the 1950s has tapered off, Americans still worship more regularly than the citizens of any other Western country: In 1970 about 62% were reported to be church members. On an average Sunday, 43% of the adult population attends church, as compared with 42% in the Netherlands, 38% in Austria, 14% in Norway, 9% in Sweden, and 5% in Finland. Americans are also more orthodox than most others: In a Gallup poll in 1968, 98% professed belief in God, as compared to 77% in Britain.

What accounts for this interest besides the cultural demand for a religious identity? It has been suggested that the voluntary nature of religious affiliation, the separation of church and state since the founding of our nation, means that each church needs enthusiastically committed laymen in order to survive. When people are free to choose, their loyalty is more enduring. But this also means that to "keep the customers coming," the churches have to accommodate their teachings and practices to the demands of laymen, and thus a certain degree of theological laxity exists. As a professor at the Yale Divinity School puts it, "American laymen [in most Protestant denominations] have not always been sure exactly what they were praying to, but they've also never been told they had to accept 'these six dogmas.' "[45]

SECULARIZATION

In the process of secularization, the realm of the sacred shrinks, the realm of the profane or ordinary grows. "Mysteries are replaced by problems."[46] The term referred originally to the removal of territory and other property from the control of ecclesiastical authorities. In a

[45]Edward B. Fiske, "God Is Alive and Well in America," *The New York Times* (Dec. 29, 1968).
[46]O'Dea, *The Sociology of Religion*, p. 86.

broader sense, secularization is "the process by which sectors of society and culture are removed from the domination of religious institutions and symbols."[47] Science has been perhaps the foremost secularizing agent, dispelling much of the mystery and hence the sacredness of the natural world. But the Protestant Reformation, says Berger, opened the world to secularization by removing mystery, miracle, and magic from religion itself and polarizing the universe between "a radically transcendent divinity and a radically 'fallen' humanity . . . [between which] lies an altogether 'natural' universe, God's creation to be sure [but] very lonely indeed," for there are no saints and angels to mediate, and man faces his God alone. "A sky empty of angels becomes open to the intervention of the astronomer—and, eventually, of the astronaut."[48]

With secularization, reverence for traditional beliefs and values is replaced by a rational–utilitarian attitude that permits them to be discarded or changed with relative ease. Some consider this paganization; others, liberation. In any case, secularization must be recognized as an empirical phenomenon of tremendous importance, "the most outstanding social and cultural development of the last several centuries."[49] Economic institutions have been almost entirely divorced from the realm of the sacred; political institutions are now regarded as man-made rather than divinely ordained. Yet we still find sacredness associated with the state; wars and new administrations are begun with prayers. The family is also largely sacred. Art, literature, and philosophy, once imbued with religious content, are increasingly secular. All over the world, the secular–rational attitude is increasing—but it is unevenly distributed. It is more apparent among men than women, city-dwellers than rural people, the middle-aged than the young and old, Protestants and Jews than Catholics, Europeans than Americans.

What happens when people become aware of the lack of fit between the traditional religious values of revelation and other-worldly salvation and the modern secular values of rationality and material success? Most fundamentalist sects withdraw, emphasizing the difference in values. Others, especially theologians, may seek radical changes in dogma. A third possible reaction is to secularize the doctrine itself in order to attract more people, whether on the sophisticated level of the European "dialogue" between Christianity and Marxism, or in the popular blessing-counting of Americans. A fourth alternative, however, seems to be more common in American churches—"to leave traditional doctrine understated and, wherever possible, unmentioned."[50] Theological discussion is considered impolite and embarrassing. In our society one can have the appearance of religiosity without the emotional commitment; "religion-in-general" is regarded as a good thing.

[47]Berger, *The Sacred Canopy*, p. 107.
[48]*Ibid.*, pp. 11–12.
[49]O'Dea, *The Sociology of Religion*, p. 80.
[50]Demerath and Hammond, *Religion in Social Context*, p. 172.

HOMOGENIZATION

This last reaction to secularization—homogenization—permits "the convergence of many religions upon a vaguely defined consensus on teaching and practice,"[51] which we noted in Chapter 10 is characteristic of American culture. American churches allied themselves with democratic principles from the start, and thus the government could ally itself with religion in general. As a result, we have developed a "civil religion" consisting of vaguely defined ideas such as belief in God: We are "one nation under God." Almost all the institutions of the society celebrate this civil religion, which promotes unity amid our diversity and allows the churches themselves to persist in their theological differences without endangering social cohesion. (Clearly this is not the case in Northern Ireland.)

COMPARTMENTALIZATION

Another process that allows religious diversity in a secular society is compartmentalization. In the modernizing process, the intertwining of different spheres of thought, action, and feeling gives way to specialization and separateness. The sacred is assigned a special "compartment" of its own—Americans may reserve one hour a week for it. Through compartmentalization one can live with the contradictions and paradoxes of a modernizing society. In India an informant told a British anthropologist, "When I put on my shirt and go to the factory I take off my caste. When I come home and take off my shirt I put on my caste." An Indian studying for a doctorate in astronomy still consults an astrologer when he wants to marry.[52]

Functions and Consequences of Religion

People may or may not find meaning and identity in religion. Nevertheless, their involvement in religion has consequences for themselves and their society—as both manifest or intended and latent or unintended consequences.

> Religion increases respect for the norms of the society by relating them to the sacred. . . . Religious rites renew the respect for the norms, and solidify the coherence of the group. Thus religion has a positive function with respect to social solidarity and social control.

[51]R. R. Alford, *Party and Society* (Chicago: Rand McNally, 1963), p. 49.

[52]Milton Singer, "The Modernization of Religious Beliefs," in Myron Weiner, ed., *Modernization* (New York: Basic Books, 1966), pp. 55–67.

But this function is obviously not the intention or purpose of those who believe in the religion and practice the rites. Their manifest purpose is concerned with an answer to the problem of meaning and with acting out in the rites a relationship to ultimacy—to God, the gods, or however the particular religion conceives the sacred object.[53]

Some sociologists believe ethics and religion are inseparable, that the notion of group welfare is not enough to make people obey any form of the Golden Rule. Supernatural rewards and punishments, they say, are necessary sanctions. "The tendency in most civilizations has been to have the ethical system supervised by religion, and in the last analysis enforced by it. When the neighbors and the police and Mrs. Grundy [gossip] have failed, there is still the all-seeing eye and the threat of eternal torment."[54]

One exception is found in Japanese culture. Their religion is subtle and vague although pervasive. A Japanese can adhere to both the Buddhist religion and the peculiarly Japanese Shinto religion; he does not belong to a congregation nor must he attend regular services. But on some national holidays the Japanese go to shrines and temples to pay their respects to the spirits of their ancestors "on the yonder shore," assuring them that they are remembered and cherished. They light candles and offer prayers, and tend the graves; but they are gay and festive, for the ancestors are still part of the family. Japanese notions of right and wrong, however, come from Confucian social ethics for right conduct in this world. They are guided not by fear of supernatural sanctions but by fear of shame if their neighbors or relatives think they have failed in some duty or obligation.

Many American Protestant churches have been charged with being mere social centers, with more emphasis on activities and clubs than worship. Taking the optimistic functionalist view, Talcott Parsons assesses the role of such churches in American society:

> Both the problem of mental health and that of religious commitment involve matters of intimate personal significance to individuals, what in a certain sense are highly "private" affairs. It is not fortuitous, therefore, that both center in the life of the local residential community and that by and large it is as family members that people are associated in churches. Both are hence somewhat withdrawn from the larger economic and political affairs of the society, and are associated together in this withdrawal. This situation has much to do with the sense in which the church . . . is a kind of substitute for the undifferentiated neighborhood, a place where "like-minded" people can get to know each other and be made to feel "at home" in contexts not specifically connected with religion.

[53]O'Dea, *The Sociology of Religion*, p. 73.
[54]Hertzler, *Social Institutions*, p. 429.

> It is not uncommon to suggest . . . that modern churchgoers are "not really" religious at all, but are only interested in sociability. In my opinion this is a misinterpretation. This associational aspect of the modern denominational parish is a predictable feature of the development of modern society when the fact is taken into account that family and church have such intimate intrinsic relations with each other. Each, in its own specialized way, involves "the whole person."[55]

By sanctifying norms and legitimating social institutions, religion obviously serves as a guardian of the status quo. But it can also be innovative, even revolutionary. In its "prophetic role," religion provides a standard of values against which institutionalized norms and values may be measured—and often found wanting. The Biblical prophets, like the charismatic leaders of dissident sects, thundered against corruption and compromise with the world. Many of today's religious leaders seek to promote social change, especially in the realm of social justice. Once guardians of the feudal order, now many Latin American priests have aligned themselves with revolutionary groups, and it is predicted that the Church will become increasingly radicalized in the 1970s. Some priests have been defrocked, others censured, and still others have left the priesthood of their own volition; but the trend appears significant.[56]

The "prophetic" role in American religion is rarely played at the parish level, because here homogeneity is valued, and many parishioners object violently to having their priests or ministers march in civil rights and peace demonstrations and preach neighborhood and school integration. Pronouncements and action along these lines come typically from those who are not bound by local congregations—from campus clergy, denominational conventions, and ecumenical meetings.

We have already mentioned several consequences of religious belief and practice for individuals: the provision of meaning, comfort in crises, identity, a sense of support and consensual validation in the fellowship of believers. Here let us touch upon two variations in the relationship of church and individual.

First, it appears that churches vary in their capacity to perform these functions for working-class people. In a study of the religious habits of a sample of Detroiters, Gerhard Lenski concluded that urban Lutheranism (and Protestantism in general) is more concerned with the healthy and wealthy than with the sick and poor; its ministers fail to reach the working class, especially men. Protestant interviewees who

[55]From "Mental Illness and 'Spiritual Malaise': The Role of the Psychiatrist and the Minister of Religion," *Social Structure and Personality* (New York: Association Press, 1964), pp. 305–13; reprinted in Birnbaum and Lenzer, *Sociology and Religion*, pp. 423–29.

[56]James Nelson Goodsell, "Church in Latin America: A Rising Tide of Challenges and Questions," *Christian Science Monitor* (Dec. 26, 1970).

felt they had experienced unusual difficulties with regard to sickness, death, or finances showed a marked decline in church attendance. Just the opposite was true of Catholics.

Second, the impact of religion on behavior in daily life varies with a person's religious orientation. Those who were highly *orthodox*, accepting traditional doctrine without question, separated religion from daily life. Those with a *devotional* orientation—who valued direct, personal communication with God through prayer and meditation and sought divine direction in their daily lives—tended to guide their behavior throughout the week by their beliefs; their devotionalism was linked with humanitarianism, although they preferred private to governmental expression of such humanitarianism.[57]

Transcendental religions and democratic societies stand in a special relationship to one another, as demonstrated in our own society. As summarized by Thomas O'Dea:

> Democratic societies require certain values, among which the worth of the individual, an ethic of social justice, and the priority of the general welfare over individual and sub-group interests are strategic. These values in the West owe much to prophetic and evangelical religion . . . and to secularized social movements whose values have been remotely derived from such religious sources. . . .
>
> However, if religion compromises with the general society . . . [it] becomes but one more institution adjusted to the prevailing winds of dominant opinion. . . . If religions of transcendence are to remain genuinely so, and if they are to continue to contribute positively to democratic society, then a degree of "healthy unadjustment" between religion and society must remain, despite the fact that this unadjustment itself will be the source of some conflict and will have some dysfunctional consequences. . . . The strain between religion and society . . . may prove in the long run to have important functional consequences of a positive character in preserving the very values which are requisite to a democratic society.[58]

The Future of Religion

It would be rash to assert that religion has not declined in influence in many spheres of life: By many empirical indices traditional orthodoxy has indeed declined. But that religion itself is at the lowest ebb ever is debatable. Christianity has gained millions of new adherents in the

[57]*The Religious Factor: A Sociological Study of Religion's Impact on Politics, Economics, and Family Life* (Garden City, N.Y.: Doubleday, 1961); reprinted in part in Birnbaum and Lenzer, *Sociology and Religion*, pp. 351–59.
[58]O'Dea, *The Sociology of Religion*, p. 106.

Third World. "In Africa, where an estimated 6000 independent churches have now sprung up either through schism from missionary-founded churches or around charismatic prophets, the number of Christians has grown from 4 million in 1900 to 97 million in 1970. . . . Asian and African churchmen have increasingly taken over influential positions in the Protestant and Orthodox World Council of Churches."[59] In the West, in fact, there is "the rather ironic situation of a spiritual revolution that has virtually nothing to do with churches."[60] Even the debate during the 1960s over the "death of God" was essentially a redefinition of meanings, and a return to the basic teachings of Jesus. Let us look at several indicators of the direction Western religion may take in the foreseeable future.

THE DECLINE OF RELIGION
AS AN INFLUENCE ON BEHAVIOR

According to the Gallup poll, more and more Americans each year think religion is losing influence in American life: In 1947 14% thought so; in 1962, 31%; in 1967, 57%; in 1969, 70%; in 1970, 75%. This may be interpreted in several ways: Is there a decline in the influence of traditional beliefs and sentiments? The answer is very likely yes. Have clergymen been active in influencing their congregations to apply the principles of individual worth and social justice in their daily lives? The answer appears to be no. As we saw above, parish clergy might find themselves preaching to empty pews if they were as daring there as those in the higher echelons of church bureaucracy can be in speaking out for racial integration, for example.

> The church's emphasis is overwhelmingly on man's relationship to God. The implications of the faith for man's relation to man are left largely to the individual to work out for himself, with God's help but without the help of the churches. . . . *How the majority of Americans behave, and what they value, is not informed by religious faith but by the norms and values of the larger society.* . . . Looking at American society as a whole [rather than particular minority religious movements] organized religion at present is neither a prominent witness to its own value system nor a major focal point around which ultimate commitments to norms, values, and beliefs are formed.[61]

[59]Edward Fiske, "Religion: More of the New, Less of the Old," in Lester Markel, ed., *World in Review* (New York: *The New York Times*/Rand McNally, 1972), pp. 130–31.

[60]*Ibid.*

[61]Charles Glock and Rodney Stark, *Religion and Society in Tension* (Chicago: Rand McNally, 1965), pp. 182–84. [Emphasis added]

ECUMENISM

Beginning among Protestants in the 1800s and joined by Catholics in recent decades, especially with the encouragement of Pope John XXIII, the ecumenical movement is aimed at achieving universal Christian accord, and to some extent action, on matters of mutual concern through international, interdenominational organizations. Ecumenism is fostered by the fact that churches are large and bureaucratized, and their administrators have similar problems, many of which can best be solved through merger or cooperation. Many communities now have interdenominational churches; in small towns, in particular, rules are worked out so no one church dominates in civic affairs; surveys are made of new suburban developments to see which church should be established there.

FERMENT IN THE CATHOLIC CHURCH

Changes have been especially great in recent years in the Roman Catholic Church.

> Emerging at last from three centuries of retrenchment that followed the Protestant Reformation, the church in effect took on the French Revolution, the Enlightenment, and technology all at once when the late Pope John XXIII convened the Second Vatican Council from 1962 to 1965. The church still faces serious problems, but it seems to have passed through a period of tearing down old structures and is entering a time of rebuilding.[62]

Unrest, innovation, and experiment characterize the Catholic Church today, especially in countries where religious interest and involvement are high, as in the United States and the Netherlands. Between 1963 and early 1971, 25,000 of the world's 540,000 ordained Catholic priests left the priesthood; the Pope implied that the main reason was their objection to the rule of mandatory celibacy. Encouraged by the Vatican II Decree on the Appropriate Renewal of the Religious Life, many orders of nuns have examined their constitutions, experimented with innovations, and followed the Council's recommendation that they become less isolated and more involved in the world. Those who stay within the orders often accept innovations such as more modern dress and more community service. Many who have left the convent live in communes with other former nuns, earn money in the helping professions, and donate their free time to family service in the slums and with the poor of their parishes. Relaxation of dietary rules, the use of the vernacular in the mass, and more audience participation

[62]Fiske, "Religion."

(such as singing hymns) are other innovations. Some groups have also experimented with masses held in private homes. As orthodoxy relaxes, devotionalism takes new forms and is expressed in humanitarian activities.

THE SEARCH FOR THE SACRED

A phenomenon of the counterculture, especially pronounced among the best students in the most elite colleges and universities—just where one might expect secularization to be strongest and science most respected—is a search for the sacred, or "neo-sacred," in directions that are often occult and bizarre. There are covens of witches and warlocks; semi-monastic cults that stress vegetarianism, meditation, and asceticism; mutual-help communities, loosely organized and not necessarily living communally; groups experimenting with extrasensory perception and other parapsychological phenomena. Many see Eastern religions as an escape from the pressures of modern society (the Krishna people). Astrology is very much in vogue, as are tarot cards and the I Ching as systems of divination that are supposed to help a person make decisions. Others find the sacred closer to home, in the Christian gospel. The "Jesus People" try to live by the simplest precepts of early Christianity.

This "return to the sacred" is seen by some as part of a general disillusionment with science and technology and with the positivist–rational approach to knowledge, which brings no inner peace and provides no "sacred canopy" of meaning. Andrew Greeley believes "that what is going on is authentically, if perhaps transiently and bizarrely, religious. Personal efficacy, meaning, community, encounter with the ecstatic and the transcendental, and the refusal to believe that mere reason can explain either life or personhood—all of these have traditionally been considered religious postures. [The religious cultists are] looking for an explanation for life and for themselves."[63] They are, in short, seeking what religion has universally provided: "definition beyond the extent of our knowledge, and security beyond the guarantees of human relationships."[64] Many agree with French priest-anthropologist Teilhard de Chardin that mankind is on the verge of a leap toward a much better form of human life.

What Is Education?

In its broadest sense, **education** is synonymous with socialization, and includes any process whereby one individual or group passes elements

[63] Andrew M. Greeley, "There's a New-Time Religion on Campus," *The New York Times Magazine* (June 1, 1969): 14–15 et passim.
[64] O'Dea, *The Sociology of Religion*, p. 9.

of culture to another. Recognizing that effective socialization is basic to the continuation of society, every society also practices education in a narrower sense: the deliberate transmission of selected knowledge, skills, and values to prepare individuals for effective membership in the society. In this chapter we are especially concerned with the formalized institution of education as embodied primarily in modern school systems.

From the standpoint of the individual, education is not synonymous with the mere acquisition of information; that may be stored in and retrieved from encyclopedias, almanacs, libraries, computers, and many other sources. Nor is it synonymous with schooling, with acquiring skills and knowledge (such as the 3 R's or history). Even learning, or deep and intensive scholarship, is not truly education. A Shakespearean scholar may know every detail of folios and quartos but fail to grasp the feeling and meaning of the plays. True education results in an ability to grasp relationships between facts and ideas, and between one idea and another; to place facts and ideas in a system of values, and to see their relevance to one's own life and to his society.[65]

Just as in the family and religion, there is great unrest, ferment, and innovation in the area of education. What should be taught? How? To whom? These are all controversial questions today. There isn't even agreement on the nature of the raw material: Is the child a blank page to be written on? A noble savage born good, who will learn if left alone? A barbarian who needs to be tamed and broken and fitted into a proper place? A pre-programmed system whose unfolding we must grasp so we can suit the content and method of teaching to the proper stage of development?

Unlike the family and religion, education is a public institution whose main directions are worked out through political processes. In modern society it is much more formal and systematically organized and bureaucratized than either family or religion. And in most modern societies it is compulsory; there is no other recognized path by which the average child may be socialized and awarded an achieved status.

THE SOCIOLOGY OF EDUCATION

The sociologist may see an educational system, first of all, as part of a total social system that both reflects and influences the social and cultural order of which it is a part. The class system, cultural values, the power structure, the balance of individual freedom and social control, the homogeneity or heterogeneity of race, religion, and nationality, the degree of urbanization and industrialization—all these factors exert a strong and inevitable influence on the school system of any community or society.

He may also look at it—and at each school within it—as a sub-

[65]Sydney Harris, *Detroit Free Press* (July 7, 1967).

system with a subculture and social organization of its own. It has a system of statuses and roles, a body of values, skills, and traditions, its own rituals, and its own special language. Each school and each classroom within the school forms an interacting social group, and social psychologists are especially interested in the relationship between the structure and atmosphere of the group and the behavior changes that result from its interaction.

In spite of its essentially conservative nature education cannot escape the effects of changes in the form and function of the family and in the size, distribution, and composition of the population; of technological changes and economic trends and crises; and of changes in political philosophy and political power. It often lags behind in adapting to such changes; but at the level of the university, especially in democratic societies, education is considered an instrument of guided social and technological change through research in many fields.

In this section we touch upon some of these questions: What are the goals, functions, and consequences of education for society and for its individual members? What is the impact of modernization on education, and what role does education play in the modernizing process? How do schools reflect and perpetuate cultural and subcultural differences and inequalities? What trends may we note and what innovations are being tried to reach the goals of education more successfully? What will education probably be like in post-industrial society?[66]

Goals, Functions, and Consequences of Education

To unravel the "functions" of education, we must distinguish between the intentions or purposes of individuals and of policy-makers, and the consequences, whether intended or not, of structures and processes. What, other than compulsion, motivates children to go to school and keep going? What do parents expect? What do educational philosophers outline as proper social goals? What do legislatures and city councils and school boards have in mind when they allocate resources? Robert Hutchins insists that the proper aim of education is "manhood, not manpower."[67] But surely society needs manpower. Harold Taylor sees the purpose of education as teaching people to think for them-

[66]We may distinguish between "educational sociology," which is usually normative, dealing with what should be, how research can best be applied within an educational system; and "the sociology of education," which is more strictly empirical, and looks at the institution from outside in order to understand it better. Both are legitimate and valid academic activities, critically important to contemporary society. See Donald A. Hansen and Joel E. Gerstl, *On Education—Sociological Perspectives* (New York: John Wiley, 1967), pp. 3–35.

[67]Robert Hutchins, "Toward a Learning Society," *The Center Magazine* 4, No. 4 (July–Aug. 1970): 42–47.

selves, for that is what it means to be free. But surely this is not the goal of education in the Soviet Union or the People's Republic of China. Education, he also asserts, should "give each person a chance to become what he is capable of becoming."[68] How many schools and how many societies come close to achieving that goal?

Somewhat arbitrarily let us divide the "functions" of education according to its contribution to social goals and to individual goals.

SOCIETY AND EDUCATION

Education plays an important role in both social stability and social change. It transmits the culture: It teaches the beliefs, values, knowledge, and skills that all members of the society presumably should share. It also trains people to do certain jobs; it screens them, places them according to ability and achievement, rejects the failures—in short, it allocates individuals to various statuses. (As we have seen in several contexts, this function is complemented by ascription according to family status by class and ethnic background.) In modern society the schools are also custodial institutions, "baby-sitters" for the younger generation—seeing, some charge, that they stay out of the mainstream of social and economic life.[69] Another latent function of modern schools —and one parents have more or less consciously in mind when they choose neighborhoods and schools for their children—is that of providing a "pool" of possible acceptable mates.

A system of education is also a source of innovation and change. A governor of the colony of Virginia said in the seventeenth century: "Thank God there are no free schools or printing; . . . for learning has brought disobedience and heresy into the world, and printing has divulged them. . . . God keep us from both." The university in particular encourages research and innovation in both the humanities and the sciences; it grants prizes and awards and funds for novelists, poets, and painters as well as for physicists, social scientists, chemists, and biologists.

THE INDIVIDUAL AND EDUCATION

Individuals may see education as an end in itself or as an instrumental means to ends. It is *the* path to success in modern society, the only way to get the skills and knowledge and credentials for a good job. Lifetime earnings in the United States are directly correlated with the amount of formal schooling. The Carnegie Commission on Higher Education reported in 1971 that median income in 1968 for heads of households with five grades of schooling or less was $2920; 6 to

---

[68]"Education: For What and For Whom?" *School and Society* 83 (Feb. 1956): 39–43.

[69]Paul Goodman, in *Summerhill: For and Against* (New York: Hart, 1970), pp. 204–22.

8 grades, $5170; 9 to 11 grades, $7260; a high school diploma, $8940; a bachelor's degree, $11,240; and an advanced or professional degree, $13,120.[70]

The same study also tried to relate amount of schooling to happiness. In reply to a questionnaire on marital happiness, 38% of those with a grade school education, 46% of those with a high school education, and 60% of those with a college education said they were "very happy." At the same time, the more schooling a person had, the more introspective he was about behavior and the more likely he was to report problems and feelings of inadequacy. He was also more sensitive to the parental role, but there was no reported difference in the recognition of parent–child problems. Schooling was also correlated with job satisfaction: 70% of those with 11 years or less, 78% of those with high school diplomas, and 89% of college graduates said they enjoyed their work. Furthermore, the Commission found that the more schooling a person had, the more liberal and tolerant he was likely to be; the less subject to unemployment; the more thoughtful and deliberate in consumer expenditures; the more likely to vote and participate in community activities; and the more informed about community, national, and world affairs.[71]

Modernization and Education

Developing nations typically are divided into an educated elite (often proud of its "high culture") and the illiterate masses. Their leaders are keenly aware "that education is the greatest instrument man has devised for his own progress."[72] Pakistani villagers, for example, disagree about almost everything, but will contribute funds toward a school. The People's Republic of China is deeply committed to education, and exercises strong central control over it. The two leading industrial nations, the United States and the Soviet Union, are also those with the most open and widespread systems of free public education.

Industrializing nations need a system of popular education to train people for industrial and commercial occupations, for political leadership and bureaucratic positions, for simply getting around a city with its numerous secondary contacts. They also need it to weld many different subcultural groups—African tribes, immigrants to America—into a nation-state. And any system of popular suffrage demands at least a minimum of literacy. A shortage of educated people is usually identified as the chief obstacle to modernization.

[70]*The New York Times* (Oct. 6, 1971).

[71]*Ibid.*

[72]John W. Hanson and Cole S. Brumbeck, eds., *Education and the Development of Nations* (New York: Holt, Rinehart & Winston, 1966), p. 32.

A system of education based on such societal requirements tends to stress verbal skills and rationality rather than emotions and expressiveness. It may seem abstract and remote, the pay-off much too far removed from what goes on in the classroom; and as modernization advances, and knowledge explodes, education takes up more and more years of the life span. As a result, there are dropouts and failures all along the line, most of whom find there is no alternative road to success in the mainstream. In the Third World, half of those who enter elementary school fail to finish fourth grade. In 1971, UNESCO estimated that there are 810 million illiterates in the world, 34% of all those over age 15. In thirty-seven African countries south of the Sahara 60% of those entering school leave before really learning to read and write.

The crisis of education in modernizing countries is two-fold. In 1972, 600,000 Brazilian high school graduates took university entrance examinations for any 200,000 places.[73] Although the proportion of Soviet citizens attending universities multiplied twenty-one times between 1914 and 1967, in 1971 there were only 900,000 places for 2.5 million university applicants. On the other side of the coin, in many developing nations there aren't enough jobs for those who do complete their education. The unevenness of education adds to unrest: Semiliterate youth flock to cities with no marketable skills, their familial and tribal bridges burned behind them.

This cultural lag in developing nations can be traced to a sharp increase in aspirations, the scarcity of resources to support mass education (aggravated by the population explosion), and the inertia of societies themselves—their traditional values and customs, their patterns of prestige and incentive.

Public policy encouraging economic expansion and the population explosion, as well as higher aspirations, has created a tremendous *social demand* for education since World War II, in industrial as well as in developing nations. Between 1950 and 1963 world-wide primary school enrollment increased over 50%, secondary and high school enrollment over 100%. Yet British universities have to turn away over one-quarter of the qualified applicants, and in West Germany 6500 qualified candidates applied for 2800 places in medical school.[74]

The American system, faced not only with the need for educating its citizens but also the need for acculturating immigrants, early established a policy of casting the net wide, of giving as many as possible from the lower classes and deprived minorities an opportunity. Statistics indicate the extent of success: In 1900 only 6% of American youngsters went through high school, 0.25% through college. By 1940, 38% of young adults had high school diplomas and 6% had college degrees; by 1970, 75% had graduated from high school and 16% from

[73]*The New York Times* (Jan. 15, 1972).
[74]Philip H. Coombs, *The World Educational Crisis: A Systems Analysis* (New York: Oxford University Press, 1968), pp. 4, 17–35.

college. At the same time, achievement as measured by standard tests had risen.[75]

Cultural Variations in Educational Systems

Although modernization leads to a certain degree of uniformity in systems of education as well as other aspects of culture, many forces make for variation from one society to another. The pattern of control may be centralized or decentralized; the relation of school and community may be distant or close; content may be varied or uniform; methods may be authoritarian or democratic, based on rote learning or problem-solving; the system of recruitment may be open or selective; a high value may be placed on education or a low one (reflected in resources committed to it rather than mere lip service). These variations may go together in unexpected ways: For example, control in the United States is extremely decentralized, with tens of thousands of local school boards taking the responsibility of hiring teachers and allocating resources; yet content displays a great degree of uniformity all over the nation due to the system of teacher training, the nation-wide textbook industry, standardized testing and college entrance requirements, and the unique Amer-

[75]Morris Janowitz, "Institution Building in Urban Education," in David Street, ed., *Innovation in Mass Education* (New York: John Wiley, 1969).

A free school.
(Photo by Richard E. Bull, from Summerhill USA, *Richard E. Bull, Penguin Books, Inc., Baltimore Maryland. Copyright © Richard E. Bull 1970.)*

A classroom in the People's Republic of China.

ican heritage, with its stress on acculturation of many immigrants.[76]

Education in China today reflects a total commitment to education and a total central control, guided by a pervasive ideology and a driving goal. China's educational endeavor "in its totality may be said to be the most extensive and ambitious attempt thus far at human engineering."[77] One indicator of the level of commitment is the rise in literacy from 20% in 1949, the year of Communist victory, to 80% two decades later. Every aspect of schooling serves the end of indoctrination. A typical arithmetic problem shows how a greedy landlord of the pre-revolutionary era loaned 5 tou (a tou being about 40 lbs.) of rice to a tenant in a famine year at 50% interest, compounded; he could not finish paying for 3 years, and had to pay nearly 17 tou. A map in a geography lesson shows China menaced by an eagle (the United States), a bear (Russia), and a lion (the British imperialism of the past century). Five-year-olds sing about unity with the peoples of Asia, Africa, and Latin America in the struggle against the imperialists. "Political power comes from the barrel of a rifle," they recite, and then drill with wooden guns.

The two goals of education are to make everyone both "red" (ideologically sound) and "expert" (trained in some field that contributes to economic development). To ensure that expertness does not produce a separate class of intelligentsia, Mao engineered the Cultural Revolution of 1966–1967, during which students were turned loose to purge the "bourgeois intellectuals" and revitalize the revolutionary spirit. Their rampages were finally subdued under army control and a new pattern of education was instituted. School terms were shortened to 5 years of primary and 5 years of secondary schooling. At age fifteen or sixteen everyone must go to work in factories or fields for a couple of years; then they may apply for a training course of 2 or 3 years at a university. The academic content of courses has been reduced and the political content increased. The "bitter remembrances" of the old society are vividly portrayed. Almost every course is taught through Mao's maxims and philosophy. School and work are amalgamated as much as possible: Schools establish factories and farms; and factories, communes, and cooperatives establish schools. Students work as responsible employees; in one school, for example, they spend part of each day making diodes for transistors, in another, steps for buses. Model citizens are held up for imitation; and all groups are trained to practice "thought reform" through criticism and self-criticism. The old education, it is said, made people think of their own fame and fortune rather

---

[76]For a good discussion of the educational heritage of the United States, see Willis Rudy, *Schools in an Age of Mass Culture: An Exploration of Selected Themes in the History of Twentieth-Century American Education* (Englewood Cliffs, N.J.: Prentice-Hall, Inc., 1965), chap. 1, "The Setting."

[77]C. T. Hu, *Aspects of Chinese Education* (New York: Columbia University, Teachers College Press, 1969), p. 1.

than the good of the society; the Cultural Revolution was therefore anti-individualistic as well as anti-intellectual.[78]

Subcultural Variations in Education

The value placed on education, the level of aspiration, access to education, the degree of adjustment and profit from schooling—all these vary with social class and ethnic background. For example, the Jews, long urbanites with a cultural–religious veneration for learning, place an extremely high value on education, both as a means to an end and an end in itself. The aspect of subcultural variation that has received the most attention, however, is the relationship between social class status and education.

The study of "Elmtown's Youth" referred to in Chapter 9 tested the hypothesis that the behavior of adolescents in and about school was significantly related to the positions their families occupied in the social class structure of the community. The hypothesis was confirmed: School-board policy, adolescent attitudes, participation in extra-curricular activities, membership in cliques, progress in school, and recognition by teachers were all determined in large part by class background.[79]

Theoretically, the American system is open as compared to the traditional class-oriented selective system in European schools, where until recently children were sorted into various kinds of schools at age ten or eleven, and thereafter destined either for trades, commercial and clerical work, or the university with its opportunities for professional standing. But some American high schools operate on the track system, which has the same effect.

> Under the track system, those from culturally deprived homes are automatically passed through the grades regardless of performance, until legal school-leaving age is reached. At that time they are dumped out on the streets, where they will spend the rest of their lives grubbing for existence through the offal of our cities. The second track is for those with low, but passable, achievement records. They are placed in the manual-arts, nonacademic track and are destined for the

[78]Joan Robinson, *The Cultural Revolution in China* (Baltimore: Penguin, 1969). See also *Report From Red China, The New York Times* (New York: Avon, 1971), chap. 5, "The Children of Chairman Mao: Education and Child-Rearing," by Tillman F. Durdin; Committee of Concerned Asian Scholars, *China! Inside the People's Republic* (New York: Bantam, 1972), chap. 7, "Education"; and Harriet C. Mills, "Thought Reform: Ideological Remolding in China," in Patricia Cayo Sexton, ed., *Readings on the School in Society* (Englewood Cliffs, N.J.: Prentice-Hall, Inc., 1968), pp. 164–74.

[79]August B. Hollingshead, *Elmtown's Youth* (New York: John Wiley, 1949), chap. 8, "The High School in Action."

menial, semiskilled trades. The highest, of course, are put into the liberal-arts, college-preparatory programs, and they inevitably will end up with college degrees and Establishment jobs. The point is that the track system reinforces—and even magnifies—the initial condition with which students begin life. Before the average child is ten years old the school system has already determined, beyond the child's ability to influence it, his entire lifetime career.[80]

Ideally, at least, the "comprehensive" high school, offering different curricula but mingling the students as much as possible and offering a maximum freedom of choice, is the type least likely to perpetuate class distinctions. But most teachers have middle-class backgrounds and unconsciously tend to discriminate against lower-class children. One aspect of this discrimination is the "self-fulfilling prophecy": They expect less of children from deprived homes, and therefore the children achieve less. The best-known study of this phenomenon—the "Rosenthal effect"—was carried out in Oak School, a public elementary school in a lower-class community of a medium-size city. About one-sixth of the pupils were Mexican-Americans. Each of the six grades was divided into one fast, one medium, and one slow classroom, primarily on the basis of reading ability, and Mexican-Americans were heavily over-represented in the slow track. To test the proposition that favorable expectations by teachers could lead to an increase in intellectual competence, all the children were given a standard nonverbal test of intelligence at the very beginning of the school year. Each of the eighteen teachers was given the names of those children in her classroom who had done well on the test. This list included about 20% of the children, and was allegedly based on the tests, but had actually been chosen according to a table of random numbers. "The difference between the special children and the ordinary children, then, was only in the mind of the teacher."[81]

Retesting showed that 19% of the control-group children of the first and second grades gained 20 or more points in IQ, while 47% of the experimental group made such a gain. Children in the medium track made the greatest improvement; and the boys who looked most Mexican—and therefore probably surprised their teachers most by showing up on a list of probable "bloomers"—benefited most from their teachers' positive prophecies. And those of the lower track who had *not* been chosen as probable intellectual bloomers, but did make spectacular gains, were viewed very negatively by their teachers. Expectations,

[80]Harvey Wheeler, "A Moral Equivalent for Riots," *Saturday Review* (May 11, 1968): 19–22 *et passim*.

[81]Robert Rosenthal and Lenore Jacobson, *Pygmalion in the Classroom: Teacher Expectation and Pupils' Intellectual Development* (New York: Holt, Rinehart & Winston, 1968); excerpts from chap. 12, "Summary and Implications," reprinted in Edgar A. Schuler *et al.*, *Readings in Sociology*, 4th ed. (New York: Crowell 1971), pp. 415–19.

then, did affect performance; but it was not made clear just how the process works. "The phenomenon of subtle interpersonal influence guiding progress in the classroom is as complex as it is fascinating."[82]

The impact of class status on educational opportunity and achievement is much greater in European countries than in the United States. In France the chances of getting a professional education are 58.5% for the children of professionals, and less than 2% for the children of agricultural and other workers.[83] Despite many educational reforms in Great Britain, more than a third leave school at age fifteen; the system has never succeeded in absorbing the working class. In the United States over 94% of those age fourteen to seventeen, nearly 48% of those age eighteen to nineteen, and 21.5% of those age twenty to twenty-four are in school.[84] Over 8 million young people were in college in 1972, and it is estimated that by 1985 there will be nearly 12 million. And many of these come from hitherto deprived groups. In the country as a whole, over 9% of freshman were blacks in 1972, as compared to 5.8% 4 years earlier. Many of these attend urban community colleges; 55–65% are not in black colleges, which enrolled most blacks until the mid-1960s.[85]

Ferment and Experiment in Education

In America especially people are seriously questioning all aspects of the educational system: social organization, the content and methods of teaching, the goals of schooling—even the very existence of a formal school system. Inside and outside the system, there is much experimentation and innovation. One anthropologist sees the ferment in American education as a symptom of cultural transformation—"a transformation that produces serious conflict. . . . The core of the change can best be conceived as a radical shift in values." Basing his generalizations on the responses of several hundred students, mainly in professional education courses, to a series of twenty-four open-ended statements, such as "The individual is —", "All men are born —", and "Intellectuals should —," and on a brief paragraph describing "The Ideal American Boy," George Spindler outlines a shift from traditional to emergent values much like that discussed in Chapter 4. Puritan morality vs. moral relativism; the work-success ethic and achievement orientation vs. sociability and hedonism; future-time orientation vs. present-time orientation; individual-

---

[82]Peter and Carol Gumpert, "The Teacher as Pygmalion: Comments on the Psychology of Expectation," *The Urban Review* 3, No. 1 (Sept. 1968): 21–25; reprinted in Schuler *et al., Readings in Sociology,* pp. 419–22.

[83]Coombs, *The World Crisis in Education,* pp. 32–33.

[84]*Information Please Almanac* (1972), p. 658.

[85]William Stief, "Blacks in College: The Most Exciting Thing Around," *The Progressive* (Sept. 1971): 32–34.

ism vs. consideration for others and conformity—these are the main outlines of traditional and emergent values. Most likely to champion traditional values are school boards, with the general public and parents close to them in conservatism. Some students also cling to traditional values, and are more conservative than school administrators. Younger teachers are more likely to hold emergent values than older ones; and emergent values are strongest of all among students from families oriented toward such values.

> In this perspective, many conflicts between parents and teachers, school boards and educators, parents and children, and between the various personages and groups within the school system (teachers against teachers, administrators against teachers, and so on) can be understood as conflicts that grow out of sharp differences in values that mirror social and cultural transformation of tremendous scope— and for which none of the actors in the situation can be held personally responsible.[86]

SOCIAL ORGANIZATION

School systems are charged with being vast, rigid bureaucracies isolated from the community and unresponsive to students. Two of the many changes suggested involve closer ties with the community and a change in student status and role.

Students are alive NOW, insists Harold Taylor; they are part of society NOW; let them get their hands dirty and their feet wet instead of sitting in an isolated classroom day after day. They should go to offices, factories, museums, hospitals, farms, police stations, and even other schools; learn about transportation, architecture, and science—in context. Many kinds of people should be brought into the classroom to talk to students.[87] Schools should prepare children not for some ideal pattern of suburban middle-class life but for their communities as they are; teachers should be aware of the problems a ghetto child faces outside the school and talk about them. An absolute moral rule like "It is wrong to fight" does a slum kid little good; more useful would be a talk on the theme "It is wrong to allow others to manipulate you into a fight." One sign that members of the community themselves want closer communication with their children's schools is the movement toward decentralization of urban systems, with neighborhood school boards overseeing some aspects of schooling.

[86]"Education in a Transforming American Culture," in George D. Spindler, ed., *Education and Culture: Anthropological Approaches* (New York: Holt, Rinehart & Winston, 1963).

[87]Harold Taylor, *Students Without Teachers: The Crisis in the University* (New York: McGraw-Hill, 1969), and *The World as Teacher* (Garden City, N.Y.: Doubleday, 1969).

The school is not a cloister; it exists in and is part of society—sometimes an intimate part, sometimes a loosely attached one. Except when there is a labor shortage or a national emergency, society "is usually negligent of its youth, insisting only that reasonable order be kept in the schools. Because youth has been largely expendable in an industrial society with labor surpluses, and because youth and those who tend them have been without real social power, schools have usually been out of the mainstream of society. This, indeed, has been the most serious problem of the schools."[88]

Students themselves are demanding greater power and participation, more control over what they are taught and how they are evaluated. Not only slum schools with their largely custodial function, but *most* schools are authoritarian. Not only do students feel they lack a meaningful function in the general socio-cultural order, they also feel powerless in their own schools. Teachers College of Columbia University concludes from studies of junior and senior high schools that students do not form an allegiance to the democratic system because they do not experience democracy in their schools.[89] A Carnegie study found the three most damaging features of United States high schools were encouragement of docility and conformity, overregulation of students' lives, and a pallid uniform curriculum. Various reform movements and experiments are designed to make the system more open, personal, and flexible. One example is Portland's John Adams High School, where students are given a great deal of freedom in designing their own curricula and even their own courses, and are allowed to study and do research with little supervision. This plan is more widespread in experimental colleges than in high schools.

Another problem is that schooling now begins earlier in life and extends later and later. It is predicted that by 1980 most people age two to twenty will be in school, and there will be numerous programs for adults. As Hutchins puts it, this trend is commendable if it is not an attempt to answer the question "How can we get everybody in schools and keep them there as long as possible?" but rather, "How can we give everybody a chance to learn all his life?"[90]

CONTENT OF EDUCATION

In a rapidly changing society, what shall we teach the young? If we give them narrowly specific skills, the advance of science and technology soon makes those skills obsolete. Some educators suggest that children must learn to learn; that they must learn to think in terms not of details but of big concepts such as the conservation of energy;

[88]Sexton, *Readings on the School in Society*, p. v.
[89]*The New York Times* (Sept. 22, 1970).
[90]Robert M. Hutchins, "Toward a Learning Society."

to see problems (other than how to con the teacher or pass the course or get a good grade). They should be encouraged to guess and brainstorm, to do their own research using basic concepts, rather than being spoon-fed information they are to learn by rote and regurgitate on command. They must not be coddled and taught some ideal world that does not exist—though ideals and values must of course be part of the content. But if the conflict and tension they see all around them are ignored in school, how will they learn to cope and understand? Classroom materials tend to be innocuous, partly because of the conflicting cross-pressures of different interest groups. This is apparent even in some universities, where the public, exerting power through legislatures, clamps down on expressions of unorthodox views and dissent, and thus frustrates some of the university's chief functions in society: criticism, research, and innovation.

A student who does not see the relevance of content to his own life will not be motivated to learn. The curriculum in most American schools has some relevance for the economic future of the advantaged, very little for the "disadvantaged." Neil Postman and Charles Weingartner suggest that children should be taught to ask and pursue questions they perceive as important to their own lives, and to go to find the answers wherever they can be found, whether or not that is in the school. They repeat "a sad little joke about a fifth-grade teacher in a ghetto school who asked a grim Negro boy, during the course of a 'science' lesson, 'How many legs does a grasshopper have?' 'Oh, man,' he replied, "I sure wish I had *your* problems!' "[91]

But everybody has one overarching problem in common: that of survival.

> Change—constant, accelerating, ubiquitous—is the most striking characteristic of the world we live in and . . . our educational system has not yet recognized this fact. . . . The abilities and attitudes required to deal adequately with change are those of the highest priority and . . . it is not beyond our ingenuity to design school environments which can help young people to master concepts necessary to survival in a rapidly changing world.[92]

GOALS AND METHODS

Closely intertwined with the content of education are its goals and methods. Do schools emphasize the lives and growth of the students, or getting through a prescribed curriculum? Do educators and

[91]*Teaching as a Subversive Activity* (New York: Dell, 1970), p. 93. See chap. 11, "Two Alternatives," for fascinating examples of curricula centered around questions and reality.

[92]*Ibid.,* pp. xii-xiv.

administrators think about WHAT they are doing, and WHY? Charles Silberman says American schools are characterized by "mindlessness," by failure to think about these fundamental things.[93]

"Free" schools, both within the system and outside it, are experimenting with goals and methods. One approach is exemplified by Summerhill, whose headmaster, A. S. Neill, operates on the conviction that if children are free of fear, if they are treated as citizens of a community, they will learn.[94] While Summerhill has aroused much controversy, and its success may depend largely on the unique personality of Neill and the particular circumstances of the school, it has served as a catalyst, prompting much debate and experimentation. In America, for example, free schools have developed outside the formal system—"street academies," such as George Dennison's short-lived First Street School,[95] and free high schools and universities based on the principle of self-regulation. Europeans have experimented with freer schools within the system, for example, the British primary schools, which adopted many innovations suggested in the Plowden Report of 1967.[96] Children are taught to work independently in an environment thoughtfully planned to permit choices from an array of materials. They help one another, move about freely, work at their individual pace; the teacher moves among them asking and answering questions as they do many different things. He or she is the organizer, catalyst, and consultant, who listens, diagnoses, advises, and introduces new ideas, words, and materials.[97] Silberman is convinced that freer, more open schools are more effective than joyless formal schools, which suppress curiosity and atrophy the senses with their emphasis on order, verbal learning, and grades.

A lot of things have happened in recent decades, and "most of them plug into walls."[98] How can schools incorporate the new means of communication and information processing without further dehumanizing the process of education? Those who dismiss television and computers as "hardware" and "gadgetry" have failed to come to terms with the fact that by the time the average American child reaches school he is already packed with information picked up from an average

[93]Charles E. Silberman, *Crisis in the Classroom: The Remaking of American Education* (New York: Random House, 1970), p. 203.

[94]A. S. Neill, *Summerhill: A Radical Approach to Child Rearing* (New York: Hart Publishing Company, 1960); and *Summerhill: For and Against.*

[95]George Dennison, *The Lives of Children: The Story of the First Street School* (New York: Random House, 1969). (One reviewer said no other book shows so well what a free and human education can be like, nor describes its philosophy more eloquently.)

[96]This report of the Central Advisory Council on Education is more formally titled "Children and Their Primary Schools."

[97]Silberman devotes sixty pages to these schools in *Crisis in the Classroom.*

[98]John M. Culkin, S.J., "A Schoolman's Guide to Marshall McLuhan," *Saturday Review* (Mar. 18, 1967): 51.

of 3,000 to 4,000 hours watching TV, and by the time he leaves high school he will have spent 10,800 hours in school as compared to 15,000 hours watching TV.[99] The success of "Sesame Street" with youngsters from three to five suggests the possibilities. Yet the danger of dehumanization remains—unless there is a live teacher in the room, a responsive human being who *uses* the master teacher on TV, or the teaching machine. The latter may be better for some students than a disapproving teacher, for it is impersonal, does not condemn, gives another chance.

The evaluation of students' potential and achievement is vital to their self-conceptions. In a school with a strict system of grading, competition rather than cooperation guides interaction. The system of evaluating the individual student, it has been argued, is a major flaw in public education. Intelligence tests are of doubtful validity, achievement tests either unfair or self-defeating for those from deprived backgrounds. A more constructive approach would be to evaluate not students but teachers, principals, school districts, and educational systems. This would lead to such questions as: How can we protect the teacher from social and administrative pressures? In spite of centralization and bureaucratization, each school is a unit in itself. Teachers are isolated from one another, principals from teachers; yet both are vulnerable to community power and hence fearful of innovation.[100]

PUBLIC SCHOOLS AND ALTERNATIVES

Some authorities say that only about 10 or 15% of the population is capable of and interested in academic pursuits; yet formal schooling in traditional subjects is made compulsory for all. As a result many are bored and alienated, made to feel that they are inadequate failures who will never make it. The monopoly of the public school system should be broken by establishing alternative paths toward participation in adult society. Says Paul Goodman:

> Society desperately needs much work, both intellectual and manual, in urban renewal, in ecology, in communications, and in the arts. All these spheres could make use of young people. . . . Our aim should be to *multiply the paths of growing up*. There should be ample opportunity for a young boy or girl to begin his career again, to cross over from one career to another, to take a moratorium, to travel, or to work on his own.[101]

Such alternatives would give nonintellectuals a chance to achieve self-respect. Among alternative plans already tried are the Job Corps, VISTA, Neighborhood Youth Corps, education within industry, the

[99]*Ibid.*
[100]Janowitz, "Institution Building in Urban Education."
[101]Goodman in *Summerhill: For and Against*, pp. 218–19.

armed forces, and labor unions. One consequence of breaking the monopoly of public education might be to jar it out of inertia.

John Fischer believes that fundamental alterations in the public school system must begin with changes in the basic assumptions underlying present policy and practice. The assumption that the basic function of schools is to screen and classify students must be abandoned; schools must truly encourage originality, inventiveness, and initiative.[102] Such changes can hardly come from within the schools themselves. It is not that they resist innovation, but that their policies are determined by the public, by political policy-makers, and by teacher-training institutions.

Education in the Post-Industrial Society

These controversies and innovations are especially relevant to the changes pointing toward the emergence of a post-industrial society. Skills and techniques quickly become obsolete: Reeducation is necessary in all fields of expertise and professionalism. Leisure time increases greatly.

As these trends accelerate, manpower becomes less important, manhood—the achievement of full human potential—more so. The post-industrial society does not need people trained to give a routine response—its machines do that. It needs imaginative, resourceful, flexible human beings. Human brains can do research and apply their findings; machines can do routine activities. Humans alone can respond richly to other humans, as teachers, parents, helpers, physicians, and friends. This response is "a critical task, for as the society becomes more interdependent, more geared to technological requirements, it is crucial that it not become alienated internally, flat emotionally, and gray."[103] Schools must go beyond teaching technical and routine subjects to cultivate the uniquely human. This may best be done through dialogue—the conversation of adult and youth.

In a rapidly changing society, this dialogue means that adults can—in fact, must—learn from youth as well as the other way around. Adults "can teach their children not what to learn, but how to learn and not what they should be committed to, but the value of commitment. . . . [The young, in turn] can lead their elders in the direction of the unknown [for they] are like the first generation born into a new country. They are at home in this time."[104]

[102]John H. Fischer, "Who Needs Schools?" *Saturday Review* (Sept. 19, 1970): 78–79 et passim.

[103]Jerome S. Bruner, "Culture, Politics, and Pedagogy," *Saturday Review* (May 18, 1968): 69 ff.

[104]Margaret Mead, *Culture and Commitment: A Study of the Generation Gap* (New York: Doubleday, 1970), pp. 58, 72, 73.

The university has always played a crucial role in storing, transmitting, and changing the culture. And "It is in the universities that lies, still, the best potential for learning to come to terms with our age. They will realize that potential fully when they succeed in bridging the current dichotomy between 'schooling' and 'adult education' with a concept of continuing education that is alive and sensitive to what will from now on in certainly be a world that will stand still no longer."[105]

Despite charges that the universities have "sold out" to the Establishment (because they accept grants for research that may be turned to the ends of the military–industrial complex, for example), they occupy a very special place in free societies. Like the progressive education movement of each generation, they foreshadow the socio-cultural order to come. Says poet Stephen Spender,

> The university is the students, the young, and in some ways their life is much in advance of the society from which they come. The students lead a life, *not just as a result of their own efforts but as an effect of the institution,* that is more egalitarian, more open to "direct democracy," more communal and certainly more civilized than that of the surrounding society. The universities are probably the institutions in our society in which freedom is most truly felt.[106]

But, he adds, the problem for students is to exercise this power of criticism without destroying the university; for if they destroy it, their power of dissent and criticism will very likely also be destroyed.

In rearing "unknown children for an unknown future," insists Margaret Mead, we must find ways of teaching and learning that keep the future open, and that recognize what the young realize better than their elders—that "for the first time human beings throughout the world, in their information about one another and responses to one another, have become a community that is united by shared knowledge and danger."[107]

Summary

In this chapter we have considered the three universal institutions that socialize members of a group, provide them with systems of meanings, and give them emotional security. All three—the family, religion, and education—vary from culture to culture; all three are affected by the

[105]Emmanuel G. Mesthene, "The University, Adult Education, and the Age of Technology," *Adult Leadership* 15, No. 4 (Oct. 1966): 113–45 *et passim.;* reprinted as "Technology Change, and Continuing Education," in Schuler *et al, Readings in Sociology,* p. 440.

[106]"What the Rebellious Students Want," *The New York Times Magazine* (Mar. 30, 1969): 56–57 ff. [Emphasis added]

[107]*Culture and Commitment,* p. 54.

processes of modernization. Each is undergoing questioning and innovation during our era of rapid social change.

Every society has a kinship system defined by cultural norms. Each family is founded by marriage, symbolizing social approval of a sexual union that is expected to persist and to serve as the basis for a family unit. A nuclear family of husband, wife, and children stresses conjugal ties, and may be seen as a constellation of dyads. A polygamous family includes more than one husband or wife. An extended family stresses consanguineal ties, and is longer-lived than a nuclear family. The most nearly universal cultural norm, the incest taboo, ensures that families will exchange or give up members to found new families, thus establishing a network of relationships among various groups.

The functions of the family are increasingly confined to consumption, the provision of emotional security, and the socialization of infants; economic, social, and religious functions have been taken over by specialized agencies. Functional sociologists see the trend toward the isolated nuclear family based on emotional ties as ideally fitted to modern industrial society, primarily because of its mobility and its freedom from nepotism. But the burden of domestic duties, the isolation of the young mother with her children for most of the day, and the heavy burden of responsibility for individual happiness placed on the marriage relationship are dysfunctional aspects of the system. The high rate of remarriage and the frequency of mutual aid among relatives and friends suggest, however, that people continue to put their faith in marriage as a primary source of satisfaction, and that functional alternatives to the traditional extended family have emerged. Like many other aspects of behavior, family life displays the consequences of social class variations in life styles.

The population explosion and contraceptive devices have contributed to redefinitions of the reproductive role and parenthood, while the fact that women live longer and have fewer children has contributed to an ongoing redefinition of their status and of husband–wife relationships. Day-care centers and communes are examples of attempts to relieve mothers of the sole burden of child care. All these influences, plus changes in definitions of stages in the life cycle, contribute to a gap between the generations, and to a shortening of the productive period of adult life.

A number of trends indicate that "the family" in post-industrial society will take varied forms, not necessarily patterned after the ideal of the middle-class American family of modern society.

While the family as an institution is grounded in escapable biological realities, religion is an attempt to give meaning to the things that lie beyond man's knowledge and control. Leaving the truth or falsity of specific beliefs to theologians and to the faithful or the doubters, sociologists study religion objectively, as a system of meaning and purpose with great consequences for society and the individual.

Religion may spring from the universal elements of the human condition—uncertainty, the need for trust in social relationships, powerlessness over death and catastrophe and misfortune, and inequality and injustice. Man cannot bear meaninglessness; he demands and constructs explanations for these conditions.

These explanations are expressed in systems of belief in the sacred, in the relationship of the sacred to mankind, in the meaning of human life. Some religions are eschatological, concerned with "last things" such as death and judgment and the after-life; judgment is tied into morality in this life. A special aspect of a religious belief system is its theodicy, which reconciles what is with what ought to be, and is typically connected with the stake its adherents have in the society.

Religious practices are typically collective, whether in the family or in a formal congregation. Church attendance, affiliation, and patterns of worship show some correlation with social class status.

Religious experience ranges from mild to ecstatic, and is difficult to measure empirically. Even the most mystical experience appears to be culturally conditioned to some extent.

The dialectical relationship between church and sect is a cycle of institutionalization and compromise with worldly values; the breaking off of a sect, usually under a charismatic leader; and frequently, its evolution into an institutionalized church that in turn compromises with the things of this world. Sects may, however, condemn society, refuse to adjust to it, and become institutionalized sects that seek to convert others like Jehovah's Witnesses; isolate themselves geographically and culturally as a protection against corruption, like the Amish; or become a subsociety, like the Mormons. By forcing established religions to reexamine their values and premises, both sects and mystics contribute to their vitality.

Modernization results in religious pluralism, with attendant hostility and conflict, or eventual cooperation and compromise. Secularization replaces mysteries with problems to be solved scientifically and rationally; the realm of the profane grows at the expense of the sacred. A tendency toward homogenization of religious belief, toward playing down differences and emphasizing religion itself as a good thing, and toward a common "civil religion" which can be shared regardless of theological niceties, is characteristic of American culture. Finally, compartmentalization, assigning religion its own time and place, makes diversity easier to manage.

The purposes for which people engage in religious practices and seek religious explanations may have no clear connection with the consequences of their religion for society. These consequences include social cohesion and social control through reinforcement of ethical norms. However, in some cultures, such as the Japanese, religion and morality are more or less distinct. Religion can be either conservative or innovative. It can be a comfort and a guide to behavior for individuals, but is not necessarily effective for either purpose in its organized form, according to empirical studies of the relation of behavior to affiliation. In a democratic society, religion, by failing to adjust entirely to secular norms and values, may make a positive contribution to the preservation of essential democratic values.

Although the influence of orthodox religious beliefs appears to be declining, there is evidence of continuing interest in religion. Ecumenism is seen as a path to understanding among different cultural and subcultural groups. A serious reexamination of norms and values is visible in the Catholic Church. The search for the sacred, even in bizarre and occult forms, has been revived, notably by college students —the very people who might be expected to be most secularized, but appear, in fact, to be most disillusioned by the failure of science and technology to provide meaning and identity and community.

Education in modern society differs from the family and religion in being both public and compulsory; but like them it manifests the impact of modernization and great unrest, experimentation, and innovation. Education is both conservative (a means of transmitting the culture) and innovative (an institutionalized system for advancing knowledge). It is the main avenue to participation and success in modern society.

Industrializing nations typically give high priority to education, but their manpower requirements and the social demand for education are not always well adjusted. Education in modern society tends to stress the verbal and rational at the expense of the expressive and creative aspects of behavior. China displays total commitment to education as a means of indoctrination and economic development.

The relationship between social class status and educational aspirations and achievements has been demonstrated by numerous empirical studies. Track systems of sorting students tend to rigidify a class system. Experiments suggest that the expectations of teachers can affect individual achievement (the "Rosenthal" effect). There are indications that the American class system, always comparatively open, is becoming more so, especially in higher education.

Unrest, experiment, and innovation are occurring in education at all levels, possibly as a result of the shift from traditional to emergent and conflicting values. Greater student participation, greater exposure to the community, and greater community control are among demands related to social organization. Content, goals, and methods are all being questioned. Experiments with "free schools," within and outside formal systems of education; debate over the use of electronic aids to teaching; a shift from evaluation of individuals to evaluation of teachers and schools and the system as a whole; and alternative paths to successful participation in society—all these indicate that people are not content with the what, why, and how of schools as they now exist.

As we enter a post-industrial stage, such controversies become increasingly relevant, for rote learning and technical skills are of little value in an automated, cybernated system of production and a rapidly changing society. Emphasis must be put on all that is uniquely human, on imagination, resourcefulness, and flexibility. The universities in particular play a crucial role in shaping the emerging society.

We turn in the final chapter to a consideration of various trends, including economic and political changes, that indicate the emergence of a world community, and we consider the implications of sociology for the moral and ethical order as well as the social structure and other aspects of culture on which such a community might be based.

QUESTIONS FOR FURTHER THOUGHT

1. All three institutions may be said to be undergoing a crisis of authority. In what ways is this crisis similar for all three? How is it different?

2. The extension of youth and the cultural revolution (expressed in part in the value conflict outlined by Spindler) have had a great impact not only on education but also on marriage and the family (including sex roles and mores) and on religion. Discuss.

3. To what extent do you believe traditional definitions of sex roles limit choices for both sexes and foster hostility?

4. Genetic engineering raises moral questions that make our traditional preoccupation with sexual morality seem trivial. What are some possible moral questions associated with the possibility that babies could be conceived and developed in test tubes; transplanted from one womb to another; sired by sperm from geniuses long dead? That new types of human beings with brains twice as large as the normal brain could be produced? That an individual could be duplicated from some of his tissue?

5. In Western civilization an attitude of contempt for the body is being replaced by a more affirmative attitude. How is this reflected in changes in the three institutions discussed here?

6. While there is apparently no single satisfactory explanation, married people all over the world have lower death rates than do unmarried, widowed, and divorced people of the same sex and age group. Construct several hypotheses that might be explored to account for the difference.

7. Parenthood has long been a prime source of a sense of worth and identity. What might take its place if almost

everyone in the future has fewer children and many have none at all?

8. A fully rounded community includes people of many kinds, especially of all ages. Group marriages in Scandinavia function best when men and women within them form exclusive sexual pairings. On the basis of these two generalizations, construct a hypothetical ideal commune for performing the functions of socialization and emotional support without the fragility of the isolated nuclear family. What other generalizations do you believe must be taken into consideration? Do you prefer the isolated nuclear family? Why or why not?

9. In American society, at least, it is very difficult for adults of different sexes who are not married to each other to develop a deep friendship without being suspected of a sexual relationship. Do you believe this is a "natural" or a "cultural" attitude? Why?

10. In a society geared to monogamy, single adults, the widowed, and the divorced are discriminated against in many ways. What are some of them? What alternative institutions have evolved in an attempt to solve the problem?

11. Religion, someone said, should comfort the afflicted and afflict the comfortable. Relate the fulfillment or nonfulfillment of these functions to ideas and data discussed in the chapter.

12. There are many definitions and descriptions of religion besides those mentioned in the text. One's religion is one's character. Religion is what one thinks about when one is alone. Science is the religion of the modern age. Organized religion in America is a form of family psychotherapy. Discuss each. Can you think of others?

13. Both Russia and China discourage pluralism and traditional religion; both may be said to have a secular religion. Discuss in terms of the concepts used in this chapter. [If you wish to pursue the subject further, see Holmes Welch, "The Deification of Mao," *Saturday Review* (Sept. 19, 1970): 25 ff.]

14. What might account for the fact that in Christianity women almost invariably participate more than men in both public worship and private devotions?

15. Many European and Latin American political parties are based on religion. Why doesn't this happen in the United States? What evidence is there that religion has a covert influence on political affairs and public policy?

16.   The orthodox in any religion, comments one observer, concentrate their hatred not on heathen or unbelievers but on the unorthodox. Discuss.

17.   Most African languages do not have a word for religion. Explain.

18.   Relate the "Jesus People" wing of the youth movement to the church-sect cycle and to the idea that the way to change society is to change individuals.

19.   Has any teacher or other school authority ever asked you, "What do you want to do with your life?" If so, what advice were you given?

20.   What is your standard of success? How do you plan to go about achieving it?

21.   How long have you been planning to attend college? How do you account for your motivation?

22.   Estimate your lifetime exposure to TV. What other non-formal sources of education have you been exposed to? Do you feel they compete or conflict with formal schooling? If so, in what ways?

23.   Do you believe "Grades Must Go"? Why or why not?

24.   The movement toward freer, more informal education has made little or no headway in France, Greece, and Spain. Construct hypotheses to account for this.

25.   When the National University of Panama was established, its Rector, a member of the upper class, was frequently told by his friends, "You are nurturing ravens to pluck out our eyes." Discuss.

26.   Coombs says agriculture was once an inefficient handicraft industry, as education is now; it was modernized mainly through research and innovation in government and universities. Do you believe education could be modernized in the same way? Why or why not?

27.   The "generation gap," according to some authorities, is really an education gap, for there has never been a generation with as much education as the present generation of American youth. The educated of all ages are more alike in attitudes toward politics, sex, childrearing, and religion than are those of similar ages with different amounts of education. What implications does this have for understanding current social and political conflict? For the future?

20

TOWARD A WORLD ORDER

Unless people believe the world is going to be better they won't make the effort to save it.

MARGARET MEAD

For the first time, all men now share the same history. Mankind is united by its very conflicts and problems, as well as by its technological skills.

RAYMOND ARON

While I am by no means an uncritical admirer of the human race, I have become rather fond of it, and would hate to see it disappear. Finding ways to save it—if we are not too late already—now strikes me as the political issue which takes precedence over all others.

JOHN FISCHER

We have met the enemy and he is us.

WALT KELLY, "POGO"

WILL WE MAKE IT TO THE YEAR 2000? Will we even make it to July 4, 1976? And if we do, will life be any "better"—freer, more fulfilling?

Nobody on Earth knows. But if we *are* to make it—as the United States of America, as Spaceship Earth—it has to be everybody or nobody. No one will be truly safe or free, until everyone is.

If there is any chance of making it, *how* will survival and freedom be assured? Nobody knows exactly; but what we have said in previous chapters clearly places us on the side of those who see man as an active agent in his own destiny. Even though problems of war and racism and population and poverty and pollution seem insurmountable, we dare not give up that "appetite for the future" that C. P. Snow calls man's greatest need. "All healthy societies are ready to sacrifice the existential moment for their children's future and for children after these. The sense of the future is behind all good policies. Unless we have it, we can give nothing either wise or decent to the world."[1]

In this final chapter we raise more questions than we try to answer. We ask, How can we achieve the ultimate goals of survival and freedom? Are there signs of an emerging world order? How can we help build one? What form should it take? How might the sociological perspective help us attain our goals?

Contributions of the Sociological Perspective

One theme of this book is the capacity of the social sciences to help us understand, preserve, and improve human life. Social philosophers contribute by depicting alternative visions of the future, often on the basis of broad theories of the past. Social critics and observers outline trends and the probable consequences of various policies. And empiricists gather data basic to sound interpretation. The greatest social scientists combine moral vision and careful research, and increasingly present their analyses with a clear sense of how they may be applied.

[1]"What Is the World's Greatest Need?" *The New York Times Magazine* (April 2, 1961).

In the pages of this book we have mentioned many of these visions, insights, theories, and data. Cultural similarities and variations demonstrate both the basic unity of mankind and the flexible limits of human nature and social arrangements. Unequal distribution of wealth, prestige, power, and freedom by social classes, racial and ethnic groups, and have and have-not nations; the promise and problems of modernization; the prospects for mankind as population grows and industry develops in a fragile and finite biosphere; the tension between social order and social change reflected in the ferment in the basic institutions of the family, religion, and education—we must take all these into account when we ask what is *possible* and *probable* in the future, as well as what is *preferable*.

Sociologists increasingly recognize that complexity, conflict, and strain are inevitable in socio-cultural systems; that numerous alternatives must be considered in order to keep as many options as possible open for future generations; that error is likely and feedback essential in any attempt to plan and guide the course of events; and that things left to themselves do not usually improve spontaneously. They are, in short, adopting a systems approach to understanding and guiding societies. Increasingly, too, they recognize the urgency of social problems— the need to use what we know now as well as to keep on learning; to work with others from many areas of specialization; and to rely on man's power to learn and adapt instead of blaming blind deterministic forces.

Goals

How can mankind ensure survival and freedom? The means to these ultimate goals are goals in themselves: (1) some kind of world order to provide for security from war and for distributive justice; and (2) a global equilibrium with both population and economic growth stabilized so that we do not overshoot the limits of our finite Earth.

The chief indicator of the urgent need for a peace-keeping order is the "arms race." In 1970 world military spending amounted to $204 billion—as much as the entire production of the poorer half of the world's people. While 90% of this amount is spent by the more "advanced" nations, the United States Arms Control and Disarmament Agency reports that between 1964 and 1970 the *increase* in military spending in "developing" countries equaled three years' expenditure on public-school education for their billion school-age children, and outstripped their annual increase in gross national product. In 1968 these poorer countries accounted for more than half the 24 million men under arms around the world.[2]

[2]Benjamin Welles, "U.S. Survey Puts World Outlay for Arms at $204-Billion Peak," *The New York Times*, May 6, 1971.

The Club of Rome has vividly demonstrated the urgency of beginning to work at once toward global equilibrium. The essential problem is exponential growth (such as the ever-faster doubling time of population) in a finite and complex system. Exponential growth means that a problem gets out of hand very quickly and suddenly if consequences are not anticipated and trends reversed in time. They illustrate the danger by a French riddle for children:

> Suppose you own a pond in which a water lily is growing. The lily plant doubles in size each day. If the lily were allowed to grow unchecked, it would completely cover the pond in 30 days, choking off the other forms of life in the water. For a long time the lily plant seems small, and so you decide not to worry about cutting it back until it covers half the pond. On what day will that be? On the twenty-ninth day, of course. You have one day to save your pond.[3]

Unrest and protest around the world force us to realize that neither a world order nor global equilibrium can be achieved and sustained without more "distributive justice"—a fairer allocation of tangible and intangible goods within and among societies, and a recognition of the dignity and worth of each human being, his right to material comfort and to opportunities for self-fulfillment.

Almost all of us would agree that these are noble goals. What, then, keeps them so far out of reach? Is it selfishness, greed, ignorance, prejudice, and other evils in the heart of man? If we phrase the question in sociological terms, we must answer, Yes, certainly. Conflicts of interests and values, lack of knowledge, outmoded and unfounded beliefs— all these must be resolved or changed somehow. Should we blame "the system" of faulty institutions, an unresponsive power structure, gaps in decision-making and conflict-reducing mechanisms? Again the answer is Yes—but a qualified yes, for men and groups *are* working to build better systems, including an international order; and a number of economic, political, and other socio-cultural trends indicate that some form of world community is emerging.

Economic Trends

Various interrelated economic trends throughout the world pull in different directions, tending to unite and divide, strengthen and weaken bonds, and to increase both affluence and inequality. Among these paradoxical trends are modernization, interdependence, an increase in

[3]Donella H. Meadows, Dennis L. Meadows, Jørgen Randers, and William H. Behrens III, *The Limits to Growth: A Report for the Club of Rome's Project on the Predicament of Mankind* (New York: Universe Books, 1972), p. 29.

the scale and scope of economic units, and the emergence of a global "political economy."

MODERNIZATION

We have discussed at length the almost universal transformation of traditional folk societies into modern urban industrial societies. While this is much more than a trend—it is a socio-cultural revolution —and while it does make societies alike in many ways, it does not inevitably result in economic affluence, nor does it cause all societies to converge toward similarity in such essential institutions as government and civil liberties. Its most conspicuous feature—the dramatic increase in production through the application of scientific knowledge to technology—is largely confined to a few advanced nations that are approaching "super-industrialism." Thus the gap grows between the have and have-not nations.

"Foreign aid" programs to narrow this gap have thus far been mere drops in the bucket. The United Nations called the 1960s the "decade of development" and urged each developed nation to give 1% of its GNP to help developing nations. But the United States has been cutting down on foreign aid, which was only about one quarter of 1% even in 1967 (for nonmilitary purposes). The percentage of GNP spent on foreign aid in recent years is: United States 0.35%; Britain, 0.39%; West Germany, 0.35%; France, 0.69%; and Japan, 0.49%.[4] In 1970, however, Japan's foreign aid reached nearly 1% of its GNP.

Soviet physicist Andrei Sakharov, in an impassioned plea for "progress, coexistence, and intellectual freedom" secretly circulated in his country and published by *The New York Times*, proposes a 15-year tax on developed nations equal to 20% of their national incomes, to be used for nonmilitary foreign aid.[5] Any foreign aid program must make use of sophisticated planning, and planners must ask first of all, "Will it benefit the *people* or only the government or some special interest group in the beneficiary country?"[6]

Demographers say the greatest return per foreign aid dollar would come from investment in population control. From 1970 to 1972 the UN allocated $40 million for such programs in about sixty countries; but it is estimated that an outlay of $3 billion is needed to stabilize world population. This works out to about $1 per person per year, or one tenth of 1% of the world's GNP. Asks one, "Is this too much to pay for survival?"[7]

[4] *The New York Times* (Jan. 29, 1971).

[5] *Progress, Coexistence, and International Freedom*, trans. *The New York Times* (New York: W. H. Norton & Company, 1968), pp. 46–47. (With Introduction, Afterword, and Notes by Harrison E. Salisbury.)

[6] Ehrlich and Ehrlich, *Population, Resources, Environment*, p. 302.

[7] William H. Draper, Jr., "Summing Up," in "Population: The U.S. Problem; the World Crisis;" Supplement to *The New York Times* (April 30, 1972).

INTERDEPENDENCE

As modernization proceeds, specialization makes the members of a society more and more interdependent. The enormous division of labor in modern society makes us "rich, not as individuals, but as members of a rich society, and our easy assumption of material sufficiency is actually only as reliable as the bonds that forge us into a social whole."[8]

A highly interdependent society is, ironically, also highly vulnerable. Slowdowns, strikes, sabotage, and mechanical failures can reduce or cut off such essential supplies as electricity. In 1970 Britain's electrical supply workers reinforced their pay claims with a slowdown, which not only cut down industrial production but also affected farmers, who had to milk their cows by hand, and poultrymen, whose chickens died of a chill; it interrupted computer-run operations such as ticketing for travel and theaters, deliveries of food, and payrolls. This relatively brief departure from routine showed what a variety of activities could be disrupted by the actions of a few hundred workers.[9]

The world, too, is increasingly interdependent in many ways. Manufacturing nations depend heavily on others for such things as oil; the less developed nations import manufactured goods. Just as a domestic economy is affected by internal politics, international trade inevitably involves national sovereignties and rivalries.[10]

BIGNESS

Economic units for the production and distribution of goods and services tend to become fewer and bigger and to enlarge the scope of their operations. In the United States, for example, according to the Federal Trade Commission, the top 100 firms owned one-half of all manufacturing assets at the end of 1968, and the top 200 owned over 60%. In 1941, in contrast, ownership of 60% of assets was spread over a thousand corporations.[11]

Many of these huge firms are "conglomerates," which have

[8]Robert L. Heilbroner, *The Economic Problem*, 3rd ed. (Englewood Cliffs, N.J.: Prentice-Hall, Inc., 1972), p. 17.

[9]Michael Banton, interview, April 1970.

[10]Karl W. Deutsch notes that "with economic progress and rising populations, the proportion of foreign trade to the gross national product [in many countries] is declining," thanks in part to the use of substitute materials—nylon for silk, for example; and to the rise in the demand for and production of "services" produced mainly within the country—schools, health services, housing, and so on—as compared to the amount of manufactured goods. *The Analysis of International Relations* (Englewood Cliffs, N.J.: Prentice-Hall, Inc., 1968), p. 4.

[11]Economic Concentration, Hearings Before the Subcommittee on Antitrust and Monopoly of the Committee on the Judiciary, U.S. Senate, 91st Congress, first session, 1969, Part 8A.

taken over other businesses that have little or no relation to the products of the parent corporation. Many are also "multi-national"; they have expanded their operations into foreign countries, where they take advantage of lower wage rates and then typically resell their products on the domestic market at regular prices. "The value of output that is produced overseas by the largest corporations by far exceeds the value of the goods they still export from the United States. . . . One estimate for 1970 places the value of all U.S. overseas output at a staggering $200 billion."[12]

One-third of American production abroad is in Canada. United States firms control 46% of Canada's manufacturing, 58% of its oil and gas, 53% of its mining and smelting. Other nations also have interests there, and the Canadians are increasingly reacting with "economic nationalism."

One-third of the American investments abroad are in Latin America. U.S. corporations and their multi-national subsidiaries control between 70% and 90% of Latin America's raw material resources and more than 60% of its industrial plant. Most of the public utilities, commerce, and foreign trade relationships are in U.S. hands.[13]

The decade of the 1960s saw enormous growth in foreign investments. As the decade began, direct U.S. foreign investment was $11.8 billion, mostly committed to the petroleum and mineral industries of Canada, Latin America, and the Middle East.[14] Ten years later, the United States accounted for $70 billion of direct foreign investment, which totaled approximately $120 billion for all countries. Other countries, notably Japan and West Germany, are now expanding their foreign operations at a faster pace than the U.S.[15] If this trend continues at the present rate, by the year 2000 the world economy will be more than one-half internationalized.

Multinational corporations have been called "immensely powerful political states, lacking only a flag." General Motors has 700,000 employees; its output exceeds the gross national product (GNP) of all but a dozen countries. Standard Oil of New Jersey has three times as many people abroad as the State Department does.[16]

POLITICAL ECONOMY

Both within and among nations, there is a trend away from the separation of government and business advocated by Adam Smith and

---

[12]Heilbroner, *The Economic Problem*, pp. 648–49, citing Judd Polk's estimate before the Subcommittee for Economic Policy of the Joint Economic Committee of Congress (July 27, 1970).

[13]*Latin America: Meditations From Afar*, Stockholm University Institute for National Economic Studies.

[14]*The Center Magazine* (May 1970): 39–40.

[15]*Fortune* (Jan. 1971): p. 54.

[16]*Detroit Free Press* (May 28, 1970).

laissez-faire capitalist philosophy. Even the most capitalist countries are now "mixed economies," in the sense that planning and government intervention and regulation have to a large extent replaced the free play of market forces. Furthermore,

> the long-term trends and the cross-sectional data show that developed non-Communist countries tend to put between 30 and 40 per cent of their gross national product through the governmental sector, and that between two-thirds and three-fourths of this (between 20 and 30 per cent of gross national product) tends to be controlled directly by the central government of each developed country. . . .
>
> In three-quarters of the countries of the world . . . the nation-state today is spending or reallocating at least one-fourth of the national product, and . . . the world's poorest countries all are moving in the same direction.[17]

But no political institutions yet exist to control the international economy. Some observers believe, however, that the rise and spread of international corporations is one of the chief stepping stones to world order. "The international system of sovereign nation-states will in time be partially superseded by some kind of global political economy. The details of that possible future system, which might combine a worldwide order under law with a worldwide economy to sustain life at a decent level, cannot even be seen dimly today. The vast interweave of private sector, crossborder, or transnational organizations and activities of many kinds, including the modern multinational corporation, now constitutes part of the indispensable social and cultural foundation of an emergent world political economy. . . ."

In the next ten to fifteen years, nation-states will slowly yield various attributes of sovereignty to the multinational and transnational corporations. The survival of the multinational corporation in the future will depend heavily upon the manning of its top posts with people who understand the dynamics of world politics and can envisage the optimum role for a global corporation in a hazardous environment.[18]

Political Trends

The government of a society is the institution which more than any other determines its balance of freedom and control and ensures its survival and cohesion. But we have no such worldwide institution, ex-

[17]Deutsch, *The Analysis of International Relations*, pp. 38–9.

[18]Richard Eells, "The Optimum Role for Transnational Corporations," *Center Report*, published by the Center for the Study of Democratic Institutions (Oct. 1971): 6.

cept in bits and pieces. In our interdependent world, with its vast potential for conflict and its awesome means of destruction, what political trends appear most relevant to a possible world order?

MASS PARTICIPATION

Just as in the economic sector, political units increase in scale and scope. Suffrage is extended to more and more people in nations old and new. For a 1972 election, officials combed the jungles of Papua New Guinea and made it possible for tribesmen with bones piercing their noses to vote. The mass media reach people all over the world with such history-making political news as President Nixon's meeting with Chairman Mao.

The other side of the coin is that as a political unit grows it inevitably embraces more and more groups with incompatible interests, values, and beliefs, and thus increases the potential for conflict and the need for control. And the awareness of all the other human beings in the world fostered by the mass media may lead to fear rather than trust.

NATIONALISM

Modern nation-states are extremely powerful; they control at least a fourth of the world's economic production, while all international organizations together spend only about 1%. "Today, and for many decades to come, the nation-states are and will be the world's main centers of power. They will remain such centers as long as the nation-state remains man's foremost practical instrument for getting things done."[19] One of these things is the provision of a sense of iden-

[19]Deutsch, *The Analysis of International Relations*, p. 39.

645

tity and belonging for transitional men torn from folk communities.

At the same time, the nature of modern warfare is making the nation-state a dangerous anachronism. In an atomic age no nation can protect its citizens; only a world government of some kind could possibly do so. But citizens of a nation-state typically regard its **sovereignty** —its complete legal and status equality with other nations and its right to control all matters within its borders—as sacred. They make the nation-state the final judge of what is right and good, and the object of their first and highest loyalty. These attitudes are out of step with the realities of warfare, the inequalities of national power, and the common problems of mankind that only global cooperation can solve.

THE BALANCE OF POWER

For many years after World War II, the United States and the Soviet Union carried on a "cold war," dividing the balance of power— and atomic terror—between them, each seeking to outdo the other in the arms race and in winning ideological and political and military allies. This uneasy bipolar balance has given way to a multi-polar one as European nations increasingly work together, Japan performs astonishing feats of production, and the People's Republic of China emerges from isolation. At the same time many foreign policy makers are abandoning the mental picture of monolithic blocs in confrontation. As they recognize the discords and differences within the "Three Worlds of Development" as well as among them, they tend to accept the idea of learning to tolerate and live with diverse beliefs and social structures— if not in harmony, at least in the "antagonistic cooperation" we call accommodation.

THE INSTITUTIONALIZATION OF WAR

There may have been some glamor in hand-to-hand combat and in the aerial dogfights of World War I; but there is only dehumanization in the body counts and five-mile-high bombing missions of modern war. And there is no victory. The first push of the nuclear button could mean mutual suicide.

Yet the idea of war as a last resort, or even an effective way of solving conflicts, persists. One reason is that it is heavily institutionalized; in nearly every nation-state a social structure including personnel, equipment, values, norms, and interests has developed. In almost all countries a military caste, class, or profession has evolved, usually with great influence over government. The prestige of its members is directly related to the presumed need for their services and the size of the establishment they administer; therefore they have a vested interest in building up armies and equipment, and large economic interests become aligned with them in promoting an arms race. "Together they work to indoctrinate the whole people in an ideology favorable to war-making,"[20] though they may have no malign conspiratorial designs, but firmly believe they are promoting the causes of peace and security. It is precisely this danger that President Eisenhower warned against in his farewell address, when he spoke of the need for civilian control of the "military-industrial complex." Massive institutionalization makes the military establishment "a juggernaut in search of a mission"[21] that will justify its existence.

In the United States perhaps 8 to 9% of the trillion-dollar GNP consists of military goods and services, including nearly $7 billion of direct and indirect military assistance to foreign nations in 1971.

> The Department of Defense (DOD) is the largest planned economy outside the Soviet Union. Its property . . . amounts to some $202 billion. . . . It rules over a population of about 4 million—direct employees or soldiers—and spends an "official" budget of over $75 billion, a budget three-quarters as large as the entire gross national product of Great Britain. This makes the DOD richer than any small nation in the world and, of course, incomparably more powerful. . . . The military establishment [is] the largest single customer in the economy.[22]

Other Socio-Cultural Trends and Innovations

Most political trends, then, are either not clearly directed toward world community or are clearly promoting international anarchy. What signs are there of a shared world culture—of knowledge, beliefs, values, norms, and social structures that might serve as a basis for community? Here again the picture is clouded, but there are indications that common myths and understandings and organizations are emerging.

SCIENCE, TECHNOLOGY, AND KNOWLEDGE

As we saw in Part One, the great bulk of any complex culture comes through contact with other cultures. Modernization hastens the process of diffusion, and modern nations share a common pool of scientific and technical knowledge and skills as well as literature, music, art, architecture, and clothing. "No people and no country in the world could have reached its present level of technology, prosperity, and health—nor could it maintain its present rate of progress—without the decisive aid of foreign discoveries and foreign contributions."[23] In

[20]R. M. MacIver, *The Web of Government*, (rev. ed.) (New York: The Macmillan Company, 1965), p. 279.

[21]*The New York Times* (April 6, 1969).

[22]Heilbroner, *The Economic Problem*, pp. 6–7.

[23]Deutsch, *The Analysis of International Relations*, p. 3.

every scientific field and in most other areas of art and learning, there are numerous international organizations and publications, as well as thousands of more informal ties. Several international commissions are working on a common set of graphic symbols for accommodation and travel, agriculture, business, communication, medicine, various sciences, recreation and safety, as well as the traffic signs long used in many nations.[24]

NORMS AND SOCIAL STRUCTURES

In many respects the norms and social structures of the two main alternative systems of political economy in the world are far apart. In "evolutionary socio-capitalist democracies" civil rights and liberties are typically cherished and protected; in "authoritarian systems of communist dictatorship"[25] they are denied. The former tend toward pluralism, encouraging many cross-cutting voluntary associations and institutions, and separating the concept of the state from that of the society; the latter demand loyalty to the state and identify it with the society. Even so, there is some agreement on norms—right and proper patterns for behavior—and some structures have emerged to exercise sanctions and enforce them, even though they fall far short of the power of nation-states, which still hold the monopoly of force.

International law.   Laws are deliberately formulated and clearly stated norms enforced by highly visible and specialized agencies. But "international law" is, in most cases, neither as clear nor as binding as the laws of nation-states. Much of it is laid down in international treaties and conventions, which "bind directly, of course, only those nations whose governments have signed and ratified each document; but if sufficiently widely accepted, notably by all the great powers, they also indicate the consensus of the international community of states. Beyond this, there are codes and collections of international law, the consensus of experts, and the precedents created by earlier international awards or acts of adjudication."[26] Examples of cases covered by such laws are disputes over boundaries, fishing rights, and the like. Social structures established to decide disputes according to international law include the panels of arbitrators named by the Permanent Court of International Justice at The Hague, and the International Court of Justice, now part of the United Nations.

Functional international organizations.   Some organizations for specific purposes are open to all or nearly all nations, have a stronger

[24]Henry Dreyfuss, *Symbol Sourcebook* (New York: McGraw-Hill, 1972).

[25]These are the two general categories into which the famous political scientist and sociologist R. M. MacIver divided nation-states. *The Web of Government*, p. 131.

[26]Deutsch, *The Analysis of International Relations*, p. 65.

permanent machinery than courts of international law, and make rules and decisions and implement and administer polices in their particular areas of concern. Some, like the International Red Cross, are nongovernmental; others, like the International Postal Union, the International Telecommunication Union, and the International Civil Aviation Organization, have governments as members. Broad functions are exercised by the International Labor Organization, the Food and Agriculture Organization, the World Health Organization, and UNESCO, the United Nations Educational, Scientific, and Cultural Organization. The United Nations Social and Economic Council, which coordinates these organizations, also discusses basic social and economic issues and sets up new norms for national and international behavior—for example, through its Convention Against Genocide and its Human Rights Convention (which have not yet, however, been ratified by many countries).

Such *functional* international organizations, many believe, are the first necessary building blocks of a world community in which war will be impossible. One proponent of this view is Elisabeth Mann Borgese, who drafted a plan for control of the oceans by a Maritime Assembly based on the principle that "the four elements of life—earth, water, air, energy—are the common property of the human race." Believing that nations should be left to do what they still can do and not be asked to do what they cannot, she proposes a widely decentralized federation based on a number of world communities, each emphasizing common action in some important area: administration of a world university; management of the atmosphere; communication and transport; energy production; world health; earth resources. These

> interlocking communities, embracing practically all human activities of worldwide scope, [would] create a peace system in which war simply has no place.
>
> Nations would remain "sovereign" self-managing entities. They would insure that the world remains culturally pluralistic. They would satisfy some of mankind's needs—just as churches do today. What is useless for these purposes—armies and huge bureaucracies—would wither away.
>
> [Under this system] the concept of human rights will have evolved to comprehend a new type of transindividual environmental rights without which the political-civic rights of the eighteenth and nineteenth centuries and the social-economic rights of the nineteenth and early twentieth centuries are today meaningless.[27]

Such visions, as we said in Chapter 14, are often dubbed Utopian and hence impractical; but they play a most important role in guiding social change. Mrs. Borgese admits that "academic or theoretical exercises alone will not change the world. Action is needed—daily, de-

[27]"The World Communities," *The Center Magazine* 4 (Sept./Oct. 1971): 10–18.

voted, dedicated action—to save what can be saved, and to keep, or find, ways open for change. But this change must be planned and projected. There must be a vision or no one will walk the open way."[28]

Functional organizations generally, however, can neither legislate, enforce, or tax; aside from some standards for air safety and health, sanctions are limited. Their members exchange views and knowledge, make studies, draft recommendations, and give technical assistance to governments requesting it. Regional organizations such as common markets and military alliances do not, according to Karl Deutsch, promise to serve any better as a basis for world order; their chief function in this respect is to accustom people to the idea of various forms of international cooperation.

Universal all-purpose organizations: the United Nations. The closest thing to a world organization working toward survival and freedom is the United Nations. Its power is limited by the strength of the nation-states, by the fear of weaker nations that the powerful ones may use it simply as a tool for exerting power, and by the lack of any deep commitment to it on the part of the great powers. Its charter is a multilateral treaty of sovereign states, designed to guard the security of each member by pledges of mutual support. It is often bypassed when its decisions would obviously not serve the perceived "national interests" of such powers as the United States and the Soviet Union.

Nonetheless, the United Nations, for all its weaknesses, has served and is serving important functions. It is a kind of "town meeting of the world," where almost all nations may be heard. One of its chief accomplishments has been to incorporate new nations into the international political order and to aid their economic development. Thus it has served as a force for peace and order in somewhat the same way that extension of the suffrage to the propertyless and uneducated citizens of Western nations helped commit them to the democratic system and endowed their governments with high legitimacy and stability. The

[28]*Ibid.*

International Communication—Delegates from Ghana and Korea confer on the floor of the U.N. General Assembly.

UN gives small nations a sense of status and thus, in a sense, "socializes" them by providing patterns and standards and appealing to their pride.

In numerous instances the UN has accommodated conflict and prevented threats to peace from developing into war. It is a world forum where injustices are aired and international standards of morality are being developed. Debate and discussion help to build the international consensus on values that may serve as the foundation of a true world community. The UN provides an accessible and acceptable structure for tackling many problems that can only be solved on a global scale. Its agenda for a conference on the environmental problem in Stockholm in 1972, for example, centered around the concept of "a planet held in trust for future generations."

Models for a World Community

If even the United Nations is not truly a world government, where can we look for models for a future one? Some advocate a *monolithic world state*, obliterating national boundaries, with a powerful policing force of its own. There might still be civil wars and revolutions within such a state; it is no guarantee of peace and harmony. Neither is the other main alternative: a *pluralistic security community*, perhaps a world federation of nation-states along the lines of the federal system of the United States of America. But if such a federation (1) allows for diversity and pluralism and (2) has some power to legislate, tax, and enforce, it might be possible to secure both peace and global equilibrium through its structure.

Just as the United States has for nearly two centuries, with no major breaks except for the Civil War, lived up fairly well to its motto, "E Pluribus Unum," ("Out of Many, One") so such a world order might achieve unity and preserve diversity. Paul and Anne Ehrlich sketch the possibility of such a combination, suggesting that some nations should be primarily agricultural producers, and some should be subsidized recreation areas (the animal parks of East Africa, for example).

> We need to create a demand for what Aborigines, Eskimos, Kenyans, and Hondurans can supply, what might be called cultural resources. These priceless resources are in short supply, they are dwindling rapidly, and they are nonrenewable. A way must be found to permit these people access to more of the fruits of industrial societies without attempting to industrialize the entire world. [The United States is overdeveloped; other nations should be helped to "semidevelop" in ways most appropriate for their cultures.]

> Certainly, ecologically sound agricultural development, rather than industrialization, should receive priority virtually everywhere. In general

the [developed countries] would, where needed, supply medical services, educational facilities and teachers, and especially technical assistance in population control.[29]

Changes in Beliefs and Values

Man's ideas and values set his goals. If we are to have a new moral and ethical order with a different set of priorities, and if we are to achieve the social structures for realizing them, then we need new myths—new constellations of beliefs and values suited to a world community. But beliefs and values are among the hardest elements of culture to change; central myths are especially stubborn and deeply rooted. Yet there are signs, especially among young people and among members of various international associations, that they are indeed changing.

CHANGES IN WORLD VIEW

To accept and work within a global community aimed at achieving global equilibrium, people must adopt a new view of the world and of man's place in it. Elements of such a world view would be: (1) biocentrism, or reverence for all life and its fragile interdependence in our global ecosystem; (2) a feeling that men are all one species, one race, whose common humanity can be felt through empathy, and whose common danger urgently requires collectivism and cooperation and outmodes many forms of ethnocentrism, individualism, and competition; (3) a conviction that all men have the right to subsistence and comfort, and to an opportunity to choose how best to fulfill themselves; and that therefore (4) we must develop a set of common norms and values regarding the taking of life and the sharing and use of resources.

CHANGES IN POLITICAL VALUES

Belief that a world community must be achieved and faith that it *can* be achieved will lead us there just as belief and faith led man to walk on the moon. But what will happen to rival "isms" and ideologies, to nationalism and patriotism? Is there only one truly moral economic or political system, which everyone must accept?

Just as people continue to follow different religious faiths and cultural traditions in societies that value pluralism, so they can continue to feel pride in and love of country, so long as they express them in constructive ways. If cultural pluralism is truly encouraged, nationalism can survive as pride in our part of the world community, just as ethnic subsocieties give Americans a sense of identity and belonging. As for

[29]*Population, Resources, Environment,* pp. 304–5.

the other "isms" that divide us, perhaps we must learn to ask if an "ism" really threatens us. French sociologist Raymond Aron says:

> Long after the world has been united by technology, men will continue to believe in rival gods. To survive, they must learn to live with their differences. This, of course, is the meaning of peaceful coexistence. But for coexistence to be genuinely peaceful, it must also be ideological. In other words, the believers must accept the principle of mutual tolerance. War, it is said, begins in men's souls. Peace transcending coexistence will begin when one side tolerates the rights and opinions of the other.[30]

CHANGES IN ECONOMIC VALUES

Survival and freedom also demand fundamental shifts in economic values concerning the distribution of goods and services and the investment of effort and resources. The idea that economic growth (in production of material goods) is the prime indicator of progress, and that more and bigger equals better, must undergo a radical shift. Not the quantity of goods (for affluent societies) but the quality of life, suggests the Club of Rome, would increase in an equilibrium state:

> Population and capital are the only quantities that need be constant in the equilibrium state. Any human activity that does not require a large flow of irreplaceable resources or produce severe environmental degradation might continue to grow indefinitely. In particular, those pursuits that many people would list as the most desirable and satisfying activities of man—education, art, music, religions, basic scientific research, athletics, and social interactions—could flourish.[31]

A closely related change in values would require, especially of Americans, a shift from the idea that private consumption is the highest good to a recognition that many goods and services can be provided only collectively. The image of the abundant economy in our society is painted almost exclusively in terms of single families with their homes and cars and television sets. The material comfort, health, and amusement of individuals and families is a prime goal of a consumer-oriented market economy. Another very important aspect of consumption, however, tends to be neglected. The goods and services essential for social and community well-being must be provided collectively if they are to be provided at all. It is not the dollar vote, but the vote in the ballot box, that makes most of these decisions, and often the American consumer fears that a "yes" vote for urban renewal, new schools, parks,

[30]*The Industrial Society: Three Essays on Ideology and Development* (New York: Simon and Schuster, 1967), p. 48.
[31]Meadows *et al., The Limits to Growth,* p. 175.

playgrounds, and hospitals will cut down on the number of dollars with which he can vote for boats and barbecue grills.

This imbalance between personal and social needs and expenditures may be accounted for in part by the persistence of faith in the market and distrust of planning. Where anything the government does, aside from space exploration and military defense, is suspect as socialistic, "social capital" is bound to be neglected. "Vacuum cleaners to ensure clean houses are praiseworthy and essential in our standard of living. Street cleaners to ensure clean streets are an unfortunate expense. Alcohol, comic books, and mouthwash all bask under the superior reputation of the market. Schools, judges, and municipal swimming pools lie under the evil reputation of bad kings."[32] This emphasis on consumer goods keeps the consumer himself from enjoying many things that can be provided only collectively—better schools, transportation systems, parks, medical care; safer water; and purer air—things he can demand only in his role as citizen, not in his role as shopper.

Inseparable from the global outlook are changes in the attitudes toward foreign aid and toward long-range planning in the interest of future generations. These would help to solve the pressures of population and poverty and pollution that threaten the rich as well as the poor; the future is, as Buckminster Fuller says, for "everybody or nobody."

CHANGES IN ATTITUDES TOWARD SCIENCE AND TECHNOLOGY

Some have utter faith in science and technology as guaranteeing solutions to all human problems. Others repudiate them as the villains of the piece, who have brought us to where we are. But those who have faith in voluntaristic theories of change, in "man's power," believe that man's *use* of scientific and technological knowledge—including its misuse—is one root of our present predicament, and that we cannot work our way out of it without fresh applications of science and technology. To deny their usefulness is to advocate a return to the cave or tribal village.

The proper use of science involves a sense of man's responsibility for the control of its applications. "The progress of scientific knowledge confers more freedom of choice and more possibilities of control over the future. It also places a greater responsibility on the shoulders of the average man"[33] as parent and citizen.

Responsibility means *we* make the choices. "The freedom to

[32]John Kenneth Galbraith, *The Affluent Society* (Boston: Houghton Mifflin, 1960), p. 135.
[33]L. B. Young, *Population in Perspective*, p. 356.

choose is the fundamental human value. To abdicate it is to become less than human."[34] To make those choices wisely means we must not "dismiss science as someone else's concern. The world today is made, it is powered by science; and for any man to abdicate an interest in science is to walk with open eyes towards slavery."[35]

Familiarity with science leads to an awareness that technological innovations have latent consequences, and often undesirable ones (as in the case of the Aswan Dam and the Interstate Highway System). Alvin Toffler insists that "The one crucial act of immorality is to do things without trying to anticipate the consequences."[36] The usual presumption according to a panel convened by the National Academy of Sciences, has been that a technological trend "ought to be allowed to continue as long as it can be expected to yield a profit for those who are exploiting it, and that any harmful consequences that might ensue either will be manageable or will not be serious enough to warrant a decision to interfere with the technology." They recommended research and monitoring by an impartial agency at the earliest possible stage of development of an innovation. If technology is not thus controlled, they fear "an unreasoned political reaction against technological innovation —a reaction that could condemn mankind to poverty, frustration, and the loss of freedom."[37]

Steps Toward a World Order

The real cultural lag has been defined as that between knowledge of a problem and its solution. Do all these trends, signs, and indicators add up to the solution of the problem—to the emergence of a world order that might bring with it freedom and fulfillment as well as survival? Only under one condition: that more people around the world feel the urgency of the goal and work to achieve it.

> Taking no action to solve these problems is equivalent to taking strong action. . . . The way to proceed is clear, and the necessary steps, although they are new ones for human society, are well within human capabilities. Man possesses, for a small moment in his history, the most powerful combination of knowledge, tools, and resources the world has ever known. He has all that is physically necessary to create a totally new form of human society—one that would be built to last for generations. The two missing ingredients are a realistic, long-

[34]Ibid.

[35]J. Bronowski, *Science and Human Values* (New York: Julian Messner, 1956).

[36]*Future Shock* (New York: Random House, 1970).

[37]Harvey Brooke and Raymond Bowers, "The Assessment of Technology," *Scientific American* 222, No. 2 (Feb. 1970): 13–20.

656 SOCIAL INSTITUTIONS IN A CHANGING WORLD

term goal that can guide mankind to the equilibrium society and the human will to achieve that goal. Without such a goal and a commitment to it, short-term goals will generate the exponential growth that drives the world system toward the limits of the earth and ultimate collapse. With that goal and that commitment, mankind would be ready now to begin a controlled, orderly transition from growth to global equilibrium.[38]

Not only social scientists, but all citizens with time, energy, and power to influence policy, must base their contributions to public opinion on as objective a study of international relations as possible:

In politics, an aroused and zealous but misinformed citizen is a menace . . . We must study international relations . . . as deeply, carefully, and responsibly as our limited time and resources permit. No other subject is as likely to have a direct bearing on . . . "a choice between the quick and the dead."[39]

Studies of social systems, goals, and policies such as those conducted by the international and interdisciplinary Club of Rome are absolutely essential. But, say prominent "social futurists," let us also "convene in each nation, in each city, in each neighborhood, democratic constituent assemblies charged with social stock-taking, charged with defining and assigning priorities to specific social goals for the remainder of the century."[40] Thus political skills in policy-making will be based on careful study, on the habit of mutual attention and communication, on responsiveness within a framework of diversity and tolerance for diversity.

U Thant, among other leaders, sees the greatest hope for changes in values and acquisition of new skills and new social structures in those now enrolled in universities and high schools, who are "the world's first truly global generation." In a message to youth he said, "It is natural for you to think and act in terms of what binds humanity rather than what divides it. Make this unique and precious gift the foundation of a new world community."

In several contexts we quoted pioneer sociologists who said that "The solid facts of life are the facts of the imagination" and that "If men think something is real, it is real in its consequences." To this we would add, "If men believe a desirable future is possible, they will work to make it come about." We might take as our creed the words of Albert Camus:

[38]Meadows *et al., The Limits to Growth*, pp. 183–84.
[39]Deutsch, *The Analysis of International Relations*, p. 5.
[40]Alvin Toffler, ed., *The Futurists* (New York: Random House, 1972).

We have no choice. Wherever we are and to the best of our abilities we must do what has to be done so that everyone can live together once again. The very fact that atomic warfare would make the future meaningless gives us back our freedom of action. We have nothing to lose—except everything. If we fail, it will be better to have taken our stand at the side of those who want to live rather than with those who destroy.[41]

QUESTIONS FOR FURTHER THOUGHT

1. What experiences have you had that indicate the emergence of a world order?

2. Do you believe you can help achieve such an order? Why or why not? If you do, how do you propose to go about it? If not, did you at one time think you might be effective? What made you abandon your commitment to action?

3. Thirty percent of college students polled in 1972 said they would rather live in some country other than the United States. Do you feel this way? Why? If we are all passengers on Spaceship Earth, with a common destiny, where on Earth is there a place to escape the great problems of mankind?

4. The same poll showed that "mainstream" students hold that social change should be achieved within the "system" —largely through "someone else's" efforts. Whom would you like to see making the decisions? To what extent do you want to participate? Why? ["Changing Values on Campus," cited in The New York Times (April 11, 1972).]

5. Refer back to the Robber's Cave experiment cited in Chapter 7, which supported the hypothesis that "Hostility gives way when groups pull together to achieve overriding goals which are real and compelling to all concerned." Relate this principle to the content of this chapter.

6. In discussing the cohesion of a group or society, we listed the following sources: consensus, control, coordination,

[41]Quoted by Robert Redfield in "Talk with a Stranger," The Gadfly (Great Books Foundation) Vol. 11, No. 7 (Jan. 1960), p. 6.

and individual commitment. How might each of these be achieved as a basis for global cohesion?

7.   Would a world community use normative, utilitarian, or coercive controls, or a combination? Give examples.

8.   Rosy dreams of everyone living in perfect peace and harmony have never come true—even in a small group or society; and advocates of a world community are often derided as unrealistic visionaries. Can accommodation or "antagonistic cooperation" rather than perfect harmony be the working principle of a world order?

9.   If the trend toward urban industrial society has brought with it an eclipse of community and a loss of identity and belonging, would a world community intensify these problems? Discuss.

10.   Are problems of war, poverty, and racism built into man's biological nature (as the ethologists who stress aggression suggest)? Are they built into present social structures? Would education in new beliefs and values solve them? Discuss.

11.   In a play by Euripides, Achilles said, "I am a man, my sword is my own, I take responsibility for my behavior. I shall not obey an immoral command." Relate to the nature of modern warfare and to the Nuremberg trials.

12.   Government measures often redistribute freedom. How?

13.   Consider the Preamble to the Constitution of the United States. Could it serve as a statement of goals for a world community?

14.   What is the responsibility of the scientist, and especially the social scientist, to society?

15.   Do you feel more free, or less free, after reading this book? Why?

We travel together, passengers on a
little spaceship. Dependent on its
vulnerable reserve of air and soil.
All committed for our safety to its
security and peace. Preserved from
annihilation only by the care, the work
and the love we give our fragile craft.

Adlai Stevenson

Bibliography

Chapter 1 THE STUDY OF SOCIETY

*BATES, ALAN P., *The Sociological Enterprise* (Boston: Houghton Mifflin Company, 1967). Sociological subject matter and careers.

*BOULDING, KENNETH, *The Meaning of the Twentieth Century: The Great Transition* (New York: Harper & Row, Publishers, 1964). Especially chap 2, "Science as the Basis of the Great Transition."

*GOULDNER, ALVIN W., *The Coming Crisis of Western Sociology* (New York: Avon Books, 1970). For those who want to go more deeply into the history of sociological theory and the trends and prospects of the discipline.

Knowledge into Action: Improving the Nation's Use of the Social Sciences. Report of the Special Commission on the Social Sciences of the National Science Board, National Science Foundation (Washington, D.C.: U.S. Government Printing Office, 1969). Recommendations for practical applications of social science.

LYND, ROBERT, *Knowledge for What? The Place of Social Science in American Culture* (Princeton, N.J.: Princeton University Press, 1948). One of the most eloquent arguments against the idea that social science can be value-free.

*MILLS, C. WRIGHT, *The Sociological Imagination* (New York: Grove Press, 1959). Provocative.

REDFIELD, ROBERT, *The Social Uses of Social Science: The Papers of Robert Redfield*, ed. Margaret Park Redfield (Chicago: University of Chicago Press, 1963). "Social science justifies itself to the extent to which it makes life comprehensible and significant."

*STEIN, MAURICE, and ARTHUR VIDICH, eds., *Sociology on Trial* (Englewood Cliffs, N.J.: Prentice-Hall, Inc., 1963). "A sociology of sociology by sociologists," arguing for the importance of the role of social critic.

*VALDES, DONALD M., and DWIGHT G. DEAN, eds., *Sociology in Use: Selected Readings for the Introductory Course* (New York: The Macmillan Company, 1965). Shows the use of sociological knowledge in visibly practical applications—medical care, community development, labor unions, religious bodies, marketing, etc.

*Available in paperback.

Chapter 2 THE CONDUCT OF SOCIAL INQUIRY

*BATTEN, THELMA F., *Reasoning and Research: A Guide for Social Science Methods* (Boston: Little, Brown and Company, 1971). Text and exercises designed to help a student evaluate evidence.

BLUMER, HERBERT, *Symbolic Interactionism: Perspective and Method* (Englewood Cliffs, N.J.: Prentice-Hall, Inc., 1969). A lucid exposition of the value of a humanist, qualitative approach to sociological research.

BRUYN, SEVERYN T., *The Human Perspective in Sociology: The Methodology of Participant Observation* (Englewood Cliffs, N.J.: Prentice-Hall, Inc., 1966). Since an empirical science must respect the nature of its subject matter, sociology must study human behavior by appropriate methods rather than by trying to emulate the physical sciences slavishly.

*CAMERON, WILLIAM BRUCE, *Informal Sociology: A Casual Introduction to Sociological Thinking* (New York: Random House, Inc., 1963). Especially five informal essays on "Theory and Methods," pp. 3–66.

*FILSTEAD, WILLIAM J., ed., *Qualitative Methodology: Firsthand Involvement with the Social World* (Chicago: Markham Publishing Co., 1970). The author intends "to provoke those who measure everything and understand nothing."

*HAMMOND, PHILLIP E., ed., *Sociologists at Work: Essays on the Craft of Social Research* (Garden City, N.Y.: Doubleday & Company, Inc., Anchor Books, 1967). Sociologists tell how actual research projects were conducted. Anecdotal and fascinating as a supplement to a study of methods.

SIMON, JULIAN L., *Basic Research Methods in Social Science: The Art of Empirical Investigation* (New York: Random House, Inc., 1969). Stresses the quantitative positivist approach.

Chapter 3 THE NATURE AND CONTENT OF CULTURE

*BOWEN, ELENORE SMITH (pseud.), *Return to Laughter* (Garden City, N.Y.: Doubleday, 1964). An engrossing not-so-fictional account of the experiences of the author, whose real name is Laura Bohannon, in a Nigerian tribe.

*CARROLL, JOHN B., ed., *Language, Thought, and Reality: Selected Writings of Benjamin Lee Whorf* (Cambridge, Mass.: M.I.T. Press, 1956). Essays by a recognized authority on language.

HAYS, H. R., *From Ape to Angel: An Informal History of Social Anthropology* (New York: Alfred A. Knopf, 1965). A breezy account of various social anthropologists and schools of thought.

HOWELLS, WILLIAM, *Mankind in the Making*, rev. ed. (Garden City, N.Y.: Doubleday, 1967). Subtitled *The Story of Human Evolution*, this book is well written and witty.

*KLUCKHOHN, CLYDE, *Mirror for Man* (New York: Fawcett World Library, 1964). A highly readable and reliable introduction to anthropology, written for the layman and specialist.

*LINTON, RALPH, *The Study of Man* (New York: Appleton-Century-Crofts, 1936). A classic of anthropology. Paperback edition, 1964.

PFEIFFER, JOHN, E., *The Emergence of Man* (New York: Harper & Row, 1969). Well written, well illustrated, comprehensive.

*POWDERMAKER, HORTENSE, *Stranger and Friend: The Way of an Anthropologist* (New York: W. W. Norton, 1966). A fascinating account of how the author came to be an anthropologist, and of her fieldwork experiences in Lesu, Mississippi, Hollywood, and Rhodesia.

Chapter 4 THE ORGANIZATION AND INTEGRATION OF CULTURE

*KLAPP, ORRIN E., *Collective Search for Identity* (New York: Holt, Rinehart & Winston, 1969). Especially chap. 4, "The Language of Ritual."

*KLUCKHOHN, FLORENCE ROCKWOOD, "Dominant and Variant Value Orientations," in James Fadiman, ed., *The Proper Study of Man* (New York: Macmillan, 1971).

*LERNER, MAX, *America as a Civilization* (New York: Simon and Schuster, 1957). Especially chap. 9, "Character and Society."

*MEANS, RICHARD L., *The Ethical Imperative: The Crisis in American Values* (Garden City, N.Y.: Doubleday, 1970). An effort to develop an objective theory of values in relation to social problems.

*REICH, CHARLES A., *The Greening of America* (New York: Random House, 1970). A popular book predicting that changes in values will bring about a social revolution.

*ROSZAK, THEODORE, *The Making of a Counter Culture* (Garden City, N.Y.: Doubleday, Anchor, 1969). Shows how some thinkers have called into question the conventional scientific world view—"the myth of objective consciousness"—and undermined the foundations of technology-dominated society.

VOGT, EVON Z., and ETHEL M. ALBERT, eds., *People of Rimrock: A Study of Values in Five Cultures* (Cambridge: Harvard University Press, 1966). A report on five neighboring communities in western New Mexico: Navaho and Zuñi Indians, Mormons, Texan homesteaders, and Spanish-Americans.

WILLIAMS, ROBIN M., JR., *American Society: A Sociological Interpretation*, 3rd ed. (New York: Alfred A. Knopf, 1970). Chap. 11, "Values in American Society," is an excellent discussion at far greater length than the one in this chapter, which is based in part on Williams' analysis.

Chapter 5 THE FUNCTIONS OF CULTURE

*FRIED, MORTON H., *Readings in Anthropology, Vol. II: Cultural Anthropology,* 2nd ed. (New York: Thomas Y. Crowell, 1968). Especially the first four selections and the section on culture and personality.

*GOODMAN, MARY ELLEN, *The Individual and Culture* (Homewood, Illinois: The Dorsey Press, 1967). Comparisons of cultural attitudes toward the individual, and of the effects of various cultures on personality.

*HALL, EDWARD, *The Hidden Dimension* (Garden City, N.Y.: Doubleday, Anchor, 1969). Brief but fascinating account of cultural differences stressing such nonverbal aspects as the uses of space.

*LEE, DOROTHY, ed., *Freedom and Culture* (Englewood Cliffs, N.J.: Prentice-Hall, 1959). Unusually provocative essays, including several on the relationship of language to ways of life and thought.

LINTON, RALPH, *The Cultural Background of Personality* (New York: Appleton-Century, 1945). A small classic by a towering figure in anthropology.

Chapter 6 THE IMPORTANCE OF THE CULTURE CONCEPT

FOSTER, GEORGE M., *Traditional Cultures and the Impact of Technological Change* (New York: Harper & Row, 1962). This fascinating account of induced change vividly points up the importance of understanding culture.

————, *Applied Anthropology* (Boston: Little, Brown, 1969). Considers the relationship between theoretical knowledge and its application by social anthropologists in guiding social change and improving human relations.

*HALL, EDWARD T., *The Silent Language* (Greenwich, Conn.: Fawcett, 1959). Written in readable and amusing style, this book describes nonverbal patterns of behavior as barriers to cross-cultural understanding.

HERSKOVITS, MELVILLE, JR., *Man and His Works* (New York: Alfred A. Knopf, 1948). See chap. 5, "The Problem of Cultural Relativism."

*JENNINGS, JESSE D., and E. ADAMSON HOEBEL, *Readings in Anthropology,* 2nd ed. (New York: McGraw-Hill, 1956). Part 10, "Applied Anthropology," contains several interesting readings. Reading No. 40 is Horace Miner's delightful "Body Ritual Among the Nacirema."

KLUCKHOHN, CLYDE, *Mirror for Man* (New York: Fawcett World Library, 1964). Especially valuable in counteracting ethnocentrism are chaps. 1, 2, 9, and 10.

WESTIN, ALAN F., JULIAN H. FRANKLIN, HOWARD R. SWEARER, and PAUL E. SIGMUND, eds., *Views of America* (New York: Harcourt Brace Jovanovich, Inc., 1966). Views from Western Europe, the Communist world, and the developing nations.

Chapter 7   SOCIAL INTERACTION AND SOCIAL STRUCTURE

BANTON, MICHAEL, *Roles: An Introduction to the Study of Social Relations* (New York: Basic Books, 1965). A highly readable book, with a somewhat different definition of status and role from ours.

BUCKLEY, WALTER, *Sociology and Modern Systems Theory* (Englewood Cliffs, N.J.: Prentice-Hall, Inc., 1967). "An exploratory sketch of a revolutionary scientific perspective and conceptual framework as it might be applied to the socio-cultural system."

*COSER, LEWIS A., *Continuities in the Study of Social Conflict* (New York: The Free Press, 1967). The functions and dysfunctions of conflict; theories of conflict and their applications to current politics.

GOFFMAN, ERVING, *Interaction Ritual: Essays in Face-to-Face Behavior* (Chicago: Aldine, 1967). The study of face-to-face interaction in natural settings, using a "drama" analogy.

*GREER, SCOTT A., *Social Organization* (Garden City, N.Y.: Doubleday, 1955). A small classic.

*LINTON, RALPH, *The Study of Man* (New York: Appleton-Century-Crofts, 1936). Chapter VIII, "Status and Role," is a classic statement on the subject. Reprinted in Schuler *et al.*, *Readings in Sociology*, 4th ed., selection 22.

*LYMAN, STANFORD M., and MARVIN B. SCOTT, *A Sociology of the Absurd* (New York: Appleton-Century-Crofts, 1970). Based on the idea that the individual, trying to make sense of a meaningless world, should be the central concern of sociology.

*MEAD, MARGARET, ed., *Cooperation and Competition Among Primitive Peoples*, rev. ed. (Boston: Beacon Press, 1961). A comparison of thirteen cultures, with emphasis on social structure and personality.

*MONANE, JOSEPH H., *A Sociology of Human Systems* (New York: Appleton-Century-Crofts, 1967). Ties sociological research into "a structural science of social system action."

Chapter 8   TYPES OF SOCIAL ORGANIZATION

*BELL, GERALD D., ed., *Organizations and Human Behavior: A Book of Readings* (Englewood Cliffs, N.J.: Prentice-Hall, Inc., 1967). Readings 4, 7–13, 16, and 17.

CARTWRIGHT, DORWIN, and ALVIN ZANDER, *Group Dynamics: Research and Theory*, 3rd ed. (New York: Harper & Row, 1968). A collection of 42 readings.

*ETZIONI, AMITAI, *Modern Organizations* (Englewood Cliffs, N.J.: Prentice-Hall, Inc., 1964). Special emphasis on structure of organizations.

*GREER, SCOTT A., *Social Organization* (Garden City, N.Y.: Doubleday, 1955). Also useful for this chapter.

HARE, A. PAUL, EDGAR F. BORGATTA, and ROBERT F. BALES, eds., *Small Groups: Studies in Social Interaction*, rev. ed. (New York: Alfred A. Knopf, 1966). Collection of readings.

HOMANS, GEORGE CASPAR, *Social Behavior: Its Elementary Forms* (New York: Harcourt, Brace & World, 1961). Defines elementary social behavior as "the face-to-face contact between individuals, in which the reward each gets from the behavior of the others is relatively direct and immediate."

*MILLS, THEODORE M., *The Sociology of Small Groups* (Englewood Cliffs, N.J.: Prentice-Hall, Inc., 1967). Emphasizes ways of thinking about groups rather than current research findings.

*OLMSTED, MICHAEL S., *The Small Group* (New York: Random House, 1959). Good descriptions of various classic studies of small groups, and some theoretical observations.

*ROSE, PETER I., ed., *The Study of Society: An Integrated Anthology*, 2nd ed. (New York: Random House, 1970). The well-chosen readings in Part Three include Redfield's "The Folk Society."

Chapter 9   SOCIAL STRATIFICATION

BENDIX, REINHARD, and SEYMOUR MARTIN LIPSET, eds., *Class, Status, and Power: Social Stratification in Comparative Perspective*, 2nd ed. (New York: The Free Press, 1966). A huge and important book of readings.

COLEMAN, RICHARD P., and BERNICE L. NEUGARTEN, *Social Status in the City* (San Francisco: Jossey-Bass, 1971). A study of Kansas City using both evaluated participation techniques and more objective indices.

*DOMHOFF, G. WILLIAM, *Who Rules America?* (Englewood Cliffs, N.J.: Prentice-Hall, Inc., 1967). Concludes that even though America is a democracy, it does have a governing class.

*FERMAN, LOUIS A., JOYCE L. KORNBLUH, and ALAN HABER, *Poverty in America*, rev. ed. (Ann Arbor: The University of Michigan Press, 1968). A comprehensive anthology with an introduction by Michael Harrington.

FICKER, VICTOR B., and HERBERT S. GRAVES, *Deprivation in America* (Beverly Hills, Calif.: Glencoe Press, 1971). This slim volume portrays vividly the housing, health, education, hunger, and hopelessness of the poor.

*HARRINGTON, MICHAEL, *The Other America: Poverty in the United States* (Baltimore: Penguin Books, 1963). The angry book that helped spark the "war on poverty."

*HOWE, LOUISE KAPP, ed., *The White Majority: Between Poverty and Affluence* (New York: Random House, Vintage Books, 1970). Readings about "average Americans" of the white lower-middle and working classes, based on the belief that they are stereotyped and misunderstood by the higher classes.

LEWIS, OSCAR, *A Death in the Sánchez Family* (New York: Random House, 1969); *La Vida: A Puerto Rican Family in the Culture of Poverty—San Juan and New York* (New York: Random House, 1965); and *The Children of Sánchez* (New York: Random House, 1961). Horowitz says Lewis fuses "the art of biography, the insight of history, and the facts of society."

MILLER, HERMAN P., *Rich Man, Poor Man*, 2nd ed. (New York: Thomas Y. Crowell, 1971). An authoritative survey of economic distribution in the United States by a Census Bureau expert.

ROACH, JACK L., LLEWELLYN GROSS, and ORVILLE R. GURSSLIN, *Social Stratification in the United States* (Englewood Cliffs, N.J.: Prentice-Hall, Inc., 1969). Survey and critique of sociological writing on stratification in the United States, especially since 1950. Theory, methodology, and empirical reports.

*TUMIN, MELVIN M., *Social Stratification: The Forms and Functions of Inequality* (Englewood Cliffs, N.J.: Prentice-Hall, Inc., 1967). An excellent text, plus social commentary.

Chapter 10   INTERGROUP RELATIONS AND AMERICAN MINORITIES

*ANDERSON, CHARLES, *White Protestant Americans: From National Origins to Religious Groups* (Englewood Cliffs, N.J.: Prentice-Hall, Inc., 1970). One of the excellent books in the "Ethnic Groups in American Life" series edited by Milton Gordon. Others are listed below.

*BARRON, MILTON L., ed., *Minorities in a Changing World* (New York: Alfred A. Knopf, 1967). Readings with world-wide perspective.

FRANKLIN, JOHN HOPE, *From Slavery to Freedom: A History of Negro Americans*, 3rd ed. (New York: Alfred A. Knopf, 1967). By a leading black historian.

*GLOCK, CHARLES Y., and ELLEN SIEGELMAN, eds., *Prejudice U.S.A.* (New York: Frederick A. Praeger, 1969). Based on the premise that the greatest promise for reducing prejudice and discrimination lies with schools, churches, mass media, industry and labor, and governmental agencies.

GOLDSTEIN, SIDNEY, and CALVIN GOLDSCHEIDER, *Jewish Americans: Three Generations in a Jewish Community* (Englewood Cliffs, N.J.: Prentice-Hall, Inc., 1968). A study in the metropolitan area of Providence, Rhode Island.

*GORDON, MILTON, *Assimilation in American Life: The Role of Race, Religion, and National Origins* (New York: Oxford University Press, 1964). Advances the theory of structural pluralism as a basic element of our social structure.

*HERBERG, WILL, *Protestant-Catholic-Jew*, rev. ed. (New York: Doubleday, 1960). A fascinating analysis of the status, history, and interrelationships of the three major religious groupings in America.

*JACOBS, PAUL, *Prelude to Riot: A View of Urban America from the Bottom* (New York: Random House, Vintage Books, 1967). About the relationships between the government and the minority poor in Los Angeles.

*KAIN, JOHN F., ed., *Race and Poverty: The Economics of Discrimination* (Englewood Cliffs, N.J.: Prentice-Hall, Inc., 1969). Readings on the interrelation of the two major domestic problems of American society.

*KITANO, HARRY H. L., *Japanese Americans: The Evolution of a Subculture* (Englewood Cliffs, N.J.: Prentice-Hall, Inc., 1969). The author calls this book a success story with all the elements of melodrama.

*KNOWLES, LOUIS L., and KENNETH PREWITT, eds., *Institutional Racism in America* (Englewood Cliffs, N.J.: Prentice-Hall, Inc., 1969). Pursues the theme of the Kerner Report that white racism is at the root of interracial conflict.

MARDEN, CHARLES F., and GLADYS MEYER, *Minorities in American Society*, 3rd ed. (New York: American Book, 1968). Deals with stabilized and dynamic aspects of intergroup relations of a majority-dominance character.

*MOORE, JOAN W., with ALFREDO CUELLAR, *Mexican Americans* (Englewood Cliffs, N.J.: Prentice-Hall, Inc., 1970). An introduction to a heterogeneous group that has been judged quickly and haphazardly.

*OSOFSKY, GILBERT, *The Burden of Race: A Documentary History of Negro-White Relations in America* (New York: Harper & Row, 1967). Documents with interpretation.

*PINKNEY, ALPHONSO, *Black Americans* (Englewood Cliffs, N.J.: Prentice-Hall, Inc., 1969). Can a society that prefers piecemeal reform avoid increased racial conflict? The author's prognosis is not favorable.

*ROSE, PETER I., ed., *The Ghetto and Beyond: Essays on Jewish Life in America* (New York: Random House, 1969). A stimulating collection of readings.

WILLIAMS, ROBIN M., JR., *Strangers Next Door: Ethnic Relations in American Communities* (Englewood Cliffs, N.J.: Prentice-Hall, Inc., 1964). In collaboration with John P. Dean and Edward A. Suchman. Demonstrates that tension and conflict grow out of established social structures and practices—not from irrational individual attitudes alone.

*WOODWARD, C. VANN, *The Strange Career of Jim Crow*, rev. ed. (London: Oxford University Press, 1966). Focuses on the history of physical segregation and does not attempt to treat all types of racial discrimination and injustice.

Chapter 11 THE PROCESS OF BECOMING HUMAN

BLUMER, HERBERT, *Symbolic Interactionism: Perspective and Method* (Englewood Cliffs, N.J.: Prentice-Hall, Inc., 1969). Essays on symbolic interactionist theory by one of its outstanding proponents.

ERIKSON, ERIK H., *Childhood and Society* (New York: W. W. Norton, 1950). A neo-Freudian view of socialization.

————, *Identity: Youth and Crisis* (New York: W. W. Norton, 1968). The life cycle theory, with special emphasis on the identity crisis of adolescence.

GORDON, CHAD, and KENNETH H. GERGEN, eds., *The Self in Social Interaction* (New York: John Wiley & Sons, 1968). Vol. 1, *Classic and Contemporary Perspectives*, includes readings from many of the theorists mentioned in this chapter.

LINDESMITH, ALFRED R., and ANSELM L. STRAUSS, *Social Psychology*, 3rd ed. (New York: Holt, Rinehart & Winston, 1968). A text written from the symbolic interactionist point of view.

*MAY, ROLLO, *Man's Search for Himself* (New York: W. W. Norton & Company, Inc., 1953). A humanist psychologist's richly suggestive discussion of the experience of becoming a person.

MEAD, GEORGE HERBERT, *Mind, Self, and Society*, Charles W. Morris, ed. (Chicago: University of Chicago Press, 1934). The landmark presentation of symbolic interactionist theory.

*SPITZER, STEPHAN P., ed., *The Sociology of Personality: An Enduring Problem in Psychology* (New York: Van Nostrand Reinhold, 1969). Especially readings 4, 5, 12, and 13.

Chapter 12   FACTORS IN PERSONALITY DEVELOPMENT

BECKER, HOWARD S., BLANCHE GEER, EVERETT C. HUGHES, and ANSELM STRAUSS, *Boys in White: Student Culture in Medical School* (Chicago: University of Chicago Press, 1961). A study of occupational socialization.

*BENEDICT, RUTH, *Patterns of Culture* (New York: Penguin Books, 1946). A classic comparison of the modal personality types of several cultures.

*BORGATTA, EDGAR F., ed., *Social Psychology: Readings and Perspective* (Chicago: Rand McNally, 1969). Readings concerning many of the topics touched upon in this chapter.

BRONFENBRENNER, URIE, *Two Worlds of Childhood: U.S. and U.S.S.R.* (New York: Russell Sage Foundation, 1970), with the assistance of John C. Condry, Jr. A challenging comparison of two systems of socialization.

LINTON, RALPH, *The Cultural Background of Personality* (New York: Appleton-Century-Crofts, 1945). An excellent assessment of the relationship of culture, society, and personality.

*MEAD, MARGARET, *Sex and Temperament in Three Primitive Societies* (New York: New American Library, 1950). Demonstrates the importance of cultural definitions of male and female roles in shaping personality.

SHIBUTANI, TOMATSU, *Society and Personality* (Englewood Cliffs, N.J.: Prentice-Hall, Inc., 1961). An interactionist approach to social psychology, attempting to employ the insights of Freud and Mead and their followers. Difficult but rewarding.

Chapter 13 VARIATIONS IN THE QUALITY AND MEANING OF LIFE: CONFORMITY, DEVIANCE, AND AUTONOMY

BECKER, HOWARD, ed., *The Other Side: Perspectives on Deviance* (New York: The Free Press of Glencoe, 1964). Provocative readings, including some that argue that deviance plays a positive role in society.

CRESSEY, DONALD R., and DAVID A. WARD, *Delinquency, Crime, and Social Process* (New York: Harper & Row, 1969). The statistical distribution of criminal and delinquent behavior in time and space; and the process by which individuals come to engage in such behavior.

*DINITZ, SIMON, RUSSELL R. DYNES, and ALFRED C. CLARKE, *Deviance: Studies in the Process of Stigmatization and Societal Reaction* (New York: Oxford University Press, 1969). Selected articles on every major aspect of deviance, illustrating recent critical issues.

*DOUGLAS, JACK D., ed., *Observations of Deviance* (New York: Random House, 1970). Insights into deviant styles and ways of life.

*GOODMAN, MARY ELLEN, *The Individual and Culture* (Homewood, Ill.: Richard D. Irwin, 1967). Discussions of autonomy in various settings.

HOWARD, JANE, *Please Touch: A Guided Tour of the Human Potential Movement* (New York: McGraw-Hill, 1970). A report of personal experience.

*JOSEPHSON, ERIC and MARY, eds., *Man Alone: Alienation in Modern Society* (New York: Dell Publishing, 1962). Readings, with an introduction discussing the conditions of modern life (as well as of other times) that have produced alienation.

*KIESLER, CHARLES A., and SARA B. KIESLER, *Conformity* (Reading, Mass.: Addison-Wesley Publishing Company, 1969). A small book on conformity—what it means and when it happens, distinguishing between compliance and private acceptance.

*LEMERT, EDWIN M., *Human Deviance, Social Problems, and Social Control* Englewood Cliffs, N.J.: Prentice-Hall, Inc., 1967). Describes the process of becoming "a deviant."

*MASLOW, ABRAHAM H., *Toward a Psychology of Being*, 2nd ed. (New York: Van Nostrand Reinhold, 1968). "This book is unmistakably a normative social psychology. That is, it accepts the search for values as one of the essential and feasible tasks of a science of society."

*RUBINGTON, EARL, and MARTIN S. WEINBERG, *Deviance: The Interactionist Perspective* (New York: Macmillan, 1968). A collection of readings that "makes sense of deviance as somehow being both product and process of social interaction," and discusses the conditions under which deviance emerges, develops, and changes over time. Stresses the importance of social perceptions and definitions of deviance.

*SCHEFF, THOMAS J., ed., *Mental Illness and Social Processes* (New York: Harper & Row, 1967). Stresses the social reaction to mental illness—that is, the recurring patterns of behavior among individuals and organizations attempting to cope with persons who are defined as mentally ill.

*SCHUR, EDWIN M., *Our Criminal Society: The Social and Legal Sources of Crime in America* (Englewood Cliffs, N.J.: Prentice-Hall, Inc., 1969). Concerned with issues of public policy, this small book also provides a systematic review of key findings and theories about crime.

*SHERIF, MUZAFER, *The Psychology of Social Norms* (New York: Harper Torchbooks, 1964). A full discussion of the classic experiment discussed in this chapter, the theory behind it, and its implications.

*SHORT, JAMES F., JR., ed., *Gang Delinquency and Delinquent Subcultures* (New York: Harper & Row, 1968). Emphasizes empirical research and its vital and creative interplay with theory.

*SILVERSTEIN, HARRY, ed., *The Social Control of Mental Illness* (New York: Thomas Y. Crowell, 1968). Six readings on mental illness in social context.

*URICK, RONALD, *Alienation* (Englewood Cliffs, N.J.: Prentice-Hall, Inc., 1970). Highly readable selections from the Beatles, Malcolm X, and more conventional sources, including a lucid statement on "What is Alienation?"

*WALKER, EDWARD L., and ROGER W. HEYNS, *An Anatomy for Conformity* (Belmont, Calif.: Brooks/Cole, 1967). Reports on laboratory experiments in producing conformity, with a discussion of their implications.

Chapter 14   PROCESSES OF SOCIAL AND CULTURAL CHANGE

*APPELBAUM, RICHARD B., *Theories of Social Change* (Chicago: Markham, 1970). A somewhat technical review.

BAUER, RAYMOND A., ed., *Social Indicators* (Cambridge: M.I.T. Press, 1966). Discussions of social systems accounting, social indicators, and social planning.

BENNIS, WARREN G., KENNETH D. BENNE, and ROBERT CHIN, eds., *The Planning of Change*, 2nd ed. (New York: Holt, Rinehart, & Winston, 1969). Seeks to "contribute to the unfinished task of merging and reconciling the arts of social practice and the sciences of human behavior."

*BREED, WARREN, *The Self-Guiding Society* (New York: The Free Press, 1971). A shorter version of Amitai Etzioni, *The Active Society* (New York: The Free Press, 1968). The central thesis is that "the post-modern society has the option to change its course."

BUCKLEY, WALTER, *Sociology and Modern Systems Theory* (Englewood Cliffs, N.J.: Prentice-Hall, Inc., 1967). Depicts the socio-cultural order as a complex adaptive system.

FOSTER, GEORGE, *Traditional Cultures and the Impact of Technological Change* (New York: Harper & Row, 1962). An interesting account of attempts to introduce change.

GROSS, BERTRAM, ed., *Social Intelligence for America's Future: Explorations in Societal Problems* (Boston: Allyn and Bacon, 1969). "Suggests an agenda for improving the quality of our social information and for creating social agencies more responsive to the needs of a developing American society."

*HAVELOCK, RONALD G., et al., *Planning for Innovation Through Dissemination and Utilization of Knowledge* (Ann Arbor: Institute for Social Research, The University of Michigan, 1971). A voluminous report that "provides a framework for understanding the processes of innovation, dissemination, and knowledge utilization, and reviews the relevant literature in education and other fields of practice within this framework."

*MANUEL, FRANK E., ed., *Utopias and Utopian Thought* (Boston: Beacon Press, 1967). Provocative readings on types of utopias and their function in social change.

MERTON, ROBERT K., and ROBERT NISBET, *Contemporary Social Problems*, 3rd ed. (New York: Harcourt Brace Jovanovich, 1971). A leading text.

MOORE, WILBERT E., *Order and Change: Essays in Comparative Sociology* (New York: John Wiley, 1967). By an expert on the subject of social change.

*MOORE, WILBERT E., *Social Change* (Englewood Cliffs, N.J.: Prentice-Hall, Inc., 1963). An excellent brief analysis.

ROGERS, EVERETT M., *Diffusion of Innovations* (New York: The Free Press, 1962). Reviews more than five hundred publications on the subject.

SILVERT, KALMAN H., *Man's Power: A Biased Guide to Political Thought and Action* (New York: Viking, 1970). Emphasizes the role of human decisions in social change.

*TOFFLER, ALVIN, *Future Shock* (New York: Random House, 1970). This best-seller is based on many studies and predictions, including sociological ones.

*———, ed., *The Futurists* (New York: Random House, 1972). "The purpose of this collection is to make accessible a few of the works of the best-known and ... most influential futurists."

*U.S. Department of Health, Education, and Welfare, *Toward a Social Report*, with an introductory commentary by Wilbur J. Cohen (Ann Arbor: The University of Michigan Press, 1970). Deals with indicators of social change useful in periodic reporting on the state of the nation and progress toward social goals.

*WIENER, NORBERT, *The Human Use of Human Beings: Cybernetics and Society* (New York: Avon, 1967). The relation between computer technology and the social sciences.

WILLIAMS, ROBIN M., JR., *American Society: A Sociological Interpretation*, 3rd ed. (New York: Alfred A. Knopf, 1970). A review and analysis of our social system.

Chapter 15   MODERNIZATION: THE GREAT TRANSFORMATION

*ARON, RAYMOND, *The Industrial Society: Three Essays on Ideology and Development* (New York: Simon and Schuster, 1967). By a leading French sociologist.

*EISENSTADT, S. N., *Modernization: Protest and Change* (Englewood Cliffs, N.J.: Prentice-Hall, Inc., 1966). Analyzes the major characteristics and problems of modern and modernizing societies, especially the ability of the institutional framework to absorb the social changes inherent in the modernization process.

*FICKETT, LEWIS P., JR., ed., *Problems of the Developing Nations: Readings and Case Studies* (New York: Thomas Y. Crowell, 1966). Concerned with sociological, economic, military, and political aspects of the developmental process; case studies of six nations.

*HOROWITZ, IRVING LOUIS, *Three Worlds of Development: The Theory and Practice of International Stratification* (New York: Oxford University Press, 1966). A qualitative study of the interaction of the three main sources of economic, political, and social power.

LERNER, DANIEL, *The Passing of Traditional Society: Modernizing the Middle East* (New York: Macmillan, 1958). Fascinating account of changes in a Turkish village, and in other societies.

*MOORE, WILBERT E., *Social Change* (Englewood Cliffs, N.J.: Prentice-Hall, Inc., 1963). Especially chap. 5, "Modernization."

*MYRDAL, GUNNAR, *The Challenge of World Poverty: A World Anti-Poverty Program in Outline* (New York: Pantheon, 1970). Stresses the urgency of institutional reform.

*SCHNEIDER, KENNETH R., *Destiny of Change: How Relevant Is Man in the Age of Development?* (New York: Holt, Rinehart & Winston, 1968). A readable, thought-provoking book about modern society and the individual's place within it.

WEINER, MYRON, ed., *Modernization: The Dynamics of Growth* (New York: Basic Books, 1966). Twenty-five scholars reflect on how modernization occurs and how it can be accelerated.

Chapter 16   CITIES AND MODERNIZATION

BREESE, GERALD, ed., *The City in Newly Developing Countries: Readings on Urbanism and Urbanization* (Englewood Cliffs, N.J.: Prentice-Hall, Inc., 1969). Readings to accompany the editor's introductory book, below.

*———, *Urbanization in Newly Developing Countries* (Englewood Cliffs, N.J.: Prentice-Hall, Inc., 1966). A vividly written exploratory discussion of the subject.

*ELIAS, C. E., JR., JAMES GILLIES, and SVEND RIEMER, eds., *Metropolis: Values in Conflict* (Belmont, Calif.: Wadsworth, 1964). Provocative readings, some representing opposed viewpoints.

*FAVA, SYLVIA FLEIS, ed., *Urbanism in World Perspective: A Reader* (New York: Thomas Y. Crowell, 1968). An excellent selection of readings on urban theory, housing, ecology, social organization, and the social psychology of urban life, in cross-cultural perspective.

GANS, HERBERT J., *The Levittowners* (New York: Random House, 1967). Report on two years of participant observation in a new suburb.

*GREEN, CONSTANCE McLAUGHLIN, *The Rise of Urban America* (New York: Harper & Row, 1965). Urban development in the United States from colonial days to the 1960s; concise, sprightly, and clear.

*GREER, SCOTT, *Governing the Metropolis* (New York: John Wiley, 1962). Lucidly written. Part I, "The Creation of a Metropolitan World," is especially pertinent to this chapter.

*HALPERN, JOEL M., *The Changing Village Community* (Englewood Cliffs, N.J.: Prentice-Hall, Inc., 1967). General ideas about contemporary change in rural areas, with concrete examples of changes in village communities throughout the world.

MUMFORD, LEWIS, *The Culture of Cities* (New York: Harcourt Brace Jovanovich, Inc., 1938). A classic.

TAYLOR, LEE, and ARTHUR R. JONES, JR., *Rural Life and Urbanized Society* (New York: Oxford University Press, 1964). The theme: that in the United States both rural and urban residents live in relation to the same pattern of social organization.

Chapter 17 POPULATION AND ENVIRONMENT

CAMPBELL, REX R., and JERRY L. WADE, eds., *Society and Environment: The Coming Collision* (Boston: Allyn and Bacon, 1972). Fifty-four classic articles on ecology.

*COMMONER, BARRY, *Science and Survival* (New York: Viking, 1966). By one of the first to sound the alarm.

*DE BELL, GARRETT, ed., *The Environmental Handbook* (New York: Ballantine/ Friends of the Earth, 1970). Prepared for the first environmental teach-in.

*DISCH, ROBERT, ed., *The Ecological Conscience: Values for Survival* (Englewood Cliffs, N.J.: Prentice-Hall, Inc., 1970). Argues that the environmental crisis is potentially lethal because it can only be met through levels of international cooperation unknown to world history.

EHRLICH, PAUL R. and ANNE H., *Population, Resources, Environment: Issues in Human Ecology* (San Francisco: W. H. Freeman, 1970). A hard-hitting book about "the damage being done by overpopulation and overdevelopment to the only life-supporting planet we know." Intended not merely to frighten or discourage, but to inform and convince readers about the elements and dimensions of the crisis.

HARTLEY, SHIRLEY FOSTER, *Population: Quantity vs. Quality* (Englewood Cliffs, N.J.: Prentice-Hall, Inc., 1972). A well-written "sociological examination of the causes and consequences of the population explosion." Highly recommended.

*HAUSER, PHILIP M., ed., *The Population Dilemma*, 2nd ed. (Englewood Cliffs, N.J.: Prentice-Hall, Inc., 1969). For the American Assembly of Columbia University. Sets forth "the key population facts, the major problems being generated by accelerating growth, the basic policy issues, and the more important policy and action alternatives."

*HEER, DAVID M., *Society and Population* (Englewood Cliffs, N.J.: Prentice-Hall, Inc., 1968). "This book is intended to reveal some of the ways in which an understanding of population is important to a proper study of sociology, and to help explain the causes and effects of the current population explosion." Heer edited an accompanying book of *Readings on Population.*

Population and the American Future (New York: New American Library, 1972). Report of the President's Commission on Population Growth and the American Future, emphasizing that unbridled growth multiplies problems of all kinds and impairs the quality of life.

REVELLE, ROGER, and HANS H. LANDSBERG, eds., *America's Changing Environment* (Boston: Beacon, 1970). A book about decision-making on environmental problems; sees ecology as an ethical science concerned with politics.

SHEPARD, PAUL, and DANIEL McKINLEY, eds., *The Subversive Science: Essays Toward an Ecology of Man* (Boston: Houghton Mifflin, 1969). An excellent anthology.

*SWATEK, PAUL, *The User's Guide to the Protection of the Environment* (New York: Ballantine/Friends of the Earth, 1971). The subtitle, "the indispensable guide to making every purchase count," indicates how life styles may be changed to harmonize with the ecological conscience.

*YOUNG, LOUISE B., ed., *Population in Perspective* (New York: Oxford University Press, 1968). Readings providing historical depth and cultural pattern, by demographers, economists, anthropologists, biologists, novelists, and poets, as well as photographs and James Thurber's picture story "The Last Flower."

Chapter 18 COLLECTIVE BEHAVIOR AND SOCIAL MOVEMENTS

*BOSKIN, JOSEPH, *Urban Racial Violence in the Twentieth Century* (Beverly Hills: Glencoe Press, 1969). Deals with conflict as expressed in two forms of violence: the urban racial riot and the racial protest riot.

*CAMERON, WILLIAM BRUCE, *Modern Social Movements: A Sociological Outline* (New York: Random House, 1966). General principles with interesting examples, and a good bibliography.

*EPSTEIN, CYNTHIA FUCHS, and WILLIAM J. GOODE, eds., *The Other Half: Roads to Women's Equality* (Englewood Cliffs, N.J.: Prentice-Hall, Inc., 1971). Brings together analyses of current issues, sociological studies of women's position in society, and historical perspectives on the present movement.

*EVANS, ROBERT R., ed., *Readings in Collective Behavior* (Chicago: Rand McNally, 1969). Theoretical, descriptive, and analytical studies of collective behavior (not including social movements).

GUSFIELD, JOSEPH R., ed., *Protest, Reform, and Revolt: A Reader in Social Movements* (New York: John Wiley, 1970). Perspectives for understanding human activity and conflict in relation to social change.

*HOROWITZ, IRVING LOUIS, ed., *The Troubled Conscience: American Social Issues* (Santa Barbara: Center for the Study of Democratic Institutions, 1971). Essays about four major social issues: the relationships of revolutionaries to reformists, the young to the old, blacks to whites, and people to their environment.

*KLAPP, ORRIN E., *Collective Search for Identity* (New York: Holt, Rinehart & Winston, 1969). Deals with identity-seeking movements of mass society: fashions, fads, poses, ritual, cultic movements, recreation, heroes and celebrities, and crusades.

*MILLER, MICHAEL V., and SUSAN GILMORE, eds., *Revolution at Berkeley: The Crisis in American Education* (New York: Dell, 1965). A collection of different points of view on one of the first student rebellions in the U.S.

*MITCHELL, J. PAUL, ed., *Race Riots in Black and White* (Englewood Cliffs, N.J.: Prentice-Hall, Inc., 1970). The historical context.

SAFILIOS-ROTHSCHILD, CONSTANTINA, ed., *Toward a Sociology of Women* (Lexington, Mass.: Xerox College Publishing, 1972).

THOMPSON, MARY LOU, ed., *Voices of the New Feminism* (Boston: Beacon, 1970). An excellent collection of essays on Women's Liberation; background, ideology, goals.

TURNER, RALPH H., and LEWIS M. KILLIAN, *Collective Behavior*, 2nd ed. (Englewood Clifs, N.J.: Prentice-Hall, Inc., 1972). An excellent text by two authorities in the field.

*WEAVER, GARY R. and JAMES H., eds., *The University and Revolution* (Englewood Cliffs, N.J.: Prentice-Hall, Inc., 1969). "The approaches and backgrounds of contributions to this anthology are as diverse and spontaneous as is the student movement itself."

Chapter 19 THE FAMILY, EDUCATION, AND RELIGION

THE FAMILY:

ADAMS, BERT N., *The American Family: A Sociological Interpretation* (Chicago: Markham, 1971). A theoretical monograph as well as an introductory text and a series of essays on the family, focusing on the American family.

*ADAMS, BERT N., and THOMAS WEIRATH, eds., *Readings on the Sociology of the Family* (Chicago: Markham, 1971). Articles and excerpts introducing "the most vital issues in the study of the American family."

*BILLINGSLEY, ANDREW, *Black Families in White America* (Englewood Cliffs, N.J.: Prentice-Hall, Inc., 1968). The central theme is that the black family can best be understood as a varied and complex institution in the black community and white society.

*CAVAN, RUTH SHONLE, ed., *Marriage and the Family in the Modern World: A Book of Readings*, 3rd ed. (New York: Thomas Y. Crowell, 1969). Sixty-four readings on many aspects of the sociology of the family.

*GEIGER, H. KENT, ed., *Comparative Perspectives on Marriage and the Family* (Boston: Little, Brown, 1968). A valuable little book drawing on Israel, Japan, China, and other societies for a comparative view of many issues in the sociology of the family.

*GOODE, WILLIAM J., *The Family* (Englewood Cliffs, N.J.: Prentice-Hall, Inc., 1964). A short introduction showing "the fruitfulness of sociological theory when applied to family relations."

*————, *World Revolution and Family Patterns* (New York: The Free Press of Glencoe, 1963). Modernization and the family.

*————, ed., *Readings on the Family and Society* (Englewood Cliffs, N.J.: Prentice-Hall, Inc., 1964). Stresses the family as an element in the larger social structure—shaping it and being shaped by it.

*HEISS, JEROLD, ed., *Family Roles and Interaction: An Anthology* (Chicago: Rand McNally, 1968). All articles are relevant to the concerns of "role theory."

KOMAROVSKY, MIRRA, *Blue-Collar Marriage* (New York: Random House, 1964). Working-class contrasted with middle-class marriages.

LESLIE, GERALD R., *The Family in Social Context* (New York: Oxford University Press, 1967). A well-written introductory text.

MARTINSON, FLOYD MANSFIELD, *Family in Society* (New York: Dodd, Mead, 1970). Describes and analyzes the American family (in its various manifestations during different periods) within the context of its involvement with society and in the lives of individuals.

*QUEEN, STUART A., and ROBERT W. HABENSTEIN, *The Family in Various Cultures*, 3rd ed. (Philadelphia: Lippincott, 1967). Comparative data about various family systems, past and present.

REISS, IRA L., *The Family System in America* (New York: Holt, Rinehart & Winston, 1971). Carefully documented generalizations.

SCHULZ, DAVID A., *The Changing Family: Its Function and Future* (Englewood Cliffs, N.J.: Prentice-Hall, Inc., 1972). Emphasizes how the family has changed and, with the aid of a cross-cultural perspective, how it might change further.

*SKOLNICK, ARLENE S. and JEROME H., *Family in Transition: Rethinking Marriage, Sexuality, Child Rearing, and Family Organization* (Boston: Little, Brown, 1971). A stimulating book of readings, challenging conventional views, both popular and professional, about marriage and the family.

TURNER, RALPH H., *Family Interaction* (New York: Wiley, 1970). Stresses the internal processes of individual families.

WILLIAMS, ROBIN M., JR., *American Society: A Sociological Interpretation* (New York: Alfred A. Knopf, 1970). Section 4, "Kinship and the Family in the United States," is a balanced assessment.

RELIGION

BERGER, PETER L., *The Sacred Canopy: Elements of a Sociological Theory of Religion* (Garden City, N.Y.: Doubleday, 1967). Religion as man's attempt to locate his life in an ultimately meaningful order.

BIRNBAUM, NORMAN, and GERTRUD LENZER, eds., *Sociology and Religion: A Book of Readings* (Englewood Cliffs, N.J.: Prentice-Hall, Inc., 1969). Stresses the role of religion in human history.

DEMERATH, N. J., III, and PHILLIP E. HAMMOND, *Religion in Social Context: Tradition and Transition* (New York: Random House, 1969). A short text focusing critically on pivotal literature and ideas in the sociology of religion.

GLOCK, CHARLES, and RODNEY STARK, *Religion and Society in Tension* (Chicago: Rand McNally, 1965). The dilemmas of organized religion in modern society.

HOULT, THOMAS FORD, *The Sociology of Religion* (New York: Holt, Rinehart & Winston, 1958). A functional analysis of religion in general, with special emphasis on the mutual interaction of religion and other social institutions.

*O'DEA, THOMAS F., *The Sociology of Religion* (Englewood Cliffs, N.J.: Prentice-Hall, Inc., 1966). A small book using empirical generalizations to present theory.

*ROBERTSON, ROLAND, ed., *Sociology of Religion* (Baltimore: Penguin, 1969). Readings center on religion as a provider—and historically the major provider —of meaning in human societies.

*SMART, NINIAN, *The Religious Experience of Mankind* (New York: Scribner's, 1969). The major world religions, the nature of religion, and contemporary manifestations.

WILLIAMS, ROBIN M., JR., *American Society: A Sociological Interpretation*, 3rd ed. (New York: Alfred A. Knopf, 1970). Section 9, "Religion in America."

EDUCATION

*COOMBS, PHILIP H., *The World Educational Crisis: A Systems Analysis* (New York: Oxford University Press, 1968). The crisis is seen as the failure of educational systems to meet the needs of a rapidly developing and changing world.

*HANSON, JOHN W., and COLE S. BREMBECK, eds., *Education and the Development of Nations* (New York: Holt, Rinehart & Winston, 1966). Deals with the capacity of education to assist in the development of nations and to bring about desirable social change.

*NEILL, A. S., *Summerhill: A Radical Approach to Child Rearing* (New York: Hart, 1960). The stimulating and controversial account of a free private school in England. See also *Summerhill: For and Against* (New York: Hart, 1970).

Articles expressing, usually in lively prose, widely varying reactions to the school and its philosophy.

*POSTMAN, NEIL, and CHARLES WEINGARTNER, *Teaching as a Subversive Activity* (New York: Dell, 1970). A hard-hitting book arguing for worthwhile goals, effective methods, and relevant content.

Saturday Review. This excellent weekly magazine, which should become part of every college student's lifetime reading, has a regular issue on education every four weeks as well as on society, science, and the arts.

*SEXTON, PATRICIA CAYO, *The American School: A Sociological Analysis* (Englewood Cliffs, N.J.: Prentice-Hall, Inc., 1967). Stresses the importance of power and the economic system, values and ideology, and urbanization; and the inefficiency and obsolescence of the school system in this context.

*———, ed., *Readings on the School in Society* (Englewood Cliffs, N.J.: Prentice-Hall, Inc., 1968). "Sociology offers educational analysis a new perspective, one that may help to bring the schools into the mainstream of American life."

*SILBERMAN, CHARLES E., *Crisis in the Classroom: The Remaking of American Education* (New York: Random House, 1970). Analyzes the successes and failures of American education, and suggests innovations, including "free schools" along the British model.

WILLIAMS, ROBIN M., JR., *American Society: A Sociological Interpretation*, 3rd ed. (New York: Alfred A. Knopf, 1970). Section 8, "American Education."

Chapter 20   TOWARD A WORLD ORDER

*DEUTSCH, KARL W., *The Analysis of International Relations* (Englewood Cliffs, N.J.: Prentice-Hall, Inc., 1968). Stresses the interdependence of peoples, all of whom are minorities in a world of "foreigners."

*EBENSTEIN, WILLIAM, *Today's Isms: Communism, Fascism, Capitalism, Socialism* Englewood Cliffs, N.J.: Prentice-Hall, Inc., 1970). Sees totalitarianism and democracy as two ways of life dividing the modern world.

HEILBRONER, ROBERT, *The Economic Problem*, 3rd ed., (Englewood Cliffs, N.J.: Prentice-Hall, Inc., 1972). Especially chaps. 1, 2, 32, 34, 35, and 36. Extremely well written.

MEADOWS, DONELLA H., DENNIS L. MEADOWS, JORGEN RANDERS, and WILLIAM F. BERHENS III, *The Limits to Growth: A Report for the Club of of Rome's Project on the Predicament of Mankind* (New York: Universe Books, 1972). Presents a systems approach to the problems of exponential growth in a finite earth, and suggests approaches to global equilibrium.

*MEANS, RICHARD L., *The Ethical Imperative: The Crisis in American Values* (Garden City, N.Y.: Doubleday, 1970). An attempt to overcome the dualism in American thought between individual and collective values.

PLANO, JACK C., and ROBERT E. RIGGS, *Forging World Order: The Politics of International Organization* (New York: Macmillan, 1967). Although global

community is still distant, functional international organizations have produced a practical approach to political integration.

*SAID, ABDUL A., ed., *America's World Role in the 70s* (Englewood Cliffs, N.J.:
Prentice-Hall, Inc., 1970). Readings emphasizing the need for change in perspectives on which our foreign policy is based.

*TOFFLER, ALVIN, ed., *The Futurists* (New York: Random House, 1972). See especially Kenneth Boulding, "The Economics of the Coming Spaceship Earth,"
comparing our obsolete "cowboy" economy with the "spaceman" economy
we must develop.

WATERS, MAURICE, *The United Nations: International Organization and Administration* (New York: Macmillan, 1967). The role of the United Nations in a
world of sovereign nation-states.

OTHER WORKS TO READ

*ALMQUIST, TERRANCE A., and GARY R. BLODICK, eds., *Readings in Con-
temporary American Society* (Englewood Cliffs, N.J.: Prentice-Hall, Inc.,
1968). The editors attempt to confront the student with competing ideologies,
contrasting views, and opinionated materials to show the importance to sociology of everyday events.

*COSER, LEWIS A., ed., *Sociology Through Literature: An Introductory Reader*
(Englewood Cliffs, N.J.: Prentice-Hall, Inc., 1963). "Literature . . . is social evi-
dence and testimony. It is a continuous commentary on manners and morals."
Selections are arranged under sixteen sociological concepts.

*FADIMAN, JAMES, *The Proper Study of Man: Perspectives on the Social Sciences*
(New York: The Macmillan Company, 1971). "The articles in each section are
intended to raise basic issues that no amount of factual information can ever
resolve."

*GOODE, WILLIAM J., ed., *The Dynamics of Modern Society* (New York: Atherton
Press, 1966). The fundamental sociological framework of ideas is tested by
application to real social behavior in many different settings; emphasis is on
the dynamics of interaction and on contemporary developments in sociology.

*LASSWELL, THOMAS E., JOHN H. BURMA, and SIDNEY H. ARONSON, *Life
in Society: Readings in Sociology*, rev. ed. (Glenview, Ill.: Scott, Foresman
and Company, 1970). Eighty-five readings tested in introductory sociology
classes.

*ROSE, PETER I., ed., *The Study of Society: An Integrated Anthology*, 2nd ed.
(New York: Random House, Inc., 1970). Selections were chosen to provide
the student with a comprehensive overview of the nature of the discipline and
a series of concrete illustrations of what sociologists have learned about the
nature of society and of how they have gone about studying it.

*SCHULER, EDGAR A., THOMAS F. HOULT, DUANE L. GIBSON, and WILBUR B. BROOKOVER, eds., *Readings in Sociology*, 4th ed. (New York, Thomas Y. Crowell Co., 1971). Selections were chosen for cogent illustration of sociological principles as well as for interest and readability.

*TRUZZI, MARCELLO, ed., *Sociology and Everyday Life* (Englewood Cliffs, N.J.: Prentice-Hall, Inc., 1968). The editor attempts to appeal to the student's natural curiosity about both the commonplace and the offbeat aspects of social life; stresses concrete data rather than abstract laws; aims at subjective understanding and insight.

The Bobbs-Merrill Reprint Series in the Social Sciences. Each of the more than 1300 reprints of scholarly articles is ready for binding in a ring notebook; thus the instructor may choose and assemble his own book of readings.

Index